Automation and Robotics

Edited by
Juan Manuel Ramos Arreguin

Automation and Robotics
Edited by Juan Manuel Ramos Arreguin

Republished by InTech
Janeza Trdine 9, 51000 Rijeka, Croatia

Technical Editor Teodora Smiljanic

Additional hard copies can be obtained from orders@intechopen.com

Automation and Robotics, Edited by Juan Manuel Ramos Arreguin
p. cm.
ISBN 978-3-902613-41-7

For EU product safety concerns:
IN TECH d.o.o., Prolaz Marije Krucifikse Kozulić 3, 51000 Rijeka, Croatia,
info@intechopen.com or visit our website at intechopen.com.

Meet the editor

Juan Manuel Ramos Arreguin . PhD in Engineering specializing in Mechatronics, he completed a Master's degree in the Faculty of Mechanical, Electrical and Electronic Engineering (FIMEE), specializing in Instrumentation and Digital Systems where he worked with embedded systems. The Bachelor's Degree in Electronic Engineering and Communications at FIMEE. He has been a professor at the Technological University of San Juan del Río and at the Center for Engineering and Industrial Development. He has held positions as President of the Academic Body of Electronics in the UTSJR until 2009. Participant with students in the National Minirobotics Competition until 2008. Member of the Mexican Mechatronics Association. Currently Professor Researcher of the Faculty of Informatics at the Autonomous University of Querétaro and member of the National System of Researchers as Candidate.

Automation and Robotics

Edited by Juan Manuel Ramos Arreguin

Republished by InTech

Janeza Trdine 9, 51000 Rijeka, Croatia

Technical Editor Teodora Smiljanic

Additional hard copies can be obtained from orders@intechopen.com

Automation and Robotics, Edited by Juan Manuel Ramos Arreguin
p. cm.
ISBN 978-3-902613-41-7

Preface

In this book, a set of relevant, updated and selected papers in the field of automation and robotics are presented. These papers describe projects where topics of artificial intelligence, modeling and simulation process, target tracking algorithms, kinematic constraints of the closed loops, non-linear control, are used in advanced and recent research.

Also, the lecturer can find some of the new methodologies applied to solve complex problems in the field of control and robotic research fields. Moreover, this book can serve as a good information source for scientific scholars, engineers and beginners who would like to start working with both automation and robotic areas. Combining the ideas of the diverse disciplines involved in such areas, this book give hints and help about how to implement them on products for industrial automation and robotics applications.

I would like to thank all the researchers who send their works to share with the scientific community. The editors are extremely grateful to all of them for their support to complete this book.

Editor

Juan Manuel Ramos Arreguin
Electronica y Automatizacion
Universidad Tecnologica de San Juan del Rio
jramos@mecamex.net

Contents

1

Tracking Control for Multiple Trailer Systems by Adaptive Algorithmic Control

Tomoaki Kobayashi, Toru Yoshida, Junichi Maenishi,
Joe Imae and Guisheng Zhai
Osaka Prefecture University
Japan

1. Introduction

In recent years, a truck-trailer system is the most useful physical distribution system. The truck-trailer systems have more convenience than coastal services or freight trains. Meanwhile, problems of the traffic jam and the air pollution in an urban area have become serious, year after year. Therefore improvement and rationalization of the transport efficiency are social needs. There are many papers suggesting a platoon system of several trucks as a part of development of ITS (Intelligent Transport System). These platoon systems consist of several unmanned trucks automatically following a truck driven by a conductor, and it is commonly believed that it brings improvements of energy efficiency along with alleviation of the traffic jam. Moreover, there is a purpose of covering insufficient workforce of truck drivers who have to do severe labors, too. In the platoon, trucks are not physically connected to each other, and thus there is much flexibility. On the other hand, even if each vehicle is physically connected by mechanical linkage, this is not important restrictions, for transport robots which are operated in the factory, because moving range and action plan are limited. Moreover, the multiple trailer system is safer than platoon system, because if each vehicle is physically connected, there is no danger of collision among trailers. In this paper, we deal with a control method for a physically connected multiple trailer robot, which is a transport system in factories.

The control method of connected vehicle has been studied for a long time (Laumond, 1986). In particular, there are many papers which studied controlling its backward motion with guaranteed stability (Sampei & Kobayashi, 1994). Moreover, kinematical model of a multiple trailer system is described by a nonholonomic system, and it is a controllable nonlinear system (Hermann & Krener, 1977). In theoretical field, it has been a hot subject of research, because asymptotic stabilization is impossible using one continuous time-invariant since the nonholonomic system does not satisfy the Brockett's necessary condition for stabilizability (Brockett, 1983). Therefore, the control problem of nonholonomic system is a theoretically difficult problem, thereupon various researches such as time-variant controller (M'Closkey & Murray, 1993) or hybrid control techniques (Matsune et al., 2005) are performed. We look at this issue from more practical point of view, then investigate a real-time control algorithm, which is based on the so called algorithmic control (Kobayashi et al., 2005a), (Imae et al., 2005) with a similar formulation of the model predictive control (MPC) technique for nonlinear continuous time system. Our algorithmic design approach is a technique for ensuring robustness by adopting a numeric solution called Riccati Equation Based (REB) algorithm using quasi linearization that includes feedback solution. Moreover, though details are described later, the control technique by algorithmic design which we proposed is an effective method for nonholonomic systems because our method is switching and applying the control strategy on a short control interval and thus the controller is discontinuous time variant, which does not violate Brockett's theorem. We showed the effectiveness of proposed method applicable to nonholonomic systems through some simulations and an experiment with a differential-driven unicycle vehicle model (Kobayashi et al., 2005b). Then, we extend our design method by incorporating numerical robustness for disturbances and parameter uncertainties and, by focusing on the switching interval of control strategy on iterative process of algorithmic design (Kobayashi et al., 2006). We discussed about effectiveness of our approach for an unstable motion control of high order nonlinear system, in this paper. In the most of conventional research, the direct-hooked type model (Lee et al., 2001) is treated. The direct-hooked model can be transformed to a canonical form called chained form (Murray & Sastry, 1993). Then, control problem for the direct-hooked model can be reduced to a canonical problem. However, the direct-hooked model has a tracking error of follow-on trailers (Fig.1). Therefore, there are many suggestions for eliminating the tracking error by model constructions or mechanical linkage design. We pick up a off-hooked model (Lee et al., 2004) which has a most simple structure and cannot be converted to canonical form (Ishikawa, 1993). Therefore, proposed algorithmic design is considered as an effective strategy for the off-hooked trailer system, because our approach can treat the general nonlinear systems. The effectiveness is discussed through a numerical simulation result.

The outline of this paper is as follows. In section 2, we describe the nonlinear optimal control problems and the Riccati Equation Based algorithm. In section 3, the algorithmic design method is described in detail. Also, we make an extension of our design method for robustness. The backward motion control problem of multiple trailer systems is formulated in section 4. In section 5, we show some simulation results in order to demonstrate the effectiveness of adaptive algorithmic design. Section 6 concludes the paper.

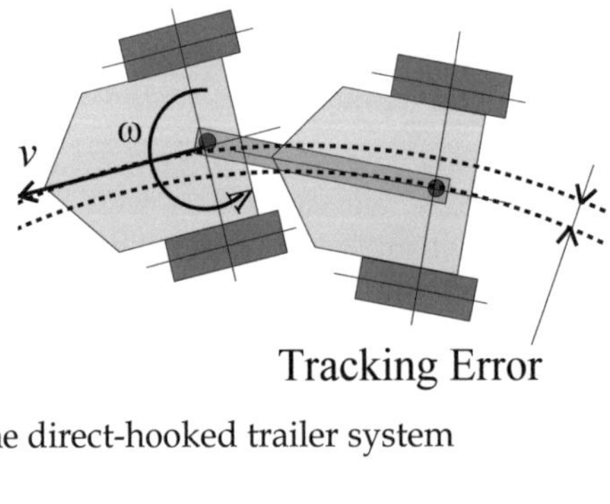

Fig. 1 Tracking error of the direct-hooked trailer system

2. Optimal control problem

2.1 Formulation

We deal with the following general nonlinear system

$$\dot{x}(t) = f(t, x(t), u(t)) \quad (1)$$

$$x(t_0) = x_0 \in \Re^n \tag{2}$$

where t_0 is initial time, x_0 is initial state given. Here, we denote the state variable by $x(t) = [x_1(t), \cdots, x_n(t)]^{\mathrm{T}} \in \Re^n$, and the input variable by $u(t) = [u_1(t), \cdots, u_r(t)]^{\mathrm{T}} \in \Re^r$. Then, the purpose is to find the controller which minimizes a performance index J over a time interval $[t_0, t_1]$.

$$J = G(x(t_1)) + \int_{t_0}^{t_1} L(t, x(t), u(t))dt \tag{3}$$

Based on the problem formulation (1) to (2), we describe our on-line computational design method, that is to say, algorithmic design method (Kobayashi et al., 2005a).
It is known that whether or not the algorithmic design method succeeds depends on how effective the algorithm is to iteratively search the numerical solutions of optimal control problems. In this paper, we adopt one of the so-called Riccati-equation based algorithms (REB algorithms (Imae & Torisu, 1998)), which is known to be reliable and effective in searching numerical solutions. Details are given later.

2.2 Riccati-equation based algorithm

Under the problem formulation (1) to (3), we describe an iterative algorithm for the numerical solutions of optimal control problems, based on Riccati differential equations. In this respect, the algorithm falls in the category of optimal control algorithms, as presented in (Nedeljkovic, 1981), (Imae et al., 1992), and so on.

[Assumptions]

Let $x : [t_0, t_1] \to \Re^n$ be an absolutely continuous function, and $u : [t_0, t_1] \to \Re^r$ be an essentially bounded measurable function. For each positive integer j, let us denote by AC^j all absolutely continuous functions: $[t_0, t_1] \to \Re^j$, and by L_∞^j all essentially bounded measurable functions: $[t_0, t_1] \to \Re^j$. Moreover, we define the following norms on AC^j and L_∞^j respectively:

$$\| x \| = \max |x(t)| \text{ for } x \in AC^j,\ t \in [t_0, t_1]$$
$$\| y \| = \text{ess sup} |y(t)| \text{ for } y \in L_\infty^j,\ t \in [t_0, t_1]$$

where the vertical bars are used to denote Euclidean norms for vectors.
Now, we make some assumptions.

i. $G : \Re^n \to \Re^1$, $f : \Re^1 \times \Re^n \times \Re^r \to \Re^n$, $L : \Re^1 \times \Re^n \times \Re^r \to \Re^1$ are continuous in all their arguments, and their partial derivatives $G_x(x)$, $f_x(t,x,u)$, $f_u(t,x,u)$, $L_x(t,x,u)$ and $L_u(t,x,u)$ exist and are continuous in all their arguments.

ii. For each compact set $U \subset \Re^r$ there exists some $M_1 \in (0, \infty)$ such that

$$|f(t,x,u)| \le M_1(|x| + 1) \tag{4}$$

for all $t \in \Re^1$, $x \in \Re^n$ and $u \in U$.

[Algorithm]

STEP A0 Let $\beta \in (0,1)$ and $M_2 \in (0,1)$. Select arbitrarily an initial input $u^0 \in L_\infty^r$.

STEP A1 $i = 0$.

STEP A2 Calculate $x^i(t)$ with $u^i(t)$ from the equation (1).

STEP A3 Select $A^i \in \Re^{n\times n}$, $B_{11}^i \in L_\infty^{n\times n}$, $B_{12}^i \in L_\infty^{n\times r}$ and $B_{22}^i \in L_\infty^{r\times r}$ so that Kalman's sufficient conditions for the boundedness of Riccati solutions (Jacobson & Mayne, 1970) hold, that is, for almost all $t \in [t_0, t_1]$,

$$\begin{aligned} &A^i(t) \geq 0 \\ &B_{22}^i(t) > 0 \\ &B_{11}^i(t) - B_{12}^i(t) B_{22}^i(t)^{-1} B_{12}^i(t)^{\mathrm{T}} \geq 0 \end{aligned} \tag{5}$$

where A^i, B_{11}^i and B_{22}^i are symmetric and $(\cdot)^{\mathrm{T}}$ means the transpose of vectors and matrices. We solve (6), (7), and (8) with respect to δx, K, r and denote the solutions as $\delta x^i(t)$, $K^i(t)$, $r^i(t)$.

$$\begin{aligned} \delta\dot{x}(t) &= \{f_x(t, x^i, u^i) + f_u(t, x^i, u^i) B_{22}^{i\ -1}(f_u^{\mathrm{T}}(t, x^i, u^i) K(t) - B_{12}^{i\ \mathrm{T}})\}\delta x(t) \\ &\quad + f_u(t, x^i, u^i) B_{22}^{i\ -1}(f_u^{\mathrm{T}}(t, x^i, u^i) r(t) - L_u^{\mathrm{T}}(t, x^i, u^i)), \\ \delta x(t_0) &= 0, \end{aligned} \tag{6}$$

$$\begin{aligned} \dot{K}(t) &= -K(t) f_x(t, x^i, u^i) - f_x^{\mathrm{T}}(t, x^i, u^i) K(t) + B_{11}^i \\ &\quad + (K(t) f_u(t, x^i, u^i) - B_{12}^i) B_{22}^{i\ -1}(B_{12}^{i\ \mathrm{T}} - f_u^{\mathrm{T}}(t, x^i, u^i) K(t)), \\ K(t_1) &= -A^i, \end{aligned} \tag{7}$$

$$\begin{aligned} \dot{r}(t) &= -f_x^{\mathrm{T}}(t, x^i, u^i) r(t) + L_x^{\mathrm{T}}(t, x^i, u^i) \\ &\quad + \{B_{12}^i - K(t) f_u^{\mathrm{T}}(t, x^i, u^i)\} B_{22}^{i\ -1}(-L_u^{\mathrm{T}}(t, x^i, u^i) + f_u^{\mathrm{T}}(t, x^i, u^i) r(t)), \\ r(t_1) &= -G(x(t_1)), \end{aligned} \tag{8}$$

and determine δu^i as follows.

$$\begin{aligned} \delta u^i(t) = B_{22}^{i\ -1}\{&(f_u^{\mathrm{T}}(t, x^i, u^i) K^i(t) - B_{12}^{i\ \mathrm{T}})\delta x^i \\ &+ f_u^{\mathrm{T}}(t, x^i, u^i) r^i(t) - L_u^{\mathrm{T}}(t, x^i, u^i)\}. \end{aligned} \tag{9}$$

STEP A4 Determine $(\tilde{x}^i, \tilde{u}^i)$ satisfying

$$\begin{aligned} &\dot{x}(t) = f(t, x(t), u(t)) \\ &x(t_0) = x_0 \in \Re^n \\ &H^i(t, (x - x^i), (u - u^i), p^i) = \max_{v \in \Re^r} H^i(t, (x - x^i), (u - u^i), p^i) \end{aligned}$$

where

$$H^i(t,\ \delta x,\ \delta u,\ p) = -\{L_x(t,\ x^i,\ u^i)\delta x + L_u(t,\ x^i,\ u^i)\delta u \\ +\frac{1}{2}(\delta x^{\mathrm{T}} B_{11}^i \delta x + 2\delta x^{\mathrm{T}} B_{12}^i \delta u + \delta u^{\mathrm{T}} B_{22}^i \delta u)\} \\ +p^{\mathrm{T}}(f_x(t,\ x^i,\ u^i)\delta x + f_u(t,\ x^i,\ u^i)\delta u)$$

and p^i is the solution of the following equation.

$$\dot{p}(t) = -f_x^{\mathrm{T}}(t, x^i, u^i)p(t) + L_x^{\mathrm{T}}(t, x^i, u^i) \\ p(t_1) = -G_x^{\mathrm{T}}(x(t_1))$$

STEP A5 $\alpha_i = 1$.

STEP A6 Set $u^{i+1}(t) = u^i(t) + \alpha_i \delta u^i(t) + \alpha_i^2(\tilde{u}^i(t) - u^i(t) - \delta u^i(t))$.
if (10) holds, go to Step A7. Otherwise, set $\alpha_i = \beta\alpha_i$ and repeat Step A6.

$$J(u^{i+1}) - J(u^i) \le \alpha_i M_2\{G(x_i(t_1))\delta x(t_1) \\ +\int_{t_0}^{t_1}(L_x(t,\ x^i,\ u^i)\delta x^i + L_u(t,\ x^i,\ u^i)\delta u^i)dt\} \tag{10}$$

STEP A7 Set $i = i+1$, and go to Step A2. Repeat Step A2 to Step A7 until the performance index J converges. Here, the integer i represents the number of iterations.

3. Algorithmic design

3.1 Real time control technique

In this section, we describe the outline of the algorithmic design for real time control of nonlinear system. See (Imae et al., 2005), (Kobayashi et al., 2005a) for more details. The basic idea of this real-time control design is the control strategy u^N is executed one by one through N iterations of the above-mentioned REB algorithm from Step A2 to Step A7. In this design method, the controller is not needed in an explicit expression, and the control strategy is decided repeatedly by the REB algorithm. After the actual states are observed, the states of the next ΔT seconds from now are predicted by the state equation (1). Then, with the predicted states set as initial states, we obtain the next control strategy u^N by N iterations of the REB algorithm from Step A2 to Step A7. Through sufficiently large number of iterations N, it could be expected to eventually reach the possible optimal solutions. However, the value of N should be decided for the iterative processing to end in the ΔT [sec]. We here describe how the algorithmic controller works. See also figure 1. Here, the feedback structure of the solution in (Imae et al., 2005) and (Kobayashi et al., 2005a) is not adopted for simplification of computation.

[Real Time Algorithm]

STEP B1 Let $k = 0$. Select arbitrarily an initial input u_k^N.

STEP B2 Measure the actual state x_{ak}, and apply the input u_k^N to the plant over the interval of the unit time of calculation ΔT. During this time interval, we proceed with two kinds of calculations: One is to predict the one-unit-time-ahead state $x_{p(k+1)}$ through the system equation (1) with the initial state x_{ak}, and the other is to calculate the N-iteration-ahead solution with the updated initial state $x_{p(k+1)}$. Then, we obtain the next control strategy u_{k+1}^{N}. If the rate of the value of performance index is less than a sufficiently small value γ, that is if following inequalities are satisfied, stop the iteration because it seems that the optimal solution was obtained.

$$\left| \frac{J(u^{i+1}) - J(u^{i})}{J(u^{i})} \right| < \gamma \ or \ \left| J(u^{i}) \right| < \gamma \tag{11}$$

STEP B3 Set $k = k+1$, and go to Step B2.

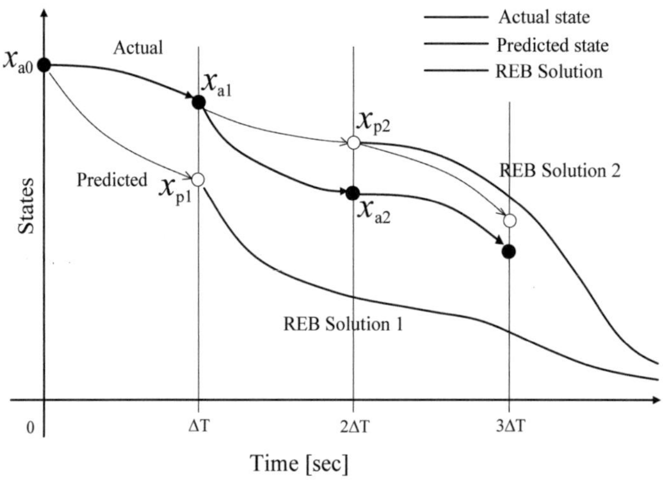

Fig. 2 Optimal / actual trajectory.

In our previous works, we verified the effectiveness of our algorithmic approach by applying to various nonlinear systems. For example, we tried a swing-up problem of inverted pendulum, or the obstacle avoidance problem for a unicycle robot. As a result, our approach gave the effective solution for these problems. The backward motion control problem for the multiple trailer system that we treat in this paper is a more difficult problem, because the system is a higher order nonlinear system. In spite of these difficulties, we confirmed the effectiveness of our algorithmic approach for such a complex problem through some numerical simulations. However, it is necessary to select carefully ΔT and N that are the design parameters of this algorithm. In the case of including disturbance, the feasibility of the algorithm depends on the combination of ΔT and N. For reducing the complexity of the method of deciding these design parameters, a simple way of computational artifice is shown in the next section. The simulation result is described in section 6.

3.2 Algorithmic design incorporating computational time

In this section, a simple computational artifice of the above-mentioned algorithmic design is pointed out. First, we describe the key notes here. In the above-mentioned algorithm, the interval of time ΔT to apply one control strategy u_k^N is called "switching time". And the maximum number of the iteration executed in a switching time N is called "maximum iteration". When the state was predicted, the obtained state trajectory is called "predictive trajectory" and actual trajectory is called "trajectory".

In our algorithmic design, the computation of maximum iteration should be done in switching interval. The search process of the optimal solution is executed in this algorithm, and the required computation time depends on the state. Therefore, it was necessary to give some margin to the switching interval. If the maximum iteration is sufficiently large, it may obtain an optimal solution in each switching interval. However, the switching interval has to set to large, because long computation time is required. Because the feedback effect is obtained by observing each switching interval, it seems that if the switching interval is as short as possible, the performance of robustness is better. The key idea of the algorithm which we propose here is to treat the switching interval as varying. It increases the maximum iteration when time is required for searching the optimal solution, and the switching interval is increased along with it. On the other hand, when long time is not required to find the optimal solution, reduce the maximum number of iteration and the switching interval for improving the robustness. The maximum iteration is decided based on Fig.2 and the computation time which was required to execute the algorithm. The maximum allowed computation time is set to τ_{max}, and the total time interval $[0,\tau_{max}]$ is divided into five sections as

$$[0,\tau_{max}] = [0,\tau_1] \cup [\tau_1,\tau_2] \cup [\tau_2,\tau_3] \cup [\tau_3,\tau_4] \cup [\tau_4,\tau_5]$$

where $t_5 = \tau_{max}$. For simplicity, let $\tau_i = \alpha i \ (i = 1,2,\cdots,5)$. Moreover, the maximum iteration N and the switching interval ΔT^N are determined as follows.

$$\Delta T^N = \beta N \tag{12}$$

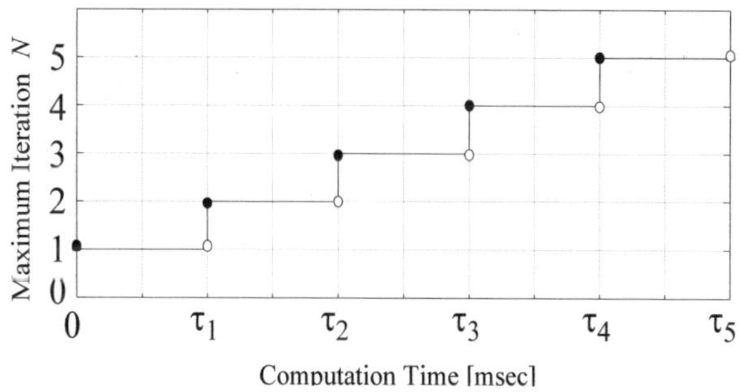

Fig. 3 Maximum iteration.

When actual calculation time is τ, the maximum iteration N is decided from Fig.2 and switching interval ΔT^N is obtained from expression (12). However, note that the present switching interval and the present maximum iteration are used in the next step. Here, based on the average computation time for one-iteration, the constants α and β are set to $\alpha = 0.02$ [sec] and $\beta = 0.03$ [sec]. In general, it is possible to decide N and ΔT^N such as $N_\sigma = g(\sigma)$ and $\Delta T_\sigma^N = h(\sigma)$ using a certain switching parameter σ.

[Robust Algorithm]

<u>STEP C1</u> Let $k = 0$. Select arbitrarily initial input u_k^N and maximum iteration N_k. Then, ΔT^{N_k} is decided.

STEP C2 Measure the actual state x_{ak}, and apply the input u_k^N to the system over the interval of the unit time of calculation ΔT^{N_k}. During this time interval, we proceed with two kinds of calculations: One is to predict the one-unit-time-ahead state $x_{p(k+1)}$ through the system equation (1) with the initial state x_{ak}, and the other is to calculate from Step A3 to Step A7 with the updated initial state $x_{p(k+1)}$.
STEP C3 The maximum iteration is N_k, and calculate the rate of the value of performance index in each iteration, similarly as the computation from Step A3 to Step A7 $(i = 1,2,\cdots,N_k)$.
STEP C4 If the rate of the value of performance index is larger than a sufficiently small value γ, that is if following inequalities are satisfied, it seems that the optimal solution was not obtained.

$$\left|\frac{J(u^{i+1}) - J(u^i)}{J(u^i)}\right| \geq \gamma \quad and \quad \left|J(u^i)\right| \geq \gamma \tag{13}$$

where $\gamma > 0$. Then, let $i = i+1$, and execute the computation from Step A3 to Step A7. Execute these iterative computations till maximum $i = N_k$.
If following inequalities are satisfied, discontinue the iteration because it seems that the optimal solution was obtained.

$$\left|\frac{J(u^{i+1}) - J(u^i)}{J(u^i)}\right| < \gamma \quad or \quad \left|J(u^i)\right| < \gamma \tag{14}$$

The computation time which was required to the above-mentioned computation is set to τ_k. Then, we obtain the next control strategy u_{k+1}^N.
STEP C5 The maximum iteration N_{k+1} and the switching interval $\Delta T^{N_{k+1}}$ for the next interval are decided based on the computation time which was required for current interval, equation (12) and Fig. 2.
STEP C6 Set $k = k+1$, and go to Step C2.

4. Modeling

The kinematical model of the multiple trailer system which we treat is shown in Fig.4. The meaning of next equation (15) is the state equation of the first vehicle (autotruck) which is driven pulling the follow-on passive trailers.

$$\begin{bmatrix} \dot{x}_0 \\ \dot{y}_0 \\ \dot{\theta}_0 \end{bmatrix} = \begin{bmatrix} \cos\theta_0 \\ \sin\theta_0 \\ 0 \end{bmatrix} v_0 + \begin{bmatrix} 0 \\ 0 \\ 1 \end{bmatrix} \omega \tag{15}$$

The control input vector of this system is denoted by $u = [v_0 \quad \omega]^{\mathrm{T}}$. Here, v_0 and ω denotes the velocity and angular velocity of the first vehicle respectively. This model is a differential-driven vehicle model which has nonholonomic constraint, and is regarded as one of the most typical nonholonomic systems. It is known that although this model has controllability, it can not be asymptotically stabilizable by any continuous time-invariant controller (Brockett, 1993). For this reason, there have been many references dealing with the stabilization problem for this model using various kinds of controllers. One successful approach is to convert it into the so-called chained form and then establish a time-varying controller. Although such an approach leads to asymptotical stabilization, it is applicable only for the case where the system's dimension is low (less than four).Since we deal with a multiple trailer system, whose dimension is obviously much larger than four, the approach of utilizing chained form with a time-varying controller can not be applied here, and more practical strategy is desirable.

The most of conventional research have treated the direct-hooked type trailer model. This model is obtained by $D_0, D_1 = 0$ in Fig.4, and the kinematics of the ith trailer is as follows.

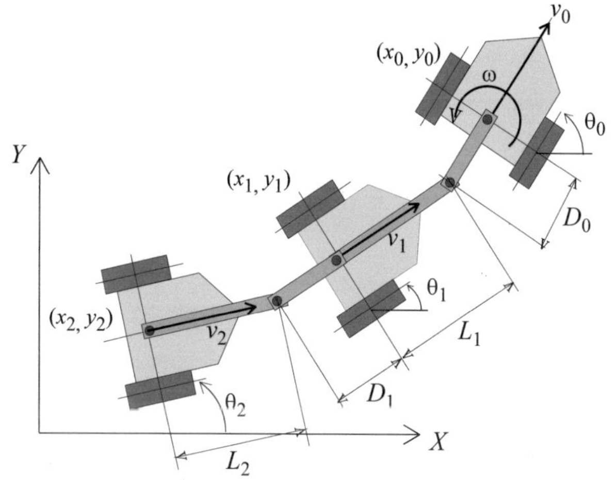

Fig. 4 Mechanical linkage design of multiple trailer system.

Only the first vehicle (truck) is driven and the following vehicles (trailers) are passively pulled by the truck.

$$\begin{aligned} \dot{\theta}_i &= \sin(\theta_{i-1} \quad \theta_i)v_{i-1} \Big/ L_i \\ v_i &= \cos(\theta_{i-1} - \theta_i)v_{i-1} \end{aligned} \tag{16}$$

where, θ_i denotes the attitude angle of the ith trailer, and L_i is the length of the ith linkage. v_i and $\dot{\theta}_i$ denote the velocity and angular velocity of ith trailer respectively.

The direct-hooked model can be transformed to a chained form. However, this model has a tracking error of follow-on trailers. Therefore, we deal with the off-hooked model ($L_i = D_{i-1} \neq 0$) which can eliminate the tracking error (Fig. 5). However, the model of off-hooked trailer system cannot be transformed to canonical form. Fig. 4 shows a off-hooked model, and the following equation denotes the ith trailer's kinematics.

$$\begin{aligned} \dot{\theta}_i &= (\sin(\theta_{i-1} - \theta_i)v_{i-1} - \cos(\theta_{i-1} - \theta_i)\dot{\theta}_{i-1}D_{i-1} \Big/ L_i \\ v_i &= \cos(\theta_{i-1} - \theta_i)v_{i-1} + \sin(\theta_{i-1} - \theta_i)\dot{\theta}_{i-1}D_{i-1} \end{aligned}$$

5. Problem formulation

Tracking control problem of the multiple trailer system is formulated as a nonlinear optimal control problem in this section. For simplicity of notation, we consider one truck and two trailers. Even if the number of the trailer increases, our control design can be extended very easily. In that case, increase of the computational cost is inevitable.

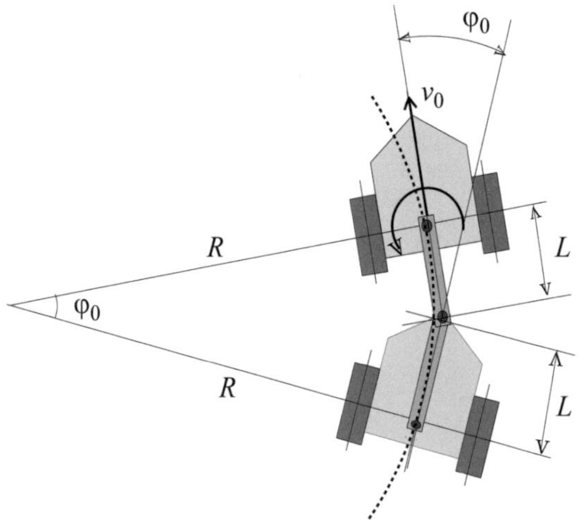

Fig. 5 Tracking path of the off-hooked trailer system.

The state equation of the 1-truck and 2-trailers model is given by

$$\dot{\xi} = A(\xi)u$$
$$\xi = [x_0 \quad y_0 \quad \theta_0 \quad \theta_1 \quad \theta_2]^{\mathrm{T}}, \quad u = [v_0 \quad \omega]^{\mathrm{T}} \tag{17}$$
$$A(\xi) = \begin{bmatrix} \cos\theta_0 & 0 \\ \sin\theta_0 & 0 \\ 0 & 1 \\ \sin(\theta_0 - \theta_1)/L & -\cos(\theta_0 - \theta_1) \\ \sin(2\theta_1 - \theta_0 - \theta_2)/L & -\cos(2\theta_1 - \theta_0 - \theta_2) \end{bmatrix}$$

The performance index is given by

$$J = (\xi(t) - \xi_f(t))^{\mathrm{T}} P(\xi(t) - \xi_f(t))\Big|_{t=t_1}$$
$$+ \frac{1}{2}\int_{t_0}^{t_1} ((\xi(t) - \xi_f(t))^{\mathrm{T}} Q(\xi(t) - \xi_f(t)) + u(t)^{\mathrm{T}} Ru(t))dt$$

where the state vector and input vector are denoted by ξ and u respectively. P, Q, R denote the weighting matrices. We set $P = 0.5I$, $Q = \mathrm{diag}[0.2 \quad 0.2 \quad 0.001 \quad 0.001 \quad 0.001]$, $R = \mathrm{diag}[0.05 \quad 0.01]$. $\xi_f(t)$ is the target state, and it is the circle of radius 0.5[m] with constant velocity. Furthermore, we treat the state constraints and input constraints by introducing the penalty term.

$$\bar{J} = J + \int_{t_0}^{t_1} \left(\sum_{i=1}^{2} \frac{r_i}{\theta_{i\lim}^2 - (\theta_{i-1} - \theta_i)^2}\right) dt + \int_{t_0}^{t_1} \frac{r_v}{v_{\lim}^2 - v^2} + \frac{r_\omega}{\omega_{\lim}^2 - \omega^2} dt \tag{18}$$

where, $\theta_{i\lim}(i=1,2)$ is an absolute value of limitation of the relative angle, and $v_{\lim}$ and $\omega_{\lim}$ are the absolute value of the limitation of the control input.

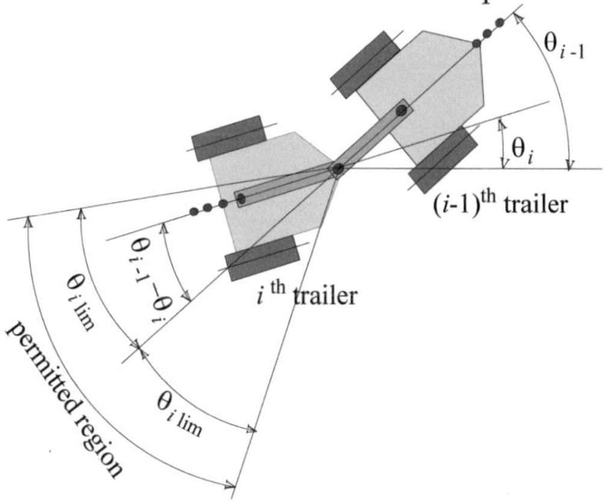

Fig. 6 Permitted region of ith trailer.

We chose $|\theta_i| < \theta_{i\lim} = 0.5$ [rad] $(i = 1,2)$, $|v| < v_{\lim} = 1.0$ [m/sec], $|\omega| < \omega_{\lim} = 4.848$ [rad/sec]. Fig. 6 shows the permitted region of follow-on trailers. The weight parameters are set to $r_i = 0.001$ $(i = 1,2)$, $r_v = 0.0001$, $r_\omega = 0.0001$.

6. Numerical simulation

The control strategy of our approach is obtained by processing the iterative calculation of the REB algorithm in each ΔT. Through sufficiently large number of iterations N, it could be expected to eventually reach the possible optimal solutions. Through some simulation results we can obtain the effective solution with roughly ΔT=100[msec] by the PC which we use. However, it is not necessarily the case that the effective solution is obtained, especially in the case of including a disturbance. The simple computational artifice described in section 3.2. partially reduces such a problem. The example of the simulation result of applying the algorithm to the case of including a disturbance is shown in the following.

Fig. 7 shows the simulation result of the computation time of each ΔT with fixed number of iterations N and switching time ΔT=100[msec]. Simulated time is 30 [sec], then average and minimum/maximum value of the computation time is shown. The solid lines are $\Delta T_k^N = \beta N_k$ with β= 0.02 [sec] and β= 0.03 [sec] respectively. According to Fig. 7, proposed algorithm is almost executable in real time with β= 0.03 [sec]. Therefore, we simply choose as α= 0.02[sec], β= 0.03 [sec]. However, real time feasibility is not guaranteed by these parameters, because the computation time varies according to running condition.

Fig. 8 - Fig. 11 show the simulation result with the initial state $\xi_0 = [0 \;\; 0 \;\; -\pi/2 \;\; -\pi/2 \;\; -\pi/2]^{\mathrm{T}}$. Impulsive disturbances on θ_1 and θ_2 have been added in this simulation at 5, 10, 15 and 20[sec], whose magnitude is 0.5[rad].

$$\theta_i(5n) = \theta_i(5n - dt) - 0.5, \ (i = 1,2, \ \ n = 1,2,3,4).$$

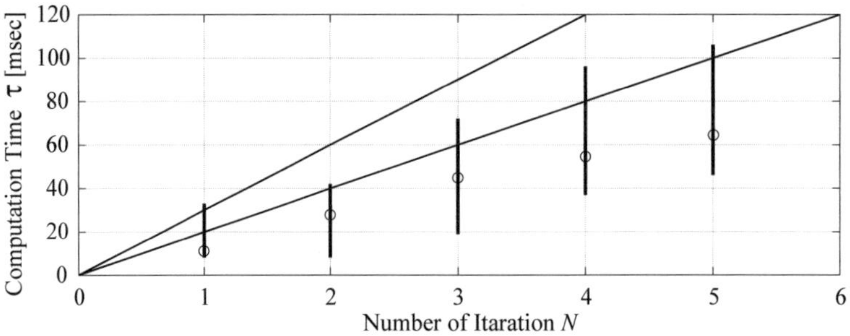

Fig. 7. Computational time. o: average of the computation time, with the maximum and minimum computation time, solid line: $\Delta T_k^N = \beta N_k$ with $\beta = 0.02$[sec] and $\beta = 0.03$[sec] respectively.

The lower part of Fig.9 shows the computation time of each switching time and its upper bound. ΔT has changed corresponding to disturbances. Also, this figure shows that this algorithm is feasible in real time, because the computation time is less than switching time ΔT .

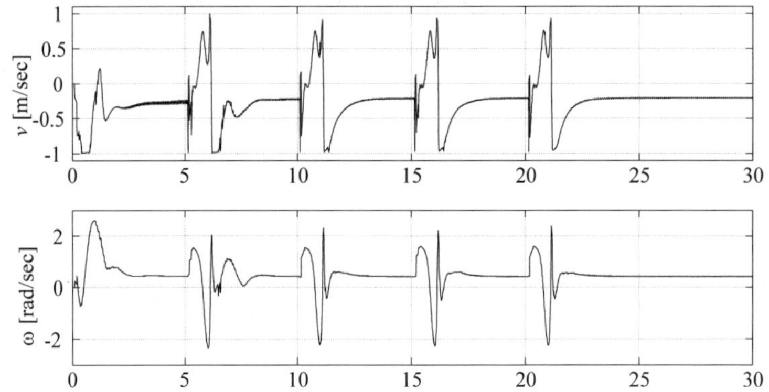

Fig. 8 Simulation results: control inputs.

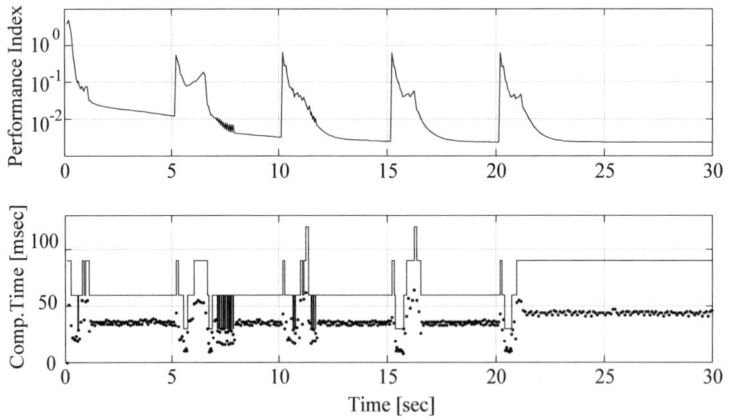

Fig. 9 Simulation results: value of performance index (upper stand). Computation time of each ΔT and its bound (lower part).

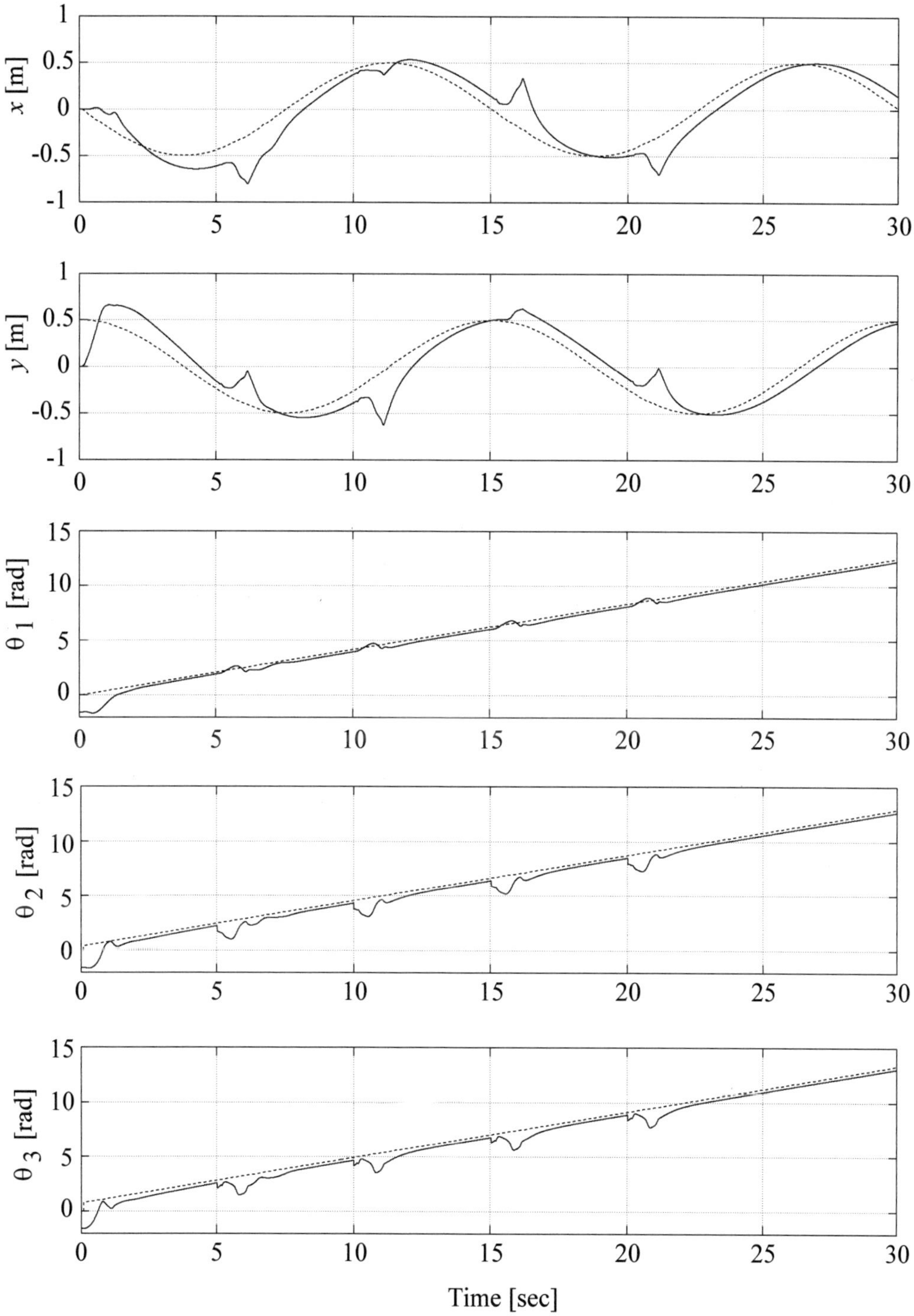

Fig. 10 Simulation results: state trajectories. (solid line: actual states, doted line: target states).

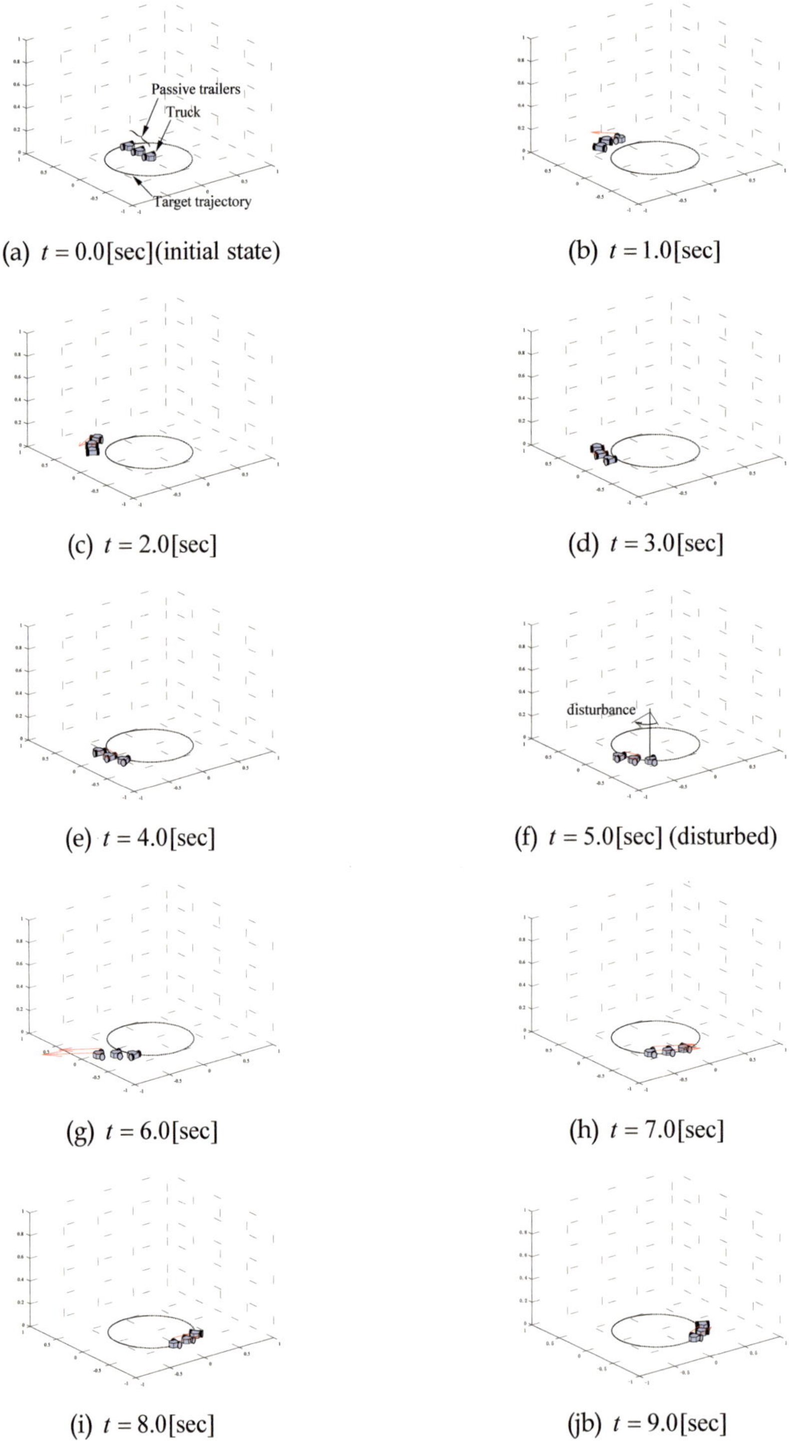

(a) $t = 0.0$[sec](initial state)
(b) $t = 1.0$[sec]
(c) $t = 2.0$[sec]
(d) $t = 3.0$[sec]
(e) $t = 4.0$[sec]
(f) $t = 5.0$[sec] (disturbed)
(g) $t = 6.0$[sec]
(h) $t = 7.0$[sec]
(i) $t = 8.0$[sec]
(jb) $t = 9.0$[sec]

Fig. 11 Simulation results.

7. Conclusions

We discussed the real time control algorithm using the numerical solution called algorithmic control. Then, we improved the conventional algorithmic design for the numerical robustness via incorporating computation time. The key idea is to adjust the maximum number of iteration with the computational time. This approach was applied to a tracking control problem of the multiple trailer system. We showed through a numerical simulation that the proposed algorithm is executable in real time, and it has robustness against disturbances.

8. Acknowledgment

This research has been supported in part by the Japan Ministry of Education, Sciences and Culture under Grants-in-Aid for Scientific Research (B) 18760326.

9. References

Brockett, R. W. (1983). Asymptotic Stability and Feedback Stabilization, *Differential Geometric Control Theory*, Vol. 27, pp. 181-191.

Hermann, R. & Krener, A. J. (1977). Nonlinear Controllability and Observability, *IEEE Transactions on Automatic Control*, Vol. 22, No. 5, pp. 728-740.

Imae, J.; Irlicht, L., Obinata, G. & Moore, J. B. (1992). Enhancing Optimal Controllers via Techniques from Robust and Adaptive Control, *International Journal of Adaptive Control and Signal Processing*, Vol. 6, pp. 413-429.

Imae, J. & Torisu, R. (1998). A Riccati-Equation Based Algorithm for Nonlinear Optimal Control Problems, *Proceedings of the 37th Conference on Decision and Control*, pp. 4422-4427.

Imae, J.; Yoshimizu, K., Kobayashi, T. & Zhai, G. (2005). Algorithmic Control for Real-time Optimization of Nonlinear Systems: Simulations and Experiments, *Proceedings of the 44th Conference on Decision and Control*, pp. 3729-3734.

Ishikawa, M. (1993). Control of Nonholonomic Systems having Complicated Controllability Structure, *Journal of The Society of Instrument and Control Engineers*, Vol. 42, No. 10, pp. 841-846.

Jacobson, D. H. & Mayne, D. Q. (1970). *Differential Dynamic Programming*, ISBN. 978-0444000705, Elsevier.

Kobayashi, T.; Magono, M., Imae, J., Yoshimizu, K. & Zhai, G. (2005a). Real-time Optimization for Nonlinear Systems Using Algorithmic Control, *Preprints of IFAC '05*, Prague, Czech Republic.

Kobayashi, T.; Maenishi, J., Imae, J. & Zhai, G. (2005b). Real-Time Optimization for Mobile Robot Based on Algorithmic Control, *Proceedings of 2005 International Conference on Control, Automation and Systems*, pp. 2102-2107.

Kobayashi, T.; Maenishi, J., Imae, J. & Zhai, G. (2006). Real Time Control for 4-wheeled Vehicles via Algorithmic Control Incorporating Computation Time, *Proceedings of 9th International Conference on Control, Automation, Robotics and Vision*, pp. 1353-1358.

Laumond, J.-P. (1986). Feasible Trajectories for Mobile Robots with Kinematic and Environment Constraints, *Proceedings of International Conference on Inteligent Autonomous Systems*, pp. 346-354.

Lee, J.; Chung, W., Kim, M., Lee, C. & Song, J. (2001). A Passive Multiple Trailer System for Indoor Service Robots, *Proceedings of 2001 IEEE/RSJ International Conference on Intelligent Robots and Systems*, pp. 827-832.

Lee, J.; Chung, W., Kim, M., Lee, C. & Song, J. (2004). A Passive Multiple Trailer System with Off-axle Hitching, *International Journal of Control, Automation, and Systems*, Vol. 2, No. 3, pp. 289-297.

Matsune, I.; Zhai, G., Kobayashi, T., & Imae, J. (2005) A Study on Hybrid Control of Nonholonomic Systems, *Proceedings of The Society of Instrument and Control Engineers Annual Conference*, pp. 211-214.

M'Closkey, R. T. & Murray, R. M. (1993). Nonholonomic Systems and Exponential Convergence: Some Analysis Tools, *Proceedings of the 32nd Conference on Decision and Control*, pp. 943-948.

Murray, R. M. & Sastry, S. S. (1993). Nonholonomic Motion Planning: Steering Using Sinusoids, *IEEE Transactions on Automatic Control*, Vol. 38, No. 5, pp. 700-716.

Nedeljkovic, N. B. (1981). New Algorithms for Unconstrained Nonlinear Optimal Control Problems, *IEEE Transactions on Automatic Control*, Vol. 26, pp. 868-884.

Sampei, M. & Kobayashi, T. (1994). Path Tracking Control of Car-Caravan Type Articulated Vehicles Using Nonlinear Control Theory, *Transactions of the Society of Instrument and Control Engineers (in Japanese)*, Vol. 30, No. 4, pp. 427-434.

2

Enhanced Motion Control Concepts on Parallel Robots

Frank Wobbe, Michael Kolbus and Walter Schumacher
Institute of Control Engineering, TU Braunschweig
Germany

1. Introduction

During the last years parallel robots have found their way into industrial applications. Though the ratio of workspace to designspace is usually worse compared to their serial counterparts, parallel robots are superior in terms of stiffness, accuracy and high-speed operation. This chapter takes the development into account and focuses on control concepts of parallel robots used for handling and assembly.

To exploit these features, an effective control system is inevitable. Since the nonlinearities of parallel structures are not negligible, control schemes have to include a precise dynamic model. This chapter presents several approaches of model-based control laws and discusses their characteristics, in theory as well as in implementation.

All discussed concepts operate on a uniform interface that takes a fully specified trajectory of position, velocity and acceleration in Cartesian space. This design of the interface can be considered as a minor restriction, since trajectories for high-speed operation usually are defined to be jerk limited (C^2-continuous) to reduce mechanical stress of the robot.

The chapter starts with a brief description of the discrete modeling scheme, afterwards a compact formulation of the robots dynamics is derived. Several control schemes using this model are presented, which can be classified into two major groups depending on the usage of the robot model as feedback or feedforward type. Based on linearization techniques the controllers for each axis are designed independently within a linear framework. The control algorithms are augmented by disturbance observers to reduce distortion of trajectory and tracking error.

Besides these classical approaches, nonlinear concepts such as sliding mode are used for control. Using a boundary layer concept and adding discontinuities to the control law ensures global asymptotic tracking with robustness against model uncertainties and disturbances. Chattering formally associated with sliding mode can be coped with modification of the control law by using continuous sliding surfaces. On contrary to the first approaches it is inherently based on nonlinear design.

Considering properties of parallel robots the control schemes of described approaches are designed. Explicit design rules are given at hand and discussed. For experiments the concepts are implemented on a planar parallel robot. The unified approaches of modeling and control guarantee transfer to more complex robots.

Evaluation of the results starts with a general comparison of control concepts. The effect of the design parameters on closed-loop system dynamics is analyzed theoretically, paying special attention to robustness and performance as essential characteristics. To substantiate the statements of the theoretical analyses, experimental results are presented and evaluated with respect to different aspects. Cartesian distortion, tracking error, drive torques and their impact are of major concern. Finally, an overall categorization is given at hand, featuring application hints for each design concept and pointing out specific drawbacks and advantages.

2. Problem statement – control concepts on parallel robots

Robot structures based on closed kinematic chains have proven to be a promising alternative to those based on serial chains. The feature of many of these so called parallel kinematic structures to allow for the drives to be fixed to the base, is especially of great interest for the design of robots for high speed handling and assembly tasks, cf. (Merlet, 2000). It enables a design with low moving masses allowing for high accelerations and achieving shorter cycle times.

Due to the nonlinearities of the manipulator a model-based control architecture is essential to ensure precise trajectory tracking, which demands a precise and compact dynamic model. Control schemes using this model are in general mainly based on centralized, decentralized or on equivalent control (Spong & Vidyasagar, 1989), (Sciavicco & Siciliano, 2001). Whereas first schemes allow an independent design of the controllers within a linear framework, the latter is refined to sliding mode control as nonlinear design-concept, which shapes the error dynamics of the system. Moreover, control design based on linearized subsystems offers a wide range of linear control design schemes.

Due to different design aspects of these concepts specific advantages and aspects of performance can be expected, which is addressed in this article.

Specific for parallel manipulators is a complex direct kinematic problem (DKP), which is in general more complex than the inverse kinematic problem (IKP), cf. (Merlet, 2000). These demands have to be met by control design: On the one hand a precise model is needed, on the other hand the complexity is limited by computational effort in real-time operation.

3. Robot dynamics

In literature many different methods of modeling parallel robots have been proposed, based on the approaches of the Newton-Euler method on the one hand (Spong & Vidyasagar, 1989) and the Lagrangian principle on the other hand (Tsai, 1999), (Murray et al., 1994). In this paper, Lagrangian equations of the second type and the formulation of Lagrange-D'Alembert (Nakamura, 1991) will be used for obtaining a compact model, guaranteeing computational efficiency in real-time control. The core idea herein is established on the use of Jacobians for discrete modeling.

3.1 Discrete modeling

Discrete modeling of parallel structures can be divided into two major steps: Derivation of manipulators Jacobian and calculation of differential equations.

The first step is discussed in (Stachera & Schumacher, 2007) and (Stachera et al., 2007), where the calculation of Jacobians bases on cutting open the parallel structure at the endeffector and applying the principle of kineto-statics (cf. section 3.3). Jacobian matrices of serial manipulators representing differential kinematic relation $\dot{\mathbf{x}} = \mathbf{J}\dot{\mathbf{q}}$ and static relation $\boldsymbol{\tau} = \mathbf{J}^{\mathrm{T}}\mathbf{f}$ are used for deduction.

The second step - deduction of an exact model for a given structure - can be done via Lagrange-D'Alembert-Formulation

$$\frac{\mathrm{d}}{\mathrm{d}t}\left(\frac{\partial L}{\partial \dot{\mathbf{q}}}\right) - \frac{\partial L}{\partial \mathbf{q}} = \boldsymbol{\tau} + \mathbf{J}^{\mathrm{T}}\mathbf{f}_{\mathrm{ext}} \tag{1}$$

with $L = T - V$ representing Lagrange function, T kinetic energy, V potential energy, $\mathbf{q}$ vector of joint space variables, $\boldsymbol{\tau}$ actuator torques and $\mathbf{J} = \mathbf{G}^{+\mathrm{T}}$ serial manipulator Jacobian on which external forces $\mathbf{f}_{\mathrm{ext}}$ are applied. Computing energy functions

$$T = \frac{1}{2}\dot{\mathbf{q}}^{\mathrm{T}}\mathbf{M}_{\mathbf{q}}(\mathbf{q})\dot{\mathbf{q}}\ , \quad V = \int_{\mathbf{q}_0}^{\mathbf{q}} \boldsymbol{\eta}_{\mathbf{q}}(\mathbf{q})\,\mathrm{d}\mathbf{q} \tag{2}$$

leads to a differential equation in joint space coordinates:

$$\mathbf{M}_{\mathbf{q}}(\mathbf{q})\ddot{\mathbf{q}} + \mathbf{C}_{\mathbf{q}}(\dot{\mathbf{q}},\mathbf{q})\dot{\mathbf{q}} + \boldsymbol{\eta}_{\mathbf{q}}(\mathbf{q}) = \boldsymbol{\tau} + \mathbf{J}^{\mathrm{T}}\mathbf{f}_{\mathrm{ext}} \tag{3}$$

Its elements can be calculated, considering a discrete model; the main idea is based upon discrete point masses m_i: Starting with the simple case of planar structures each link can be replaced by a combination of at least three single point masses without neglecting and disturbing properties concerning mass, center of mass and moment of inertia, thus guaranteeing correct dynamical behavior (Dizioglu, 1966). Without loss of generality this concept can be transferred to more complex structures. With growing complexity in structure the number of discrete elements increases, resulting in the finite element method. The concept of discrete point masses leads to

$$\begin{aligned}
\mathbf{M}_{\mathbf{q}} &= \sum_i m_i \mathbf{J}_i^{\mathrm{T}}\mathbf{J}_i + \mathrm{diag}\{I_m, I_m\} \\
\mathbf{C}_{\mathbf{q}} &= \frac{\partial \mathbf{M}_{\mathbf{q}}}{\partial t} - \frac{1}{2}\frac{\partial(\dot{\mathbf{q}}^{\mathrm{T}}\mathbf{M}_{\mathbf{q}})}{\partial \mathbf{q}} \\
\boldsymbol{\eta}_{\mathbf{q}} &= \sum_i m_i \mathbf{J}_i^{\mathrm{T}}\mathbf{g}
\end{aligned} \tag{4}$$

with drive inertia I_m and $\mathbf{g}$ being vector of gravity. All Jacobians $\mathbf{J}_i$ can be described by a linear combination of endeffector- and passive joints Jacobians.

The choice of Coriolis-Matrix is not unique: Using Christoffel-Symbols and following the notation of (Vetter, 1973) and (Weinmann, 1991) with discussion in (Bohn, 2000) leads to

$$\mathbf{C}_{\mathbf{q}} = \frac{1}{2}\left\{\left(\dot{\mathbf{q}}^{\mathrm{T}} \otimes \mathbf{I}_{n_{\mathbf{q}}}\right) - \left(\mathbf{I}_{n_{\mathbf{q}}} \otimes \dot{\mathbf{q}}^{\mathrm{T}}\right)\right\}\frac{\partial \mathbf{M}_{\mathbf{q}}}{\partial \mathbf{q}} + \frac{1}{2}\left\{\left(\mathbf{I}_{n_{\mathbf{q}}} \otimes \dot{\mathbf{q}}^{\mathrm{T}}\right)\frac{\partial \mathbf{M}_{\mathbf{q}}}{\partial \mathbf{q}}\right\}^{\mathrm{T}} \tag{5}$$

where $\otimes$ denotes the Kronecker-product, $n_\mathbf{q}$ is the number of degrees of freedom of the parallel structure and

$$\frac{\partial \mathbf{M_q}}{\partial \mathbf{q}} = m_i \frac{\partial \left(\mathbf{J}_i^{\mathrm{T}} \mathbf{J}_i\right)}{\partial \mathbf{q}} = \frac{\partial \mathbf{J}_i^{\mathrm{T}}}{\partial \mathbf{q}} \mathbf{J}_i + \left(\mathbf{I}_{n_\mathbf{q}} \otimes \mathbf{J}_i^{\mathrm{T}}\right) \frac{\partial \mathbf{J}_i}{\partial \mathbf{q}} \tag{6}$$

A basic feature of this rearranging is skew-symmetry of $\dot{\mathbf{M}}_\mathbf{q} - 2\mathbf{C_q}$, e.g.

$$\mathbf{w}^{\mathrm{T}} \left(\dot{\mathbf{M}}_\mathbf{q} - 2\mathbf{C_q}\right)\mathbf{w} = 0 \ , \qquad \mathbf{w} \in \Re^{(n_\mathbf{q} \times 1)} \tag{7}$$

which simplifies matrix usage for control algorithms (Sciavicco & Siciliano, 2001).
Without loss of generality this formalism can be enhanced for more complex structures featuring elasticities or redundancies. It thus can be used for generalized parallel structures considering an adequate discrete mass distribution.

3.2 Dynamics equations

Control in operational space requires coordinate transformation, resulting in

$$\mathbf{M_x}(\mathbf{q})\ddot{\mathbf{x}} + \mathbf{C_x}(\dot{\mathbf{q}},\mathbf{q})\dot{\mathbf{x}} + \boldsymbol{\eta}_\mathbf{x}(\mathbf{q}) = \mathbf{G}\boldsymbol{\tau} + \mathbf{f}_{\mathrm{ext}} \tag{8}$$

with

$$\begin{aligned}
\mathbf{M_x} &= \mathbf{J}^{-\mathrm{T}} \mathbf{M_q} \mathbf{J}^{-1} = \mathbf{G} \mathbf{M_q} \mathbf{G}^{\mathrm{T}} \\
\mathbf{C_x} &= \mathbf{J}^{-\mathrm{T}} \left(\mathbf{C_q} \mathbf{J}^{-1} + \mathbf{M_q} \dot{\overline{\mathbf{J}^{-1}}} \right) = \mathbf{G}\left(\mathbf{C_q} \mathbf{G}^{\mathrm{T}} + \mathbf{M_q} \dot{\mathbf{G}}^{\mathrm{T}}\right) \\
\boldsymbol{\eta}_\mathbf{x} &= \mathbf{J}^{-\mathrm{T}} \boldsymbol{\eta}_\mathbf{q} = \mathbf{G} \boldsymbol{\eta}_\mathbf{q}
\end{aligned} \tag{9}$$

where (7) still holds. Matrix-dependence on joint space variables can be noted as advantageous. These are measured and used for computation of the direct kinematic problem (DKP).

3.3 Planar parallel manipulator FIVEBAR

For experimental setup a planar parallel structure with $n_\mathbf{q} = 2$ degrees of freedom, named FIVEBAR (cf. fig. 1), is used. The end effector of the manipulator is connected to the drives by two independent kinematic chains. Cranks and rods of the manipulator are made of carbon fiber to reduce the weight of moved masses, thus being well-suited for high-speed operation with a maximum velocity v = *5 m/s* and acceleration a = *70 m/s²* in Cartesian space. The control system consists of a PC running QNX and an IEEE 1394 FireWire link to the inverters ensuring short cycle time and sufficient bandwidth for control purposes.
Applying deduced discrete modeling scheme requires determination of manipulators Jacobian, which can be calculated via internal link forces $\mathbf{f}_\mathrm{B} = \left[f_{\mathrm{B}_1} \quad f_{\mathrm{B}_2}\right]^{\mathrm{T}}$. Use of static relations of the end effector results in

$$\mathbf{f}_\mathrm{B} = \left[s_1 \quad s_2\right]^{-1} \mathbf{f}_{\mathrm{ext}} = \mathbf{S}^{-1} \mathbf{f}_{\mathrm{ext}} \tag{10}$$

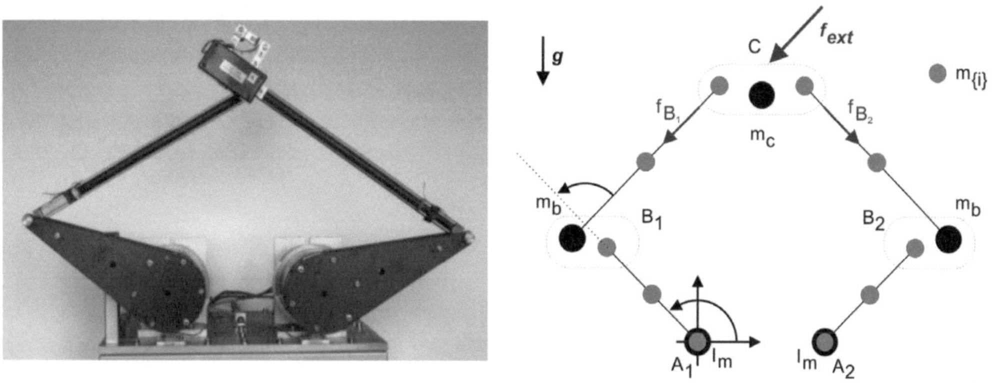

Fig. 1: Planar parallel manipulator FIVEBAR and its discrete model

Considering that the links connected to the end effector do not transmit transverse forces (no elasticities featured), the Jacobian of the end effector point C can be deduced as

$$\mathbf{G}^{+} = \operatorname{diag}\{\mathbf{J}_{B_1}, \mathbf{J}_{B_2}\}^{T} \operatorname{diag}\{\mathbf{s}_1, \mathbf{s}_2\} \mathbf{S}^{-1} = \mathbf{J}_C^{T} = \mathbf{J}^{T} \tag{11}$$

representing the Jacobian of the parallel manipulator. Moreover, Jacobians of passive joints can be determined via analytical differentiation of passive joint position in operational space, which enables calculation of all other Jacobians as a linear combination. Hence the discrete modeling scheme can be applied.

4. Control design

Control design is based on a torque driven interface to the inverters at bottom layer. Its concepts first and foremost aim at tracking a trajectory specified by position, velocity and acceleration $\{\mathbf{x}_{ref}, \dot{\mathbf{x}}_{ref}, \ddot{\mathbf{x}}_{ref}\}$ in the base frame of the robot.

In general two different approaches for design of the subordinated drive-controller can be noted: linear control concepts based upon linearization techniques on the one hand and nonlinear ones such as sliding mode control on the other hand. Both provide a uniform trajectory interface for the top layer, which ensures hybrid control within the task-frame formalism, as discussed in (Kolbus et al., 2005), (Finkemeyer, 2004). Thus the manipulator is not restricted to position control, but extendable to force control in operational space.

4.1 Linearization techniques: Feedback vs. Feedforward

Classical linear control concepts can be applied, if linearization techniques are used. These can be distinguished between exact feedback linearization and computed torque feedforward linearization (Isidori, 1995), (Spong & Vidyasagar, 1989), (Sciavicco & Siciliano, 2001).

The implementation of the inverse dynamic control is illustrated in fig. 2 where the manipulator is assumed to be nonredundant. In case of redundancy the principle remains the same, where additional actuator degrees of freedom can be used for internal pre-stressing of mechanical structure (Kock, 2001). The model derived in section 3 is used to set the input to

$$\tau = \mathbf{G}^{-1}\mathbf{M}_x\mathbf{u} + \mathbf{G}^{-1}\xi_x, \quad \xi_x = \mathbf{C}_x\dot{\mathbf{x}} + \eta_x \tag{12}$$

where **u** is the new external reference input. Its basic feature is the use of measured values for linearization. Equation (12) renders the closed loop dynamical behavior of the overall system to a set of decoupled double integrators in Cartesian space.
Computed torque feedforward linearization to the contrary uses reference values instead of measured values. In implementation (cf. fig. 3) derived model is used to calculate the input as

$$\boldsymbol{\tau} = \mathbf{G}^{-1}\mathbf{M}_x\ddot{\mathbf{x}}_{\text{ref}} + \mathbf{G}^{-1}\boldsymbol{\xi}_{x,\text{ref}} + \mathbf{M}_q\mathbf{v}\,,\quad \boldsymbol{\xi}_{x,\text{ref}} = \mathbf{C}_x\dot{\mathbf{x}}_{\text{ref}} + \boldsymbol{\eta}_x\,,\quad \mathbf{M}_q = \mathbf{G}^{-1}\mathbf{M}_x\mathbf{G}^{-T} \tag{13}$$

where **v** represents the new reference input, analogues to exact feedback linearization. A set of double integrators is obtained by eq. (13) for closed loop dynamics, this time, however, in joint space.

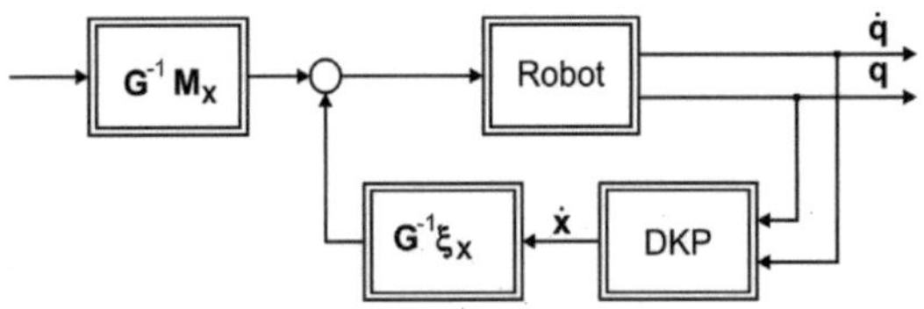

Fig. 2: Feedback linearization

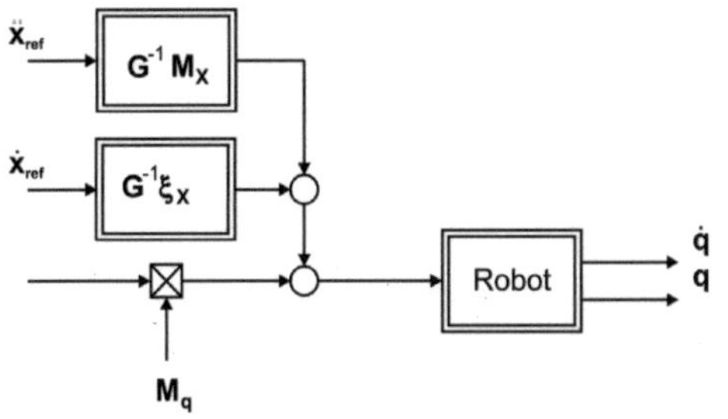

Fig. 3: Feedforward linearization

The delay of the inverters affects the described linearization. Instead of a set of double integrators, feedback (eq. (12)) and feedforward linearization (eq. (13)) results in

$$T_{\text{V}}u_i = T_{\text{el}}x_i^{(3)} + x_i^{(2)}\,,\quad T_{\text{V}}v_i = T_{\text{el}}q_i^{(3)} + q_i^{(2)}\,,\quad i \in \{1,\dots,n_{\mathbf{q}}\} \tag{14}$$

as description for the linearized subsystem, respectively, where T_{el} denotes the delay of the inverter and T_{V} represents the virtual inertia of the linearized mechanical system. In absence of model uncertainties linearization techniques yield $T_{\text{V}} = 1$. Nonlinear terms have been neglected here, but are taken into account as disturbances for the design of the top layer axis controller.
Comparing both concepts reveals important aspects: Whereas feedback linearization results in control in operational space, e.g. centralized control, feedforward linearization leads to decentralized control in joint space. The fact, that in general for parallel structures the IKP is easier to solve than the DKP, suggests the use of computed torque feedforward linearization for parallel manipulators. The advantage of feedback linearization on the other hand is the decoupling of axes - single controllers do not compete.
In case of FIVEBAR the direct kinematic problem is of nearly the same complexity as the inverse one, thus both concepts will be shown.

4.2 Linear cascaded control schemes: Centralized vs. Decentralized

Based upon linearization techniques described in former section, cascaded control schemes can be developed. Following (Sciavicco & Siciliano, 2001) due to their difference in linearization, they can be denoted as centralized control in case of feedback linearization on the one hand and decentralized control or computed torque control on the other hand.

Design is based upon the linearized subsystem given by eq. (14), resulting in a cascaded control scheme, see fig 4. and fig. 5.

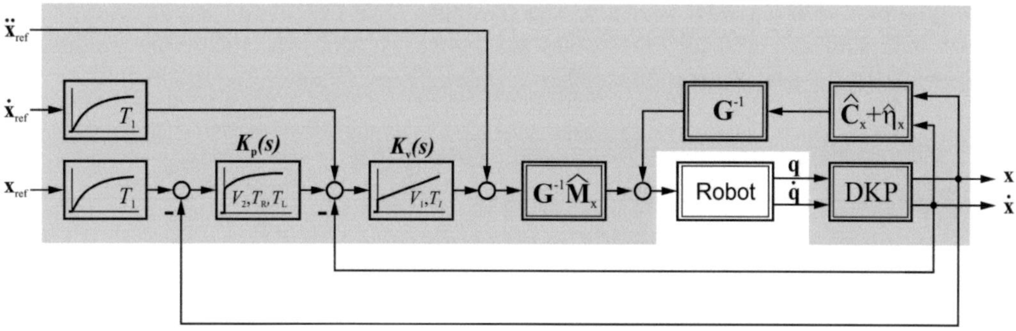

Fig. 4: Cascade control / centralized control

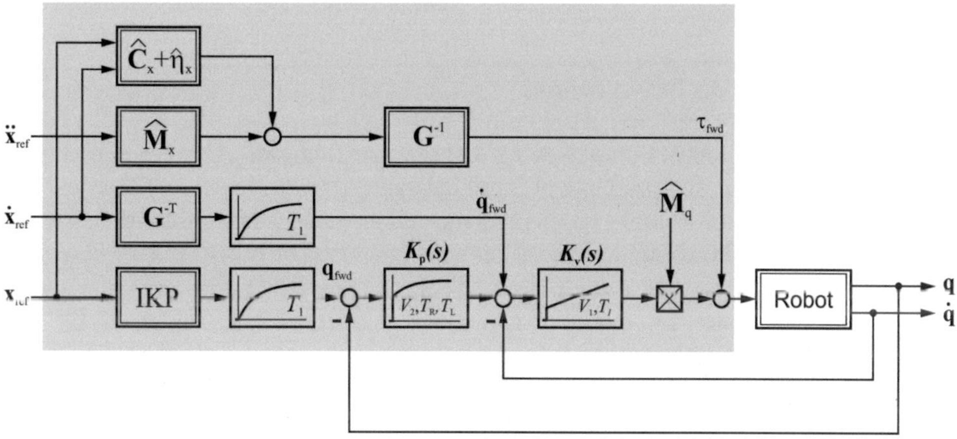

Fig. 5: Computed torque control / decentralized control

The control laws - common for both control schemes - are described by transfer functions

$$K_v(s) = V_1 \frac{T_i s + 1}{T_i s}, \quad K_p(s) = V_2 \frac{T_R s + 1}{T_L s + 1} \tag{15}$$

The parameters can be derived by symmetrical optimum design (Leonhard, 1996), which maximizes the phase margin of control system and ensures stability in presence of model uncertainties. The inherent overshoot of the velocity controller needs to be compensated by the outer loop. Therefore, a simple proportional control law is insufficient and replaced by a PTD-controller that suppresses the overshot and offers better performance. By using the damping $D_p = D_v = 1$ as parameter for closed loop design of velocity- and position-cascade one obtains

$$\begin{aligned} V_1 &= \frac{1}{3T_{el}}, \quad T_i = 9T_{el} \\ V_2 &= \frac{4}{81T_{el}}, \quad T_R = 3T_{el}, \quad T_L = T_i \end{aligned} \tag{16}$$

A more detailed discussion can be found in (Leonhard, 1996).
Alternatively, parameters can be determined by comparing the denominator of the closed loop dynamics with a model function. The damping D of one complex pole pair can be chosen independently and all other poles are placed on real axis. Following the idea of minimizing the integral of disturbance step response, the parameters are obtained as

$$\begin{aligned} V_1 &= \frac{5D^2+1}{16D^2 T_{\mathrm{el}}}, & T_i &= \frac{4T_{\mathrm{el}}(5D^2+1)}{1+2D^2} & & \\ V_2 &= \frac{1}{4T_{\mathrm{el}}(1+2D^2)}, & T_R &= 4T_{\mathrm{el}}, & T_L &= T_i \end{aligned} \tag{17}$$

which is discussed more widely in (Brunotte, 1999).
Whereas first design aims at maximizing phase margin and therefore targets robustness, the second one tends to optimize feedforward dynamics and disturbance rejection. The second design is preferable on parallel robots due to their high accelerations.

4.3 Disturbance observer based control

To improve disturbance rejection the concept of disturbance observers is well known in literature. This method focuses on observing disturbances and using them as a feedforward signal. A special concept, the principle of input balancing as introduced by (Brandenburg & Papiernik, 1996) offers advantages on tracking as well as disturbance rejection. Its core idea consists of a direct feed-through in forward control amended by a disturbance observer. In contrast to classical observers (Luenberger, 1964), (Lunze, 2006) this principle uses the controlled velocity plant as model for observing disturbances, which leads to an improvement in command action with improved robustness against external disturbances. Formerly intended for linear systems the linearization techniques presented in section 4.1 ensure using input balancing for robot control. Based on the linearized subsystem given by eq. (14) the control structure is illustrated in fig. 6.

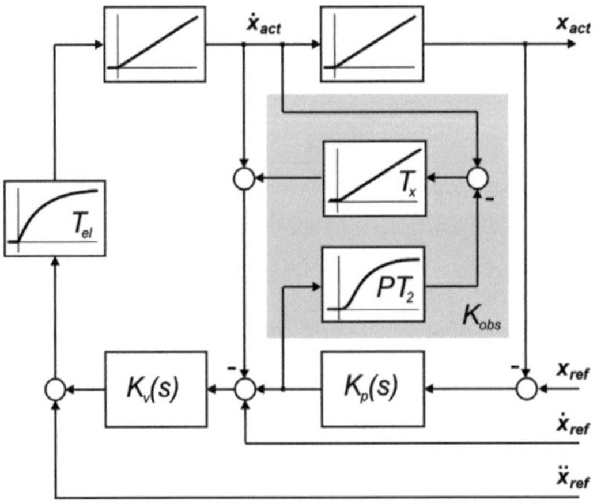

Fig. 6: Input balancing with centralized control

For computed torque control operational space references and measured values have to be replaced by joint space variables.

The control laws are described by transfer functions

$$\begin{aligned} &K_v(s) = V_1, && K_p(s) = V_2 \\ &K_{PT_2}(s) = \frac{1}{\left(\frac{s}{\omega_0}\right)^2 + \frac{2D_v}{\omega_0}s + 1}, && K_x(s) = \frac{1}{T_x s} \end{aligned} \tag{18}$$

Here $K_{PT_2}(s)$ represents the model of the closed loop velocity cascade, the disturbance-model is matched by an integrator $K_x(s)$. Using $D_p = 1$ for damping in position control loop leads to parameters

$$\begin{aligned} &V_1 = \frac{1}{3T_{\mathrm{el}}}, \quad V_2 = \frac{1}{9T_{\mathrm{el}}} \\ &\frac{2D_v}{\omega_0} = 3T_{\mathrm{el}}, \quad \frac{1}{\omega_0^2} = 3T_{\mathrm{el}}^2, \quad T_x = 9T_{\mathrm{el}} \end{aligned} \tag{19}$$

for control.

Using this control concept, an improvement in trajectory tracking compared to classical cascaded control schemes can be expected - due to the observer. On the other hand model uncertainties nonetheless have impact on the dynamical behavior (Wobbe et. al., 2006).

4.4 Sliding mode control

An approach to address an uncertain model is sliding mode control. The basic concept has been discussed by (Utkin, 1977) and was taken up by (Slotine, 1983) with a general definition of sliding surfaces and boundary layers to lessen the effect of chattering. This section focuses on control via sliding mode of first order, see fig. 7 - an extension to higher order sliding modes to reduce chattering can be found in the works of (Levant & Friedman, 2002).

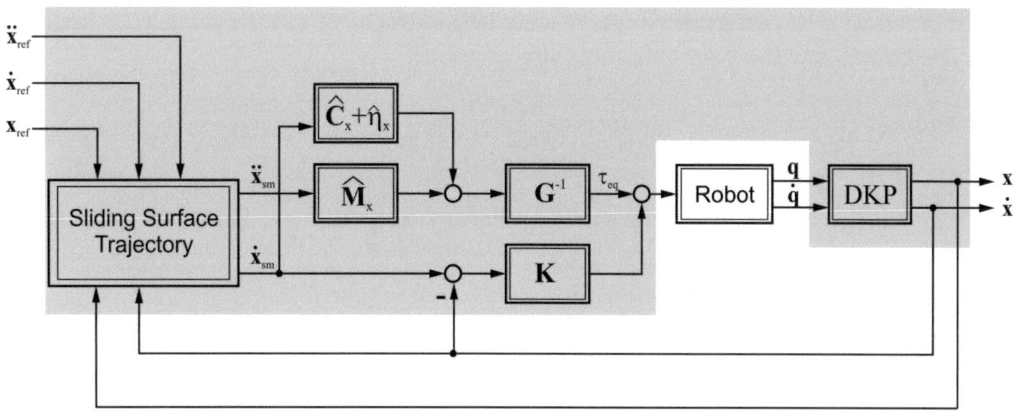

Fig. 7: Sliding mode control using continuous sliding surfaces

On contrary to linear design concepts as cascade control and input balancing sliding mode control is based on nonlinear design and focuses on the dynamics of the tracking-error (Wobbe et al., 2007), considered and defined by a sliding surface

$$\mathbf{s} = \dot{\tilde{\mathbf{x}}} + \mathbf{\Lambda}\tilde{\mathbf{x}}\,, \quad \tilde{\mathbf{x}} = \mathbf{x}_{\text{act}} - \mathbf{x}_{\text{ref}} \tag{20}$$

with a positive definite matrix $\mathbf{\Lambda}$. The error is restricted to the sliding surface by modifying the reference trajectory and computing a virtual trajectory $\{\mathbf{x}_{\text{sm}}, \dot{\mathbf{x}}_{\text{sm}}, \ddot{\mathbf{x}}_{\text{sm}}\}$ with

$$\mathbf{x}_{\text{sm}} = \mathbf{x}_{\text{ref}} - \mathbf{\Lambda}\int_0^t \tilde{\mathbf{x}}\,\mathrm{d}t \tag{21}$$

This trajectory definition is used for the computation of the control law under use of equivalent dynamics set point $\boldsymbol{\tau}_{\text{eq}}$ in Filippov's sense (Slotine & Li, 1991), (Filippov, 1988)

$$\boldsymbol{\tau} = \boldsymbol{\tau}_{\text{eq}} - \mathbf{u} = \mathbf{G}^{-1}(\hat{\mathbf{M}}_{\mathbf{x}}\ddot{\mathbf{x}}_{\text{sm}} + \hat{\mathbf{C}}_{\mathbf{x}}\dot{\mathbf{x}}_{\text{sm}} + \hat{\boldsymbol{\eta}}_{\mathbf{x}}) - \mathbf{K}\mathbf{s} \tag{22}$$

where $\hat{\mathbf{M}}_{\mathbf{x}}$, $\hat{\mathbf{C}}_{\mathbf{x}}$ and $\hat{\boldsymbol{\eta}}_{\mathbf{x}}$ denote estimates of manipulator dynamics. The additional input $\mathbf{u}$ ensures stability and precise tracking in the presence of model uncertainties. It copes chattering formally associated with sliding mode control by the continuous sliding surface. The control law features no discontinuities such as switching terms. The reduced tendency of chattering is gained at the price of slightly reduced - but still outstanding - performance compared to original switching concept.

The performance of control by sliding surfaces depends on matrix $\mathbf{\Lambda}$ with the delay of the inverter being its most limiting factor. Thus parameters of sliding mode control are obtained by

$$\mathbf{\Lambda} = \frac{1}{3T_{\text{el}}}\begin{bmatrix} 1 & 0 \\ 0 & 1 \end{bmatrix}, \quad \mathbf{K} = \mathbf{G}^{-1}\hat{\mathbf{M}}_{\mathbf{x}}\mathbf{\Lambda} \tag{23}$$

An improvement in performance can be obtained by focusing on the integral of tracking error. Redefinition of the corresponding sliding surface

$$\mathbf{s} = \dot{\tilde{\mathbf{x}}} + 2\mathbf{\Lambda}\tilde{\mathbf{x}} + \mathbf{\Lambda}^2\int_0^t \tilde{\mathbf{x}}\,\mathrm{d}t \tag{24}$$

forces integral action and thus improves disturbance rejection.

5. Comparison of control concepts

Presented design concepts feature different characteristics. As essential among others the performance of feedforward-dynamic, i.e. command action on the one hand and the robustness against parameter variation, i.e. disturbance rejection are paid special attention, revealing hints for range of application. Theoretical analysis here is based on the closed loop dynamics considering applied linearization techniques.

5.1 Performance

Performance of control concepts can be subdivided into groups: the linearization technique and closed loop system dynamics of an equivalent linear system.

Referring to linearization three different methods have been presented: decentralized, centralized and equivalent control. Performance analysis is widely spread in literature (Whitcomb et al., 1993), (Slotine, 1985) and kept rather short for sake of simplicity. Main characteristics are - referring to weak points of each technique - an influence of measurement noise for centralized control, drift of linearization in case of trajectory following error in decentralized control and both - however to a far lesser extend - for equivalent control.

Closed loop system dynamics reveal different aspects on command action and disturbance rejection, see tab.1

	Cascade (1)	Cascade (2)	Input balancing
FF	$\frac{4}{(9T_{el}s+1)^2(9T_{el}s+4)}$	$\frac{1}{(4T_{el}s+1)^3}$	$\frac{1}{(3T_{el}s+1)^3}$
DIST	$\frac{2187T_{el}^3 s(T_{el}s+1)}{(9T_{el}s+1)^2(9T_{el}s+4)(3T_{el}s+1)}$	$\frac{256T_{el}^3 s(T_{el}s+1)}{(4T_{el}s+1)^4}$	$\frac{243T_{el}^3 s(T_{el}s+1)(3T_{el}^2 s^2+3T_{el}s+1)}{(3T_{el}s+1)^6}$

Tab. 1: Closed Loop Dynamics - Feedforward (FF) and Disturbance (DIST) of linear control schemes

Input balancing offers a good bandwidth for command action, firstly presented control design for cascade control (1) ranging up to 33% compared to this, which can be optimized up to 75% with optimized parameters (2). Static disturbances are rejected by each control scheme, with optimized cascade control providing good damping - outperformed just slightly by input balancing.

Sliding mode control in comparison to linear control schemes possesses nonlinear closed loop dynamics that can be subdivided into two parts. In case of absence of disturbances and model uncertainties, its dynamics are described by sliding, i.e. referring to eq. (20) and (24) the system output error $\tilde{\mathbf{x}}$ exponentially - with time constant $\frac{1}{\lambda}$ ($\frac{2}{\lambda}$ in case of integral action) - slides to zero. The system dynamics are matched by dynamics on the sliding surface. In case of disturbances, model uncertainties or improper initial conditions, additional dynamics are present, describing the reaching phase towards the sliding surface. Its convergence mainly depends on **K**, considering eq. (23) leads to a time constant $\frac{1}{\lambda}$.

The overall dynamics in case of disturbances **d** can thus be described by

$$\mathbf{M_x}\ddot{\tilde{\mathbf{x}}} + (2\mathbf{M_x}\mathbf{\Lambda} + \mathbf{C_x})\dot{\tilde{\mathbf{x}}} + (\mathbf{M_x}\mathbf{\Lambda} + \mathbf{C_x})\mathbf{\Lambda}\tilde{\mathbf{x}} = \mathbf{d} \tag{25}$$

for classical sliding mode control and

$$\mathbf{M_x}\dddot{\tilde{\mathbf{x}}} + (3\mathbf{M_x}\mathbf{\Lambda} + \mathbf{C_x})\ddot{\tilde{\mathbf{x}}} + (3\mathbf{M_x}\mathbf{\Lambda} + 2\mathbf{C_x})\mathbf{\Lambda}\dot{\tilde{\mathbf{x}}} + (\mathbf{M_x}\mathbf{\Lambda} + \mathbf{C_x})\mathbf{\Lambda}^2\tilde{\mathbf{x}} = \dot{\mathbf{d}} \quad (26)$$

for sliding mode control with integral action. For sake of simplicity inverter dynamics have been neglected. A consideration can be found in (Levant & Friedman, 2002) showing that dynamics are pushed to sliding of order two with similar dynamics.
Comparing sliding mode to linear control design reveals an offset in disturbance rejection for classical sliding mode control, which can be coped with integral action, cf. eq. (25) and (26). It can be seen that chosen parameters lead to similar closed loop dynamics as input balancing, however being nonlinear.

5.2 Robustness against model uncertainties

Robustness of the selected control scheme is an important issue when dealing with parallel robots. The control concepts that base on linearization techniques use an underlying linear controller to compensate model uncertainties and reject disturbances. Considering the control laws introduced in section 4 each drive is treated individually. Important system parameters for controller design are the inertia of the mechanical system T_v and the delay introduced by the inverter and communication T_el, cf. eq. (14).
The virtual inertia comprises the drive and parts of the structure. Although compensated by both linearization concepts, it varies in case of model uncertainties and payload changes. Considering the structure of the cascaded controller, as introduced in fig. 4 and 5, the transfer function for command action yields to

$$G_c(s) = \frac{G_\mathrm{PTD} G_\mathrm{PI} G_\mathrm{I1} G_\mathrm{PT1} G_\mathrm{I2}}{1 + G_\mathrm{PI} G_\mathrm{I1} G_\mathrm{PT1} + G_\mathrm{PTD} G_\mathrm{PI} G_\mathrm{I1} G_\mathrm{PT1} G_\mathrm{I2}} \quad (27)$$

The parameter uncertainties are included by an additional factor to the properties. The systems inertia and delay are thus described by $k_\mathrm{Tel} T_\mathrm{el}$ and $k_\mathrm{Tv} T_\mathrm{v}$, where T_el and T_v represent the values used for controller design. Thus, the transfer function, eq. (27), can be simplified by using eq. (17) to

$$\begin{aligned} G_C(s) &= \frac{4T_\mathrm{el}s + 1}{256T_\mathrm{el}^4 k_\mathrm{Tv} k_\mathrm{Tel} s^4 + 256T_\mathrm{el}^3 k_\mathrm{Tv} s^3 + 96T_\mathrm{el}^2 s^2 + 16T_\mathrm{el}s + 1} \\ &= \frac{a + 1}{k_\mathrm{Tel} k_\mathrm{Tv} a^4 + 4k_\mathrm{Tv} a^3 + 6a^2 + 4a + 1} \end{aligned} \quad (28)$$

To avoid the explicit solution of the fourth-order polynomial, the stability of the loop is analyzed using Hurwitz' criteria. This yields to the determinant of the matrix

$$|\mathbf{H}_3| = \left\| \begin{bmatrix} 256T_\mathrm{el}^3 k_\mathrm{Tv} & 16T_\mathrm{el} & 0 \\ 256T_\mathrm{el}^4 k_\mathrm{Tv} k_\mathrm{Tel} & 96T_\mathrm{el}^2 & 1 \\ 0 & 256T_\mathrm{el}^3 k_\mathrm{Tv} & 16T_\mathrm{el} \end{bmatrix} \right\| = 2^{16} T_\mathrm{el}^6 k_\mathrm{Tv} \left(6 - k_\mathrm{Tel}\right) \quad (29)$$

The inequalities derived from the matrix are linearly dependent. To ensure stability there is no limitation to factor k_Tv, whereas the variation of the delay T_el is restricted by

$$|\mathbf{H}_3| > 0 \Leftrightarrow 6 - k_{\mathrm{Tel}} > 0 \Leftrightarrow k_{\mathrm{Tel}} < 6 \tag{30}$$

which is illustrated in fig. 10. Besides stability, dynamic behavior of the control structure is important. It is analyzed by the root locus of the system. Eq. (28) shows the general structure of denominator. The pole placement is independent of T_{v} and scaled by the delay T_{el}. Thus, the location of the poles with respect to the parameters k_{Tel} and k_{Tv} is examined in a normalized diagram. The results are shown in fig 8.

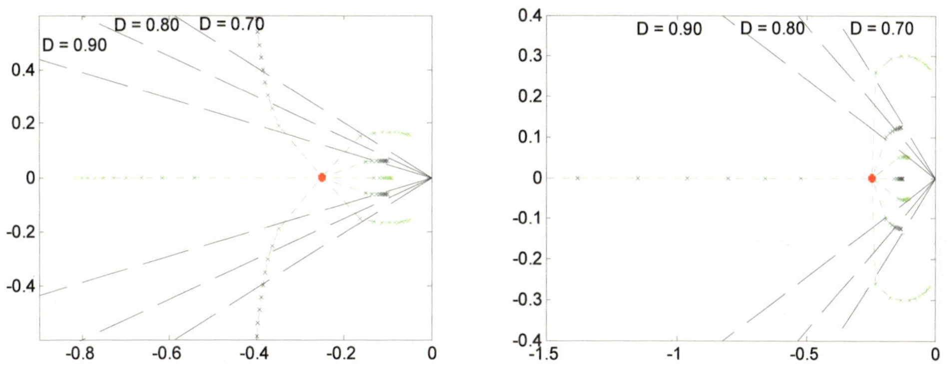

Fig. 8: Map of poles. Left: Mass is varied, right: Variation of delay. Green indicates that the real value is larger then that used for controller design. The red dot marks the location in case of no variation.

Since the factors k_{Tel} and k_{v} are linearly scaled the plots reveal the sensitivity to parameter variation. The actual damping of the outer loop is affected heavily by parameter mismatch. The step response in fig. 9 illustrates the performance loss. Errors in the delay are again more critical.

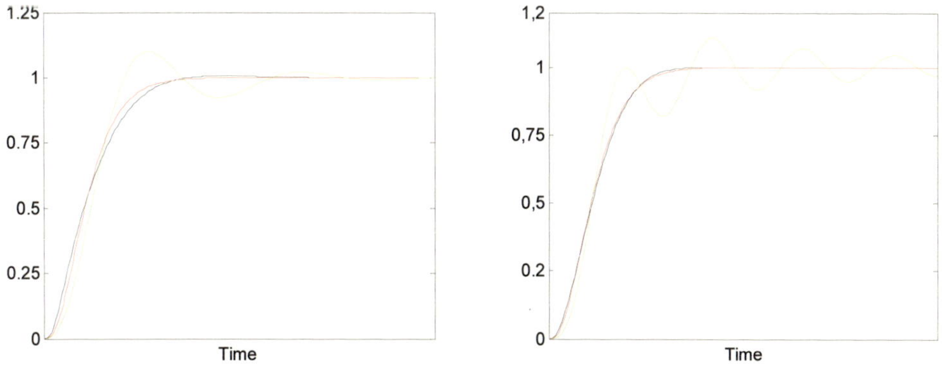

Fig. 9: Step response of closed loop. Left: Variation of mass. Right: Variation of delay. The response with correct parameters is plotted in red. Green indicates that the real value is larger then that used for controller design, black marks the opposite.

Assuming parameter variation in case of input balancing the transfer function can be expressed by

$$G_{\mathrm{IB}}(s) = \frac{a^3 + 3a^2 + 3a + 1}{k_{\mathrm{Tv}}k_{\mathrm{Tel}}a^6 + 3k_{\mathrm{Tv}}(1 + k_{\mathrm{Tel}})a^5 + 3(1 + k_{\mathrm{Tv}}k_{\mathrm{Tel}} + 3k_{\mathrm{Tv}})a^4 + (3k_{\mathrm{Tv}} + 11)a^3 + 15a^2 + 6a + 1} \quad (31)$$

where $a = 3T_{\mathrm{el}}s$ and controller parameters are set according to eq. (19). Though, the relative degree of the system is still three, no poles and zeros are cancelled out, which leads to a more complex dynamic. The stability limits are analyzed by Hurwitz criteria again

$$\mathbf{H}_5 = \begin{bmatrix} 3k_{\mathrm{Tv}}(1 + k_{\mathrm{Tel}}) & 9k_{\mathrm{Tv}} + 11 & 6 & 0 & 0 \\ k_{\mathrm{Tv}}k_{\mathrm{Tel}} & 3(1 + k_{\mathrm{Tv}}k_{\mathrm{Tel}} + 3k_{\mathrm{Tel}}) & 15 & 1 & 0 \\ 0 & 3k_{\mathrm{Tv}}(1 + k_{\mathrm{Tel}}) & 9k_{\mathrm{Tv}} + 11 & 6 & 0 \\ 0 & k_{\mathrm{Tv}}k_{\mathrm{Tel}} & 3(1 + k_{\mathrm{Tv}}k_{\mathrm{Tel}} + 3k_{\mathrm{Tel}}) & 15 & 1 \\ 0 & 0 & 3k_{\mathrm{Tv}}(1 + k_{\mathrm{Tel}}) & 9k_{\mathrm{Tv}} + 11 & 6 \end{bmatrix} \quad (32)$$

$|\mathbf{H}_i| > 0, i \in \{2,3,4,5\}$, where $\mathbf{H}_i$ are the upper left submatrices of $\mathbf{H}_5$

Due to the high system order several inequalities have to be taken into account that lead to the stability area shown in fig. 10. Compared to cascade control input balancing tolerates lesser parameter uncertainties. Moreover, stability depends on the accuracy of inertia, mirrored in parameter k_{Tv}, as well.

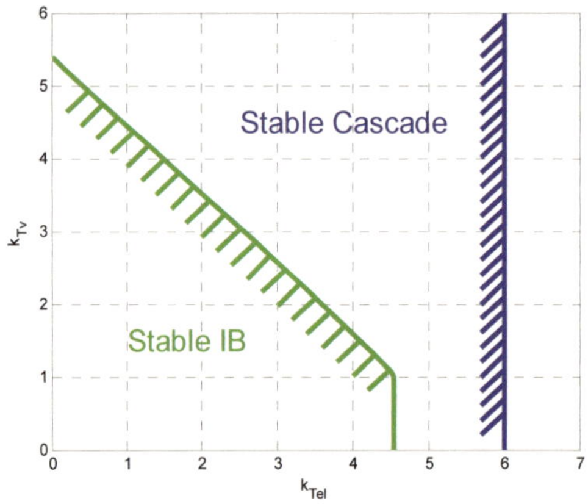

Fig. 10: Stability of linear control schemes dependent on variation

The pole-zero map of the transfer function, eq (31), is presented in fig. 11. Both parameters, inertia and delay, have significant impact on system dynamics. In line with cascade control scheme input balancing is more sensitive to variations, when parameters are assumed smaller than in reality. This is substantiated by the step response of the system, see fig. 12, which points out the lack of damping in case of wrong parameters. Both step responses (fig. 9, 12) are computed with the same parameter mismatch.

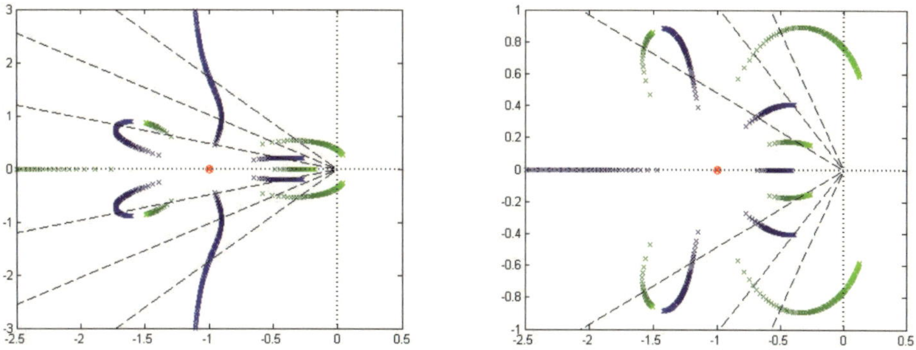

Fig 11: Map of poles. Left: Mass is varied, right: Variation of delay. Green indicates that the real value is greater than that used for controller design, whereas blue marks the opposite. The red dot marks the location in case of no variation. The dashed line indicates the damping cone for D=0.9, D=0.7 and D=0.5, respectively.

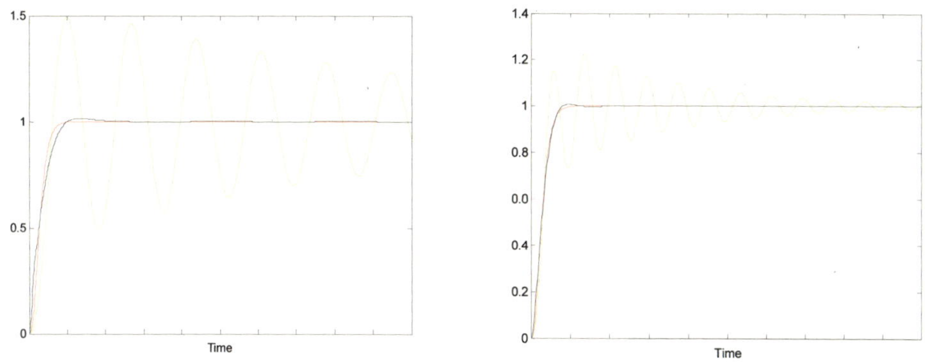

Fig. 12: Step response of closed loop (input balancing). Left: Variation of mass. Right: Variation of delay. The response with correct parameters is plotted in red. Green indicates that the real value is larger then that used for controller design, black marks the opposite.

Sliding mode control is more robust in view of parameter variation than control based upon linearized subsystems; it features consideration of parameter uncertainties $\tilde{\mathbf{M}}_\mathbf{x} = \hat{\mathbf{M}}_\mathbf{x} - \mathbf{M}_\mathbf{x}$, $\tilde{\mathbf{C}}_\mathbf{x} = \hat{\mathbf{C}}_\mathbf{x} - \mathbf{C}_\mathbf{x}$ and $\tilde{\boldsymbol{\eta}}_\mathbf{x} = \hat{\boldsymbol{\eta}}_\mathbf{x} - \boldsymbol{\eta}_\mathbf{x}$ in design. For a detailed analysis see (Slotine, 1985) where one can see that sliding mode control guarantees robustness against parameter uncertainties in case of integral action and is more robust than control schemes based upon linearization techniques.

6. Experimental results

For experimental evaluation, controller designs are implemented to the planar parallel manipulator FIVEBAR. For the sake of clarity a selection of the control schemes and design parameters presented in section 4 has been made. The focus is on centralized and decentralized control (with optimized parameters) and its comparison to disturbance observer based control via input balancing. Sliding mode control with integral action is presented as nonlinear control scheme to compare nonlinear design performance to linearization techniques based ones.

6.1 Experimental setup and performance criteria

For control purposes the concept of skill primitives is used. The main idea consists of specifying a task and a terminating condition that lead to execution of next skill primitive. We here use the position accuracy ε_{pos} as terminating condition for each axis separately.

Workspace of the parallel robot FIVEBAR is illustrated in fig 13. A common trajectory for all setups is used to guarantee comparable results. The selected path covers the workspace almost completely, including positions close to singularities. It consists of 6 parts, each resembled by a skill primitive. The trajectory is generated piecewise and terminates with both axes fulfilling specified position accuracy.

For evaluation of controller performance different criteria are used: Concerning tracking error, a time-integral of absolute tracking error (ITAE) $\Delta_{t,\mathbf{x}_i}$ is used. It is defined for each axis in Cartesian coordinates,

$$\Delta_{t,\mathbf{x}_i} = \int_{t_0}^{t_1} \left|\mathbf{x}_{i,\text{ref}} - \mathbf{x}_{i,\text{act}}\right| \mathrm{d}t \qquad (33)$$

respectively and gives a benchmark of in-time execution of trajectory.

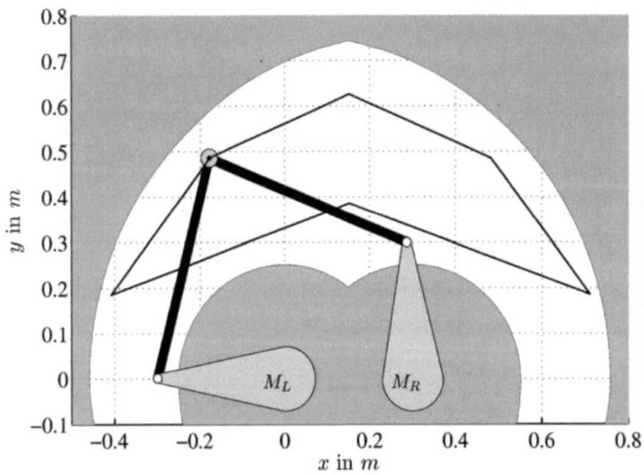

Specification of trajectory		
Velocity	$\lvert\dot{\mathbf{x}}\rvert_{\max}$	2 m/s
Acceleration	$\lvert\ddot{\mathbf{x}}\rvert_{\max}$	40 m/s^2
Jerk	$\lvert\dddot{\mathbf{x}}\rvert_{\max}$	600 m/s^3
Position accuracy	ε_{pos}	300 μm

Fig. 13: Workspace and experimental setup of FIVEBAR in initial position

Secondly, a position-integral of absolute Cartesian distortion (IACD) Δ_{A} is defined for benchmarking path-accuracy in operational space

$$\Delta_{\text{A}} = \oint_{x_{\text{ref}}} \left|y_{\text{ref}}(x_{\text{ref}}) - y_{\text{act}}(x_{\text{ref}})\right| \mathrm{d}x_{\text{ref}} \qquad (34)$$

It represents the absolute size of distortion areas and thus indicates accuracy of the end effector path with respect to the trajectory.

Moreover, settling time

$$t_{\text{settling}} = t_{\text{nextSKP}} - t_{\text{endSKP}} \tag{35}$$

is considered, where t_{endSKP} denotes time when the actual skill primitive ends and t_{nextSKP} represents the point of next skill primitive starting. They are defined by

$$\left|\tilde{\mathbf{x}}_i(t \geq t_{\text{nextSKP}})\right| \leq \varepsilon_{\text{pos}}, \quad t_{\text{endSKP}} = t \mid \left(\left|\dot{\mathbf{x}}_{\text{ref}}\right| = 0 \wedge \left|\ddot{\mathbf{x}}_{\text{ref}}\right| = 0\right) \tag{36}$$

In addition maximum tracking error $\Delta_{\text{trk},i}$ and maximum overshooting during settling time $\Delta_{\text{set},i}$ defined by

$$\begin{aligned} \Delta_{\text{trk},i} &= \max\left\{\left|\tilde{\mathbf{x}}_i(t)\right|\right\}, \quad t \in \{t_{\text{nextSKP}} \ldots t_{\text{endSKP}}\} \\ \Delta_{\text{set},i} &= \max\left\{\left|\tilde{\mathbf{x}}_i(t)\right|\right\}, \quad t \in \{t_{\text{endSKP}} \ldots t_{\text{nextSKP}}\} \end{aligned} \tag{37}$$

are evaluated.

Performance criteria could easily be extended - selected set is sufficient for an overview of performance instead of a claim to be overarching.

6.2 Data presentation

Plots of experimental results and data concerning trajectory are given in fig. 15-19, and used for benchmarks in the following.

It can be seen that overshooting during trajectory follow up is in general of higher value than during settling time, due to chosen high dynamics. Examining average settling time on centralized and decentralized control reveals that disturbance observers improve this property as expected by theoretical analysis in section 5. Furthermore maximum overshooting during trajectory follow up is reduced, which is also reflected in Cartesian distortion error, cf. fig. 14(b).

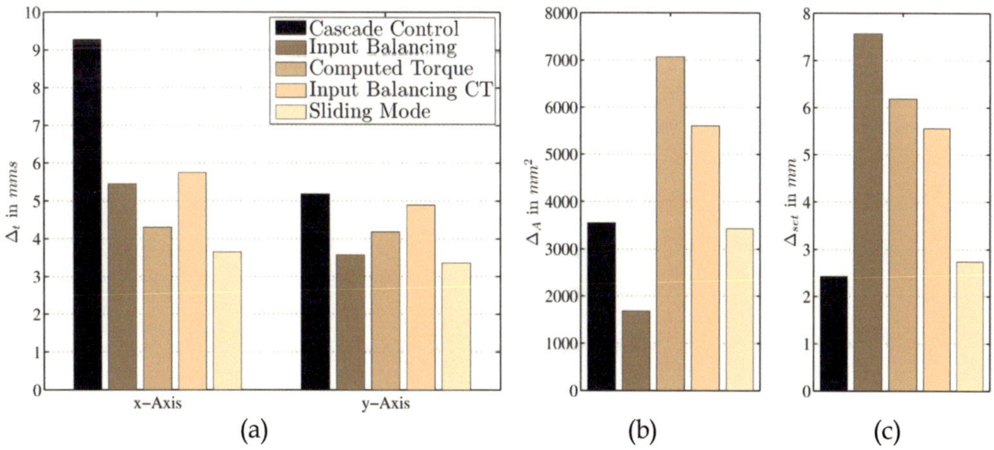

Fig. 14: Time integral of tracking error (a), Cartesian distortion (b) and maximum overshooting during settling time (c)

In comparing both linearization techniques with respect to Cartesian distortion, cf. fig. 14(a), and maximum overshooting during settling time, cf. fig. 14(c), it can be seen that cascade control with exact feedback linearization seems of better quality than computed torque control. The reason can be found in focus of control. While cascade control is operating in Cartesian space, computed torque addresses joint space. Thus an appropriate error in joint space is nonlinear (depending on position) transformed into Cartesian space.
Concerning nonlinear control design it can be seen that sliding mode control exhibits an overall up to best performance. All criteria except settling time range in high performance being only outperformed by input balancing concerning Cartesian distortion (fig. 14(b)). This is met by a far lesser overshooting during settling time (fig 14(c)) which substantiates the performance of sliding mode control. Due to inclusion of uncertainties in design its disturbance rejection during trajectory following up equals observer performance via input balancing. Its advantage compared to linear based controller design lies within its robustness against model uncertainties. As seen in section 5, linear design - especially input balancing - is more sensitive to variation of parameters, cf. fig. 11. This leads to loss of damping and can clearly be seen in settling times here (fig. 16). Input balancing shows large values in overshooting, indicating a parameter mismatch, while sliding mode control with same model-parameters offers far less overshooting. However, problems in positions close to workspace boundaries arise, which are indicated by a longer settling time after trajectory part 3 and 5, cf. fig. 19. In case of linear control schemes on the contrary these positions do not seem to have a significant impact on settling time, cf. fig. 15-18. The reasons can be found in nonlinear design, resulting in nonlinear closed loop dynamics and in design of sliding surface dynamics with integral action. Therefore a higher average settling time in case of sliding mode control can be seen. However, on other parts of the trajectory settling time is smaller than in case of all other control schemes.

	x	y
Δ_{trk}	10.7 mm	7.8 mm
Δ_{set}	1.7 mm	2.4 mm
$\bar{t}_{\text{settling}}$	0.75 s	

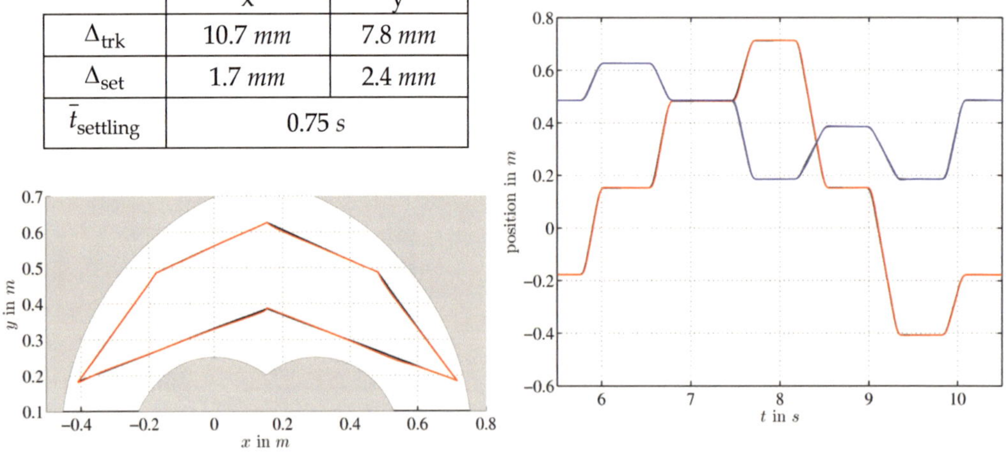

Fig. 15: Experimental Results on cascade control

	x	y
Δ_{trk}	8.1 mm	7.2 mm
Δ_{set}	7.6 mm	6.4 mm
$\bar{t}_{\text{settling}}$	0.43 s	

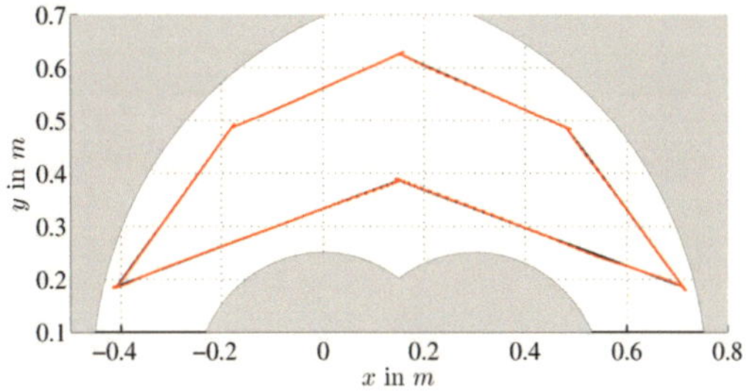

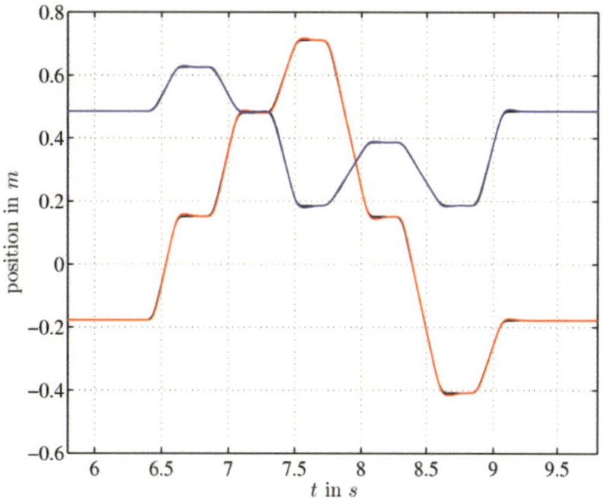

Fig. 16: Experimental Results on input balancing

	x	y
Δ_{trk}	14.2 mm	9.4 mm
Δ_{set}	1.6 mm	6.2 mm
$\bar{t}_{\text{settling}}$	0.91 s	

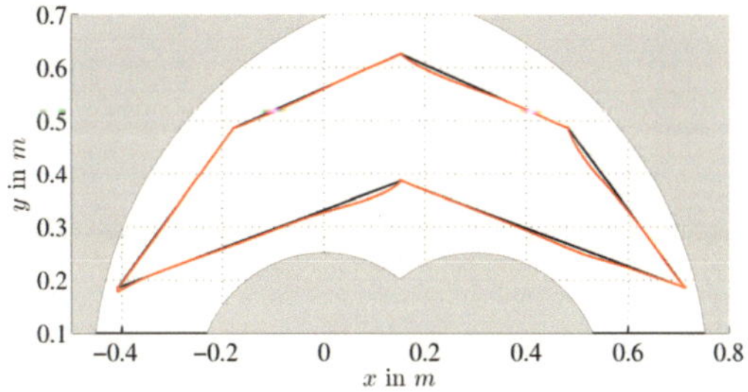

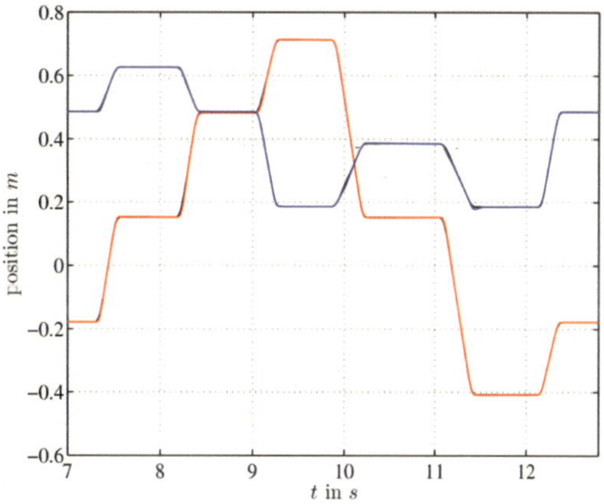

Fig. 17: Experimental Results on computed torque control

	x	y
Δ_{trk}	12.9 mm	9.7 mm
Δ_{set}	5.5 mm	2.8 mm
$\bar{t}_{\text{settling}}$	0.67 s	

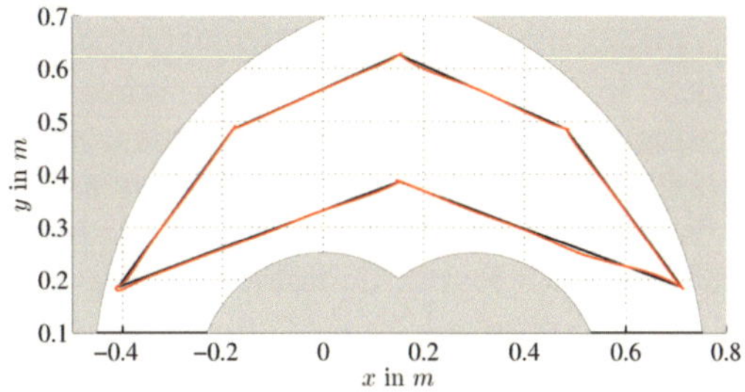

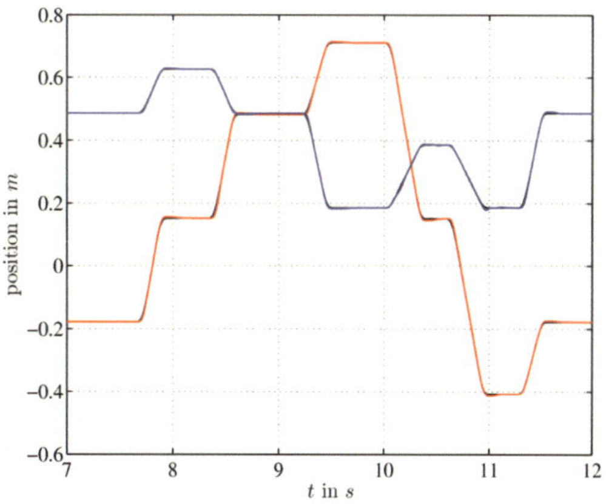

Fig. 18: Experimental Results on computed torque with input balancing

	x	y
Δ_{trk}	3.9 mm	6.6 mm
Δ_{set}	2.7 mm	1.8 mm
$\bar{t}_{\text{settling}}$	3.37 s	

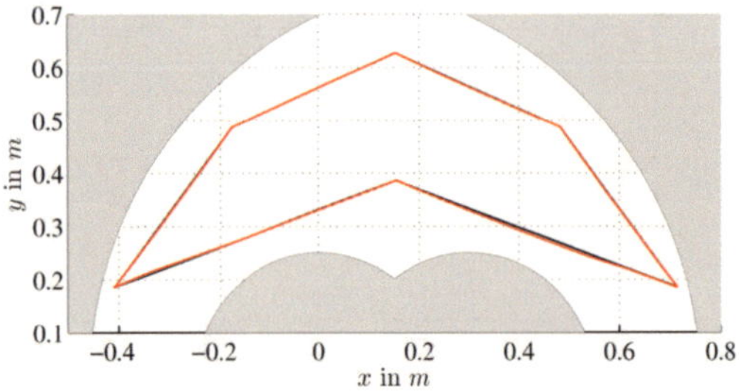

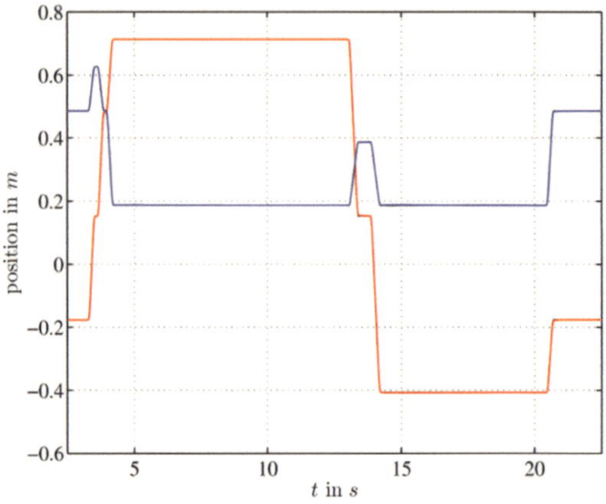

Fig. 19: Experimental Results on sliding mode control

Towards chattering associated with sliding mode control the continuous control lessens this tendency as can be seen in fig. 20. Here a single drive torque during a trajectory part is compared to cascade control. Although frequency analysis reveals energy in frequencies next to the characteristic ones of cascade control, it can be seen that these are damped well in contrast to classical sliding mode control with discontinuous control law.

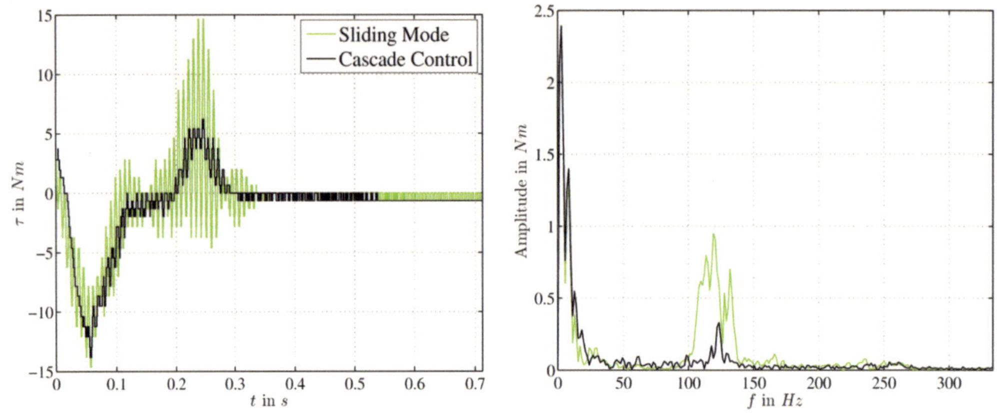

Fig. 20: Comparison of torques of linear and nonlinear design

Comparing presented results it can be seen that each control scheme features specific advantages, cf. tab. 2. The performance of each controller lies within its concept of design. Centralized, i.e. cascade control with feedback linearization guarantees tracking whereas disturbance rejection is not explicitly included in design process. Thus parameter uncertainties in modeling result in cross coupling of axes by inverse dynamic control scheme, cf. eq. (12) and (13). This can be matched by use of disturbance observers as the concept of input balancing, reducing Cartesian distortion and time integral of tracking error. As a drawback, however, a parameter mismatch leads to a loss of damping resulting in a higher overshooting during settling time. This can be improved by explicitly considering model- and parameter-uncertainties via sliding mode control at the cost of position dependent settling dynamics.

Decentralized, i.e. computed torque control reveals a good performance, and becomes handy when the direct kinematic problem is not computational efficient anymore. For control concepts considering wide range parameter variation other concepts have to be focused - such as adaptive control, which is discussed in (Hesselbach et al., 2004) with experimental benchmarking.

	CC	CT	IB	SMC
Path accuracy	+	o	++	+
Tracking	o	+	+	++
Axis coupling	-	-	-	+
Robustness against model uncertainties	o	o	-	+
Disturbance rejection	o	o	+	++
Axis independent design	+	o	+	+
Velocity noise	+	++	++	o
Chattering	++	++	+	o
Execution time	+	o	++	- (++)

Tab. 2: Properties of different control approaches: CC - cascade control, CT - computed torque control, IB - input balancing, SMC - sliding mode control

7. Conclusion

Different model based control architectures have been analyzed and compared by experimental studies. Experiments were carried out on a planar parallel robot optimized for high-speed operation.

Starting with a generalized scheme for discrete modeling of parallel structures, design of controllers are given at hand and discussed with respect to performance and robustness. Performance of each control design was analyzed and compared. In experimental results design concepts are validated, revealing that sliding mode control is a promising alternative to classical linear design concepts on parallel robots. Its main advantage is explicit inclusion of uncertainties to the design of the controller, whereas centralized and decentralized control just consider the nonlinearities on the innermost level.

Control by sliding surfaces demands a trajectory specified in position, velocity and acceleration. In the fields of robotics, however, providing a full trajectory is no real restriction, because these are planned jerk-bounded to prevent the mechanical structure from being damaged.

Nonetheless centralized and decentralized control feature certain advantages. Computed torque control is the best solution in case of complex direct kinematics, guaranteeing real-time execution. Best suppression of noisy velocity signals is featured since these do not influence the feedforward-linearization. Centralized control provides good path accuracy and is worth to be extended by input balancing in case of absence of parameter uncertainties improving Cartesian distortion. It is optimized towards disturbance rejection, however lacks robustness against parameter uncertainties.
In case of large parameter variations - for example caused by payloads - presented methods can be extended to parameter adaption, which sliding mode control and computed torque control fit best for.

8. Acknowledgements

This work was funded by the German Research Foundation (DFG) within the framework of the Collaborative Research Center SFB 562 "Robotic Systems for Handling and Assembly". We would like to thank QNX for providing licenses of the real-time operating system.

9. References

Bohn, C. (2000), Recursive parameter estimation for nonlinear continuous-time systems through sensitivity model-based adaptive filters, Ph.D. dissertation, Ruhr-Universität Bochum, 2000.

Brandenburg, G.; Papiernik, W. (1996). Feedforward and Feedback Strategies Applying the Principle of Input Balancing for Minimal Tracking Errors in CNC Machine Tools, Proc. of 4th International Workshop on Advanced Motion Control (AMC '96), pp. 612-618 vol.2., Mie, March 1996, Japan.

Brunotte, Ch. (1999). Regelung und Identifizierung von Linearmotoren fuer Werkzeugmaschinen, Ph.D. dissertation, University of Braunschweig (in German).

Dizioglu, B. (1966). Getriebelehre. Bd. 3. Dynamik. Vieweg, Braunschweig (in German).

Filippov, A.F. (1988). Differential equations with discontinuous right-hand sides, Springer, ISBN: 978-9027726995, Netherlands.

Finkemeyer, B. (2004). Robotersteuerungsarchitektur auf Basis von Aktionsprimitiven, Ph.D. dissertation, University of Braunschweig (in German).

Hesselbach, J.; Pietsch, I.T., Bier, C.C, Becker, O.T. (2004). Model-based Control of Plane Parallel Robots - How to Choose the Appropriate Approach?, *Proc. of 4th Chemnitz Parallel Kinematics Seminar (PKS2004)*, pp. 211-231, Chemnitz, April 2004, Germany.

Isidori, A. (1995). Nonlinear Control Systems, Springer, ISBN: 978-3540199168, London.

Kock, S. (2001). Parallelroboter mit Antriebredundanz, Ph.D. dissertation, Fortschritt-Berichte VDI, Duesseldorf - Braunschweig (in German).

Kolbus, M.; Reisinger, T.; Maaß, J. (2005). Robot Control Based on Skill Primitives, Proc. of IASTED Conf. on Robotics and Applications, pp. 260-266, Camebridge, October 2005, USA.

Leonhard, W. (1996). Control of Electrical Drives, Springer, ISBN: 978-3540418207, Berlin - Heidelberg - New York.

Levant, A.; Friedman, L. (2002). Higher Order Sliding Modes, In: Sliding Mode Control in Engineering (Control Engineering Series, 11), Perruquetti, W.; Barbot, J.-P. pp. 53-101, Marcel Dekker, Inc., ISBN: 978-0824706715, New York.

Luenberger, D.G. (1964). Observing the state ov a linear system, IEEE Transactions on Military Electronics, pp. 74-80.

Lunze, J. (2006). Regelungstechnik 2: Mehrgrößensysteme, Digitale Regelung, Springer, ISBN: 978-3540323358, Berlin

Merlet, J.-P. (2000). Parallel Robots, Kluwer Academic Publishers, Springer, ISBN: 978-1402041327, Netherlands.

Murray, R.M., Li, Z., Sastry, S.S. (1994), A mathematical introduction to robotic manipulation. CRC Press LLC, ISBN: 978-0849379819, USA.

Nakamura, Y. (1991). Advanced robotics: redundancy and optimization, Addison-Wesley Publishing Company, Inc., ISBN: 978-0201151985.

Sciavicco, L.; Siciliano, B. (2001). Modelling and Control of Robot Manipulators, Springer, ISBN: 978-1852332211, Berlin.

Stachera, K.; Schumacher, W. (2007). Simultaneous calculation of the direct dynamics of the elastic parallel manipulators, Proc. of the 13th IEEE IFAC International Conference on Methods and Models in Automation, pp. 863-868, Szczecin, August 2007, Poland.

Stachera, K.; Wobbe, F.; Schumacher, W. (2007). Jacobian-based derivation of dynamics equations of elastic parallel manipulators, Proc. of the IASTED Asian Conference on Modelling and Simulation (AsiaMS 2007), pp. 47-54, Beijing, October 2007, China.

Spong, M. W.; Vidyasagar, M. (1989). Robot dynamics and control, John Wiley & Sons, Inc., ISBN: 978-0471612438, USA.

Slotine, J.-J. (1983). Tracking Control of Nonlinear Systems Using Sliding Surfaces, Doctoral Dissertation, Massachusetts Institute of Technology.

Slotine, J.-J. (1985). The Robust Control of Robot Manipulators, International Journal of Robotics Research, vol. 4, no. 2, pp. 49-64, 1985.

Slotine, J.-J.; Li, W. (1991). Applied Nonlinear Control, Prentice Hall, ISBN: 978-0130408907, New Jersey.

Tsai, L.-W. (1999), Robot Analysis, Wiley-Interscience; ISBN: 978-0471325932, New York.

Utkin, V.I. (1977). A Survey: Variable Structure Systems with Sliding Modes, IEEE Transactions on Automatic Control , vol. 22, no. 2, pp. 212-222, April 1977.

Vetter, W. (1973). Matrix calculus operations and taylor expansions, SIAM Review, vol. 15, pp. 352–369, 1973.

Weinmann, A. (1991).Uncertain mod and robust control, Springer, ISBN: 978-3-211-82299-9, Wien.

Whitcomb, L.L.; Rizzi, A.; Koditschek, D.E. (1993), Comparative Experiments with a New Adaptive Controller for Robot Arms, IEEE Transactions on Robotics and Automation, vol. 9, no. 1, pp 59-70, Februar 1993.

Wobbe, F.; Schumacher, W.; Böske, W. (2006). Optimierte Antriebsreglerstrukturen zur Störunterdrückung, SPS/IPC/DRIVES 2006, Nürnberg (in German)

Wobbe, F.; Kolbus, M.; Schumacher, W. (2007). Continuous Sliding Surfaces versus Classical Control Concepts on Parallel Robots, Proc. of the 13th IEEE IFAC International Conference on Methods and Models in Automation, pp. 869-874, Szczecin, August 2007, Poland.

3

Vision Guided Robot Gripping Systems

Zdzislaw Kowalczuk and Daniel Wesierski
Gdansk University of Technology
Poland

1. Description of the past and recent trends in robot positioning systems

Industrial robots are used customary without any embedded sensors. They rely on a predictable pose of an object (position and orientation in 6 degrees of freedom, 6DOF) when performing the task of gripping parts located for instance on palettes or assembly lines. In practice though, a part can easily deviate from its ideal nominal location and a robot having no embedded sensors can miss or crash into the object. This would lead to damages and downtime of such an assembly line.

1.1 Manual and automated part acquisition

Manual part acquisition involves human employment. Clearly, it is not a good solution because humans are exposed to possible injuries, what increasing medical and social costs. Parts are often sharp and heavy. Yet, they are not sterile. Contamination (for instance, dust, oil, hair etc.) transferred to critical areas of the object leads to reduction in the quality of assembly (inevitably followed by product recalls).

Conventionally, automated gripping relied on intricate mechanical and electromechanical devices known as precision fixtures, which were utilized to ensure that the part was always at the programmed pose with respect to the robot. The design of such fixtures is though expensive, imposes design constraints, requires frequent maintenance, and has a reduced flexibility.

1.2 2D and 3D robot positioning

Over the years a variety of techniques have been developed to automate the process of gripping parts as an alternative to the existing manual part acquisition. Due to the rapidly evolving machine vision technology, vision sensors are playing today a key role in the three-dimensional robot positioning systems. They are not only cheaper but also far more effective.

A robot with an embedded vision sensor can have greater 'awareness' of the scene. It can grip objects, which can be non-fixtured, stacked or loosely located. Thus, it enables the robot to grip objects that are provided in racks, bins, or on pallets. Regardless of the presentation, a vision-guided robot can locate an object for further processing. This generic application of robotic guidance is applied in industries such as automotive for the location of power train components, sheet metal body parts, complete car bodies, and other parts used in assembly. Other industries such as food, pharmaceutical, glass and daily products apply vision guided robotic technology to their applications, as well.

As a response to the industry needs two major techniques have emerged: 2D and 3D machine vision. Two-dimensional machine vision is a well-developed technique and has been successfully implemented in the past years. 2D robotic vision systems locate the object in 3 degrees of freedom (x, y, and roll angle) based on one image. Consequently, the main limitation of 2D vision is its inability to compute part's rotation outside of a single plane. Unfortunately, this does not suffice in many applications that aim to eliminate, for instance, the precision fixtures in order to achieve greater versatility. 2D vision systems have proved to be very useful in picking objects from moving conveyors. Calibration of such robotic systems requires relatively simple methods.

The problem of creating a vision-guided robot positioning system for 3D part acquisition has apparently been studied before. 3D machine vision systems locate the object in 6 degrees of freedom (x, y, z and yaw, pitch, roll). We can distinguish here single-image systems which compute the object's pose iteratively using only one image, stereo systems which compute the pose analytically based on two overlapping images, and multi-vision systems, which combine the stereo-systems in a conventional manner to increase robustness and precision.

The 3D vision applications, which can position the robot to grip a rigid object using information derived only from one image, are gaining an increasing attention. The distances between the object features have to be known to the system beforehand for the purpose of computing the object's pose iteratively based on some minimized criteria. This information can be taken from a CAD model of the object in a model-based approach. Since only one camera is required, the cost of the whole plant is reduced, the cycle time is decreased, and the calibration process is made easier. Yet, finding features in one image (and not in multiple images) is simpler for image processing applications (IPAs). However, one-image methods have several drawbacks. One of them is that there are some critical configurations of points in 3D space, which could limit the number of potential features of the object for IPA. Another disadvantage is that these methods give good results if more than 5 points are found on the object what increases the processing time of IPA, and, more importantly, it increases the risk that not all points are found by IPA what can bring about stopping the plant and the entire assembly line.

Stereovision is thus far more often used in 3D positioning systems as it is simple to be implemented due to its analytical form. It computes the distance between the object features and the vision sensors, and derives all 3 coordinates of a feature. Having computed at least 3 features, the pose of the object can be determined. Commonly, more points are used to provide a certain degree of redundancy. This method has several disadvantages though: it is relatively sensitive to noise, identification of the corresponding features in two images can be very difficult (although the epipolar geometry of stereo cameras is very helpful here), and its application is confined to small objects due to a relatively small field of view. Multi-stereo-systems are used to compute the pose of bigger objects as they can examine them from opposite sides.

1.3 Retrieving information based on laser vision

Laser vision plays a vital role in 3D part acquisition tasks, as well. By painting a part's surface with a laser beam (coherent light), a laser triangulation sensor can determine the depth and the orientation of the surface observed. Although such measurements are very precise, the use of lasers has several drawbacks, such as long process of relating the features to the 'point cloud' data, shadowing/occlusion, as well as ergonomic issues when deployed near human operators. Moreover, lasers require using sophisticated interlock mechanisms, protective curtains, and goggles, which is very expensive.

1.4 Flexible assembly systems

Apart from integrating robots with machine vision, the assembly technology takes yet another interesting course. It aims to develop intelligent systems supporting human workers instead of replacing them. Such an effect can be gained by combining human skills (in particular, flexibility and intelligence) with the advantages of machine systems. It allows for creating a next generation of flexible assembly and technology processes. Their objectives cover the development of concepts, control algorithms and prototypes of intelligent assist robotic systems that allow workplace sharing (assistant robots), time-sharing with human workers, and pure collaboration with human workers in assembly processes. In order to fulfill these objectives new intelligent prototype robots are to be developed that integrate power assistance, motion guidance, advanced interaction control through sophisticated human-machine interfaces as well as multi-arm robotic systems, which integrate human skillfulness and manipulation capabilities.

Taking into account the above remarks, an analytical robot positioning system (Kowalczuk & Wesierski, 2007) guided by stereovision has been developed achieving the repeatability of ±1 mm and ±1 deg as a response to rising demands for safe, cost-effective, versatile, precise, and automated gripping of rigid objects, deviated in three-dimensional space (in 6DOF). After calibration, the system can be assessed for gripping parts during depalletizing, racking and un-racking, picking from assembly lines or even from bins, in which the parts are placed randomly. Such an effect is not possible to be obtained by robots without vision guidance. The Matlab Calibration Toolbox (MCT) software can be used for calibrating the system. Mathematical formulas for robot positioning and calibration developed here can be implemented in industrial tracking algorithms.

2. 3D object pose estimation based on single and stereo images

The entire vision-guided robot positioning system for object picking shall consist of three essential software modules: image processing application to retrieve object's features, mathematics involving calibration and transformations between CSs to grip the object, and communication interface to control the automatic process of gripping.

2.1 Camera model

In this chapter we explain how to map a point from a 3D scene onto the 2D image plane of the camera. In particular, we distinguish several parameters of the camera to determine the point mapping mathematically. These parameters comprise a model of the camera applied.

In particular, such a model represents a mathematical description of how the light reflected or emitted at points in a 3D scene is projected onto the image plane of the camera. In this Section we will be concerned with a projective camera model often referred to as a pinhole camera model. It is a model of a pinhole camera having its aperture infinitely small (reduced to a single point). With such a model, a point in space, represented by a vector characterized by three coordinates $\vec{r}^C = \begin{bmatrix} x^C & y^C & z^C \end{bmatrix}^T$, is mapped to a point $\vec{r}^S = \begin{bmatrix} x^S & y^S \end{bmatrix}^T$ in the sensor plane, where the line joining the point $\vec{r}^C$ with a center of projection O_C meets the sensor plane, as shown in Fig.1. The center of projection O_C, also called the camera center, is the origin of a coordinate system (CS) $\{\hat{X}_c, \hat{Y}_c, \hat{Z}_c\}$ in which the point $\vec{r}^C$ is defined (later on, this system we will be referred to as the Camera CS). By using the *triangle similarity rule* (confer Fig.1) one can easily see that the point $\vec{r}^C$ is mapped to the following point:

$$\vec{r}^C = \left[-f_C \frac{x_C}{z^C} \quad -f_C \frac{y_C}{z^C} \right]^T$$

that means that

$$\vec{r}^C = \left[-f_C \frac{x^C}{z^C} \quad -f_C \frac{y^C}{z^C} \right]^T \tag{1}$$

which describes the central projection mapping from Euclidean space $\mathbf{R}^3$ to $\mathbf{R}^2$. As the coordinate z^C cannot be reconstructed, the depth information is lost.

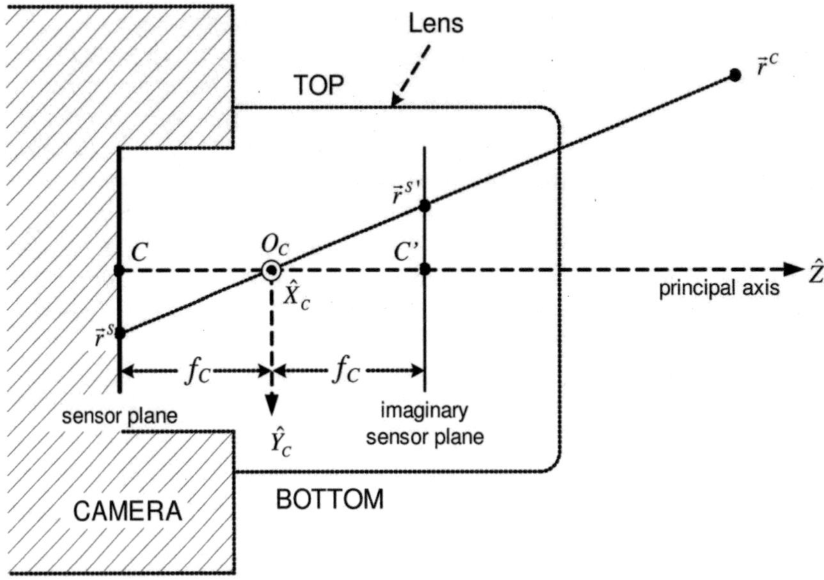

Fig. 1. Right side view of the camera-lens system

The line passing through the camera center O_C and perpendicular to the sensor plane is called the *principal axis* of the camera. The point where the principal axis meets the sensor plane is called a *principal point,* which is denoted in Fig. 1 as *C*.

The projected point $\vec{r}^S$ has negative coordinates with respect to the positive coordinates of the point $\vec{r}^C$ due to the fact that the projection inverts the image. Let us consider, for instance, the coordinate y^C of the point $\vec{r}^C$. It has a negative value in space because the axis $\hat{Y}_C$ points downwards. However, after projecting it onto the sensor plane it gains a positive value. The same concerns the coordinate x^C. In order to omit introducing negative coordinates to point $\vec{r}^S$, we can rotate the image plane by 180 deg around the axes $\hat{X}_C$ and

$\hat{Y}_C$ obtaining a non-existent plane, called an *imaginary sensor plane*. As can be seen in Fig. 1, the coordinates of the point $\vec{r}^{S'}$ directly correspond to the coordinates of point $\vec{r}^{C}$, and the projection law holds as well. In this Chapter we shall thus refer to the imaginary sensor plane.

Consequently, the central projection can be written in terms of matrix multiplication:

$$\begin{bmatrix} x^C \\ y^C \\ z^C \end{bmatrix} \rightarrow \begin{bmatrix} f_C \dfrac{x^C}{z^C} \\ f_C \dfrac{y^C}{z^C} \\ 1 \end{bmatrix} = \begin{bmatrix} f_C & 0 & 0 \\ 0 & f_C & 0 \\ 0 & 0 & 1 \end{bmatrix} \begin{bmatrix} \dfrac{x^C}{z^C} \\ \dfrac{y^C}{z^C} \\ 1 \end{bmatrix} \tag{2}$$

where $M = \begin{bmatrix} fc & 0 & 0 \\ 0 & fc & 0 \\ 0 & 0 & 1 \end{bmatrix}$ is called a *camera matrix*.

The pinhole camera describes the ideal projection. As we use CCD cameras with lens, the above model is not sufficient enough for precise measurements because factors like rectangular pixels and lens distortions can easily occur. In order to describe the point mapping more accurately, *i.e.* from the 3D scene measured in millimeters onto the image plane measured in pixels, we extend our pinhole model by introducing additional parameters into both the camera matrix M and the projection equation (2). These parameters will be referred to as *intern camera parameters*.

Intern camera parameters The list of intern camera parameters contains the following components:

- distortion
- focal length (also known as a camera constant)
- principal point offset
- skew coefficient.

Distortion In optics the phenomenon of distortion refers to lens and is called *lens distortion*. It is an abnormal rendering of lines of an image, which most commonly appear to be bending inward (*pincushion distortion*) or outward (*barrel distortion*), as shown in Fig. 2.

Fig. 2. Distortion: lines forming pincushion (left image) and lines forming a barrel (right image)

Since distortion is a principal phenomenon that affects the light rays producing an image, initially we have to apply the distortion parameters to the following normalized camera coordinates

$$\vec{r}^{\,C}_{Normalized} = \begin{bmatrix} \dfrac{x^C}{z^C} & \dfrac{y^C}{z^C} \end{bmatrix}^T = \begin{bmatrix} x_{norm} & y_{norm} \end{bmatrix}^T$$

Using the above and letting $h = x^2_{norm} + y^2_{norm}$, we can include the effect of distortion as follows:

$$\begin{aligned} x_d &= \left(1 + k_1 h^2 + k_2 h^4 + k_5 h^6\right) x_{norm} + dx_1 \\ y_d &= \left(1 + k_1 h^2 + k_2 h^4 + k_5 h^6\right) y_{norm} + dy_1 \end{aligned} \tag{3}$$

where x_d and y_d stand for normalized distorted coordinates and dx_1 and dx_2 are tangential distortion parameters defined as:

$$\begin{aligned} dx_1 &= 2k_3 x_{norm} y_{norm} + k_4\left(h^2 + 2x^2_{norm}\right) \\ dx_2 &= 2k_3\left(h^2 + 2y^2_{norm}\right) + 2k_4 x_{norm} y_{norm} \end{aligned} \tag{4}$$

The distortion parameters k_1 through k_5 describe both radial and tangential distortion. Such a model introduced by Brown in 1966 and called a "Plumb Bob" model is used in the MCT tool.

Focal length Each camera has an intern parameter called focal length f_c, also called a camera constant. It is the distance from the center of projection O_C to the sensor plane and is directly related to the focal length of the lens, as shown in Fig. 3. Lens focal length f is the distance in air from the center of projection O_C to the focus, also known as focal point.

In Fig. 3 the light rays coming from one point of the object converge onto the sensor plane creating a sharp image. Obviously, the distance d from the camera to an object can vary. Hence, the camera constant f_c has to be adjusted to different positions of the object by moving the lens to the right or left along the principal axis (here $\hat{Z}_c$-axis), which changes the distance $|OC|$. Certainly, the lens focal length always remains the same, that is $|OF| = const.$

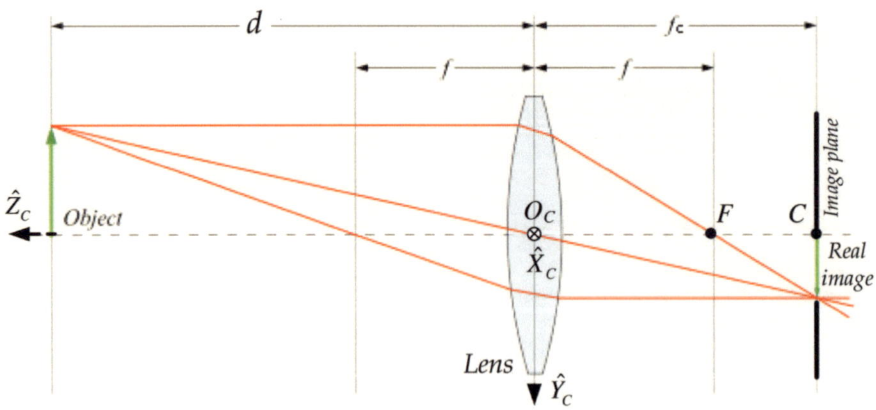

Fig. 3. Left side view of the camera-lens system

The camera focal length f_c might be roughly derived from the *thin lens formula*:

$$\frac{1}{f_C}+\frac{1}{d}=\frac{1}{f}\Rightarrow f_C=\frac{f\,d}{d-f} \tag{5}$$

Without loss of generality, let us assume that a lens has its focal length of f = 16 mm. The graph below represents the camera constant $f_C(d)$ as a function of the distance d.

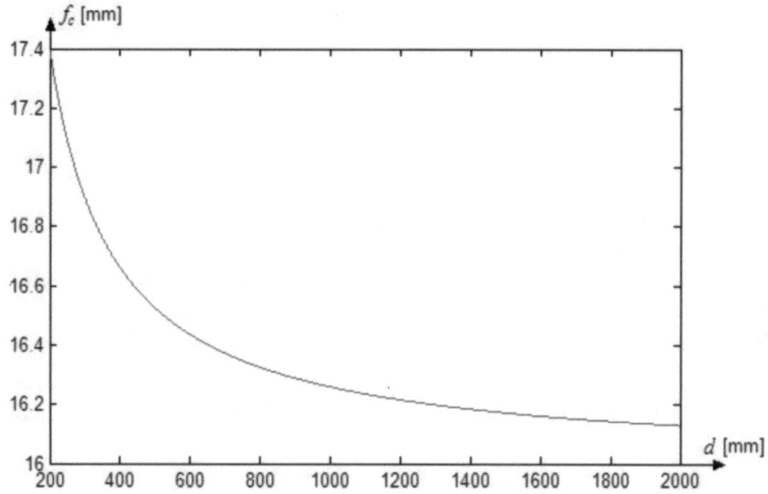

Fig. 4. Camera constant f_c in terms of the distance d

As can be seen from equation (5), when the distance goes to infinity, the camera constant equals to the focal length of the lens, what can be inferred from Fig. 4, as well. Since in industrial applications the distance ranges from 200 to 5000 mm, it is clear that the camera constant is always greater than the focal length of the lens. Because physical measurement of the distance is overly erroneous, it is generally recommended to use calibrating algorithms, like MCT, to extract this parameter. Let us assume for the time being that the camera matrix is represented by

$$K=\begin{bmatrix} f_C & 0 & 0 \\ 0 & f_C & 0 \\ 0 & 0 & 1 \end{bmatrix}$$

Principal point offset The location of the principal point C on the sensor plane is most important since it strongly influences the precision of measurements. As has already been mentioned above, the principal point is the place where the principal axis meets the sensor plane. In CCD camera systems the term principal axis refers to the lens, as shown in both Fig. 1 and Fig. 3. Thus it is not the camera but the lens mounted on the camera that determines this point and the camera's coordinate system.

In (1) it is assumed that the origin of the sensor plane is at the principal point, so that the Sensor Coordinate System is parallel to the Camera CS and their origins are only the camera constant away from each other. It is, however, not truthful in reality. Thus we have to compute a principal point offset $\begin{bmatrix} C_{0x} & C_{0y} \end{bmatrix}^{\mathrm{T}}$ from the sensor center, and extend the camera matrix by this parameter so that the projected point can be correctly determined in the Sensor CS (shifted parallel to the Camera CS). Consequently, we have the following mapping:

$$\begin{bmatrix} x^C & y^C & z^C \end{bmatrix}^{\mathrm{T}} \rightarrow \begin{bmatrix} f_C \dfrac{x^C}{z^C} + C_{Ox} & f_C \dfrac{x^C}{z^C} + C_{Oy} \end{bmatrix}^{\mathrm{T}}$$

Introducing this parameter to the camera matrix results in

$$K = \begin{bmatrix} f_C & 0 & C_{Ox} \\ 0 & f_C & C_{Oy} \\ 0 & 0 & 1 \end{bmatrix}$$

As CCD cameras are never perfect, it is most likely that CCD chips have pixels, which are not of the shape of a square. The image coordinates, however, are measured in square pixels. This has certainly an extra effect of introducing unequal scale factors in each direction. In particular, if the number of pixels per unit distance (per millimeter) in image coordinates are m_x and m_y in the directions x and y , respectively, then the camera transformation from space coordinates measured in millimeters to pixel coordinates can be gained by pre-multiplying the camera matrix M by a matrix factor diag(m_x, m_y, 1). The camera matrix can then be estimated as

$$K = \begin{bmatrix} m_x & 0 & 0 \\ 0 & m_y & 0 \\ 0 & 0 & 1 \end{bmatrix} \begin{bmatrix} f_c & 0 & C_{Ox} \\ 0 & f_c & C_{Oy} \\ 0 & 0 & 1 \end{bmatrix} \Rightarrow K = \begin{bmatrix} f_{cp1} & 0 & C_{Oxp} \\ 0 & f_{cp2} & C_{Oyp} \\ 0 & 0 & 1 \end{bmatrix}$$

where $f_{cp1} = f_c m_x$ and $f_{cp2} = f_c m_y$ represent the focal length of the camera in terms of pixels in the x and y directions, respectively. The ratio f_{cp1} / f_{cp2} , called an *aspect ratio*, gives a simple measure of regularity meaning that the closer it is to 1 the nearer to squares are the pixels. It is very convenient to express the matrix M in terms of pixels because the data forming an image are determined in pixels and there is no need to re-compute the intern camera parameters into millimeters.

Skew coefficient Skewing does not exist in most regular cameras. However, in certain unusual instances it can be present. A skew parameter, which in CCD cameras relates to pixels, determines how pixels in a CCD array are skewed, that is to what extent the x and y axes of a pixel are not perpendicular. Principally, the CCD camera model assumes that the image has been stretched by some factor in the two axial directions. If it is stretched in a non-axial direction, then skewing results. Taking the skew parameter into considerations yields the following form of the camera matrix:

$$K = \begin{bmatrix} f_{Cp1} & 0 & C_{Oxp} \\ 0 & f_{Cp2} & C_{Oyp} \\ 0 & 0 & 1 \end{bmatrix}$$

This form of the camera matrix (M) allows us to calculate the pixel coordinates of a point $\vec{r}^C$ cast from a 3D scene into the sensor plane (assuming that we know the original coordinates):

$$\begin{bmatrix} x^S \\ y^S \\ 1 \end{bmatrix} = \begin{bmatrix} f_{Cp1} & 0 & C_{Oxp} \\ 0 & f_{Cp2} & C_{Oyp} \\ 0 & 0 & 1 \end{bmatrix} \begin{bmatrix} x_d \\ y_d \\ 1 \end{bmatrix} \tag{6}$$

Since images are recorded through the CCD sensor, we have to consider closely the image plane, too. The origin of the sensor plane lies exactly in the middle, while the origin of the Image CS is always located in the upper left corner of the image. Let us assume that the principal point offset is known and the resolution of the camera is $\mathrm{N}_x \times \mathrm{N}_y$ pixels. As the center of the sensor plane lies intuitively in the middle of the image, the principal point offset, denoted as $[cc_x \quad cc_y]^{\mathrm{T}}$, with respect to the Image CS is $\begin{bmatrix} \frac{\mathrm{N}_x}{2} + C_{Oxp} & \frac{\mathrm{N}_y}{2} + C_{Oyp} \end{bmatrix}^{\mathrm{T}}$.

Hence the full form of the camera matrix suitable for the pinhole camera model is

$$M = \begin{bmatrix} f_{cp1} & s & cc_x \\ 0 & f_{cp2} & cc_y \\ 0 & 0 & 1 \end{bmatrix} \tag{7}$$

Consequently, a complete equation describing the projection of the point $\vec{r}^C = \begin{bmatrix} x^C & y^C & z^C \end{bmatrix}^{\mathrm{T}}$ from the camera's three-dimensional scene to the point $\vec{r}^I = \begin{bmatrix} x^I & y^I \end{bmatrix}^{\mathrm{T}}$ in the camera's Image CS has the following form:

$$\begin{bmatrix} x^I \\ y^I \\ 1 \end{bmatrix} = \begin{bmatrix} f_{cp1} & 0 & cc_x \\ 0 & f_{cp2} & cc_y \\ 0 & 0 & 1 \end{bmatrix} \begin{bmatrix} x_d \\ y_d \\ 1 \end{bmatrix} \tag{8}$$

where x_d and y_d stand for the normalized distorted camera coordinates as in (3).

2.2 Conventions on the orientation matrix of the rigid body transformation

There are various industrial tasks in which a robotic plant can be utilized. For example, a robot with its tool mounted on a robotic flange can be used for welding, body painting or gripping objects. To automate this process, an object, a tool, and a complete mechanism itself have their own fixed coordinate systems assigned. These CSs are rotated and translated w.r.t. each other. Their relations are determined in the form of certain mathematical transformations T.

Let us assume that we have two coordinate systems $\{F1\}$ and $\{F2\}$ shifted and rotated w.r.t. to each other. The mapping ${}_{F1}T^{F2} = \left({}_{F1}R^{F2}, {}_{F1}K^{F2}\right)$ in a three-dimensional space can be represented by the following 4×4 homogenous coordinate transformation matrix:

$${}_{F1}T^{F2} = \begin{bmatrix} {}_{F1}R^{F2} & {}_{F1}K^{F2} \\ 0_{[1\times 3]} & 1 \end{bmatrix} \tag{9a}$$

where ${}_{F1}R^{F2}$ is a 3×3 orthogonal *rotation* matrix determining the orientation of the {*F*2} CS with respect to the {*F*1} CS and ${}_{F1}K^{F2}$ is a 3×1 translation vector determining the position of the origin of the {*F*2} CS shifted with respect to the origin of the {*F*1} CS.
The matrix ${}_{F1}T^{F2}$ can be divided into two sub-matrices:

$$ {}_{F1}R^{F2} = \begin{bmatrix} r11_{F1F2} & r12_{F1F2} & r13_{F1F2} \\ r21_{F1F2} & r22_{F1F2} & r23_{F1F2} \\ r31_{F1F2} & r32_{F1F2} & r33_{F1F2} \end{bmatrix}, \quad {}_{F1}K^{F2} = \begin{bmatrix} kx_{F1F2} \\ ky_{F1F2} \\ kz_{F1F2} \end{bmatrix} \tag{9b} $$

Due to its orthogonality, the rotation matrix *R* fulfills the condition $R^{\mathrm{T}}R = I$, where *I* is a 3×3 identity matrix.
It is worth noticing that there are a great number (about 24) of conventions of determining the rotation matrix *R*. We describe here two most common conventions, which are utilized by leading robot-producing companies, i.e. the ZYX-Euler-angles and the unit-quaternion notations.
Euler angles notation The ZYX Euler angles representation can be described as follows. Let us first assume that two CS, {*F*1} and {*F*2}, coincide with each other. Then we rotate the {*F*2} CS by an angle *A* around the $\hat{Z}_{F2}$ axis, then by an angle *B* around the $\hat{Y}'_{F2}$ axis, and finally by an angle *C* around the $\hat{X}''_{F2}$ axis. The rotations refer to the rotation axes of the {*F*2} CS instead of the fixed {*F*1} CS. In other words, each rotation is carried out with respect to an axis whose position depends on the previous rotation, as shown in Fig. 5.

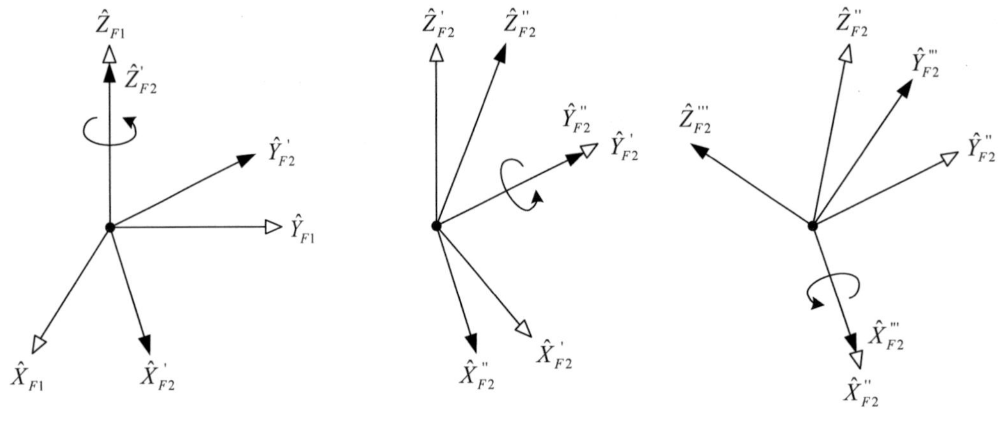

Fig. 5. Representation of the rotations in terms of the ZYX Euler angles

In order to find the rotation matrix ${}_{F1}R^{F2}$ from the {*F*1} CS to the {*F*2} CS, we introduce indirect {*F*2'} and {*F*2"} CSs. Taking the rotations as descriptions of these coordinate systems (CSs), we write:

$$ {}_{F1}R^{F2} = {}_{F1}R^{F2'}\,{}_{F2'}R^{F2''}\,{}_{F2''}R^{F2} $$

In general, the rotations around the $\hat{Z}, \hat{Y}, \hat{X}$ axes are given as follows, respectively:

$$R_{\hat{Z}} = \begin{bmatrix} \cos(A) & -\sin(A) & 0 \\ \sin(A) & \cos(A) & 0 \\ 0 & 0 & 1 \end{bmatrix} \quad R_{\hat{Y}} = \begin{bmatrix} \cos(B) & 0 & \sin(B) \\ 0 & 1 & 0 \\ -\sin(B) & 0 & \cos(B) \end{bmatrix} \quad R_{\hat{X}} = \begin{bmatrix} 1 & 0 & 0 \\ 0 & \cos(C) & -\sin(C) \\ 0 & \sin(C) & \cos(C) \end{bmatrix}$$

By multiplying these matrices we get a compose formula for the rotation matrix $R_{\hat{Z}\hat{Y}\hat{X}}$:

$$R_{\hat{Z}\hat{Y}\hat{X}} = \begin{bmatrix} \cos(A)\cos(B) & \cos(A)\sin(B)\sin(C)-\sin(A)\cos(C) & \cos(A)\sin(B)\cos(C)+\sin(A)\sin(C) \\ \sin(A)\cos(B) & \sin(A)\sin(B)\sin(C)+\cos(A)\cos(C) & \sin(A)\sin(B)\cos(C)-\cos(A)\sin(C) \\ -\sin(B) & \cos(B)\sin(C) & \cos(B)\cos(C) \end{bmatrix} \quad (10)$$

As the above formula implies, the rotation matrix is actually described by only 3 parameters, *i.e.* the Euler angles *A*, *B* and *C* of each rotation, and not by 9 parameters, as suggested (9b). Hence the transformation matrix *T* is described by 6 parameters overall, also referred to as a *frame*.

Let us now describe the transformation between points in a three-dimensional space, by assuming that the {*F2*} CS is moved by a vector $K = \begin{bmatrix} kx_{F1F2} & ky_{F1F2} & kz_{F1F2} \end{bmatrix}^T$ w.r.t. the {*F1*} CS in three dimensions and rotated by the angles *A*, *B* and *C* following the ZYX Euler angles convention. Given a point $\vec{r}^{F2} = \begin{bmatrix} x^{F2} & y^{F2} & z^{F2} \end{bmatrix}^T$, a point $\vec{r}^{F1} = \begin{bmatrix} x^{F1} & y^{F1} & z^{F1} \end{bmatrix}^T$ is computed in the following way:

$$\begin{bmatrix} x^{F1} \\ y^{F1} \\ z^{F1} \\ 1 \end{bmatrix} = \begin{bmatrix} \cos(A)\cos(B) & \cos(A)\sin(B)\sin(C)-\sin(A)\cos(C) & \cos(A)\sin(B)\cos(C)+\sin(A)\sin(C) & kx_{F1F2} \\ \sin(A)\cos(B) & \sin(A)\sin(B)\sin(C)+\cos(A)\cos(C) & \sin(A)\sin(B)\cos(C)-\cos(A)\sin(C) & ky_{F1F2} \\ -\sin(B) & \cos(B)\sin(C) & \cos(B)\cos(C) & kz_{F1F2} \\ 0 & 0 & 0 & 1 \end{bmatrix} \begin{bmatrix} x^{F2} \\ y^{F2} \\ z^{F2} \\ 1 \end{bmatrix} \quad (11)$$

Using (9) we can also represent the above in a concise way:

$$\begin{bmatrix} x^{F1} \\ y^{F1} \\ z^{F1} \\ 1 \end{bmatrix} = \begin{bmatrix} r11_{F1F2} & r12_{F1F2} & r13_{F1F2} & kx_{F1F2} \\ r21_{F1F2} & r22_{F1F2} & r23_{F1F2} & ky_{F1F2} \\ r31_{F1F2} & r32_{F1F2} & r33_{F1F2} & kz_{F1F2} \\ 0 & 0 & 0 & 1 \end{bmatrix} \begin{bmatrix} x^{F2} \\ y^{F2} \\ z^{F2} \\ 1 \end{bmatrix} = {}_{F1}T^{F2} \begin{bmatrix} x^{F2} \\ y^{F2} \\ z^{F2} \\ 1 \end{bmatrix} \quad (12)$$

After decomposing this transformation into rotation and translation matrices, we have:

$$\begin{bmatrix} x^{F1} \\ y^{F1} \\ z^{F1} \end{bmatrix} = \begin{bmatrix} r11_{F1F2} & r12_{F1F2} & r13_{F1F2} \\ r21_{F1F2} & r22_{F1F2} & r23_{F1F2} \\ r31_{F1F2} & r32_{F1F2} & r33_{F1F2} \end{bmatrix} \begin{bmatrix} x^{F2} \\ y^{F2} \\ z^{F2} \end{bmatrix} + \begin{bmatrix} kx_{F1F2} \\ ky_{F1F2} \\ kz_{F1F2} \end{bmatrix} = {}_{F1}R^{F2} \begin{bmatrix} x^{F2} \\ y^{F2} \\ z^{F2} \end{bmatrix} + {}_{F1}K^{F2} \quad (13)$$

There from, knowing the rotation *R* and the translation *K* from the first CS to the second CS in the three-dimensional space and having the coordinates of a point defined in the second CS, we can compute its coordinates in the first CS.

Unit quaternion notation Another notation for rotation, widely utilized in machine vision industry and computer graphics, refers to unit quaternions. A quaternion, $p = (p_0, p_1, p_2, p_3) = (p_0, \vec{p})$, is a collection of four components, first of which is taken as a scalar and the other three form a vector. Such an entity can thus be treated in terms of complex numbers what allows us to re-write it in the following form:

$$p = p_0 + i \cdot p_1 + j \cdot p_2 + k \cdot p_3$$

where i, j, k are imaginary numbers. This means that a real number (scalar) can be represented by a purely real quaternion and a three-dimensional vector by a purely imaginary quaternion. The conjugate and the magnitude of a quaternion can be determined in a way similar to the complex numbers calculus:

$$p^* = p_0 - i \cdot p_1 - j \cdot p_2 - k \cdot p_3 \quad , \qquad \|p\| = \sqrt{p_0^2 + p_1^2 + p_2^2 + p_3^2}$$

With another quaternion $q = (q_0, q_1, q_2, q_3) = (q_0, \vec{q})$ in use, the sum of them is

$$p + q = (p_0 + q_0, \vec{p} + \vec{q})$$

and their (non-commutative) product can be defined as

$$p \cdot q = (p_0 q_0 - \vec{p}\vec{q}, p_0 \vec{q} + q_0 \vec{p} + \vec{p}\vec{q})$$

The latter can also be written in a matrix form as

$$p \cdot q = \begin{bmatrix} p_0 & -p_1 & -p_2 & -p_3 \\ p_1 & p_0 & -p_3 & p_2 \\ p_2 & p_3 & p_0 & -p_1 \\ p_3 & -p_2 & p_1 & p_0 \end{bmatrix} \cdot q = P \cdot q$$

or

$$q \cdot p = \begin{bmatrix} p_0 & -p_1 & -p_2 & -p_3 \\ p_1 & p_0 & p_3 & -p_2 \\ p_2 & -p_3 & p_0 & p_1 \\ p_3 & p_2 & -p_1 & p_0 \end{bmatrix} \cdot q = \overline{P} \cdot q$$

where P and $\overline{P}$ are 4×4 orthogonal matrices.
Dot product of two quaternions is the sum of products of corresponding elements:

$$p \circ q = p_0 q_0 + p_1 q_1 + p_2 q_2 + p_3 q_3$$

A unit quaternion $\|p\| = 1$ has its inverse equal its conjugate:

$$p^{-1} = \left(\frac{1}{p \circ p} \right) p^* = p^*$$

as the square of the magnitude of a quaternion is a dot product of the quaternion with itself:

$$\|p\|^2 = p \circ p$$

It is clear that the vector's length and angles relative to the coordinate axes remain constant after rotation. Hence rotation also preserves dot products. Therefore it is possible to represent the rotation in terms of quaternions. However, simple multiplication of a vector by a quaternion would yield a quaternion with a real part (vectors are quaternions with imaginary parts only). Namely, if we express a vector $\vec{q}$ from a three-dimensional space as a unit quaternion $q = (0, \vec{q})$ and perform the operation with another unit quaternion p

$$\vec{q}' = p \cdot q = (q_0', q_1', q_2', q_3')$$

then we attain a quaternion which is not a vector. Thus we use composite product in order to rotate a vector into another one while preserving its length and angles:

$$\vec{q}' = p \cdot q \cdot p^{-1} = p \cdot q \cdot p^* = (0, q_1', q_2', q_3')$$

We can prove this by the following expansion:

$$p \cdot q \cdot p^* = (Pq)p^* = \overline{P}^{\mathrm{T}}(Pq) = (\overline{P}^{\mathrm{T}}P)q$$

where

$$\overline{P}^{\mathrm{T}}P = \begin{bmatrix} p \circ p & 0 & 0 & 0 \\ 0 & (p_0^2 + p_1^2 - p_2^2 - p_3^2) & 2(p_1p_2 - p_0p_3) & 2(p_1p_3 - p_0p_2) \\ 0 & 2(p_1p_2 - p_0p_3) & (p_0^2 - p_1^2 + p_2^2 - p_3^2) & 2(p_2p_3 - p_0p_1) \\ 0 & 2(p_3p_1 - p_0p_2) & 2(p_3p_2 - p_0p_1) & (p_0^2 - p_1^2 - p_2^2 + p_3^2) \end{bmatrix}$$

Therefore, if q is purely imaginary then q' is purely imaginary, as well. Moreover, if p is a unit quaternion, then $p \circ p = 1$, and P and $\overline{P}$ are orthonormal. Consequently, the 3×3 lower right-hand sub-matrix is also orthonormal and represents the rotation matrix as in (9b).
The quaternion notation is closely related to the axis-angle representation of the rotation matrix. A rotation by an angle θ about a unit vector $\hat{\omega} = [\omega_x \quad \omega_y \quad \omega_z]^{\mathrm{T}}$ can be determined in terms of a unit quaternion as:

$$p = \cos\frac{\theta}{2} + \sin\frac{\theta}{2}(i\omega_x + j\omega_y + k\omega_z)$$

In other words, the imaginary part of the quaternion represents the vector of rotation and the real part along with the magnitude of the imaginary part provides the angle of rotation.
There are several important advantages of unit quaternions over other conventions. Firstly, it is much simpler to enforce the constraint on the quaternion to have a unit magnitude than to implement the orthogonality of the rotation matrix based on Euler angles. Secondly, quaternions avoid the *gimbal lock* phenomenon occurring when the pitch angle is 90°. Then yaw and roll angles refer to the same motion what results in losing one degree of freedom. We postpone this issue until Section 3.3.
Finally, let us study the following example. In Fig. 6 there are four CSs: {A}, {B}, {C} and {D}. Assuming that the transformations ${}_AT^B$, ${}_BT^C$ and ${}_AT^D$ are known, we want to find the

other two, ${}_{A}T^{C}$ and ${}_{D}T^{C}$. Note that there are 5 loops altogether, *ABCD, ABC, ACD, ABD* and *BCD,* that connect the origins of all CSs. Thus there are several ways to find the unknown transformations. We find ${}_{A}T^{C}$ by means of the loop *ABC,* and ${}_{D}T^{C}$ by following the loop *ABCD*. Writing the matrix equation for the first loop we immediately obtain:

$${}_{A}T^{C} = {}_{A}T^{B}\,{}_{B}T^{C}$$

Writing the equation for the other loop we have:

$${}_{A}T^{B}\,{}_{B}T^{C} = {}_{A}T^{D}\,{}_{D}T^{C} \Rightarrow {}_{D}T^{C} = \left({}_{A}T^{D}\right)^{-1}\,{}_{A}T^{B}\,{}_{B}T^{C}$$

To conclude, given that the transformations can be placed in a closed loop and only one of them is unknown, we can compute the latter transformation based on the known ones. This is a principal property of transformations in vision-guided robot positioning applications.

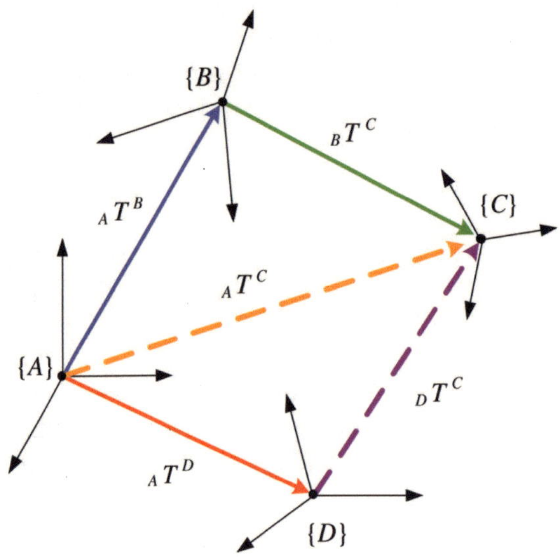

Fig. 6. Transformations based on closed loops

2.3 Pose estimation – problem statement

There are many methods in the machine vision literature suitable for retrieving the information from a three-dimensional scene with the use of a single image or multiple images. Most common cases include single and stereo imaging, though recently developed applications in robotic guidance use 4 or even more images at a time. In this Section we characterize few methods of pose estimation to give the general idea of how they can be utilized in robot positioning systems.

Why do we compute the pose of the object relative to the camera? Let us suppose that we have a robot-camera-gripper positioning system, which has already been calibrated. In robot positioning applications the vision sensor acts somewhat as a medium only. It determines the pose of the object that is then transformed to the Gripper CS. This means that the pose of the object is estimated with respect to the gripper and the robot 'knows' how to grip the object.

In another approach we do not compute the pose of the object relative to the camera and then to the gripper. Single or multi camera systems calculate the coordinates of points at the calibration stage, and then perform the calculation at each position while the system is running. Based on the computed coordinates, a geometrical motion of a given camera from the calibrated position to its actual position is processed. Knowing this motion and the geometrical relation between the camera and the gripper, the gripping motion can then be computed so that the robot 'learns' where its gripper is located w.r.t to the object, and then the gripping motion can follow.

2.3.1 Computing 3D points using stereovision

When a point in a 3D scene is projected onto a 2D image plane, the depth information is lost. The simplest method to render this information is stereovision. The 3D coordinates of any point can be computed provided that this point is visible in two images (1 and 2) and the intern camera parameters together with the geometrical relation between stereo cameras are known.

Rendering 3D point coordinates based on image data is called *inverse point mapping*. It is a very important issue in machine vision because it allows us to compute the camera motion from one position to another. We shall now derive a mathematical formula for rendering the 3D point coordinates using stereovision.

Let us denote the 3D point $\vec{r}$ in the Camera 1 CS as $\vec{r}^{C1} = \begin{bmatrix} x^{C1} & y^{C1} & z^{C1} & 1 \end{bmatrix}^T$. The same point in the Camera 2 CS will be represented by $\vec{r}^{C2} = \begin{bmatrix} x^{C2} & y^{C2} & z^{C2} & 1 \end{bmatrix}^T$. Moreover, let the geometrical relation between these two cameras be given as the transformation from Camera 1 to Camera 2 ${}_{C1}T^{C2} = \left({}_{C1}R^{C2}, {}_{C1}K^{C2}\right)$, their calibration matrices be M_{C1} and M_{C2}, and the projected image points be $\vec{r}^{I1} = \begin{bmatrix} x^{I1} & y^{I1} & 1 \end{bmatrix}^T$ and $\vec{r}^{I2} = \begin{bmatrix} x^{I2} & y^{I2} & 1 \end{bmatrix}^T$, respectively.

There is no direct way to transform distorted image coordinates into undistorted ones because (3) and (4) are not linear. Hence, the first step would be to solve these equations iteratively. For the sake of simplicity, however, let us assume that our camera model is free of distortion. In Section 5 we will verify how these parameters affect the precision of measurements. In the considered case, the normalized distorted coordinates match the normalized undistorted ones: $x_d = x_{norm}$ and $y_d = y_{norm}$. As the stereo images are related with each other through the transformation ${}_{C1}T^{C2}$, the pixel coordinates of Image 2 can be transformed to the plane of Image 1. Thus combining (8) and (13), and eliminating the coordinates x and y yields:

$$M_{C1}^{-1}\vec{r}^{I1}z^{C1} = {}_{C1}R^{C2}M_{C2}^{-1}\vec{r}^{I2}z^{C2} + {}_{C1}K^{C2} \tag{14}$$

This overconstrained system is solved by the linear least squares method (LS) and computation of the remaining coordinates in {C1} and {C2} comes straightforward. Such an approach based on (14) is called *triangulation.*

It is worth mentioning that the stereo camera configuration has several interesting geometrical properties, which can be used, for instance, to inform the operator that the system needs recalibration and/or to simplify the implementation of the image processing application (IPA) used to retrieve object features from the images. Namely, the only constraint of the stereovision systems is imposed by their epipolar geometry. An epipolar plane and an epipolar line represent epipolar geometry. The epipolar plane is defined by a

3D point in the scene and the origins of the two Camera CSs. On the basis of the projection of this point onto the first image, it is possible to derive the equation of the epipolar plane (characterized by a *fundamental matrix*) which has also to be satisfied by the projection of this point onto the second image plane. If such a plane equation condition is not satisfied, then an error offset can be estimated. When, for instance, the frequency of the appearance of such errors exceeds an *a priori* defined threshold, it can be treated as a warning sign of the necessity for recalibration. The epipolar line is also quite useful. It is the straight line of intersection of the epipolar plane with the image plane. Consequently, a 3D point projected onto one image generates a line in the other image on which its corresponding projection point must lie. This feature is extremely important when creating an IPA. Having found one feature in the image reduces the scope of the search for its corresponding projection in the other image from a region to a line. Since the main problem of stereovision IPAs lies in locating the corresponding image features (which are projections of the same 3D point), this greatly improves the efficiency of IPAs and yet eases the process of creating them.

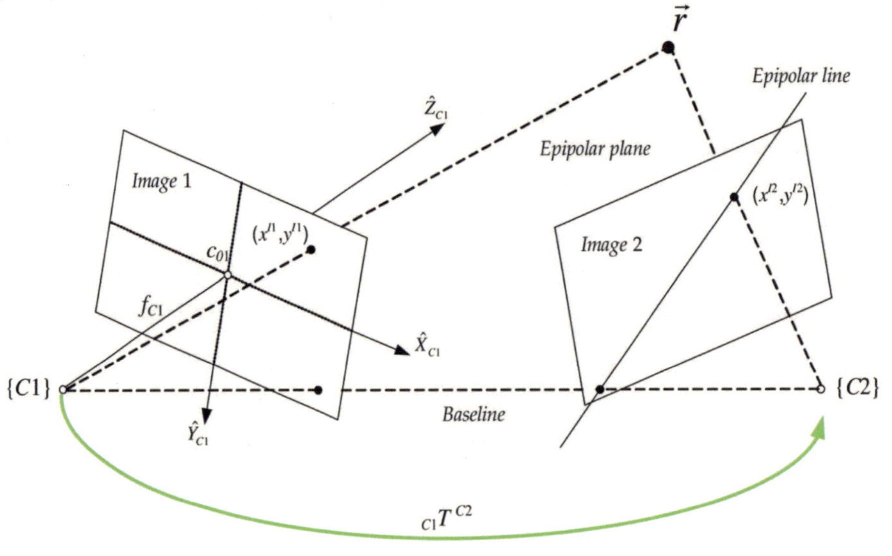

Fig. 7. Stereo–image configuration with epipolar geometry

2.3.2 Single image pose estimation

There are two methods of pose estimation utilized in 3D robot positioning applications. A first one, designated as *3D-3D estimation*, refers to computing the actual pose of the camera either w.r.t. the camera at the calibrated position or w.r.t. the actual position of the object. In the first case, the 3D point coordinates have to be known in both camera positions. In the latter, the points have to be known in the Camera CS as well as in the Object CS. Points defined in the Object CS can be taken from its CAD model (therefore called *model points*).

The second type of pose estimation is called *2D-3D estimation* and is used only by the gripping systems equipped with a single camera. It consists in computing the pose of the object with respect to the actual position of the camera given the 3D model points and their projected pixel coordinates. The main advantage of this approach over the first one is that it does not need to calculate the 3D points in the Camera CS to find the pose. Its disadvantage lies in only iterative implementations of the computations. Nevertheless, it is widely utilized in camera calibration procedures.

The assessment of camera motions or else the poses of the camera at the actual position relative to the pose of the camera at the calibration position are also known as *relative orientation*. The estimation of the transformation between the camera and the object is identified as *exterior orientation*.

Relative orientation

Let us consider the following situation. During the calibration process we have positioned the cameras, measured n 3D object points ($n \geq 3$) in a chosen Camera CS $\{Y\}$, and taught the robot how to grip the object from that particular camera position. We could measure the points using, for instance, stereovision, linear n-point algorithms, or structure-from-motion algorithms. Let us denote these points as $\vec{r}_1^{\,Y},...,\vec{r}_n^{\,Y}$. Now, we move the camera-robot system to another (actual) position in order to get another measurement of the same points (in the Camera CS $\{X\}$). This time they have different coordinates as the Camera CS has been moved. We denote these points as $\vec{r}_1^{\,X},...,\vec{r}_n^{\,X}$, where for an i-th point we have: $\vec{r}_i^{\,Y} \leftrightarrow \vec{r}_i^{\,X}$, meaning that the points correspond to each other. From Section 2.2 we know that there exists a mapping which transforms points $\vec{r}^{\,X}$ to points $\vec{r}^{\,Y}$. Note that this transformation implies the rigid motion of the camera from the calibrated position to the actual position. As will be shown in Section 3.2, knowing it, the robot is able to grip the object from the actual position. We can also consider these pairs of points as defined in the Object CS ($\vec{r}_1^{\,X},...,\vec{r}_n^{\,X}$) and in the Camera CS ($\vec{r}_1^{\,Y},...,\vec{r}_n^{\,Y}$). In such a case the mapping between these points describes the relation between the Object and the Camera CSs. Therefore, in general, given the points in these two CSs, we can infer the transformation between them from the following equation:

$$\vec{r}^{\,Y}_{[4\times n]} = T_{[4\times 4]}\vec{r}^{\,X}_{[4\times n]}$$

After rearranging and adding noise η to the measurements, we obtain:

$$\vec{r}_n^{\,Y} = R \cdot \vec{r}_n^{\,X} + K + \eta_n$$

One of the ways of solving the above equation consists in setting up a least squares equation and minimizing it, taking into account the constraint of orthogonality of the rotation matrix. For example, Haralick *et al.* (1989) describe iterative and non-iterative solutions to this problem. Another method, developed by Weinstein (1998), minimizes the summed-squared-distance between three pairs of corresponding points. He derives an analytic least squares fitting method for computing the transformation between these points. Horn (1987) approaches this problem using unit quaternions and giving a closed-form solution for any number of corresponding points.

Exterior orientation

The problem of determining the pose of an object relative to the camera based on a single-image has found many relevant applications in machine vision for object gripping, camera calibration, hand-eye calibration, cartography, etc. It can be easily stated more formally: given a set of (model) points that are described in the Object CS, the projections of these points onto an image plane, and the intern camera parameters, determine the rotation R and translation K between the object centered and the camera centered coordinate system. As has been mentioned, this problem is labeled as the *exterior orientation* problem (in the photogrammetry literature, for instance). The dissertation by Szczepanski (1958) surveys

nearly 80 different solutions beginning with the one given by Schrieber of Karlsruhe in the year 1879. A first robust solution, identified a *RANSAC paradigm*, has been delivered by Fischler and Bolles (1981), while Wrobel (1992) and Thomson (1966) discuss configurations of points for which the solution is unstable. Haralick *et al.* (1989) introduced three iterative algorithms, which simultaneously compute both object pose w.r.t. the camera and the depths values of the points observed by the camera. A subsequent method represents rotation using Euler angles, where the equations are linearized by a Newton's first-order approximation. Yet another approach solves linearized equations using M-estimators.
It has to be emphasized that there exist more algorithms for solving the 2D-3D estimation problem. Some of them are based on minimizing the error functions derived from the collinearity condition of both the object-space and the image-space error vector. Certain papers (Schweighofer & Pinz, 2006; Lu *et al.*, 1998; Phong *et al.*, 1995) provide us with the derivation of these functions and propose iterative algorithms for solving them.

3. 3D robot positioning system

The calibrated vision guided three-dimensional robot positioning system, able to adjust the robot to grip the object deviated in 6DOF, comprises the following three consecutive fundamental steps:

1. Identification of object features in single or multi images using a custom image processing application (IPA).
2. Estimation of the relative or exterior orientation of the camera.
3. Computation of the transformation determining the gripping motion.

The calibration of the vision guided gripping systems involves three steps, as well. In the first stage the image processing software is taught some specific features of the object in order to detect them at other object/robot positions later on. The second step performs derivation of the camera matrix and hand-eye transformations through calibration relating the camera with the flange (end-effector) of the robot. This is a crucial stage, because though the camera can estimate algorithmically the actual pose of the object relative to itself, the object's pose has to be transformed to the gripper (also calibrated against the end-effector) in order to adjust the robot gripper to the object. This adjustment means a motion of the gripper from the position where the object features are determined in the images to the position where the object is gripped. The robot knows how to move its gripper along the motion trajectory because it is calibrated beforehand, what constitutes the third step.

3.1 Coordinate systems

In order do derive the transformations relating each component of the positioning system it is necessary to fix definite coordinate systems to these components. The robot positioning system (Kowalczuk & Wesierski, 2007) presented in this chapter is guided by stereovision and consists of the following coordinate systems (CS):

1. Robot CS, $\{R\}$
2. Flange CS, $\{F\}$
3. Gripper CS, $\{G\}$
4. Camera 1 CS, $\{C1\}$
5. Camera 2 CS, $\{C2\}$
6. Sensor 1 CS of Camera 1, $\{S1\}$
7. Sensor 2 CS of Camera 2, $\{S2\}$
8. Image 1 CS of Camera 1, $\{I1\}$

9. Image 2 CS of Camera 2, {*I2*}
10. Object CS, {*W*}.

The above CSs, except for the Sensor and Image CSs (discussed in Section 2.1), are three-dimensional Cartesian CSs translated and rotated with respect to each other, as depicted in Fig. 8. The Robot CS has its origin in the root of the robot. The Flange CS is placed in the middle of the robotic end-effector. The Gripper CS is located on the gripper within its origin, called Tool Center Point (TCP), defined during the calibration process. The center of the Camera CS is placed in the camera projection center O_C. As has been shown in Fig.1, the Camera principal axis determines the $\hat{Z}_C$-axis of the Camera CS pointing out of the camera in positive direction, the $\hat{Y}_C$-axis pointing downward and the $\hat{X}_C$-axis pointing to the left as one looks from the front. Apart from the intern parameters, the camera has extern parameters as well. They are the translation vector *K* and the three Euler angles *A, B, C*. The extern parameters describe translation and rotation of the camera with respect to any CS, and, in Fig. 8, with respect to the Flange CS, thus forming the hand-eye transformation. The Object CS has its origin at an arbitrary point/feature defined on the object. The other points determine the object's axes and orientation.

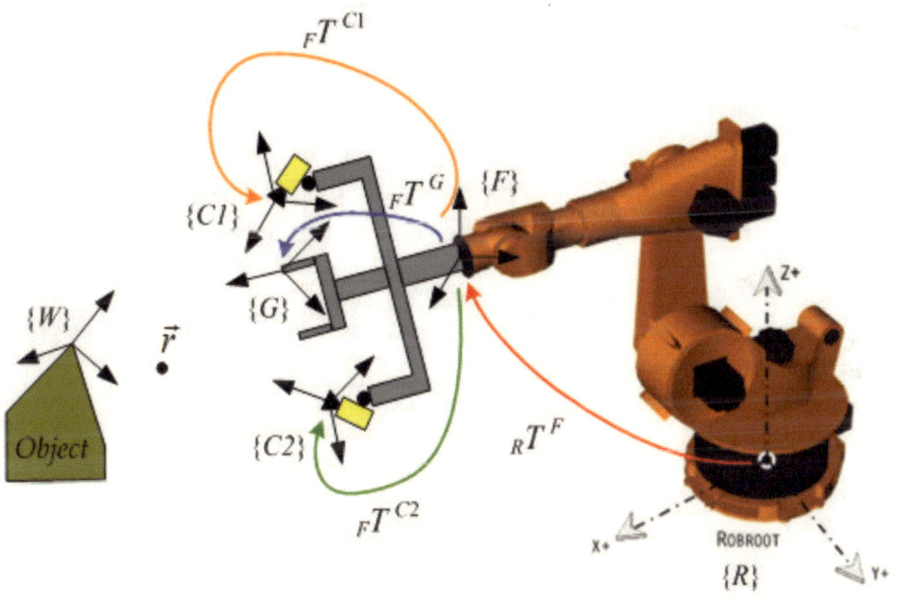

Fig. 8. Coordinate systems of the robot positioning system

3.2 Realization of gripping

In Section 2.3.2 we have shortly described two methods for gripping the object. We refer to them as the exterior and the relative orientation methods. In this section we explain how these methods are utilized in vision guided robot positioning systems and derive certain mathematical equations of concatenated transformations.

In order to grip an object at any position the robot has to be first taught the gripping motion from a position at which it can identify object features. This motion embraces three positions and two partial motions, first, a point-to-point movement (PTP), and then a linear

movement (LIN). The point-to-point movement means a possibly quickest way of moving the tip of the tool (TCP) from a current position to a programmed end position. In the case of linear motion, the robot always follows the programmed straight line from one point to another.
The robot is jogged to the first position in such a way that it can determine at least 3 features of the object in two image planes {*I*1} and {*I*2}. This position is called Position 1 or a *'Look-Position'*. Then, the robot is jogged to the second position called a *'Before-Gripping-Position'*, denoted as *Gb*. Finally, it is moved to the third position called an *'After-Gripping-Position'*, symbolized by *Ga*, meaning that the gripper has gripped the object. Although the motion from the *'Look-Position'* to the *Gb* is programmed with a PTP command, the motion from *Gb* to *Ga* has to be programmed with a LIN command because the robot follows then the programmed linear path avoiding possible collisions. After saving all these three calibrated positions, the robot 'knows' that moving the gripper from the calibrated *'Look-Position'* to *Ga* means gripping the object (assuming that the object is static during this gripping motion).
For the sake of conceptual clarity let us assume that the positioning system has been fully calibrated and the following data are known:

- transformation from the Flange to the Camera 1 CS: ${}_{F}T^{C1}$
- transformation from the Flange to the Camera 2 CS: ${}_{F}T^{C2}$
- transformation from the Flange to the Gripper CS: ${}_{F}T^{G}$
- transformation from the Gripper CS at Position 1 (*'Look-Position'*) to the *'Before-Gripping-Position'*: ${}_{G}T^{Gb}$
- transformation from the *'Before-Gripping-Position'* to the *'After-Gripping-Position'*: ${}_{Gb}T^{Ga}$
- the pixel coordinates of the object features in stereo images when the system is positioned at the *'Look-Position'*.

Having calibrated the whole system allows us to compute the transformation from the Camera 1 to the Gripper CS ${}_{C1}T^{G}$ and from the Camera 1 to the Camera 2 CS. We find the first transformation using the equation below:

$${}_{C1}T^{G} = \left({}_{F}T^{C1}\right)^{-1} {}_{F}T^{G}$$

To find the latter transformation, we write:

$${}_{C1}T^{C2} = \left({}_{F}T^{C1}\right)^{-1} {}_{F}T^{C2}$$

Based on the transformation ${}_{C1}T^{C2}$ and on the pixel coordinates of the projected points, the system uses the triangulation method to calculate the 3D points in the Camera 1 CS at Position 1.
We propose now two methods to grip the object, assuming that the robot has changed its position from Position 1 to Position N, as depicted in Fig. 9.
Exterior orientation method for robot positioning This method is based on computing the transformation ${}_{C1}T^{W}$ from the camera to the object using the 3D model points determined in the Object CS {*W*1} and the pixel coordinates of these points projected onto the image. The exterior orientation methods described in Section 2.3.2 are used to obtain ${}_{C1}T^{W}$.

The movement of the positioning system, shown in Fig. 9, from Position 1 to an arbitrary Position N can be presented in three ways:

- the system changes its position relative to a constant object position
- the object changes its position w.r.t. a constant position of the system
- the system and the object both change their positions.

Note that, as the motion of the gripper between the *Gb* to the *Ga* Positions is programmed by a LIN command, the transformation ${}_{Gb}T^{Ga}$ remains constant.

Regardless of the current presentation, the two transformations ${}_{C1}T^{W}$ and ${}_{G}T^{Gb}$ change into ${}_{C1p}T^{W}$ and ${}_{Gp}T^{Gb}$, respectively, and they have to be calculated. Having computed ${}_{C1p}T^{W}$ by using exterior orientation algorithms, we write a *loop equation* for the concatenating transformations at Position N:

$${}_{C1}T^{W} = {}_{C1}T^{G}\,{}_{G}T^{Gb}\left({}_{Gp}T^{Gb}\right)^{-1}\left({}_{C1}T^{G}\right)^{-1}\,{}_{C1p}T^{W}$$

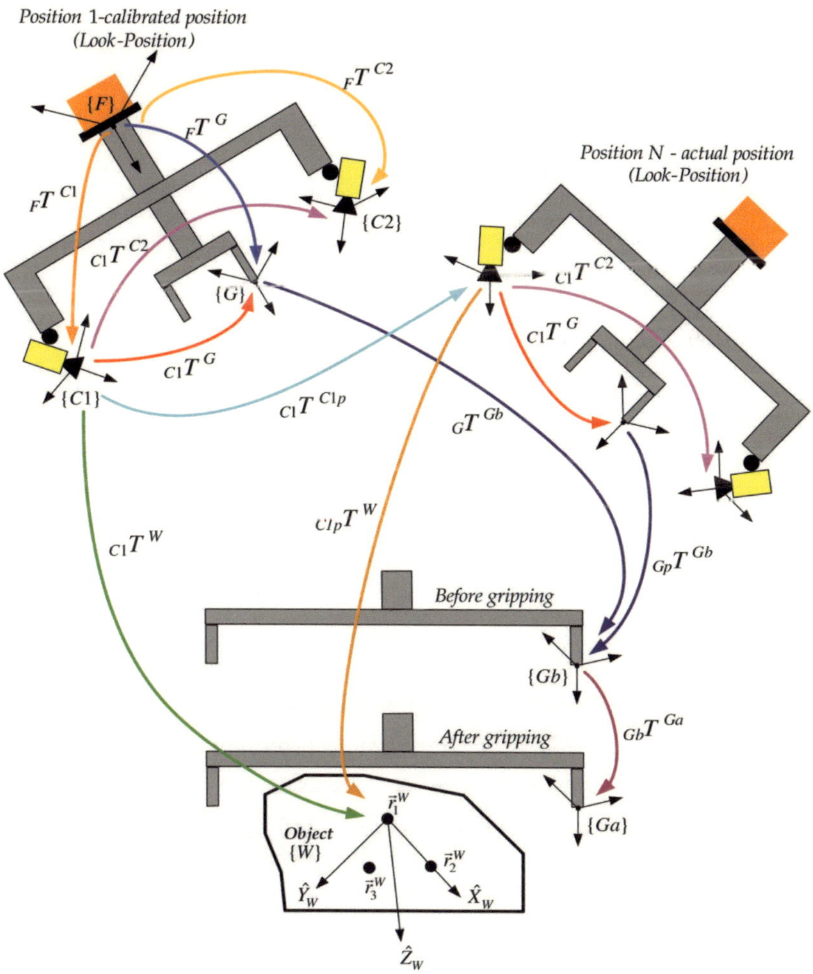

Fig. 9. Gripping the object

After rearranging, a new transformation from the Gripper CS at Position N to the Gripper CS at Position *Gb* can be shown as:

$$ {}_{Gp}T^{Gb} = \left({}_{C1}T^{G}\right)^{-1} {}_{C1p}T^{W} \left({}_{C1}T^{W}\right)^{-1} {}_{C1}T^{G}\, {}_{G}T^{Gb} \tag{15a} $$

Relative orientation method for robot positioning After measuring at least three 3D points in the Camera 1 CS at Position 1 and at Position N, we can calculate the transformation ${}_{C1}T^{C1p}$ between these two positions of the camera (confer Fig. 9), using the methods mentioned in Section 2.3.2. A straightforward approach is to use 4 points to derive ${}_{C1}T^{C1p}$ analytically. It is possible to do so based on only 3 points (which cannot be collinear) since the fourth one can be taken from the (vector) cross product of two vectors representing the 3 points hooked at one of the primary points. Though we sacrifice here the orthogonality constraint of the rotation matrix.
We write the following *loop equation* relating the camera motion, constant camera-gripper transformation, and the gripping motions:

$$ {}_{C1}T^{G}\, {}_{G}T^{Gb} = {}_{C1}T^{C1p}\, {}_{C1}T^{G}\, {}_{Gp}T^{Gb} $$

And after a useful rearrangement,

$$ {}_{Gp}T^{Gb} = \left({}_{C1}T^{G}\right)^{-1} \left({}_{C1}T^{C1p}\right)^{-1} {}_{C1}T^{G}\, {}_{G}T^{Gb} \tag{15b} $$

The new transformation ${}_{Gp}T^{Gb}$ determines a new PTP movement at Position N from *Gp* to *Gb*, while a final gripping motion LIN is determined from the constant transformation ${}_{Gb}T^{Ga}$. Consequently, equations (15a) and (15b) determine the sought motion trajectory which the robot has to follow in order to grip the object.
Furthermore, the transformations described by (15a, b) can be used to position the gripper while the object is being tracked. In order to predict the 3D image coordinates of at least three features one or two sampling steps ahead, a tracking algorithm can be implemented. With the use of such a tracking computation and based on the predicted points, the transformations ${}_{C1}T^{W}$ or ${}_{C1}T^{C1p}$ can be developed and substituted directly into equations (15a, b) so that the gripper could adjust its position relative to the object in the next sampling step.

3.3 Singularities

In systems using the Euler angles representation of orientation the movement ${}_{Gp}T^{Gb}$ has to be programmed in a robot encoder using the frame representation of the transformation ${}_{Gp}T^{Gb}$. The last column of the transformation matrix is the translation vector, directly indicating the first three parameters of the frame (*X*, *Y* and *Z*). The last three parameters *A*, *B* and *C* have to be computed based on the rotation matrix of the transformation. Let us assume that the rotation matrix has the form of (10). First, the angle *B* is computed in radians as

$$ B_1 = \pi + \arcsin(r31) \quad \vee \quad B_2 = -\arcsin(r31) \tag{16a} $$

Then, the angles A and C, based on the angle B, can be computed from the following recipes:

$$A_1 = a\tan 2\left(\frac{r21}{\cos(B_1)}, \frac{r11}{\cos(B_1)}\right) \quad \vee \quad A_2 = a\tan 2\left(\frac{r21}{\cos(B_2)}, \frac{r11}{\cos(B_2)}\right) \tag{16b}$$

$$C_1 = a\tan 2\left(\frac{r32}{\cos(B_1)}, \frac{r33}{\cos(B_1)}\right) \quad \vee \quad C_2 = a\tan 2\left(\frac{r32}{\cos(B_2)}, \frac{r33}{\cos(B_2)}\right) \tag{16c}$$

The above solutions results from solving the sine/cosine equations of the rotation matrix in (10). As the sine/cosine function is a multi-value function over the interval $(-\pi,+\pi)$, the equations (16a-16c) have two sets of solutions: $\{A_1, B_1, C_1\}$ and $\{A_2, B_2, C_2\}$. These two sets give the very same transformation matrix when substituted into (9b). Another common method of rendering these angles from the rotation matrix represents the Nonlinear Least Squares Fitting algorithm. Although its accuracy is higher than that of the technique (16a-16c), applying the NLSF algorithm to the positioning system guided by stereovision obviously deprives the system of its fully analytical development.

As (16a-16c) imply, the singularity of the system occurs in the case when the pitch angle equals ±90 deg, that is $r31$ equals ±1, since it results in zero values of the denominators. This case is called a *gimbal lock* and is a well-known problem in aerospace navigation systems. That is also why unit quaternions notation is preferred against the Euler angles notation.

Another singularity refers to the configuration of object features. Considering the relative orientation algorithms, the transformation between camera positions can only be computed under the condition that at least three not collinear object features are found (as has been discussed above the points have to span a plane in order to render the orientation). The exterior orientation algorithms have drawbacks, as well. Namely, there exist certain critical configurations of points for which the solution is unstable, as already mentioned in Section 2.3.2.

4. Calibration of the system – outline of the algorithms

There are many calibration methods able to find the transformation from the flange of the robot (hand) to the camera (eye). This calibration is called a hand-eye calibration. We demonstrate a classical approach initially introduced by Tsai & Lenz (1989). It states that when the camera undergoes a motion from Position i to Position i+1, described by the transformation ${}_{Ci}T^{Ci+1} = \left({}_{Ci}R^{Ci+1}, {}_{Ci}K^{Ci+1}\right)$, and the corresponding flange motion is ${}_{Fi}T^{Fi+1} = \left({}_{Fi}R^{Fi+1}, {}_{Fi}K^{Fi+1}\right)$, then they are coupled by the following hand-eye transformation ${}_{F}T^{C} = \left({}_{F}R^{C}, {}_{F}K^{C}\right)$, depicted in Fig. 10. This approach yields the subsequent equation:

$${}_{Fi}T^{Fi+1}\,{}_{F}T^{C} = {}_{F}T^{C}\,{}_{Ci}T^{Ci+1} \tag{17}$$

where ${}_{Ci}T^{Ci+1}$ is estimated from the images of the calibration rig using the MCT software, for instance, ${}_{Fi}T^{Fi+1}$ is known with the robot precision from the robot encoder, and ${}_{F}T^{C}$ is the unknown. This equation is also known as the Sylvester equation in systems theory. Since each transformation can be split into rotation and translation matrices, we easily land at

$${}_{Fi}R^{Fi+1}\,{}_{F}R^{C} = {}_{F}R^{C}\,{}_{Ci}R^{Ci+1} \tag{18a}$$

$$ {}_{Fi}R^{Fi+1}\,{}_{F}K^{C} + {}_{Fi}K^{Fi+1} = {}_{F}R^{C}\,{}_{Ci}K^{Ci+1} + {}_{F}R^{C} \tag{18b}$$

Tsai and Lenz proposed a two-step method to solve the problem resented by (18a) and (18b). At first, they solve (18a) by least-square minimization of a linear system, obtained by using the axis-angle representation of the rotation matrix. Then, once ${}_{F}R^{C}$ is known, the solution for (18b) follows using the linear least squares method.

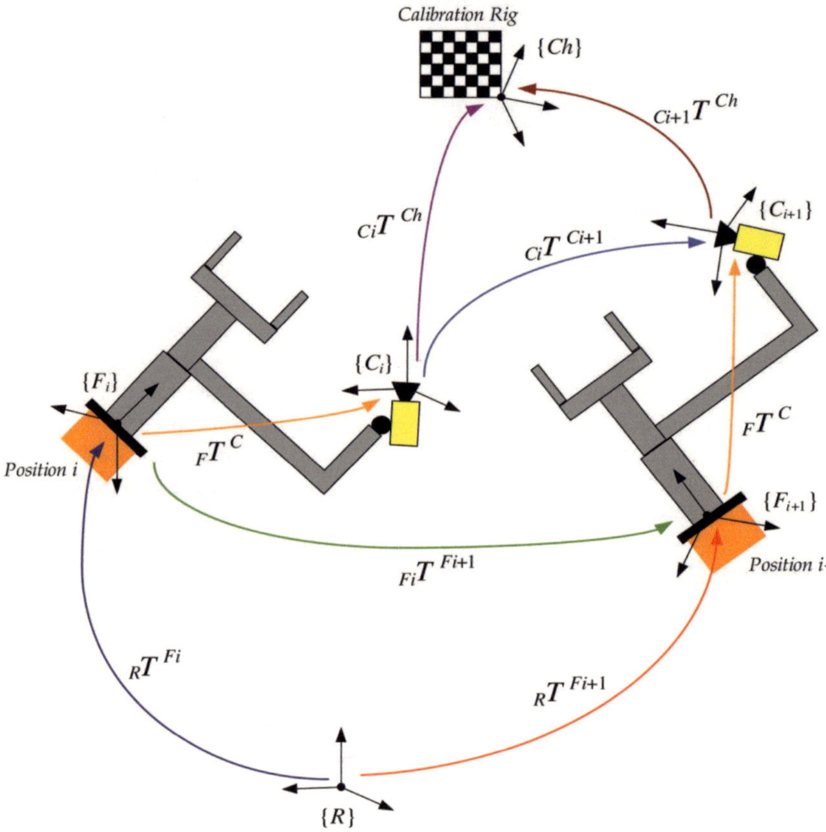

Fig. 10. Hand-Eye Calibration

In order to obtain a unique solution, there have to be at least two motions of the flange-camera system giving accordingly two pairs $({}_{F1}T^{F2}, {}_{C1}T^{C2}), ({}_{F2}T^{F3}, {}_{C2}T^{C3})$. Unfortunately, noise is inevitable in the measurement-based transformations ${}_{Fi}T^{Fi+1}$ and ${}_{Ci}T^{Ci+1}$. Hence it is useful to make more measurements and form a number of the transformations pairs $\{({}_{F1}T^{F2}, {}_{C1}T^{C2}), ({}_{F2}T^{F3}, {}_{C2}T^{C3}), \ldots, ({}_{Fi}T^{Fi+1}, {}_{Ci}T^{Ci+1}), \ldots, ({}_{Fk-1}T^{Fk}, {}_{Ck-1}T^{Ck})\}$, and, consequently, to find a transformation ${}_{F}T^{C}$ that minimizes an error criterion:

$$ \varepsilon = \sum_{i=1}^{k} d({}_{Fi+1}T^{Fi}\,{}_{C}T^{F}, {}_{C}T^{F}\,{}_{Ci+1}T^{Ci}) $$

where $d(\cdot,\cdot)$ stands for some distance metric on the Euclidean group. With the use of the Lie algebra the above minimization problem can be recast into a least squares fitting problem that admits an explicit solution. Specifically, given vectors $x_1,\ldots,x_k$, $y_1,\ldots,y_k$ in a Euclidean n-space, there exist explicit expressions for the orthogonal matrix R and translation K that minimize:

$$\varepsilon = \sum_{i=1}^{k} \left\| Rx_i + K - y_i \right\|^2$$

The best values of R and K turn out to depend on only the matrix $M = \sum_{i=1}^{k} x_i y_i^T$, while the rotation matrix R is then given by the following formula:

$$R = \left(M^T M\right)^{-1/2} M^T$$

Thus ${}_F R^C = \left(M^T M\right)^{-1/2} M^T$ represents in that case the computed rotation matrix of the hand-eye transformation ${}_F T^C$. After straightforward matrix operations on (18b), we acquire the following matrix equation for the translation vector ${}_F K^C$:

$$\begin{bmatrix} {}_{F1}K^{F2} - I \\ {}_{F2}K^{F3} - I \\ \vdots \\ {}_{Fk-1}K^{Fk} - I \end{bmatrix} = {}_F K^C \begin{bmatrix} {}_F R^C \, {}_{C1}K^{C2} - {}_{F1}K^{F2} \\ {}_F R^C \, {}_{C2}K^{C3} - {}_{F2}K^{F3} \\ \vdots \\ {}_F R^C \, {}_{Ck-1}K^{Ck} - {}_{Fk-1}K^{Fk} \end{bmatrix}$$

Using the least-squares method we obtain the solution for ${}_F K^C$.

Although simple to implement, the idea has a disadvantage as it solves (17) in two steps. Namely, the rotation matrix derived from (18a) propagates errors onto the translation vector derived from (18b). In the literature there is a large collection of hand-eye calibration methods, which have proved to be more accurate than the one discussed here. For instance, Daniilidis (1998) solves equation (17) simultaneously using dual quaternions. Andreff *et al.* (2001) uses the structure-from-motion algorithm to find the camera motion ${}_{Ci}T^{Ci+1}$ based on unknown scene parameters, and not by finding the transformations ${}_{Ci}T^{Ch}$ relating the scene (the calibration rig, here) with the camera. This is an interesting approach as it allows for a fully automatic calibration and thus reduces human supervision.

4.1 Manual hand-eye calibration – an evolutionary approach

After having derived the hand-eye transformations for both cameras (using MCT and Tsai method, for instance), it is essential to test their measurement accuracy. Based on images of a checkerboard, the MCT computed the transformation ${}_{Ci}T^{Ch}$ for each robot position with the estimation errors of ±2 mm. This has proved to be too large, as the point measurements resulted then in the repeatability error of even ±6 mm, which was unacceptable. Therefore, a genetic algorithm (GA) was utilized to correct the hand-eye parameters of both cameras, as they have a major influence on the entire accuracy of the system. We aimed to obtain the repeatability error of ±1 mm for each coordinate of all 3D points when compared to the points measured at the first vantage point.

Correcting the values of the hand-eye frames involves the following calibration steps: jogging the camera-robot system to K positions and saving pixel coordinates of N features seen in stereo images. Assuming that the accuracy of K measurements of N points

$(P_{1,1},\ldots,P_{N,1},\ldots,P_{1,K},\ldots,P_{N,K})$ depends only on the hand-eye parameters (actually it depends also on the robot accuracy), the estimated values of both frames have to be modified by some yet unknown corrections:

$$(kx_{FC1}+\Delta kx_{FC1},ky_{FC1}+\Delta ky_{FC1},kz_{FC1}+\Delta kz_{FC1},A_{FC1}+\Delta A_{FC1},B_{FC1}+\Delta B_{FC1},C_{FC1}+\Delta C_{FC1})$$

and

$$(kx_{FC2}+\Delta kx_{FC2},ky_{FC2}+\Delta ky_{FC2},kz_{FC2}+\Delta kz_{FC2},A_{FC2}+\Delta A_{FC2},B_{FC2}+\Delta B_{FC2},C_{FC2}+\Delta C_{FC2}).$$

The corrections, indicated here by Δ, have to be found based on a certain criterion. Thus, a sum of all repeatability errors $f(\Delta)$ of each coordinate of N=3 points has been chosen as a criterion to be minimized. The robot was jogged to K=10 positions. It is clear that the smaller the sum of the errors, the better the repeatability. Consequently, we seek for such corrections, which minimize the following function of the error sum:

$$\varepsilon = f(\Delta)=\sum_{n=1}^{N}\sum_{k=2}^{K}\left|P_{n1}(\Delta)-P_{nk}(\Delta)\right|, \qquad N=3, K=10 \tag{19}$$

As genetic algorithms effectively maximize the criterion function, while we wish to minimize (19), we transform it to:

$$g(\Delta)=C-f(\Delta)$$

The fitness function $g(\Delta)$ can then be maximized, with C being a constant scale factor ensuring that $g(\Delta)>0$,

$$\min f(\Delta)=\max g(\Delta)=\max\{-f(\Delta)\}$$

The function $g(\Delta)$ has 12 variables (6 corrections for each frame). Let us assume that the corrections for both translation vectors $dK=\{\Delta kx_{FC1},\Delta ky_{FC1},\Delta kz_{FC1},\Delta kx_{FC2},\Delta ky_{FC2},\Delta kz_{FC2}\}$ are within a searched interval $D_{dK}=[k_1,k_2]\subseteq R$ and the corrections for the Euler angles of both frames $dR=\{\Delta A_{FC1},\Delta B_{FC1},\Delta C_{FC1},\Delta A_{FC2},\Delta B_{FC2},\Delta C_{FC2}\}$ are within the interval $D_{dR}=[r_1,r_2]\subseteq R$, where $\Delta=\{dK,dR\}$ and $\forall_{dK\in D_{dK}}\ \forall_{dR\in D_{dR}}\ g(\Delta)>0$. Our desire is to maximize $g(\Delta)$ with a certain precision for dK and dR, say 10^{-n} and 10^{-m}, respectively. It means that we have to divide D_{dK} and D_{dR} into $(k_2-k_1)\cdot 10^n$ and $(r_2-r_1)\cdot 10^m$ equal intervals, respectively. Denoting a and b as the least numbers satisfying $(k_2-k_1)\cdot 10^n\le 2^a$ and $(r_2-r_1)\cdot 10^m\le 2^b$ implies that when the values $dK_i, i=1,\ldots,6$ and $dR_i, i=1,\ldots,6$ are coded as binary chains $(ch_i)_{bin},\ i=1,\ldots,6$ and $(ch_j)_{bin},\ j=1,\ldots,6$ of length a and b, respectively, then the binary representation of these values will satisfy the precision constraints. The decimal value of such binary chains can then be expressed as

$$dK_i = k_1 + \frac{decimal\ [(ch_i)_{bin}]\cdot(k_2-k_1)}{2^a} \quad \text{and} \quad dR_i = r_1 + \frac{decimal\ [(ch_j)_{bin}]\cdot(r_2-r_1)}{2^b} \tag{20}$$

Putting binary representations of the corrections $dK_i, i = 1,...,6$ and $dR_i, i = 1,...,6$ into one binary chain leads to a chromosome:

$$v = \{ch_i, ch_j\}, \qquad i, j = 1,...,6$$

A reasonable number of chromosomes, forming a population, have to be defined to guarantee the effectiveness of a GA. The population is initiated completely randomly, *i.e.* bit by bit for each chromosome. In each generation we evaluate all chromosomes by first separating the chains ch_i and ch_j, then computing their decimal values using (20), and finally substituting the final results into $g(\Delta)$. The error function producing a sum of measurement errors for each chromosome, is used to compute the suitability of each chromosome in terms of the fitness function (in effect, by minimizing the repeatability error both frames are optimized). After evaluation, we select a new population according to the probability distribution based on suitability of each chromosome and with the use of recombination and mutation.
The most challenging part of creating a GA lies in determining the fitness function. Suitable selection, recombination and mutation processes are also very important as they form the GA structure and affect convergence to the right results. In spite of a wealth of GA modifications (Kowalczuk & Bialaszewski, 2006), we have implemented classical forms of the procedures of selection, recombination, and mutation (Michalewicz, 1996). Additionally, in order to increase the effectiveness of convergence, though, we did not recombine the five best chromosomes at each selection step (elitism).
After these steps the new population is ready for another evaluation, which is used to determine the distribution of the probability for new selection. The algorithm terminates when the number of generations reaches a certain/given epoch (number). Then the final, sought result is represented by one chromosome characterized by a minimal value of $f(\Delta)$. The chromosome is then divided into 12 binary chains, which are transformed into their decimal values. They represent the computed phenotype, or the optimized corrections, which are then added to the hand-eye frames.
Technical values of the parameters of the genetic algorithm have been as follows:

- generation epoch (number of populations): 300
- population of chromosomes: 40
- recombination probability: 0.5
- mutation probability: 0.05
- precision of corrections: 10^{-4}
- interval for corrections of the translation vectors: [-5, +5] mm
- interval for corrections of the Euler angles: [-0.5, +0.5] deg.

Our genetic algorithm might not converge to the desired error bounds of ±1 mm in the first trial. If this is the case, one has to run the algorithm few times with changed or unchanged parameters.

4.2 Automated calibration

Apart from the pose calibration methods (like the one of Tsai and Lenz), there are also structure-from-motion algorithms that can be applied to calibrate the system without any calibration rig (self hand-eye calibration). Andreff *et al.* (2001) have developed one of such effective calibration methods. They allow for a mobile autonomic robot or robot space applications equipped with vision sensors to recalibrate themselves based on only the actual surrounding scene. By performing programmed movements and using 2D image matching algorithms, the translation vector between the origins of the moving Camera CSs can be estimated and used as a further input to the main algorithm. One of such image matching techniques, based on an adaptive least squares correlation, has been proposed by Gruen (1985).

A fully automatic hand-eye calibration algorithm is a great challenge (with or without a calibration rig) because it would certainly simplify and speed up the calibration process. The time factor is of high importance because it happens quite often that the robotic systems with vision guidance have to be recalibrated. The hand-eye relations change easily during the assembly process due to vibrations during a permanent gripping process. The measurement accuracy does then decrease and the assembly line needs to be stopped (declining efficiency). The faster the system is recalibrated, the sooner the assembly line resumes its work.

5. Experimental results

The experimental system consisted of the following hardware and optical components:

- Kuka robot with 6DOF, model KR 60-3
- Siemens camera, model SIMATIC VS723, resolution of 640×480 pixels
- Cognex camera, model In-Sight 1100, resolution of 640×480 pixels
- Fujinon TV lens, focal length of 16 mm
- Pentax TV lens, focal length of 16 mm

In this research a KUKA robot was utilized which is a six-axis robot with a maximum payload of 60 kg at a maximum range of 2429 mm and a repeatability of ±0.25 mm.

We calibrated the entire stereo system using the classical Tsai and Lenz method and corrected the hand-eye parameters (translation plus rotation based on the Euler angles) with the GA algorithm. We then performed three tests to verify the system's ability to compute the object's pose with repeatable results w.r.t. the static Robot CS based on measured 3 object features. The verification procedure was performed as follows. The robot-stereo system was calibrated for 3 baselines (Baseline 1 was 450 mm, Baseline 2 was 330 mm, and Baseline 3 was 220 mm) and for each one the object was placed at 3 object positions (OPs). The robot was jogged to 10 vantage points (VPs) for each OP. The Euler angles were computed using the NLSF algorithm. As our aim was to create the positioning system with the pose repeatability error of ±1 mm and ±1 deg, the GA was run three times for each camera baseline until it obtained satisfactory results. Each time the computation took about 5 min. The values of the GA parameters listed in Section 4.1 were applied.

Furthermore, we analyzed the influence of the distortion parameters on the system's performance. Three types of verification were used for each baseline. A first method verified the performance of the system with the distortion parameters and with the corrected hand-eye frames of both cameras, a second approach was without the distortion parameters and with the hand-eye corrections, while a third verification was without hand-eye corrections and with the distortion parameters.

As depicted in Fig. 11 after adding the corrections (computed by the GA) to the hand-eye parameters the repeatability error was significantly diminished. Satisfactory results were obtained with and without the distortion parameters. Although distortions seemed not to influence the accuracy for the lens focal length of 16 mm, the authors suggest that they should be included in the camera model when the camera is equipped with lenses of shorter focal lengths.

The figures show that the measuring accuracy of the system without the corrected hand-eye parameters is unsatisfactory for Baselines 1 and 3. The desired accuracy was achieved for Baseline 2, though here the camera-checkerboard transformations computed by MCT had very small errors as compared to those obtained for the other two baselines. Yet, the system with Baseline 2 had the best accuracy because the distances from the Camera 1 to the Object CS were relatively smaller in this configuration. Fig. 12 shows the distances between these two CSs varying from 250 mm to 600 mm, while we set the focus of the cameras at the distance of 400 mm. Although images were blurred at minimal and maximal distances, such deviations proved to be acceptable. Not surprisingly, Baseline 3, the shortest one, produced the worst accuracy.

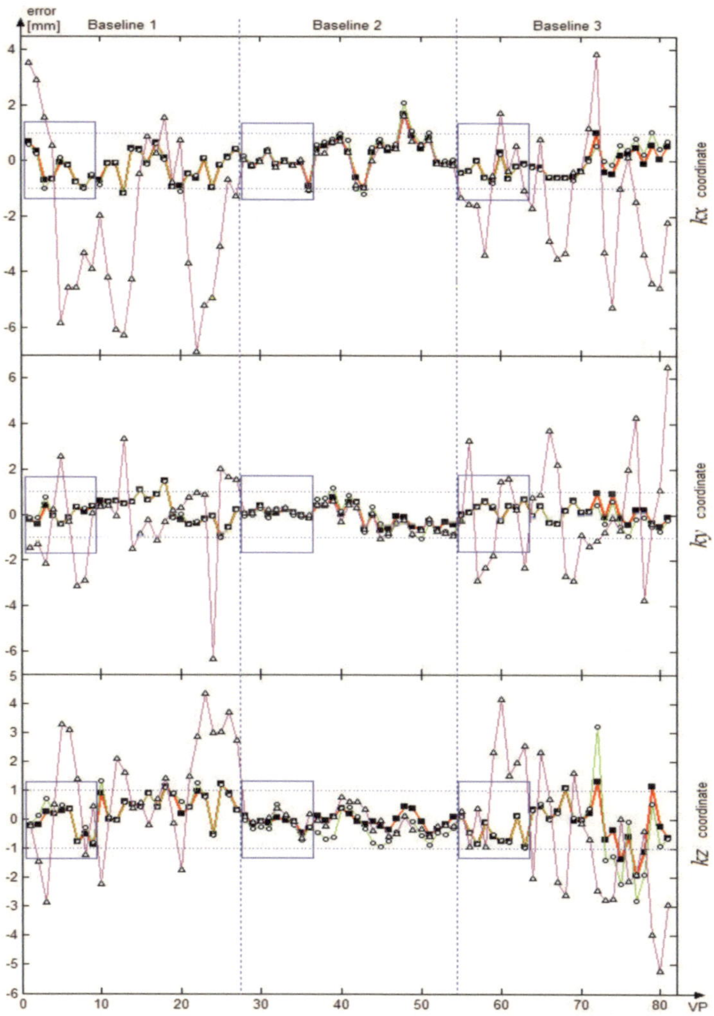

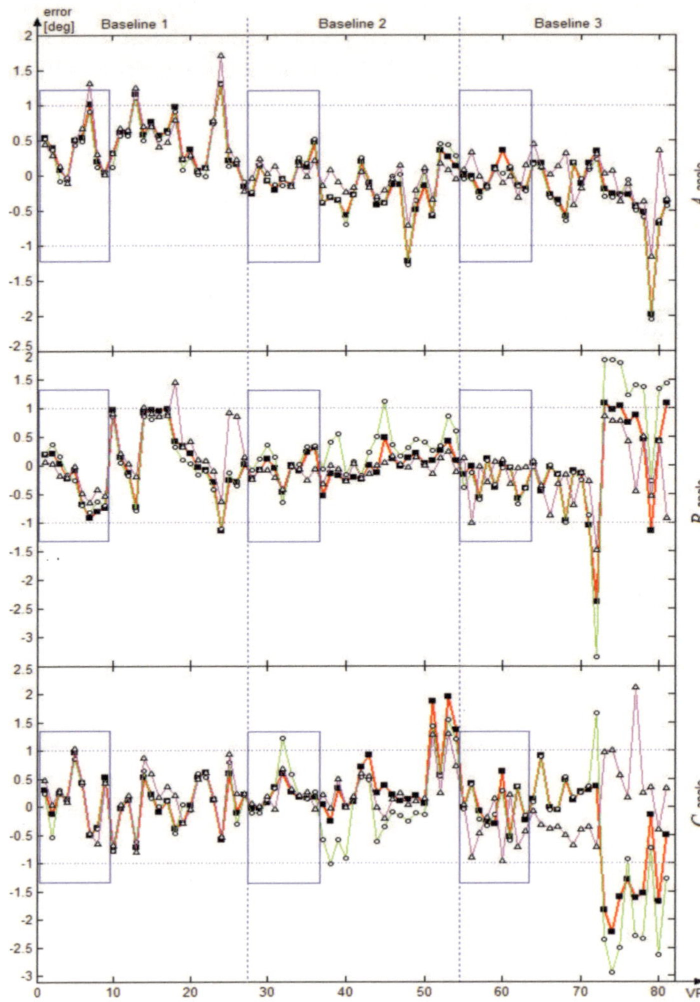

Fig. 11. Repeatability error of the *kx*, *ky*, *kz* coordinates and the *A*, *B*, *C* angles for Baselines 1, 2, 3 : *square* - with the distortion coefficients and with hand-eye corrections; *circle* - without the distortion coefficients and with the hand-eye corrections; *triangle* - with the distortion coefficients and without the hand-eye corrections

The proposed manual calibration of the stereovision system satisfied the criterions of repeatability of measurements. Although there are some errors shown in Fig. 11 that exceed the desired accuracy, it has to be noticed that some pictures were taken at very acute angles. In overall, the camera's yaw angle varied between -50 and +100 deg and the pitch angle varied between -60 and +40 deg throughout the whole test, what far exceeds the real working conditions. Moreover, the image data were collected for GA only at the first OP for each baseline (marked as blue rectangles in the figures) and they were very noisy in several cases. We suppose that noise must have decreased the GA's efficiency in searching for the best solutions, but the evolutionary approach itself allowed preserving stability and robustness of the ultimate robotic system.

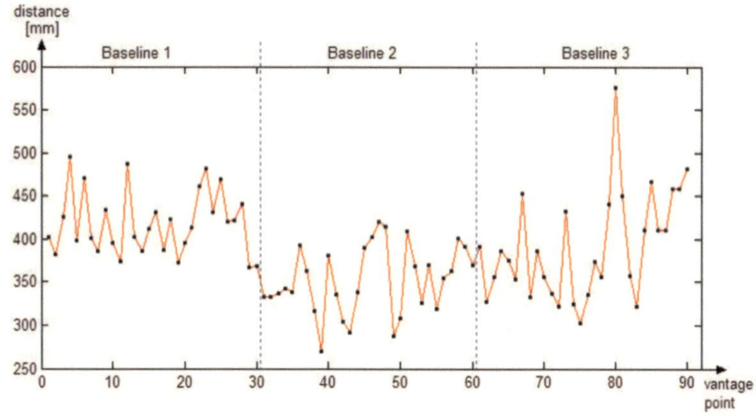

Fig. 12. Distance between the origins of the Object CS and the Camera 1 CS for each VP

6. Conclusion and future work

A manipulator equipped with vision sensors can be 'aware' of the surrounding scene, what admits of performing tasks with higher flexibility and efficiency. In this chapter a robotic system with stereo cameras has been presented the purpose of which was to release humans from handling (picking, moving, *etc.*) non-constrained objects in a three-dimensional space.
In order to utilize image data, a pinhole camera model has been introduced together with a "Plumb Bob" model for lens distortions. A precise description of all parameters has been given. Two conventions (*i.e.* the Euler-angle and the unit quaternion notations) have been presented for describing the orientation matrix of rigid-body transformations that are utilized by leading robot manufacturers. The problem of 3D object pose estimation has been explained based on retrieved information from single and stereo images. Epipolar geometry of stereo camera configurations has been analyzed to explain how it can be used to make image processing more reliable and faster. We have outlined certain pose estimation algorithms to provide the reader with a wide integrated spectrum of methods utilized in robot positioning applications when considering specific constraints (like analytical, or iterative). Moreover, we have also supplied various references to other algorithms. Two methods for a three-dimensional robot positioning system have been developed and bridged with the object pose estimation algorithms. Singularities of the robot positioning systems have been indicated, as well.
A challenging task has been to find a hand-eye transformation of the system, *i.e.* the transformation between a camera and a robot end-effector. We have explained the classic approach by Tsai and Lenz solving this problem and have used a Matlab Calibration Toolbox to perform calibration. We have extended this approach by utilizing a genetic algorithm (GA) in order to improve the system measurement precision in the sense of satisfactory repeatability of positioning the robotic gripper. We have then outlined other calibration algorithms and suggested an automated calibration as a step towards making the entire system autonomous and reliable.
The experimental results obtained have proved that our GA-based calibration method yields the system precision of ±1 mm and ±1 deg, thus satisfying the industrial demands on the accuracy of automated part acquisition. A future research effort should be placed on (•) optimization of the mathematical principles for positioning the robot through some orthogonality constraints of rotation to increase the system's accuracy, (•) development of a

method for computing 3D points using two non-overlapping images (to be utilized for large objects), (•) implementation of a hand-eye calibration method based on the structure-from-motion algorithms, and (•) implementation of algorithms for tracking objects.

7. References

Andreff, N.; Horaud, R. & Espiau, B. (2001). Robot hand-eye calibration using structure-from-motion. *The International Journal of Robotics Research*, vol. 20, no. 3, pp. 228-248

Daniilidis, K. (1998). *Hand-Eye Calibration Using Dual Quaternions*, GRASP Laboratory, University of Pennsylvania, PA (USA)

Fischler, M.A. & Bolles, R.C. (1981). Random sample consensus: A paradigm for model fitting with applications to image analysis and automated cartography. *Graphics and Image Processing*, vol. 24, no. 6, pp. 381-395

Gruen, A.W. (1985). Adaptive least squares correlation: A powerful image matching technique. *South African Journal of Photogrammetry, Remote Sensing and Cartography*, vol. 14, no. 3, pp. 175-187

Haralick, R.M.; Joo, H.; Lee, C.; Zhuang, X.; Vaidya, V.G. & Kim, M.B. (1989). Pose estimation from corresponding point data. *IEEE Transactions on Systems, Man and Cybernetics*, vol. 19, no. 6, pp. 1426-1446

Horn, B.K.P. (1987). Closed-form solution of absolute orientation using unit quaternions. *Journal of the Optical Society of America A*, vol. 4, no.4, pp. 629-642

Kowalczuk, Z. & Bialaszewski, T. (2006) Niching mechanisms in evolutionary computations. *International Journal of Applied Mathematics and Computer Science*, vol. 16, no. 1, pp. 59-84

Kowalczuk, Z. & Wesierski, D. (2007). Three-dimensional robot positioning system with stereo vision guidance. *Proc. 13th IEEE/IFAC Int. Conf. on Methods and Models in Automation and Robotics*, Szczecin (Poland), CD-ROM, pp. 1011-1016

Lu, C.P.; Hager, G.D. & Mjolsness, E. (1998). Fast and globally convergent pose estimation from video images. *IEEE Transactions on Pattern Analysis and Machine Intelligence*, vol. 22, no. 6, pp. 610-622

Michalewicz, Z. (1992). *Genetic Algorithms + Data Structures = Evolution Programs*. Springer, New York

Phong, T.Q.; Horaud, R.; Yassine, A. & Tao, P.D. (1995). Object pose from 2D to 3D point and line correspondences. *International Journal of Computer Vision*, vol. 15, no. 3, pp. 225-243

Schweighofer, G. & Pinz, A. (2006). Robust pose estimation from planar target. *IEEE Transactions on Pattern Analysis and Machine Intelligence*, vol. 28, no. 12, pp. 2024-2030

Szczepanski, W. (1958). Die Lösungsvorschläge für den räumlichen Rückwärtseinschnitt. *Deutsche Geodätische Komission*, Reihe C: Dissertationen-Heft, No. 29, pp. 1-144

Thompson, E. H. (1966). Space resection: Failure cases. *Photogrammetric Record*, vol. X, no. 27, pp. 201-204

Tsai, R. & Lenz, R. (1989). A new technique for fully autonomous and efficient 3D robotics hand/eye calibration. *IEEE Transactions on Robotics and Automation*, vol. 5,, no. 3, pp. 345-358

Weinstein, D.M. (1998). The analytic 3-D transform for the least-squared fit of three pairs of corresponding points. *Technical Report*, Dept. of Computer Science, University of Utah, UT (USA)

Wrobel, B.P. (1992). Minimum solutions for orientation. *Proc. IEEE Workshop Calibration and Orientation Cameras in Computer Vision*, Washington D.C. (USA)

4

Closed-Loop Feedback Systems in Automation and Robotics, Adaptive and Partial Stabilization

G. R. Rokni Lamooki
Center of Excellence in Biomathematics, Faculty of mathematics statistics and Computer Science, College of Science, University of Tehran
Iran

1. Introduction

Feedback controls have applications in various fields including engineering, mechanics, biomathematics, and mathematical economics; see (Ogata, 1970), (de Queiroz, et al. 2000), (Murray, 2002), and (Seierstad & Sydsaeter, 1987) for more details. Lyapunov based control of mechanical system is a well-known technique. This includes Lyapunov direct/indirect methods. Such techniques can be employed to control the whole state variables or a part of the state variables. Sometimes there are some uncertainties or some reference trajectories which requires adaptive control. Back-stepping is a yet powerful approach to design the required controller. However, this approach leads to a complicated controller, especially when the chain of integrators is long. Back-stepping can also be used when the aim of control is the stability with respect to a part of the variables. These three concepts emerge in a mechanical system like a robot. Adaptive control can be carried out through two different approaches: indirect and direct adaptive control. Nevertheless there are some drawbacks in such control systems which are a matter of concern. For example, when there is the possibility of fault or it is considered to turn off the adaptation for saving energy, when the system seems to be relaxed at its equilibrium situation, the outcome can be dramatically destructive. Adaptively controlled systems with unknown parameters exhibit partial stability phenomenon when the persistence of excitation is not assumed to be satisfied by the designed controllers. Partial stability technique is most useful when a fully stabilized system losses some control engine or some phase variables are not actively controlled. Such situation is most applicable for automatic systems which need to work remotely without a proper access to maintenance; e.g., satellite, robots to work on other planets or under hard conditions which are required to continue their mission even if some fault happens, or when a minimum of controller is required. It is also applicable to biped robots when one of the engines is turned off, or weakened, for lack of energy or fault or when the robot is passively designed. It is worth noting that another useful aspect of partial stability and control is the possibility of controlling the required part of the phase variables without spending energy to control the part of the variables which is not relevant to the mission of the designed system. These concepts will be explained through some examples. The results will be illustrated by numerical computations. This chapter is organized as follows. In section 2 the notion of stability and partial stability will be briefly discussed. In section 3 the adaptive back stepping design will be introduced with two examples of fully stabilized and partially stabilized systems. The notion of single-wedge bifurcation will be discussed. In section 4, the question is: whether in mechanical system single-wedge bifurcation is likely to appear or not? If so, what sort of instability may occur when such bifurcation takes place? In this section an example of a simple mechanical system with unknown parameter will be studied. This mechanical system is a pendulum with one unknown parameter. The reason of considering such simple system is to emphasize that such undesirable situation is more likely to take place in more complicated mechanical systems when that is possible in a simple case. In section 5 a robot will be studied where only one of the phase variables is actively controlled while there are a reference trajectory and some unknown parameters. This falls into the category of adaptive stabilization with respect to a part of the variables. Such technique does not always leads to the objective of the control. We would like to see that how the geometric boundedness of the system can lead to a successful design.

2. Stability and partial stability

Consider the differential equation

$$\dot{x} = f(x). \tag{1}$$

For any initial value x_0 the solution $\phi_t(x_0) = x(t, x_0)$ is called the flow of the system (1). The point x^* is called an equilibrium for (1) if $\phi_t(x^*) = x^*$ for all $t \geq 0$. Such points satisfy $f(x^*) = 0$. Suppose that the vector field f is complete so that the solutions exist for all time. We call x^* an asymptotic stable equilibrium if for any neighborhood U around x^* there is another neighborhood V such that all solutions starting in V are bounded by U and converge to x^* asymptotically. In order to check the stability, one needs to resort different techniques. Lyapunov has developed important techniques for the problem of stability, so-called *direct* and *indirect* methods. Lyapunov indirect method basically guarantees local stability of the nonlinear system. Here, the eigenvalues of the linearization of the system, about the equilibrium x^* are examined. If all of them have negative real parts then the linearized system is globally stable. However, the original nonlinear system is typically stable only for small perturbations of initial conditions around the equilibrium. The set of admissible initial perturbations is usually a difficult task to determine. On the other hand, Lyapunov direct method examines the vector field directly. It is based on the existence of a so-called Lyapunov function, a positive-definite function defined in a neighborhood of the equilibrium x^*, with a negative-definite time derivative. This guarantees the stability of the system in a neighborhood of x^*.

The case where the Lyapunov function is not negative-definite, but just negative can only guarantees the stability, but not asymptotic stability. However, through some invariant properties we can have asymptotic stability too. This is formulated in La' Salle invariant principle (Khalil, 1996).

Now, we consider the system

$$\dot{x} = f(x,w), \qquad x = (y,z) \in R^{p+q}, \qquad w \in R^s, p+q = n. \tag{2}$$

Here, $f(0,0)=0$, x is the state and $w = w(x)$ is the feedback controller such that $w(0)=0$. The vector field f is considered smooth. In the standard Lyapunov based stabilization with respect to all variables $x=(y,z)$ around the equilibrium, lets say $x=0$, we choose a control $w(x)$ such that there exists a positive-definite Lyapunov function with a negative-definite time derivative in a domain around the equilibrium, which then guarantees the asymptotic stability of $x=0$. In the problem of stabilization with respect to a part of the variables the notion of $y-$positive-definite Rumyantsev function (Rumyantsev, 1957) plays a key role. The domain of a Rumyantsev function is a cylinder

$$D = \{(y,z) \mid \quad \| y \| \le H, \quad \| z \| \le \infty \ \}, \tag{3}$$

for some $H > 0$.

Definition: The function $V : D \to R$ is called a $y-$positive definite Rumyantsev function if there exists a continuous function $W(y)$ with $W(0)=0$ which is positive in cylinder (2) so that $V(y,z) \ge W(y)$ for all $(y,z) \in D$.

Definition: The system $\dot{x} = f(x,w(x))$ is called $y-$stable or stable with respect to y if for any $\varepsilon > 0$ there exists $\delta > 0$ such that for all initial conditions x_0 with $\| x_0 \| < \delta$ the solution $y(t)$ satisfies $\| y(t) \| < \varepsilon$. The system $\dot{x} = f(x,w(x))$ is called asymptotically $y-$stable or asymptotically stable with respect to y if, in addition, there exists a number $\Delta > 0$ such that for all initial condition x_0 with $\| x_0 \| < \Delta$ the solution $y(t)$ satisfies $\lim_{t\to\infty} y(t) = 0$.

There are several approaches towards analyzing the partial stability. These approaches are given by (Rumyantsev, 1957); (Rumyantsev, 1970); and (Rumyantsev & Oziraner, 1987); see also (Vorotnikov, 1998).

There are two major directions to prove asymptotic $y-$stability: the method of sign-definite time derivative Rumyantsev function and the method of sign-constant time derivative Rumyantsev function. The former requires a Rumyantsev function with a $y-$negative-definite time-derivative, whereas the later considers a Rumyantsev function with a $y-$negative time-derivative. For simplicity, we refer to these methods by terms sign-definite and sign-constant method respectively. See (Rumyantsev, 1957), (Rumyantsev, 1970) and (Vorotnikov, 1998) for more details. The method of the sign-constant is based on two concepts of the boundedness and precompactness; see (Andreev, 1991), (Andreev, 1987) and (Oziraner, 1973).

3. Adaptive back-stepping design

Consider the following system with one fixed unknown parameter

$$\begin{cases} \dot{x} = f_1(x,y,\theta^*), \\ \dot{y} = f_2(x,y,u). \end{cases} \tag{4}$$

Assume $f_1(0,0,\theta)=0$ for all θ. Adaptive back-stepping has two steps. First a feedback $y=\kappa(x,\hat{\theta})$ is designed with $\kappa(0,\hat{\theta})=0$ for all $\hat{\theta}$, using an estimation $\hat{\theta}$ for the unknown parameter θ^*. The estimation $\hat{\theta}$ is updated according to the adaptation $\dot{\hat{\theta}}=G(x,\theta)$ such that the $x-$equation is stabilized. In the next step we need to specify the actual controller u and parameter adaptation so that $\varsigma(t)=y(t)-\kappa(x(t),\hat{\theta}(t))$ and $x(t)$ converge to zero as time goes to infinity. As an example, consider the system

$$\begin{cases}\dot{x}=y+\theta^*\varphi(x),\\ \dot{y}=u.\end{cases} \tag{5}$$

Here, $x,y\in R$ are state variables, u is the controller and $\theta^*\in R$ is the unknown parameter. Suppose ϕ is smooth and $\phi(0)=0$. Using the back-stepping technique, one can construct the following controller and parameter adaptation.

$$\begin{cases}u=-\nu(\varsigma)-x-\left(\mu'(x)+\phi'(x)\hat{\phi}\right)\left(-\mu(x)+\varsigma\right)-\phi(x)\hat{\theta},\\ \dot{\hat{\theta}}=\phi(x)\left[x+\varsigma\left(\mu'(x)+\phi'(x)\hat{\theta}\right)\right]\end{cases} \tag{6}$$

to achieve the following closed-loop system.

$$\begin{cases}\dot{x}=-\mu(x)+\varsigma+\tilde{\theta}\phi(x),\\ \dot{\varsigma}=-x-\nu(\varsigma)+\left(\mu'(x)+\phi'(x)(\theta^*-\tilde{\theta}\right)\tilde{\theta}\phi(x),\\ \dot{\tilde{\theta}}=-\phi(x)\left(x+\varsigma\left(\mu'(x)+\phi'(x)(\theta^*-\tilde{\theta}\right)\right)\end{cases} \tag{7}$$

Here, $\tilde{\theta}=\theta-\hat{\theta}$ is the error of estimation. One can observe that in such system $\tilde{\theta}$ is bounded and indeed converges to some fixed value depends on initial cinditions. This fixed value defines a non-adaptive controlle so called limit controller which is accordingly corresponding to a non-adaptive closed system so called limit system. Surprisingly, such limit system is not guaranteed to be stabilized. Sometimes such limit system attracts a large subset of all initial conditions. The occurrence of this situation is called single-wedge bifurcation. The term single-wedge reffers to the fact that the shape of all initial conditions absorbed to such destabilized non-adaptive limit systems looks like a wedge. The system (7), dramatically undergoes a singl-wedge bifurcation; that is a transcritical bifurcation corresponding to a destabilized limit system, possibly with finite escape time, and with a large basin of attraction; see (Townley, 1999) and (Rokni, et al. 2003) for more details on this issue and derivation of (6)-(7). The problem is not merely about the destabilizing limit system, that is also about the finite escape time.

Now, we focus on the system

$$\begin{cases}\dot{x}=f\ (x,w,\theta^*),\\ \dot{w}=h\ (x,w,u),\end{cases} \qquad x=(y,z)\in R^{p+q}, \qquad w\in R^s, p+q=n. \tag{8}$$

Here x, w are the phase variables, θ^* is a vector of unknown parameters, and $u \in R^m$ is the controller. Suppose $f(0,0,\theta)=0, h(0,0,0)=0$ for all θ. The aim is to design a controller u such that the closed-loop system is stabilized with respect to y while other variables including parameter adaptation stay bounded. We use the back-stepping design, but at each step we only aim to stabilize y. We use the partial stability approach described in section 2 to design a controller u together with a $y-$positive definite function V with $y-$negative-definite $\dot{V}$. In case of sign constant $\dot{V}$, we also need the boundedness property of non-stabilized variables. Consider the following example.

$$\begin{cases} x = [y \quad z]^T \in R^2, \\ \dot{y} = bw + \theta^* \phi^1(y,z), \\ \dot{z} = cw + \theta^* \phi^2(y,z) \\ \dot{w} = u. \end{cases} \tag{9}$$

Suppose ϕ is smooth and $\phi(0,0)=0$. The adaptive partial stabilization of this system has two stages. First we stabilize the $x-$equation with respect to y by assuming that w is the controller. At this stage we can define $w = \kappa(x,\hat{\theta}) = -b^{-1}(\hat{\theta}\phi^1 + h(y))$ where $\hat{\theta}$ is the estimation for θ. Here h satisfies $yh(y) > 0$. Next, we stabilize two variables $\varsigma = w - \kappa(x,\hat{\theta})$ and y using a suitable controller u. This leads to

$$\begin{cases} u = -\left[by + b^{-1}\phi^1\hat{\theta} + b^{-1}\hat{\theta}\left(\dfrac{\partial \phi^1}{\partial y} + h'\right)(b\varsigma - h(y))\right] \\ \qquad - \left[b^{-1}\hat{\theta}\dfrac{\partial \phi^1}{\partial z}\left(c\varsigma - cb^{-1}\hat{\theta}\phi^1 - cb^{-1}h(y) + \hat{\theta}\phi^2\right)\right] - \mu(\varsigma), \\ \dot{\hat{\theta}} = \varsigma\left(b^{-1}\hat{\theta}\left(\dfrac{\partial \phi^1}{\partial y} + h'\right)\phi^1 + b^{-1}\hat{\theta}\dfrac{\partial \phi^1}{\partial z}\phi^2\right) + y\phi^1. \end{cases} \tag{10}$$

Here, μ is another function satisfying $\varsigma\mu(\varsigma) > 0$. It can be shown that under some mild conditions on ϕ, in this closed-loop system, the error of parameter estimation $\tilde{\theta} = \theta - \hat{\theta}$ converges to some value depending on initial conditions. The variable w converges to zero and z stay bounded. This system exhibits destabilized limit systems, but no single-wedge type behavior.

Partial stability phenomena frequently appear in mechanical systems, for example, in rotating bodies. One classical example is Euler's equations for tumbling box when one or more controller is omitted. Another well-known case of partially stabilized systems is adaptively controlled systems without persistence of excitation. Sometimes the system capability requires partial stabilization and sometimes the control strategy implies that. In mathematical model of certain biological systems of $n-$ spices a chain of integrators appears with the controller located at the last integrator; see (Murray, 2002). Such systems are referred to as strict feedback form and are locally asymptotically stabilizable about the nominal equilibrium via a recursive design. Such controller is usually very complicated and contains many unnecessary cancellations; see (Krstić, et al. 1995) for some techniques for avoiding unnecessary cancellations. However, it might not be necessary to stabilize all the spices. If that is required, or enough, to fully control a part of these spices while the other stay bounded, then the designed controller will be simpler and more economic. In these types of systems, unknown parameters are likely to appear. Therefore, that is vital to study the possibility of single-wedge bifurcation to avoid destabilizing when the adaptation turns off. In this chapter we focus on mechanical cases, but the method can be applied to other fields too.

4. Simple pendulum

A simple pendulum with fixed given length and mass can be represented by

$$\ddot{\phi} + \alpha\dot{\phi} - k\sin\phi = u, \tag{11}$$

Here, ϕ is the angle between the rod and the vertical axis, and $\alpha > 0$ represents the friction. The pendulum is inverted when $k > 0$ and is not inverted when $k < 0$. We assume $k \in R$ to cover both situations. The absolute value of k is proportional to the gravitation constant which is assumed to be fixed but unknown. The aim is to design an adaptive controller which works for any value of k. Note that the case $k = 0$, no gravity, is not generic. The purpose of the control is $(\phi, \dot{\phi}) \to 0$ asymptotically. The focus is the possibility of single-wedge bifurcation. Suppose that there is no friction; that is $\alpha = 0$. Suppose $\hat{k}$ is the estimation of k and $\tilde{k} = k - \hat{k}$ is the error of the estimation. Through a recursive back-stepping design we can find an adaptive controller with a tuning function for parameter adaptation. We denote $x = \phi$ and $y = \dot{\phi}$. Then, the equation (11) becomes

$$\begin{cases} \dot{x} = y, \\ \dot{y} = k\sin x - \alpha y + u. \end{cases} \tag{12}$$

It needs to remind that we assumed $\alpha = 0$. We use the adaptive back-stepping approach to design an adaptive controller. At first step, we consider y as the controller for $x-$equation. Using $2V_1 = x^2$ as the Lyapunov function the time derivative of V_1 is negative definite by choosing $y = -h(x)$, where h satisfies $xh(x) > 0$. Then, we apply the change of variable $\varsigma = y + h(x)$. In the new system of coordinate, the equation (12) becomes

$$\begin{cases} \dot{x} = \varsigma - h(x), \\ \dot{\varsigma} = (\hat{k} + \tilde{k})\sin x + (\varsigma - h(x))h'(x)) + u. \end{cases} \tag{13}$$

Now, we propose the Lyapunov function $2V = x^2 + \varsigma^2 + \tilde{k}^2$. The time derivative of V is

$$\dot{V} = -xh(x) + \varsigma\left[x + \hat{k}\sin x + \varsigma h'(x) - h(x)h'(x) + u\right] + \tilde{k}\left[\varsigma\sin x - \dot{\hat{k}}\right]. \tag{14}$$

We choose

$$\begin{cases} u = -\mu(\varsigma) - x - \hat{k}\sin x - \varsigma h'(x) + h(x)h'(x), \\ \dot{\hat{k}} = \varsigma \sin x. \end{cases} \tag{15}$$

Here, μ is a function satisfying $\varsigma\mu(\varsigma) > 0$, then

$$\dot{V} = -xh(x) - \varsigma\mu(\varsigma). \tag{16}$$

The three-dimensional auxiliary closed-loop system is

$$\begin{cases} \dot{x} = \varsigma - h(x), \\ \dot{\varsigma} = \tilde{k}\sin x - x - \mu(\varsigma), \\ \dot{\tilde{k}} = -\varsigma \sin x. \end{cases} \tag{17}$$

The closed-loop system (17) is partially asymptotically stabilized with respect to (x,ς) . To see this, one can observe that the auxiliary closed loop system (17) is $\tilde{k}-$ bounded. This boundedness property together with the fact that V is $(x,\varsigma,\tilde{k})-$ positive definite while $\dot{V}$ is sign constant results the required partial stability. Therefore, the origin of the actual closed-loop system (11) and (15) is partially asymptotically stabilized with respect to $(\phi,\dot{\phi})$ regardless the actual value of k and its initial condition. This stabilization is global. In Fig. 1 $x(t)$ and $\varsigma(t)$ are drawn for $h(x) = x + x^2 + x^3$ and $\mu(\varsigma) = \varsigma + \varsigma^2 + \varsigma^3$ for initial condition $(x,\varsigma,\tilde{k}) = (2,6,-6)$.

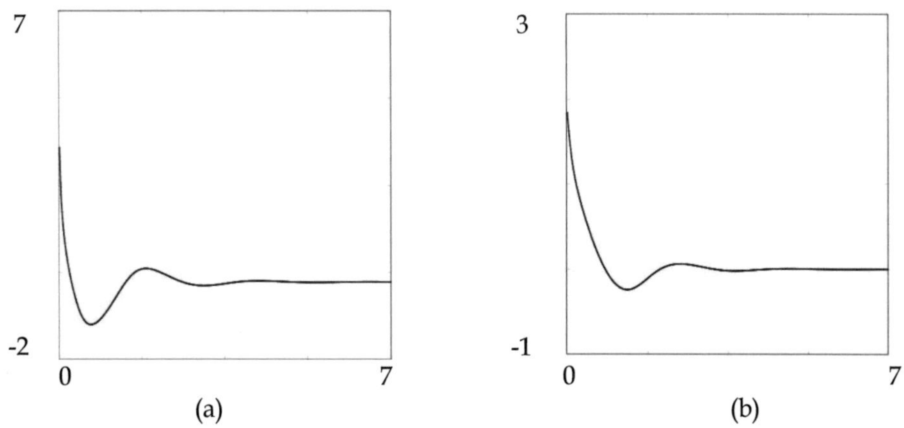

Fig. 1. $x(t)$ and $\varsigma(t)$ are drawn for $h(x) = x + x^2 + x^3$ and $\mu(\varsigma) = \varsigma + \varsigma^2 + \varsigma^3$ for initial condition $(x,\varsigma,\tilde{k}) = (2,6,-6)$. The horizontal axis is time. The vertical axis in (a) is $\varsigma(t)$ and in (b) is $x(t)$.

The closed-loop system (17) has a one dimensional manifold of equilibria defined by $(x,\varsigma)=0$. Every equilibrium on this manifold has one zero eigenvalue due to the degeneracy appeared in $\tilde{k}-$ equation as a result of adaptive back-stepping design. The stability type of equilibria on this manifold is characterized by two more eigenvalues given by the linearization of the vector field around those equilibria. One can observe that the arbitrary equilibrium $(0,0,\tilde{k}_\infty)$ has two eigenvalues given by the polynomial

$$\lambda^2+(h_1+\mu_1)\lambda+h_1\mu_1+1-\tilde{k}_\infty=0, \tag{18}$$

where $h_1=h'(0)$ and $\mu_1=\mu'(0)$. The single-wedge bifurcation may take place when $h_1\mu_1+1-\tilde{k}_\infty=0$, and $h_1+\mu_1>0$. This later condition is always the case as long as both linear parts of h and μ are not simultaneously zero. We denote this critical equilibrium with $(0,0,\tilde{k}_c)$. We use the change of variables

$$\begin{bmatrix} x \\ \varsigma \end{bmatrix}=M^{-1}\begin{bmatrix} p \\ q \end{bmatrix}, \quad M=\begin{bmatrix} 1 & 1 \\ -\mu_1 & -h_1 \end{bmatrix}. \tag{19}$$

Here, the column of M are the eigenvectors of the linearization matrix of the $(x,\varsigma)-$ part of the vector field (17) around the critical equilibrium corresponding to the eigenvalues $\lambda_1=-h_1-\mu_1<0$ and $\lambda_2=0$ respectively. Such transformation keeps $\tilde{k}$ invariant. In order to analyze the closed-loop system (17) around its critical equilibrium, we first represent the system (17) in terms of $(p,q,\tilde{k})$ and then reduce the resultant system to the center manifold. Here, the center manifold is given by $p=H(q,\tilde{k})$. The center manifold is invariant and tangent to the linear eigenspace corresponding to the eigenvalue $\lambda_2=0$. Therefore,

$$\dot{p}=\frac{\partial H}{\partial q}\dot{q}+\frac{\partial H}{\partial \tilde{k}}\dot{\tilde{k}}. \tag{20}$$

The lengthy, but straightforward procedure of center manifold calculation leads to the following truncation of the reduced system

$$\begin{cases} \dot{q}=\beta_1 q^2+\beta_2 q\tilde{k}+qO(|q,\tilde{k}|^2), \\ \dot{\tilde{k}}=\gamma_1 q^2+qO(|q,\tilde{k}|^2). \end{cases} \tag{21}$$

Here,

$$\beta_1=\frac{\mu_1 h_2+h_1^2\mu_2}{h_1+\mu_1}, \quad \beta_2=\frac{1}{h_1+\mu_1}, \quad \gamma_1=-h_1, \tag{22}$$

where, $2h_2 = h''(0)$ and $2\mu_2 = \mu''(0)$. It can be observed that the reduced system (21) is degenerate. We utilize the singular time reparametrization (Dumortier & Roussarie, 2000); that is $t = \frac{1}{q}\tau$ to achieve the divided out system

$$\begin{cases} \frac{dq}{d\tau} = q' = \beta_1 q + \beta_2 \tilde{k} + O(|q,\tilde{k}|^2), \\ \frac{d\tilde{k}}{d\tau} = \tilde{k}' = \gamma_1 q + O(|q,\tilde{k}|^2), \end{cases} \tag{23}$$

which is generically hyperbolic around the origin. The singular time reparametrization keeps the orbits but the direction of which are reversed when $q < 0$. In order to have single-wedge bifurcation for the closed-loop system (17), it is sufficient that the origin of the system (23) become a node, either stable or unstable. The characteristic equation of the origin of the system (23) is

$$\lambda^2 - \beta_1\lambda - \beta_2\gamma_1 = 0. \tag{24}$$

The sign of the discriminant of this algebraic equation is equivalent to the sign of

$$\delta = A\mu_2^2 + Bh_2^2 + C\mu_2 h_2 - \omega, \tag{25}$$

where,

$$A = h_1^4, \quad B = \mu_1^2, \quad C = 2\mu_1 h_1^2, \quad \omega = 4h_1^2 + 4h_1\mu_1. \tag{26}$$

The origin of the divided out system (23) is a center when $\delta < 0$. This implies that the center manifold (21) has a semi-center at the origin. This causes that the critical equilibrium of the closed-loop system (17) to have a semi-center. However, when $\delta > 0$, the origin of the divided out system (23) is a node; therefore, the critical equilibrium of the closed-loop system (17) undergoes a single-wedge bifurcation. It can be observed that $\delta < 0$ is corresponding to the stripe

$$-\frac{2}{h_1}\sqrt{1+\frac{\mu_1}{h_1}} < \mu_2 + \frac{C}{2A}h_2 < \frac{2}{h_1}\sqrt{1+\frac{\mu_1}{h_1}}, \tag{27}$$

in $(\mu_2, h_2)-$ parameter space. It is worth noting that the second order derivatives of h and μ control the occurrence of the single-wedge bifurcation. When $\mu_2 = h_2 = 0$, we have $\delta < 0$ and there will be no single-wedge bifurcation. When $\|(\mu_2, h_2)\|$ is large enough, that is $|\mu_2 + C/(2A)h_2| > 2/h_1(1+\mu_1/h_1)^{0.5}$, the parameter δ become positive and single-wedge bifurcation takes place. With $\mu_2 = 0$, the critical values of h_2 are $h_2^c = \pm 2h_1/\mu_1(1+h_1/\mu_1)^{0.5}$, and for $h_2 = 0$, the critical values of μ_2 are $\mu_2^c = \pm 2/h_1(1+\mu_1/h_1)^{0.5}$.

In Fig. 2, the single-wedge bifurcation appeared in the reduced system (23) is shown for the case $h(x)=x+2x^2+x^3$ and $\mu(\varsigma)=\varsigma+2\varsigma^2+\varsigma^3$. Here $\beta_1=4$, $\beta_2=0.5$, $\gamma_1=-1$. The wedge region is the set of all initial conditions attracting to the origin where the limit system is unstable. The black curves are orbits converging the bifurcation point. The wedge is the lower right area limited by the border, tick horizontal line and one of the orbits.

Remark 1: The single-wedge bifurcation generically appears due to the nonlinear terms in feedbacks. One might argue that by applying linear feedbacks such situation can be avoided. However, linear feedbacks are applying through devices which may introduce some amount of nonlinearities. The width of the stripe defined by (27) depends on h_1 and μ_1 and is bounded by $\eta=4/h_1(1+\mu_1/h_1)^{0.5}$. The linear coefficients h_1 and μ_1 determine the local convergence. When they are small the convergence will slow down. One can observe that if we expect similar rate of local convergence for both x and ς, then $\eta=4\sqrt{2}/h_1$ approximately. For large enough h_1 the area where the single-wedge bifurcation does not take place will narrow down. To extend this region one needs to slow down the convergence process which may not be desirable. Another reason to consider this situation is to illustrate that how such behavior happens in a simple system. In a more complicated case, such dramatic behavior may occur generically.

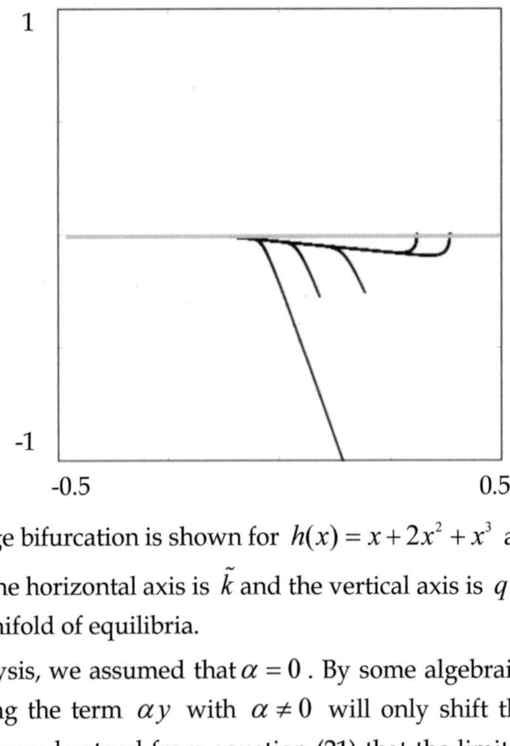

Fig. 2. The single-wedge bifurcation is shown for $h(x)=x+2x^2+x^3$ and $\mu(\varsigma)=\varsigma+2\varsigma^2+\varsigma^3$. The horizontal axis is $\tilde{k}$ and the vertical axis is q. The tick horizontal line represents the manifold of equilibria.

Remark 2: In our analysis, we assumed that $\alpha=0$. By some algebraic calculation, it can be observed that including the term αy with $\alpha\neq 0$ will only shift the value of μ_1 by the amount of α. It can be understood from equation (21) that the limit system corresponding to $\tilde{k}_\infty>0$ is unstable, but due to the linear part $\beta_2\tilde{k}_\infty q$, the limit system will be only unstable and finite escape time will not arise. It suggests that the closed-loop inverted pendulum with limit controller and without parameter adaptation can stay stabilized if it will not fall into the basin of attraction of the equilibrium $(0,0,\tilde{k}_c)$.

5. Biped robots

A passive bipedal robot with elastic elements has been studied in (Asano & Wei Luo, 2007), where a feedback control has been designed. Here we consider the same model when there is an unknown parameter. The governing equation is

$$M(q)\ddot{q} + h(q,\dot{q}) + \frac{\partial Q}{\partial q} = Su. \tag{28}$$

Here $q = [\theta_1 \quad \theta_2 \quad b_2]$ are the geometrical variables of the robot, $M(q)$ is the inertia matrix, $h(q,\dot{q})$ is the vector of Coriolis centrifugal and gravity forces. The elastic energy is defined as

$$Q = \frac{1}{2}k(b_2 - b_0)^2, \tag{29}$$

where, b_0 is the normal length of the leg and k is an unknown parameter; see (Asano & Wei Luo, 2007) for more details.

The vector $S = [0 \quad 0 \quad 1]^T$ requires that the walk is passive and only the elastic element is under control. We introduce the following variables

$$X = [x_1 \quad x_2 \quad x_3] = [\theta_1 \quad \theta_2 \quad b_2], \qquad Y = \dot{X}, \qquad X_0 = b_0 S. \tag{30}$$

This leads to

$$\begin{cases} \dot{X} = Y, \\ \dot{Y} = -M^{-1}h - kM^{-1}(X - X_0) + M^{-1}Su. \end{cases} \tag{31}$$

We omitted the arguments of the functions for simplicity, but all changes in variables need to be applied in functions arguments. Suppose $X_d = Sx_d$ is the reference signal. We define the error by $e = X_d - X$. The equation (31) becomes

$$\begin{cases} \dot{e} = \dot{X}_d - Y, \\ \dot{Y} = -M^{-1}h - kM^{-1}(X_d - e - X_0) + M^{-1}Su. \end{cases} \tag{32}$$

We proceed with adaptive back-stepping technique to partially stabilize the system with respect to $(e_3, \dot{e}_3)$. Suppose $|e_3|^2 \le V_1$ is an e_3 – positive definite Rumyantsev function with time derivative

$$\dot{V}_1 = \frac{\partial V_1}{\partial e}\dot{e} = \frac{\partial V_1}{\partial e}(\dot{X}_d - Y). \tag{33}$$

The first step of back-stepping approach can be proceeded by considering Y as the controller of $X-$equation. We can choose

$$Y = \dot{X}_d + \mu(e). \tag{34}$$

The time derivative of V_1 will become

$$\dot{V}_1 = -\frac{\partial V_1}{\partial e}\mu(e) = -w(e). \tag{35}$$

By choosing a suitable function μ we achieve an e_3-positive definite w. Now, we introduce an auxiliary variable

$$\varsigma = Y - (\dot{X}_d + \mu(e)). \tag{36}$$

For simplicity we take

$$V_1 = \frac{1}{2}e_3^2 \tag{37}$$

In this new coordinates we get the following auxiliary system

$$\begin{cases} \dot{e}_3 = -\varsigma_3 - \mu(e_3), \\ \dot{\varsigma}_3 = S^T\left[-M^{-1}h - kM^{-1}(X_d - e - X_0) - \ddot{X}_d - \mu'(e)\dot{e}\right] + \eta u. \end{cases} \tag{38}$$

Here, $\eta = S^T M^{-1} S$. Suppose $k = \hat{k} + \tilde{k}$, where $\hat{k}$ is the estimation of k and $\tilde{k}$ is the error of estimation. We introduce the following Rumyantsev function

$$V = V_1(e) + V_2(\varsigma) + V_3(\tilde{k}). \tag{39}$$

Without loss of generality we can take

$$V_2 = \frac{1}{2}\varsigma_3^2, \quad V_3 = \frac{1}{2}\tilde{k}^2. \tag{40}$$

The time derivative of V becomes

$$\begin{aligned} \dot{V} &= -e_3\mu(e_3) \\ &+ \varsigma_3\left[S^T[-M^{-1}h - \hat{k}M^{-1}(X_d - e - X_0) - \ddot{X}_d - \mu'\mu + \mu'\varsigma - e_3] + \eta u\right] \\ &+ \tilde{k}\left[-\dot{\hat{k}} - \varsigma_3 S^T M^{-1}(X_d - e - X_0)\right]. \end{aligned} \tag{41}$$

We choose the controller and the parameter adaptation as

$$\begin{aligned}\eta u &= -\nu(\varsigma_3) \\ &\quad - S^T\left(-M^{-1}h - \hat{k}M^{-1}(X_d - e - X_0) - \ddot{X}_d - \mu'\mu + \mu'\varsigma - e_3\right) \\ \dot{\hat{k}} &= -\varsigma S^T M^{-1}(X_d - e - X_0).\end{aligned} \tag{42}$$

We choose a suitable function ν such that $\eta\varsigma_3\nu > 0$. These leads to

$$\dot{V} = -\frac{\partial V}{\partial e}\mu(e) - \eta\varsigma_3\nu(.\varsigma_3). \tag{43}$$

The function V is positive definite with respect to $(e_3, \varsigma_3, \tilde{k})$, but (43) states that its time derivative is negative semidefinite, because $\tilde{k}$ is not included in (43). One can observe that two angels θ_1, θ_2 are always bounded; see (Asano & Wei Luo, 2007). It is also clear that the vector field (31) is smooth. We can also assume that feedbacks are smooth. Therefore, the non-stabilized variables stay bounded. So we can construct the cylinder (3) and employ the boundedness property stated in section 2 to achieve the required partial stability.

6. Conclusion

We have seen that in relatively simple mechanical systems like a pendulum, having an unknown parameter may leads to an adaptive controller which undergoes an undesirable behaviour, dramatically. According to the questions addressed in introduction of this chapter, we have found that the destabilising limit system with a large basin of attraction does not perform a finite escape time. Instead, that will be only unstable. It is clear that when the pendulum is not inverted, we do not expect to see such situation. That is apparent from the centre manifold analysis too. It is worth noting that, lack of adaptation, does not mean that there is no control. It only means that the controller is converged to a limit controller, but the system is still closed-loop. For inverted pendulum, such non-adaptive limit controller works perfectly, as long as the system does not fall into the region of attraction of the critical limit system. This shows a drawback of back-stepping approach. There is still a question: how such situation can be overcome without further knowledge of the system?

When we design a partially stabilized system, the method of sign definite and sign constant work in two different ways. When the time derivative of Rumyantsev function is not negative definite, one would employ boundedness or precompactness. None of them can be directly applied to the system, without any further knowledge of the system's dynamics or geometry. In case of section 5, assuming that two angels are both bounded during procedure and that the vector field is smooth, we can conclude that the closed-loop system is indeed stabilized with respect to leg's length. Otherwise, such conclusion would not be straightforward. The difficulty relates to differences between the appearance of non-stabilized variables and the unknown parameters. One can assume that non-stabilized variables satisfy the precompactness property. In another assumption, one can observe that the parameter estimation stay bounded if the controller is designed properly. However, in many systems, these two sets of non-stabilized variables and parameter estimation may belong to different categories satisfying precompactness or boundedness. In the example of section 5, both stayed bounded and we achieved the aim of stabilization. However, this method has a drawback. Stabilization with respect to one variable and the boundedness of others does not guarantee that the system works properly, since they are just bounded. One would not worry about the parameter estimation as long as that is bounded and converges to some value depending on initial conditions, but the phase variables may exceed the mechanical capacity of the system. Therefore, after designing a partially adaptive controller for a system, one needs to work out on mechanical advantage and disadvantage of the closed-loop system. Such procedure is not accomplished in section 5. Another issue in controller designed by (42) is the asymptotic convergence. This is always the case when we have some unknown parameter.

7. References

Andreev, A. S. (1987) Investigation of partial asymptotic stability and instability based on the limiting equations, *J. Appl. Maths. Mechs.*, 2, 51, 196--201.

Andreev, A. S. (1991). An investigation of partial asymptotic stability, *J. Appl. Maths. Mechs.*, 4, 5, 429-435.

Asano, F. & Wei Luo, Zh. (2007) Parametrically excited dynamic bipedal walking, in Habib, M. K. (2007) *Bioinspiration and Robotics: Walking and Climbing Robots*, I-Tech Education and Publishing, Vienna, Austria, 1-14.

Dumortier, F. & Roussarie, R. (2001) Geometric singular perturbation theory beyond normal hyperbolicity, in Jones, C. K. R. T. and Khibnik, A. I. (editors) Multiple-time-scale dynamical systems, Springer-Verlag, New York, 29-63.

Khalil, H. K. (1996) *Nonlinear systems*, Prentice-Hall, London.

Krstić, M. & Kanellakopoulos, I. & Kokotović (1995) *Nonlinear and Adaptive Control Design*, John-Wiley & Sons, New York.

Murray, J. D. (2002) *Mathematical biology*, 3rd ed., Springer, Berlin.

Ogata, K. (1970) *Modern control engineering*, Prentice-Hall, London.

Oziraner, A. S. (1973) On asymptotic stability and instability relative to a part of variables, *J. Appl. Maths. Mechs*, 37, 659-665.

de Queiroz, M. S. & Dawson, D. M. & Nagarkatti, S. P. & Zhang, F. (2000) *Lyapunov-based control of mechanical systems*, Birkhauser, Boston.

Rokni Lamooki, G. R. & Townley, S. & Osinga, H. M. (2003) Bifurcation and limit dynamics in adaptive control systems, *Int. J. Bif. Chaos*, 15, 5, 1641-1664.

Rumyantsev, V. V. (1957) On the stability of motion with respect to the part of the variables, *Vestnik Moscow. Univ. Ser. Mat. Mech Fiz. Astron. Khim.*, 4, 9-16.

Rumyantsev, V. V. (1970) On the optimal stabilization of controlled systems, *J. Appl. Maths. Mechs*, 3, 34, 440-456.

Rumyantsev, V. V. and Oziraner, A. S. (1987) *The Stability and Stabilization of Motion with Respect to some of the Variables*, Nauka, Moscow.

Seierstad, A. & Sydsaeter, K. (1987) *Optimal control theory with economic applications*, North-Holland, Netherland.

Townley, S. (1999) An example of a globally stabilizing adaptive controller with a generically destabilizing parameter estimate, *IEEE Trans. Automat. Control*, 44, 11, 2238-2241.

Vorotnikov, V. I. (1998) *Partial Stability and Control*, Birkhauser , Boston, MA.

Nonlinear Control Law for Nonholonomic Balancing Robot

Alicja Mazur and Jan Kędzierski
Institute of Computer Engineering, Control and Robotics,
Wrocław University of Technology,
ul. Janiszewskiego 11/17, 50-372 Wrocław,
Poland

1. Introduction

In the paper a new control algorithm for special mobile manipulator, namely for nonholonomic balancing robot, has been presented. A mobile manipulator is defined as a robotic system composed of a mobile platform equipped with non-deformable wheels and a manipulator mounted on the platform. Balancing robot is in fact a mobile robot, which platform can be considered as an inverted pendulum (i.e. rigid manipulator) mounted on the axis with two conventional fixed wheels. Such the axis it is called in the literature a mobile robot with structure of unicycle (Canudas de Wit et al., 1996). The balancing robot considered in this work is presented in Fig. 1.

Taking into account the type of mobility of their components, there are 4 possible configurations of mobile manipulators: type (h,h) - both the platform and the manipulator holonomic, type (h,nh) - a holonomic platform with a nonholonomic manipulator, type (h,nh) - a nonholonomic platform with a holonomic manipulator, and finally type (nh,nh) - both the platform and the manipulator nonholonomic. The balancing robot is a mobile manipulator of (nh,h) type because nonholonomic constraints occur only in the motion of the mobile part (wheels) and the motion of the inverted pendulum (rigid manipulator with only one degree of freedom) is holonomic.

In the literature it can be found control laws for balancing robot but all solutions to this problem use either local linearization of the model (Segbot, 2004) or linear controllers (R. Chi Ooi, 2003). Such linear models and controllers are valid only local, near the desired configuration and therefore their application is limited only to stabilization of the pendulum about $\alpha_d = 0$. However, if the fully nonlinear character of the dynamics is explored, then it is possible to obtain other nonlinear control laws preserving not only point stabilization of the pendulum but the trajectory tracking, too. In this work a new nonlinear control algorithm for balancing robot guaranteeing trajectory tracking for the inverted pendulum is introduced.

This paper is organized as follows. In Section 2 a mathematical model of nonholonomic balancing robot is obtained. Nonholonomic constraints in the model come from an assumption about frictionless motion of robot's wheels. In Section 3 control problem is formulated. Section 4 is devoted to the design of nonlinear control algorithm. The proof of the convergence of this algorithm is included. Section 5 contains simulation results which illustrate proper working of the proposed nonlinear controller. In Section 6 some conclusions are presented.

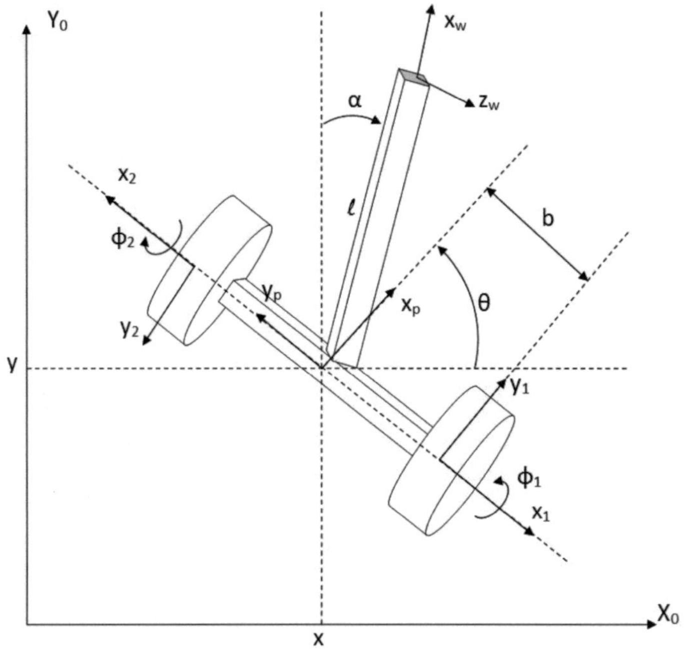

Fig. 1. Balancing robot: inverted pendulum with two fixed wheels on common axis

2. Mathematical model of nonholonomic balancing robot

We consider the mobile manipulator which consists of two subsystems, namely of rigid manipulator (inverted pendulum) and mobile platform (two fixed wheels located on common axis – unicycle).

2.1 Nonholonomic constraints

The motion of wheels can be described using generalized coordinates $q_m \in R^5$ and generalized velocities $\dot{q}_m \in R^5$.

$$q_m^T = \begin{pmatrix} x & y & \theta & \phi_1 & \phi_2 \end{pmatrix}$$

where (x, y) denote Cartesian coordinates of the center of the axis relative to the basic frame X_0Y_0, θ is an angle between X_p and X_0 axis and ϕ_i is a rotation angle of *i*th wheel. The mobile subsystem should move without slipping of wheels. This assumption implies the existence of 3 independent nonholonomic constraints which can be expressed in the so-called Pfaff's form

$$A(q_m)\dot{q}_m = 0\,, \tag{1}$$

where $A(q_m)$ is a full rank matrix of (3 x 5) size. Due to (1), since the platform velocity is always in the null space of A, it is always possible to find a vector of special auxiliary velocities $\eta \in R^m$, $m = 5 - 3 = 2$, such that

$$\dot{q}_m = G(q_m)\eta, \tag{2}$$

where $G(q_m)$ is an 5 x 2 full rank matrix satisfying $A(q_m)G(q_m) \equiv 0$.

2.2 Dynamic model of the mobile manipulator of (*nh*, *h*) type

Let a vector of generalized coordinates of the mobile manipulator be denoted as

$$q = \begin{pmatrix} q_m \\ \alpha \end{pmatrix} \in R^6,$$

where $q_m \in R^5$ is a vector of generalized coordinates for the mobile platform and $\alpha \in R$ describes an angle between the inverted pendulum (axis X_w) and vertical direction. Because of the nonholonomic character of constraints, to obtain the dynamic model of the balancing robot, the d'Alembert Principle should be used

$$M(q)\ddot{q} + C(q,\dot{q})\dot{q} + D(q) = A(q_m)\lambda + B(q)\tau. \tag{3}$$

The model of dynamics (3) can be expressed in more detail as

$$\begin{bmatrix} M_{11} & M_{12} \\ M_{21} & M_{22} \end{bmatrix}\begin{pmatrix} \ddot{q}_m \\ \ddot{\alpha} \end{pmatrix} + \begin{bmatrix} C_{11} & C_{12} \\ C_{21} & C_{22} \end{bmatrix}\begin{pmatrix} \dot{q}_m \\ \dot{\alpha} \end{pmatrix} + \begin{pmatrix} 0 \\ D \end{pmatrix} = \begin{pmatrix} A^T\lambda \\ 0 \end{pmatrix} + \begin{pmatrix} B\tau \\ 0 \end{pmatrix}$$

where

$M(q) = \begin{bmatrix} M_{11}(q) & M_{12}(q) \\ M_{21}(q) & M_{22} \end{bmatrix}$ - inertia matrix,

$C(q,q) = \begin{bmatrix} C_{11}(q,\dot{q}) & C_{12}(q,\dot{q}) \\ C_{21}(q,\dot{q}) & 0 \end{bmatrix}$ - matrix coming from Coriolis and centrifugal forces,

$D(q) = \begin{pmatrix} 0 \\ D \end{pmatrix}$ - vector of gravity,

$\lambda \in R^3$ - vector of Lagrange multipliers,

$B(q) = \begin{bmatrix} B(q_m) & 0 \\ 0 & 0 \end{bmatrix}$ - input matrix,

$\tau = \begin{pmatrix} \tau_m \\ 0 \end{pmatrix}$ - vector of controls.

The model of dynamics (3) of the (nh,h) mobile manipulator is often called a model in generalized coordinates.

Now we want to express the dynamics using auxiliary velocities (2) for the mobile platform. We compute

$$\ddot{q}_m = G(q_m)\dot{\eta} + \dot{G}(q_m)\eta$$

and eliminate from the model (3) the vector of Lagrange multipliers (using the condition $G^T(q_m)A^T(q_m) \equiv 0$) by left-sided multiplying the mobile platform equations by $G^T(q_m)$ matrix. After substituting for $\dot{q}_m$ and $\ddot{q}_m$ we get

$$\begin{bmatrix} G^T M_{11} G & G^T M_{12} \\ M_{21} G & M_{22} \end{bmatrix} \begin{pmatrix} \dot{\eta} \\ \ddot{\alpha} \end{pmatrix} + \begin{bmatrix} G^T \left(C_{11} G + M_{11} \dot{G} \right) & G^T C_{12} \\ C_{21} G & C_{22} \end{bmatrix} \begin{pmatrix} \eta \\ \dot{\alpha} \end{pmatrix} + \begin{pmatrix} 0 \\ D \end{pmatrix} = \begin{pmatrix} G^T B \tau_m \\ 0 \end{pmatrix} \tag{4}$$

We introduce a new symbol covering centrifugal and Coriolis forces as well as gravity. Then we obtain the model expressed in more compact form as follows

$$\begin{bmatrix} M_{11}^* & M_{12}^* \\ M_{21}^* & M_{22}^* \end{bmatrix} \begin{pmatrix} \dot{\eta} \\ \ddot{\alpha} \end{pmatrix} + \begin{pmatrix} F_1^* \\ F_2^* \end{pmatrix} = \begin{pmatrix} B^* \tau_m \\ 0 \end{pmatrix} \tag{5}$$

where the arguments of matrices and vectors are omitted for the sake of simplicity. We will refer to the model (5) as the model of dynamics of the (nh, h) mobile manipulator expressed in auxiliary variables.

2.3 Partial global linearization

The dynamic model of nonholonomic balancing robot can be considered as a mobile manipulator with one passive degree of freedom (degree of freedom without actuator). The role of this passive joint plays the inverted pendulum. For such the object it is possible to introduce due to (De Luca et al., 2001) partial global linearization, which transforms the model in auxiliary velocities to a form more convenient from control's point of view. For this reason we extract $\ddot{\alpha}$ from the second matrix equation of (5)

$$\ddot{\alpha} = -\left(M_{22}^*\right)^{-1}\left(M_{21}^* \dot{\eta} + F_2^*\right) \tag{6}$$

and put it into the first equation, (Ratajczak & Tchoń, 2007). Then we get the following expression

$$\overline{M}(q)\dot{\eta} + \overline{F}(q, \dot{q}) = B^* \tau_m \,, \tag{7}$$

where

$$\overline{M}(q) = M_{11}^* - M_{12}^*(q) M_{22}^*(q)^{-1} M_{21}^*(q)$$

$$\overline{F}(q, \dot{q}) = F_1^* - M_{12}^*(q) M_{22}^*(q)^{-1} F_2^*(q, \dot{q})$$

Now a linearizing control law with a new control input u should be introduced

$$\tau_m = \left(B^*\right)^{-1}\left\{\overline{M}(q)u + \overline{F}(q, \dot{q})\right\} \tag{8}$$

to get a model (5) defined as a partially linearized control system

$$\begin{cases} \ddot{\alpha} = -\left(M_{22}^{*}\right)^{-1}\left(M_{21}^{*}\dot{\eta} + F_{2}^{*}\right) \\ \dot{\eta} = u \end{cases} \tag{9}$$

Such a system is a point of departure to design a new nonlinear control algorithm preserving not only point stabilization but trajectory tracking as well.

3. Control problem statement

In the paper we will find a control law guaranteeing the proper behaviour of the balancing robot. The task of the robot is to follow the desired trajectory $\alpha_d(t)$ (trajectory tracking or point stabilization) of the inverted pendulum without slipping of platform's wheels.
A goal of this paper will be to address the following control problem for balancing robot given by the model (9):

Find control law u such that the balancing robot with the known dynamics follows a desired trajectory $\alpha_d(t)$ without slippage of platform's wheels and tracking errors converge against zero.

To design a controller for the such the mobile manipulator, it is necessary to observe that complete nonholonomic system (9) is a cascade with two subsystems. For this reason the structure of the controller is divided into two parts due to backstepping-like procedure (Krstić et al., 1995):

1. kinematic level - η_r represents an embedded control input, which ensures the convergence the real trajectory α of the inverted pendulum to the desired trajectory $\alpha_d(t)$ for the equation of constraints (6) if the dynamics were not present,
2. dynamic level - as a consequence of cascaded structure of the system model, the pendulum's angle α cannot be commanded directly, as is assumed in the design of control on kinematic level, and instead it must be realized as the output of the partially linearized dynamics driven by u. The dynamic input u intends to regulate η toward the embedded control input η_r, and therefore, attempts to provide control input necessary to track the desired trajectory.

Because there exists a difference between the real velocity of the mobile platform η and the embedded control input η_r at the start position, it is necessary to account for the influence of the error $e_\eta = \eta - \eta_r$ on the behaviour of the full mathematical model of the nonholonomic balancing robot.

4. Nonlinear control law

4.1 Reference auxiliary velocities η_r

Let some reference functions describing desired accelerations of platform's wheels will be defined as follows

$$-\left(M_{22}^{*}\right)^{-1}\left(M_{21}^{*}\dot{\eta}_r + F_{2}^{*}\right) = \ddot{\alpha}_d - K_d\dot{e}_\alpha - K_p e_\alpha, \quad K_d, K_p > 0, \tag{10}$$

where

$$e_\alpha = \alpha - \alpha_d$$

is a tracking error of the inverted pendulum. It is obvious that η_r is not unique defined, because this equation is scalar and $\eta_r \in R^2$. However, it is possible to assume some relationship between η_{1r} and η_{2r} (for instance $\eta_{1r} = \eta_{2r}$) and to get unique solution of (10). The motion of wheels with velocities η_r preserves convergence of the inverted pendulum to the desired constant configuration α_d or to the desired trajectory $\alpha_d(t)$. The main problem is that the real velocities of wheels η are not equal to the reference velocities η_r at the beginning of the motion. It means that some errors occur on the dynamic level and disturb the behaviour of the balancing robot. Therefore we want to prove using Lyapunov-like function that the properly chosen control law on dynamic level can guarantee the asymptotic convergence of these errors to zero. As a consequence we obtain stabilization of the pendulum about the desired trajectory (or configuration).

4.2 Nonlinear controller

We consider the model of the balancing robot (9) expressed in auxiliary variables. We assume that we know the solution η_r to the constraints equation (10), which preserves a convergence of real coordinate $\alpha(t)$ of the inverted pendulum to the desired trajectory $\alpha_d(t)$. Then we propose a new control algorithm guaranteeing asymptotic trajectory tracking for all coordinates of the mobile manipulator. This control law is defined by expression

$$u = \dot{\eta}_r - K_m e_\eta, \qquad K_m > 0 \tag{11}$$

where K_m is some diagonal regulation matrix and

$$e_\eta = \eta - \eta_r = \begin{pmatrix} \eta_1 - \eta_{1r} \\ \eta_2 - \eta_{2r} \end{pmatrix} = \begin{pmatrix} e_{\eta 1} \\ e_{\eta 2} \end{pmatrix}$$

is an error appearing on dynamic level, if real velocities of wheels are not equal to reference velocities, i.e. $\eta(0) \neq \eta_r(0)$. In such a situation, on the dynamic level we have the dynamic of the closed-loop error given by

$$\dot{e}_\eta + K_m e_\eta = 0 \tag{12}$$

which due to positive definiteness of K_m matrix is exponentially fast convergent to 0. On the other side, on kinematic level (the equation describing constraint, i.e. trajectory of a passive joint) the motion of the inverted pendulum is disturbed in the following way

$$\ddot{\alpha} = -\left(M_{22}^*\right)^{-1} M_{21}^* \left(\dot{\eta}_r - K_m e_\eta\right) - \left(M_{22}^*\right)^{-1} F_2^* = \ddot{\alpha}_d - K_d \dot{e}_\alpha - K_p e_\alpha + \left(M_{22}^*\right)^{-1} K_m e_\eta \,. \tag{13}$$

4.3 Proof of convergence of the control algorithm

Lets consider trajectories of the disturbed closed-loop system (12) and (13). We choose the following Lyapunov-like function

$$V(e_\alpha, \dot{e}_\alpha, e_\eta) = \frac{1}{2}(e_\alpha + \dot{e}_\alpha)^2 + e_\eta^T e_\eta . \tag{14}$$

Now we calculate the time derivative of V

$$\dot{V} = (e_\alpha + \dot{e}_\alpha)(\dot{e}_\alpha + \ddot{e}_\alpha) + e_\eta^T \dot{e}_\eta$$

which along solutions of the closed-loop system (12)-(13) is equal to

$$\begin{aligned} \dot{V} &= (e_\alpha + \dot{e}_\alpha)(\dot{e}_\alpha - K_d \dot{e}_\alpha - K_p e_\alpha + (M_{22}^*)^{-1} M_{21}^* K_m e_\eta) - e_\eta^T K_m e_\eta \\ &= -e_u \dot{e}_u K_2 - K_p e_u^2 - (K_d - 1)\dot{e}_u^2 - e_\eta^T K_m e_\eta + e_\alpha K_1 e_\eta + \dot{e}_\alpha K_1 e_\eta \end{aligned} . \tag{15}$$

with parameters defined in the following way

$$K_1 = \left(M_{22}^*\right)^{-1} M_{21}^* K_m = \frac{\cos\alpha}{I_p}[K_{m11}, K_{m22}], \qquad K_2 = K_p + K_d - 1$$

where I_p is a moment of inertia of the inverted pendulum. Then the time derivative of the V function can be evaluated by the expression

$$\begin{aligned} \dot{V} &\le -e_\alpha \dot{e}_\alpha K_2 - K_p e_u^2 - (K_d - 1)\dot{e}_u^2 - K_{m11} e_{\eta 1}^2 - K_{m22} e_{\eta 2}^2 + K_3 (e_\alpha + \dot{e}_\alpha)(e_{\eta 1} + e_{\eta 2}) \\ &= \frac{K_2^2}{4}\dot{e}_\alpha^2 + e_\alpha^2 - \left(\frac{K_2}{2}\dot{e}_\alpha + e_\alpha\right)^2 - K_p e_\alpha^2 - (K_d - 1)\dot{e}_\alpha^2 - K_{m11} e_{\eta 1}^2 - K_{m22} e_{\eta 2}^2 + K_3 (e_\alpha + \dot{e}_\alpha)(e_{\eta 1} + e_{\eta 2}) \\ &\le -(K_p - 1)e_\alpha^2 - \left(K_d - 1 - \frac{K_2^2}{4}\right)\dot{e}_\alpha^2 - K_{m11} e_{\eta 1}^2 - K_{m22} e_{\eta 2}^2 + K_3 (e_\alpha + \dot{e}_\alpha)(e_{\eta 1} + e_{\eta 2}) \end{aligned}$$

with

$$K_3 = \max_{\forall \alpha}\left(\frac{\cos\alpha}{I_p} K_{m11}; \frac{\cos\alpha}{I_p} K_{m22}\right)$$

Using the same method of estimation, we can obtain the following formula

$$\dot{V} \le -\left(K_p - 1 - \frac{K_3^2}{2}\right)e_\alpha^2 - \left(K_d - 1 - \frac{K_2^2}{2}\right)\dot{e}_\alpha^2 - (K_{m11} - 1)e_{\eta 1}^2 - (K_{m22} - 1)e_{\eta 2}^2 \le 0 . \tag{15}$$

If the regulation parameters K_m, K_p, K_d are properly chosen, i.e.

$$K_{m11} > 1, \qquad K_{m22} > 1, \qquad K_p > 1 + \frac{K_3^2}{2}, \qquad K_d > 1 + \frac{K_2^2}{2},$$

then from LaSalle invariance principle we can deduce that all errors, i.e. $(e_\alpha, \dot{e}_\alpha, e_\eta)$ converge to 0 asymptotically.

5. Simulations

As the object of simulations we have chosen a model of the inverted pendulum on two fixed wheels presented in Fig. 1. The goal of simulations is to examine the behaviour of the presented control algorithm using a full knowledge about the dynamics. The motion of the closed loop system has been examined by simulations which have run with the MATLAB package and the SIMULINK toolbox.

- First, the desired trajectory for inverted pendulum was chosen as a constant configuration $\alpha_d = \pi/3$. The start position of the platform was equal to $(x(0), y(0), \theta(0)) = (0,0,0)$ and start position of the manipulator $\alpha(0) = 0$. In Fig. 2b tracking terror $e_{\eta 1}$ for the mobile platform have been shown. The relationship between reference velocities is selected as $\eta_{1r} = \eta_{2r}$ (straightforward motion). Figure 2a presents tracking error e_α for the inverted pendulum. The gains of control parameters used for getting plots presented in Figure 2 are equal to

$$K_m = 50, \qquad K_p = 100, \qquad K_d = 50.$$

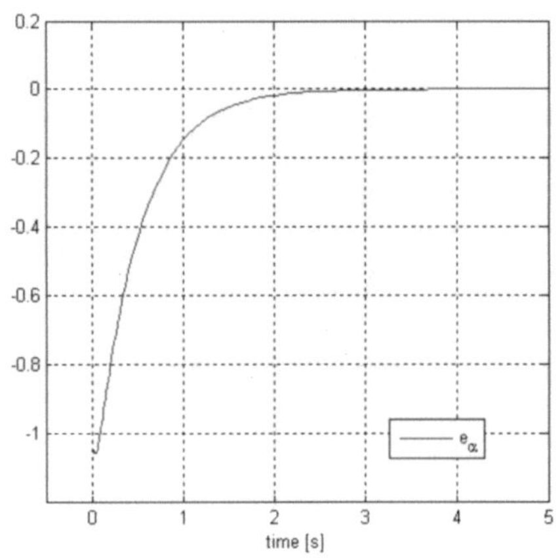

a)

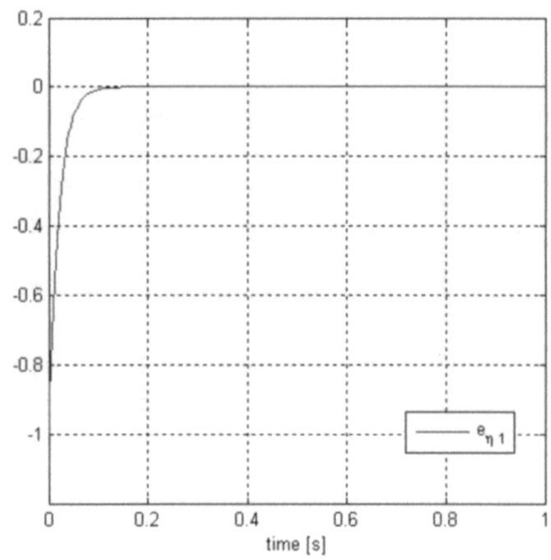

b)

Fig. 2. Tracking errors occurring in the balancing robot during tracking constant configuration: a) e_α b) $e_{\eta 1}$

- Next, the desired trajectory for inverted pendulum was chosen as a slowly changing periodic function $\alpha_d(t) = 0.05\sin(t/10)$. The start position of the platform was equal to $(x(0), y(0), \theta(0)) = (0,0,0)$ and start position of the manipulator $\alpha(0) = 0$. In Fig. 3b tracking error $e_{\eta 1}$ for the mobile platform has been shown. The relationship between reference velocities is selected as $\eta_{1r} = \eta_{2r}$. Figure 3a presents tracking error e_α for the inverted pendulum. The gains of control parameters used for getting plots presented in Fig. 3 are equal to

$$K_m = 50, \qquad K_p = 100, \qquad K_d = 50.$$

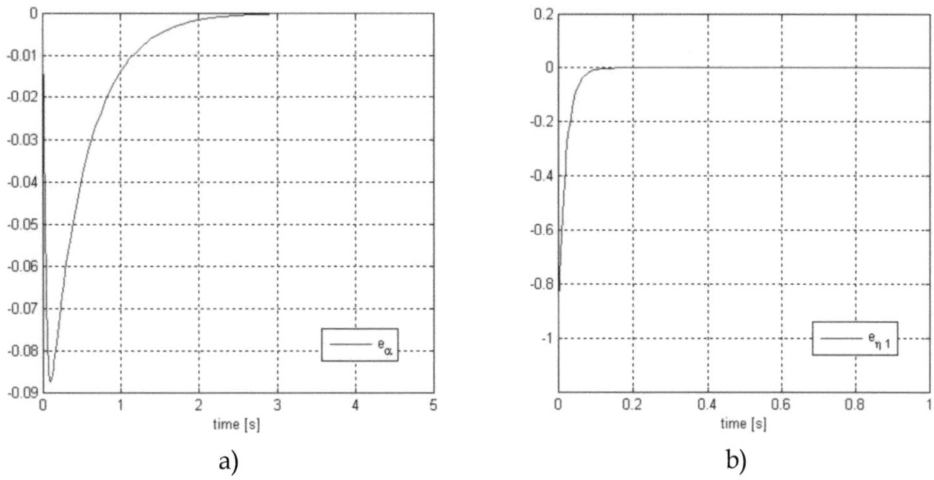

Fig. 3. Tracking errors occurring in the balancing robot during tracking periodic trajectory: a) e_α b) $e_{\eta 1}$

6. Concluding remarks

In the paper a new control algorithm for nonholonomic balancing robot (inverted pendulum mounted on a two fixed conventional wheels) has been introduced. The algorithm covers not only stabilization of the pendulum about a desired constant configuration α_d, not necessary 0, but the tracking of some time-dependent trajectory as well. Differently from previous works presenting control problem of the balancing robot, the motion of the robot is not restricted to straight-line motion but it is possible to realize more complicated manoeuvres on XY plane without slipping of robot's wheels. It depends on the selection of relationship between reference velocities designed for the wheels, what case of robot's motion will be realized in practice.

In our forthcoming research we will focus on extending the presented approach to other cases of mobile manipulators (nh, h) with different structures of passive joints.

8. References

C. Canudas de Wit & B. Siciliano & G. Bastin. Theory of Robot Control, Springer-Verlag, London, 1996.

A. De Luca & S. Iannitti & G. Oriolo. Stabilization of the PR planar underactuated robot. Proc. IEEE International Conference on Robotics and Automation (ICRA 2001), pp. 2090–2095, 2001.

M. Krstić & I. Kanellakopoulos & P. Kokotović, *Nonlinear and Adaptive Control Design*, J. Wiley and Sons, New York, 1995.

A. Ratajczak & K. Tchoń. Control of underactuated robotic manipulators: an endogenous configuration space approach. Proc. IEEE Conf. on Methods and Models in Automation and Robotics MMAR 2007, pp. 985–990, Szczecin, 2007.

Rich Chi Ooi, *Balancing a Two-wheeled Autonomus Robot*, The University of Western Australia; Final Year Thesis, 2003.

Segbot - Final project for the Introduction to Mechatronics class at the University of Illinois http://coecsl.ece.uiuc.edu/ge423/spring04/group9/index.htm, 2004.

6

Deghosting Methods for Track-Before-Detect Multitarget Multisensor Algorithms

Przemyslaw Mazurek
Szczecin University of Technology
Poland

1. Introduction

Track-Before-Detect (TBD) algorithms are very powerful for tracking applications. In comparison to classical (Detect-Before-Track) algorithms they are computationally demanding but allow achieving incredible SNR (Signal-to-Noise Ratio) performance. For classical systems SNR should be greater then one. If this condition is fulfilled classical tracking algorithms does not need a lot of computations and they process acquired data by filtering, detection and estimation algorithms. Typical detection algorithms based on fixed or adaptive threshold fails for SNR<1 because if signal is below noise floor a lot of false measurements occurs or target can not be detected correctly. Improving performance for low SNR systems is very important from applications point of view and it is research very active area using alternative approaches and improved algorithms.

Track-Before-Detect algorithms are excellent alternative for low SNR signals because signal (target) detection is processed after intensive testing set of hypotheses related to possible signal states (e.g. object trajectories). Even if there are no any signal from target complete search is used for best performance. Huge discrete state-space needs a lot of computations mostly not related to real state of target. Today available computing devices like fast processors, specialized VLSI circuits and distributed computing methods allows gives a possibility of using real-time TBD algorithms for dim target tracking. It is worth to be noted that computation cost for TBD algorithms is serious disadvantage because it significantly influent on financial cost of system but it can be meaningful for military applications (air, naval or space surveillance) where plane, ship or political costs are much more significant.

There are two groups of TBD algorithms. The first one group contains deterministic TBD algorithms statistical computations oriented for results calculation. All hypotheses are tested and computation cost is usually constant. The second one group contains nondeterministic TBD algorithms. Such algorithms do not test all hypotheses only use statistical methods for finding most probable results but optimality of results is not guarantied. For example particle filters are statistical search based and they gives results sometimes faster in comparison to first group of algorithms (Gordon et al., 1993; Doucet et al., 2001; Arulampalam et al., 2002; Ristic et al., 2004), but deterministic group is much more reliable for many application and is only considered in this chapter. For real-time applications first group has advantages of results quality and constant processing time - very important for

every system developer. It is worth to be noted that useful TBD algorithms for practically applications are not optimal. There is optimality in some sense for particular algorithms but only bath processing is optimal from detection quality point-of-view. Bath algorithm tests all hypotheses (all object trajectories) using all information from beginning up to actual time moment (Blackman & Popoli, 1999). Unfortunately bath processing is not feasible for real-time applications because memory and computation cost is growing. Much more popular are recurrent TBD algorithms and last results and actual measurements are used for computations (like 1'st order IIR filter). There are also popular algorithms based on FIR filters and they use N-time moments for computation results.
Independently on computation cost of TBD there are other limitations that are challenges for developers. Classical and TBD algorithms are quite simple for single object tracking but more complex approach is necessary if there are multiple targets or false target due to measurement errors. A false measurement occurs due to occasional high noise peaks that are detected as targets. Assignment, targets track live control, targets separation algorithms and multiple sensors are considered for multiple target tracking. Excellent books (Blackman, 1986; Bar-Shalom & Fortmann, 1988; Bar-Shalom ed. 1990; Bar-Shalom ed. 1992; Bar-Shalom & Li, 1993; Bar-Shalom & Li, 1995; Brookner, 1998; Blackman & Popoli, 1999; Bar-Shalom & Blair eds. 2000) includes thousand references to much more specific topic related papers are available but there is a lot of to discover, measure and investigate.
Most multiple target tracking algorithms are related to classical systems but there are also well fitted algorithms for improving TBD trackers. Simple method is using TBD algorithm results as input for high level data fusion algorithm that should be tolerant for redundant information from TBD algorithms. Very important part of TBD is state-space that should be adequate for application and decide about algorithm properties significantly. In this chapter is assumed strength correspondence of state-space to the measurement space. It allows simplify description of behaviours of TBD algorithms using kinematics properties. The measurement space depends on sensor type. From Bayesian point of view different sensors outputs can be mixed for calculation joint measurements. This data fusion approach is very important because there are sensors superior for angular (bearing) performance like optical based and sensors superior for distance measurements like radar based. Diversification of sensors for measurement for tracking systems improvements is contemporary active research area. Progress in optical sensors development for visible and infrared spectrum gives passive measurements ability that is especially important for military applications and linear and two-dimensional optical sensors (cameras) are used. Unfortunately distance measurement using single sensor without additional information about target state is not possible. Another disadvantages of optical sensors is an atmospheric condition so dust, clouds, atmospheric refraction can limits measurement and tracking abilities for particular applications. Because targets move between sensors and background (for example moving clouds) background estimation is a very important for improving SNR. Another problem is optical occlusion that limits tracking possibilities (for example aircraft tracking between or above clouds layer). Such limitations related to optical measurement sensors are related to single and multiple targets tracking also, but there is another non-trivial multiple target related problem known as a ghosting (Pattipati et al, 1992). For every bearing only system ghosting should be considered and suppression methods should be used or obtained tracking results are false.

2. Ghosting and basic methods of ghost suppression

2.1 Ghosting

In this chapter are considered sources of ghosts and methods for suppression them using illustrative examples for usually hard to visualize high dimensionality state spaces. For single or multiple targets positions estimation two or more sensors are necessary. Using LOS (Line-of-Sight) triangulation target position and distance estimation is possible.

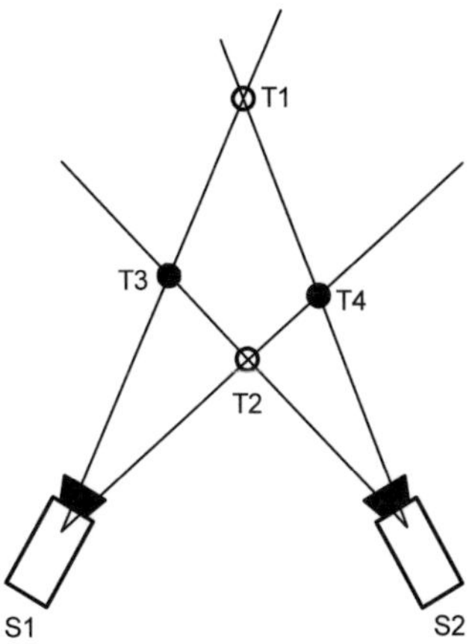

Fig. 1. Two targets and two ghosts

Assuming two targets and two sensors triangulation fails because there are two possible solutions:

T1 and T2 - true targets,
T3 and T4 - false targets (ghosts)

or

T1 and T2 - false targets (ghosts),
T3 and T4 - true targets.

If there is no available additional information there is no answer which solution is correct. This problem is not related to tracking method only to geometrical properties of bearing only sensors and common to classical and TBD tracking systems. Many methods can be used for finding solution or eliminate some false assignments.

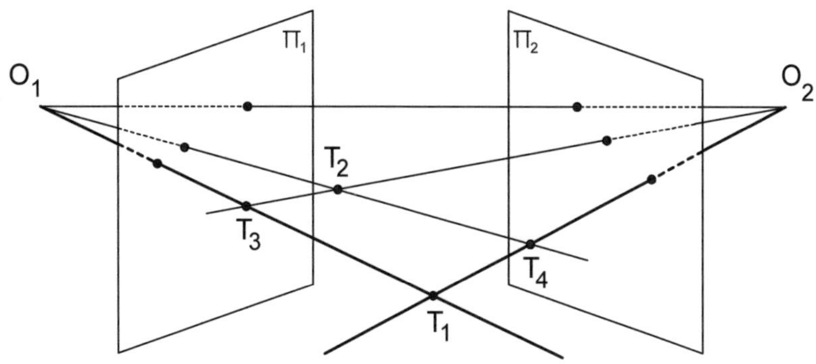

Fig. 2. Ghosting in 3D observation space

If two targets are on common plane (O_1, O_2, T_1 and O_1, O_2, T_2) ghost effect occurs (Fig.2). It can be little surprising that number of ghosts is smaller for 3D space in comparison to 2D space. If one of the targets is placed outside second plane ghost effect does not occur (Fig.3). For 2D space ghosts are always (Fig.1).

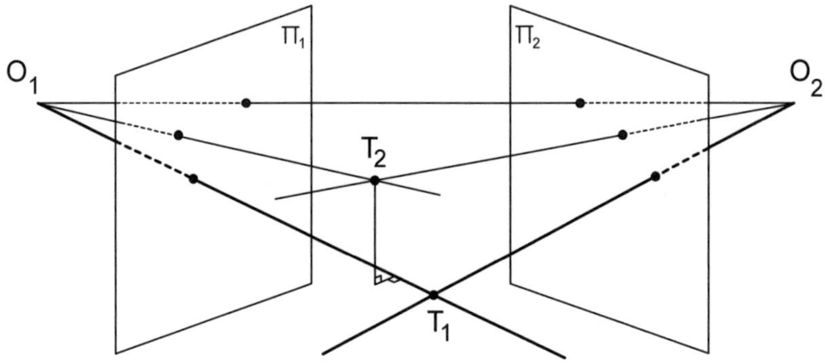

Fig. 3. Two targets and no ghosts in 3D space

2.2 Influence of measurement errors

Angle measurement errors can influent on results for trivial cases. Due to calibration errors and measurements noises all LOS for single target do not cross in single point (Fig.4). For 2D object plane all LOS are crossed but not in single point but for 3D space practically they almost never cross and approximation is required. If there are multiple closely located targets problem arises.

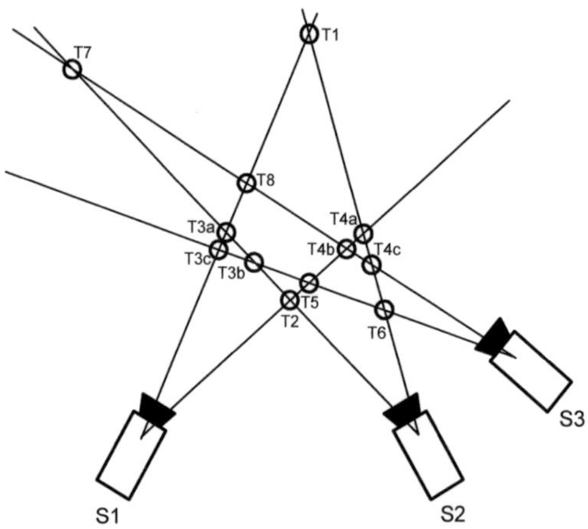

Fig. 4. True objects T3 and T4 are dispersed due to measurement errors

Increasing number of sensors is probably most popular solution, because for true targets number of LOS crosses increases also. Unfortunately number of ghosts increases also.
Using additional information about targets is promising because it allows eliminate some ghosts. Amount of eliminated ghosts depends on sensors and object position. Even if not all ghosts are eliminated it can helps for estimation proper positions of targets using other algorithms.

Constraints oriented deghosting methods uses typically knowledge about allowed position, maximal or minimal velocity, maximal acceleration, direction of movements and others (Mazurek, 2007). If it is possible all constraints can be used together for best performance.

2.3 Counting and accumulative strategies

For classical methods for every target position (true or ghost) constraints using is straightforward even if constraints tests are performed for every scan separately. Much more reliable is extensive tracking where ghosts are tracked and constraints are used for marking them as ghosts if they forbid constraints limit.

Because TBD algorithms are signal accumulation oriented algorithms they do not consider LOS crossing as sum of number of crosses but they accumulate signals for particular state space cell where crossing occurs. It following example is assumed availability of two targets and three sensors. Signal values registered by sensors for targets are P1=1 and P2=0.5 equal. True targets are located in T1 and T4 positions. It is worth to be noted that all noises are omitted so this is very comfortable for any algorithm case.

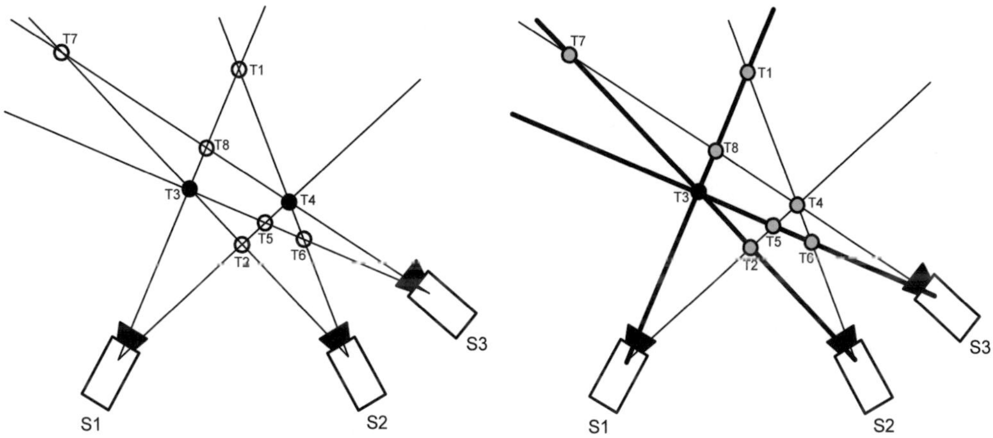

Fig. 5. Counting strategy (left) and accumulative strategy (right) for two targets and three sensors

LOS cross point	LOS value Counting strategy	LOS value Accumulative strategy
T1	2	1.5
T2	2	1.5
T3	3	3
T4	3	1.5
T5	2	1.5
T6	2	1.5
T7	2	1.5
T8	2	1.5

Table 1. LOS values for Fig.5

This example shows how counting and accumulative strategy algorithms differ. For counting strategy maximal values corresponding to most probable position of targets and three sensors help to solve ghosting problem if we know maximal number of targets.
Accumulative strategy fails because T4 value is equal to ghosts' values and only one target (T3) is detected as a true target. Even knowledge about number of targets can not help to solve this simple example.
Only one way for improving accumulative strategy is increasing number of sensors and in next example is assumed four sensors availability (Fig.6).

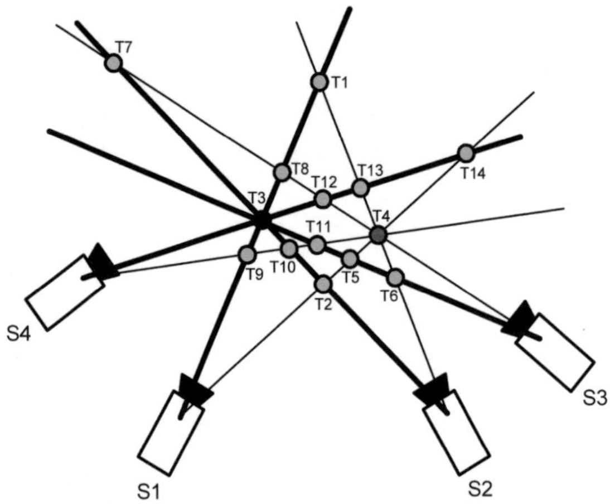

Fig. 6. Improving accumulative strategy using additional sensor

LOS cross point	LOS value Counting strategy	LOS value Accumulative strategy
T1	2	1.5
T2	2	1.5
T3	4	4
T4	4	2
T5	2	1.5
T6	2	1.5
T7	2	1.5
T8	2	1.5
T9	2	1.5
T10	2	1.5
T11	2	1.5
T12	2	1.5
T13	2	1.5
T14	2	1.5

Table 2. LOS values for Fig.6

Counting methods gives correct results and maximal values correspond to true targets. Accumulative methods give two largest values corresponding to true targets but T4 cross point has only 50% higher value over ghosts. Counting strategy work better but it needs detection of correct LOS so if SNR>1 it is recommended to use. Accumulative strategy inherently available in TBD algorithms can be used also and it will be discussed in next examples.

2.4 Accumulative strategy examples

Examples of results for noiseless and noised measurements space will be shown. For simplification instead of projective cameras are used orthographic cameras. First example shows how number of sensors improves results for accumulative strategy. Selected part of state space is shown and some ghosts are outside image.

For two target T1=1.0 and T2=0.5 the 3x3 matrix values filled by target value and filtered by 3x3 low pass filter (all values of filter are equal) so small size blurred targets are available.

Values for every case are normalized separately. Black value is zero level and white corresponds to maximal value.

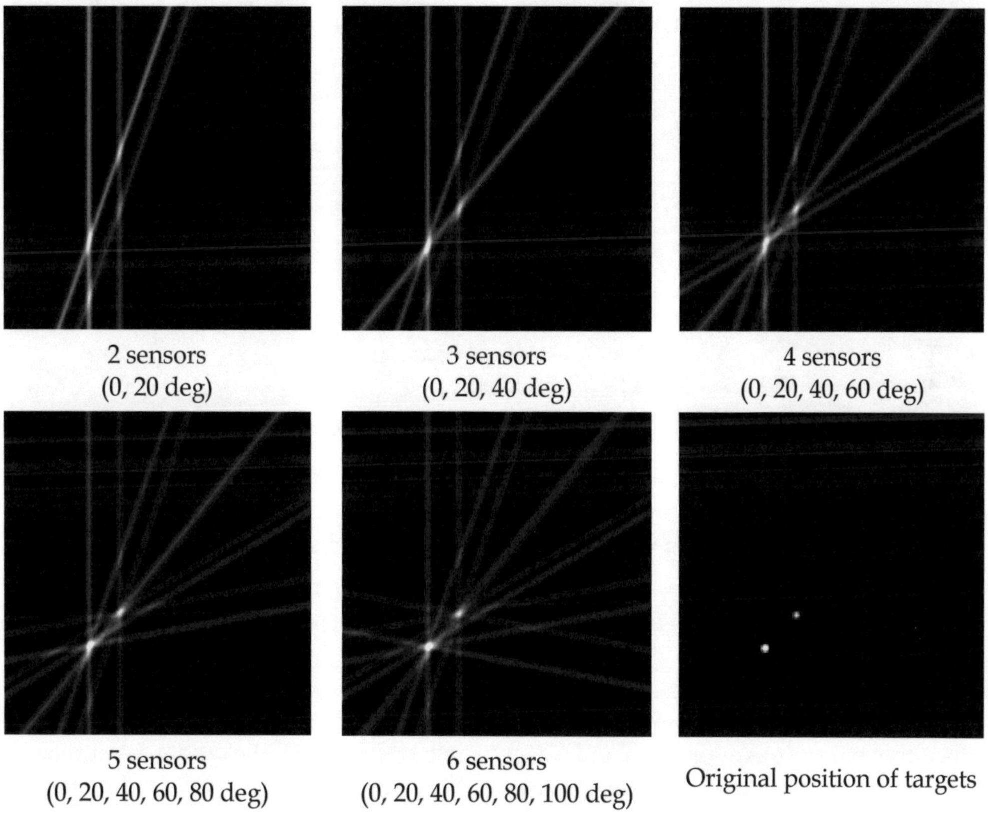

Fig. 7. Measurement spaces for two targets and variable number of sensors

For two sensors ghosting effect is well visible and there is one large value (true target), two medium values (ghosts) and one small (true target). Increasing number of sensors improves value for true targets and reduces values of ghosts. A lot of LOS is sources of many lines.

Shape of target blob and ghosts depends on sensors placement and number of them. If small number of sensors is used and they are close together targets blobs are elliptical. If sensors are much more dispersed blobs are more circular and better recognized.
In next example five true targets are placed in this space and they have following values: T1=1.0 (bottom); T2=0.8; T3=0.6; T4=0.2 and T5=0.4 (upper). The order of values T4 and T5 is intentional for reducing human related adaptive effects of results observation for image blobs series.

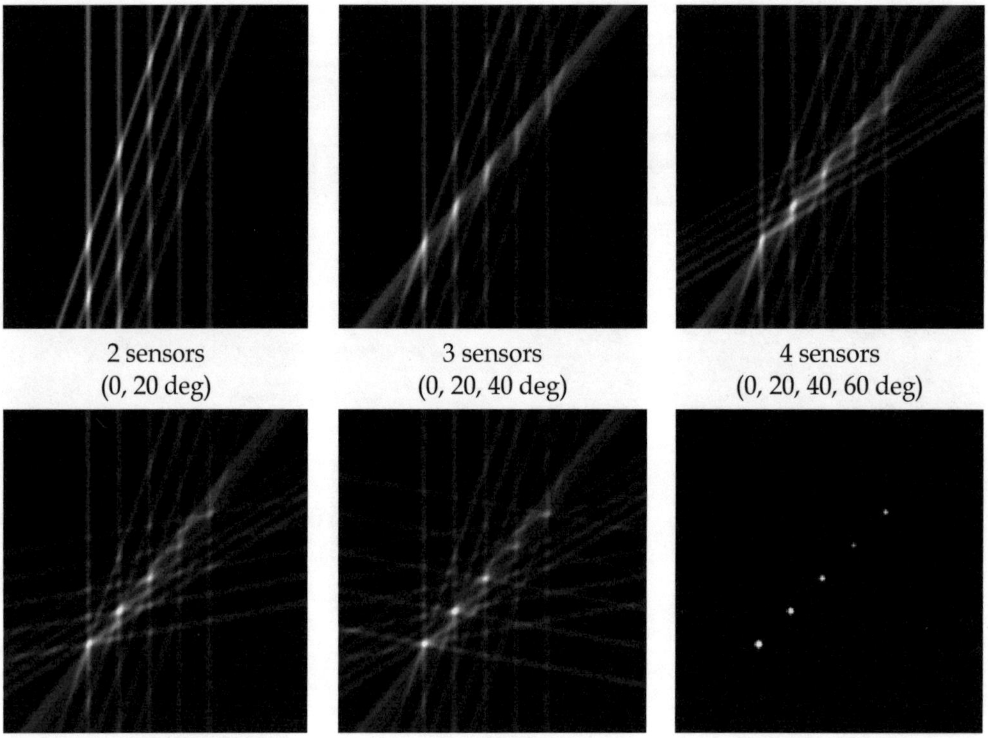

2 sensors (0, 20 deg)

3 sensors (0, 20, 40 deg)

4 sensors (0, 20, 40, 60 deg)

5 sensors (0, 20, 40, 60, 80 deg)

6 sensors (0, 20, 40, 60, 80, 100 deg)

Original position of targets

Fig. 8. Measurement spaces for five targets and variable number of sensors

For two sensors a lot of ghosts are and some of them are outside image and it is not possible to find solution. Different values of targets are mixed and generate a lot of different ghosts' values.
Sensor 40 gives well visible thick line that occurs if targets are collinear (it is well visible in examples for 3 and more sensors). Increasing number of sensors positioned at other angles reduce this effect. In subfigures 4 and 5 is a visible strength blob below target number T2 that shows sensitivity of this strategy – a lot LOS can accumulate in bad conditioned case and ghost appear.
Dim target T4 is visually recognized when there are 5 sensors because humans expect position in proper place but from computation point of view there are also a lot similar value blobs (ghosts). Increasing number sensors improves results for dim targets but it is worth to be noted that problem of detection is also related to collinear placement of targets.

Accumulative strategy work well if there is similar values of targets but in real applications it can not be guaranteed especially if there is measurement noise.

In next example noises is added. There can be two sources of noise. The first one is measurement noise like Gaussian noise that is sources of giant amount of visible parallel lines in figures (Fig.9). The second one is related to observation space of additional objects that is projected onto all sensors and in this chapter is omitted.

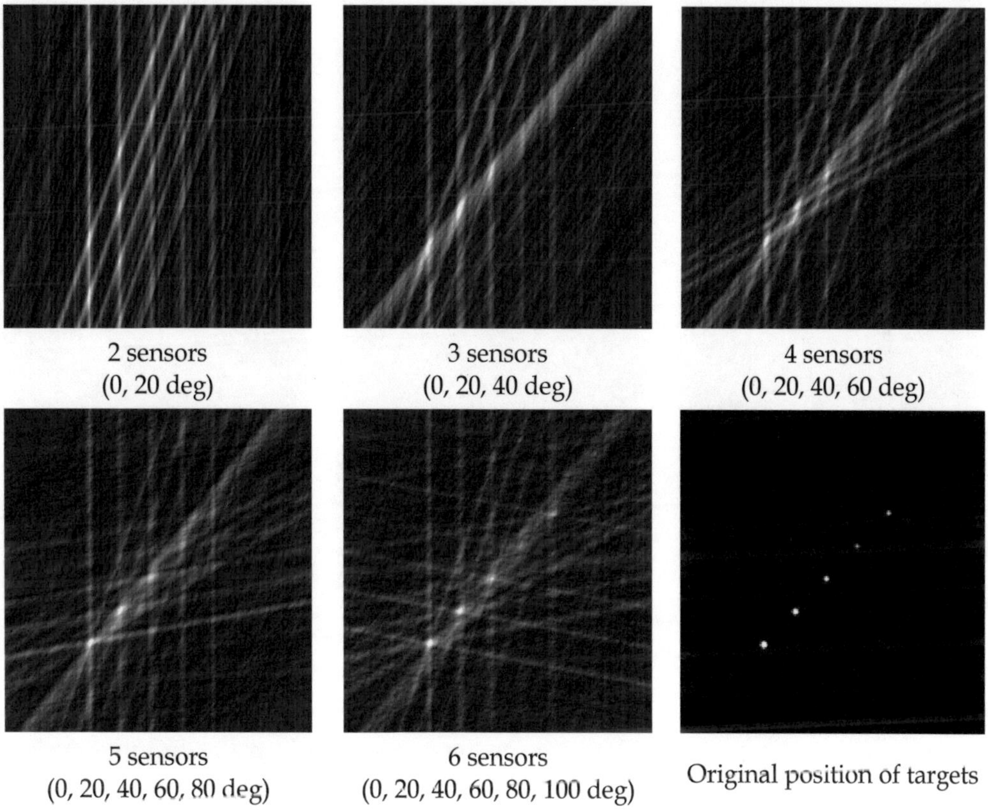

Fig. 9. Measurement spaces for five targets and variable number of sensors. Noise is added to measurements

It is interesting to compare this and previous example. For 5 sensors only three targets are visible for human. Targets T4 and T5 are missing in noise and as is expected due to accumulation from different direction increasing number of sensors helps to find such targets. For 6 sensors target T5 is visible but dim target T4 is still missing.

Noise effects can be reduced by multiple measurements what is a kind of the simplest TBD algorithm. If targets are not moving measurements averaging reduce noise and increase SNR. This is well known noise reduction techniques that can be approved for tracking. This technique correspondence to FIR based TBD. Class of TBD algorithms can be derived from this technique if set of motion vectors is incorporated for averaging. Advantages of averaging for statically placed targets and sensors are shown in next example. This method reduces noise and suppresses values of ghosts also (Fig.10).

For single measurements noises gives a lot of noise in LOS and crossing them gives ghosts. Averaging stabilizes values for cross measurement cells and it is especially visible as lower values for every LOS line between two neighborhoods cross points (ghosts).

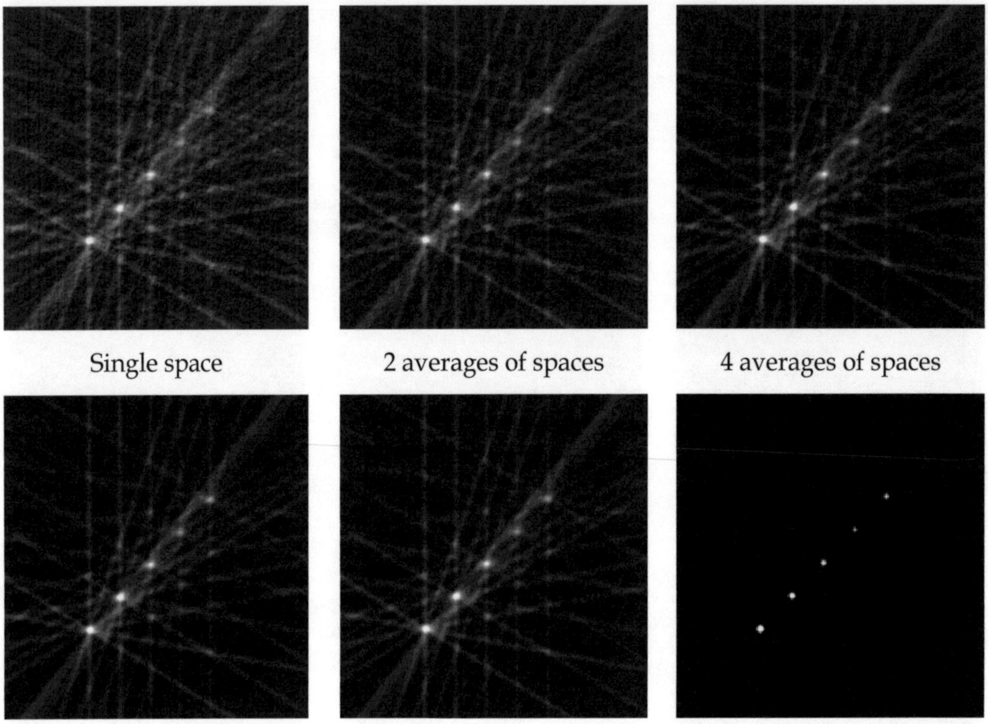

Fig. 10. Measurement spaces for five targets and variable number of averaging. Noise is added to measurements

Averaging of measurements can be used for improving signal quality and two methods should be considered in real applications. The first one is a sensor related averaging by registration time extending and the second one method is numerical averaging based. For real applications both should be considered because TBD algorithms are very good but work much better if signal strength as high as possible. Tracking effort and requirements for additional ghosts suppression algorithms can be reduced by proper designed system. Optical sensor noises can be greatly reduced by cooling and careful analog front-end design what is non trivial for dim targets signal acquisition.

It is worth to be noted that averaging technique can be implemented by parallel sensors. It is interesting method because extending registration time can not be used at any cost. If registration time is long time resolution is usually reduced also. For proper tracking of maneuvering targets and high frame rates linear approximation of movement can be used. Additionally long registration time is not correct for today available sensors because signal accumulated in one sensor cell (pixel) influent on values of neighborhoods pixels.

An additionally parallel sensor averaging is important for dim targets because sensors can be bombarded by high energy particles from space and register very high values for some frames. Using signal processing filters like median filters high values can be detected and removed before averaging and significantly improving overall acquisition process, because TBD algorithms are accumulation oriented.

3. Track-Before-Detect algorithms

Two recursive algorithms can be used as examples of TBD algorithms. Spatio-temporal TBD based on fading memory (exponential smoothing) and simplified version of LLR TBD (Stone et al., 1999). Main difference is that LLR TBD use strict Bayesian approach and spatio-temporal not, but both have similar algorithm structure and they have similar behaviors in a case of ghosting. Spatio-temporal TBD with exponential smoothing can be written as a following pseudoalgorithm:

Start

$P(k=0,s)=0$ //Initial value (1a)

For $k \geq 1$ **and** $s \in S$

$$P^{-}(k,s)=\int_{S} q_k(s \mid s_{k-1}) P(k-1,s_{k-1}) ds_{k-1} \quad \text{//Motion update} \quad (1b)$$

$$P(k,s)=\alpha P^{-}(k,s)+(1-\alpha)X_k \quad \text{//Information update} \quad (1c)$$

EndFor

End

S - state space (2D position and motion vectors Vx, Vy in this chapter),

s - state (spatial and velocity components in this chapter),

k - step number or time moment,

α - smoothing coefficient $\alpha \in (0,1)$,

X_k - measurements (input image),

$P(k,s)$ - estimated value of targets,

$q_k(s \mid s_{k-1})$ - state transitions (Markov matrix).

Simplified LLR TBD can be written as a following pseudoalgorithm:

Start

$$\Lambda(k=0,s)=\frac{p(k=0,s)}{p(k=0,\phi)} \text{ for } s \in S \quad \text{//Initial likelihood ratio} \quad (2a)$$

For $k \geq 1$ **and** $s \in S$

$$\Lambda^{-}(k,s)=\int_{S} q_k(s \mid s_{k-1}) \Lambda(k-1,s_{k-1}) ds_{k-1} \quad \text{//Motion update} \quad (2b)$$

$$\Lambda(k,s)=L_k(y_k \mid s)\Lambda^{-}(k,s) \quad \text{//Information update} \quad (2c)$$

EndFor

End

$\Lambda(k,s)$ - likelihood ratio (LLR),

$\Lambda^{-}(k,s)$ - motion update likelihood ratio,

$L_k(y_k \mid s)$ - measurement likelihood, usually calculated using target signal model,

y_k - measurement.

It is worth to be noted that LLR TBD is very attractive from computational point of view because logarithmic implementation allows reduce number of computation and is very useful in analytical analysis (Stone et al., 1999). Initial likelihood ratio value can be fixed value.
As was mentioned state space in this chapter correspond to measurement space. It allows simplifying analysis and testing TBD algorithms in convenient way. State space is divided on to set of subspaces. Every subspace correspond to measurement space in represents objects positions for specific motion vector and number of subspaces is dependent on number of different velocities and movement directions.
Unidirectional graph show in Fig.11 describes possible target movements - velocity and direction. This graph can be position dependent but in this chapter is assumed as a fixed.

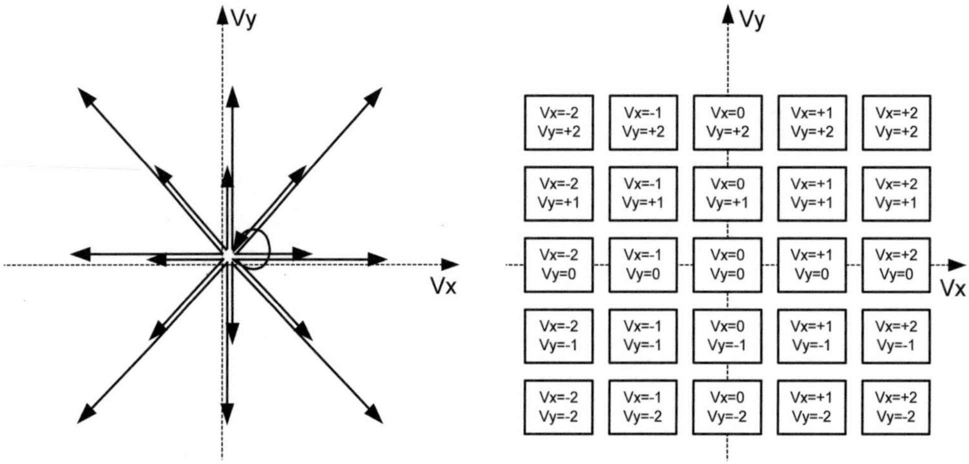

Fig. 11. Motion vectors (left) and corresponding subspaces of TBD algorithm (right)

For assumed motion graph Markov matrix can be prepared directly or implemented in another computational efficient way but there is other important application of motion vectors. Due to high dimensionality visualization of results is complicated especially if after TBD processing there is not available another data fusion algorithm. Joint space can be used but for multiple targets and different directions and velocities only position of targets is visible. The second one visualization method (Mazurek, 2007) is based on placement of multiple subspaces corresponding to motion vector like in Fig. 11 for selected time moment. Central position (looped vector in Fig.11) is very similar to averaging of input measurement (Fig.10) but is not exact average, because there are Markov transitions from other motion vector states and from this state to others.

4. Ghost suppression and Track-Before-Detect Algorithms

4.1 Ghost suppression by accumulative strategy

In following example results for spatio-temporal algorithm for two moving targets and $\alpha = 0.95$ are shown. There are 21 motion vectors and 6 sensors. The first one target starts from left-down area and has assigned Vx=+1, Vy=+1 motion vector. The second one target start from right-up area and has assigned Vx=-1, Vy=-1 motion vector. Target trajectories crosses own trajectories.

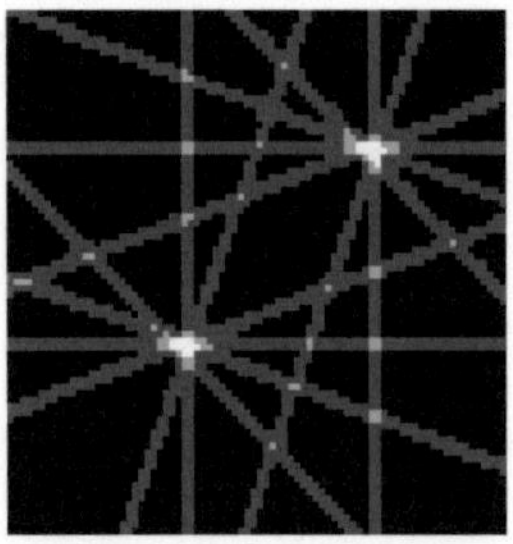

Measurement space for time moment k=20 without noises

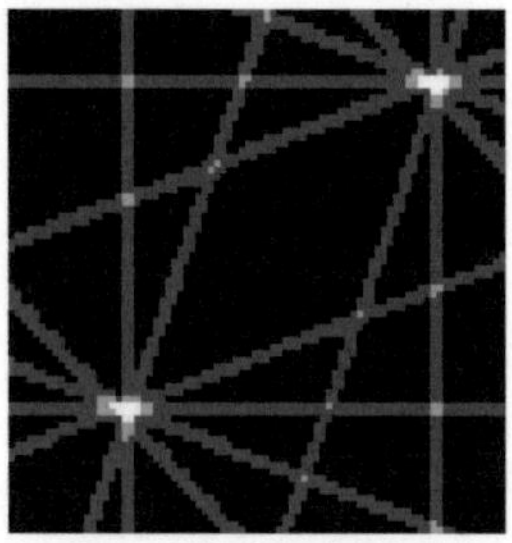

Measurement space for time moment k=60 without noises

Measurement space for time moment k=20 with noises

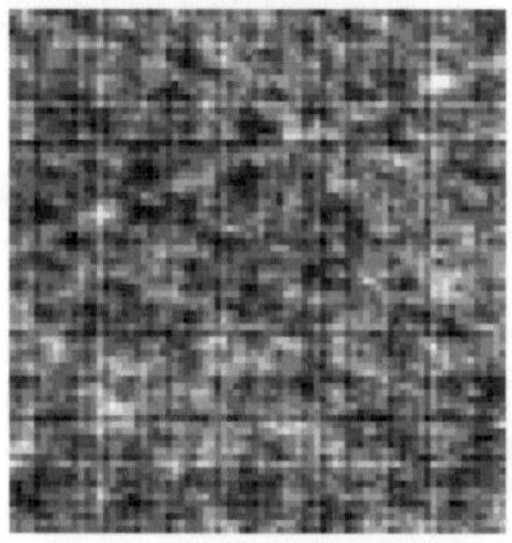

Measurement space for time moment k=60 with noises

TBD state space for time moment k=20 with noises and motion analysis

TBD state space for time moment k=60 with noises and motion analysis

Fig. 12. State spaces for two time moments

Noiseless input measurements show well visible positions of targets but due to noise in input measurements such parameters like positions and number of targets or ghosts are not possible to estimate. Comparing measurement spaces with and without noise shows how it is hard to find targets and classical threshold based algorithms are useless for detection. Targets separated by TBD algorithms motion vectors are the largest values in state spaces for Vx=+1,Vy=+1 and Vx=-1,Vy=-1 subspaces (Fig.13). Due to averaging of multiple sensors measurements ghosts are almost at LOS levels.

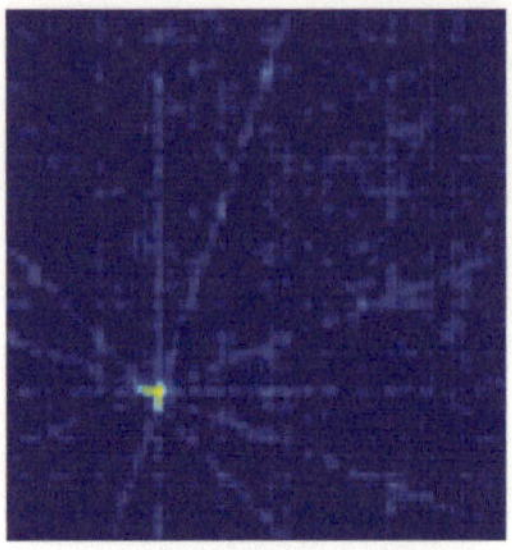

Vx=-1,Vy=-1

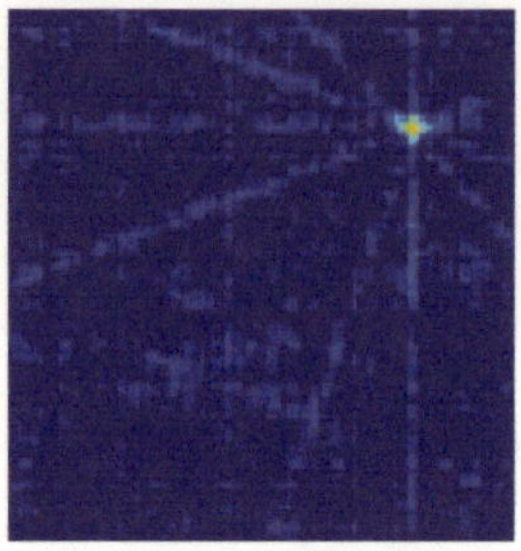

Vx=+1,Vy=+1

Fig. 13. Enlarged selected subspaces for time moment k=60

The Markov matrix describe dispersion of values from particular subspace to neighborhoods subspaces that is necessary for tracking if target changes own motion vector or if target motion vectors is not well fitted to motion vectors defined by motion graph so additional blobs in neighborhoods subspaces surrounding largest one. Using average of all subspaces it is possible obtaining joint space without motion vectors but it is not recommended for good trackers because motion should use for better separating crossing targets.

4.2 Ghost suppression by additional dimension measurements

It was mentioned very interesting behavior of angular sensors that are very sensitive in 1D measurement (2D observation space) and always generate ghosts (Fig.4). In the case of 2D measurements (3D observation space) and proper position of sensors in relation to targets separation (Fig.3) can be obtained. Such forced separation reduces number of ghosts or even completely eliminate them if targets and sensors are not coplanar. In real applications should be considered such technique for example instead of two linear (1D) IR sensitive sensors in marine surveillance two 2D sensors properly placed can help if one of them is at some high over sea surface (e.g. aircraft). This example shows how cooperative measurements and data fusion from many and distance sensors can solve unsolvable problems. This technique can be used in TBD but direct implementation increases computation cost significantly. TBD algorithms for 3D space can be used in two ways:

- Full processing 3D space by TBD needs state space for position only as 3D so even for small state space cost is huge. For example if 2D measurement space has 100x100 cells and full 3D tracking is assumed state space for position has 100x100x100 cells for two orthogonal sensors. Number of computations increases additionally because not only spatial component is much larger but also movement direction (velocity component) increases and amount of computations is gigantic (Barniv, 1990). In near future using optical or electro-optical processing tracking in real-time for such spaces will be possible or it is already possible in today available secret military trackers because optical technology is well suited for TBD algorithms. Unfortunately research papers related to available military applications of TBD are not available.
- Partial TBD processing where only 2D image frames are processed by TBD algorithms for every sensor separately. After targets detection classical assignment or other ghost elimination algorithms are used. This method is very useful because number of computation is exactly proportional to number of sensors.

4.3 Ghost suppression by using positions constraints

This technique is very popular because possible spatial position of targets can be simple measured and used as constraint for reducing number of ghosts. For example as shown in Fig. 14 three targets (T1, T7, T14) should be a ghosts because they are outside of area where targets are.

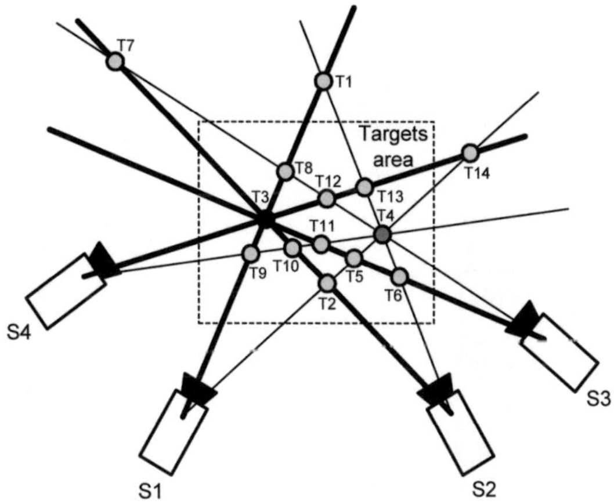

Fig. 14. Ghost suppression by using positions constraints

4.4 Ghost suppression by using proper placement of sensors

This technique is very useful but is not well emphasized in literature and usually it is assumed no target area constraints. Such assumption is important in some cases but if there is possibility of control measurement scenario by experiment planning knowledge about possible trajectories allows finding much better position of sensors and reduce or even eliminate ghosts (Fig.15).

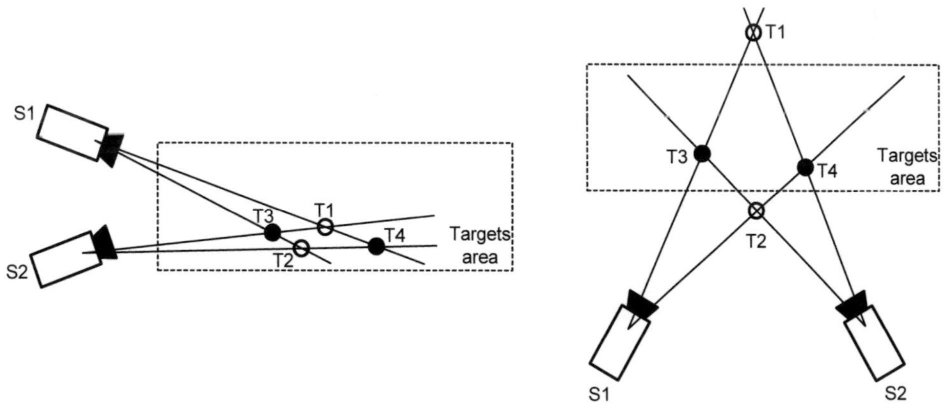

Fig. 15. Two examples same targets positions in area

In left figure bad sensor placement and in right figure solution are shown. For know target are there is possible place ghosts outside area of interest. Proper placement is very interesting from application and research point of view. Using optimization techniques before measurements ghost elimination can be obtained. For simple cases optimization is even not required and geometrical analysis can be used.

4.5 Ghost suppression by using velocity constraints

Very often mentioned in literature are velocity constraints for ghost detection. Usually is emphasized case where projective sensors are used and for two sensors and targets one of the ghosts has much higher velocity in measurement space.

In following example will be show results for two targets and two sensors that can not be solved in general case. Assuming knowledge about targets velocities and movement direction motion graph gives reduced Markov matrix and reduced number of subspaces because some state transitions are forbidden. Due to orientation of sensors or direction of movements of targets the fist one ghost has highest velocity and second one has zero velocity.

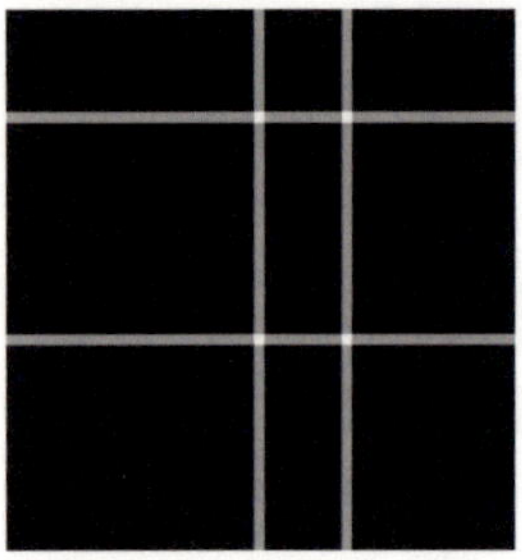

Measurement space for time moment k=20 without noises

Measurement space for time moment k=60 without noises

TBD state space for time moment k=20 without noises and with motion analysis

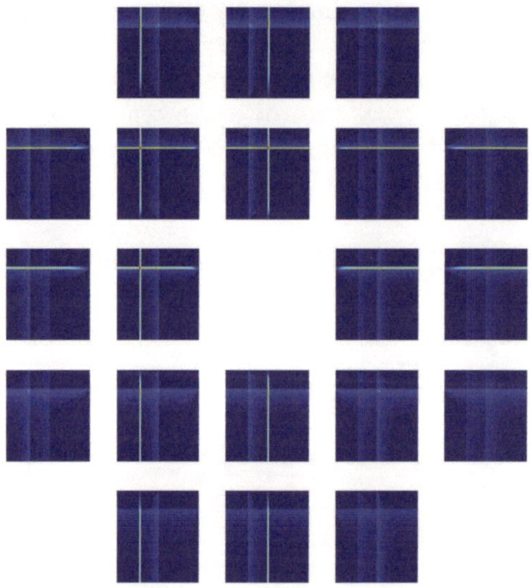

TBD state space for time moment k=60 without noises and with motion analysis

Fig. 16. Selected state spaces for two time moment

Usually velocity constraints are recognized in literature as a maximal velocity limitation, but as shown in this example (Fig.16) minimal velocity can be used for ghost suppression also. Without TBD motion analysis ghosts' elimination is not possible but only one ghost is eliminated (Fig.16). The first one ghost has similar values to target (Fig.17).

Vx=-1,Vy=+1 (ghost) Vx=-1,Vy=0 (true target)

Fig. 17. Zoom of motion separated targets for time moment k=20

4.6 Ghost suppression by using motion direction constraints

This technique allows reducing values for ghosts if they are not moving in proper direction. If there is knowledge available about object trajectory even for small number of sensors like two for two targets can be used. In following noiseless example there are motion vectors ($Vx \geq 0$ and $Vy \geq 0$) and ($Vx \leq 0$, $Vy \leq 0$) allowed for targets (the first one starts from left-up corner and move towards to right-down corner and the second one use opposite direction).

Measurement space for time moment k=20 without noises Measurement space for time moment k=60 without noises

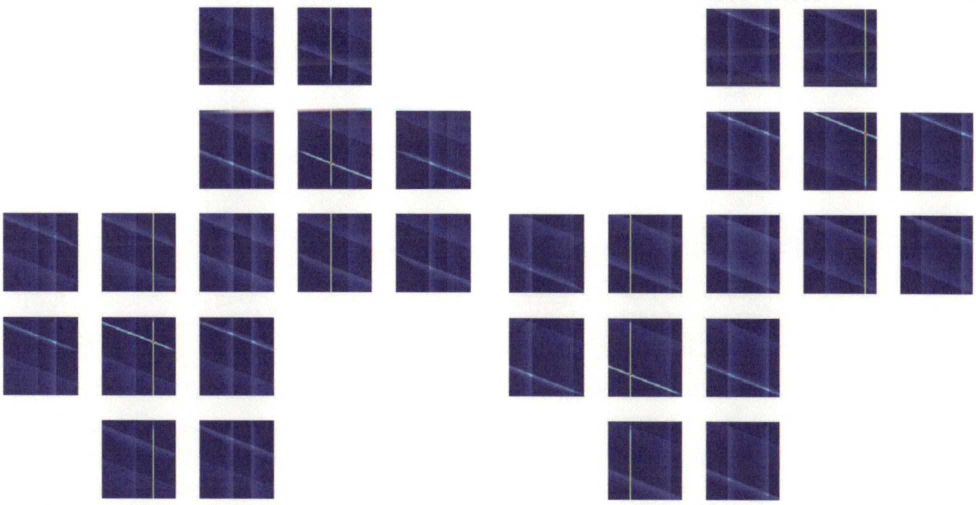

TBD state space for time moment k=20 with motion analysis TBD state space for time moment k=60 with motion analysis

Fig. 18. Selected state spaces for two time moment

As show in Fig.18 there are two ghosts in measurement spaces and they have similar values in comparison to the true targets.

Vx=0,Vy=+1 (left blob is a weak ghost) Vx=+1,Vy=+1 (true target)

Fig. 19. Zoom of motion separated targets for time moment k=60

Ghost values are suppressed (Fig.19) but results depend on number and configuration of sensors and targets trajectories.

There is additional advantages of this and previous method because TBD algorithms need a lot of computation and subspaces reduction decrease computation cost.

4.7 Ghost suppression by increasing angular resolution

Not only coplanar targets and sensors position is source of ghost effect. Angular measurements are sensitive for noises that influent on position measurements even for single target. There almost always errors and ideal triangulation is not possible so two LOS are not crossed in single point for 3D space. Triangulation algorithm estimate (Hartley & Sturm, 1997) target position by minimal distance search between two or more LOS, so approximated position of target P_E is obtained.

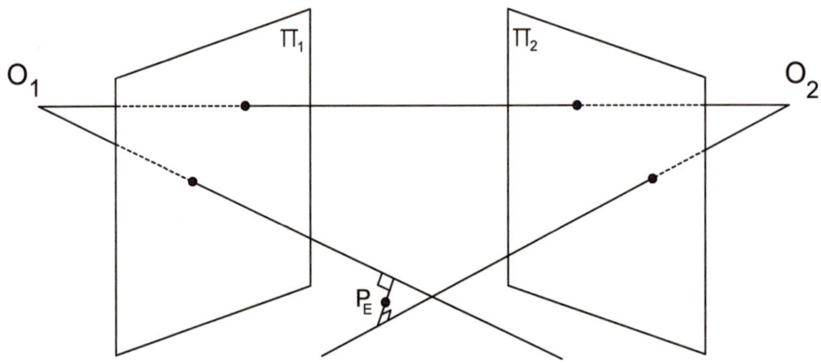

Fig. 20. Triangulation error in 3D observation space

If there are more targets and some of them are closely spaced measurement errors are source of ghosts depending on sensor resolution and measurement noise. Classical track maintenance algorithms can reduce such effect but improving sensor resolution can reduce noise and separate closely located targets also. Optical sensors have resolution dependent on number of optical elements (sensor pixels) and field of view (FOV). Using variable focal length controlled by tracking algorithm is very interesting for improving angular resolution performance.

Spatial errors that induce ghost effect can be reduced by proper placement of sensors. Uncertainly of target position can be modeled as a cone from focal point of sensors. If distance between sensor and target is small position errors are smaller also and ghosts occurrence is less probable. Tracking distant target using bearing only sensors is always challenging.

4.8 Ghost suppression by using additional attributes of targets

This idea uses diversification measurements and allows extend measurement space. For example instead simple IR measurements can be used: two wavelengths for IR measurements, IR and visible light wavelengths, or color light (RGB) measurements.

Good multispectral approach can improves separation between targets significantly and if targets are separated ghosts effect does not occur or is reduced.

The first one technique that use additional attributes uses them directly inside TBD processing.

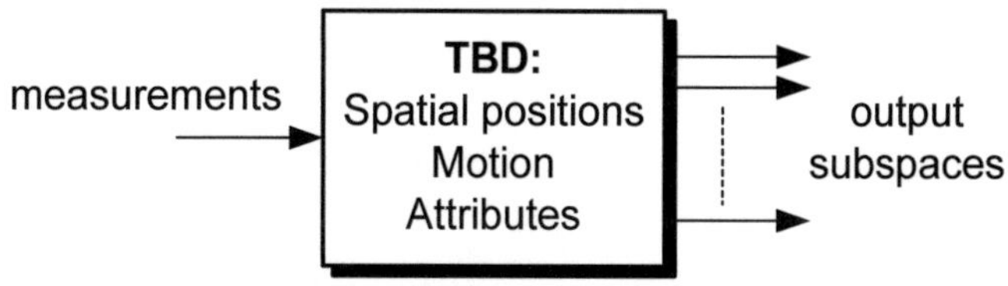

Fig. 21. Additional attributes TBD - combined processing

The second one technique where additional attributes can reduce ghost effect is implementation divide-and-conquer approach using set of filter fitted to attributes for extraction important signal from measurement.

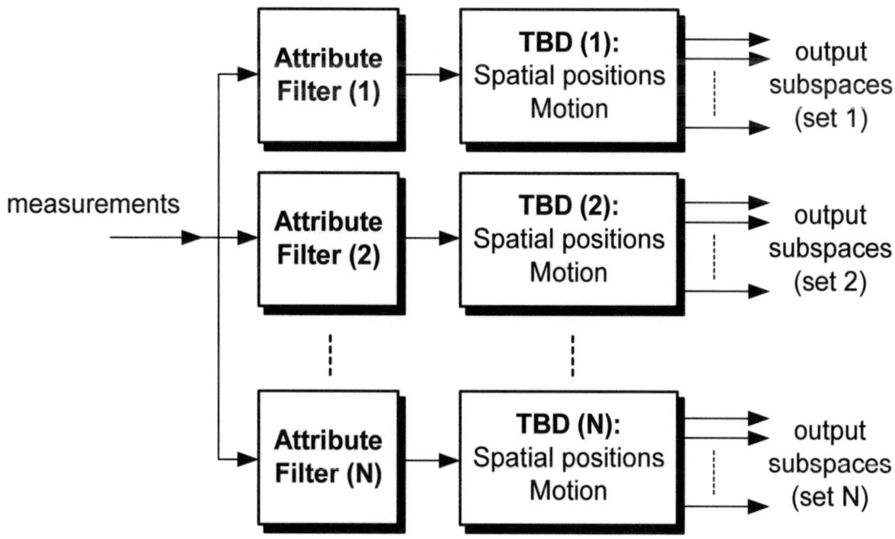

Fig. 22. Additional attributes TBD - separate processing

Attribute based TBD algorithms are very interesting research area because this approach greatly improves tracking and can be used for many practical systems.
In this chapter is considered example of separate processing TBD for tracking colored targets. In this case measurement space is greatly extended because for every measurement cells (pixels) is available more then one value representing spectral data like three R, G and B components. This method is general approach and has very efficient parallel implementation. Unfortunately separate processing does not have ability of using information between spectral components and if target color evolves in time obtained measurements in some channel can not be used by another directly by TBD algorithm. For such situation combined processing TBD approach can be used or additional data fusion algorithms for tracks maintenance are necessary.
Assuming constant color for every target and Gaussian noise filters can be designed using geometric properties of color space. It is assumed typical RGB color space where all color components are orthogonal so point target (pixel size) is a vector in such space and noise can be represented as 3σ radius sphere like in Fig.23 and noise is additive for target signal.

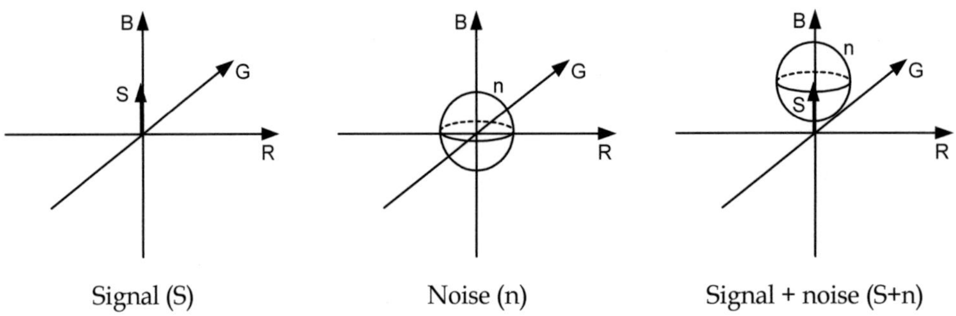

Fig. 23. Single pixel vector representation

In Fig.23 is shown blue color only target and if target color is any but known, transformation using rotation matrix is necessary and signal vector should be parallel to the one of the space vectors (X,Y,Z) for example parallel to the X (Fig.24).

$$\begin{bmatrix} x \\ y \\ z \end{bmatrix} = \begin{bmatrix} a_{11} & a_{12} & a_{13} \\ a_{21} & a_{22} & a_{23} \\ a_{31} & a_{32} & a_{33} \end{bmatrix} \begin{bmatrix} r \\ g \\ b \end{bmatrix} \tag{3}$$

Because only one space vector X is important previous formula can be rewritten to more compact and useful form:

$$[x] = [a_{11} \quad a_{12} \quad a_{13}] \begin{bmatrix} r \\ g \\ b \end{bmatrix} = \frac{1}{\|s\|} [s_r \quad s_g \quad s_b] \begin{bmatrix} sn_r \\ sn_g \\ sn_b \end{bmatrix} \tag{4}$$

where *sn* is any signal plus noise and *s* is expected signal without noise. Such formula can be simple extended to any multispectral case if color space is orthogonal.

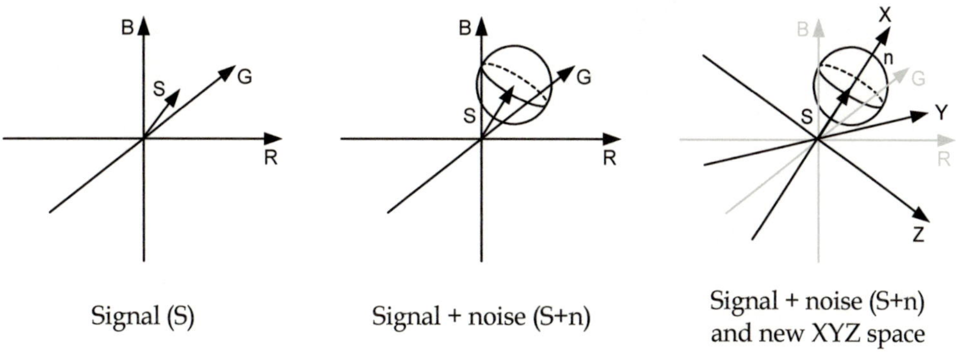

Fig. 24. Single pixel vector representation

Three noised targets are for following example: red (1,0,0), yellow (0.707, 0.707, 0) and green (0,1,0) and three s vectors are used for separation for three measurement spaces. Values for targets are intentionally selected because length of all target vectors is equal so all of them have equal strength.

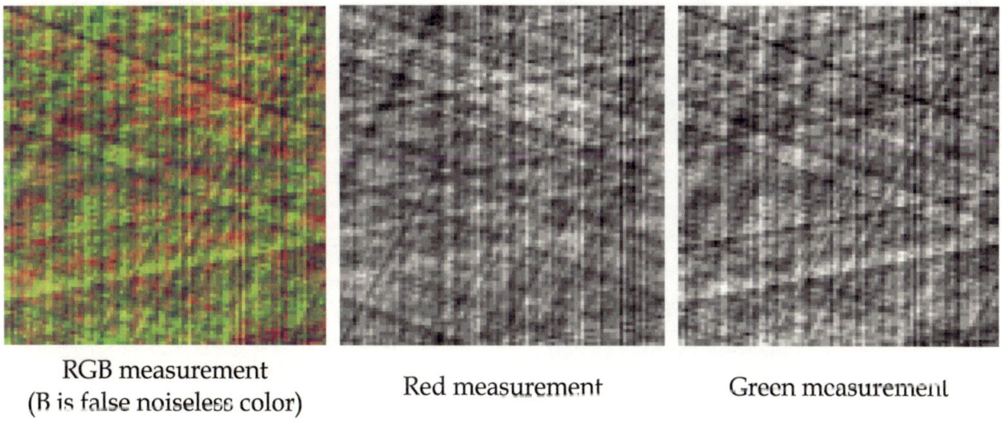

Fig. 25. Input signal for time moment k=60

Blue subspaces are omitted in TBD process because blue component is orthogonal to noiseless target signals. There is only noise in blue color component of RGB space and for separate processing strategy this component is not important.

Full or partial separation between color components is not only related to the targets but LOS also and cross points values are also reduced. Red target use Vx=0, Vy=+1; yellow target use Vx=+1, Vy=+1; green target use Vx=-1, Vy=-1 motion vector.

Without multispectral approach a lot of ghosts should be visible. Separation helps for eliminate ghosts or reduce them. Because yellow target consist component from red and green components there are some signals from this target in both components. Red and green components of target are visible in yellow component also. Crosstalk between nonorthogonal components is a result of simple method of separation but obtained results shows that ghost are weak.

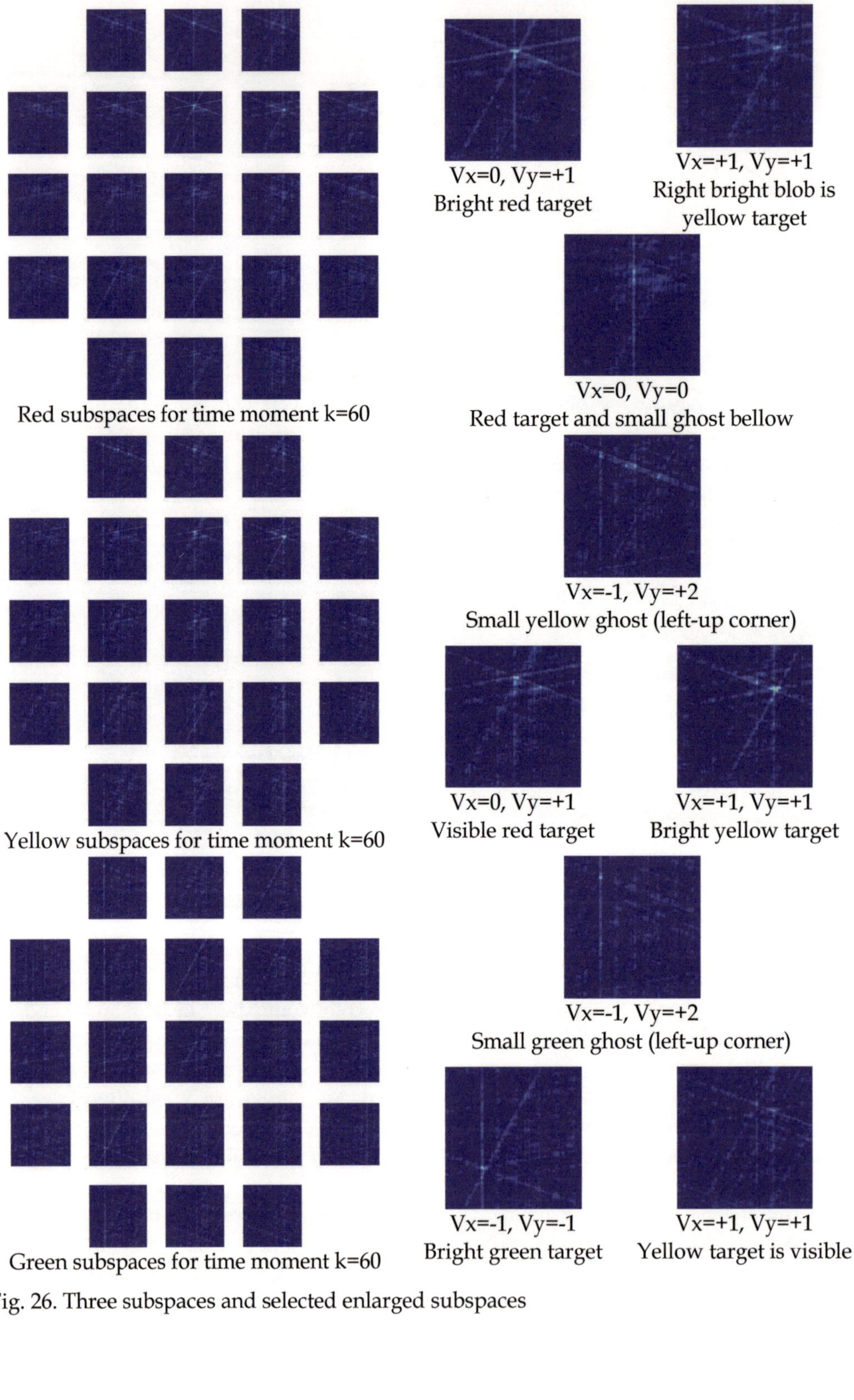

Fig. 26. Three subspaces and selected enlarged subspaces

5. Conclusions

Ghosts are phenomenon that occurs for bearing only sensors and many methods can be used for elimination or reduction them. For accumulative algorithms like considered group of TBD are presented and discussed possible solution.
Comparing discussed deghosting methods is not possible because every method uses another approach and different knowledge about targets. For specific case one method can be better in comparison to others but can fail in another case and all of them should be used carefully. In this chapter are proposed deghosting methods using TBD algorithms directly without additional postprocessing and some of them are used in classical deghosting algorithms.
This approach based on deghosting in TDB algorithms together with main tracking purpose is correct but serious developer should consider other methods also as an additional improvement of systems or even if necessary as replacement for considered in this chapter methods. Ghosting is very serious problem for serious applications. Using suggested method of state space implementation allows design and test systems. Decomposition of 4D state space allows visualize results of TBD for human also. Very popular Monte Carlo based tests for determine system quality is good idea also but it should be used carefully.
Extension of deghosting directly in TBD algorithms is possible but there a lot of interesting question for future researches, for example influence of projective measurements on ghosts because measurement space is not rectangular and approximation is necessary. Measurement likelihood has knowledge about sensor properties and also influent on ghost values and real sensors needs good description of this function additionally so there is question about this influence on ghosts.

6. Acknowledgments

This work is supported by the MNiSW grant N514 004 32/0434 (Poland)

7. References

Arulampalam, M. S.; Maskell, S.; Gordon, N. & Clapp, T. (2002). A Tutorial on Particle Filters for Online Nonlinear/Non-Gaussian Bayesian Tracking, *IEEE Transactions on Signal Processing*, Vol. 50, No.2, February 2002 pp.174-188, ISSN 1053-587X

Bar-Shalom, Y. & Fortmann, T.E. (1988). *Tracking and Data Association*, Academic Press, ISBN 978-0120797608

Bar-Shalom, Y. (ed.) (1990). *Multitarget-Multisensor Tracking: Advanced Applications*, Artech House, ISBN 0-89006-377-X, Boston, London

Bar-Shalom, Y. (ed.) (1992), *Multitarget-Multisensor Tracking: Applications and Advances Vol. II*, Artech House, ISBN 0-89006-517-9, Boston, London

Bar-Shalom, Y. & Li, X-R. (1993). *Estimation and Tracking: Principles, Techniques, and Software*, Artech House, ISBN 0-89006-643-4, Norwood

Bar-Shalom, Y. & Li, X-R. (1995). *Multitarget-Multisensor Tracking: Principles and Techniques*, YBS, ISBN 0-9648312-0-1

Bar-Shalom, Y. & Blair, W. D. (eds.) (2000), *Multitarget-Multisensor Tracking: Applications and Advances Vol. III*, Artech House, ISBN 1-58053-091-5, Boston, London

Barniv, Y. (1990). Dynamic Programming Algorithm for Detecting Dim Moving Targets, In: Bar-Shalom, Y. (ed.) (1992), *Multitarget-Multisensor Tracking: Applications and Advances Vol. II*, Artech House, ISBN 0-89006-517-9, Boston, London

Blackman, S. S. (1986). *Multiple-Target Tracking with Radar Applications*, Artech House, ISBN 978-0890061794

Blackman, S. S. & Popoli, R. (1999). *Design and Analysis of Modern Tracking Systems,* Artech House, ISBN 1-58053-006-0, Boston, London

Brookner, E. (1998). *Tracking and Kalman filtering made easy*, Wiley-Interscience, ISBN 0-471-18407-1, New-York

Doucet, A.; Freitas, N. & Gordon, N. (eds.) (2001), *Sequential Monte Carlo Methods in Practice,* Springer , ISBN 978-0387951461

Gordon, N. J.; Salmond, D. J. & Smith, A. F. M. (1993). Novel approach to nonlinear/non-Gaussian Bayesian state estimator, *IEE Proceedings-F*, Vol. 140, No. 2, April 1993, pp 107-113, ISSN 0956-375X

Hartley, R. I. & Sturm, P. (1997). Triangulation, *Computer Vision and Image Understanding,* Vol. 60, No. 2, November 1997, pp 146-157, ISSN 1077-3142

Mazurek, P. (2007). Deghosting Methods for Likelihood Ratio Track-Before-Detect Algorithm, *Proceedings of the 13-th IEEE/IFAC International Conference on Methods and Models in Automation and Robotics - MMAR'2007*, Szczecin, pp 1227-1232, ISBN 978-83-751803-3-6

Pattipati, K. R.; Deb, S.; Bar-Shalom, Y. & Washburn, R. B. (1992). A New Relaxation Algorithm and Passive Sensor Data Association. *IEEE Transaction on Automatic Control*, Vol. 37, No. 2, February 1992 pp. 198-213, ISSN 00189286

Ristic, B.; Arulampalam, S. & Gordon, N. (2004). *Beyond the Kalman Filter. Particle Filters for Tracking Applications*, Artech House, ISBN 1-58053-631-X, Boston, London

Stone, L. D.; Barlow, C. A. & Corwin, T. L. (1999). *Bayesian Multiple Target Tracking,* Artech House, ISBN 1-58053-024-9, Boston, London

7

Identification of Dynamic Systems & Selection of Suitable Model

Mohsin Jamil, Dr. Suleiman M Sharkh and Babar Hussain
School of Engineering Sciences, University of Southampton
England

1. Introduction

Process Industry is growing very rapidly. To tackle this fast growth, current control methods need to be replaced to produce product with compatible quality & price. Normally the systems are described by suitable mathematical models. These models are replaced by actual process later on. Actually controllers are designed on behalf of suitable models to control the process effectively. So suitable models are very crucial. Different purposes demand for different types of models where the objective could be: (Bjorn Sohlberg, 2005)

- Construction of controllers to control the process.
- Simulation of control system to analyze the effect of changing reference
- Simulate the behaviour of system during different production situations.
- Supervise different parts of process which properties change due subjected to wear or changing product quality.

The exact model of any system will reflect detailed description. A simple feedback controller demands a simple process description than a process description which is going to be used for supervision of wear. Often a more advanced application, demand for a more complex model. The relation between the purpose of the model and its complexity is shown below.

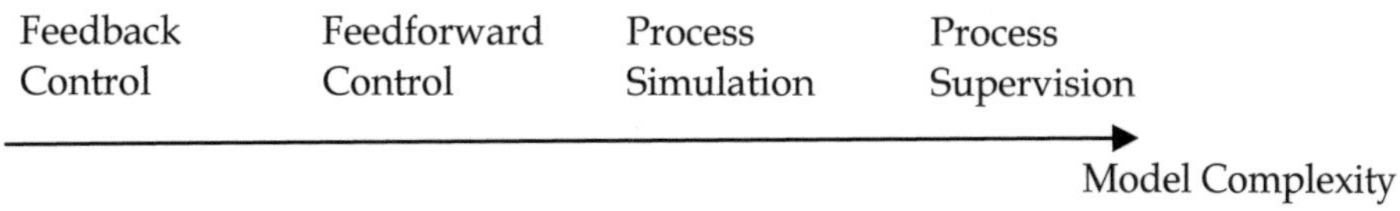

Fig. 1. Model Complexity

The development of information technology has opened new prospective in modelling and simulation of processes used in different scientific applications. There are different types of models which will be discussed in next section. In this chapter we will discuss different types of models, Identification techniques using matlab identification toolbox & different examples. Several aspects on experimental design for identification purposes will be also discussed. In a nutshell this chapter will be useful especially for those who want to do linear black box identification. For any given system/process modelling & identification techniques would be useful to apply after proper understanding of this chapter.

1.1 Types of models

To describe a process or a system we need a model of system. This is nothing new, since we use models daily, without paying this any thoughts. For example, when we drive a car and approaching a road bump, we slow down because we fell intuitively that when this speed is too high we will hit the head in the roof. So from experiences we have developed a model of car driving. We have a feeling of how the car will behave when reach the bump and how we will be affected. Here the model of situation can be considered as a mental model. We can also describe the model by linguistic terms. For example if we drive the car faster than 110km/h then we will hit the head at the roof. This is linguistic model, since the model uses words to describe what happens. (Bjorn Sohlberg, 2005)

A third way of describing the systems is to use scientific relations to make a mathematical model , which describes in what way output signals respond due to changes in input signal. There are different types of models to represent the systems.

1. **White Box Modelling**: When a model is developed by modelling, we mean that model is constructed completely from mathematical scientific relations, such as differential equations, difference equations, algebraic equations and logical relations. The resulting model is called white box or a simulation model.

   Example: For example a model of electrical network using Kirchhoff's laws and similar theorems:

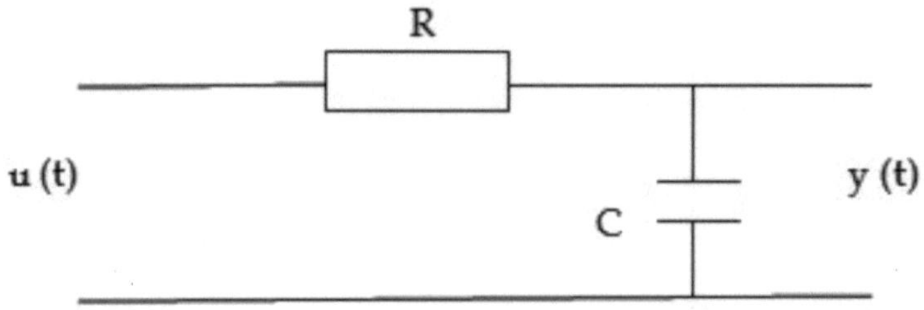

Fig. 2. RC Circuit

   In above RC-circuit where the relation between the input signal u(t) and output signal y(t) is given by Ohm's law. The resulting model would be a linear differential equation with the unknown parameter M=RC, which can be estimated form an experiment with the circuit or formal nominal values of the resistor and the capacitor. A mathematical model is given by:

$$M.\dot{y}(t) + y(t) = u(t) \tag{1}$$

   Similarly other processes can be modelled using scientific relations.

2. **Black Box Modelling:** When a model is formed by means of identification, we consider the process completely unknown. The process is considered black box with inputs and outputs. Thus it is not necessary to use any particular model structure which reflects the physical characteristics of the system. Normally we use a model which given from a group of standard models. Unknown model parameters are estimated by using measurement data which is achieved from an experiment with the process. In this way model shows input-output relation.

Identification using black box models have been used for industrial, economic, ecological and social systems. Within industry, black box models have been used for adaptive control purposes.
Example: Consider a standard model given by equation 2.The process consists of one input signal u(k) and one output signal y(k).Here there two unknown parameters a and b. These parameters are estimated using identification from measured data of process.

$$y(k)+a.y(k-1)=b.u(k-1) \tag{2}$$

We want the model output to look like the process output as good as possible. The difference between the process and model outputs, the error e (t) will be a measure to minimise to find the values of the parameters that is a and b.

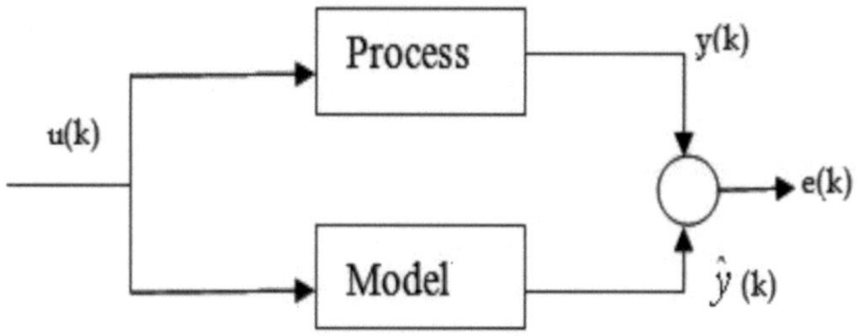

Fig. 3. Black Box Identification

3. **Grey Box Modelling**: For many processes there is some but incomplete knowledge about the process. The amount of knowledge varies from one process to another. Between the white box and black box models there is grey zone.

Type of Model	Application Area
Black Box Models	Process Control
Grey Box Models	Economical Systems, Hydrological Systems
White Box Models	Electronic Circuits

Table. 1. Grey Box Models

The other two common terms in modelling are deterministic and stochastic models. In deterministic models we neglect the influence of disturbance. It is not realistic to make a perfect deterministic model of a real system. The model would be too expensive to develop and would probably be too complex to use. Therefore it is good idea to divide the model into two parts; one deterministic part and one stochastic.

2. Linear black box identification

Black box identification deals with identification of a system using linear models from a family of standard models. The tentative black box model consists of unknown parameters, needed to be estimated from measured data. Some linear models are ARX, ARMAX and similar types of other models. Prerequisite for black box identification is measured data, which are achieved from an experiment with the system. Experimental design will be discussed in next section. During the identification of the model procedure, we normally let three models ARX, ARMAX and OUTPUT-ERROR to find the best model.

2.1 ARX models:

The most common black box model identification is named as ARX-model (Bjorn Sohlberg, 2005).ARX stands for auto regression exogenous. By using the shift operator q^{-1}, the model is reformulated in the following form:

$$A(q^{-1})y(k)=B(q^{-1})u(k)+e(k) \tag{3}$$

The following polynomials $A\left(q^{-1}\right)$ and $B(q^{-1})$ are given by equations (4) and (5), where na and nb are positive number which define the order of the polynomials.

$$A(q^{-1})=1+a_1 q^{-1}+\dots\dots\dots\dots\dots\dots+a_{na}q^{-na} \tag{4}$$

$$B(q^{-1})=b_1 q^{-1}+\dots\dots\dots\dots\dots\dots+b_{nb}q^{-nb} \tag{5}$$

Observations while using ARA Model:

- Easy to use
- Models the disturbance as an regression process (output is non-white even when input=0)
- Better disturbance models than that in Output-Error
- Poles of the dynamic model and poles of the disturbance model coincide; as a result, modelling is not very flexible.

2.2 ARMAX –model:

The model given by equations (6) can be augmented to include a model of the disturbance. ARMAX stands for auto regression moving average exogenous model. Mathematically, this can be introducing a polynomial $C(q^{-1})$:

$$A(q^{-1})y(k)=B(q^{-1})u(k)+C(q^{-1})e(k) \tag{6}$$

$$A(q^{-1})=1+a_1 q^{-1}+\dots\dots\dots\dots\dots\dots+a_{na}q^{-na} \tag{7}$$

$$B(q^{-1})=b_1 q^{-1}+\dots\dots\dots\dots\dots\dots+b_{nb}q^{-nb} \tag{8}$$

$$C(q^{-1})=1+c_1 q^{-1}+\dots\dots\dots\dots\dots\dots+c_{nc}q^{-nc} \tag{9}$$

Observations while using ARMAX Model:

- More complex than ARX model
- Poles of dynamic model and disturbance model are same, as in ARX, but provides extra flexibility with an MA model of disturbance

2.3. Output-Error model

When the disturbances mainly influence the measurements of the output signal, the general model can be transformed to the output error model:

$$F(q^{-1})y(k) = B(q^{-1})u(k) + e(k) \tag{10}$$

The simulation and use of these models will be shown in case study section.

3. Parameter estimation

There are different estimators available. To estimate the parameters one should keep following in the mind:

- The model is never an exact representation of the system
- Undesirable noise always contaminates the measured data
- The system itself may contain sources of disturbance
- Error between the measured output(s) and the model output(s) is unavoidable
- A good identification is one that minimizes this error

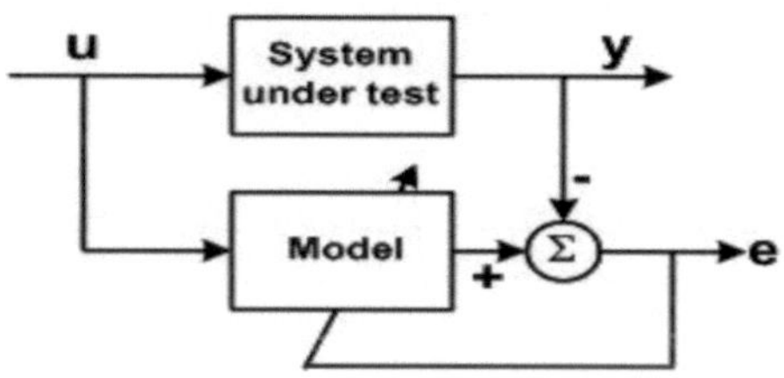

Fig. 4. Difference between the process and model output

3.1 Least squares estimation

Parameter estimation using lease minimization is an early applied method to estimate unknown parameters in mathematical models. The theory was developed in the beginning of 1800 century by Gauss and Legendre. The parameters are estimated such that the sum of the squares of errors is minimized. For an error vector $[e]_{N\times1}$, the LSE minimizes the following sum

$$V = \frac{1}{N}\sum_{i=1}^{N} e_i^2 = \frac{1}{N} e^T e \tag{11}$$

This sum is also known as the Loss Function. Next, we shall generalize the least squares estimation problem for a system with any arbitrary relationship between input & output. Relation exists between the response (dependent variable) of the system under test and regressor (independent variables) via some function. This is represented by linear regression model as:

$$y = f\left(\varphi_1, \varphi_2, \ldots, \varphi_p; \theta\right) + v \tag{12}$$

The relationship is known except for the constants or coefficients θ called parameters and a possible disturbance v. The term φ_i could be taken as regressor. An important special case for the function f is linear regression based on the model:

$$y = \varphi^T \theta + v \tag{13}$$

We will show its implementation in our research work later on.
In case of colour noise affecting the process we use pseudo least square method.
Example: Estimating the parameters of a 2nd order ARX model of the following order:

$$y(k) + a_1 y(k-1) = b_1 u(k-1) + b_2 u(k-2) + e(k) \tag{14}$$

Using matlab system identification toolbox we can do it in following way:

```
>> z  = iddaat(y u)  % From measured data
>> nn = [1 2 1]      % Configure the order of the model
>> m  = arx (z, nn)  % Estimate unknown parameters
>> present (m)       % Present values and accuracy of estimates.
```

4. Model analysis

After the model parameters have been estimated by using measured data, the model has to be analysed. It is important to investigate the quality of model and how well the model is adapted to measured data. By model analysis we will study in what way the model describes the static and dynamic characteristics of the process. Further we will study if the parameter estimates are reproducible. This is done by using two or more different measurement sequences and comparing the estimates by each of them. It is also interesting to calculate residual.
The value of the loss function is also used when we are going to choose between different model candidates. Usually the model having lower loss function is preferred. Moreover we check the frequency characteristics. Below is short summary of steps:

4.1 Simulation

The model is simulated using the inputs from the experiment and the outputs from the model and process are plotted in the same diagram and study if the curves are about the same. In short dynamics of the curves should be same and follow the same trajectory. A systematic difference in the levels is possible to compensate by using regulator.
Example: Below is one example for simulation of model and real process. Both curves are matched in this case.

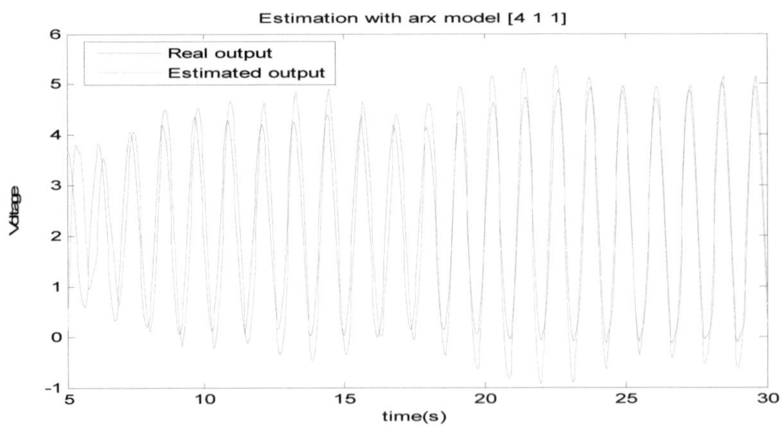

Fig. 5. Simulation

4.2 Statistical analysis

There are several tests which can be used to study whether the residual sequence is white noise. The most important are autocorrelation of the residuals, cross correlation between the residuals. A simple and fast way to get an opinion about the residual is to make a plot in time diagram. Trends in signal will get clear overview. In short we take care of following points while doing statistical analysis.

- Autocorrelation
- Cross correlation
- Normal Distribution
- Residual Plot

4.3 Model structure analysis

When a model is constructed, it should describe the behaviour of the system as perfect as possible. As a measure of perfectness of the model we can use the loss function, since a better model will generate smaller residuals than a worse model. It is observed from experiments that loss function will decrease with the in increase in number of parameters. This means accuracy of estimated parameters will decrease.

4.4 Parameter analysis

If possible, the experiment is repeated so we will have two different measurements sequences. The circumstances around the experiments should be as similar as possible. During these conditions, we investigate whether it is possible to reproduce the same value of the estimates.

The results from estimation can also be presented by a pole/zero plots. We can find whether the model is over determined and too many parameters are estimated. In case of overlapping the two poles and zeros upon each other, the order of system should be reduced.

Example: Pole Zero Diagram of system which is not over determined.

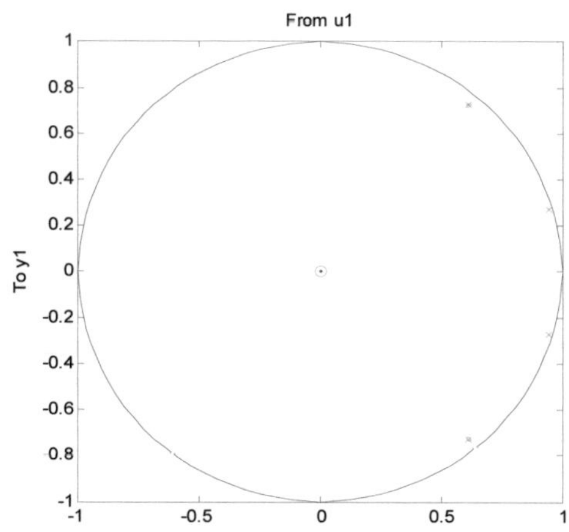

Fig. 6. Pole Zero Diagram

4.5 Frequency analysis

The frequency analysis is a complement to the analysis in time space. It is used to give information about whether the frequency relation between inputs and outputs is covered by model.

The method gives possibility to investigate whether the model can describe the characteristics of the process within a specific interesting frequency range. The frequency plot based on an estimated model and spectrum from measured input/output signals is performed by using Matlab system identification tool box. This is shown in Fig. 16.

5. Model appraisal

During the model appraisal, the model is evaluated based on the purpose of model. This model will be used in some way in feedback control, Feedforward control, model predictive control supervision or failure detection. Following points could be useful during model appraisal.

- When the model is going to be used for designing PID-controllers, then dynamical properties are most important. This can be analysed by plotting the outputs from the process and the model in same diagram. It is important that the model outputs should follow the variations in the process outputs while it is not necessary that both are same.
- When the model is going to be used for simulation purposes, then statistical properties of the model and process are important.
- When the model is going to be used for supervision of parameters within the process which are not possible to measure by a transducer it is necessary to have a model which contains white box parts.

6. Case study: active control of tall structure building

Considerable attention has been paid to active structural control research in recent years; with particular emphasis on alleviation of wind and seismic response. There have been numerous investigations, both analytical and experimental, into the area of passive vibration control of tall buildings in previous decades. Passive vibration control devices such as tuned mass dampers (TMD) have proven to be effective for certain applications but they are limited in the magnitude of motion reduction they can achieve. These limitations have led to the development of active control devices. This device uses a control algorithm which analyses the dynamic structural feedback to create a control force which drives a mass. The theory for active control has been extensively investigated for the past two decades and it has been found to be a superior method of vibration control.

6.1 Background

In recent years, innovative means of enhancing structural functionality and safety against natural and man-made hazards have been in various stages of research and development. By and large, they can be grouped into three broad areas: (i) base isolation; (ii) passive damping; and (iii) active control (Y. Fujino et al., 1996). Of the three, base isolation can now be considered a more mature technology with wider applications as compared with the other two. Implementation of passive energy dissipation systems, such as tuned mass dampers (TMDs), to reduce vibration response of civil engineering structures started in the

U.S.A. in the 1970s and in Japan in the 1980s. In parallel, research and development of active control progressed greatly during the 80's in both the U.S.A. and Japan (R.J Facian et al., 1995).

It has been shown in field studies that tall buildings that are subjected to wind induced oscillations usually oscillate at the fundamental frequency of the building. In some cases this is coupled with torsion motion, when the torsion and lateral oscillation frequencies are close. One of the most common control schemes used to correct these oscillations is a TMD system. Basically, TMD consists of a mass attached to a building, such that it oscillates at the same frequency of the structure but with a phase shift. The mass is attached to the building via a spring-dashpot system and the energy is dissipated by the dashpot as relative motion develops between the mass and structure (R.J Facian et al., 1995).

In the mid 1960s it was studies by Banning and others that the dynamic characteristics of sloshing liquid which eventually initiated the development of a series of natural dampers. The rotation dampers have some unique advantages such as low cost ,easy installation and adjustment of liquid frequency, and little maintenance etc. which are unmatched by the traditional TMD system. The rotation dampers work by absorbing and dissipating energy through the sloshing or oscillating mechanisms of liquid inside a container. Two of the major devices developed in this category include the tuned liquid damper (TLD) and the tuned liquid column damper (J.T.P.Yao, 1972).Both these devices provide excellent overview in the development and application.

Dynamic loads that act on large civil structures can be classified into two main types: environmental, such as wind, wave, and earth quake; and man-made, such as vehicular and pedestrian traffic and those caused by reciprocating and rotating machineries. The response of these structures to dynamic loads will depend on the intensity and duration of the excitation, the structural system, and the ability of the structural system to dissipate the excitations energy. The shape of the structure also has a significant effect on the loading and resulting response from wind excitation. The advent of high strength, light and more flexible construction materials has created a new generation of tall buildings. Due to the smaller amount of damping provided by these modern structures, large deflection and acceleration responses result when they are subjected to environmental loads. Such large responses, in turn, can cause human discomfort or illness and some times, unsafe conditions. Passive, semi active, and active vibration control schemes are becoming an integral part of the system of the next generation of tall buildings (Mohsin Jamil et al., 2007)

6.2 Selection of strategy:

The available strategies are:

- --Active Tuned Mass Damper (ATMD)
- --Sinusoidal Reference Strategy (SRS)
- --Mass dampers and their optimal designs

Comparing all the above strategies, most results are similar with very few differences. The efficiency and robustness of SRS strategy and ATMD are similar to that of LQG (linear quadratic Gaussian) sample controller. Due to lack of help from the passive method, the control forces are much larger than that using the ATMD actuation system. So for this experiment LQG controller is suitable to apply and easy to develop. In the case of active tuned control devices, an actuator is required; the installation cost of the actuator is more. So the operation cost of the active tuned mass dampers is more than the LQG controller. Here we selected active tuned mass damper for implementation.

6.3 Process identification and selection of suitable model

The knowledge about the dynamic characteristics of a system is one of the most important aspects of control system design. An accurate mathematical model of the system determines whether a controller works properly or becomes unstable. Because of the practical unavailability of wind force measurement, the system identification in this study is processed without them. The active control force and wind forces are the actual exciting input forces to the structure.

A linear black box model shall be developed for this process.

The steps followed to develop the model are:

- Make an experiment
- Data processing
- Model selection
- Parameter estimation
- Model Analysis
- Model appraisal

6.3.1 Experimental setup

A model of a flexible tall building structure is designed in the laboratory (see fig7) in order to study and design of a semi active control system with ATMD i.e. active tune mass damper. Dynamic parameters collected through system identification as described in the following section, and controller performance is simulated through MATLAB. An accelerometer is placed on top of the model to measure the response of the structure with nominal dimensions 1m x 0.05m.

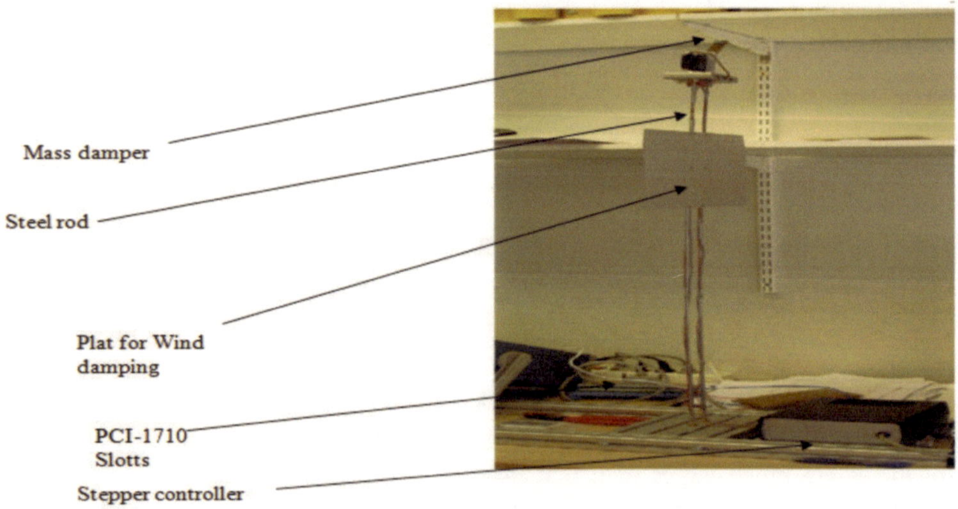

Fig. 7. Experimental Setup

In the fig 7, we can see the mass damper attached on the top of the system to reduce the vibration of the structure .The mass damper having the variable mass but we can change the mass in the initial stage i.e. before the system to run. This mass damper i.e. (TMD) tune mass damper operate with the help of a linear servo motor. For more broad view of the mass damper, servo motor and accelerator meter is shown in the fig.8 below.

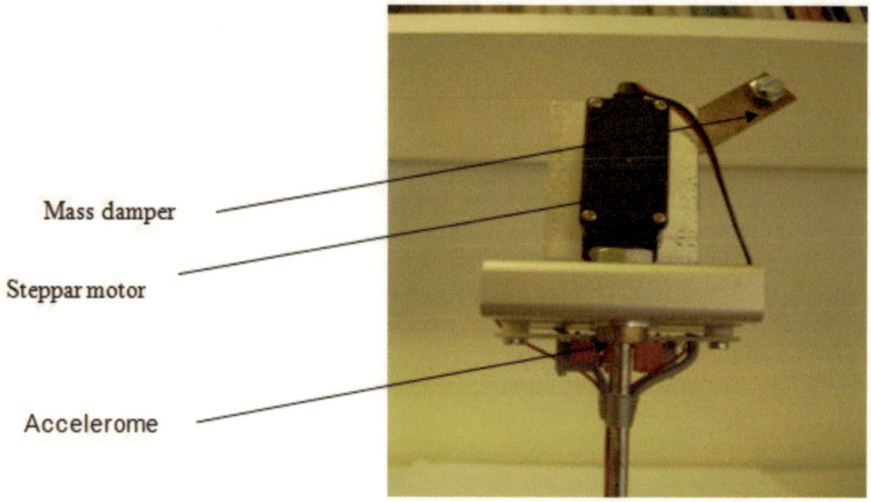

Fig. 8. Closer View of Setup

In the fig.8, we can see the steel rod of one meter height attached in the base of the steel structure stands for the height of the building. The steel rod attached is quite light weight and flexible to allow it vibrate with the impact of the external force. The motion of the structure is just like a pendulum. It vibrates with its natural frequency whose acceleration in terms of voltages is roundabout (+0.02) to (- 0.03) voltages if even without any external force. As it is described previously that voltages output represent the acceleration of the system. The natural movement graph is given below in fig. 9.

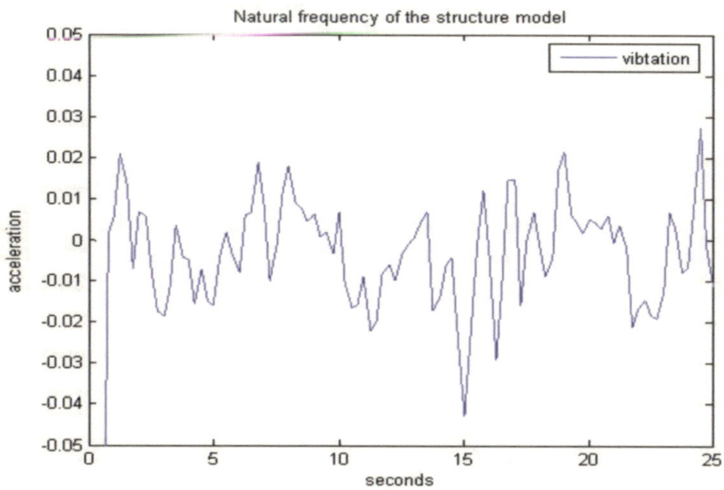

Fig. 9. Natural frequency graph of the structure model.

So as this vibration of the system is due to the natural frequency or natural movement, we can't reduce this vibration more than this low frequency or acceleration.
The length of steel rod made our system model high degree of robust and fast vibrating. So reduction of the vibration is harder and required more time to stop to natural frequency as compare to the actual system. As shown in the fig.7, the plate for wind damping is used to create the effect of linearization of the wind effect. It also tries to create real conditions as in our steel structure rods having between empty spaces to pass the air as compare to the high structure building. So to create the filled effect of the building, we use this board sheet as show in fig7. It also creates the linear effect for the air force.
PCI-1710, I/O card (Input and output) is used to get the output of the model structure acceleration in term of the analogue voltages. With the A/D converter (analogue to digital converter), voltages from the accelerometer is converted to digital form to communicate with the matlab. This voltages to use for control, i.e., for taking the measurements feedback, computing the control command and then sending out back the voltages to the servo motor through the PCI I/O card. D/A conversion are used for the voltages coming out from the computer to the structure model's servo motor. The schematic diagram of the PCI-1710(12/16 bit multifunction card) is shown in appendix. In PCI-1710 series four pins i.e. 57, 58, 60 and 68 are used. Pin57 and 60 are grounded, Pin58 (D/A) is the output from the system and Pin 68(A/D) is the output from the setup.
The basic idea behind this control of the structure model against the external forces is to operate the mass attached on the top (tuned mass damper) in opposite direction to the motion of the structure

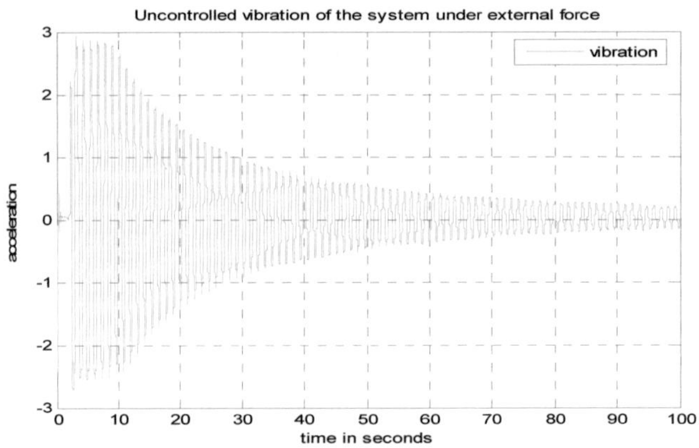

Fig. 10. Uncontrolled vibration due to single external of the structure model.

The figure 10 shows the behavior of the tall structure prototype model under external force without controlling it in open loop. This shows that the system vibrates like a pendulum and even after 100 seconds the vibration is more than 0.1 units of acceleration. This figure provides good reference for us to compare between the controlled and uncontrolled system. It also shows that after 30 seconds system comes to high vibration level as 1.00 units of acceleration. And after 60 seconds the vibration comes in the range of 0.5 voltages.

6.3.2 Experiment design

The goal of experiment is to affect all frequencies of interest with as much as possible of the available input energy. When a process model is constructed by using identification methods, measured data is necessary when unknown model parameters are estimated. This means both the input and the output variables have to be collected when process is running. Several aspects have to be considered when designing an experiment to achieve informative measurements from the process. First of all there are practical considerations in what way we can affect the process. We have to realise when the process is affected by external signal, the process will be disturbed. Hence the output of the process will deviate from a desired result. This situation will limit the amplitude of input signal and the length of the experiment. When designing the signal is that the inputs shall influence the process in a way so the interesting frequencies are affected. Further to keep the relative error constant, we need a signal with constant signal/noise ratio (Bjorn Sohlberg, 2005). Much commercial process cannot be exposed by an open loop experiment. It is not possible to run the experiment without proper controller. There may also be problem with running the process safely, which means it is necessary to keep important process variables with in specified limits. From the discussion, we have that a suitable wave form is a pseudo random binary signal.

Generation of PRBS Signal:

This kind of signal has the lowest crest factor and is easy to implement. This signal has also the advantages to be piece wise constant, which makes it suitable to identify discrete time linear models. The PRBS signal is generated from the matlab routine named makeprbs. PRBS signal is applied at the input of the system. For this purpose it is necessary to define its parameters. (Bjorn Sohlberg, 2004)

```
>> PRBS= makeprbs (tstop, ts, tmin, tmax, umin, umax);
```

Stop time: the experiment have to take place during a time long enough to achieve estimation of the unknown parameters. The given process is vibration process so 30 seconds more enough to estimation of unknown parameters. So we take: tstop=30 seconds;

Sample time: when the sample time is long, we will have high variance values of the estimated parameters. When the sample time is too short, the change of the outputs may be small compared to the measurement disturbances. When the sample time is h=0.05 seconds, we will have three samples during the transport time.

Thus we select: ts=0.05 seconds;

Time at the same level of the input signal: the input signal must affect the process longer than a shortest time period which influences the outputs considerable. The signal length on the same level must be long enough to influence the dynamic of the process. Long duration on the same level give no more information about the behaviour of the process. Hence between the shortest and longest time periods the signal change levels with a random distribution of the time duration on the same level. The longest time of the input signal can be chosen as 0.7seconds, if the value more than this the output of the process is not follow the input, means when the signal is constant at that moment is also system is oscillating. The shortest time of the input signal at the same level can be chosen as 0.5 seconds, if the value less than this the output of the process is slow than the input of the process, means when the input signal varying the output is varied slowly.

tmin =0.5 seconds, tmax =0.7 seconds;

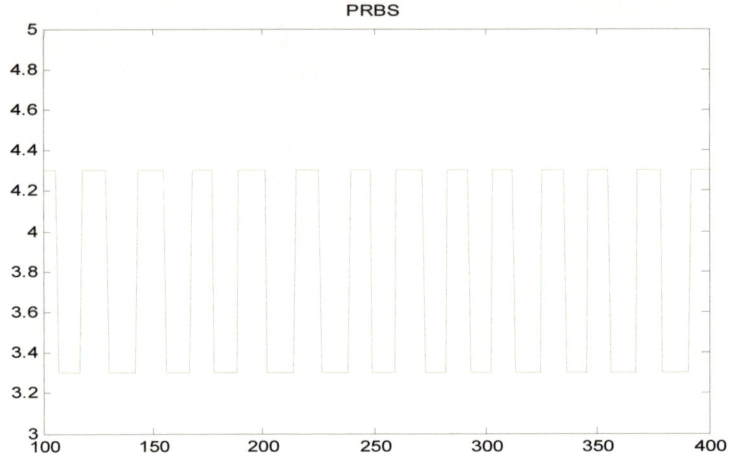

Fig. 11. PRBS Signal

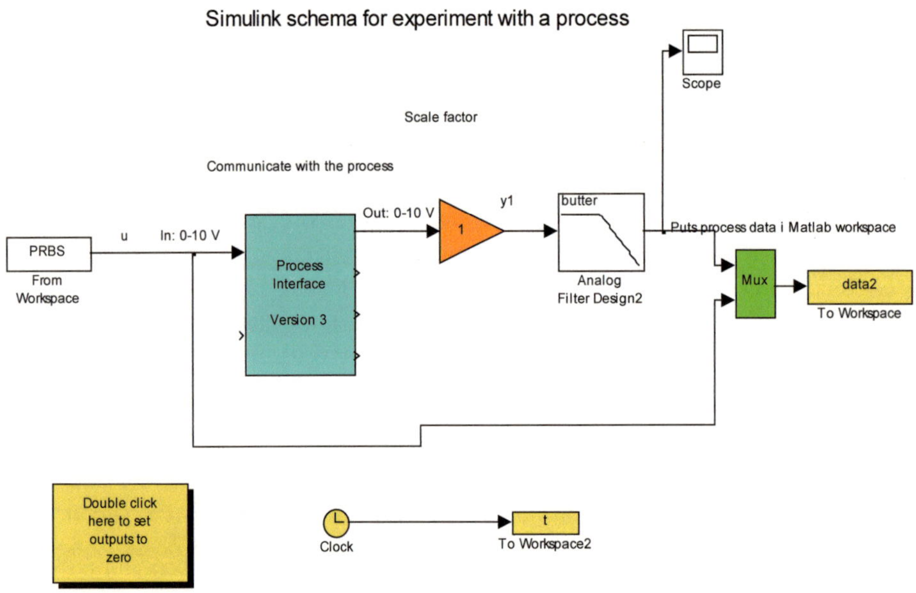

Fig. 12. Simulink Window of the Process

Amplitude values of the PRBS: large amplitudes may also increase the influence of process non linearity's, which makes the system identification, based on a linear model, more difficult. We should avoid using values of the inputs at the ends of its range. In our process, the input signal can be affected within the range [2.4 - 4.6]. The input signal must not produce non-linear characteristics. The system is to be controlled in a steady state; hence, the small oscillations in transient time must be avoided. For this reason we have limitations in control signal, Umax=4.3 volts and Umin=3.3 volts; the change in the input signal should not be large because linear model would turn to be nonlinear model. The parameters are estimated from the different experimental trails and then decide the values are suitable for this process. Finally we have:

>> PRBS= makeprbs (30, 0.05, 0.5, 0.7, 3.3, 4.3);

Let the input signal be PRBS; the sample time in all appropriate blocks in the simulink window has to be changed at the start of the experiment. The stop time for the simulink window must be same as the experiment stop time.

After the experimentation the system will record the measured data through sensors. For this data will help to make mathematical model.

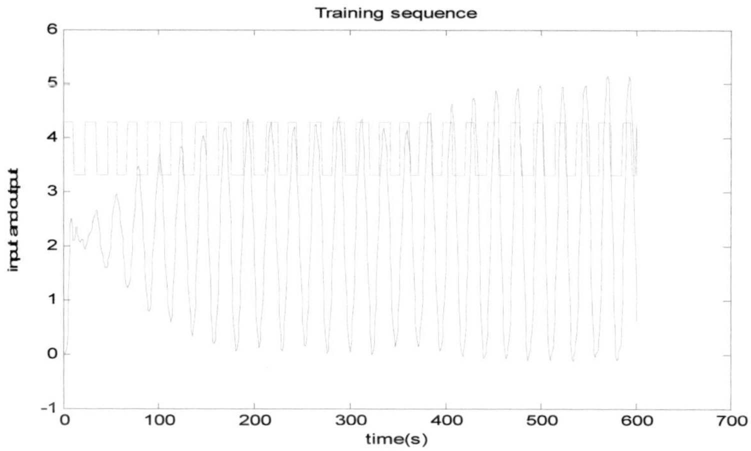

Figure. 13. Input and Output of the Process

The results from the experiment are shown in fig.13. It shows both the input and output of the process. From the experiment it can be concluded that the variation in the amplitude of the output is same as input. It also shows the output follows the input with little delay.

6.3.3 Data processing

After this idealised experiment, there is no need for any data processing. From fig. 13, we can see there are no outliers, or filtering or low and high frequency disturbances needed to be eliminated. The stationary point for the output is 2.24 and input is 3.75. Hence we need to eliminate mean values from the measurements.

>>data_d=dtrend (dat); %removing mean values

>>data_d=dtrend (dat, 1); % removing trend values

6.3.4 Parameter estimation

During the identification of the model procedure, we let three models ARX, ARMAX and Output-Error to find the best model. Details of these models have been already explained earlier. So we just apply and show the research results.

Model Parameter	ARX-3	ARX-4	ARX-5	ARMAX-3	ARMAX-4
A1	-2.519 (±0.03516)	-3.111(±0.01927)	-3.267 (±0.03743)	-2.661 (±0.03138)	-3.099 (±0.02297)
A2	2.167(±0.06646)	4.176(±0.05036)	5.849 (±0.1174)	2.433 (±0.05957)	4.118 (±0.06053)
A3	-0.6157(±0.03421)	-2.882(±0.04939)	-5.248 (±0.1605)	-0.7544 (±0.03065)	-2.808 (±0.05999)
A4		0.8708(±0.01815)	2.582 (±0.1133)		0.8388 (±0.02226)
A5			-0.53 (±0.03479)		
B1	0.01872(±0.001846)	0.0309(±0.0008174)	0.01499 (±0.001243)	0.00968 (±0.001587)	0.02928 (±0.001005)
Loss fcn	0.00150523	0.000265366	0.00028017	0.00054384	0.0001517
FPE	0.00152941	0.000270705	0.00028453	0.00056146	0.00016517

Model Parameter	ARMAX-5	OE-3	OE-4	OE-5
A1	-3.642 (±0.03699)	0.2612 (±0.7533)	0.3144 (±0.502)	0.8788 (±0.1729)
A2	5.875 (±0.1166)	1.395 (±0.9609)	0.2596 (±0.4368)	-0.3017 (±0.1248)
A3	-5.306 (±0.16)	-1.598 (±0.6474)	0.8884 (±0.3116)	0.0144 (±0.0684)
A4	2.667 (±0.1132)		-1.392 (±0.4393)	0.5596 (±0.1175)
A5	-0.5745 (±0.03478)			-1.123 (±0.1684)
B1	0.01171 (±0.001239)	-0.8989 (±0.0914)	-0.8811 (±0.06313)	-0.952 (±0.0474)
Loss fcn	0.00015433	1.49666	1.35876	0.740544
FPE	0.00016944	1.52094	1.38649	0.773725

Table. 2. Parameter estimation

Percentage of Error:
Now we check percentage of error in estimated models. All the values are given below in table 3.

Model Parameter	ARX-3	ARX-4	ARX-5	ARMAX-3	ARMAX-4	ARMAX-5	OE-3	OE-4	OE-5
A1	1.4%	0.6%	1.1%	1.2%	0.7%	1%	288%	159%	19.6%
A2	3.1%	1.2%	2%	2.45%	1.5%	2%	68%	168%	415%
A3	5.6%	1.7%	3%	4.1%	2.14%	3%	40%	35%	475%
A4		2.08%	4.4%		2.7%	4.2%		31.5%	21%
A5			6.5%			6.1%			15%
B1	9.86%	2.6%	8.3%	16.4%	3.4%	1.1%	10%	7.2%	5%

Table. 3. Percentage of error of the estimated parameters

It clearly shows which model represents the process. Every parameter is estimated given by its margin of errors as the standard deviation.

Discussion on Loss Function: The loss function decreases relatively slowly between the models ARX-3 and ARX-4. The smallest value is achieved from for the ARX-4 model. However we can see that the smallest value of FPE is achieved for ARX-4. Hence, the results from the loss function and the number of estimated parameters favours model ARX-4.The loss function decreases relatively much between the models ARMAX-3 and ARMAX-5. The smallest value achieved from for the ARMAX-4 model. However we can see that the smallest value of FPE is achieved for ARMAX-4. Hence the results from the loss function and the number of estimated parameters favour model ARMAX-4.The loss function decreases relatively much between the models OE-4 and OE-5. The smallest value achieved from for the OE-5 model. However we can see that the smallest value of FPE is achieved for OE-5. Hence the results from the loss function and the number of estimated parameters more.

Discussion on Parameter Estimation: Every parameter estimate is given by its margin of errors, i.e. the standard deviation. For the model ARX-4, the margin of errors is small compared to the model ARX-3 and ARX-5.For the model ARMAX-4, the margin of errors is small compared to the model ARMAX-3 and ARMAX-5.For the model OE-5, the margin of errors is small compared to the model OE-3 and OE-4.Compare all three models ARX-4, ARMAX-4 and OE-5; among these ARX-4 has less parameter error and less parameters compared to ARMAX-4 model.

6.3.5 Model analysis

The ARX [4 1 1] model is simulated using the outputs from the process. The output of the model is compared with the output of the process. The result is shown in following figure.

Simulation:

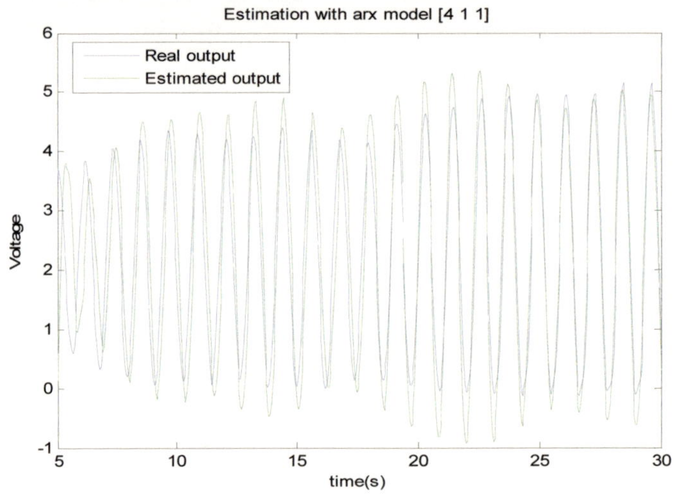

Fig 14: Simulation Results

From the simulation it can be seen that the model ARX [4 1 1] is able to describe the measurements from the process well.

Auto and Cross Correlation Analysis: The next step in the model analysis is to figure it out the residuals of auto and cross correlation results.

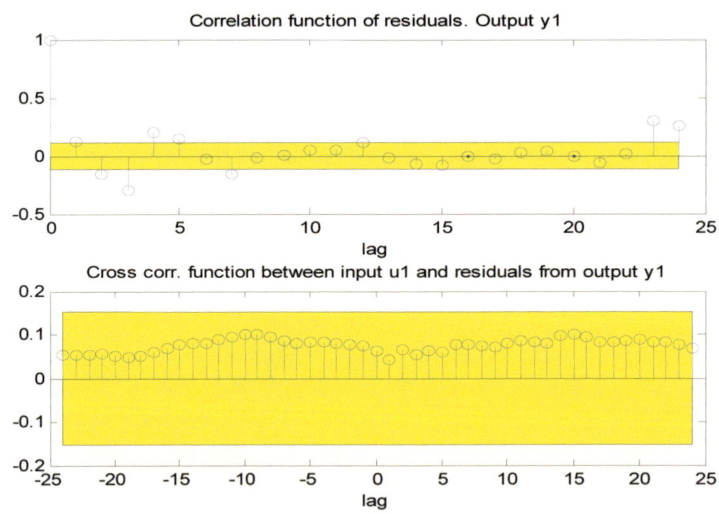

Fig 15: Auto and Cross Correlation

The curves show that no value of cross correlation and very few values of auto correlation coming out of the defined boundaries of the standard deviation and the residual is independent between two or more samples. The residual is also independent of the control signal. So there is no more information left to be gathered from the process.

Frequency Analysis

The frequency characteristics are investigated by plotting the bode diagrams for the measured data and the models. The Upper bode plot shows the gain (amplitude) and the lower shows the phase of model ARX [4 1 1]

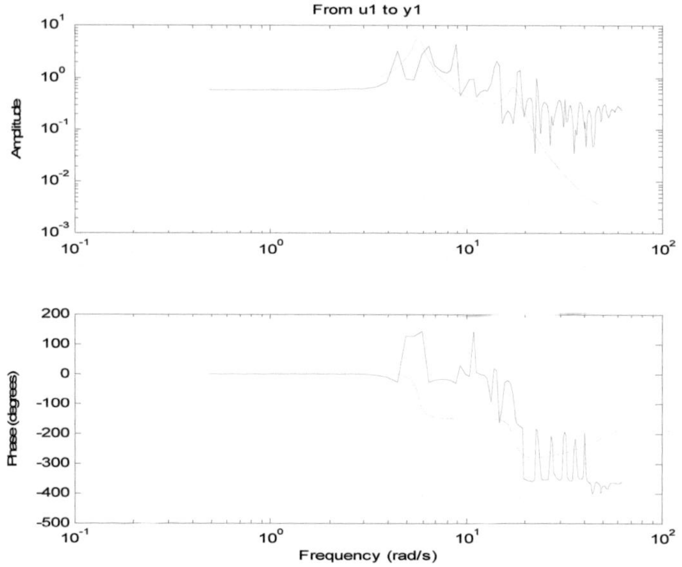

Fig 16: Frequency Diagram

The frequency plot based on an estimated model and spectrum from measured input/ output signals is performed by using Matlab SITB, the plot shown in fig 3.6 provides the information, whether the frequency relation between input and outputs is covered by the model.

The above figure is showing that the model and process have similar dynamic curves. So the model is representing the process well.

Pole-zero analysis: The following figure shows the poles and zero of the model.

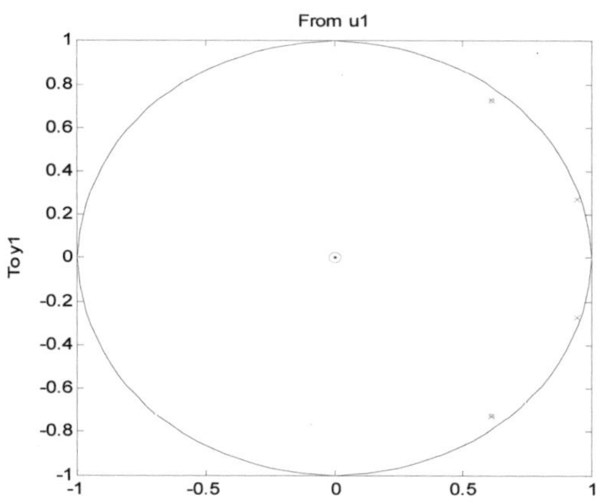

Figure 17: Pole-Zero Diagram

The above figure of poles and zero shows that, the model is not over determined and it is also shows that the pole is far away from the area of the zero. From fig3.9 the uncertainty plot from poles and zeros are not overlapping each other. So there is no pole/zero cancellation. Furthermore the poles/zeros lay insight the unit circle, so the system is stable.

6.3.6 Model appraisal

During the model appraisal, we are going to make an in all analysis concerning which model is best suitable to describe the process. From the model analysis, we have that the model ARX-4 is favoured from the analysis of Loss function, FPE and parameter estimation. The values from the parameter estimate are significant for models ARX-4 and ARMAX-4. But OE-3, OE-4 and OE-5 have overestimated parameters. ARX-4 has fewer margins of errors compared to ARMAX-4.The extra parameters are estimated for the model OE model. Hence some of the parameters for OE are not significant. From the model simulation, it is seen that the models are ARX [4 1 1] are able to describe the measurements from the process. From the correlation, it is obvious that ARX-3, ARX-5, ARMAX-3, ARMAX-4, ARMAX-5, OE_3, OE-4, and OE-5 give a result which is more outside the confidence interval. The ARX-4 fulfils the tests for both the auto and cross correlations. Further, the frequency analysis contradicts the remaining models except ARX-4 model. While pole zero plot shows that ARX-4 is better among the others. It can be conclude that most of the model analysis favours the model ARX [4 1 1]. It is not necessary to expand or use another model type.

6.3.7 Simulated mathematical model of a process

From the chosen mathematical model, the simulink diagram is made in the matlab. In the fig.3.10 the mathematical model is tested for its suitability for the system

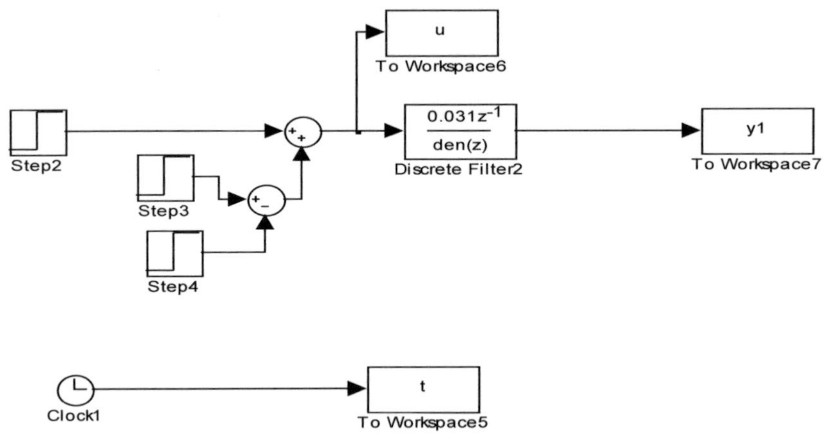

Fig 18: Selected Mathematical Model in Simulink Window

Generally the system is an oscillating system, so the output must be a sine curve. To check this result a reference signal is given as step input and its value is set to zero, adding step signal at step time 1sec and after 0.1 sec the signal is removed. The above fig. 19 represents the input and output of the mathematical model. From the results the mathematical model satisfies the original process. Firstly the controller for our mathematical model is designed to replace original process instead of model. Among the various controllers available the pole placement controller and state space pole placement controller are chosen.

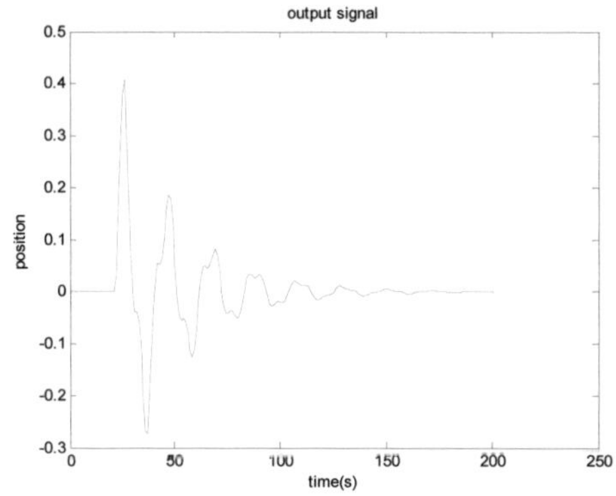

(a)

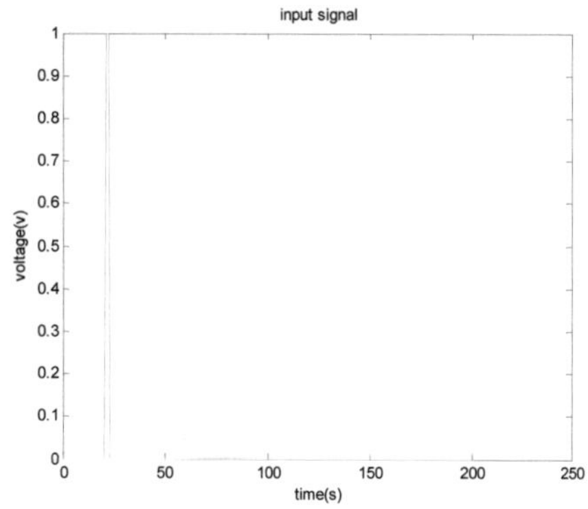

(b)

Fig 19: (a) output signal and (b) input signal

7. Summary

From the results of above experiments, PRBS signal is defined, using this as input to the system and obtaining their corresponding output. For the output obtained, three different matlab scripts were built for model estimation (which calculate the model parameters and represent its behaviour of the system), one for each sort of model (arx, armax, output-error). Using matlab scripts, two of the models are discarded. The order of the chosen one (ARX) was defined by successive limitations of the range and elimination of the least effect parameters. From the analysis of simulation, parameter estimation, pole-zero analysis, frequency diagram, auto and cross correlation, the final model resulted is arx [4 1 1]. It defines the process with 5 parameters with a delay of one sample; the other two models are discarded from the model analysis. All the model analysis is shown in the report. Thus identification of real process was done successfully and then model is selected, it will be used for design of controller in next phase. It has been tested that control design for this model is perfect.

8. References

Banning DA, Hengeveld LD, Modi VJ (1966), "Apparatus for demonstrating dynamics of sloshing liquids", *bulletin mechanical engineering education*, p.p5:65-70.

Bjorn Sohlberg (2005). Book: *Applied Modelling & Identification*, Dalarna University, Sweden.

Bjorn Sohlberg (2005). Book: *Applied model based control systems*, Dalarna University, Sweden.

Jong-Cheng wu, Bo-chen Pan (2002) "Wind tunnel verification of actively controlled high rise building in along-wind motion", *journal of wind engineering and industrial aero dynamics* 90, p.p 1933-1950, 2002.

Jin Zhang, Paul N.Roschke (1999) "Active control of a tall structure excited by wind", *journal of engineering and industrial aero dynamics* 83, p.p 209-223, 1999.

J.T.P.Yao (1972), Concept of structural control, *Journal structural division ASCE 98* (ST7) p.p1567-1574, 1972.

Mohsin Jamil , G.Murtaza Hashmi ,Nagendra, & Bjorn Sohlberg (2007) "Modelling & Identification For Active Control Of Tall Structure Excited By External Forces" *Proceeding of 13th IEEE/IFAC Conference on Methods & Models In Automation & Robotics(MMAR 2007)*,pp.1203-1208,August 27-30,2007 ,Szczecin Poland.

R.J Faciani, K.C.S.Kwok, B.Samali (1953) "Wind tunnel investigation of an active vibration control of tall buildings", *Journal of Wind engineering and industrial aerodynamics*, p.p. 397-412, 1995.

Y. Fujino, T.T. Soong, and B.F. Spencer Jr. (1996), "Structural Control: Basic Concepts and Applications " *Proceedings of the ASCE Structure Congress, Chicago, Illinois*, and April 15-18, 1996.

8

Towards an Automated and Optimal Design of Parallel Manipulators

Marwene Nefzi, Martin Riedel and Burkhard Corves
Department of Mechanism Theory and Dynamics of Machines,
RWTH Aachen University
Germany

1. Introduction

The development of parallel manipulators involves new challenges related to the design of the mechanical, actuating and information-processing subsystems. In this chapter, we limit ourselves to the design of the mechanical subsystem. It typically includes a structural and a dimensional synthesis. Whereas the first one consists in finding the *a priori* most appropriate mechanical architecture, i.e. the types and the arrangements of the joints and the links that make up the robot, the latter deals with the determination of its dimensions in order to match the requirements of the task at hand as closely as possible. Structural synthesis may be achieved either by combining in a systematic way the different types of joints and links allowed by the task in order to obtain all possible arrangements, or by considering pre-existing solutions and customizing them. Clearly, this step relies on engineers' intuition, whereas dimensional synthesis can more easily be automated. Still, it remains a very delicate task, especially for parallel manipulators. Indeed, the performances of these manipulators heavily depend on the chosen geometry. As underlined by many authors (Gosselin, 1988; Merlet, 2006), they also possess kinematic features that vary in opposite directions when their dimensions are modified. In this chapter, we propose an approach to the optimal design of parallel manipulators that helps the designer to find the appropriate dimensions of the mechanical structure he has opted for. For the sake of clarity, we illustrate our approach by a practical example: the design of a guidance mechanism to be used in a stitching unit.

This challenging task results from the continuous demand for speeding up the assembly process of reinforcement textiles needed for the manufacture of fibre composites This demand has led to an increased automation over the last decade in the textile industry. In order to reduce the process duration and to improve both the productivity and the quality of the assembly seam, robot stitching units have been introduced. Recently, we have proposed a new sewing technology in (Kordi *et al.*, 2006). In contrast to conventional ones, all mechanical parts of the proposed sewing head are arranged only on one side of the work pieces. This enhances chances for the automation of the assembly process, as the free side can be more easily attached to manipulators. The next step is to design an appropriate manipulator that takes into consideration the peculiarities of this technology.

(a) (b)

Fig.1 Perspective view of the CAD model (a) The stitching unit (b)

We have already established a systematic procedure for the generation of all the structures having the number of degrees of freedom required by the task. We have also defined a list of evaluation criteria to asses the generated architectures. Without being exhaustive about this methodology, we show a CAD model of the resulting mechanical structure in figure 1a: a hybrid manipulator with seven degrees of freedom. Figure 1b depicts the finished stitching unit. It consists of a fully parallel robot with five degrees of freedom (Mbarek *et.al*, 2005), whose moving platform is equipped with a drive that amplifies the rotation of the sewing head about its longitudinal axis. This large rotation is required for tracking circular seam paths. Furthermore, this unit is mounted on a linear axis to achieve large translations in one direction. The development of such a stitching unit implies a careful design of the parallel manipulator to be used. Indeed, its kinematic performances will be decisive for the overall performances of the stitching unit.

So far, we have only considered the number of degrees of freedom. Further stages of the design process have to involve other requirements such as the workspace volume, the positioning accuracy of the sewing head, its maximal translation and angular velocities etc.... To this end, we first review some available design methodologies for parallel manipulators. Then, we investigate the kinematic and Jacobian analysis of the parallel manipulator to be considered. In the fourth section, we list the requirements of the task and associate to each of them a performance index that indicates whether the requirement is satisfied by the manipulator or not. Once these performance indices can be evaluated numerically, we will develop a numerical procedure that guarantees the generation of design solutions that meet all prescribed requirements simultaneously. Finally, we will give graphical representations of the prescribed performances and the obtained ones.

2. Available design methodologies

Many approaches have already been proposed in a rich literature about the design of parallel robots. The parameter space approach has often been proposed by Merlet (Merlet, 1997; Merlet, 2006). It consists in finding sets of robot geometries by considering successively two requirements, i.e. the workspace requirement and the articular velocities. The intersection of these sets defines all designs that satisfy these two requirements simultaneously. The obtained set of design solutions is then sampled to determine the best compromise with regard to other requirements, which were not considered yet. An implementation of the parameter space approach based on interval analysis has also been proposed in (Merlet, 2005a; Hao and Merlet, 2005). Interval analysis has appealing advantages, such as generating certified solutions and finding all possible mechanisms for a given list of design requirements. Yet, it remains very time consuming and requires a lot of storage. It should be pointed out, however, that some improvements can speed up the algorithm, see (Merlet, 2005b).

Another way to deal with the optimal design of parallel robots is the cost function approach. Some authors focused on the synthesis of parallel manipulators whose workspace complies as closely as possible with a prescribed one (Gosselin and Boudreau, 2001; Ottaviano and Ceccarelli, 2001). Later, the design problem becomes a multi objective optimisation problem (Ceccarelli, 2002; Arsenault and Boudreau, 2006). Many of these formulations have, however, the drawback of providing one design solution, which is generally a trade off between the design objectives. Having one design solution may confine the end user at many stages of the design process. In our formulation, we will define lower bounds for each performance. If a robot features kinematic characteristics that are better than the prescribed ones, then it will be retained. Hence, many design solutions are possible. Furthermore, if these bounds are chosen adequately, the proposed formulation ensures the generation of many solutions that satisfy all prescribed requirements. Our formulation can, therefore, be seen as an alternative between the parameter space approach that provides a set of infinite solutions and usual formulations that find one design solution.

3. Jacobian analysis

Prior to the quantification of the manipulator's kinematic performances, we review its kinematics without being exhaustive, for more details see (Mbarek *et.al*, 2005). As depicted in figure 2, the parallel manipulator consists of five kinematic chains. Four of them have the same topology and are composed of a universal joint on the base, a moving link, an actuated prismatic joint, a second moving link and a spherical joint attached to the platform. In reality, universal joints have also been used for the platform, since the slider of the actuators can rotate about its longitudinal axis. The fifth kinematic chain can be distinguished by the anti-twist device. This special leg restricts the motion of the platform to five degrees of freedom so that only five of the six Cartesian coordinates can be prescribed independently. The remaining rotational coordinate ψ cannot be controlled; it corresponds to a constrained rotation of the platform due to the special leg. The first step in achieving the kinematic analysis is, therefore, the computation of this angle by considering the supplementary constraint in the special leg.

Referring to figure 1, a vector-loop equation can be written for the ith leg of the mechanism as:

$$\mathbf{p}_i = -\mathbf{a}_i + \mathbf{r} + \mathbf{Q}\mathbf{b}_i^{'} \quad (1)$$

where Q denotes the Euler rotation matrix and pi represents the vector from the joint centre point Ai to the joint centre point Bi. The vector r = $(x, y, z)^T$ designates the position of O′ with respect to the frame of coordinates (O, x, y, z). Furthermore, we denote by a and by b the radii of the base and the platform.

Differentiating (1) with respect to time for each leg leads to six equations that can be written in this form:

$$\dot{\boldsymbol{\rho}} = \mathbf{J}_p \dot{\boldsymbol{\chi}} \tag{2}$$

where $\dot{\boldsymbol{\chi}} = \begin{pmatrix} x & y & z & \omega_x & \omega_y & \omega_z \end{pmatrix}^T$ is the velocity vector of the end effector and $\mathbf{J}_p$ denotes the Jacobian matrix of the parallel manipulator. It has been shown in (Mbarek *et.al*, 2005) that:

$$\mathbf{J}_p = \begin{pmatrix} \mathbf{s}_1^T & (\mathbf{Q}\mathbf{b}_1' \times \mathbf{s}_1)^T \\ \vdots & \vdots \\ \mathbf{s}_5^T & (\mathbf{Q}\mathbf{b}_5' \times \mathbf{s}_5)^T \\ \mathbf{0} & \mathbf{s}_5^T \end{pmatrix} \tag{3}$$

The vector $\mathbf{s}_i$ denotes the unit vector along the ith leg. The last row of $\mathbf{J}_p$ corresponds to the additional constraint in the special leg. Hence, the first five elements of the vector $\dot{\boldsymbol{\rho}}$ are the actuators velocities and the sixth element corresponds to the component of the platform's angular velocity along the unit vector s_5. The interrelation between an external wrench **F** exerted on the platform and the vector of the actuators' forces $\boldsymbol{\tau}$ is provided by following equation:

$$\mathbf{F} = \mathbf{J}_p^T \boldsymbol{\tau} \tag{4}$$

The sixth element of the vector $\boldsymbol{\tau}$ corresponds to the moment exerted by the additional constraint.

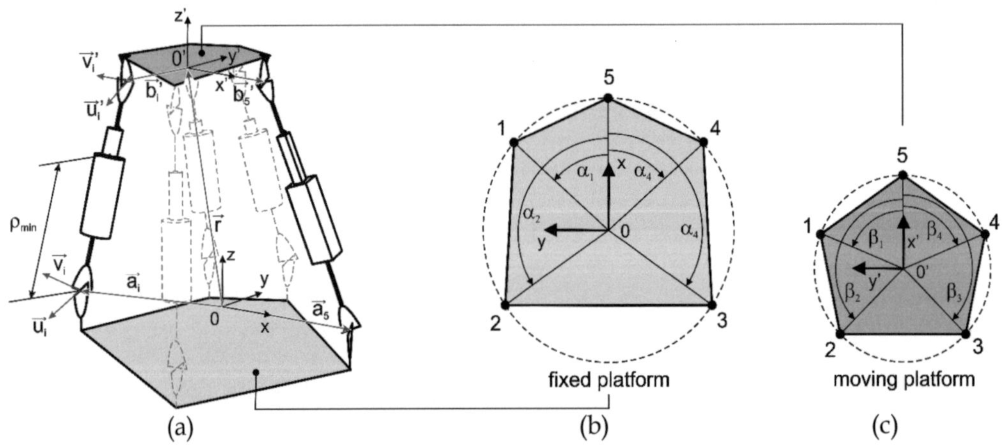

Fig. 2. Schematic representation of the parallel manipulator (a), the base (b) and the platform (c)

3. The design requirements and the optimisation of the robot's performances

The starting point of the design process is usually a list that tabulates the requirements of the task, as shown in table 1. These may be categorized according to their importance as demands or wishes. Whereas demands are those requirements that must be met to obtain a satisfactory design, wishes can be used to make the final choice between different feasible solutions. The corresponding values of the manipulator's performances can be seen as lower bounds to be met. In other words, each manipulator that features at least these values is considered as an appropriate design. In this way, many design solutions can be generated. Besides, the search for an appropriate design is more straightforward.

Requirements of the stitching process			**Performance index**	
Geometry	Size of the work pieces	400 x 400 x 200 mm³	Constant orientation Workspace	400 x 400 x 200 mm³
	Shape of the work pieces	Three-.dimensional	Rotation ranges	±20°
Motion parameters	Stitching speed	1000 stitches per minute	Translation velocity	0.3 m/s
			Angular velocity	п/2 rad/s
Machining quality	Allowed deviation from the desired seam shape	0.1 mm	Positioning accuracy	0.1 mm
			Orientation accuracy	0.05°

Table 1: Requirements list and the corresponding performance indices

As shown in Table 1, we associate to every demand one or more kinematic performances of the manipulator. In the following, we attach an index to each performance in order to quantify to what extent each requirement is satisfied or violated. Once the derived indices can be evaluated numerically, we present a formulation of the optimal design problem able to provide many design solutions that satisfy all demands of the requirements list. Since the corresponding performances of the manipulator may differ from each other in both unit and value, we derive functions whose values range from 0 to 1. 0 indicates that the manipulator satisfies the design criterion. On the other hand, the index converges to 1, if the kinematic performances of the manipulator are far away from the prescribed values.

3.1 The design parameters

Prior to the formulation of the objective functions, we should identify the geometric parameters that have to be modified in order to meet the requirements. Previous works of different research groups showed that the accuracy of parallel manipulators is sensitive to the angles a_i and β_i. Moreover, the radii of the base and the platform, the minimal and maximal leg lengths affect the workspace's volume of the manipulator. We may also assume that the joint centre points A_i and B_i are symmetrically disposed on a circle, i.e. $a_1 = a_4$, $a_2 = a_3$, $\beta_1 = \beta_4$ and $\beta_2 = \beta_3$. The attachment points A_5 and B_5 of the special leg should not be modified. Indeed, a modification of these points complicates the computation of the constrained rotation; and thereby the solution of the inverse kinematic problem. A further design parameter could be the height z_0 of the platform's start position. In this way, we end up with 9 design parameters that can be defined as a vector:

$$\Pi = \begin{pmatrix} \rho_{max} & \rho_{min} & a_1 & a_2 & a & \beta_1 & \beta_2 & b & z_0 \end{pmatrix}$$

3.2 The workspace requirement

The seam path to be achieved should entirely fit in the workspace of the manipulator. As we intend to join small and medium sized fibre composites, the required workspace should be a parallelepiped of 400mm x 400mm x 200mm. In order to join 3D structures of fibre composites, the needles of the sewing head should always be perpendicular to the seam path. Hence, a rotation of the sewing head of 1000 stitches per minute, and thereby of the manipulator's platform should be possible. For every point in this parallelepiped, each leg length $\|\mathbf{p_i}\|$ must neither exceed the maximal available stroke ρ_{max}, nor be lower than a length offset ρ_{min}, which corresponds to the stator length.

Accordingly, the objective function F_1 corresponding to the workspace criterion can be formulated for each ith leg as:

$$\mathbf{F}_{1,i}^{n}(\boldsymbol{\chi}_{n,}\boldsymbol{\pi})=\begin{cases} 1-\dfrac{\rho_{max}}{\|\mathbf{p}_i\|}, & \text{if } \|\mathbf{p}_i\|>\rho_{max} \\ 0, & \text{if } \rho_{min}\le\|\mathbf{p}_i\|\le\rho_{max} \\ 1-\dfrac{\|\mathbf{p}_i\|}{\rho_{min}}, & \text{if } \|\mathbf{p}_i\|<\rho_{min} \end{cases} \tag{5}$$

where $\boldsymbol{\chi}_n=(x_n \;\; y_n \;\; z_n \;\; \varphi_n \;\; \theta_n \;\; \psi_n)^T$ represents the vector of the actual pose. The workspace is defined as a set of N finitely separated poses that result from the discretisation of the prescribed parallelepiped. As formulated in (5), the objective function F_1 to be minimized has numerical values between 0 and 1. If the leg length is within the range ρ_{min} and ρ_{max}, the workspace requirement is satisfied and F_1 returns 0. It converges to 1, if the leg length is greater than the maximal stroke ρ_{max} of one actuator or lower than ρ_{min}.

Furthermore, the rotation of the passive joints should not exceed the operating angles for every configuration of the manipulator in the prescribed parallelepiped.

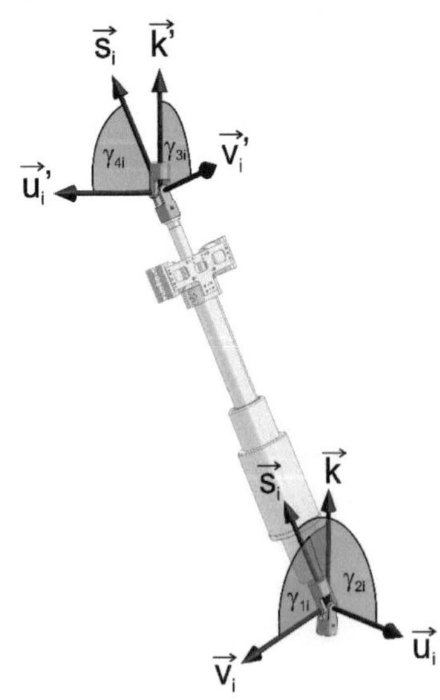

Fig. 3: Operating angles of the universal joints

To this end, the resulting angles in the universal joints on the base and on the platform should be within a range of ±45°. An additional objective function is therefore necessary to guarantee that every configuration in the prescribed workspace is feasible with regard to the passive joints:

$$\mathbf{F}^{n}_{2,ij}(\chi_n,\pi)=\begin{cases}1-\left|\dfrac{\gamma_{max}}{\gamma_{ji}}\right|, & \text{if } \gamma_{ji}>\gamma_{max}\\ 0, & \text{if } \gamma_{min}\le\gamma_{ji}\le\gamma_{max}\\ 1-\left|\dfrac{\gamma_{ji}}{\gamma_{min}}\right|, & \text{if } \gamma_{ji}<\gamma_{min}\end{cases} \tag{6}$$

γ_{ji} denotes the rotation angles of the passive joints in each leg. The computation of these angles is straightforward and is not reported in this work.

3.3 The accuracy requirement

Position and orientation errors of the tool centre point are, mainly, due to the bounded resolution of the encoders. The amplification of these errors is given by (8) in each direction of the Cartesian space.

$$\delta\boldsymbol{\rho}=\mathbf{J}_p\delta\boldsymbol{\chi} \tag{8}$$

In order to avoid the time consuming inversion of the Jacobian matrix, we specify the desired accuracy of the platform and try to match the known resolution of the encoders, i.e. 10 μm. The minimal position and orientation accuracy should not be lower than 0.1 mm in x, y and z direction and 0.05° for the angles φ and θ.

A possible design objective is therefore the maximization of $\delta\boldsymbol{\rho}$ over the workspace. Hence, the corresponding function can be written as:

$$\mathbf{F}^{n}_{4,i}(\chi_n,\pi)=\begin{cases}1-\dfrac{\delta\rho_i}{\delta\rho_{min}}, & \text{if } \delta\rho_i<\delta\rho_{min}\\ 0, & \text{if } \delta\rho_i\ge\delta\rho_{min}\end{cases} \tag{9}$$

3.4 The stiffness requirement

External forces and moments acting on the moving platform cause a compliant displacement that depends on the stiffness of the legs k_1, k_2, k_3, k_4 and k_5 and the additional constraint in the special leg k_6, i.e. the stiffness of the universal joint on the platform. In this work, we are not interested in evaluating the stiffness matrix $K = \mathrm{diag}(k_1, k_2, k_3, k_4, k_5, k_6)$. Rather, the parameters $k_1, \ldots, k_6$ correspond to scaling factors. Consequently, the compliant displacements differ from the displacements that may occur in reality. Even though, it's still important to consider this design criterion, since it guarantees that the compliant displacements in each direction are bounded. It should be noted, however, that the parameter k_6 has been chosen larger than the other stiffness parameters.

For a given displacement of the actuators and the constraint in the special leg, the resulting forces in the actuators are

$$\boldsymbol{\tau}=\mathbf{K}\delta\boldsymbol{\rho} \tag{10}$$

After substituting $\boldsymbol{\tau}$ and $\delta\boldsymbol{\rho}$ in (10) by $\mathbf{J}_p^{-T}\mathbf{F}$ and $\mathbf{J}_p\delta\boldsymbol{\chi}$ from (4) and (8), we obtain an interrelation between the external wrench and a compliant displacement:

$$\mathbf{F} = \mathbf{J}_p^T\mathbf{K}\mathbf{J}_p\delta\boldsymbol{\chi} \tag{11}$$

In order to avoid the time consuming inversion of the Jacobian matrix, we specify the minimal external forces and moments in each direction and strive to find design geometries whose compliant displacements are lower than 0.1 mm in each direction and 0.05° about the direction of the reference frame. For simplicity of exposition, we denote by F_{min} both the minimal external forces and moments. The corresponding function can be written as:

$$\mathbf{F}_{5,i}^{n}(\boldsymbol{\chi}_{n},\boldsymbol{\pi}) = \begin{cases} 1-\dfrac{F_i}{F_{min}}, & \text{if } F_i < F_{min} \\ 0, & \text{if } F_i \geq F_{min} \end{cases} \tag{12}$$

3.5 The velocity requirement

Owing to the fact that actuators velocities are bounded, it is important to find a design that can achieve the required Cartesian velocities throughout the workspace without exceeding the allowable actuators velocities. The velocity transmission relation is given by (2). Clearly, the maximal required velocity in each actuator for a given velocity of the platform is:

$$\dot{\rho}_i = \sum_{i=1}^{6} \left|J_{pij}\right| \dot{\chi} \tag{9}$$

where $\left|J_{pij}\right|$ is the absolute value of the ith row and jth column of the Jacobian. A possible design objective is therefore the minimisation of $\dot{\rho}_i$ over the workspace. In this case, the corresponding function can be written as:

$$F_{6,i}^{n}(\chi_{n},\pi) = \begin{cases} 1-\dfrac{\dot{\rho}_{max}}{\dot{\rho}_i}, & \text{if } \dot{\rho}_i > \dot{\rho}_{max} \\ 0, & \text{if } \dot{\rho}_i \leq \dot{\rho}_{max} \end{cases} \tag{10}$$

In order to achieve our objective of 1000 stitches per minute, the manipulator's platform should reach a translation velocity of 0.3 m/s in x, y and z direction and an angular velocity of $\pi/2$ rad/s about the y axis for any pose in the prescribed workspace. The actuators velocities $\dot{\rho}_{max}$ should not exceed 1 m/s. Whereas the accuracy requirement consists in maximizing $\delta\rho$, thereby maximizing the components of the Jacobian matrix, the velocity requirement consists in minimizing these components.

3.6 The dexterity criterion

One major drawback of parallel manipulators is singular configurations within the workspace. In these configurations the manipulator gains or looses some degrees of freedom and becomes uncontrollable. Also ill conditioned configurations, i.e. configurations close to a singularity, have to be avoided. Indeed, in these configurations large actuators forces are required to support even reasonable loads. In order to avoid these regions, an upper bound for the condition number of the Jacobian matrix should be specified $\kappa_{max} = 70$. It should be noted that this criterion can not be associated to an explicit design requirement. The corresponding objective function can be formulated as:

$$\mathbf{F}_{7,i}^{n}(\chi_{n},\mathbf{\pi})=\begin{cases}1-\frac{\kappa_{max}}{\kappa}, & \text{if } \kappa>\kappa_{max}\\ 0, & \text{if } \kappa\leq\kappa_{max}\end{cases} \tag{7}$$

The condition number κ is defined as the ratio of the maximal singular value to the minimal singular value of the Jacobian matrix. It can be computed by the Matlab function cond.

4. Results

It's increasingly apparent that minimizing the derived objective functions to 0 throughout the manipulator's workspace yields a manipulator whose geometry satisfies all prescribed requirements. Hence, the optimal design problem can be formulated as:

$$\min_{\pi} \mathbf{F}(\pi)=\min_{\pi}\left[\mathrm{F}_1(\chi_1,\mathbf{\pi}),\cdots,\mathrm{F}_1(\chi_N,\mathbf{\pi}),\cdots,\mathrm{F}_C(\chi_N,\mathbf{\pi})\right] \tag{11}$$

subject to $\mathbf{\pi}\in\left[\mathbf{\pi}_{min},\mathbf{\pi}_{max}\right]$

where C denotes the number of the performance indices. Additional constraints for the design parameters have been included to obtain manipulator sizes within practical values. After the formulation of the optimal design problem, we may now derive a numerical procedure to find the optimal design according to the requirements of section 4.

4.1 The numerical procedure

The numerical procedure adopted in this paper is based on trust region methods, as implemented in the Matlab function *lsqnonlin* for large scale optimisation problems , see figure 4.

Basically, an objective function F to be minimized is approximated at each step with a simpler function: $J_F s+F$ in a neighbourhood N of the current point (the trust region). J_F is the Jacobian matrix of the objective function. A trial step s is computed by minimizing the new function over the trust region. If an improvement of the objective function, i.e. a lower function value, is achieved, the current point is updated using the computed step. Otherwise, the current point remains unchanged and the region is contracted, see also (The Math Works Inc., 2006).

In order to generate many design solutions, the final algorithm chooses randomly different initial guesses within the specified ranges of the design parameters, see figure 4. If all objective functions are reduced to 0, the design parameters are stored and another initial guess is selected. We ran this optimization algorithm with p_{limit} = 500 different initial guesses. The computation time was less than 4 hours, and more than 300 feasible design solutions have been found.

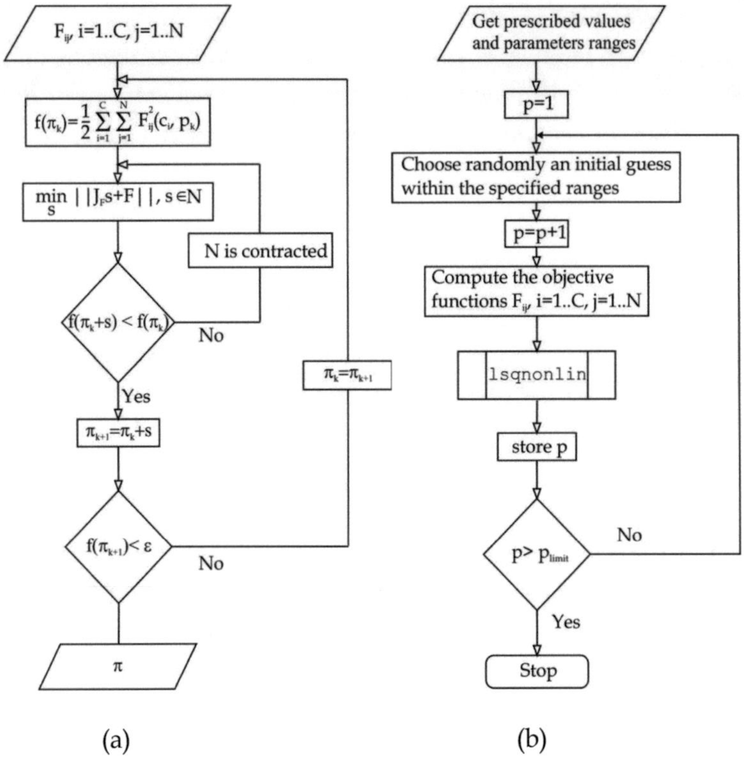

Fig. 4: A flow chart of the MATLAB function lsqnonlin (a) Flow-chart of the overall numerical procedure (b)

Many design solutions are very close to each other and can be gathered in different groups of solutions. Table 2 shows a list of five design solutions sorted into ascending value of the maximal leg length.

ρ_{max} [m]	ρ_{min} [m]	α_1 [°]	α_2 [°]	a [m]	β_1 [°]	β_2 [°]	b[m]	z_0 [m]
1.15	0.67	106	162	0.55	125	151	0.21	0.73
1.3	0.80	109	143	0.57	133	160	0.21	0.87
1.22	0.66	135	148	0.6	127	160	0.17	0.85
1.34	0.83	131	148	0.6	106	168	0.38	0.94

Table 2: Four feasible design solutions

4.2 Simulation results

In this section, we show the simulation results of the first solution of table 2. Figure 5 and 6 depict an isometric view and a view of the x, y plane of both the prescribed and the constant orientation workspace of the selected solution. As shown by figure 7 and 8 an orientation of $\theta = 20°$ is also feasible without violating the workspace requirement.

Figure 9 and 10 depict the displacement of the first actuator for a position error of 0.1 mm in each direction and an orientation error of 0.05° in the two first Euler angles, as defined in (Mbarek et.al, 2005). Moreover, figure 11 and 12 demonstrate that these errors induce a displacement of 1e-4 m

Fig. 4: Flow-chart of the overall numerical procedure

throughout the workspace for $\theta = 20°$. The accuracy requirement is therefore satisfied for this actuator, since the resolution of the encoders is 1e-5 m. For simplicity of exposition, the displacements of the other actuators are not represented in this work.

The velocity requirement is also satisfied. Indeed, the actuators velocities of each actuator is less than the prescribed limit 1 m/s. Figure 13-16, depict the required velocities of the fifth actuator. Finally, figure 17-20 depict the distribution of the condition number throughout the workspace.

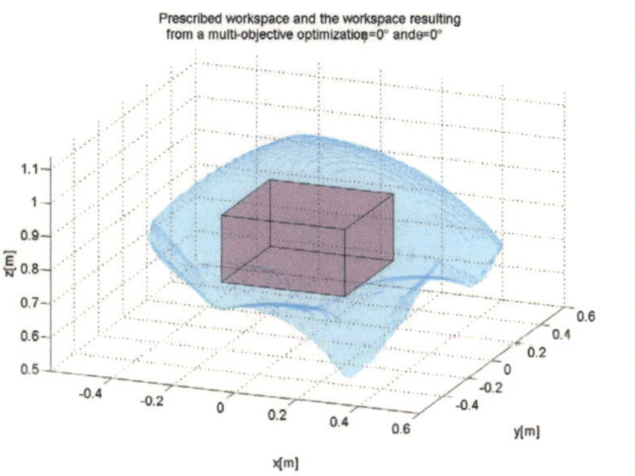

Fig 5: The prescribed workspace and the workspace of the selected design solution for $\varphi = 0, \theta = 0°$

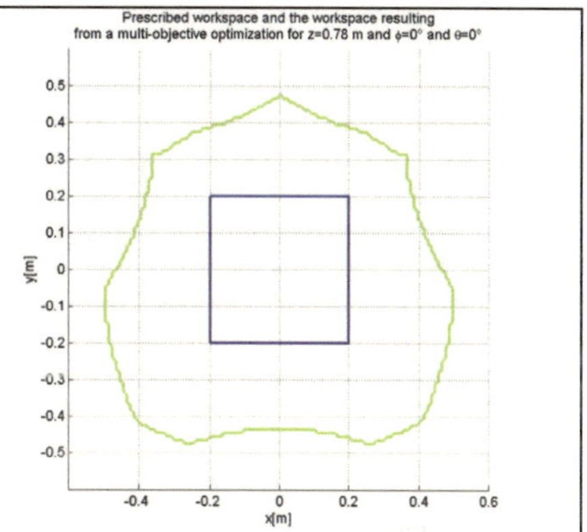

Fig 6: The prescribed workspace and the workspace of the selected design solution for $z = 0.78m, \varphi = 0, \theta = 0°$

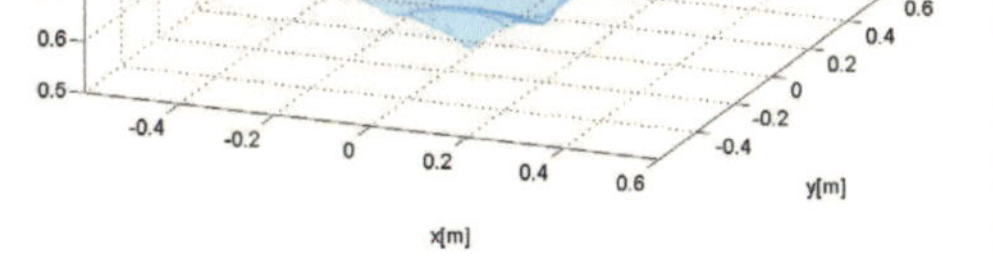

Fig 7: The prescribed workspace and the workspace of the selected design solution for $\varphi = 0, \theta = 20°$

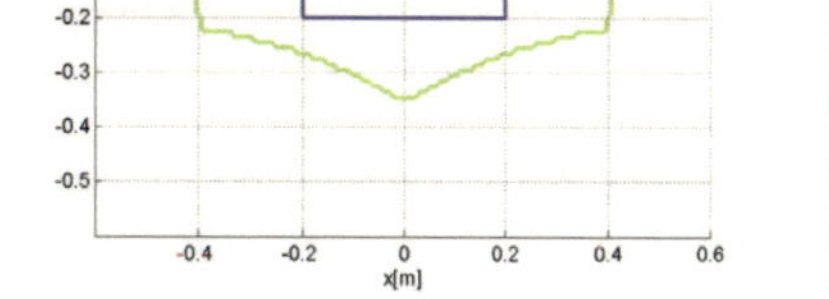

Fig 8: The prescribed workspace and the workspace of the selected design solution for $z = 0.78m, \varphi = 0, \theta = 20°$

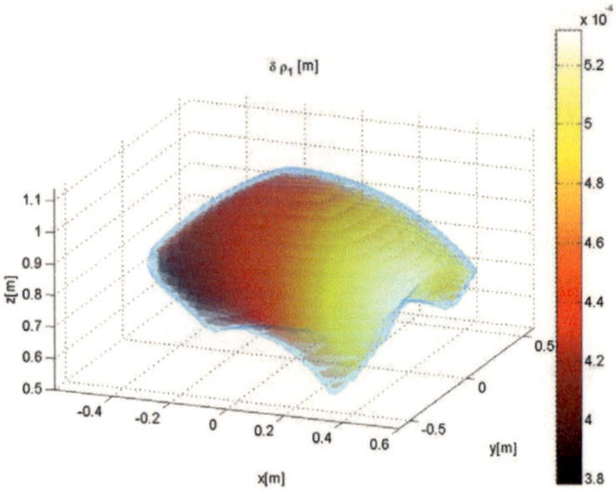

Fig 9: $\delta\rho_1$ for $\varphi = 0, \theta = 0°$

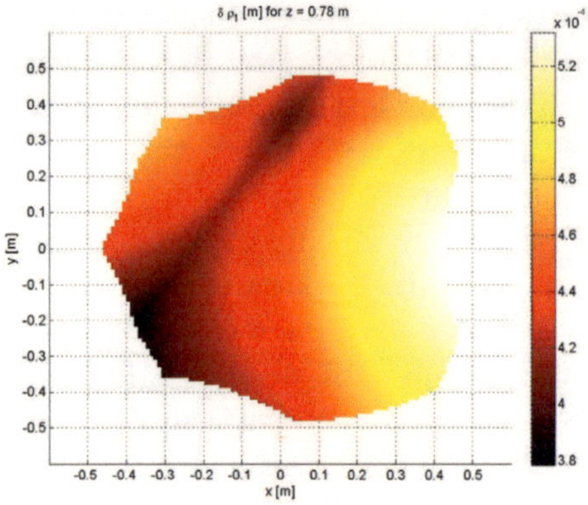

Fig 10: $\delta\rho_1$ for $z = 0.78m, \varphi = 0, \theta = 0°$

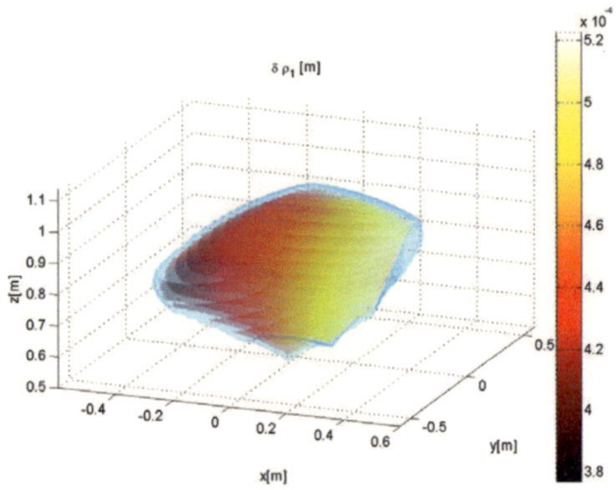

Fig 11: $\delta\rho_1$ for $\varphi = 0, \theta = 20°$

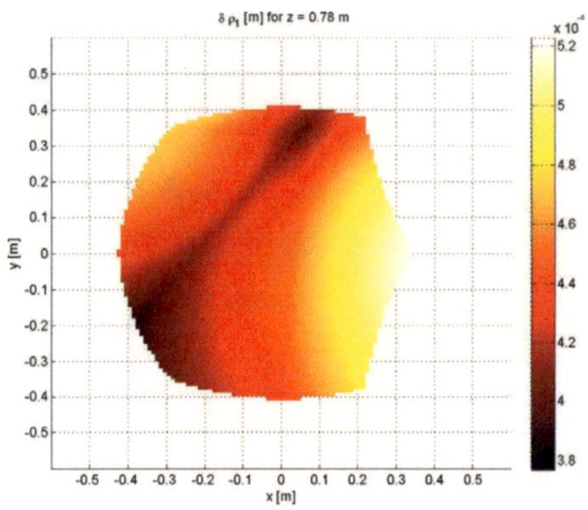

Fig 12: $\delta\rho_1$ for $z = 0.78m, \varphi = 0, \theta = 20°$

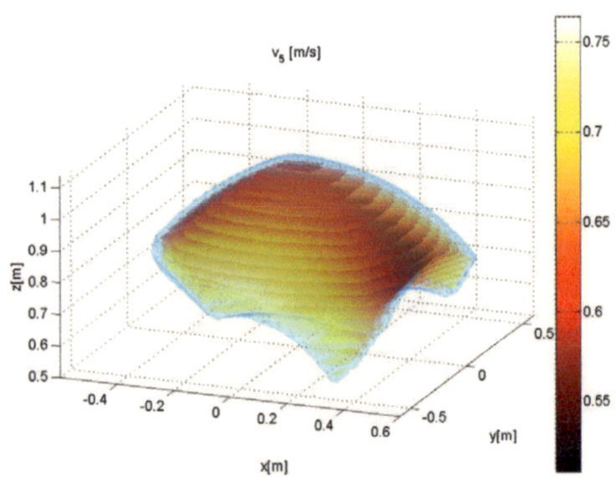

Fig 13: v_5 for $\varphi = 0, \theta = 0°$

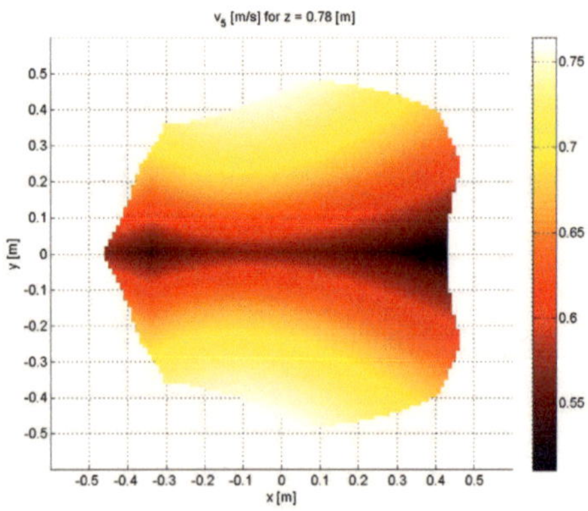

Fig 14: v_5 for $z = 0.78m, \varphi = 0, \theta = 0°$

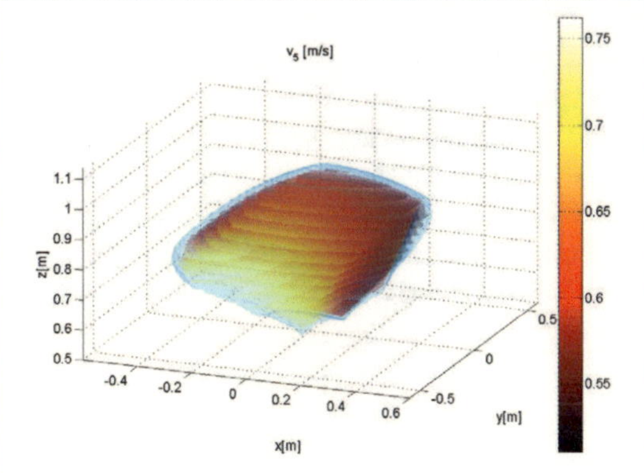

Fig 15: v_5 for $\varphi = 0, \theta = 20°$

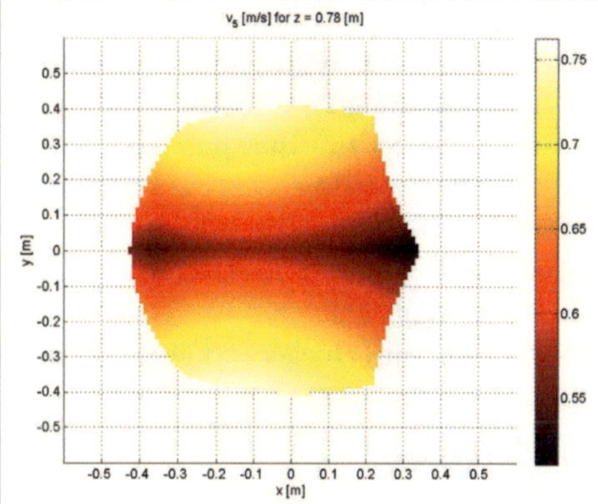

Fig 16: v_5 for $z = 0.78m, \varphi = 0, \theta = 20°$

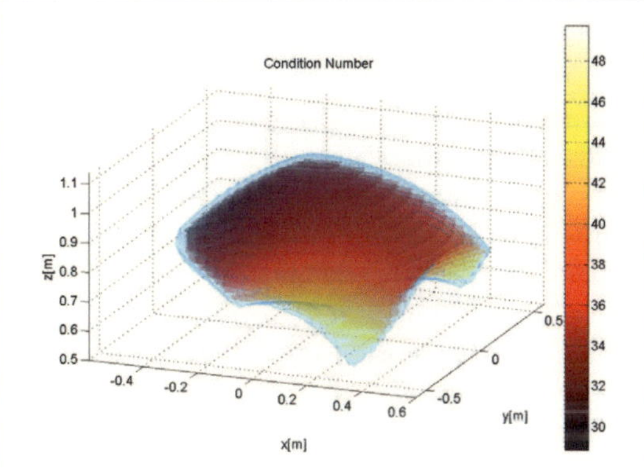

Fig 17: The condition number distribution for $\varphi = 0, \theta = 0°$

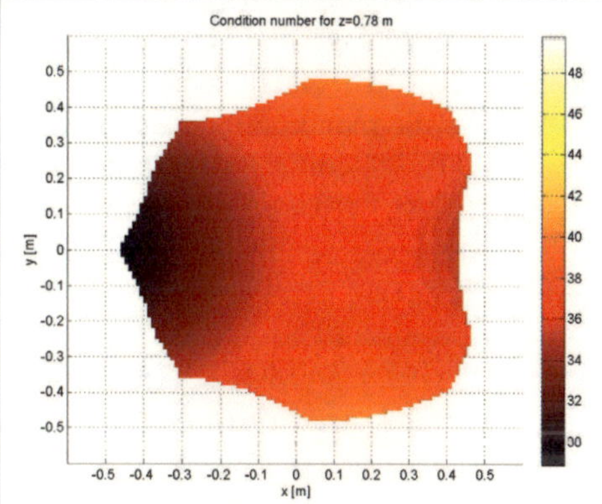

Fig 18: The condition number distribution for $z = 0.78m, \varphi = 0, \theta = 0°$

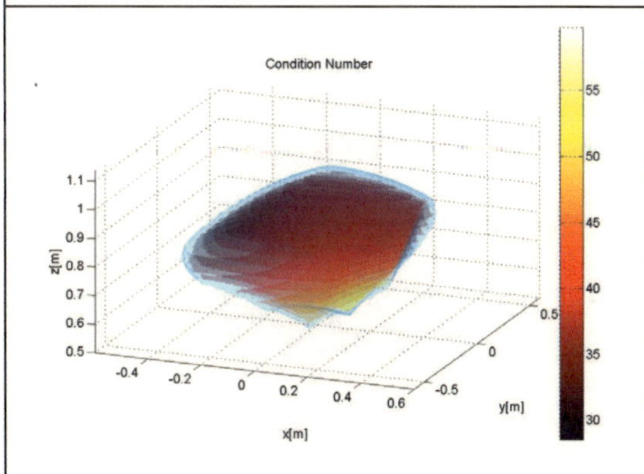

Fig 19: The condition number distribution for $\varphi = 0, \theta = 20°$

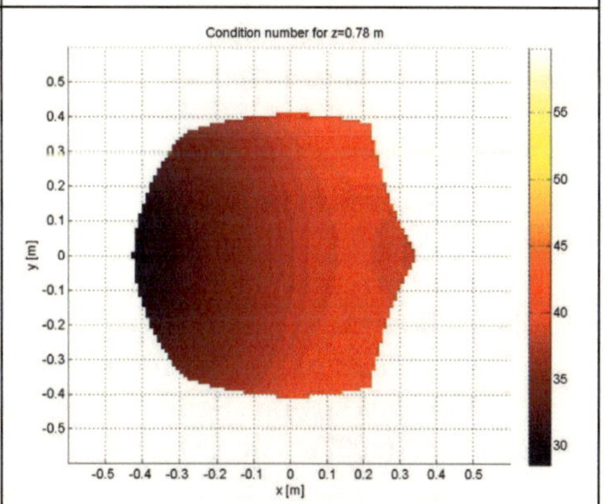

Fig 20: The condition number distribution for $z = 0.78m, \varphi = 0, \theta = 20°$

5. Conclusion

In this chapter, we investigated the optimal design problem of a parallel manipulator with five degrees of freedom that will be used in a high-speed stitching unit as a guidance mechanism for a novel sewing head. First, we reviewed the kinematics of the manipulator. Starting from the requirements list, we derived performance indices that allowed us to evaluate the adequacy of the manipulator for this application. Finally, we developed a numerical procedure that provides many design solutions, which satisfy all requirements. Owing to the iterations that may occur during the design process, the designer may consider different solutions. This allows one to take into account other requirements, such as manufacturing capabilities, available actuators on the market, costs etc ... The presented robot stitching unit can be used to assemble reinforcement textiles for the aerospace, automotive, rail vehicles and shipbuilding industry.

6. References

Kordi, M.T., T. Mbarek and B. Corves (2006). Synthesis of a new mechanism for needle guidance in a sewing machine with single-sided sewing technique. In: *Proceedings of EuCoMes, the first European Conference on Mechanism Science. Obergurgl. Austria.*

Mbarek, T., M. Nefzi and B. Corves (2005). Prototypische Entwicklung eines Parallelmanipulators mit dem Freiheitsgrad fünf. In: *Proceedings of Mechatronik 2005: Innovative Produktentwicklung.* Wiesloch (Germany).

Gosselin, C.M. (1988). Kinematic Analysis and Programming of Parallel Robotic Manipulators. Ph.D. Thesis, McGill University, Montréal, Canada.

Merlet, J.P. (2006). Parallel Robots (Solid Mechanics and Its Applications). Second Edition. Springer, 2006.

Merlet, J.P. (1997). DEMOCRAT: A DEsign MethOdology for the Conception of Robot with parallel ArchiTecture. In: *Proceedings of the International Conference on Intelligent Robots and Systems, IROS.* Grenoble. France. Pp. 1630-1636

Merlet, J.P. (2005a). The necessity of optimal design for parallel machines and a possible certified methodology. In: *Proceedings of the 2nd International Colloqium of the Collaborative Research Center 562, Robotic Systems for Handling and Assembly.* Braunschweig. Germany. Pp. 7-20

Hao, F. and J.P. Merlet (2005). Multi-Criteria optimal design of parallel manipulators based on interval analysis. *Mechanism and Machine Theory* 40.

Merlet, J.P. (2005b) Optimal design of robots. In: *Online Proceedings of Robotics: Science and Systems.* Boston. USA.

Boudreau, R. and C.M. Gosselin (2001). La synthèse d'une plate-forme de Gough-Stewart pour un espace atteignable prescrit. *Mechanism and Machine Theory* 36. Pp. 327-342

Ottaviano, E. and M. Ceccarelli (2001). Optimal design of CAPAMAN (Cassino parallel manipulator) with prescribed workspace. In: *Proceedings of Computational Kinematics.* Seoul. South Corea. Pp. 35-44.

Cecarelli, M. (2002). An Optimum Design of Parallel Manipulators: Formulation and Experimental Validation. In: *Proceedings of Collaborative Research Centre 562: Robotic Systems for Handling and Assembly.* Braunschweig. Germany. Pp. 47-64.

Lou, Y., Z. Dongjun and L. Zexiang (2005). Optimal Design of a Parallel Machine Based on Multiple Criteria. In: *Proceedings of the 2005 IEEE International Conference on Robotics and Automation.* Barcelona. Spain. Pp. 3219-2224

The Math Works, Inc. (2006). Optimization Toolbox. User's Guide, Version 3. Pp. 4-12.

9

Identification of Continuous-Time Systems with Time Delays by Global Optimization Algorithms and Ant Colony Optimization

Janusz P. Paplinski
Technical University of Szczecin
Poland

1. Introduction

There are systems which have inherent time delay. If the time delay used for controller design does not coincide with the real process time delay, than a close-loop system can be unstable, or may cause efficiency lost (Bjorklund & Ljung, 2003; Boukas, 2003; Li & Wan, 2002). The identification of linear systems with unknown time delay is important and should be treated as first task during system analysis and control design. This problem can become more complicated for the multi-input single-output (MISO) system, where the solution space is multi-modal.

The most of conventional system identification techniques, such as those based on the non-linear estimations method, for example separable nonlinear least squares (SEPNLS) method, are in essence gradient-guided local search methods. They require a smooth search space or a differentiable performance index. The conventional approaches in the multi-modal optimisation can easily fail in obtaining the global optimum and may be stopped at a local optimum (Chen & Hung, 2001; Harada et al., 2003). One of the possible solution of this problem is use of a SEPNLS methods with global optimisation elements (Chen & Wang, 2004), for example Global SEPNLS (GSEPNLS), known from the literature (Previdi & Lovera, 2004).

New possibility in identification of systems with multi modal solution space is opened by application of the computational intelligence methods (Papliński, 2004; Path & Savkin, 2002; Shaltaf, 2004; Yang et al., 1997). Ant Colony Optimization (ACO) is one among them. Ants are known as a social insects. They exhibit adaptive and flexible collective behavior to achieve various tasks. The macro-scale complex behavior emerges as a result of cooperation in micro-scale.

This paper considers the problem of parameter estimation for continuous-time systems with unknown time delays from sampled input-output data. The iterative separable nonlinear least-squares (SEPNLS) method and global separable nonlinear least-squares (GSNLS) method (Westwick & Kearney, 2001) are presented. We have extended this method by using the ACO. The ACO proposed in the paper is looking for the time delays. Another parameters of linear system are obtained during evaluation of leaving pheromone, by using the SEPNLS method.

2. Problem description

The dynamic of continuous-time MISO system with unknown time delays can be described as:

$$\sum_{i=0}^{n} a_i p^{n-i} x(t) = \sum_{j=1}^{r} \sum_{k=1}^{m_j} b_{jk} p^{m_j - k} u_j(t-\tau_j) \tag{1}$$

where

$a_0 = 1$; $b_{j1} \neq 0$;

p - differential operator;
$u_j(t)$ - j-th input;
τ_j - time delay of *j-th* input;
x - non-disturbed output of system;
We assume the parameters n and m_j are known.
The measurement output is disturbed by stochastic noise:

$$y(t) = x(t) + v(t) \tag{2}$$

The zero order hold is used

$$u_j(t) = \tilde{u}_j(k) \quad \text{for} \quad (k-1)T \le t < kT, \tag{3}$$

where T – sampling period.
The problem studied here is as follows: how to estimate the time delays and the system parameters from sampled data representation of the inputs and the noisy output.

3. SEPNLS estimation method

The low-pass pre filter Q(p) is used in order to obtain direct signal derivatives (Iemura et al., 2004):

$$Q(p) = \frac{1}{(\alpha p + 1)^n} \tag{4}$$

where α is the parameter of the Q(p).
Using the pre-filter Q(p) and bilinear transformation in the system (1) we can obtain an approximated discrete-time estimation model of the original system:

$$\xi_{0\bar{y}}(k) = \sum_{i=1}^{n} a_i \xi_{i\bar{y}}(k) = \sum_{j=1}^{r} \sum_{l=1}^{m_j} b_{jl} \xi_{(n-m_j+1)\bar{u}_j}\left(k - \bar{\tau}_j\right) + r(k) \tag{5}$$

where

$$r(k) = \sum_{i=0}^{n} a_i \xi_{i\bar{v}}(k), \tag{6}$$

$$\tilde{\tau}_j = \frac{\tau_j}{T} = \rho + \frac{\Delta}{T}, \qquad 0 \le \Delta < T \tag{7}$$

and

$$\xi_{i\gamma_i}(k) = \frac{\left(\frac{T}{2}\right)^i \left(1+z^{-1}\right)^i \left(1-z^{-1}\right)^{n-i}}{\left(\alpha\left(1-z^{-1}\right)+\frac{T}{2}\left(1+z^{-1}\right)\right)^n} \frac{1+z^{-1}}{2} \gamma_j(k), \qquad \gamma = [y, \ u, \ v] \tag{8}$$

The model (5) can be written in the vector form:

$$\xi_{0\bar{y}}(k) = \varphi^T(k,\tau)\theta + r(k) \tag{9}$$

where

$$\begin{aligned}\varphi^T(k,\tau) = [&-\xi_{1\tilde{y}}(k),\ldots,-\xi_{n\tilde{y}}(k), \xi_{(n-m_j+1)\tilde{u}_1}(k-\tilde{\tau}_1),\ldots,\\ &\xi_{n\tilde{u}_1}(k-\tilde{\tau}_1),\ldots,\xi_{(n-m_j+1)\tilde{u}_r}(k-\tilde{\tau}_r),\ldots,\xi_{n\tilde{u}_r}(k-\tilde{\tau}_r)]\end{aligned} \tag{10}$$

$$\theta^T = \left[a_1,\ldots,a_n, b_{11},\ldots,b_{1m_j},\ldots,b_{r1},\ldots,b_{rm_j}\right] \tag{11}$$

The parameters of the model can be estimated as the minimizing arguments of the LS criterion

$$V_N(\theta,\tau) = \frac{1}{N-k_s} \sum_{k=k_s+1}^{N} \frac{1}{2}\varepsilon^2(k,\theta,\tau) \tag{12}$$

$$\varepsilon(k,\theta,\tau) = \xi_{0\bar{y}}(k) - \varphi^T(K,\tau)\theta \tag{13}$$

The vectors of the time delays τ and linear parameters θ are estimated in a separable manner. The linear parameters, when the time delays are known, can be obtained from linear LS method:

$$\hat{\theta}_N(\tau) = R^{-1}(N,\tau) f(N,\tau) \tag{14}$$

where

$$R(N,\tau) = \frac{1}{N-k_s} \sum_{k=k_s+1}^{N} \varphi(k,\tau)\varphi^T(k,\tau) \tag{15}$$

$$f(N,\tau) = \frac{1}{N-k_s} \sum_{k=k_s+1}^{N} \varphi(k,\tau)\xi_{0\bar{y}}(k) \tag{16}$$

The time delays $\boldsymbol{\tau}$ can be estimated as the minimizing arguments of the criterion

$$\hat{\tau} = \arg\min_{\tau} \breve{V}_N(\tau) \tag{17}$$

where

$$\breve{V}_N(\tau) = \frac{1}{N-k_s} \sum_{k=k_s+1}^{N} \frac{1}{2} \breve{\varepsilon}^2(k,\tau) \tag{18}$$

and

$$\breve{\varepsilon}(k,\tau) = \xi_{0\bar{y}}(k) - \varphi^T(k,\tau) R^{-1}(N,\tau) f(N,\tau) \tag{19}$$

The all time delays occurring in the system can be computed by the iterative algorithm

$$\hat{\tau}_j^{l+1} = \hat{\tau}_j^l + \Delta\hat{\tau}_j^{l+1} \tag{20}$$

where

$$\Delta\hat{\tau}_j^{l+1} = -\mu \left[\breve{R}_j\left(\hat{\tau}_j^l\right) \right]^{-1} \breve{V}_j'\left(\hat{\tau}_j^l\right) \tag{21}$$

The parameter μ determines the step size of the algorithm. The Hessian of the LS criterion $\breve{R}_j(\tau)$, which permits to use information about the local curvature of the error-surface (Westwick & Kearney, 2001), may be calculated as

$$\breve{R}_j(\tau) = \frac{1}{N-k_s} \sum_{k=k_s+1}^{N} \psi_j^2(k,\tau), \tag{22}$$

and the gradient of LS criterion $\breve{V}_j'(\tau)$ can be obtained from:

$$\breve{V}_j'(\tau) = -\frac{1}{N-k_s} \sum_{k=k_s+1}^{N} \psi_j(k,\tau) \breve{\varepsilon}(k,\tau) \tag{23}$$

The derivatives $\psi_j(k,\tau)$ are defined as

$$\begin{aligned} \psi_j(k,\tau) &= \frac{\partial \breve{\varepsilon}(k,\tau)}{\partial \tau_j} = \frac{\partial \varphi^T(k,\tau)}{\partial \tau_j} R^{-1}(N,\tau) f(N,\tau) \\ &+ \varphi^T(k,\tau) \frac{\partial R^{-1}(N,\tau)}{\partial \tau_j} f(N,\tau) \\ &+ \varphi^T(k,\tau) R^{-1}(N,\tau) \frac{\partial f(N,\tau)}{\partial \tau_j} \end{aligned} \tag{24}$$

After suitable differentiations:

$$\begin{aligned}&\varphi_{\tau_j}(k,\tau)=\frac{\partial\varphi^T(k,\tau)}{\partial\tau_j}=\left[0_{1xm},0_{1xm},\ldots,0_{1xm},\right.\\&-\xi_{(n-m)\bar{u}}(k-\tilde{\tau}),-\xi_{(n-m+1)\bar{u}}(k-\tilde{\tau}),\ldots,\\&\left.-\xi_{(n-1)\bar{u}}(k-\tilde{\tau}),0_{1xm},\ldots,0_{1xm}\right]\end{aligned}\tag{25}$$

$$\begin{aligned}&R_{\tau_j}(N,\tau)=\frac{\partial R^{-1}(N,\tau)}{\partial\tau_j}\\&R_{\tau_j}(N,\tau)=\frac{1}{N-k_s}\sum_{k=k_s+1}^{N}\varphi_{\tau_j}(k,\tau)\varphi^T(k,\tau)\end{aligned}\tag{26}$$

$$\begin{aligned}&f_{\tau_j}(N,\tau)=\frac{\partial f(N,\tau)}{\partial\tau_j}\\&f_{\tau_j}(N,\tau)=\frac{1}{N-k_s}\sum_{k=k_s+1}^{N}\varphi_{\tau_j}(k,\tau)\xi_{0\bar{y}}(k)\end{aligned}\tag{27}$$

finally we can get

$$\begin{aligned}&\psi_j(k,\tau)=\varphi^T_{\tau_j}(k,\tau)R^{-1}(N,\tau)f(N,\tau)\\&-\varphi^T(k,\tau)R^{-1}(N,\tau)\left[R_{\tau_j}(N,\tau)+R^T_{\tau j}(N,\tau)\right]R^{-1}(N,\tau)f(N,\tau)\\&+\varphi^T(k,\tau)R^{-1}(N,\tau)f_{\tau_j}(N,\tau)\end{aligned}\tag{28}$$

I. The SEPNLS algorithm

1. Let l = 0. Set the initial estimate of the time delays $\hat{\tau}_j^{(l)}=\hat{\tau}_j^{(0)}$.
2. Compute Hessian $R(N,\tau)$ and gradient $f(N,\tau)$ of the linear LS criterion, for the assumed time delays $\hat{\tau}_j^{(l)}$ - expressions (15) – (16)
3. Compute Hessian $\breve{R}_j(\tau)$ and gradient $\breve{V}_j'(\tau)$ of LS criterion by harness equations (22) – (28)
4. Compute new value of the time delays $\hat{\tau}_j^{l+1}$ by using the equation (20) and (21)
5. Check if the new time delays belong to permissible area. If not, let decrease the increment of time delays $\Delta\hat{\tau}_j^{l+1}=\upsilon\Delta\hat{\tau}_j^{l+1}$, where υ is a random variable, and go back to step 4.
6. Check if the new value of LS criterion $\breve{V}_N\left(\hat{\tau}_N^{(l)}\right)$ is smaller than the anterior $\breve{V}_N\left(\hat{\tau}_N^{(l+1)}\right)\le\breve{V}_N\left(\hat{\tau}_N^{(l)}\right)$. If not, decrease the increment of the time delays

$$\Delta\hat{\tau}_j^{l+1}=\upsilon\Delta\hat{\tau}_j^{l+1},\tag{29}$$

where υ is a random variable, and go back to step 4.
7. If the stopping condition is satisfied, go to the next step 7, else let l = l + 1 and go back to step 2.
8. Compute the linear parameter vector from linear LS criterion (14), and terminate algorithm.

4. The global SEPNLS estimation method (GSNLS)

The SEPNLS method can converges to the local optimum. It is possible to apply stochastic approximation (Bhart & Borkar, 1999) with convolution smoothing to the SEPNLS method in order to reach the global optimum (Iemura et al., 2004). The estimate of the time delay in GSNLS can be obtain as

$$\hat{\tau}_j^{(l+1)} = \hat{\tau}_j^{(l)} - \mu^{(l)}\left(\left(\breve{R}_j\left(\hat{\tau}_j^{(l)}\right)\right)^{-1} \breve{V}_j'\left(\hat{\tau}_j^{(l)}\right) + \beta^{(l)}\eta\right) \tag{30}$$

where $\eta \in R^r$ is a random vector used to perturb τ. The values of η are generated by Gaussian, uniform, or Cauchy distribution probability density function. The values of μ and β control its variance.

The value of β has to be chosen large at the start of the iterations and decreased to zero when the global minimum is reached (Yang et al., 2005). It can be obtain for

$$\beta^{(l)} = \beta_0 \breve{V}_N\left(\hat{\tau}_N^{(l)}\right) \tag{31}$$

where the LS criterion $\breve{V}_N\left(\hat{\tau}_N^{(l)}\right)$ is given by equation (18). The value of $\breve{V}_N\left(\hat{\tau}_N^{(l)}\right)$ decreases during the sequence of iterations, which cases that disturbances of τ decrease too.

5. Ant colony optimization (ACO)

Recently, researchers in various fields have showed interest in the behaviour of social creatures to solve various tasks. The ants exhibit collective behaviour to perform task as foraging, building a nests. These tasks can not be carried out by one individual. The macro-scale complex behaviour emerges as a result of cooperation in micro-scale. This appears with out any central or hierarchical control. A way of communicating between individuals in colony is chemical substances called pheromones (Agosta, 1992; Bonabeau et al., 1999). Ants looking for food lay the way back to their nest with a specific type of pheromone. Other ants can follow the pheromone trail and find the way to the aliments. Pheromones remain in the some way superimpose and intensify, concurrently the pheromones evaporate in time and their intensity decreases. A specific map of pheromones is created on the search space. This map is not unalterable and can bring into line with ambient. Each ant looks for food independently of the others and moves from nest to source of food. There are a lot of ways in which ants can go. Ants choose a way for theirs leverage three sources of information

- the own experience
- the local information
- the pheromone trail.

The own experience permits to recognize place when it already was and avoid looping of the way. For the artificial ant it permits to allocate particular value to appropriate seeking parameters.
The local information determines permissible way. Ants can recognize and sidestep hindrances. In the artificial ant colony it is responsible for the search space constraint.
The pheromone trail permits to come back to the nest and find the source of food found earlier by another individuals from colony. Ants prefer this way in which intensity of pheromones is the biggest.
The intensity of the pheromone is given by the equation:

$$\tau_i(t+1) = \tau_i(t) * \rho + \frac{n}{m} \frac{J_i}{\sum_{k=1}^{n} J_i} \tag{32}$$

where:

$\tau_i(t)$ - the intensity of the pheromone at the time t

ρ - a coefficient such that $(i-\rho)$ represents the evaporation rate of the pheromone between time t and t+1.

n - an amount of ant in the nest;

m - an amount of rows in the matrix of pheromone;

The value of ρ must be set to a value less than 1 to avoid unlimited accumulation of the pheromone. The investigation where obtained for $\rho = 0,95$.
The quality function J is divided by the sum of all quality functions in order to uniform it to one. The quotient the number of ants to the number of rows in the matrix of pheromone conforms the lied intensity of pheromone to the existing pheromone.
The amount of pheromone traces was limited to specified number by removing the worst traces.
The investigations was made with the amount of pheromone trace equal double of amount of ants in the colony:

$$m = 2 * n \tag{33}$$

Every ants live in one iteration and they died after updating the pheromone trace. The new ants are created in another iteration. The time delays of the model (2) are interpreted as a decision tie inside a way of ants. It is a place where an ant has to decide about next direction of motion. The direction is randomly chosen with the probability distribution specified by the pheromone traces. The half of population of ants has disturbed direction:

$$c_{ij} = \zeta_{ijn}\beta + \zeta_{ijs}(1-\beta) \tag{34}$$

where:

i - the number of ants

j - the number of parameter – tie

ζ_{ijn} - the random number with normal distribution, inside the solution space

ζ_{ijs} - the random number with distribution defined by pheromone trace

β - a randomly coefficient of ratio of averaging.

The ants are looking only for the time delays of a model. The residual parameters of the model are obtained from SEPNLS during calculation the quality function J. It can be do because these parameters are linear and SEPNLS works efficiently with them.

6. Simulation example

The algorithm presented in the previous sections has been tested on the MISO example. We consider the following system (Papliński, 2007):

$$\ddot{y}(t)+a_1\dot{y}(t)+a_2y(t)=b_{11}u_1(t-\tau_1)+b_{21}u_2(t-\tau_2) \tag{35}$$

where
$a_1=3.0$; $a_2=4.0$; $b_{11}=2.0$; $b_{21}=2.0$
$\tau_1=9.15$; $\tau_2=2.57$;
The inputs and output signals are converted by zero-order-hold operation with sampling period $T=0.05$. The pre-filter $Q(p)$ with $\alpha=0.4$ is used. As a input signals are used independent sequence of uniform distribution between 0 and 1. The signal to measurement noise ratio SNR is 5%. A data set of 1000 samples was generated for the identification process. The algorithms are implemented for 250 iterations. The initial values of time delays $\tau^{(0)}$ are randomly chosen between 0 and 25.
All algorithms, presented in the paper were running 200 times. The GSNLS was used with variance coefficient $\mu=10^6$.
The solution space of time delays is multimodal and the global optimum is not reached in every time. Therefore the percentages of identified time delays, with error les than 10%, can be treated as a main quality function and they are presented in Fig. 1

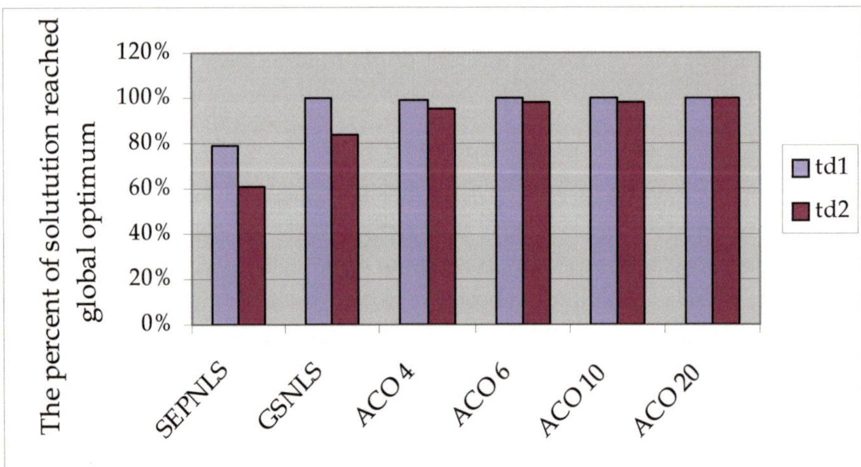

Fig. 1. The percent of identified time delays τ_1, τ_2 which are reached global optimum for SEPNLS, GSNLS and ACO with 4, 6, 10 and 20 ants in the colony

For the SEPNLS the global optimum are reached only at 60% of trials. These results strongly depend on the initial values, because algorithm can not miss the attraction area of the local minimum. The GSNLS works better, but still more than 16% of solution is bed. The AM gave the best solution. The results depend on the number of ants in computational colony. Bigger number of individuals make better accuracy. But even small colony wit 4 ants gave better results than SEPNLS and GSNLS.

The Table 1 presents the mean value of identified time delay and references standard deviation. The ACO algorithm gave much better results than SEPNLS and GSNLS. The augmentation of amount of ants in ACO only little improves obtained results. It confirms the conclusion obtained from Fig. 1. If we look only for solution laying in the global optimum, all algorithms give similar accuracy. This is presented in the Table 2.

	The amount of ants	t_1 of the plant	td1 (identified)	t_2 of the plant	td2 (identified)
SEPNLS	-	9,13	$9{,}88 \pm 5{,}02$	2,57	$7{,}17 \pm 8{,}04$
GSNLS	-	9,13	$9{,}27 \pm 0{,}04$	2,57	$5{,}22 \pm 6{,}64$
ACO	4	9,13	$9{,}26 \pm 0{,}18$	2,57	$2{,}66 \pm 0{,}18$
ACO	6	9,13	$9{,}24 \pm 0{,}07$	2,57	$2{,}66 \pm 0{,}13$
ACO	10	9,13	$9{,}26 \pm 0{,}05$	2,57	$2{,}67 \pm 0{,}11$
ACO	20	9,13	$9{,}25 \pm 0{,}04$	2,57	$2{,}68 \pm 0{,}08$

Table 1. The mean value of identified time delay and references standard deviation

	The amount of ants	t_1 of the plant	td1 (identified)	t_2 of the plant	td2 (identified)
SEPNLS	-	9,13	$9{,}88 \pm 5{,}02$	2,57	$7{,}17 \pm 8{,}04$
GSNLS	-	9,13	$9{,}27 \pm 0{,}04$	2,57	$5{,}22 \pm 6{,}64$
ACO	4	9,13	$9{,}26 \pm 0{,}18$	2,57	$2{,}66 \pm 0{,}18$
ACO	6	9,13	$9{,}24 \pm 0{,}07$	2,57	$2{,}66 \pm 0{,}13$
ACO	10	9,13	$9{,}26 \pm 0{,}05$	2,57	$2{,}67 \pm 0{,}11$
ACO	20	9,13	$9{,}25 \pm 0{,}04$	2,57	$2{,}68 \pm 0{,}08$

Table 2. The mean value of identified time delay and standard deviation of it for the solution laying in the global optimum

The time of computation is one of the parameters indicating the performance of iterative algorithms. These times are presented in the Fig. 2. For the ACO algorithms the time of computation depends linearly on the amount of ants. For the colony with 12 ants and less, this time is not bigger than for SEPNLS and GSNLS. For these two last, the time is comparable. The standard deviation of the time of computation is shown in the Fig. 2. The ACO with a few ants has the smallest deviation of time of computation. For the SEPNLS and GSNLS the number of repetition in every iteration is variable and depends on indirect solutions.

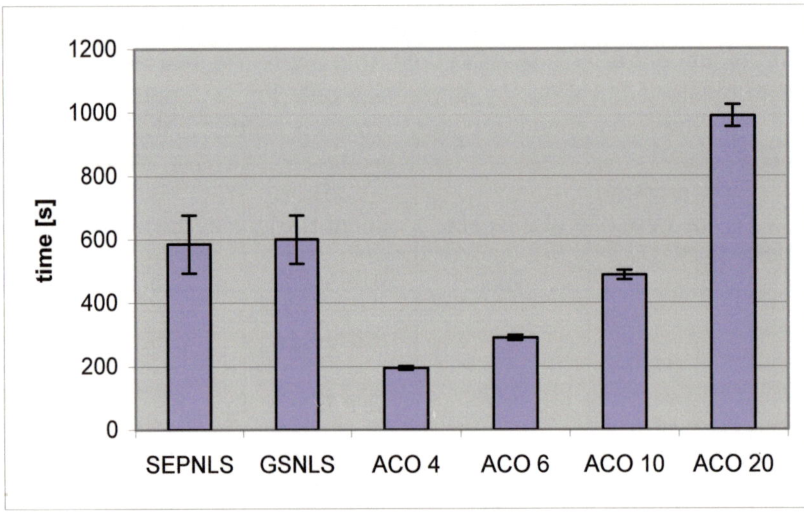

Fig. 2. The time of computation with standard deviation

7. Conclusion

In this paper a separable nonlinear least squares method is developed for identification of systems with time delays. The SEPNLS is vulnerable to local minima in the error surface. The solution depends on the initial values used for identification. The efficiency of this algorithm is poor.

The GSNLS applies the stochastic approximation to the SEPNLS method. It permits to leave the attraction area of a local minimum and reach the global optimum. The efficiency of this algorithm is good.

The ACO has the best performance even for small amount of ants. The algorithm with four ants is fast and quite good. We obtain solution tree times faster and better than from SEPNLS and GSNLS The augmentation of amount of ants permits to improve slightly accuracy of identification of time delay, but the time of identification is increasing linearly too.

8. References

Agosta W.C. (1992). *Chemical communication – the Language of Pheromone.* W.H. Freeman and Company, ISBN 0716750368, New York

Bharth B., Borkar V. S. (1999). Stochastic approximation algorithms: overview and resent trends. *Sādhanā*, Vol. 24, Parts 4 & 5, pp. 425-452, India

Bonabeau E., M. Dorigo & G. Theraulaz (1999). *Swarm Intelligence: From Natural to Artificial Systems.*: Oxford University Press, ISBN 0195131592, New York

Bjorklund S., Ljung L. (2003). A Review of Time-Delay Estimation Techniques *Proceedings of the IEEE Conference on Decision and Control* 2003, Vol. 3, pp. 2502-2507, ISBN: 0-7803-7925-X, Maui, Hawaii, USA

Boukas E. K. (2003). Stochastic output feedback of uncertain time-delay system with saturing actuators. *Journal of optimization theory and applications* 2003, Vol. 118, No. 2, pp. 255-273, ISSN 0022-3239

Chen B.-S., Hung J.-C. (2001). A global estimation for multichannel time-delay and signal parameters via genetic algorithm. *Signal Processing* 2001, Vol. 81 (5), pp. 1061-1067.

Chen X., Wang M. (2004) Global optimization methods for time delay estimation. *Proceedings of the World Congress on Intelligent Control and Automation (WCICA)*, Vol. 1 pp. 212-215, ISBN: 0-7803-8273-0

Harada K., Kobayashi Y., Okita T. (2003). Identification of Linear Systems With Time Delay and Unknown Order Electrical. *Engineering in Japan (English translation of Denki Gakkai Ronbunshi)* 2003, Vol. 145 (3), pp. 61-68,

Iemura H., Yang Z., Kanae S., Wada K. (2004). Identification of continous-time systems with unknow time delays by global nonlinear least-squares method. *IFAC Workshop on adaptation and lerning in control and signal processing*. Yokohama, Japan 2004

Li Z.-S., Wan Y.-C. (2002). Suboptimal control for plants with pure time delay based on state feedback. *Shanghai Jiaotong Daxue Xuebao/Journal of Shanghai Jiaotong University* 2002, Vol. 36 (SUPPL.), pp. 138-140.

Papliński J.P. (2004). An evolutionary algorithm for identification of non-stationary linear plants with time delay. *Proceedings of the First International Conference of Informatics in Control, Automation and Robotics (ICINCO)* 2004, Vol. 1 pp. 64-69. ISBN 972-8865-12-0

Papliński J.P., (2007), Identification of continous-time system with time delays by nonlinear least-squares method with global optimization elements. *Proceedings of the 12th IEEE IFAC Internationa Conference Methods and Models in Automation and Robotics (MMAR)*, pp 601-606, Szczecin, Poland, August 2007, ISBN 978-83-751803-3-6

Phat V.N., Savkin A.V. (2002) Robust state estimation for a class of uncertain time-delay systems. *Systems and Control Letters* 2002, Vol. 47 (3), pp. 237-245, ISSN 0167-6911

Previdi F., Lovera M. (2004). Identification of non-linear parametrically varying models using separable least squares. *Int. J. Control*, 2004, Vol. 77, no. 16, pp. 1382-1392, ISSN: 1366-5820

Shaltaf S. (2004). Neural-Network-Based Time-Delay Estimation *Eurasip Journal on Applied Signal Processing*, 2004, Vol. 3, pp. 378-385

Westwick D. T., Kearney R. E. (2001). Separable least squares identification of nonlinear Hammerstein models: application to stretch reflex dynamics. *Annals of Biomedical Engineering*, 2001, Vol. 29, pp. 707-718, ISSN 0090-6964

Yang Z., Hachino T., Tsuji T. (1997). On-line identification of continous time delay systems combining least-squares techniques with a genetic algorithm. *Int. J. Control.* 1997, Vol. 66, No. 1, pp. 23-42, ISSN: 1366-5820

Yang Z., Iemura H., Kanae S., Wada K. (2005). A global nonlinear instrumental variable method for identification of continous-time systems with unknow time delays. *IFAC Wold Congres*, Prague, Czech Republic, July 4-8, 2005

10

Linear Lyapunov Cone-Systems

Przemysław Przyborowski and Tadeusz Kaczorek
Warsaw University of Technology – Faculty of Electrical Engineering,
Institute of Control and Industrial Electronics,
Poland

1. Introduction

In positive systems inputs, state variables and outputs take only non-negative values. Examples of positive systems are industrial processes involving chemical reactors, heat exchangers and distillation columns, storage systems, compartmental systems, water and atmospheric pollution models. A variety of models having positive linear behavior can be found in engineering, management science, economics, social sciences, biology and medicine, etc.

Positive linear systems are defined on cones and not on linear spaces. Therefore, the theory of positive systems in more complicated and less advanced. An overview of state of the art in positive systems theory is given in the monographs (Farina L. & Rinaldi S., 2000; Kaczorek T., 2001). The realization problem for positive linear systems without and with time delays has been considered in (Benvenuti L. & Farina L., 2004; Farina L. & Rinaldi S.,2000; Kaczorek T., 2004a; Kaczorek T., 2006a; Kaczorek T., 2006b; Kaczorek T. & Busłowicz M, 2004a).

The reachability, controllability to zero and observability of dynamical systems have been considered in (Klamka J., 1991). The reachability and minimum energy control of positive linear discrete-time systems have been investigated in (Busłowicz M. & Kaczorek T., 2004). The positive discrete-time systems with delays have been considered in (Kaczorek T., 2004b; Kaczorek T. & Busłowicz M., 2004b; Kaczorek T. & Busłowicz M., 2004c). The controllability and observability of Lyapunov systems have been investigated by Murty Apparao in the paper (Murty M.S.N. & Apparao B.V., 2005). The positive discrete-time and continuous-time Lyapunov systems have been considered in (Kaczorek T., 2007b; Kaczorek T. & Przyborowski P., 2007a; Kaczorek T. & Przyborowski P., 2008; Kaczorek T. & Przyborowski P., 2007e). The positive linear time-varying Lyapunov systems have been investigated in (Kaczorek T. & Przyborowski P., 2007b). The continuous-time Lyapunov cone systems have been considered in (Kaczorek T. & Przyborowski P., 2007c). The positive discrete-time Lyapunov systems with delays have been investigated in (Kaczorek T. & Przyborowski P., 2007d).

The first definition of the fractional derivative was introduced by Liouville and Riemann at the end of the 19th century (Nishimoto K., 1984; Miller K. S. & Ross B., 1993; Podlubny I., 1999). This idea by engineers has been used for modelling different process in the late 1960s (Bologna M. & Grigolini P., 2003; Vinagre B. M. et al., 2002; Vinagre B. M. & Feliu V., 2002; Zaborowsky V. & Meylanov R., 2001). Mathematical fundamentals of fractional calculus are given in the monographs (Miller K. S. & Ross B., 1993; Nishimoto K., 1984; Oldham K. B. &

Spanier J, 1974; Podlubny I., 1999; Oustaloup A., 1995). The fractional order controllers have been developed in (Oldham K. B. & Spanier J., 1974; Oustaloup A., 1993; Podlubny I.,2002). A generalization of the Kalman filter for fractional order systems has been proposed in (Sierociuk D. & Dzieliński D., 2006). Some others applications of fractional order systems can be found in (Ostalczyk P., 2000; Ostalczyk P., 2004a; Ostalczyk P., 2004b; Ferreira N.M.F. & Machado I.A.T., 2003; Gałkowski K., 2005; Moshrefi-Torbati M. & Hammond K.,1998; Reyes-Melo M.E. et al., 2004; Riu D. et al., 2001; Samko S. G. et al., 1993; Dzieliński A. & Sierociuk D., 2006). In (Ortigueira M. D., 1997) a method for computation of the impulse responses from the frequency responses for the fractional standard (non-positive) discrete-time linear systems is proposed. The reachability and controllability to zero of positive fractional systems has been considered in (Kaczorek T.,2007c; Kaczorek T., 2007d). The reachability and controllability to zero of fractional cone-systems has been considered in (Kaczorek T., 2007e). The fractional discrete-time Lyapunov systems has been investigated in (Przyborowski P., 2008a) and the fractional discrete-time cone-systems in (Przyborowski P., 2008b).
The chapter is organized as follows, In the Section 2, some basic notations, definitions and lemmas will be recalled. In the Section 3, the continuous-time linear Lyapunov cone-systems will be considered. For the systems, the necessary and sufficient conditions for being the cone-system, the asymptotic stability and sufficient conditions for the reachability and observability will be established. In the Section 4, the discrete-time linear Lyapunov cone-systems will be considered. For the systems, the necessary and sufficient conditions for being the cone-system, the asymptotic stability, reachability, observability and controllability to zero will be established. In the Section 5, the fractional discrete-time linear Lyapunov cone-systems will be considered. For the systems, the necessary and sufficient conditions for being the cone-system, the reachability, observability and controllability to zero and sufficient conditions for the stability will be established. In the Section 6, the considerations will be illustrated by numerical examples.

2. Preliminaries

Let R^{nxm} be the set of real $n \times m$ matrices , $R^n = R^{n\times 1}$ and let R_+^{nxm} be the set of real $n \times m$ matrices with nonnegative entries. The set of nonnegative integers will be denoted by Z_+.

Definition 1.

The Kronecker product $A \otimes B$ of the matrices $A = [a_{ij}] \in R^{mxn}$ and $B \in R^{pxq}$ is the block matrix (Kaczorek T.,1998):

$$A \otimes B = [a_{ij}B]_{\substack{i=1,\dots,m \\ j=1,\dots,n}} \in R^{mp\times nq} \tag{1}$$

Lemma 1.

Let us consider the equation:

$$AXB = C \tag{2}$$

where: $A \in R^{m\times n}, B \in R^{q\times p}, C \in R^{m\times p}, X \in R^{n\times q}$

Equation (2) is equivalent to the following one:

$$(A \otimes B^T)x = c \tag{3}$$

where $x := \begin{bmatrix} x_1 & x_2 & \dots & x_n \end{bmatrix}^T$, $c := \begin{bmatrix} c_1 & c_2 & \dots & c_m \end{bmatrix}^T$, and x_i and c_i are the i th rows of the matrices X and C respectively.

Proof: See (Kaczorek T., 1998)

Lemma 2.

If $\lambda_1, \lambda_2, \dots \lambda_n$ are the eigenvalues of the matrix A and $\mu_1, \mu_2, \dots \mu_n$ the eigenvalues of the matrix B, then $\lambda_i + \mu_j$ for $i, j = 1, 2, \dots, n$ are the eigenvalues of the matrix:

$$\bar{A} = A \otimes I_n + I_n \otimes B^T$$

Proof: See (Kaczorek T.,1998)

Definition 2.

Let $P = \begin{bmatrix} p_1 \\ \vdots \\ p_n \end{bmatrix} \in R^{n \times n}$ be nonsingular and p_k be the k th $(k = 1, \dots, n)$ its row. The set:

$$\mathrm{P} := \left\{ X(t) \in R^{n \times n} : \bigcap_{k=1}^{n} p_k X_i(t) \geq 0 \right\} \tag{4}$$

where $X_i(t)$, $i = 1, \dots, n$ is the i th column of the matrix $X(t)$,is called a linear cone of the state variables generated by the matrix P. In the similar way we may define the linear cone of the inputs:

$$\mathrm{Q} := \left\{ U(t) \in R^{m \times n} : \bigcap_{k=1}^{m} q_k U_i(t) \geq 0 \right\} \tag{5}$$

generated by the nonsingular matrix $Q = \begin{bmatrix} q_1 \\ \vdots \\ q_m \end{bmatrix} \in R^{m \times m}$ and the linear cone of the outputs

$$\mathrm{V} := \left\{ Y(t) \in R^{p \times n} : \bigcap_{k=1}^{p} v_k Y_i(t) \geq 0 \right\} \tag{6}$$

generated by the nonsingular matrix $V = \begin{bmatrix} v_1 \\ \vdots \\ v_p \end{bmatrix} \in R^{p \times p}$.

3. Continuous-time linear Lyapunov cone-systems

Consider the continues-time linear Lyapunov system (Kaczorek T. & Przyborowski P., 2007a) described by the equations:

$$\dot{X}(t) = A_0 X(t) + X(t)A_1 + BU(t) \tag{7a}$$

$$Y(t) = CX(t) + DU(t) \tag{7b}$$

where, $X(t) \in R^{nxn}$ is the state-space matrix, $U(t) \in R^{mxn}$ is the input matrix, $Y(t) \in R^{pxn}$ is the output matrix, $A_0, A_1 \in R^{nxn}, B \in R^{nxm}, C \in R^{pxn}, D \in R^{pxm}$.

The solution of the equation (1a) satisfying the initial condition $X(t_0) = X_0$ is given by (Kaczorek T. & Przyborowski P., 2007a):

$$X(t) = e^{A_0(t-t_0)} X_0 e^{A_1(t-t_0)} + \int_{t_0}^{t} e^{A_0(t-\tau)} BU(\tau) e^{A_1(t-\tau)} d\tau \tag{8}$$

Lemma 3.
The Lyapunov system (7) can be transformed to the equivalent standard continuous-time, nm -inputs and pn -outputs, linear system in the form:

$$\dot{\tilde{x}}(t) = \tilde{A}\tilde{x}(t) + \tilde{B}\tilde{u}(t) \tag{9a}$$

$$\tilde{y}(t) = \tilde{C}\tilde{x}(t) + \tilde{D}\tilde{u}(t) \tag{9b}$$

where, $\tilde{x}(t) \in R^{n^2}$ is the state-space vector, $\tilde{u}(t) \in R^{(nm)}$ is the input vector, $\tilde{y}(t) \in R^{(pn)}$ is the output vector, $\tilde{A} \in R^{n^2xn^2}, \tilde{B} \in R^{n^2x(nm)}, \tilde{C} \in R^{(pn)xn^2}, \tilde{D} \in R^{(pn)x(nm)}$.
Proof:
The transformation is based on Lemma 1. The matrices X, U, Y are transformed to the vectors:

$$\tilde{x} = \begin{bmatrix} X_1 & X_2 & \dots & X_n \end{bmatrix}^T, \tilde{u} = \begin{bmatrix} U_1 & U_2 & \dots & U_m \end{bmatrix}^T, \tilde{y} = \begin{bmatrix} Y_1 & Y_2 & \dots & Y_p \end{bmatrix}^T$$

where X_i, U_i, Y_i denotes the i th rows of the matrices X, U, Y, respectively.
The matrices of (9) are:

$$\tilde{A} = (A_0 \otimes I_n + I_n \otimes A_1^T), \tilde{B} = B \otimes I_n, \tilde{C} = C \otimes I_n, \tilde{D} = D \otimes I_n \tag{10}$$

3.1 Cone-systems

Definition 3.
The Lyapunov system (7) is called $(\mathrm{P},\mathrm{Q},\mathrm{V})$-cone-system if $X(t) \in \mathrm{P}$ and $Y(t) \in \mathrm{V}$ for every $X_0 \in \mathrm{P}$ and for every input $U(t) \in \mathrm{Q}$, $t \ge t_0$.

Note that for $\mathrm{P} = R_+^{n\times n}, \mathrm{Q} = R_+^{m\times n}, \mathrm{V} = R_+^{p\times n}$ we obtain $(R_+^{n\times n}, R_+^{m\times n}, R_+^{p\times n})$ -cone system which is equivalent to the positive Lyapunov system (Kaczorek T. & Przyborowski P., 2007c).

Theorem 1.

The Lyapunov system (7) is $(\mathrm{P},\mathrm{Q},\mathrm{V})$-cone-system if and only if :

$$\hat{A}_0 = PA_0P^{-1},\ \hat{A}_1 = A_1 \tag{11}$$

are the Metzler matrices and

$$\hat{B} = PBQ^{-1} \in R_+^{nxm},\ \hat{C} = VCP^{-1} \in R_+^{pxn}, \hat{D} = VDQ^{-1} \in R_+^{pxm}. \tag{12}$$

Proof:

Let:

$$\hat{X}(t) = PX(t),\ \hat{U}(t) = QU(t),\ \hat{Y}(t) = VY(t) \tag{13}$$

From definition 2 it follows that if $X(t) \in \mathrm{P}$ then $\hat{X}(t) \in R_+^{n\times n}$, if $U(t) \in \mathrm{Q}$ then $\hat{U}(t) \in R_+^{m\times n}$, and if $Y(t) \in \mathrm{V}$ then $\hat{Y}(t) \in R_+^{p\times n}$.

From (7) and (13) we have:

$$\begin{aligned}\dot{\hat{X}}(t) &= P\dot{X}(t) = PA_0X(t) + PX(t)A_1 + PBU(t) = PA_0P^{-1}\hat{X}(t) + PP^{-1}\hat{X}(t)A_1 + \\ &+PBQ^{-1}\hat{U}(t) = \hat{A}_0\hat{X}(t) + \hat{X}(t)A_1 + \hat{B}\hat{U}(t)\end{aligned} \tag{14a}$$

and

$$\hat{Y}(t) = VY(t) = VCX(t) + VDU(t) = VCP^{-1}\hat{X}(t) + VDQ^{-1}\hat{U}(t) = \hat{C}\hat{X}(t) + \hat{D}\hat{U}(t) \tag{14b}$$

It is known (Kaczorek T. & Przyborowski P., 2007a) that the system (14) is positive if and only if the conditions (11) and (12) are satisfied. □

3.2 Asymptotic stability

Consider the autonomous Lyapunov $(\mathrm{P},\mathrm{Q},\mathrm{V})$-cone-system:

$$\dot{X}(t) = A_0X(t) + X(t)A_1,\quad X(t_0) = X_0 \tag{15}$$

where, $X(t) \in \mathrm{P}$ and $PA_0P^{-1}, A_1 \in R^{n\times n}$ are the Metzler matrices.

Definition 4.

The Lyapunov $(\mathrm{P},\mathrm{Q},\mathrm{V})$-cone-system (15) is called asymptotically stable if:

$$\lim_{t\to\infty} X(t) = 0 \text{ for every } X_0 \in \mathrm{P}$$

***Theorem* 2.**

Let us assume that $\lambda_1, \lambda_2, \ldots \lambda_n$ are the eigenvalues of the matrix A_0 and $\mu_1, \mu_2, \ldots \mu_n$ the eigenvalues of the matrix A_1. The system (15) is stable if and only if:

$$\mathrm{Re}(\lambda_i + \mu_j) < 0 \text{ for } i, j = 1, 2, ..., n \tag{16}$$

Proof:

The theorem results directly from the theorem for asymptotic stability of standard systems (Kaczorek T., 2001), since by Lemma 2 eigenvalues of matrix $\tilde{A}$ are the sums of eigenvalues of the matrices A_0 and A_1. □

3.3 Reachability

***Definition* 5.**

The state $X_f \in \mathrm{P}$ of the the Lyapunov $(\mathrm{P,Q,V})$-cone-system (7) is called reachable at time t_f, if there exists an input $U(t) \in \mathrm{Q}$ for $t \in [t_0, t_f]$, which steers the system from the initial state $X_0 = 0$ to the state X_f.

***Definition* 6.**

If for every state $X_f \in \mathrm{P}$ there exists $t_f > t_0$, such that the state is reachable at time t_f, then the system is called reachable.

***Theorem* 3.**

The $(\mathrm{P,Q,V})$-cone-system (7) is reachable if the matrix:

$$R_f := \int_{t_0}^{t_f} e^{PA_0P^{-1}(t_f-\tau)}(PBQ^{-1})(PBQ^{-1})^T e^{(PA_0P^{-1})^T(t_f-\tau)} d\tau \tag{17}$$

is a monomial matrix (only one element in every row and in every column of the matrix is positive and the remaining are equal to zero).

The input, that steers the system from initial state $X_0 = 0$ to the state X_f is given by:

$$U(t) = Q^{-1}[(PBQ^{-1})^T e^{(PA_0P^{-1})^T(t_f-t)} R_f^{-1} PX_f e^{A_1(t-t_f)}] \tag{18}$$

for $t \in [t_0, t_f]$.

Proof:

If R_f is the monomial matrix, then there exists $R_f^{-1} \in R_+^{n\times n}$ and the input (18) is well-defined.

Using (8) and (18) we obtain:

$$X(t_f) = P^{-1}[\int_{t_0}^{t_f} e^{PA_0P^{-1}(t_f-\tau)}(PBQ^{-1})(PBQ^{-1})^T e^{(PA_0P^{-1})^T(t_f-\tau)} R_f^{-1} PX_f e^{A_1(\tau-t_f)} e^{A_1(t_f-\tau)} d\tau] = \tag{19}$$

$$= P^{-1}[\int_{t_0}^{t_f} e^{PA_0P^{-1}(t_f-\tau)}(PBQ^{-1})(PBQ^{-1})^T e^{(PA_0P^{-1})^T(t_f-\tau)} d\tau R_f^{-1} PX_f] = P^{-1}PX_f = X_f$$

since $e^{A_1(\tau-t_f)} e^{A_1(t_f-\tau)} = I_n$. □

3.4 Dual Lyapunov cone-systems

Definition 7.

The Lyapunov system described by the equations:

$$\dot{X}(t) = A_0^T X(t) + X(t) A_0^T + C^T U(t) \tag{20a}$$

$$Y(t) = B^T X(t) + DU(t) \tag{20b}$$

is called the dual system with respect to the system (7). The matrices $A_0, A_1, B, C, D,$ $X(t), U(t), Y(t)$ are the same as in the system (7).

3.5 Observability

Definition 8.

The state X_0 of the Lyapunov $(\mathrm{P,Q,V})$ -cone- system (7) is called observable at time $t_f > 0$, if X_0 can be uniquely determined from the knowledge of the output $Y(t)$ and input $U(t)$ for $t \in [0, t_f]$.

Definition 9.

The Lyapunov $(\mathrm{P,Q,V})$-cone- system (7) is called observable, if there exists an instant $t_f > 0$, such that the system (7) is observable at time t_f.

Theorem 4.

The Lyapunov $(\mathrm{P,Q,V})$-cone-system (7) is observable if the dual system (20) is reachable i.e. if the matrix:

$$O_f := \int_{t_0}^{t_f} e^{(PA_0P^{-1})^T(t_f-\tau)}(VCP^{-1})^T(VCP^{-1})e^{(PA_0P^{-1})(t_f-\tau)} d\tau \tag{21}$$

is a monomial matrix.

Proof:

The Lyapunov $(\mathrm{P,Q,V})$-cone-system (7) is observable if and only if the equivalent standard system (9) is observable and this implies that dual system with respect to the system (9) must be reachable thus the dual system (20) with respect to the system (7) also must be reachable. Using Theorem 3. we obtain the hypothesis of the Theorem 4. □

4. Discrete-time linear Lyapunov cone-systems

Consider the discrete-time linear Lyapunov system (Kaczorek T., 2007b; Kaczorek T. & Przyborowski P., 2007e; Kaczorek T. & Przyborowski P., 2008) described by the equations:

$$X_{i+1} = A_0 X_i + X_i A_1 + BU_i \tag{22a}$$

$$Y_i = CX_i + DU_i \tag{22b}$$

where, $X_i \in R^{nxn}$ is the state-space matrix, $U_i \in R^{mxn}$ is the input matrix, $Y_i \in R^{pxn}$ is the output matrix, $A_0, A_1 \in R^{nxn}, B \in R^{nxm}, C \in R^{pxn}, D \in R^{pxm}, i \in Z_+$.

The solution of the equation (22a) satisfying the initial condition X_0 is given by (Kaczorek T.,2007b):

$$X_i = \sum_{k=0}^{i} \frac{i!}{k!(i-k)!} A_0^k X_0 A_1^{i-k} + \sum_{j=0}^{i-1}\sum_{k=0}^{j} \frac{j!}{k!(j-k)!} A_0^k BU_{i-j-1} A_1^{i-k}, i \in Z_+ \tag{23}$$

Lemma 4.
The Lyapunov system (22) can be transformed to the equivalent standard discrete-time, nm-inputs and pn-outputs, linear system in the form:

$$\overline{x}_{i+1} = \overline{A}\overline{x}_i + \overline{B}u_i \tag{24a}$$

$$\overline{y}_i = \overline{C}\overline{x}_i + \overline{D}u_i \tag{24b}$$

where, $\overline{x}_i \in R^{n^2}$ is the state-space vector, $\overline{u}_i \in R^{(nm)}$ is the input vector, $\overline{y}_i \in R^{(pn)}$ is the output vector, $\overline{A} \in R^{n^2 x n^2}, \overline{B} \in R^{n^2 x(nm)}, \overline{C} \in R^{(pn)xn^2}, \overline{D} \in R^{(pn)x(nm)}, i \in Z_+$.
Proof:
The proof is similar to the one of Lemma 3.
The matrices of (24) have the form:

$$\overline{A} = (A_0 \otimes I_n + I_n \otimes A_1^T), \overline{B} = B \otimes I_n, \overline{C} = C \otimes I_n, \overline{D} = D \otimes I_n \tag{25}$$

4.1 Cone-systems

Definition 10.
The Lyapunov system (22) is called $(\mathrm{P},\mathrm{Q},\mathrm{V})$-cone-system if $X_i \in \mathrm{P}$ and $Y_i \in \mathrm{V}$ for every $X_0 \in \mathrm{P}$ and for every input $U_i \in \mathrm{Q}$, $i \in Z_+$.

Note that for $\mathrm{P} = R_+^{n\times n}, \mathrm{Q} = R_+^{m\times n}, \mathrm{V} = R_+^{p\times n}$ we obtain $(R_+^{n\times n}, R_+^{m\times n}, R_+^{p\times n})$-cone system which is equivalent to the positive Lyapunov system (Kaczorek T., 2007b).

***Theorem* 5.**
The Lyapunov system (22) is $(\mathrm{P},\mathrm{Q},\mathrm{V})$-cone-system if and only if :

$$\hat{A}_0 = PA_0P^{-1} = \left[\hat{a}_{ij}^0\right]_{\substack{i=1,\dots,n\\ j=1,\dots,n}}, \hat{A}_1 = A_1 = \left[\hat{a}_{ij}^1\right]_{\substack{i=1,\dots,n\\ j=1,\dots,n}} \tag{26}$$

are the Metzler matrices satisfying

$$\hat{a}_{kk}^0 + \hat{a}_{ll}^1 \geq 0 \;\; \textit{for every} \;\; k,l = 1,\dots,n \tag{27}$$

and

$$\hat{B} = PBQ^{-1} \in R_+^{n\times m}, \hat{C} = VCP^{-1} \in R_+^{p\times n}, \hat{D} = VDQ^{-1} \in R_+^{p\times m} \tag{28}$$

Proof:
Let:

$$\hat{X}_i = PX_i,\; \hat{U}_i = QU_i,\; \hat{Y}_i = VY_i \tag{29}$$

From definition 2 it follows that if $X_i \in \mathrm{P}$ then $\hat{X}_i \in R_+^{n\times n}$, if $U_i \in \mathrm{Q}$ then $\hat{U}_i \in R_+^{m\times n}$, and if $Y_i \in \mathrm{V}$ then $\hat{Y}_i \in R_+^{p\times n}$.
From (22) and (29) we have:

$$\begin{aligned}\hat{X}_{i+1} &= PX_{i+1} = PA_0X_i + PX_iA_1 + PBU_i = PA_0P^{-1}\hat{X}_i + PP^{-1}\hat{X}_iA_1 + \\ &+PBQ^{-1}\hat{U}_i = \hat{A}_0\hat{X}_i + \hat{X}_iA_1 + \hat{B}\hat{U}_i\end{aligned} \tag{30a}$$

and

$$\hat{Y}_i = VY_i = VCX_i + VDU_i = VCP^{-1}\hat{X}_i + VDQ^{-1}\hat{U}_i = \hat{C}\hat{X}_i + \hat{D}\hat{U}_i \tag{30b}$$

The Lyapunov system (30) is positive if and only if, the equivalent standard system is positive. By the theorem for the positivity of the standard discrete-time systems, the matrices $(\hat{A}_0 \otimes I_n + I_n \otimes \hat{A}_1^T), (\hat{B} \otimes I_n), (\hat{C} \otimes I_n), (\hat{D} \otimes I_n)$ have to be the matrices with nonnegative entries , so from (30) follows the hypothesis of the Theorem 5. □

4.2 Asymptotic stability

Consider the autonomous Lyapunov $(\mathrm{P},\mathrm{Q},\mathrm{V})$-cone-system:

$$X_{i+1} = A_0X_i + X_iA_1 \tag{31}$$

where, $X_i \in \mathrm{P}$, $\mathrm{i} \in \mathrm{Z}_+$.

***Definition* 11.**
The Lyapunov $(\mathrm{P},\mathrm{Q},\mathrm{V})$-cone-system (15) is called asymptotically stable if:

$$\lim_{i\to\infty} X_i = 0 \text{ for every } X_0 \in \mathrm{P}$$

Theorem 6.

Let us assume that $\lambda_1, \lambda_2, \ldots \lambda_n$ are the eigenvalues of the matrix A_0 and $\mu_1, \mu_2, \ldots \mu_n$ the eigenvalues of the matrix A_1. The system (31) is stable if and only if:

$$\left|\lambda_i + \mu_j\right| < 1 \text{ for } i, j = 1, 2, \ldots, n \tag{32}$$

Proof:

The theorem results directly from the theorem for asymptotic stability of standard systems (Kaczorek T., 2001), since by Lemma 2 eigenvalues of matrix $\overline{A}$ are the sums of eigenvalues of the matrices A_0 and A_1. □

4.3 Reachability

Definition 12.

The Lyapunov $(\mathrm{P,Q,V})$-cone-system (22) is called reachable if for any given $X_f \in \mathrm{P}$ there exist $q \in Z_+, q > 0$ and an input sequence $U_i \in \mathrm{Q}, q = 0, 1, \ldots, q-1$ that steers the state of the system from $X_0 = 0$ to X_f, i.e. $X_q = X_f$.

Theorem 7.

The Lyapunov $(\mathrm{P,Q,V})$-cone-system (22) is reachable:

a) For A_1 satisfying the condition $XA_1 = A_1X$, i.e. $A_1 = aI_n, a \in R$, if and only if the matrix:

$$R_n = [PBQ^{-1} \quad \overline{A}_0(PBQ^{-1}) \quad \cdots \quad \overline{A}_0^{n-1}(PBQ^{-1})] \tag{33}$$

contains n linearly independent monomial columns, $\overline{A}_0 = PA_0P^{-1} + A_1$.

b) For $A_1 \neq aI_n, a \in R$, if and only if the matrix PBQ^{-1} contains n linearly independent monomial columns.

Proof:

From (26),(28),(29) and from the definitions 2 and 12, we have that the discrete-time Lyapunov $(\mathrm{P,Q,V})$-cone-system (22) is reachable if and only if the positive discrete-time Lyapunov system, with the matrices $\hat{A}_0, \hat{A}_1, \hat{B}, \hat{C}, \hat{D}$, is reachable – so from the theorem for the reachability of positive discrete-time Lyapunov systems (Kaczorek T. & Przyborowski P., 2007e; Kaczorek T. & Przyborowski P., 2008) follows the hypothesis of the theorem 7. □

4.4 Controllability to zero

Definition 13.

The Lyapunov $(\mathrm{P,Q,V})$-cone-system (22) is called controllable to zero if for any given nonzero $X_0 \in \mathrm{P}$ there exist $q \in Z_+, q > 0$ and an input sequence $U_i \in \mathrm{Q}, q = 0, 1, \ldots, q-1$ that steers the state of the system from X_0 to $X_q = X_f = 0$.

Theorem 8.

The Lyapunov $(\mathrm{P,Q,V})$-cone-system (22) is controllable to zero:

a) in a finite number of steps (not greater than n^2) if and only if the matrix $(PA_0P^{-1} \otimes I_n + I_n \otimes A_1^T)$ is nilpotent, i.e. has all zero eigenvalues.

b) in an infinite number of steps if and only if the system is asymptotically stable.

Proof:

From (26),(28),(29) and from the definitions 2 and 13, we have that the discrete-time Lyapunov $(\mathrm{P,Q,V})$-cone-system (22) is controllable to zero if and only if the positive discrete-time Lyapunov system, with the matrices $\hat{A}_0, \hat{A}_1, \hat{B}, \hat{C}, \hat{D}$, is controllable to zero - so from the theorem for the controllability to zero of positive discrete-time Lyapunov systems (Kaczorek T. & Przyborowski P., 2007e; Kaczorek T. & Przyborowski P., 2008) follows the hypothesis of the theorem 8. □

Lemma 5.

If the matrices PA_0P^{-1} and A_1 are nilpotent then the matrix $(PA_0P^{-1} \otimes I_n + I_n \otimes A_1^T)$ is also nilpotent with the nilpotency index $\nu \leq 2n$.

Proof: See (Kaczorek T. & Przyborowski P, 2008).

4.5 Dual Lyapunov cone-systems

Definition 14.

The Lyapunov system described by the equations:

$$X_{i+1} = A_0^T X_i + X_i A_1^T + C^T U_i \tag{34a}$$

$$Y_i = B^T X_i + DU_i \tag{35b}$$

is called the dual system respect to the system (22). The matrices A_0, A_1, B, C, D, X_i, U_i, Y_i are the same as in the system (22).

4.6 Observability

Definition 15.

The Lyapunov $(\mathrm{P,Q,V})$-cone-system (22) is called observable in q-steps, if X_0 can be uniquely determined from the knowledge of the output Y_i and $U_i = 0, i \in Z_+$ for $i \in [0, q]$.

Definition 16.

The Lyapunov $(\mathrm{P,Q,V})$-cone-system (22) is called observable, if there exists a natural number $q \geq 1$, such that the system (22) is observable in q-steps.

Theorem 9.

The Lyapunov $(\mathrm{P,Q,V})$-cone-system (22) is observable:

a) For A_1 satisfying the condition $XA_1 = A_1X$, i.e. $A_1 = aI_n, a \in R$, if and only if the matrix:

$$O_n = \begin{bmatrix} VCP^{-1} \\ (VCP^{-1})\overline{A}_0 \\ \vdots \\ (VCP^{-1})\overline{A}^{n-1} \end{bmatrix} \tag{33}$$

contains n linearly independent monomial rows, $\overline{A}_0 = PA_0P^{-1} + A_1$.

b) For $A_1 \neq aI_n, a \in R$, if and only if the matrix VCP^{-1} contains n linearly independent monomial rows.

Proof:

From (26),(28),(29) and from the definitions 2 and 15, we have that the discrete-time Lyapunov (P,Q,V) -cone-system (22) is observable if and only if the positive discrete-time Lyapunov system, with the matrices $\hat{A}_0, \hat{A}_1, \hat{B}, \hat{C}, \hat{D}$, is observable – so from the theorem for the observability of positive discrete-time Lyapunov systems (Kaczorek T. & Przyborowski P., 2007e; Kaczorek T. & Przyborowski P., 2008) follows the hypothesis of the theorem 9. □

5. Fractional discrete-time linear Lyapunov cone-systems

Consider the fractional discrete-time linear Lyapunov system (Przyborowski P., 2008a; Przyborowski P., 2008b) described by the equations:

$$\Delta^N X_{i+1} = A_0 X_i + X_i A_1 + BU_i \tag{34a}$$

$$Y_i = CX_i + DU_i \tag{34b}$$

where, $X_i \in R^{nxn}$ is the state-space matrix, $U_i \in R^{mxn}$ is the input matrix, $Y_i \in R^{pxn}$ is the output matrix, $A_0, A_1 \in R^{nxn}, B \in R^{nxm}, C \in R^{pxn}, D \in R^{pxm}, i \in Z_+$ and

$$\Delta^N X_i = \frac{1}{h^N}\sum_{j=0}^{i}(-1)^j \binom{N}{j} X_{i-j} \quad , \quad \binom{N}{j} = \begin{cases} 1 & \text{for } j = 0 \\ \dfrac{N(N-1)\cdots(N-j+1)}{j!} & \text{for } j = 1,2,\ldots \end{cases}$$

is the Grünwald-Letnikov N -order ($N \in R, 0 < N \leq 1$) fractional difference, and h is the sampling interval.

The equations (34) can be written in the form:

$$X_{i+1} + \sum_{j=1}^{i+1}(-1)^j \binom{N}{j} X_{i-j+1} = A_0 X_i + X_i A_1 + BU_i \tag{35a}$$

$$Y_i = CX_i + DU_i \tag{35b}$$

Lemma 6.
The fractional Lyapunov system (34) can be transformed to the equivalent fractional discrete-time, nm-inputs and pn-outputs, linear system in the form:

$$\Delta^N \widehat{x}_{i+1} = \widehat{A}\widehat{x}_i + \widehat{B}\widehat{u}_i \tag{36a}$$

$$\widehat{y}_i = \widehat{C}\widehat{x}_i + \widehat{D}\widehat{u}_i \tag{36b}$$

where, $\widehat{x}_i \in R^{n^2}$ is the state-space vector, $\widehat{u}_i \in R^{(nm)}$ is the input vector, $\widehat{y}_i \in R^{(pn)}$ is the output vector, $\widehat{A} \in R^{n^2 x n^2}, \widehat{B} \in R^{n^2 x(nm)}, \widehat{C} \in R^{(pn)xn^2}, \widehat{D} \in R^{(pn)x(nm)}, i \in Z_+$.
Proof:
The proof is similar to the one of Lemma 3.
The matrices of (36) have the form:

$$\widehat{A} = (A_0 \otimes I_n + I_n \otimes A_1^T), \widehat{B} = B \otimes I_n, \widehat{C} = C \otimes I_n, \widehat{D} = D \otimes I_n \tag{37}$$

5.1 Cone-systems

Definition 17.
The fractional Lyapunov system (22) is called $(\mathrm{P},\mathrm{Q},\mathrm{V})$-cone-system if $X_i \in \mathrm{P}$ and $Y_i \in \mathrm{V}$ for every $X_0 \in \mathrm{P}$ and for every input $U_i \in \mathrm{Q}$, $i \in Z_+$.
Note that for $\mathrm{P} = R_+^{n\times n}, \mathrm{Q} = R_+^{m\times n}, \mathrm{V} = R_+^{p\times n}$ we obtain $(R_+^{n\times n}, R_+^{m\times n}, R_+^{p\times n})$-cone system which is equivalent to the fractional positive Lyapunov system (Przyborowski P., 2008a).
Theorem 10.
The fractional Lyapunov system (34) is $(\mathrm{P},\mathrm{Q},\mathrm{V})$-cone-system if and only if :

$$\hat{A}_0 = PA_0P^{-1} = \left[\hat{a}_{ij}^0\right]_{\substack{i=1,\dots,n\\ j=1,\dots,n}}, \hat{A}_1 = A_1 = \left[\hat{a}_{ij}^1\right]_{\substack{i=1,\dots,n\\ j=1,\dots,n}} \tag{38}$$

are the Metzler matrices satisfying

$$\hat{a}_{kk}^0 + \hat{a}_{ll}^1 + N \geq 0 \text{ for every } k,l = 1,\dots,n \tag{39}$$

and

$$\hat{B} = PBQ^{-1} \in R_+^{n\times m}, \hat{C} = VCP^{-1} \in R_+^{p\times n}, \hat{D} = VDQ^{-1} \in R_+^{p\times m} \tag{40}$$

Proof:
Let:

$$\hat{X}_i = PX_i,\ \hat{U}_i = QU_i,\ \hat{Y}_i = VY_i \tag{41}$$

From definition 2 it follows that if $X_i \in \mathrm{P}$ then $\hat{X}_i \in R_+^{n\times n}$, if $U_i \in \mathrm{Q}$ then $\hat{U}_i \in R_+^{m\times n}$, and if $Y_i \in \mathrm{V}$ then $\hat{Y}_i \in R_+^{p\times n}$.

From (34) and (41) we have:

$$\begin{aligned}&\hat{X}_{i+1}+\sum_{j=1}^{i+1}(-1)^j\binom{N}{j}\hat{X}_{i-j+1}=PX_{i+1}+\sum_{j=1}^{i+1}(-1)^j\binom{N}{j}PX_{i-j+1}=\\&=PA_0X_i+PX_iA_1+PBU_i=PA_0P^{-1}\hat{X}_i+PP^{-1}\hat{X}_iA_1+PBQ^{-1}\hat{U}_i=\\&=\hat{A}_0\hat{X}_i+\hat{X}_iA_1+\hat{B}\hat{U}_i\end{aligned} \tag{41a}$$

and

$$\hat{Y}_i=VY_i=VCX_i+VDU_i=VCP^{-1}\hat{X}_i+VDQ^{-1}\hat{U}_i=\hat{C}\hat{X}_i+\hat{D}\hat{U}_i \tag{42b}$$

It is known (Przyborowski P., 2008a) that the system (34) is positive if and only if the conditions (41a) and (42b) are satisfied. □

5.2. Stability

Consider the autonomous fractional Lyapunov (P,Q,V) -cone-system:

$$\Delta^N X_{i+1}=A_0X_i+X_iA_1 \tag{43}$$

where, $X_i\in \mathrm{P}$, $\mathrm{i}\in \mathrm{Z}_+$.

Definition 18. (Dzieliński A. & Sierociuk D., 2006)

The fractional Lyapunov (P,Q,V)-cone- system (43) is called stable in finite relative time if for $\alpha,\beta\in R_+,\ \alpha<\beta,\ \alpha,\beta<\infty,\ k=1,\dots,n;\ M,N\in Z_+$:

$$\left\|X_i^k\right\|<\alpha \quad for \quad i=0,-1,\dots,-N$$

implies

$$\left\|X_i^k\right\|<\beta \quad for \quad i=0,1,\dots,M$$

where X_i^k is the k th column of the matrix X_i.

Theorem 11.

The fractional Lyapunov (P,Q,V)-cone- system (34) is stable in the meaning of the definition 18 if:

$$\left\|\widehat{A}+I_{n^2}N\right\|+\sum_{j=2}^{i+1}\left\|(-1)^j\binom{N}{j}I_{n^2}\right\|<1 \tag{44}$$

where $\widehat{A}=A_0\otimes I_n+I_n\otimes A_1^T$ and $\left\|W\right\|$ denotes the norm of the matrix W, defined as $\max_l\left|\lambda_l\right|$, where λ_l is the l th eigenvalue of the matrix W.

Proof:

The theorem results directly from the theorem of asymptotic stability of standard fractional systems (Dzieliński A. & Sierociuk D., 2006). □

5.3 Reachability

Definition 19.

The fractional Lyapunov $(\mathrm{P},\mathrm{Q},\mathrm{V})$-cone-system (34) is called reachable if for any given $X_f \in \mathrm{P}$ there exists $q \in Z_+, q > 0$ and an input sequence $U_i \in \mathrm{Q}, q = 0,1,\ldots,q-1$ that steers the state of the system from $X_0 = 0$ to X_f, i.e. $X_q = X_f$.

Theorem 12.

The fractional Lyapunov $(\mathrm{P},\mathrm{Q},\mathrm{V})$-cone-system (34) is reachable:

a) For A_1 satisfying the condition $XA_1 = A_1X$, i.e. $A_1 = aI_n, a \in R$, if and only if the matrix:

$$R_n = \left[PBQ^{-1}, \quad (\overline{A}_0 + I_nN)PBQ^{-1}\right] \tag{45}$$

contains n linearly independent monomial columns, $\overline{A}_0 = PA_0P^{-1} + A_1$.

b) For $A_1 \neq aI_n, a \in R$, if and only if the matrix PBQ^{-1} contains n linearly independent monomial columns.

Proof:

From (38),(39),(40) and from the definitions 2 and 19, we have that the fractional discrete-time Lyapunov $(\mathrm{P},\mathrm{Q},\mathrm{V})$-cone-system (34) is reachable if and only if the fractional positive discrete-time Lyapunov system, with the matrices $\hat{A}_0, \hat{A}_1, \hat{B}, \hat{C}, \hat{D}$, is reachable - so from the theorem for the reachability of positive discrete-time Lyapunov systems (Przyborowski P.,2008a). follows the hypothesis of the theorem 12. □

5.4 Controllability to zero

Definition 20.

The fractional Lyapunov $(\mathrm{P},\mathrm{Q},\mathrm{V})$-cone-system (34) is called controllable to zero if for any given nonzero $X_0 \in \mathrm{P}$ there exist $q \in Z_+, q > 0$ and an input sequence $U_i \in \mathrm{Q}, q = 0,1,\ldots,q-1$ that steers the state of the system from X_0 to $X_q = X_f = 0$.

Theorem 13.

The fractional Lyapunov $(\mathrm{P},\mathrm{Q},\mathrm{V})$-cone-system (34) is controllable to zero if and only if $q = 2$ and:

$$PA_0P^{-1} \otimes I_n + I_n \otimes A_1^T + (I_nN) \otimes I_n = 0 \tag{46}$$

Proof:

From (38),(39),(40) and from the definitions 2 and 19, we have that the fractional discrete-time Lyapunov $(\mathrm{P},\mathrm{Q},\mathrm{V})$-cone-system (34) is controllable to zero if and only if the fractional positive discrete-time Lyapunov system, with the matrices $\hat{A}_0, \hat{A}_1, \hat{B}, \hat{C}, \hat{D}$, is controllable - so from the theorem for the controllability of positive discrete-time Lyapunov systems (Przyborowski P., 2008a). follows the hypothesis of the theorem 13. □

5.5 Dual fractional Lyapunov cone-systems

Definition 21.

The fractional Lyapunov system described by the equations:

$$\Delta^N X_{i+1} = A_0^T X_i + X_i A_1^T + C^T U_i \tag{47a}$$

$$Y_i = B^T X_i + DU_i \tag{47b}$$

is called the dual system respect to the system (34). The matrices $A_0, A_1, B, C, D,$ X_i, U_i, Y_i are the same as in the system (34).

5.6 Observability

Definition 22.

The fractional Lyapunov (P,Q,V)-cone-system (34) is called observable in q -steps, if X_0 can be uniquely determined from the knowledge of the output Y_i and $U_i = 0, i \in Z_+$ for $i \in [0, q]$.

Definition 23.

The fractional Lyapunov (P,Q,V)-cone-system (34) is called observable, if there exists a natural number $q \geq 1$, such that the system (34) is observable in q -steps.

Theorem 14.

The fractional Lyapunov (P,Q,V) -cone-system (34) is observable:

a) For A_1 satisfying the condition $XA_1 = A_1X$, i.e. $A_1 = aI_n, a \in R$, if and only if the matrix:

$$O_n = \begin{bmatrix} VCP^{-1} \\ VCP^{-1}(\overline{A}_0 + I_n N) \end{bmatrix} \tag{48}$$

contains n linearly independent monomial rows, $\overline{A}_0 = PA_0P^{-1} + A_1$.

b) For $A_1 \neq aI_n, a \in R$, if and only if the matrix VCP^{-1} contains n linearly independent monomial rows.

Proof:

From (38),(39),(40) and from the definitions 2 and 20, we have that the fractional discrete-time Lyapunov (P,Q,V)-cone-system (34) is controllable to zero if and only if the fractional positive discrete-time Lyapunov system, with the matrices $\hat{A}_0, \hat{A}_1, \hat{B}, \hat{C}, \hat{D}$, is observable - so from the theorem for the observability of positive discrete-time Lyapunov systems (Przyborowski P., 2008a). follows the hypothesis of the theorem 14. □

6. Examples

Consider the state, input and output cones generated by the matrices

$$P = \begin{bmatrix} -1 & 2 \\ 1 & 1 \end{bmatrix}, \; Q = \begin{bmatrix} 1 & 0 \\ 0 & 1 \end{bmatrix}, \; V = \begin{bmatrix} 1 & 0 \\ 0 & 1 \end{bmatrix} \tag{49}$$

6.1 Example 1

Consider the continuous-time Lyapunov system (7) with the matrices

$$A_0 = \frac{1}{3}\begin{bmatrix} -7 & -4 \\ -2 & -5 \end{bmatrix},\ A_1 = \begin{bmatrix} -4 & 0 \\ 0 & -1 \end{bmatrix}, B = \frac{1}{3}\begin{bmatrix} -1 & 2 \\ 1 & 1 \end{bmatrix},$$
$$C = \begin{bmatrix} -2 & 4 \\ 1 & 1 \end{bmatrix}, D = \begin{bmatrix} 0 & 0 \\ 0 & 0 \end{bmatrix} \tag{50}$$

This system is $(\mathrm{P,Q,V})$-cone-system with P,Q and V defined by (49) since:

$$\hat{A}_0 = \begin{bmatrix} -1 & 2 \\ 1 & 1 \end{bmatrix}\frac{1}{3}\begin{bmatrix} -7 & -4 \\ -2 & -5 \end{bmatrix}\begin{bmatrix} -1 & 2 \\ 1 & 1 \end{bmatrix}^{-1} = \begin{bmatrix} -1 & 0 \\ 0 & -3 \end{bmatrix}$$
$$\hat{A}_1 = \begin{bmatrix} -4 & 0 \\ 0 & -1 \end{bmatrix}$$

are the Metzler matrices and

$$\hat{B} = \begin{bmatrix} -1 & 2 \\ 1 & 1 \end{bmatrix}\frac{1}{3}\begin{bmatrix} -1 & 2 \\ 1 & 1 \end{bmatrix}\begin{bmatrix} 1 & 0 \\ 0 & 1 \end{bmatrix}^{-1} = \begin{bmatrix} 1 & 0 \\ 0 & 1 \end{bmatrix}$$
$$\hat{C} = \begin{bmatrix} 1 & 0 \\ 0 & 1 \end{bmatrix}\begin{bmatrix} -2 & 4 \\ 1 & 1 \end{bmatrix}\begin{bmatrix} -1 & 2 \\ 1 & 1 \end{bmatrix}^{-1} = \begin{bmatrix} 2 & 0 \\ 0 & 1 \end{bmatrix}$$
$$\hat{D} = \begin{bmatrix} 1 & 0 \\ 0 & 1 \end{bmatrix}\begin{bmatrix} 0 & 0 \\ 0 & 0 \end{bmatrix}\begin{bmatrix} 1 & 0 \\ 0 & 1 \end{bmatrix}^{-1} = \begin{bmatrix} 0 & 0 \\ 0 & 0 \end{bmatrix}$$

are matrices with nonnegative entries.

A_0 has the eigenvalues: $\lambda_1 = -1, \lambda_2 = -3$ and A_1 has the eigenvalues: $\mu_1 = -4$, $\mu_2 = -1$ therefore the system is asymptotically stable, since all the sums of the eigenvalues:

$$(\lambda_1 + \mu_1) = -5,\ (\lambda_1 + \mu_2) = -2,\ (\lambda_2 + \mu_1) = -7,\ (\lambda_2 + \mu_2) = -4$$

have negative real parts.

For this system the reachability matrix

$$R_f = \int_0^{t_f} \begin{bmatrix} e^{(-t_f+\tau)^2} & 0 \\ 0 & 4e^{3(-t_f+\tau)^2} \end{bmatrix} d\tau$$

and the observability matrix

$$O_f = \int_0^{t_f} \begin{bmatrix} 4e^{(-t_f+\tau)^2} & 0 \\ 0 & e^{3(-t_f+\tau)^2} \end{bmatrix} d\tau$$

are the monomial matrices for every $t_f > 0$. Therefore, the system is reachable and observable.

6.2 Example 2

Consider the discrete-time Lyapunov system (22) with the matrices

$$\begin{aligned} A_0 &= \begin{bmatrix} 0.3 & 0.2 \\ 0.1 & 0.2 \end{bmatrix}, A_1 = \begin{bmatrix} 0.2 & 0 \\ 0 & 0.5 \end{bmatrix}, B = \frac{1}{3}\begin{bmatrix} -1 & 2 \\ 1 & 1 \end{bmatrix}, \\ C &= \begin{bmatrix} -2 & 4 \\ 1 & 1 \end{bmatrix}, D = \begin{bmatrix} 0 & 0 \\ 0 & 0 \end{bmatrix} \end{aligned} \quad (50)$$

This system is (P,Q,V)-cone-system with P, Q and V defined by (49) since:

$$\hat{A}_0 = \begin{bmatrix} -1 & 2 \\ 1 & 1 \end{bmatrix}\begin{bmatrix} 0.3 & 0.2 \\ 0.1 & 0.2 \end{bmatrix}\begin{bmatrix} -1 & 2 \\ 1 & 1 \end{bmatrix}^{-1} = \begin{bmatrix} 0.1 & 0 \\ 0 & 0.4 \end{bmatrix}, \hat{A}_1 = \begin{bmatrix} 0.2 & 0 \\ 0 & 0.5 \end{bmatrix}$$

are the Metzler matrices satisfying conditions:

$$\begin{aligned} \hat{a}_{11}^0 + \hat{a}_{11}^1 &= 0.3 + 0.2 = 0.5 > 0, \quad \hat{a}_{22}^0 + \hat{a}_{11}^1 = 0.2 + 0.2 = 0.4 > 0 \\ \hat{a}_{11}^0 + \hat{a}_{22}^1 &= 0.3 + 0.5 = 0.8 > 0, \quad \hat{a}_{22}^0 + \hat{a}_{22}^1 = 0.2 + 0.5 = 0.7 > 0 \end{aligned}$$

and

$$\hat{B} = \begin{bmatrix} -1 & 2 \\ 1 & 1 \end{bmatrix}\frac{1}{3}\begin{bmatrix} -1 & 2 \\ 1 & 1 \end{bmatrix}\begin{bmatrix} 1 & 0 \\ 0 & 1 \end{bmatrix}^{-1} = \begin{bmatrix} 1 & 0 \\ 0 & 1 \end{bmatrix}, \hat{C} = \begin{bmatrix} 1 & 0 \\ 0 & 1 \end{bmatrix}\begin{bmatrix} -2 & 4 \\ 1 & 1 \end{bmatrix}\begin{bmatrix} -1 & 2 \\ 1 & 1 \end{bmatrix}^{-1} = \begin{bmatrix} 2 & 0 \\ 0 & 1 \end{bmatrix}$$

$$\hat{D} = \begin{bmatrix} 1 & 0 \\ 0 & 1 \end{bmatrix}\begin{bmatrix} 0 & 0 \\ 0 & 0 \end{bmatrix}\begin{bmatrix} 1 & 0 \\ 0 & 1 \end{bmatrix}^{-1} = \begin{bmatrix} 0 & 0 \\ 0 & 0 \end{bmatrix}$$

are matrices with nonnegative entries.

A_0 has the eigenvalues: $\lambda_1 = 0.1, \lambda_2 = 0.4$ and A_1 has the eigenvalues: $\mu_1 = 0.2$, $\mu_2 = 0.5$ therefore the system is asymptotically stable, since all the eigenvalues:

$$(\lambda_1 + \mu_1) = 0.3, \ (\lambda_1 + \mu_2) = 0.6, \ (\lambda_2 + \mu_1) = 0.6, \ (\lambda_2 + \mu_2) = 0.9$$

have moduli less than one.

The system is reachable and observable because the matrix PBQ^{-1} has $n=2$ monomial columns, and the matrix VCP^{-1} has $n=2$ monomial rows.
The system is not controllable to zero in finite number of steps since the matrix

$$(PA_0P^{-1} \otimes I_n + I_n \otimes A_1^T) = \begin{bmatrix} 0.3 & 0 & 0 & 0 \\ 0 & 0.6 & 0 & 0 \\ 0 & 0 & 0.6 & 0 \\ 0 & 0 & 0 & 0.9 \end{bmatrix}$$

is not a the nilpotent matrix, but the system is controllable to zero in the infinite number of steps since it is asymptotically stable.

6.3 Example 3

Consider the discrete-time Lyapunov system (34) with $N = \frac{1}{4}$ and the matrices

$$A_0 = \begin{bmatrix} -0.5 & -0.8 \\ 0.6 & 0.9 \end{bmatrix},\ A_1 = \begin{bmatrix} 0.17 & 0 \\ 1 & 0.4 \end{bmatrix},\ B = \begin{bmatrix} -\frac{1}{3} & \frac{2}{3} \\ \frac{1}{3} & \frac{1}{3} \end{bmatrix},$$
$$C = \begin{bmatrix} -2 & 4 \\ 1 & 1 \end{bmatrix}, D = \begin{bmatrix} 0 & 0 \\ 0 & 0 \end{bmatrix} \quad (n=2) \tag{51}$$

This system is (P,Q,V)-cone-system with P, Q and V defined by (49) since:

$$\hat{A}_0 = \begin{bmatrix} 0.3 & 2 \\ 0 & 0.1 \end{bmatrix},\ \hat{A}_1 = \begin{bmatrix} 0.17 & 0 \\ 1 & 0.4 \end{bmatrix},\ \hat{B} = \begin{bmatrix} 1 & 0 \\ 0 & 1 \end{bmatrix},\ \hat{C} = \begin{bmatrix} 2 & 0 \\ 0 & 1 \end{bmatrix},\ \hat{D} = \begin{bmatrix} 0 & 0 \\ 0 & 0 \end{bmatrix}$$

The system is (P,Q,V) -cone-system because:

$$\hat{a}_{11}^0 + \hat{a}_{11}^1 + N = 0.3 + 0.17 + 0.25 = 0.72 > 0, \hat{a}_{22}^0 + \hat{a}_{11}^1 + N = 0.1 + 0.17 + 0.25 = 0.52 > 0$$
$$\hat{a}_{11}^0 + \hat{a}_{22}^1 + N = 0.3 + 0.4 + 0.25 = 0.95 > 0, \hat{a}_{22}^0 + \hat{a}_{22}^1 + N = 0.1 + 0.4 + 0.25 = 0.75 > 0$$

and the matrices $\hat{B}, \hat{C}, \hat{D}$ have nonnegative entries.
For the instant $i = 100$ we have

$$\left\| \overline{A} + I_{n^2} N \right\| + \sum_{j=2}^{i+1} \left\| (-1)^j \binom{N}{j} I_{n^2} \right\| = 0.8268 < 1$$

so the system is stable in the meaning of the the definition 18.

The system is reachable and observable because the matrix PBQ^{-1} has $n=2$ monomial columns, and the matrix VCP^{-1} has $n = 2$ monomial rows.
The system is not controllable to zero in finite number of steps since the matrix

$$(PA_0P^{-1} \otimes I_n + I_n \otimes A_1^T + (I_nN) \otimes I_n) = \begin{bmatrix} 0.72 & 0 & 0 & 0 \\ 0 & 0.52 & 0 & 0 \\ 0 & 0 & 0.95 & 0 \\ 0 & 0 & 0 & 0.75 \end{bmatrix}$$

is not a zero matrix.

7. Conclusions

In this paper three types of systems have been considered. For the continuous-time linear Lyapunov cone-systems, the necessary and sufficient conditions for being the cone-system, the asymptotic stability and sufficient conditions for the reachability and observability have been be established. For the discrete-time linear Lyapunov cone-systems, the necessary and sufficient conditions for being the cone-system, the asymptotic stability, reachability, observability and controllability to zero have been established. For the fractional discrete-time linear Lyapunov cone-systems, the necessary and sufficient conditions for being the cone-system, the reachability, observability and controllability to zero and sufficient conditions for the stability have been established. The considerations have been illustrated on the numerical examples.

8. References

Benvenuti L. & Farina L. (2004). A tutorial on positive realization problem, *IEEE Trans. Autom. Control,* vol. 49, No 5, pp. 651-664.

Bologna M. & Grigolini P. (2003). *Physics of Fractal Operators.* Springer-Verlag, New York.

Busłowicz M. & Kaczorek T. (2004). Reachability and minimum energy control of positive linear discrete-time systems with one delay, *Proceedings of 12th Mediterranean Conference on Control and Automation,* June 6-9, Kusadasi, Izmir, Turkey.

Dzieliński A. & Sierociuk D.. Stability of discrete fractional order state-space systems., *Proceedings of 2nd IFAC Workshop on Fractional Differentiation and its Applications. IFAC FDA'06.*

Farina L. & Rinaldi S. (2000). *Positive Linear Systems; Theory and Applications,* J. Wiley, New York.

Ferreira N.M.F. & Machado I.A.T.(2003). Fractional-order hybrid control of robotic manipulators. *Proceedings of 11th Int. Conf. Advanced Robotics, ICAR'2003,* Coimbra, Portugal, pp. 393-398.

Gałkowski K. (2005). Fractional polynomials and nD systems. *Proceedings of IEEE Int. Symp. Circuits and Systems, ISCAS'2005,* Kobe, Japan.

Kaczorek T. (1998). *Vectors and Matrices in Automation and Electrotechnics,* Wydawnictwo Naukowo-Techniczne, Warszawa (in Polish).

Kaczorek T. (2001). *Positive 1D and 2D systems,* Springer Verlag, London.

Kaczorek T. (2004a). Realization problem for positive discrete-time systems with delay, *Systems Science*, vol. 30, No. 4, pp.117-130.

Kaczorek T. (2004b). Stability of positive discrete-time systems with time-delay, *Proceedings of The 8th World Multi-Conference on Systemics, Cybernetics and Informatics*, July 18-21, Orlando, Florida, USA.

Kaczorek T. (2006a). Realization problem for positive multivariable discrete-time linear systems with delays in the state vector and inputs, *Int. J. Appl. Math. Comp. Sci.*, vol. 16, No. 2, pp. 101-106.

Kaczorek T. (2006b). A realization problem for positive continuous-time systems with reduced number of delays, *Int. J. Appl. Math. Comp. Sci.* , vol. 16, No. 3, pp. 101-117.

Kaczorek T. (2007a). New reachability and observability tests for positive linear discrete-time systems, *Bull. Pol. Acad. Sci. Techn.* vol. 55, No. 1.

Kaczorek T. (2007b). Positive discrete-time linear Lyapunov systems, *Proceedings of The 15th Mediterranean Conference of Control and Automation – MED 2007*, 27-29 June, Athens.

Kaczorek T. (2007c). Reachability and controllability to zero of positive fractional discrete-time systems, *Machine Intelligence and Robotics Control*, vol. 6, No. 4, 2007.

Kaczorek T. (2007d). Reachability and controllability to zero tests for standard and positive fractional discrete-time systems, *Submitted to Journal European Systems Analysis.*

Kaczorek T. (2007e). Reachability and controllability to zero of cone fractional linear systems, *Archives of Control Sciences*, vol. 17, 2007, No.3, pp. 357-367.

Kaczorek T. & Busłowicz M. (2004a). Minimal realization problem for positive multivariable linear systems with delay, *Int. J. Appl. Math. Comp. Sci.*, vol. 14, No. 2, pp. 181-187.

Kaczorek T. & Busłowicz M. (2004b). Recent developments in theory of positive discrete-time linear systems with delays – stability and robust stability, *Pomiary, Automatyka, Kontrola*, No 9, pp. 9-12

Kaczorek T. & Busłowicz M. (2004c). Recent developments in theory of positive discrete-time linear systems with delays – reachability, minimum energy control and realization problem. *Pomiary, Automatyka, Kontrola*, No 9, pp. 12-15.

Kaczorek T. & Przyborowski P. (2007a). Positive continues-time linear Lyapunov systems, *Proceedings of The International Conference on Computer as a Tool EUROCON 2007*, 9-12 September, Warsaw , pp. 731-737.

Kaczorek T. & Przyborowski P. (2007b). Positive continuous-time linear time-varying Lyapunov systems, *Proceedings of The XVI International Conference on Systems Science*, 4-6 September 2007, Wroclaw – Poland , vol. I, pp. 140-149.

Kaczorek T. & Przyborowski P. (2007c). Continuous-time linear Lyapunov cone-systems, *Proceedings of The 13th IEEE IFAC International Conference on Methods and Models in Automation and Robotics*, 27 - 30 August 2007, Szczecin – Poland, pp. 225-229.

Kaczorek T. & Przyborowski P. (2007d). Positive discrete-time linear Lyapunov systems with delays, *Proceedings of The International Workshop "Computational Problems of Electrical Engineering* September 14th-16th, 2007, Wilkasy, Poland, *Electrical Review (Przegląd Elektrotechniczny)*, 2k/2007, pp. 12-15.

Kaczorek T. & Przyborowski P. (2007e). Positive linear Lyapunov systems, *FNA-ANS International Journal - Problems Of Nonlinear Analysis In Engineering Systems Journal, No.2(28), vol.13, 2007, pp. 35-60.*

Kaczorek T. & Przyborowski P. (2008) Reachability, controllability to zero and observability of the positive discrete-time Lyapunov systems, *Submitted to The Control and Cybernetics Journal.*

Klamka J. (1991). *Controllability of dynamical systems*, Kluwer Academic Publ. Dordrcht.

Miller K. S. & Ross B. (1993). *An Introduction to the Fractional Calculus and Fractional Differential Equations*. Willey, New York.

Moshrefi-Torbati M. & Hammond K. (1998). Physical and geometrical interpretation of fractional operators,. *J. Franklin Inst.*, Vol. 335B, no. 6, 1998, pp. 1077-1086.

Murty M.S.N. & Apparao B.V. (2005). Controllability and observability of Lyapunov systems, *Ranchi University Mathematical Journal*, vol. 32, pp. 55-65.

Nishimoto K. (1984). *Fractional Calculus*. Koriyama: Decartes Press.

Oldham K. B. & Spanier J. (1974). *The Fractional Calculus*. New York: Academic Press.

Ortigueira M. D. (1997). Fractional discrete-time linear systems, *Proceedings of the IEE-ICASSP 97*, Munich, Germany, IEEE, New York, vol. 3, 2241-2244.

Ostalczyk P. (2000). The non-integer difference of the discrete-time function and its application to the control system synthesis. *Int. J. Syst, Sci*. vol. 31, no. 12, pp. 1551-1561.

Ostalczyk P. (2004a). Fractional-Order Backward Difference Equivalent Forms Part I - Horner's Form. *Proceedings of 1-st IFAC Workshop Fractional Differentation and its Applications, FDA'04*, Enseirb, Bordeaux, France, pp. 342-347.

Ostalczyk P. (2004b). Fractional-Order Backward Difference Equivalent Forms Part II - Polynomial Form. *Proceedings of 1st IFAC Workshop Fractional Differentation and its Applications, FDA'04*, Enseirb, Bordeaux, France, pp. 348-353.

Oustaloup A. (1993). *Commande CRONE*. Paris, Hermés.

Oustaloup A. (1995). *La dérivation non entiére*. Paris: Hermés.

Podlubny I. (1999). *Fractional Differential Equations*. San Diego: Academic Press.

Podlubny I. (2002). Geometric and physical interpretation of fractional integration and fractional differentation. *Fract. Calc. Appl. Anal.* Vol. 5, no. 4, 2002, pp. 367-386.

Podlubny I., Dorcak L., Kostial I. (1997). On fractional derivatives, fractional-order systems and PIλDμ-controllers. *Proceedings of 36th IEEE Conf. Decision and Control*, San Diego, CA, 1997, pp. 4985-4990.

Przyborowski P. (2008a). Positive Fractional Discrete-time Lyapunov Systems, Archives of Control Sciences,vol.18(LIV), 2008, No. 1, pp. 5-18.

Przyborowski P. (2008b). Fractional discrete-time Lyapunov cone-systems, Electrical Review (Przegląd Elektrotechniczny), 5/2008, pp. 47-52.

Reyes-Melo M.E., Martinez-Vega J.J., Guerrero-Salazar C.A., Ortiz-Mendez U. (2004). Modelling and relaxation phenomena in organic dielectric materials. Application of differential and integral operators of fractional order. *J. Optoel. Adv. Mat.* Vol. 6, no. 3, 2004, pp. 1037-1043.

Riu D., Retiére N., Ivanes M. (2001). Turbine generator modeling by non-integer order systems. *Proceedings of IEEE Int. Electric Machines and Drives Conference, IEMDC* 2001, Cambridge, MA, 2001, pp. 185-187.

Samko S. G., Kilbas A.A., Maritchev O.I. (1993). *Fractional Integrals and Derivative. Theory and Applications*. London: Gordon&Breach.

Sierociuk D. & Dzieliński D. (2006). Fractional Kalman filter algorithm for the states, parameters and order of fractional system estimation. *Int. J. Appl. Math. Comp. Sci.*, 2006, vol. 16, no. 1, pp. 129-140.

Vinagre B. M., Monje C. A., Calderon A.J. (2002). Fractional order systems and fractional order control actions. *Lecture 3 IEEE CDC'02 TW#2: Fractiional calculus Applications in Autiomatic Control and Robotics*.

Vinagre B. M. & Feliu V. (2002). Modeling and control of dynamic system using fractional calculus: Application to electrochemical processes and flexible structures. *Proceedings of 41st IEEE Conf. Decision and Control*, Las Vegas, NV, 2002, pp. 214-239.

11

Pneumatic Fuzzy Controller Simulation vs Practical Results for Flexible Manipulator

Juan Manuel Ramos-Arreguin[1], Jesus Carlos Pedraza-Ortega[2], Efren Gorrostieta-Hurtado[2], Rene de Jesus Romero-Troncoso[3], Jose Emilio Vargas-Soto[4] and Francisco Hernandez-Hernandez[1]

[1]*Universidad Tecnológica de San Juan del Río,*
[2]*Universidad Autónoma de Querétaro,*
[3]*Universidad de Guanajuato,*
[4]*Universidad Anáhuac del Sur,*
México

1. Introduction

The flexible manipulators have many industrial applications; but most of the reported works are using electrical or hydraulic actuators. These actuators have a linear behaviour and the control is easier than pneumatic actuators; but the pneumatic position control is a highly non linear problem, due to the air compressibility behaviour and internal friction (Moore & Pu, 1993). Because of these conditions, there are certain difficulties in pneumatics cylinder control design. The main disadvantage of electrical actuators is the low power-weight rate, the high current related with its load and it is heavy. The hydraulic actuators are not ecological, needs hydraulic oil and return lines to the pump is needed. By the other hand, the pneumatic actuators are clean, economy, light, faster, have a great power-weight rate and return lines are not needed. However, pneumatic actuators are not used into flexible manipulators developed due to their highly non linear behaviour. It is important to note that research lines; such as pneumatic control, embedded systems and flexible manipulators, are used in separate way.

As a matter of fact, most of manipulators robots use electric or hydraulic actuators; however, the pneumatic actuators are being used in recent years (Ramos at al, 2006a; Ramos et al, 2006b) to control a flexible manipulator arm. This is the beginning of a project which involves the use of a pneumatic cylinder to control a flexible manipulator robot. Our first approach is to use one degree of freedom, but the main goal is to have a two degree of freedom flexible manipulator.

Several pneumatic controllers had been developed; for example, the Model Reference Adaptive Control, MRAC (Suarez & Luis, 2005); however, the pneumatic model used for the control design, have the next considerations; a lineal actuator, a lineal valve, without damping systems at the sides, ideal gas, adiabatic changes and constant viscous friction.

Other works have been focused in friction parameter identification techniques of cylinder pneumatic (Wang & Wang, 2004), dynamic modelling and simulation (Jozsef & Claude,

2003), analytic and experimental research (Henri & Hollerbach, 1998) and the development of robotic hands using cylinder pneumatics.

Flexible manipulators can be used only under two conditions: a) when the robot weight must be minimized, and b) when the collisions in the work space need to be avoided (Feliu et al, 2001). The modelling of flexible manipulators has been developed almost 35 years ago (Mirro, 1972; Whitney et al, 1974), where, almost in all cases, they used electric or hydraulic actuators, and pneumatic cylinders are discouraged due to their non linear behavior.

Pneumatic control started in 1968 with Burrows (1968), and recent works are focused mainly with adaptive control methods (Suarez & Luis, 2005; Quiles et al, 2004), some of them use a computer to implement the control (Burbano et al, 2003). Other researches are focused on mechanical system modelling using pneumatic actuators (Perez, 2003), from these kind of works, a Flexible Manipulator Model with pneumatic cylinder -called Thermo-Mechanical model- was developed, then the mechanical system is involved to give the movement for the flexible arm (Kiyama & Vargas, 2004). By other hand, electric actuators are used in the development of flexible manipulators (Feliu & Garcia, 2001), where the motor speed is considered for the control implementation along with the motor effects and the mechanical structure.

In our prototype we are using a flexible manipulator robot with a pneumatic actuator, where the damping systems in both sides and the mechanical dynamics for control are considered. The full Thermo-Mechanical model is used as a starting point, later it is simplified and the results are used for the control development. One contribution of this work is the position control of a flexible manipulator using a pneumatic actuator and a simplified Thermo-Mechanical model (Ramos et al, 2006).

The simplified Thermo-Mechanical model of pneumatic actuators allows us to predict its behavior, considering the air compressibility effects, internal friction forces, damping effects in both extremes of the cylinder, massic flow and energy conservation; also, gives us the instant pressure that depends on the rod position. From the engineering control point of view, this model let us predict the variable behavior, involved in the physical process, and can be used for control purposes.

This chapter is important, because the innovation of this work is the application of three research lines to obtain a flexible manipulator light, ecological and fast with great power-weight rate. The contribution of this chapter is the reported behaviour of the one-link flexible manipulator with pneumatic actuator with practical control results. Simulations of several controllers have been reported to learn about the pneumatic manipulator behaviour with one-link. The simulation and practical results are discussed. Later, the graphical simulation is important, because let us to obtain the control parameters in few time, and learn about the pneumatic manipulator behaviour before implementation. Finally, the control algorithm is implemented in Matlab language, and digital interfaces are implemented into field programmable gate array (FPGA), obtaining an embedded digital system with serial communication (RS232) protocol. The control algorithm implemented is a PD controller and results are compared with Fuzzy-Controller simulation results.

2. The pneumatic system

The complete system is showed in figure 1, and we call the PLANT. The output plant is θ_6, corresponding to the arm elevation. The arm movement depends of the rod displacement

and the cylinder force generated by the air pressure and the valve position, according with the figure 2.
The 5/2 electro valve is used to control the rod direction, using two proportional valves, represented by A1 and A3. The pneumatic system of the figure 2 has a mathematical model, and is called Simplified Thermo-Mechanical Model (Ramos et al., 2006).

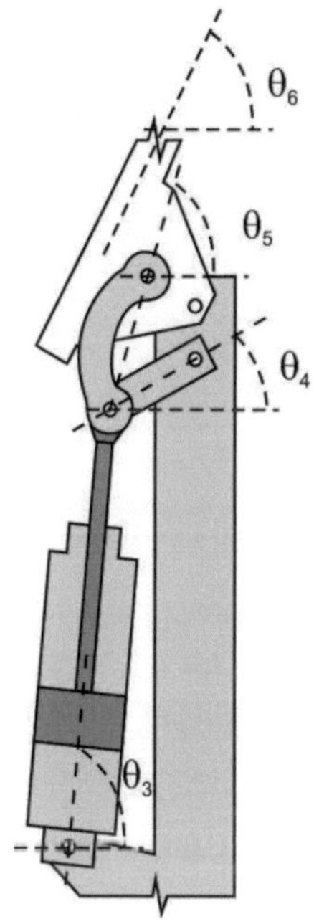

Fig. 1. Mechanical-Pneumatic system for the flexible manipulator.

The Thermo-Mechanical controller developed previously (Ramos et al., 2006) includes a PID, discrete PID and a speed change feedback proposals. In this works a fuzzy control simulation is proposed and compared with practical results of fuzzy control implementation with personal computer support, considering the pneumatic system as shown in figure 2.

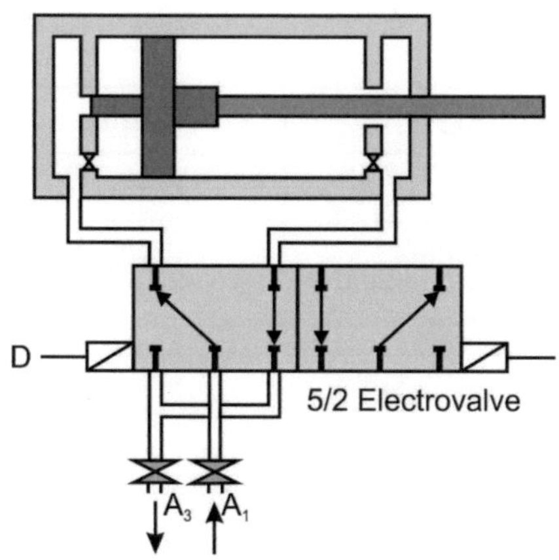

Fig. 2. Pneumatic system for the flexible arm manipulator.

3. The fuzzy algorithm

The Thermo-Mechanical Model has the next control inputs: the valve effective area air flow, eq. (1).

$$u = [A_1, A_2, A_3] \tag{1}$$

Where A_1, A_2 and A_3, are the valve area of cylinder side, rod side, and air return, respectively. However the value of A_1 and A_2 are the same.

3.1 The fuzzy algorithm proposal

Figure 3 shows the control block diagram used for the pneumatic actuator system, taking the θ angle as the mechanical system output.

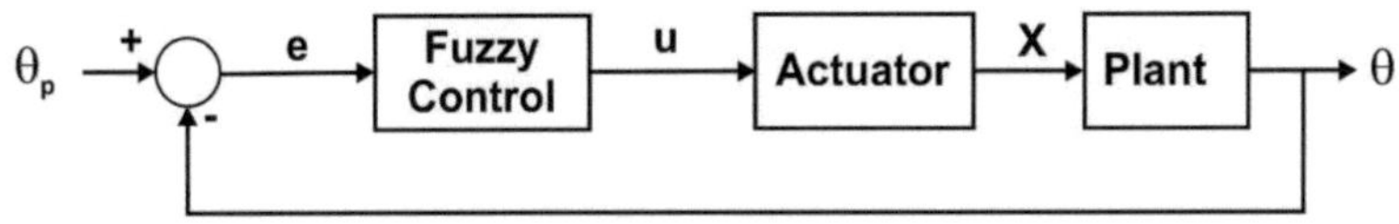

Fig. 2. The fuzzy controller proposal for pneumatic position.

Equation (2), shows the error equation; the eqs. (3) and (4) shows the proportional valve open level, obtained with a fuzzy logic method, where θ_p is the reference and θ is the actual position of the arm.

$$e = \theta_p - \theta \tag{2}$$

$$[A_1, A_3] = \text{fuzzy}(\theta_p, \theta, e) \tag{3}$$

$$A_2 = A_1 \tag{4}$$

Next, the fuzzy rules used to solve the problem are presented.

3.2 The fuzzy rules

Before the rule settings, both inputs and outputs variables were specified, and are showed in table 1.

Input	Output
Reference, θ_p	Valve 1, A_1
Angle, θ	Valve 2, A_3
Error, *e*	

Table 1. Fuzzy rules, inputs and outputs.

The membership functions used in the fuzzy process are showed in figures 3 to 5. The used membership functions for the input variables, called reference and angle are the same; and the membership functions for the output variables called valve open A_1 and A_2, are the same.

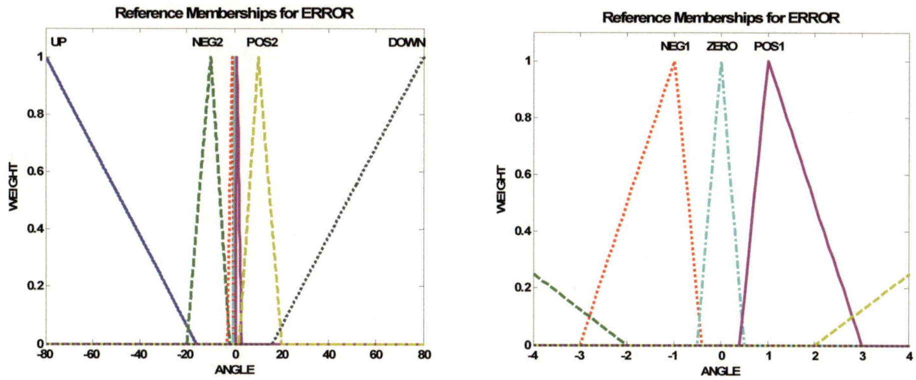

(a) (b)

Fig. 3. Membership functions for ERROR input. (a) The external part. (b) The internal interval.

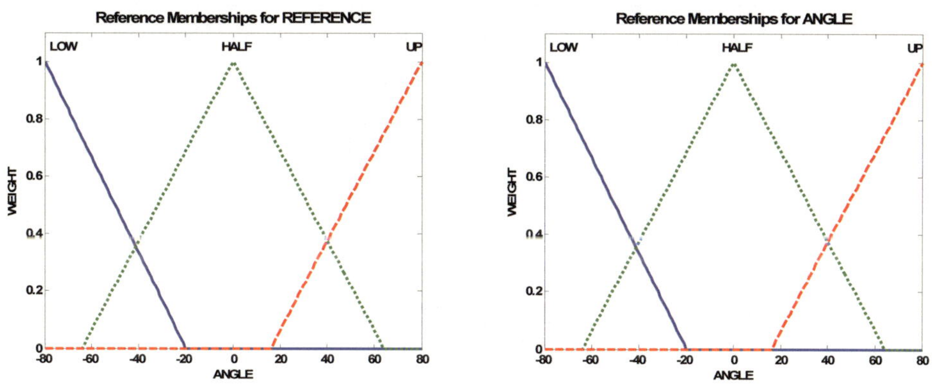

(a) (b)

Fig. 4. Memberships functions. (a) Reference input. (b) Angle input

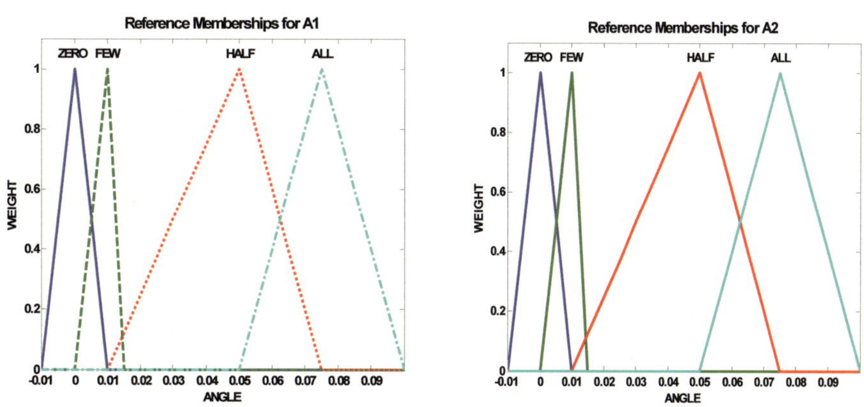

(a) (b)

Fig. 5. Membership functions for the valve values. (a) Valve 1. (b) Valve 2.

These membership functions are used to control the pneumatic actuator on the manipulator system. In the fuzzy process, the control needs 26 rules, and those rules are distributed depending of the interval of each variable. Table 5 shows the fuzzy rules used to control the pneumatic actuator position. The values for A_1 and A_3 are normalized, that is, a value of 1.0 represents a 100% open valve (completely open); a 0.5 represents a 50% open valve and 0% means the valve is completely closed.

INPUT			OUTPUT	
Reference	Angle	Error	A_1	A_2
LOW	LOW	NEG2	FEW	FEW
LOW	LOW	NEG1	FEW	ZERO
LOW	LOW	ZERO	ZERO	ZERO
LOW	LOW	ZERO	ZERO	ZERO
LOW	LOW	POS1	FEW	ZERO
LOW	LOW	POS2	FEW	FEW
LOW	HALF	DOWN	HALF	FEW
LOW	UP	DOWN	ALL	HALF
HALF	LOW	UP	HALF	FEW
HALF	HALF	UP	FEW	FEW
HALF	HALF	NEG2	FEW	FEW
HALF	HALF	NEG1	FEW	ZERO
HALF	HALF	ZERO	ZERO	ZERO
HALF	HALF	POS1	FEW	FEW
HALF	HALF	POS2	FEW	FEW
HALF	HALF	DOWN	HALF	FEW
HALF	UP	DOWN	HALF	HALF
UP	UP	UP	FEW	FEW
UP	UP	NEG1	FEW	ZERO
UP	UP	NEG2	FEW	FEW
UP	UP	ZERO	ZERO	ZERO
UP	UP	POS1	FEW	ZERO
UP	UP	POS2	FEW	FEW
UP	HALF	UP	HALF	HALF
UP	LOW	UP	HALF	HALF

Table 2. Set of fuzzy rules used in the control process.

3.3 Experimental description

Figure 6 shows a functionally block diagram of the system. The ADC is a 12-bit ADS7841 device, with a synchronous serial interface communication, 4-channel and up to 200 KHz conversion rate. The DAC is a 12-bit DAC7624 device, with quad voltage output, parallel input data and 10 μs of settling time. Both DAC and ADC are manufactured by Texas Instruments. The DAC is used to control the proportional valve, and the ADC is used to read the flexible arm position with a 10KΩ resistive sensor, which output value has an interval of 0 to 2 V. Finally, an FPGA is used to implement the digital interfaces with the personal computer, and the PD FPGA based controller.

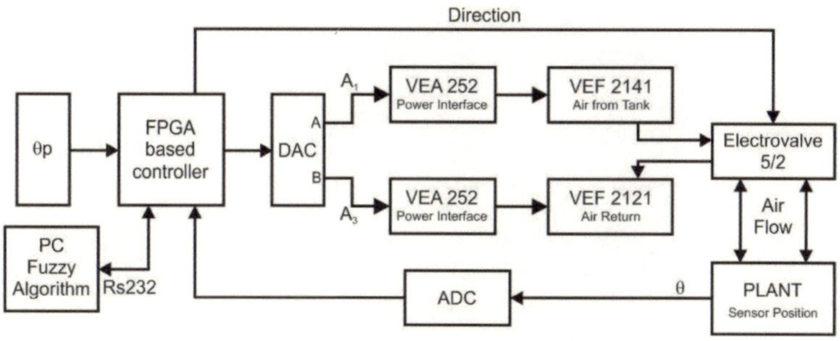

Fig. 6. Control block diagram for single-link flexible manipulator with pneumatic actuator.

Figure 7 shows a block diagram of hardware description to be implemented into FPGA, such as DAC driver, ADC driver, 50 ms sample time generator, communication protocol controller (RS232 driver), a register to load the DAC input (Register) and the finite state machine to synchronize each module (FSM control).

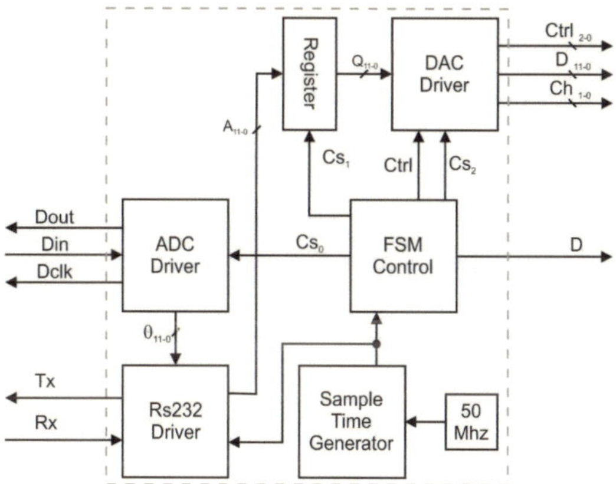

Fig. 7. Hardware description for FPGA block diagram.

The FPGA is used to implement the digital interface to control the flexible manipulator robot prototype that is shown in figure 8. Figure 9 shows the hardware used to control the flexible manipulator development.

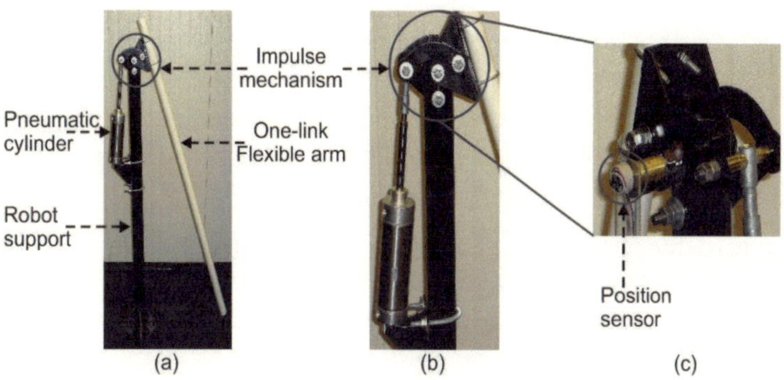

Fig. 8. Flexible manipulator robot prototype. (a) General view. (b) Impulse mechanism. (c) Position sensor.

Fig. 9. Hardware used for flexible manipulator control.

VEA252 power board must be supplied with 24 V dc and the control signal should have ground isolation. For that, an HCNR200 device, manufactured by Hewlett Packard, is used.

4. Results

To test the behavior of the system, a set points vector was used, as shows the eq. (2).

$$\theta_P = [8, 40, 70, 95] \tag{2}$$

Figure 10 shows the fuzzy control simulation results, in comparison with practical results. The values for open valve are small, due to the air pressure; if the valve open are high, the actuator goes up too fast and arrive to the top in less than one second; in simulation way, the maximum value for the valves was established in 10%. This result was compared with practical results of the Fuzzy control.

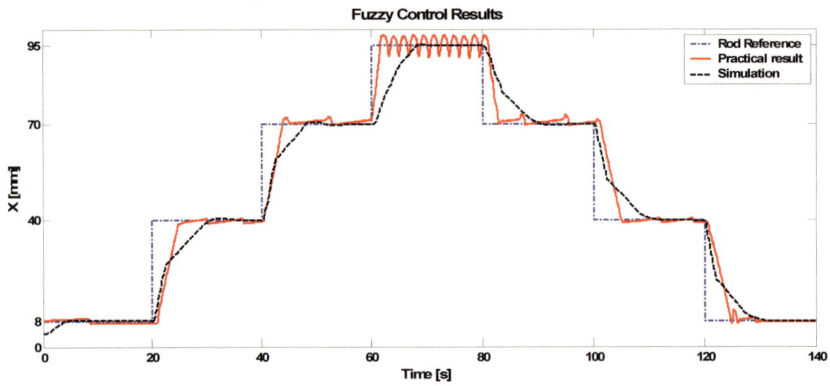

Fig. 10. Fuzzy control behavior of the flexible arm.

The pneumatic actuator is used to generate a flexible manipulator arm displacement in radial way. To control the air flow through the cylinder, a fuzzy logic algorithm was implemented. In figure 10, the system response at the end of cylinder, must be improved. That behaviour is due to the gravity influence on the arm, the valves response and mechanical structure. The behaviour of figure 10 shows several step responses, and speed profile must be developed to obtain better results.

5. Conclusions and future work

The pneumatic actuator is used for the arm position, and to control the air flow through the cylinder, a fuzzy logic algorithm was tested in simulation and practical process, with satisfactory results. The Fuzzy control works only with the percent of valve open, to limit the air flow from the compressor trough the cylinder chambers. The values for A1 and A2 are the same, but different for A_3. Actually A_3 must be small than A1 to get a better system response. In this case, we can see that a single Fuzzy Logic control is not enough to get a soft behaviour of the system, and a PID algorithm must be used.
The system has been tested using several step functions, but a speed profile developing is necessary to improve the system response.
The innovation of this work is the application of artificial intelligence control for one-link flexible arm position, with pneumatic cylinder, instead of electrical or hydraulic actuator. The contribution is the base of the knowledge about flexible manipulators with pneumatic actuator and fuzzy logic application.
As future work, is considering the use of reference frame, neuronal networks and maybe a combination of those controllers. By other hand, a speed profile should be developed.

9. References

Moore P. y J. Pu; Progression of servo pneumatics toward advanced applications; Fluid Power Circuit, Component and System Design; K. Edge and C. Burrows, Eds. Boldock, U. K.: Research Studies Press; pages 347 to 365; 1993.

Ramos, J.M.; Gorrostieta, E.; Vargas, E.; Pedraza, J.C.; Romero, R.J.; Piñeiro, B. Pneumatic cylinder control for a flexible manipulator robot. 12th IEEE International Conference on Methods and Model in Automation and Robotics, Miedzyzdroje, Poland, 28 - 31 August 2006a; ISBN 978-83-60140-88-8.

Ramos, J.M.; Vargas, E.; Gorrostieta, E.; Romero, R.J.; Pedraza, J.C. Pneumatic Cylinder Control PID for Manipulator Robot; 2006 International Conference on Dynamics, Instrumentation and Control; Queretaro, México, August 13-16 2006b.

Suarez, L.; Luis, S. Estrategias de Control Adaptable para el posicionamiento continuo de Cilindros Neumáticos. XI Convencion Informatica 2005; La Habana, Cuba; ISBN 959-7164-87-6; 2005.

Wang, J.; Wang, J. D. Identification of Pneumatic Cylinder Friction Parameters using Genetic Algorithms. IEEE Transactions on Mechatronics; vol. 9, no. 1; pages 100 to 107; 2004.

Jozsef, K.; Claude, J. Dynamics Modelling and Simulation of Constrained Robotic System. EEE/ASME Transactions on Mechatronics; vol. 8, no. 2; pages 165 to 177; 2003.

Henri, P.; Hollerbach, J.M. An Analytical and Experimental Investigation of a Jet Pipe controlled electro-pneumatic Actuator. IEEE Transactions on Robotics and Automation; vol. 14, no. 4; pages 601 to 611; 1998.

Feliu, V.; García, A.; Somolinos, J.A. Gauge-Based Tip Position Control of a New Three - Degree-Freedom Flexible Robot. The International Journal of Robotics Research; vol. 20, no. 8; pp. 660-675; August 2001.

Mirro, J.; Automatic Feedback Control of a Vibrating Flexible Beam; MS Thesis, Department of Mechanical Engineering, Massachussets Institute of Technology, August 1972.

Whitney, D.E.; Book, W.J.; Lynch, P.M. Design and Control Considerations for Industrial and Space Manipulators; Proceedings of the Joint Automatic Control Conference, June, 1974.

Burrows, C.R.; Webb C.R. Simulation of an On - Off Pneumatic Servomechanism; Automatic Control Group, 1968.

Quiles, E.; Morant, F.; García, E.; Blasco, R.; Correcher, A. Control Adaptivo de un Sistema de Control Neumatico. 3ra. Conferencia Iberoamericana en Sistemas, Cibernetica e Informatica CISCI, Julio 2004.

Burbano, J.C.; Bacca, G.; Hoyos, M. Control de Posicion y Presion para Manipulador Neumatico a traves de PC. Scientia Et Tecnica, UTP; vol. 21, pp. 71-76; 2003.

Pérez, J. Analisis Dinamico de Mecanismos Accionados Neumaticamente. Ph.D. Thesis; Facultad de Ingeniería Mecanica, Electrica y Electronica, FIMEE; Salamanca, Gto.; March 2003.

Kiyama, F.; Vargas, J. Modelo Termo-Mecanico para un Manipulador tipo Dielectrico. Informacion Tecnologica; vol. 15; no 5; pages 23 to 31; 2004; ISSN 0716-8756.

Feliu, V.; Garcia, A. Gauge-Based tip Position Control of a New Three Degree of Freedom Flexible Robot. The International Journal of Robotics Research; vol. 20, no. 8; pp. 660-675; 2001.

Ramos, J.M.; Vargas, J.E.; Gorrostieta, E.; Pedraza, J.C. Nuevo Modelo Polinomial del Comportamiento de un Cilindro Neumatico. Revista Internacional Informacion Tecnologica; vol. 17, no. 3; ISSN 0716-8756; 2006.

12

Nonlinear Control Strategies for Bioprocesses: Sliding Mode Control versus Vibrational Control

Dan Selişteanu, Emil Petre, Dorin Popescu and Eugen Bobaşu
Department of Automation and Mechatronics, University of Craiova
Romania

1. Introduction

Nowadays, the domain of biotechnology is characterized by rapid changes in terms of novelty and by highly complex processes that require advanced procedures for design, operation and control. From the engineering point of view, the control of bioprocesses poses a number of challenging problems. These problems arise from the presence of living organisms, the high complexity of the interactions between the micro-organisms, as well as the high complexity of the metabolic reactions. Moreover, for monitoring and control applications, only a few measurements are available, either because the measuring devices do not exist or are too expensive, or because the available devices do not give reliable measurements. Therefore, we can deduce that the main difficulties arising in the control of bioprocesses arrive from two main sources: the process complexity and the difficulty to have reliable measurements of bioprocess variables (Bastin & Dochain, 1990; Selişteanu et al., 2007a).

In order to overcome these difficulties several strategies for the control of bioprocesses were developed, such as adaptive approach (Bastin & Dochain, 1990; Mailleret et al., 2004), vibrational control (Selişteanu & Petre, 2001; Selişteanu et al., 2007a), sliding mode control (Selişteanu et al., 2007a; Selişteanu et al., 2007b), fuzzy and neural strategies etc.

Sliding mode control (SMC) has been widely accepted as an efficient method for control of uncertain nonlinear systems (Utkin, 1992; Slotine & Li, 1991; Edwards & Spurgeon, 1998). The classical applications of SMC (such as robotics, electrical machines etc.) were extended to SMC of chemical processes (Sira-Ramirez & Llanes-Santiago, 1994) and to SMC of bioprocesses (Selişteanu et al., 2007a; Selişteanu et al., 2007b). The well-known advantages of the SMC are the robustness, controller order reduction, disturbance rejection, and insensitivity to parameter variations. The main disadvantage of the SMC strategies used in real applications remains the chattering phenomenon, even if some techniques of chattering reduction were developed (Slotine & Li, 1991; Edwards & Spurgeon, 1998).

Vibrational control (VC) is a non-classical open-loop control method proposed by Bellman, Bentsman and Meerkov (Meerkov, 1980; Bellman et al., 1986a; Bellman et al., 1986b). Applications of the vibrational control theory can be found for: stabilization of plasma, lasers, chemical reactors, biotechnological processes (Selişteanu et al., 2007a) etc. The VC technique is applied by oscillating an accessible system component at low amplitude and high frequency. Therefore, this technique can be considered, like the SMC, a form of high-frequency control (obviously high-frequency relative to the natural frequency of the system).

But, unlike the SMC, the amplitude and the frequency of the control input are constants and independent of the state of the system, so this technique is a form of open-loop control.
In this chapter, which is an extended work of (Selişteanu et al., 2007a), two nonlinear control strategies for bioprocesses are designed: a feedback SMC law and a vibrational control strategy. First, a class of bioprocesses is briefly analysed and a nonlinear prototype model is presented in detail. Then, the design of a feedback control law for a prototype bioprocess is developed. The design is based on a combination between exactly linearization, sliding mode control, and generalized observability canonical forms. In order to implement this SMC law, asymptotic observers (Bastin & Dochain, 1990) will be used for the reconstruction of unmeasured states. The next paragraph deals with the presentation of most important results of vibrational control theory. Also, a VC strategy for a continuous bioprocess is developed. The existence and the choice of stabilizing vibrations, which ensure the desired behaviour of the bioprocess are analysed. Some simulations results, comparisons of the proposed nonlinear control strategies, and final remarks are also presented.

2. Nonlinear dynamical models of the bioprocesses

2.1 The dynamical model of a class of bioprocesses

In bioindustry, the bioprocesses take place in biological reactors, also called bioreactors. A bioreactor is a tank in which several biological reactions occur simultaneously in a liquid medium (Bastin & Dochain, 1990). These reactions can be classified into two classes: microbial growth reactions and enzyme-catalysed reactions. The bioreactors can operate in three modes: the continuous mode, the fed-batch mode and the batch mode. For example, a Fed-Batch Bioreactor (FBB) initially contains a small amount of substrates and micro-organisms and is progressively filled with the influent substrates. When the FBB is full the content is harvested. By contrast, in a Continuous Stirred Tank Bioreactor (CSTB) the substrates are fed to the bioreactor continuously and an effluent stream is continuously withdrawn from the reactor such that the culture volume is constant.
In practice, the bioprocess control is often limited to regulation of the temperature and pH at some constant values favourable to the microbial growth.
There is however no doubt that the control of the biological state variables (biomass, substrates, products) can help to increase the bioprocess performance. In order to develop and apply advanced control strategies for these biological variables, obviously is necessary to obtain a useful dynamical model. The modelling of bioprocesses is a difficult task; however, using the mass balance of the components inside the bioreactor and obeying some modelling rules, a dynamical state-space model can be obtained (Bastin & Dochain, 1990; Bastin, 1991).
A process carried out in a bioreactor can be defined as a set of m biochemical reactions involving n components (with $n \geq m$). The reaction scheme of a bioprocess (the reaction network) contains n components and m reactions. The concentrations of the physical components will be denoted with the notations $\xi_i, i = \overline{1,n}$. The reaction rates will be denoted as $\varphi_j, j = \overline{1,m}$. The evolution of each component is described by the differential equation (Bastin & Dochain, 1990):

$$\dot{\xi}_i = \sum_{j \sim i} (\pm) k_{ij} \varphi_j - D\xi_i + F_i - Q_i \tag{1}$$

where $\dot{\xi}_i$ is the time derivative of the concentration ξ_i (g/l) and the notation $j \sim i$ indicates that the sum is done in accordance with the reactions j that involve the component i. The positive and dimensionless constants k_{ij} are yield coefficients. The sign of the first term of (1) is given by the type of the component ξ_i : plus (+) when the component is a reaction product and minus (-) otherwise. D is the specific volumetric rate (h^{-1}), usually called dilution rate. F_i represents the rate of supply of the component ξ_i (external substrate) to the bioreactor per unit of volume (g/lh). When this component is not an external substrate, then $F_i \equiv 0$. Q_i represents the rate of removal of the component ξ_i from the bioreactor in gazeous form per unit of volume (g/lh).

In order to obtain a dynamical state-space model of the entire bioprocess, we denote $\xi = [\xi_1 \;\; \xi_2 \;\; \cdots \;\; \xi_n]^T$, where ξ is the n-dimensional vector of the instantaneous concentrations, also is the state of the model. The vector of the reaction rates (the reaction kinetics) is denoted $\varphi = [\varphi_1 \;\; \varphi_2 \;\; \cdots \;\; \varphi_m]^T$. The reaction rate vector is m-dimensional. Usually, a reaction rate is represented by a non-negative rational function of the state ξ. The yield coefficients can be written as the $(n \times m)$ - dimensional yield matrix $K = [K_{ij}]$, $i = \overline{1,n}; j = \overline{1,m}$, where $K_{ij} = (\pm)k_{ij}$ if $j \sim i$ and 0 otherwise. Next, we introduce the notations $F = [F_1 \;\; F_2 \;\; \cdots \;\; F_n]^T$, $Q = [Q_1 \;\; Q_2 \;\; \cdots \;\; Q_n]^T$, where F is the vector of rates of supply and Q is the vector of rates of removal of the components in gazeous form.

From (1), with the above notations, the global dynamics can be represented by the dynamical state-space model (Bastin & Dochain, 1990):

$$\dot{\xi} = K \cdot \varphi(\xi) - D\xi + F - Q \tag{2}$$

This model describes in fact the behaviour of an entire class of biotechnological processes and is referred to as the general dynamical state-space model of this class of bioprocesses (Bastin & Dochain, 1990; Bastin, 1991). In (2), the term $K \cdot \varphi(\xi)$ is in fact the rate of consumption and/or production of the components in the reactor, i.e. the reaction kinetics. The term $-D\xi + F - Q$ represents the exchange with the environment, i.e. the dynamics of the component transportation through the bioreactor. The strongly nonlinear character of the model (2) is given by the reaction kinetics. In many situations, the yield coefficients, the structure and the parameters of the reaction rates are partially known or unknown.

Remark 1. In a FBB, the term $D\xi_i$ represents the dilution of a component due to the increase in volume. In this case D is the specific rate of volume increase ($\dot{V} = D \cdot V$, with V the liquid volume in the FBB and $\dot{V}$ its time derivative). In a CSTB, $D\xi_i$ represents the rate of removal of a component in liquid form (in a CSTB, $\dot{V} = 0$).

Often in practice, the bioprocess control goal is to regulate a scalar output y, which can be defined as a linear combination of the state variables. Usually, this control objective is reached using as a control input one of the components of F, i.e. a rate of supply of an external substrate: $u = F_i$. Consequently, the vector F can be written as $F = b \cdot u + \widetilde{F}$, with

$b=[b_1 \; b_2 \; \cdots \; b_n]^T$; $b_i=1, \; b_j=0, \; i \neq j$; and $\widetilde{F}=[\widetilde{F}_1 \; \widetilde{F}_2 \; \cdots \; \widetilde{F}_n]^T$; $\widetilde{F}_i=0, \; \widetilde{F}_j=F_j, j \neq i$.
Then, the model (2) can be rewritten as

$$\begin{aligned} \dot{\xi} &= K \cdot \varphi(\xi) - D\xi + \widetilde{F} - Q + b \cdot u = f(\xi) + b \cdot u \\ y &= h(\xi) \end{aligned} \tag{3}$$

2.2 The model prototype of a continuous bioprocess

A model prototype of a continuous bioprocess that takes place inside a CSTB is described by the following nonlinear system (Bastin & Dochain, 1990; Dochain & Vanrolleghem, 2001):

$$\frac{d\xi_1}{dt} = \mu(\xi_1, \xi_2) \cdot \xi_1 - D \cdot \xi_1 \tag{4}$$

$$\frac{d\xi_2}{dt} = -k_1 \mu(\xi_1, \xi_2) \cdot \xi_1 - D \cdot \xi_2 + D \cdot S_{in} \tag{5}$$

where ξ_1, ξ_2 represent the biomass and the limiting substrate concentrations (g/l). S_{in} is the influent substrate concentration, and D is the dilution rate (h^{-1}). In (4), (5) μ is the specific growth rate and $k_1 > 0$ the yield coefficient.

The bioprocess (4), (5) is in fact a fermentation process, which usually occurs in a bioreactor. A compact representation of (4), (5) is:

$$\dot{\xi} = f(\xi) \tag{6}$$

with $f(\xi) = [f_1(\xi_1, \xi_2), \; f_2(\xi_1, \xi_2)]^T$ and $\xi = [\xi_1 \; \xi_2]^T$ the state vector.

The equilibrium states of (4), (5) are of two types:

E1. Wash-out state, defined by:

$$\xi_s = [\xi_{s1} \; \xi_{s2}]^T = [0 \quad S_{in}]^T \tag{7}$$

This equilibrium is a state when the bacterial life has disappeared; therefore, the wash-out state has not practical interest.

E2. Operational equilibrium states, implicitly defined by:

$$\begin{cases} \mu(\xi_{s1}, \xi_{s2}) = D \\ k_1 \mu(\xi_{s1}, \xi_{s2}) \xi_{s1} + D\xi_{s2} = DS_{in} \end{cases} \tag{8}$$

These equilibria can be attractive or repulsive depending on the particular form of $\mu(\xi_1, \xi_2)$. Only these equilibria have a practical interest. Let's assume that the specific growth rate is of the form:

$$\mu(\xi_1, \xi_2) = \mu(\xi_2) = \mu_0 \frac{\xi_2}{K_M + \xi_2 + \xi_2^2 / K_i} \tag{9}$$

This is the Haldane kinetic model of the specific growth rate (Bastin & Dochain, 1990), where K_M is the Michaelis-Menten constant, K_i the inhibition constant and μ_0 the maxim specific growth rate.

Let's analyse the stability of the equilibria (E2) for given constant inputs D and S_{in}. The linear approximation of the system (4), (5) around the equilibrium point (E2) is:

$$\frac{d}{dt}(\xi - \xi_s) = A(\xi_s)(\xi - \xi_s) \tag{10}$$

where $A(\xi_s)$ is the matrix of the linearized system, which takes for the specific rate (6) the form:

$$A(\xi_s) = A(\xi_{s1}, \xi_{s2}) \stackrel{\Delta}{=} J(\xi_{s1}, \xi_{s2}) = \begin{bmatrix} \frac{\partial f_1}{\partial \xi_1} & \frac{\partial f_1}{\partial \xi_2} \\ \frac{\partial f_2}{\partial \xi_1} & \frac{\partial f_2}{\partial \xi_2} \end{bmatrix}_{\xi=\xi_s} = \begin{bmatrix} 0 & \rho \\ -k_1\mu(\xi_{s2}) & -k_1\rho - D \end{bmatrix} \tag{11}$$

where $\rho \stackrel{N}{=} \xi_{s1} \left[\frac{d\mu(\xi_2)}{d\xi_2}\right]_{\xi_2=\xi_{s2}} = \xi_{s1}\mu_0 \frac{K_M - \xi_{s2}^2 / K_i}{\left(K_M + \xi_{s2} + \xi_{s2}^2 / K_i\right)^2}$.

The eigenvalues of the matrix (11) are $\lambda_1 = -D < 0$ (D is positive) and $\lambda_2 = -k_1\rho$. The equilibrium state is stable only if $\rho > 0$, i.e.:

$$0 \le \xi_{s2} < \sqrt{K_M K_i} = \max_{\xi_2}\{\mu(\xi_2)\} \tag{12}$$

Two possibilities appear for the equilibria (E2):
a) - if the condition (12) is achieved:

$$\xi_{s1} = \frac{S_{in} - \xi_{s2}}{k_1} \stackrel{N}{=} \xi_{s1,1} = \frac{S_{in} - \xi_{s2,1}}{k_1}; \qquad \xi_{s2} \stackrel{N}{=} \xi_{s2,1} \tag{13}$$

b) - or contrarily:

$$\xi_{s1} = \frac{S_{in} - \xi_{s2}}{k_1} \stackrel{N}{=} \xi_{s1,2} = \frac{S_{in} - \xi_{s2,2}}{k_1}; \qquad \xi_{s2} \stackrel{N}{=} \xi_{s2,2} \tag{14}$$

The case a) corresponds to a stable equilibrium point (stable node) with $\lambda_1 < 0, \lambda_2 < 0$. The case b) leads to a saddle type for the equilibria (E2): $\lambda_1 < 0, \lambda_2 > 0$. The phase plane of the system (4), (5) for the values of the parameters: $\mu_0 = 6h^{-1}$, $K_M = 10g/l$, $K_i = 100g/l$, $D = 3.6h^{-1}$, $k_1 = 1$, $S_{in} = 100g/l$ and for different initial conditions is represented in Fig. 1. From this picture it can be seen that when the substrate inhibition appears, the process can exhibit unstable or, maybe worse, the evolution leads to wash-out steady-state, for which the microbial life has disappeared and the reactor is stopped. In these situations, the bioprocess requires control to stabilize the CSTB. Moreover, in many cases, the stable equilibrium point corresponding to a) is not technological operable (requires a big initial amount of biomass).

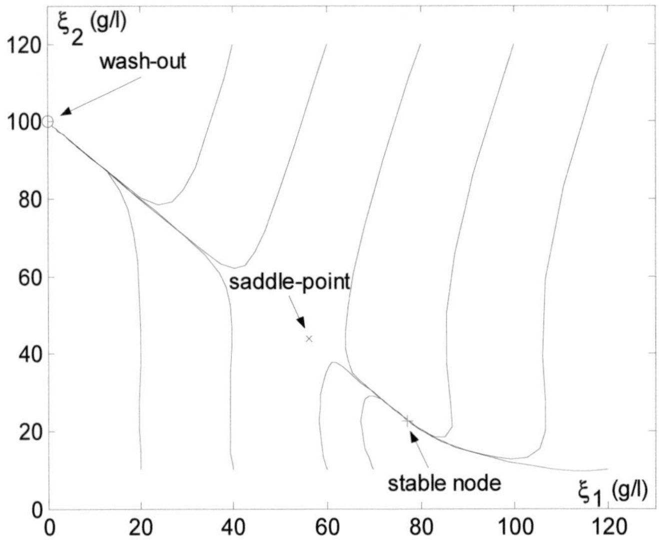

Fig. 1. Phase portrait of the continuous bioprocess – state trajectories and equilibrium points

The model (4), (5) is a prototype model for some bioprocesses, as the activated sludge bioprocess, anaerobic digestion process for wastewater treatment etc. (Dochain & Vanrolleghem, 2001) and for other biotechnological applications. For instance, the control objective for the waste treatment processes is to control the concentration of some pollutants at a constant (low) level. Various control strategies were developed for this prototype bioprocess: exact linearizing strategy (Bastin & Dochain, 1990), adaptive control (Bastin & Dochain, 1990; Bastin, 1991; Dochain & Vanrolleghem, 2001) and so on. The exact linearizing control does not work when the kinetics are imprecisely known because the exact cancellation of the nonlinearities would not be possible. The performance of adaptive control decreases when large and abrupt changes occur in bioprocess parameters.

Viable alternatives are the sliding mode control (Fossas et al., 2001; Stanchev, 2003; Tham et al., 2003) and adaptive sliding mode control strategies (Selişteanu & Petre, 2005; Selişteanu et al., 2007b) with good performance in the presence of parameter uncertainties and external disturbances. Another possible strategy is the open-loop vibrational control (Selişteanu et al., 2007a); in this situation, on-line measurements of the state variables are no more needed.

3. Sliding mode control design

3.1 Linearizing sliding mode control law design

In order to implement a viable SMC strategy for the continuous bioprocess, the control goal is to design a discontinuous feedback law by using the exactly linearization of the system (Isidori, 1995) and by imposing a SMC action that stabilize the output. The control strategy is obtained by repeated output differentiation and by imposing a discontinuous feedback controller, which drives the output of the system to satisfy a stable linearized dynamics; for details see (Sira-Ramirez, 1992; Sira-Ramirez & Llanes-Santiago, 1994; Selişteanu et al., 2007b). Let's define the output of the system (4), (5) as

$$y = h(\xi) = \xi_1 - C \tag{15}$$

The control variable is the rate of supply of substrate to the reactor per unit of volume, i.e. $u = D \cdot S_{in}$ (g/lh). The control goal for the biological process (4), (5), (15) is to regulate the concentration error y towards zero so that the biomass concentration value ξ_1 converges to a prescribed setpoint value specified by the constant C. It is assumed that the control variable u is naturally bounded in the interval $[0, U_{max}]$. This SMC strategy can be applied for the nonlinear bioprocess (4), (5), (15) if the so-called observability matrix

$$\mathbf{O} = \begin{bmatrix} \frac{\partial h(\xi)}{\partial \xi} & \frac{\partial h^{(1)}(\xi)}{\partial \xi} \end{bmatrix}^T \tag{16}$$

is full rank (Fliess, 1990; Sira-Ramirez, 1992; Sira-Ramirez & Llanes-Santiago, 1994). It is easy to verify, after some straightforward calculations, that the rank of the observability matrix is equal to 2 (full rank), except on line $\xi_1 = 0$, which is devoid of practical significance (ξ_1 represents the biomass concentration; so $\xi_1 = 0$ means no micro-organisms and the life in the bioreactor is stopped).

Assume that $u = u_s$, $\xi = \xi_s(u_s)$ expresses a constant equilibrium point for the system (4), (5), (15) such that $h(\xi_s(u_s))$ is zero. The stability nature of an equilibrium point $u = u_s$ of the zero dynamics (Sira-Ramirez, 1992; Sira-Ramirez & Llanes-Santiago, 1994) determines the minimum or non-minimum phase character of the system (4), (5), (15). Next, the constant equilibrium point of this system is represented as $(\xi_s(u_s), u_s, y_s = 0) = (\xi_s(u_s), u_s, 0)$. A stable constant equilibrium point for (4), (5), (15) is given by (13), if the condition (12) is achieved. In this case, the system is locally minimum phase around this equilibrium point (i.e. the zero dynamics is locally asymptotically stable to the equilibrium point).

The following input-dependent state coordinate transformation:

$$\begin{aligned} z_1 &= y = \xi_1 - C \\ z_2 &= \dot{y} = \dot{\xi}_1 = \mu(\xi_2)\xi_1 - D\xi_1 \end{aligned} \tag{17}$$

allows one to obtain an observability canonical form for the system (4), (5), (15) (for details about the generalized observability canonical forms see (Fliess, 1990)). The inverse of this transformation is obtained by solving (17) with respect to ξ_1 and ξ_2. One can obtain also the transformed system equations, which are of the form:

$$\begin{aligned} \dot{z}_1 &= z_2 \\ \dot{z}_2 &= \psi(z_1, z_2, u) \\ y &= z_1 \end{aligned} \tag{18}$$

where ψ is a nonlinear function of state variables and of the input.

For the design of SMC, consider now the auxiliary output function (the sliding surface):

$$\sigma = z_2 + \gamma_1 z_1 = \dot{y} + \gamma_1 y = \mu(\xi_2)\xi_1 - D\xi_1 + \gamma_1(\xi_1 - C) \tag{19}$$

If (19) is zeroed by means of a discontinuous control strategy, then it follows that the time response of the controlled output y is ideally governed by an asymptotically stable linear time-invariant dynamics $\dot{z}_1 = -\gamma_1 z_1$ (for the design parameter $\gamma_1 > 0$).

Proposition 1. The following discontinuous feedback control law (sliding mode control law):

$$u(t) = k_1\mu(\xi_2)\xi_1 + D\xi_2 - \frac{(\mu(\xi_2) - D)^2}{\mu'(\xi_2)} - \frac{1}{\mu'(\xi_2)\xi_1} \cdot [\gamma_1(\mu(\xi_2) - D)\xi_1 + k \cdot \mathrm{sgn}(\sigma)] \tag{20}$$

imposes to the output of the system (18), in finite time, a linearized dynamics of the form $\dot{y} + \gamma_1 y = 0$. In (20), k is a strictly positive scalar, "sgn" stand for the signum function, $\gamma_1 > 0$, and $\mu'(\xi_2) \overset{\Delta}{=} \frac{d\mu(\xi_2)}{d\xi_2}$.

Proof. The proof is immediate considering the auxiliary output function (19) and imposing on this auxiliary output the discontinuous dynamics $\dot{\sigma} = -k \cdot \mathrm{sgn}(\sigma)$, which leads to the implicit discontinuous equation $\psi(z_1, z_2, u) = -\gamma_1 z_2 - k\,\mathrm{sgn}(\sigma)$. Then the control law (20) is easily obtained using the original state coordinates. This discontinuous system globally exhibits a sliding regime on $\sigma = 0$. Any trajectory starting on the value $\sigma = \sigma(0)$ at time 0 reaches the condition in finite time T given by $T = k^{-1}|\sigma(0)|$ (see (Utkin, 1978; Sira-Ramirez & Llanes-Santiago, 1994)).

The basic idea for the design of the SMC law (20) is to use the auxiliary output $\sigma = 0$ as a sliding surface, and so to force the system trajectories to remain on this surface.

Remark 2. In the case of a static SMC law, the inherent chattering can be reduced using various continuous approximations of the SMC (Slotine & Li, 1991; Edwards & Spurgeon, 1998; Bartoszewicz, 2000), which are designed to make a boundary layer attractive such that the trajectories started off the boundary layer will be attracted to this region in a finite time. A possibility is to use the so-called sampled SMC (Sira-Ramirez & Llanes-Santiago, 1994). To reach a good compromise between small chattering and tracking precision a range of other compensation strategies have been proposed, such as integral sliding mode control, sliding mode control with time-varying boundary layers (Slotine & Li, 1991), fuzzy sliding mode control (Palm et al., 1997) and complementary SMC (Su & Wang, 2002).

3.2 Design of state observers for bioprocesses

The SMC law presented in the previous paragraph can be implemented only if the measurements of state variables are available on-line. However, in many practical applications, only a part of the concentrations of the components involved are measurable on-line. In such cases, an alternative is the use of state observers. An important difficulty when applying state observers to bioprocesses is related to the uncertainty of models describing their dynamics. Presently two classes of state observers for bioprocesses can be found in the literature (Bastin & Dochain, 1990; Bastin, 1991; Dochain & Vanrolleghem, 2001).

The first class of observers (including classical observers like Luenberger and Kalman observers, nonlinear observers) are based on a perfect knowledge of the model structure. A

disadvantage of this class is that the uncertainty in the model parameters can generate possibly large bias in the estimation of the unmeasured states. A second class of observers, called asymptotic observers, is based on the idea that the uncertainty in process models lies in the process kinetics models. The design of these observers is based on the mass and energy balances without the knowledge of the process kinetics being necessary. The potential drawback of the asymptotic observers is that the rate of estimation convergence depends on the operating conditions (Selişteanu et al., 2007b).
A general class of observers for bioprocesses of the form (2) is (Bastin & Dochain, 1990):

$$\dot{\hat{\xi}} = K\varphi(\hat{\xi}) - D\cdot\hat{\xi} + F - Q + \Omega(\hat{\xi})\cdot(\zeta_1 - \hat{\zeta}_1) \tag{21}$$

where $\hat{\xi}$ is the estimated state vector, $\Omega(\hat{\xi})$ is a gain matrix, and ζ_1 is the vector of measurable state variables: $\zeta_1 = L\cdot\xi$, L being a selection matrix. The design of observer lies in the choice of the gain matrix.
If in the model (2) the reaction rate $\varphi(\xi)$ is completely known, it is possible to design the so-called exponential observers, such as extended Luenberger or Kalman observers based on the general form (21). But the reaction rates are usually incompletely known (uncertainties of parametric or structural nature); therefore it is not possible to design and to use such observers. A possibility is to use an asymptotic observer (Bastin & Dochain, 1990; Bastin, 1991; Dochain & Vanrolleghem, 2001), which can be designed even without knowledge of kinetic reaction. The design of an asymptotic observer is based on some useful changes of coordinates, which lead to a submodel of (2) which is independent of the kinetics. In order to achieve the change of coordinates, a partition of the state vector ξ in two parts is considered. This partition denoted (ξ_a, ξ_b) induces partitions of the yield matrix K: (K_a, K_b), also of the rate vectors F and Q: (F_a, F_b), (Q_a, Q_b) accordingly. We suppose that a state partition is chosen such that the submatrix K_a is full rank and $\dim(\xi_a) = \mathrm{rank}(K_a)$ $= \mathrm{rank}(K)$. Then a linear change of coordinates can be defined as follows: $z = G\cdot\xi_a + \xi_b$, with z an auxiliary state vector and G the solution of the matrix equation $G\cdot K_a + K_b = 0$. In the new coordinates, model (2) can be rewritten as

$$\begin{aligned} \dot{\xi}_a &= K_a\varphi(\xi_a, z - G\xi_a) - D\cdot\xi_a + F_a - Q_a \\ \dot{z} &= -D\cdot z + G\cdot(F_a - Q_a) + F_b - Q_b \end{aligned} \tag{22}$$

The main achievement of the change of coordinates is that the dynamics of the auxiliary state variables z is independent of the reaction kinetics. Now z can be rewritten as a linear combination of the vectors of measured states ζ_1 and unmeasured states ζ_2:

$$z = G_1\cdot\zeta_1 + G_2\cdot\zeta_2 \tag{23}$$

with G_1 and G_2 well defined matrices. If the matrix G_2 is left invertible, the asymptotic observer equations for (2) derive from the structure of equations (22) and (23):

$$\begin{aligned} \dot{\hat{z}} &= -D\cdot\hat{z} + G\cdot(F_a - Q_a) + F_b - Q_b \\ \hat{\zeta}_2 &= G_2^{+}\cdot(\hat{z} - G_1\zeta_1) \end{aligned} \tag{24}$$

where $G_2^+ = (G_2^T G_2)^{-1} G_2^T$. The asymptotic observer is indeed independent of the kinetics. The asymptotic observer (24) has good convergence and stability performance (Bastin & Dochain, 1990; Bastin, 1991; Dochain & Vanrolleghem, 2001).

Concerning the continuous bioprocess (4), (5), (15), a possible practical situation, which can appear when the sliding mode control law (20) is implemented, is that the only measurement on-line available is the biomass concentration inside of CSTB. In this case, the unmeasured variable ξ_2 (the substrate concentration) can be estimated by using an asymptotic state observer. For that, let us define the auxiliary variable ζ as follows:

$$\zeta = k_1\xi_1 + \xi_2$$

In the new coordinates, the model (4), (5), (15) can be rewritten

$$\begin{aligned} \dot{\xi}_1 &= \mu(\zeta - k_1\xi_1)\xi_1 - D\xi_1 \\ \dot{\zeta} &= -D\zeta + u \\ y &= \xi_1 - C \end{aligned}$$

The asymptotic observer equations derive from the above model:

$$\begin{aligned} \frac{d\hat{\zeta}}{dt} &= -D\cdot\hat{\zeta} + u \\ \hat{\xi}_2 &= \hat{\zeta} - k_1\xi_1 \end{aligned} \tag{25}$$

The dynamics of the auxiliary variable ζ is independent of the reaction kinetics. The estimations of ξ_2 obtained using this asymptotic observer can be used in the sliding mode control law (20), which takes the form:

$$u(t) = k_1\mu(\hat{\xi}_2)\xi_1 + D\hat{\xi}_2 - \frac{\left(\mu(\hat{\xi}_2) - D\right)^2}{\mu'(\hat{\xi}_2)} - \frac{1}{\mu'(\hat{\xi}_2)\xi_1}\cdot\left[\gamma_1\left(\mu(\hat{\xi}_2) - D\right)\xi_1 + k\cdot \mathrm{sgn}(\sigma)\right] \tag{26}$$

4. Vibrational control design

4.1 Vibrational control theory fundaments

The general theory of vibrational control was developed by Bellman, Bentsman and Meerkov (Meerkov, 1980; Bellman et al., 1986a; Bellman et al., 1986b), who presented the criteria for vibrational stabilizability and vibrational controllability of linear and nonlinear systems. Consider a nonlinear system given by the equation:

$$\dot{x} = f(x, \alpha) \tag{27}$$

with $f:\Re^n \times \Re^m \to \Re^n$, $x \in \Re^n$ is a state and $\alpha \in \Re^m$ is a parameter, in fact a vector that contains the system parameters. Suppose that for a fixed $\alpha = \alpha_0$ the system (27) has the equilibrium $x_s = x_s(\alpha)$. Let introduce now in (27) parametric vibrations according to the law:

$$\alpha(t) = \alpha_0 + g(t) \tag{28}$$

where α_0 is a constant vector and g(t) is an almost periodic vector function with average equal to zero (APAZ vector). Then (27) becomes:

$$\dot{x} = f(x, \alpha_0 + g(t)) \tag{29}$$

Definition 1 (Bellman et al., 1986a). An equilibrium point $x_s(\alpha_0)$ of (27) is vibrationally stabilizable if for any $\delta > 0$ there exists an APAZ vector g(t) such that (29) has an asymptotically stable almost periodic solution $x^s(t)$ characterized by $\left\|\overline{x}^s - x_s(\alpha_0)\right\| < \delta$, $\overline{x}^s = \overline{x^s(t)} \overset{\Delta}{=} \lim_{T\to\infty} \frac{1}{T}\int_0^T x^s(\tau)d\tau$.

Definition 2 (Bellman et al., 1986a). An equilibrium point $x_s(\alpha_0)$ of (27) is totally vibrationally stabilizable if it is vibrationally stabilizable and in addition we have $x^s(t) = \text{const} = x_s(\alpha_0)$, $\forall t \in \Re$.

The vibrational stabilizability problem consists of finding conditions for existence of stabilizable vibrations. Meerkov has demonstrated since 1980 (Meerkov, 1980) that for linear systems, vibrational stabilizability implies total stabilizability. If the matrix A of the linear system $\dot{x} = Ax$ is a nonderogatory matrix, i.e. the minimal and characteristic polynomials coincide, a sufficient condition of v-stabilizability is $tr(A) < 0$.

Considered now a class of nonlinear systems such that (29) is represented as:

$$\dot{x}(t) = f(x, \alpha_0) + f_v(g(t), x) \tag{30}$$

with $f_v(\cdot,\cdot)$ a vector function linear with respect to its first argument and $f(x) \overset{N}{=} f(x, \alpha_0)$ (α_0 fixed).

For this large class of nonlinear systems with parametric oscillations, a classification can be done with respect to the form of $f_v(\cdot,\cdot)$:

i) $f_v(g(t), x) = L(t)$, where $L(t)$ is an APAZ vector and the vibrations are called *vector additive*. If $L(t) = [0 \;\; 0 \;\; \cdots \;\; l(t)]^T$, i.e. all but the last components of $L(t)$ are zero, the vibrations are *AP – forcing*;

ii) $f_v(g(t), x) = B(t)x$, with $B(t)$ an APAZ matrix. These vibrations are *linear multiplicative*;

iii) $f_v(g(t), x) = B(t)\Gamma(x)$ - vibrations are *nonlinear multiplicative*. $B(t)$ is an APAZ matrix.

In (Bellman et al., 1986a; Bellman et al., 1986b) the existence of stabilizing vibrations for the class of the nonlinear system (30) is analyzed and it is shown in what sense and under which conditions an equilibrium of (30) can be stabilized. The general conclusion of (Bellman et al., 1986a; Bellman et al., 1986b) is that the VC with vibrations of the form i) and ii) is not feasible if the Jacobian matrix has a positive trace. The case of nonlinear multiplicative vibrations iii) was studied for a subclass of nonlinear systems in (Bentsman, 1987). Once the conditions for existence of vibrational stabilizability are settled for a system, it is necessary to solve another important problem: finding the specific form of stabilizing vibrations. This problem is referred as vibrational controllability (Bellman et al., 1986b).

Consider the general solution of

$$\dot{x}(t) = f_v(g(t), x) \tag{31}$$

denoted as $x(t)=\vartheta(t,c)$, where $c\in\Re^n$ is a constant uniquely defined for every initial condition (x_0,t_0) and assume that this general solution is almost periodic. The substitution $x(t)=\vartheta(t,\tilde{x}(t))$ transforms the nonlinear system (30) into $\dot{\tilde{x}}=\left[\frac{\partial\vartheta}{\partial\tilde{x}}\right]^{-1}\cdot f(\vartheta(t,\tilde{x}))\overset{\Delta}{=}X(t,\tilde{x})$. Then, the averaging of this system is:

$$\dot{x}_a=\overline{X}(x_a)=\overline{X(t,\tilde{x})}\overset{\Delta}{=}\lim_{T\to\infty}\frac{1}{T}\int_0^T X(t,\tilde{x})dt \tag{32}$$

Consider $x_{a,s}$ an equilibrium of (32), and the linearization of (32) around $x_{a,s}$:

$$\dot{x}_a=\left[\frac{\partial\overline{X}(x_a)}{\partial x_a}\right]_{x_a=x_{a,s}}\cdot x_a \tag{33}$$

The goal is to find an APAZ vector g(t) that induces a dynamic equivalence between systems (30) and (32). Assume that the equilibrium x_s of (30) satisfies the equality $x_s=\overline{\vartheta(t,x_{a,s})}$. Then, for the equilibrium $x_{a,s}$ corresponding to x_s, the linearization (33) can be represented as:

$$\dot{x}_a=(J+H)\cdot x_a \tag{34}$$

where J is the Jacobian matrix of (30) for the equilibrium x_s and H is a constant $n\times n$ matrix.

Definition 3 (Bellman et al., 1986b). An element j_{ij} of matrix J is vibrationally controllable if there exists an APAZ vector g(t) such the corresponding element h_{ij} of H is nonzero.

The type of vibrations and their parameters depend of the particular nonlinear system that is analysed. Calculation formulas have been obtained in (Bellman et al., 1986b). Assume that the Jacobian matrix J of the nonlinear system (30) has negative trace. Then the calculation formula for *linear multiplicative vibrations* applied to the nonlinear system is:

$$H=R-J,\quad R=\overline{\Phi^{-1}(t,0)\cdot J\cdot\Phi(t,0)} \tag{35}$$

where $\Phi(t,0)$ is the state transition matrix of the system (30), in the particular case of the linear multiplicative vibrations ii): $f_v(g(t),x)=B(t)x$.

4.2 The vibrational control strategy for the continuous bioprocess

The basic idea of vibrational controlled CSTB is to vibrate the flow rates and in this way to operate the bioreactor at *average conversion rates* which were previously unstable. By using this technique is possible to eliminate significant expenses associated with feedback. Since the vibrations depend only on time and not on the value of states, there no longer was a need to take measurements of concentrations.

In order to apply the vibrational control we have three possibilities: additive vibrations, linear multiplicative vibrations or nonlinear multiplicative vibrations. The general conclusion of (Selişteanu & Petre, 2001) is that the additive vibrations and AP-forcing VC are not applicable to the bioprocess described in Section 2. A study about the linear multiplicative VC of the CSTB is achieved next.

Consider the bioprocess (4), (5) with the equilibria (E1) or (E2). From operational point of view, only the equilibrium (E2) is interesting. With the Haldane kinetic model of the specific rate (9), we have two possibilities for the equilibrium (E2): stable equilibrium point (13) - a stable nod - if $\rho > 0$ and saddle type of equilibrium point (14), i.e. instability, if $\rho < 0$ (see also Fig. 1). In those situations when the substrate inhibition appears, the bioprocess can exhibit unstable or can go to the wash-out; in these cases the system requires control in order to stabilize the CSTB.

The trace condition for the Jacobian matrix (11) of the bioprocess (4), (5) is achieved if:

$$\mathrm{tr}(J) = -k_1\rho - D < 0 \tag{36}$$

Assume that (36) is respected. The vibrational controlled bioprocess is of the form:

$$\dot{\xi} = f(\xi) + B(t)\cdot\xi \tag{37}$$

where B(t) is an APAZ matrix.

There exists positive $\varepsilon_0 = \text{const.}$ such that vibrations $(1/\varepsilon)\cdot B(t/\varepsilon)$, $0 < \varepsilon \le \varepsilon_0$, induce a dynamic equivalence between the linearized averaged system of the form (32), denoted here $\dot{\bar{\xi}} = \Xi(\bar{\xi})$, and the vibrationally controlled process $\dot{\xi} = f(\xi) + (1/\varepsilon)\cdot B(t/\varepsilon)\cdot\xi$. In order to apply the VC, it is important to find the particular form of B(t) such that this dynamical equivalence is achieved. Consider B(t) of the form:

$$B(t) = \begin{bmatrix} 0 & 0 \\ b(t) & 0 \end{bmatrix} \tag{38}$$

Then the state transition matrix of $\dot{\xi} = B(t)\xi$ is: $\Phi(t) = \begin{bmatrix} 1 & 0 \\ \varphi(t) & 1 \end{bmatrix}$, with $\varphi(t) = \int_0^t b(\tau)d\tau$.

Assuming that $\overline{\varphi(t)} = 0$ we obtain from (35):

$$R = \begin{bmatrix} 0 & \rho \\ -k_1\mu(\xi_{s2}) - \rho\overline{\varphi^2(t)} & -k_1\rho - D \end{bmatrix} \tag{39}$$

For b(t) - an APAZ function - we consider the cosinusoidal form: $b(t) = \beta\cos(t)$. Consequently we have $\overline{\varphi^2(t)} = \lim_{T\to\infty}\frac{1}{T}\int_0^T \varphi^2(\tau)d\tau = \beta^2/2$, and finally R and then H using the calculation formula (35) are obtained:

$$R = \begin{bmatrix} 0 & \rho \\ -k_1\mu(\xi_{s2}) - \rho\cdot\beta^2/2 & -k_1\rho - D \end{bmatrix} \tag{40}$$

$$H = R - J = \begin{bmatrix} 0 & 0 \\ -\rho \cdot \beta^2 / 2 & 0 \end{bmatrix} \tag{41}$$

For β chosen such that R is Hurwitz, and for ε sufficiently small, the vibrations (38) stabilize the equilibrium (14) of (4), (5). A theoretical value for ε_0 is complicated to obtain, but a practical value can be obtained via simulation.

Remark 3. Because the equilibrium (14) is nonzero (nontrivial), in fact it is stabilizable by a combination of linear multiplicative and vector additive vibrations $B(t) \cdot (\xi - \xi_s)$.

5. Simulation results

Sliding mode control. Simulation were performed for a continuous stirred tank bioreactor (CSTB) described by the model (4), (5), (15) with the parameters from paragraph 2. Two simulation cases are considered:

i) The simulated control task considered the problem of stabilizing the output y to $y^* = 0$, using the SMC law (20). In fact, the closed loop system was tested for a step profile of the external substrate reference C. The final reference value is achieved in two steps: first the reference is set to 70 g/l; the next reference is set to the value $\xi_1^* = C = 80 g/l$. The SMC law parameters are $\gamma_1 = 1$ and $k = 3$.

Figure 2 presents the time evolution of the concentrations, and Fig. 3 depicts the output and the control input.

The behaviour of the concentrations is good, but it can be seen that the control action exhibits a chattering, which can be unacceptable in practice. The profile of the auxiliary output function (the "sliding surface") and a magnification of this auxiliary output are depicted in Fig. 4. In order to obtain a smoothed control input, a saturation function is used and the results are presented in Fig. 5.

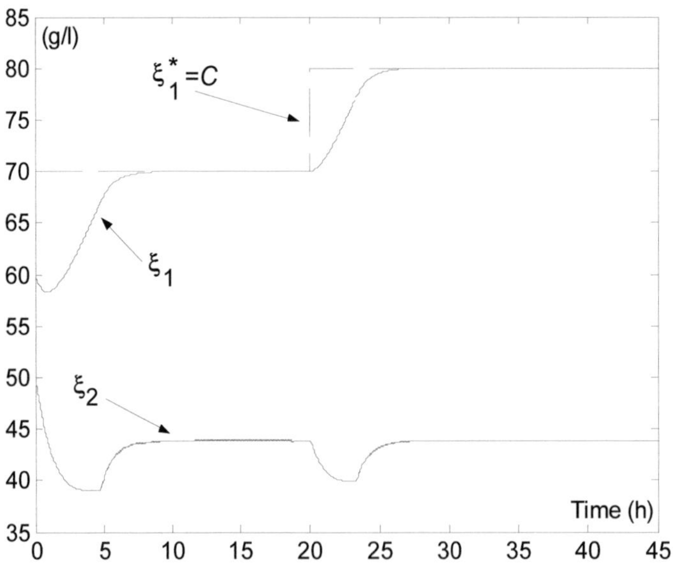

Fig. 2. Time evolution of the substrate and biomass concentrations – SMC case

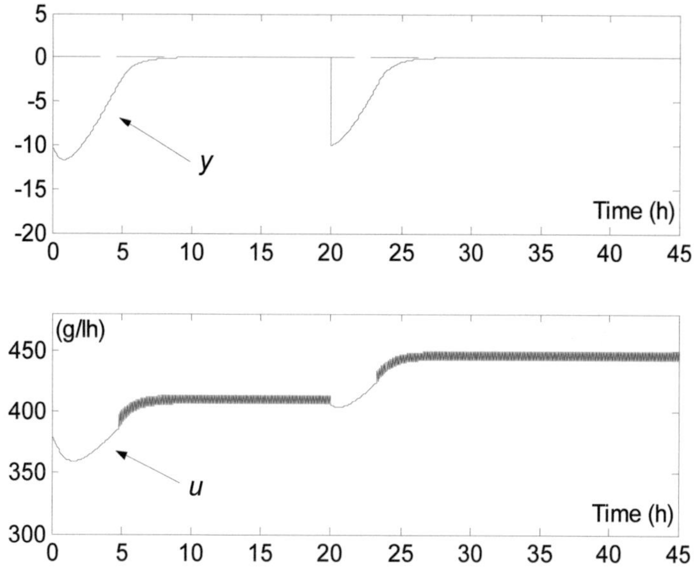

Fig. 3. Profiles of output and control input (rate of supply of substrate per unit of volume)

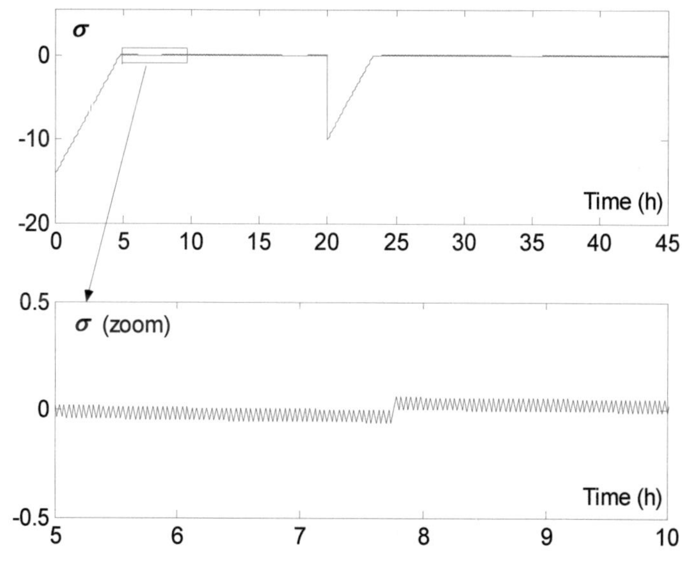

Fig. 4. The evolution of the auxiliary output (the sliding surface), including a zoom area

ii) In order to test the robustness properties of the controlled bioprocess and to add realism to the simulation, a parametric disturbance in the yield coefficient k_1 was considered (a 50% variation from the nominal value); this coefficient is uncertain in practice. The disturbance occurs once in the simulation time interval, about 1 h in duration (time interval 30h - 31h). Also, in this simulation case, only the biomass concentration is considered on-line measurable.

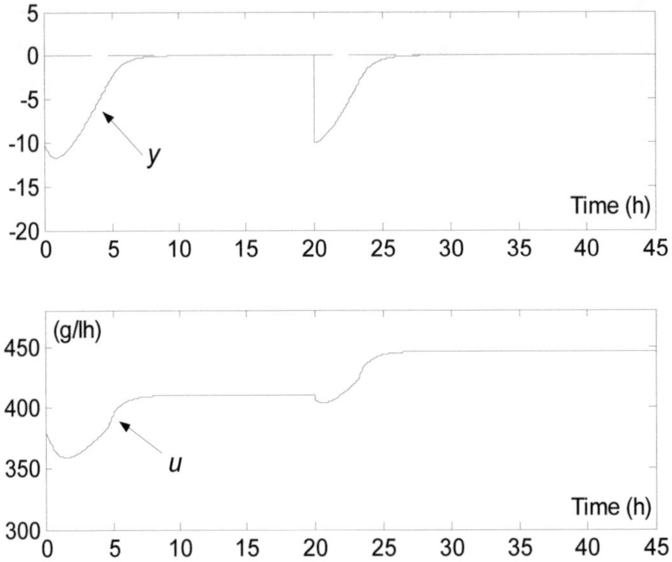

Fig. 5. Time evolution of the output and the control input – the chattering reduction case

Therefore, the SMC law (26) was implemented, using the estimations $\hat{\xi}_2$ provided by the asymptotic observer (25). The profile of the reference is the same as in the first simulation case. The performance of the asymptotic observer can be noticed in Fig. 6, where the substrate concentration and its estimate are depicted. Fig. 7 shows that in this simulation case, the controlled process exhibits a good behaviour and the SMC law can cope with the parametric disturbance.

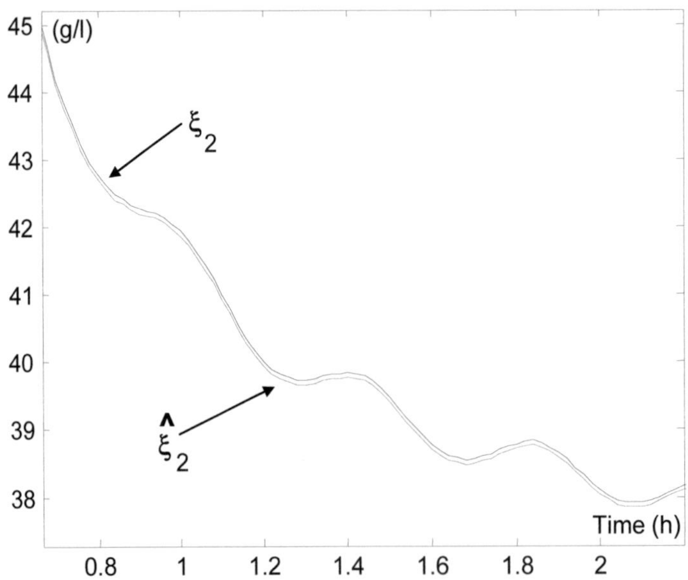

Fig. 6. Profiles of the substrate concentration and its estimate (magnification of a small area)

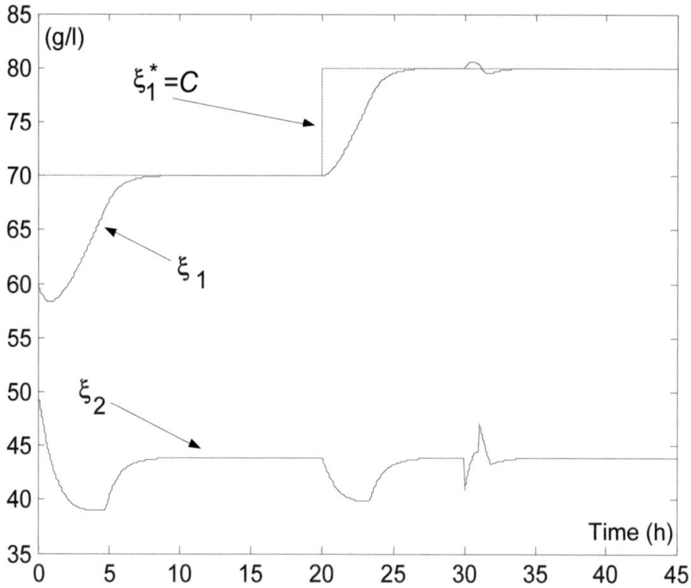

Fig. 7. Time evolution of the concentrations - the SMC parametric disturbance case

Remark 4. In practice, there exist the so-called parasitic or unmodelled dynamics, along with the principal dynamics of the plant (Boiko, 2005; Boiko & Fridman, 2006). The principal dynamics are used for the SMC design. On the other hand, to implement the designed algorithms, some equipment such as actuators, sensors etc. are needed. Hence it is required to take into consideration the parasitic dynamics, introduced mainly by the actuators. Often, a first-order (plus time lag) model of the actuator is used, with the transfer function $H_a(s) = K_a e^{-\tau s} / (T_a s + 1)$, where K_a, T_a are the parameters of the actuator, and τ is the time lag. However, for our CSTB, the dynamics of the actuator are faster than the principal dynamics and the time lag is negligible, hence their contribution to the overall system dynamics is small. Nevertheless, some supplementary simulation results show that the performance of the sliding mode controlled process is deteriorated in this case (in comparison with the ideal sliding mode controlled bioprocess) - for example the chattering of the control input is increasing and the setpoint regulation performance is deteriorated.

Remark 5. A problem in the case of SMC is that the robustness of the sliding surface (used in the SMC design procedure) with respect to the parametric uncertainties is valid only for small variations of the parameters. If the parameters are imprecisely known, then the switchings cannot take place with precision on the switching manifold and furthermore the stability of the closed loop system can be affected. In that case, an adaptive dynamical SMC law can be used in order to improve the performance of the controlled bioprocess (Selişteanu et al., 2007b).

Vibrational control. The simulation is given for the same bioprocess parameters. The value of the control parameter $\beta = 5$ is chosen such that the matrix R is Hurwitz. In Figure 8, the averaged phase portrait of the vibrationally controlled bioprocess (the averaged state trajectories) is presented. It can be seen that the previously unstable equilibrium (see Fig. 1) is stabilized into a stable node.

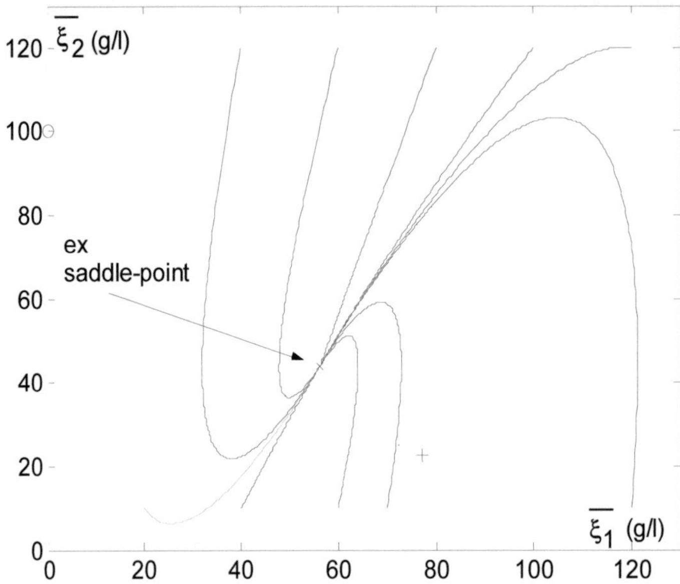

Fig. 8. The averaged phase portrait of the vibrationally controlled continuous bioprocess

The time evolution of concentrations and the averaged time trajectories are provided in Fig. 9. This picture gives a comparison of $\xi(t)$ (solid curves) and the averaged state variables $\overline{\xi(t)}$ (dashed curves) for $\varepsilon = 0.066$. To test the robustness of the vibrationally controlled bioprocess, the same parametric disturbance in the yield coefficient like in the SMC case was considered (in the time interval 10h - 11h). The simulation results are presented in Fig. 10.

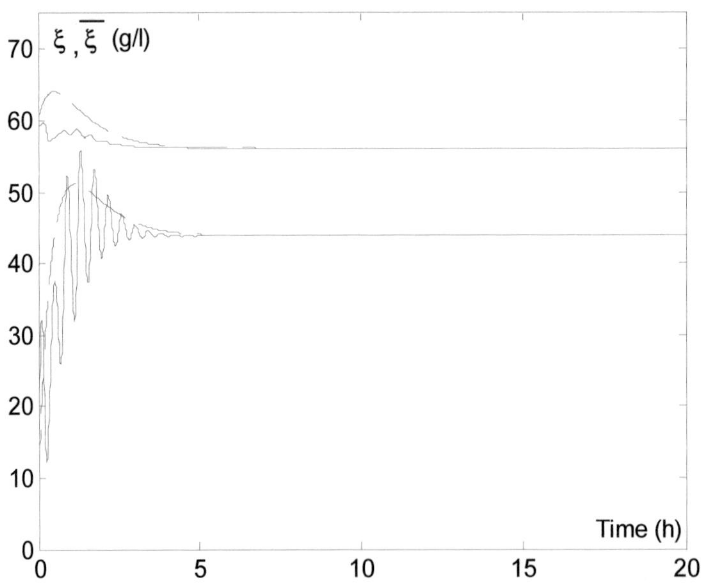

Fig. 9. Time evolution of the biomass and substrate concentrations – VC strategy

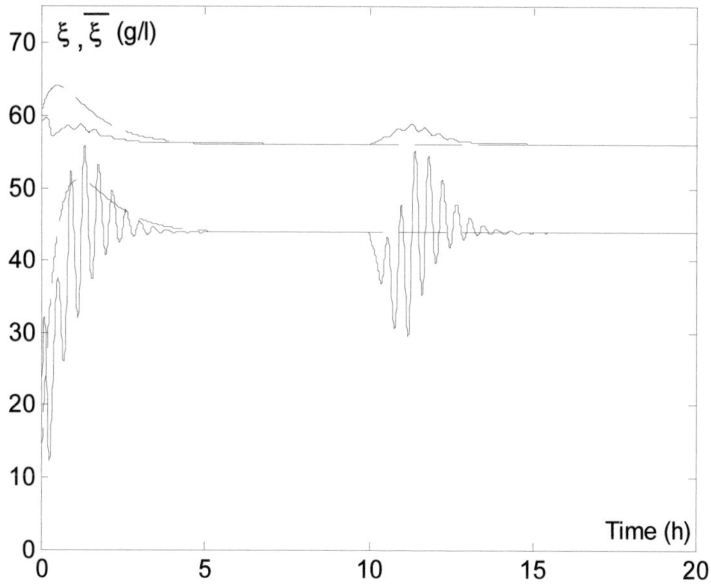

Fig. 10. Time profiles of the concentrations – VC parametric disturbance case

6. Conclusion

In this work, two nonlinear high-frequency control strategies for bioprocesses are proposed: a feedback sliding mode control law and a vibrational control strategy. In order to implement these strategies, a prototype bioprocess that is carried out in a Continuous Stirred Tank Bioreactor was considered. First, a discontinuous feedback law was designed using the exact linearization and by imposing a SMC that stabilizes the output of the bioprocess. When some state variables used in the control law are not measurable on-line, an asymptotic state observer was used in order to reconstruct these states. Second, using the vibrational control theory, a VC strategy for the continuous bioprocess was developed. The existence and the choice of stabilizing vibrations, which ensure the desired behaviour of the bioprocess are widely analysed.

Some discussions and comparisons regarding the application of the sliding mode control and vibrational control techniques to bioprocesses can be done. Both the SMC and VC strategies are high-frequency methods, obviously high frequency relative to the natural frequency of the bioprocess. A main difference between VC and SMC is that in vibrational case, no measurements of state variables are required.

The idea of vibrational stabilization is to determine vibrations such the unstable equilibrium point of a bioprocess bifurcates into a stable almost periodic solution. The practical engineering VC problem can be described as a three steps technique: first it is necessary to find the conditions for existence of stabilizing vibrations, second to find which parameter or component is physically possible to vibrate and finally to find the parameters of vibrations that ensure the desired response.

From the simulations, the conclusion is that both methods can deal with some parametric disturbances. However, from this point of view, the behaviour of the feedback SMC is better. For the vibrational technique to be effective, one needs to have an accurate

description of system dynamics. This fact together with physical limitation on the magnitude and the frequency of vibrations in some cases are the disadvantages of the vibrational technique. A drawback of the SMC strategy is the chattering phenomenon. This chattering can be reduced using various techniques, but it cannot be eliminated, due to the inherent presence of the so-called parasitic dynamics, which are introduced principally by the actuator.
The proposed high-frequency techniques were tested using a prototype of a continuous bioprocess. For that reason, the presented results cannot be extended without intensive studies to other bioprocesses.
However, there exist some studies and implementations of the SMC strategy for fed-batch bioprocesses (Selişteanu & Petre, 2005). On another hand, using the results obtained by (Lehman & Bentsman, 1992; Lehman et al., 1994), the vibrational control theory can be extended for time lag systems with bounded delay. Such systems are the bioprocesses that take place inside the CSTB with delay in the recycle stream (Selişteanu et al., 2006).
The obtained results are quite encouraging from a simulation viewpoint and show the robustness of the controllers and good setpoint regulation performance. These results must to be verified in the laboratory using some real bioreactors. Further research will be focused on this real implementation. Also, some theoretical approaches will be the development of the high-frequency control strategies for multivariable bioprocesses and of some hybrid control strategies for these bioprocesses, like the closed-loop vibrational control (see for example (Kabamba et al., 1998)) and the adaptive sliding mode techniques.

7. Acknowledgment

This work was supported by the National University Research Council - CNCSIS, Romania, under the research projects ID 786, 358/2007 and ID 686, 255/2007 (PNCDI II), and by the National Authority for Scientific Research, Romania, under the research projects SICOTIR, 05D7/2007 (PNCDI II) and APEPUR, 717/P1/2007 (CEEX).

8. References

Bartoszewicz, A. (2000). Chattering attenuation in sliding mode control systems. *Control and Cybernetics*, Vol. 29, No. 2, pp. 585-594, ISSN 0324-8569

Bastin, G. & Dochain, D. (1990). *On-line Estimation and Adaptive Control of Bioreactors.* Elsevier, ISBN 978-0-444-88430-5

Bastin, G. (1991). Nonlinear and adaptive control in biotechnology: a tutorial, *Proceedings of the European Control Conference ECC'91*, pp. 2001–2012, Grenoble, France, 1991

Bellman, R.E.; Bentsman, J. & Meerkov, S.M. (1986a). Vibrational control of nonlinear systems: vibrational stabilizability. *IEEE Transactions on Automatic Control*, Vol. 31, No. 8, pp. 710-716, ISSN 0018-9286

Bellman, R.E.; Bentsman, J. & Meerkov, S.M. (1986b). Vibrational control of nonlinear systems: vibrational controllability and transient behavior. *IEEE Transactions on Automatic Control*, Vol. 31, No. 8, pp. 717-724, ISSN 0018-9286

Bentsman, J. (1987). Vibrational control of a class of nonlinear systems by nonlinear multiplicative vibrations. *IEEE Transactions on Automatic Control*, Vol. 32, No. 8, pp. 711-716, ISSN 0018-9286

Boiko, I. (2005). Analysis of the sliding modes in frequency domain. *International Journal of Control*, Vol. 78, No. 13, pp. 969-981, ISSN 0020-7179

Boiko, I. & Fridman, L. (2006). Frequency domain analysis of second order sliding modes, *Proceedings of the American Control Conference*, pp. 5390-5395, Minneapolis, Minnesota, USA, 2006

Dochain, D. & Vanrolleghem, P. (2001). *Dynamical Modelling and Estimation in Wastewater Treatment Processes*. IWA Publishing, ISBN 1900222507

Edwards, C. & Spurgeon, S.K. (1998). *Sliding Mode Control: Theory and Applications*. Taylor and Francis, ISBN 0748406018

Fliess, M. (1990). Generalized canonical forms for linear and nonlinear systems. *IEEE Transactions on Automatic Control*, Vol. 35, No. 9, pp. 994–1001, ISSN 0018-9286

Fossas, E.; Ros, R.M. & Fabregat, J. (2001). Sliding mode control in a bioreactor model. *Journal of Mathematical Chemistry*, Vol. 30, No. 2, pp. 203-218, ISSN 0259-9791

Isidori, A. (1995). *Nonlinear Control Systems*. Springer Verlag, ISBN 3540199160, New York

Kabamba, P.T.; Meerkov, S.M. & Poh E.-K. (1998). Pole placement capabilities of vibrational control. *IEEE Transactions on Automatic Control*, Vol. 43, No. 9, pp. 1256-1261, ISSN 0018-9286

Lehman, B. & Bentsman, J. (1992). Vibrational control of linear time lag systems with arbitrarily large but bounded delays. *IEEE Transactions on Automatic Control*, Vol. 37, No. 10, pp. 576-582, ISSN 0018-9286

Lehman, B.; Bentsman, J.; Lunel, S.V. & Verriest, E.I. (1994). Vibrational control of nonlinear time lag systems with bounded delay: averaging theory, stabilizability, and transient behavior *IEEE Transactions on Automatic Control*, Vol. 39, No. 5, pp. 898-912, ISSN 0018-9286

Mailleret, L.; Bernard, O. & Steyer J.P. (2004). Nonlinear adaptive control for bioreactors with unknown kinetics. *Automatica*, Vol. 40, No. 8, pp. 1379-1385, ISSN 0005-1098

Meerkov, S.M. (1980). Principle of vibrational control: theory and applications. *IEEE Transactions on Automatic Control*, Vol. 25, No. 4, pp. 755-762, ISSN 0018-9286

Palm, R; Driankov, D. & Hellendoorn, H. (1997). *Model Based Fuzzy Control: Fuzzy Gain Schedulers and Sliding Mode Fuzzy Controllers*. Springer-Verlag, ISBN 978-3540614715, Berlin

Selişteanu, D. & Petre, E. (2001). Vibrational control of a class of bioprocesses. *Control Engineering and Applied Informatics*, Vol. 3, no. 1, pp. 39–50, ISSN 1454-8658

Selişteanu, D. & Petre, E. (2005). On adaptive sliding mode control of a fed-batch bioprocess, *Proceedings of the 11th IEEE International Conference on Methods and Models in Automation and Robotics MMAR 2005*, pp. 243-248, ISBN 83-60140-90-1, Miedzyzdroje, Poland, August-September 2005

Selişteanu, D.; Petre, E.; Hamdan, H. & Popescu, D. (2006). Modelling and vibrational control of a continuous stirred tank bioreactor with delay in the recycle stream. *WSEAS Transaction on Biology and Biomedicine*, Issue 5, Vol. 3, pp. 331-338, ISSN 1109-9518.

Selişteanu, D.; Petre, E.; Popescu, D. & Bobaşu, E. (2007a). High frequency control strategies for a continuous bioprocess: sliding mode control versus vibrational control, *Proceedings of the 13th IEEE/IFAC International Conference on Methods and Models in Automation and Robotics MMAR 2007*, pp. 77-84, ISBN 978-83-751803-2-9, Szczecin, Poland, August 2007

Selişteanu, D.; Petre, E. & Răsvan, V. (2007b). Sliding mode and adaptive sliding-mode control of a class of nonlinear bioprocesses. *International Journal of Adaptive Control and Signal Processing*, Vol. 21, No. 8-9, pp. 795-822, ISSN 0890-6327

Sira-Ramirez, H. (1992). On the sliding mode control of nonlinear systems. *Systems and Control Letters*, Vol. 19, No. 4, pp. 302–312, ISSN 0167-6911

Sira-Ramirez, H. & Llanes-Santiago, O. (1994). Dynamical discontinuous feedback strategies in the regulation of nonlinear chemical processes. *IEEE Transactions on Control Systems Technology*, Vol. 2, No. 1, pp. 11–21, ISSN 1063-6536

Slotine, J.-J.E. & Li, W. (1991). *Applied Nonlinear Control*. Prentice-Hall, ISBN 978-0-130-40890-7, Englewood Cliffs, NJ

Stanchev, S.P. (2003). A variant of an (combined) adaptive controller design introducing sliding regime in Lyapunov derivative, *Proceedings of the American Control Conference*, pp. 909-914, Denver, USA, 2003

Su, J.-P. & Wang, C.-C. (2002). Complementary sliding control of non-linear systems. *International Journal of Control*, Vol. 75, No. 5, pp. 360–368, ISSN 0020-7179

Tham, H.J.; Ramachandran, K.B. & Hussain, M.A. (2003). Sliding mode control for a continuous bioreactor. *Chemical and Biochemical Engineering*, Vol. 17, No. 4, pp. 267-275, ISSN 0352-9568

Utkin, V.I. (1978). *Sliding Regimes and their Applications in Variable Structure Systems*. MIR Publ., ISBN 978-0714712130, Moscow

Utkin, V.I. (1992). *Sliding Modes in Control Optimization*. Springer Verlag, ISBN 978-0-387-53516-6, Berlin

13

Sliding Mode Observers for Rotational Robotics Structures

Dorin Sendrescu, Dan Selişteanu, Emil Petre and Cosmin Ionete
Department of Automation and Mechatronics, University of Craiova
Romania

1. Introduction

The problem of controlling uncertain dynamical systems subject to external disturbances has been an issue of significant interest over the past several years. Most systems that we encounter in practice are subjected to various uncertainties such as nonlinearities, actuator faults parameter changes etc. Many of the proposed control strategies suppose that the state variables are available; this fact is not always true in practice, so the state vector must be estimated for use in the control laws. In the past, several types of observers have been designed for the reconstruction of state variables: Kalman filter (Kalman, 1976), adaptive observers (Gevers & Bastin, 1986), high gain observers (Gauthier et al., 1992), sliding mode observers (SMO) (Utkin, 1992; Walcott & Zak, 1986; Edwards & Spurgeon, 1994) and so on - see (Thein & Misawa, 1995) for some comparisons. Depending upon the particular application, all these observers can be used with suitable results. Sliding mode observers differ from more traditional observers in that there is a non-linear discontinuous term injected into the observer depending on the output estimation error. These observers are known to be much more robust than Luenberger observers, as the discontinuous term enables the observer to reject disturbances (Tan & Edwards, 2000). The observers based on the variable structure systems theory and sliding mode concept can be classified in two categories (Xiong & Saif, 2000): 1) the equivalent control based methods and 2) sliding mode observers based on the method of Lyapunov. The analysis of these two types of SMO (Edwards & Spurgeon, 1994; Xiong & Saif, 2000) shows that there exist some differences in terms of robustness properties. From practical point of view, the selection of the switched gain for the equivalent control based SMO is difficult (in order to obtain a sliding mode without excessive chattering) (Edwards & Spurgeon, 1994). Also, there exists bounded estimation error for bounded modelling errors (the estimation will not be accurate when uncertainties are presented) (Xiong & Saif, 2000). The Lyapunov based SMO (the so-called Walcott-Zak observer) provides exact estimation for certain class of nonlinear systems under existence of certain class of uncertainties. However, the difficulty in finding the design and gain matrices is the main drawback of this observer. Consider the effect of adding a negative output feedback term to each equation of the Utkin observer. This results in a new error system. The addition of a Luenberger type gain matrix, feeding back the output error, yields the potential to provide robustness against certain classes of uncertainty.

In order to test the performances of SMO, this work addresses the design and the implementation of SMO for two rotational Quanser experiments: flexible link and inverted pendulum experiments. Growing needs for advanced and precise robot manipulators in space industry and mechanically flexible constructions result in new and complicated problems of modelling, identification and control of flexible structures, i.e. flexible beams, robot arms, etc. Dealing with flexible systems one is faced with inherent infinite dimensionality of the systems, light damping, nonlinearities, influence of variable environment etc. One of the most important factors is to establish a suitable mathematical model of the system to make analysis as realistic as possible. Therefore, inclusion of the dynamics of electrical devices (i.e. DC servomotors, tachogenerators, etc.) to a mechanical model may be required. In recent years, various strategies were developed in order to control flexible beams: adaptive control, robust control (Gosavi & Kelkar, 2001), different sliding-mode control strategies (Drakunov & Ozguner, 1992; Jalili et al., 1997; Selisteanu et al., 2006), fuzzy control and some combined methods (Ionete, 2003; Gu & Song, 2004). The control goal is to achieve the flexible link position control, and to damp the arm vibrations. In spite of the simplicity of the structure, an inverted pendulum system is a typical nonlinear dynamic control object, which includes a stable equilibrium point when the pendulum is at pending position and an unstable equilibrium point when the pendulum is at upright position. When the pendulum is raised from the pending position to the upright position, the inverted pendulum system is strongly nonlinear with the pendulum angle. The inverted pendulum is a classic problem in dynamics and control theory and widely used as benchmark for testing control algorithms (PID controllers, neural networks, genetic algorithms, etc). Variations on this problem include multiple links, allowing the motion of the cart to be commanded while maintaining the pendulum, and balancing the cart-pendulum system on a see-saw. The inverted pendulum is related to rocket or missile guidance, where thrust is actuated at the bottom of a tall vehicle. The inverted pendulum exists in many different forms. The common thread among these systems is to balance a link on end using feedback control. In the rotary configuration, the first link, driven by a motor, rotates in the horizontal plane to balance a pendulum link, which rotates freely in the vertical plane. The real mathematical models of these systems are very complicated, so for control purpose simplified models are typically used. In general, the models of the rotational experiments are derived using Lagrange's energy equations, and consequently generalized dynamic equations are obtained. In order to obtain useful models for control design, approximations of these models can be derived (represented by nonlinear ordinary differential equations). Moreover, a linear approximation can be also obtained. Even the linear models have unknown or partially known parameters; therefore identification procedures are needed. The control strategies require the use of state variables; when the measurements of these states are not available, it is necessary to design a state observer.

The LQG/LTR (Linear Quadratic Gaussian/Loop Control Recovery) method is used in order to obtain feedback controllers for the benchmark Quanser experiments (Selisteanu et al., 2006). The aim of these controllers is to achieve robust stability margins and good performance in step response of the system. LQG/LTR method is a systematic design approach based on shaping and recovering open-loop singular values. Because the control laws necessitate the knowledge of state variables, the equivalent control method SMO and the modified Utkin SMO are designed and implemented. Some numerical simulations and real experiments are provided.

2. The models of quanser rotational experiments

The Quanser experimental set-up contains the following components (Apkarian, 1997): Quanser Universal Power Module UPM 2405/1503; Quanser MultiQ PCI data acquisition board; Quanser Flexgage - Rotary Flexible Link Module; Quanser SRV02-E servo-plant; PC equipped with Matlab/Simulink and WinCon software.

WinCon™ is a real-time Windows 98/NT/2000/XP application. It allows running code generated from a Simulink diagram in real-time on the same PC (also known as local PC) or on a remote PC. Data from the real-time running code may be plotted on-line in WinCon Scopes and model parameters may be changed on the fly through WinCon Control Panels as well as Simulink. The automatically generated real-time code constitutes a stand-alone controller (i.e. independent from Simulink) and can be saved in WinCon Projects together with its corresponding user-configured scopes and control panels.

WinCon software actually consists of two distinct parts: WinCon Client and WinCon Server. WinCon Client runs in hard real-time while WinCon Server is a separate graphical interface, running in user mode. WinCon Server is the software component that performs the following functions: conversion of a Simulink diagram to C source code, starting and stopping the real-time code on WinCon Client, making changes to controller parameters using user-defined Control Panels and plotting the data streamed from the real-time code. WinCon supports two possible configurations: the local configuration (i.e. a single machine) and the remote configuration (i.e. two or more machines). In the local configuration, WinCon Client, executing the real-time code, runs on the same machine and at the same time as WinCon Server (i.e. the user-mode graphical interface). In the remote configuration, WinCon Client runs on a separate machine from WinCon Server. The two programs always communicate using the TCP/IP protocol. Each WinCon Server can communicate with several WinCon Clients, and reciprocally, each WinCon Client can communicate with several WinCon Servers. The local configuration was used to perform the real time experiments and is shown below in Fig. 1. The data acquisition card, in this case the MultiQ PCI, is used to interface the real-time code to the plant to be controlled. The user interacts with the real-time code via either WinCon Server or the Simulink diagram. Data from the running controller may be plotted in real-time on the WinCon scopes and changing values on the Simulink diagram automatically changes the corresponding parameters in the real-time code. The real-time code, i.e. WinCon Client, runs on the same PC. The real-time code takes precedence over everything else, so hard real-time performance is still achieved.

The PC running WinCon Server must have a compatible version of The MathWorks' MATLAB installed, in addition to Simulink, and the Real-Time Workshop toolbox.

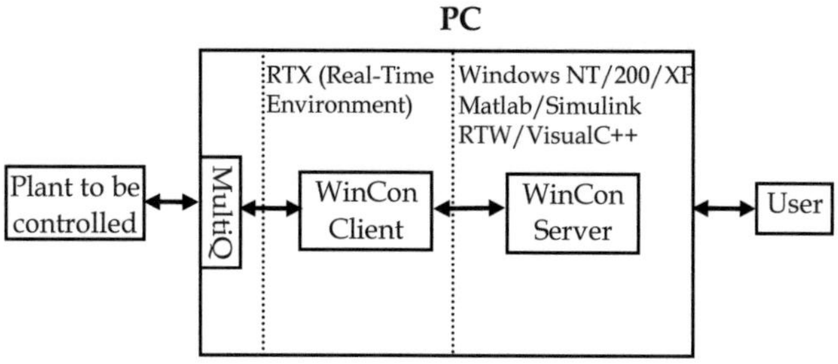

Fig. 1. The WinCon local configuration: WinCon Client and WinCon Server on same PC

A. Rotating Flexible Beam Model

The rotary motion experiments are based on the Rotary Servo Plant SRV02-E. It consists of a DC servomotor with built in gearbox whose ratio is 70 to 1. The output of the gearbox drives a potentiometer and an independent output shaft to which a load can be attached. The flexible link experiment consists of a mechanical and an electrical subsystem. The modelling of the mechanical subsystem consists in describing the tip deflection and the base rotation dynamics. The electrical subsystem involves modelling of DC servomotor that dynamically relates voltage to torque.

The Flexible Link module consists of a flat flexible arm at the end of which is a hinged potentiometer (Fig. 2). The flexible arm is mounted to the hinge. Measurement of the flexible arm deflection is obtained using a strain gage. The gage is calibrated to output 1 volt per 1 inch of tip deflection.

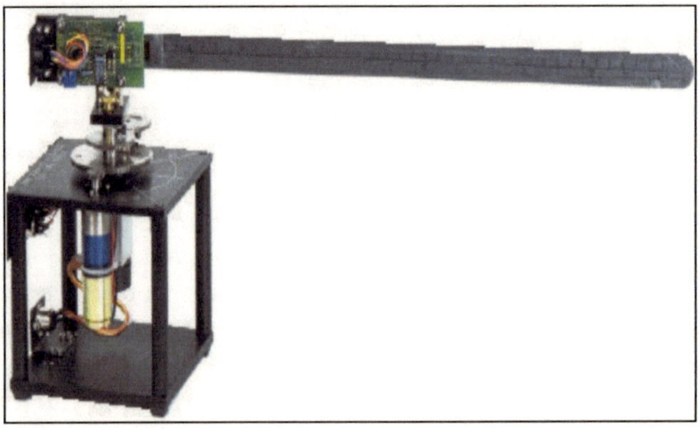

Fig. 2. Quanser Flexible Beam Experiment: SRV02-E servo plant and rotary flexible link module

The equations of motion involving a rotary flexible link imply modelling the rotational base and the flexible link as rigid bodies. As a simplification to the partial differential equation describing the motion of a flexible link, a lumped single degree of freedom approximation is used. We first start the derivation of the dynamic model by computing various rotational moment of inertia terms. The rotational inertia for a flexible link and a light source attachment is given respectively by

$$J_{link} = \frac{1}{3} m_{link} L^2 \tag{1}$$

where m_{link} is the total mass of the flexible link, and L is the total flexible link length. For a single degree of freedom system, the natural frequency is related with torsional stiffness and rotational inertia in the following manner

$$\omega_n = \sqrt{\frac{K_{stiff}}{J_{link}}} \tag{2}$$

where ω_n is found experimentally and K_{stiff} is an equivalent torsion spring constant as delineated through the following figure

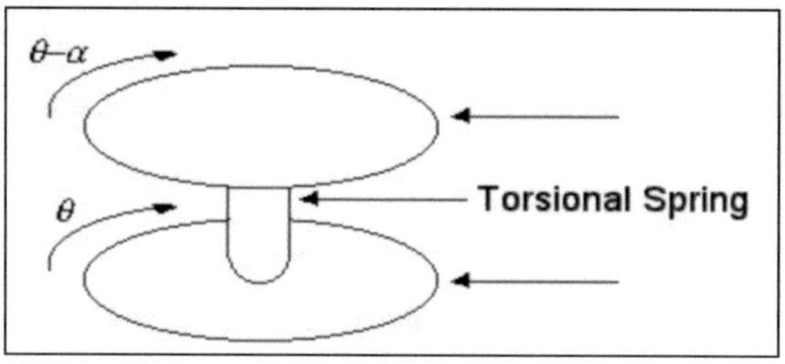

Fig. 3. Torsional spring

In addition, any frictional damping effects between the rotary base and the flexible link are assumed negligible. Next, we derive the generalized dynamic equation for the tip and base dynamics using Lagrange's energy equations in terms of a set of generalized variables α and θ, where α is the angle of tip deflection and θ is the base rotation given in the following

$$\begin{aligned} \frac{\partial}{\partial t}\left(\frac{\partial T}{\partial \dot{\theta}}\right) - \frac{\partial T}{\partial \theta} + \frac{\partial P}{\partial \theta} = Q_\theta \\ \frac{\partial}{\partial t}\left(\frac{\partial T}{\partial \dot{\alpha}}\right) - \frac{\partial T}{\partial \alpha} + \frac{\partial P}{\partial \alpha} = Q_\alpha \end{aligned} \tag{3}$$

where T is the total kinetic energy of the system, P is the total potential energy of the system, and Q_i is the ith generalized force within the ith degree of freedom. Kinetic energy of the base and the flexible link are given respectively as

$$T_{base} = \frac{1}{2} J_{base} \dot{\theta}^2 \tag{4}$$

$$T_{link} = \frac{1}{2} J_{link} \left(\dot{\theta} - \dot{\alpha}\right)^2 \tag{5}$$

The total kinetic energy of the mechanical system is computed as the sum of (4) and (5)

$$T = \frac{1}{2} J_{base} \dot{\theta}^2 + \frac{1}{2} J_{link} \left(\dot{\theta} - \dot{\alpha}\right)^2 \tag{6}$$

Potential energy of the system provided by the torsional spring is given as

$$P = \frac{1}{2} K_{stiff} \alpha^2 \tag{7}$$

Applying equation (6) and (7) into (3) results in the following dynamic equations

$$\begin{aligned} (J_{base} + J_{link})\ddot{\theta} - J_{link}\ddot{\alpha} = Q_\theta \\ -J_{link}\ddot{\theta} + J_{link}\ddot{\alpha} + K_{stiff}\alpha = Q_\alpha \end{aligned} \tag{8}$$

Next we compute the amount of virtual work, W, applied into the system. The amount of virtual work is given to be

$$\delta W = \tau\delta\theta + 0\delta\alpha \tag{9}$$

where τ is the torque applied to the rotational base. Rewriting equation (9) into a general form of virtual work given as

$$\delta W = Q_\theta \delta\theta + Q_\alpha \delta\alpha \tag{10}$$

one obtains the virtual forces applied onto the generalized coordinates Q_θ and Q_α respectively to be

$$Q_\theta = \tau, Q_\alpha = 0 \tag{11}$$

After decoupling the acceleration terms of (8), the dynamic equations for the mechanical subsystem are

$$\begin{aligned} \ddot{\theta} &= -\frac{K_{stiff}}{J_{base}}\alpha + \frac{1}{J_{base}}\tau; \\ \ddot{\alpha} &= -K_{stiff}\left(\frac{1}{J_{link}} + \frac{1}{J_{base}}\right)\alpha + \frac{1}{J_{base}}\tau \end{aligned} \tag{12}$$

Next, rewriting equations (12) into a state space form gives

$$\begin{bmatrix} \dot{\theta} \\ \dot{\alpha} \\ \ddot{\theta} \\ \ddot{\alpha} \end{bmatrix} = \begin{bmatrix} 0 & 0 & 1 & 0 \\ 0 & 0 & 0 & 1 \\ 0 & -\frac{K_{stiff}}{J_{base}} & 0 & 0 \\ 0 & -K_{stiff}\left(\frac{1}{J_{link}} + \frac{1}{J_{base}}\right) & 0 & 0 \end{bmatrix} \begin{bmatrix} \theta \\ \alpha \\ \dot{\theta} \\ \dot{\alpha} \end{bmatrix} + \begin{bmatrix} 0 \\ 0 \\ \frac{1}{J_{base}} \\ \frac{1}{J_{base}} \end{bmatrix} \tau \tag{13}$$

Since the control input into the mechanical model of equation (13) is a torque τ, an electrical dynamic equation relating voltage to torque is needed.

First, the torque applied to the rotational base, on the right hand side of equation (13), is converted to the torque applied to the gear train by the DC servomotor by means of a gear ratio K_g given as $\tau = K_g \tau_m$, where τ_m is the torque applied by the servomotor.

The DC servomotor is an electromechanical device that relates torque to current through a proportionality gain K_T. Applying Kirchoff's voltage law to the DC circuitry of the motor, and after some calculations, we obtain a state space model of (13), rewritten to utilize an electrical control voltage as input (Ionete, 2003):

$$\begin{bmatrix} \dot{\theta} \\ \dot{\alpha} \\ \ddot{\theta} \\ \ddot{\alpha} \end{bmatrix} = \begin{bmatrix} 0 & 0 & 1 & 0 \\ 0 & 0 & 0 & 1 \\ 0 & -\frac{K_{stiff}}{J_{base}} & -\frac{K_T K_b K_g^2}{J_{base} R_m} & 0 \\ 0 & -K_{stiff}\left(\frac{1}{J_{link}} + \frac{1}{J_{base}}\right) & -\frac{K_T K_b K_g^2}{J_{base} R_m} & 0 \end{bmatrix} \begin{bmatrix} \theta \\ \alpha \\ \dot{\theta} \\ \dot{\alpha} \end{bmatrix} + \underbrace{\begin{bmatrix} 0 \\ 0 \\ \frac{K_T K_g}{J_{base} R_m} \\ -\frac{K_T K_g}{J_{base} R_m} \end{bmatrix}}_{b} V \tag{14}$$

where K_b is a proportional constant between angular velocity of the motor and the voltage applied by the motor shaft, R_m is the resistance of the resistor of DC circuitry and V is the voltage supplied by the data acquisition board.
Next, a transformation between relative angular position and relative displacement about a neutral axis is used within the state space model. The relative angular position and the velocity with respect to the rotating base are proportional to the relative displacement and to the velocity of the flexible link tip (i.e. $\sin(\alpha) \approx \alpha$, for α small) respectively: $d = \alpha \cdot L$, $\dot{d} = \dot{\alpha} \cdot L$, where d is the relative displacement and L is the length of the flexible link. The Fig. 4 shows the relationship of these three parameters. Substituting the above equations into the state space dynamics previously obtained gives the following state space equation:

$$\begin{bmatrix} \dot{\theta} \\ \dot{d} \\ \ddot{\theta} \\ \ddot{d} \end{bmatrix} = \begin{bmatrix} 0 & 0 & 1 & 0 \\ 0 & 0 & 0 & 1 \\ 0 & -\frac{K_{stiff}}{J_{base} L} & -\frac{K_T K_b K_g^2}{J_{base} R_m} & 0 \\ 0 & -\frac{K_{stiff}}{L}\left(\frac{1}{J_{link}} + \frac{1}{J_{base}}\right) & -\frac{K_T K_b K_g^2}{J_{base} R_m} & 0 \end{bmatrix} \begin{bmatrix} \theta \\ d \\ \dot{\theta} \\ \dot{d} \end{bmatrix} + bV \qquad (15)$$

The Quanser flexible beam parameters are: length of link: $L = 0.45\text{m}$; mass of link m = 0.0008 kg; link inertia moment: J_{link} = 0.0042 kgm^2; mass of base: m_b = 0.05 kg; resistance of motor circuit: R_m = 2.6 Ω; gear ratio of rotary base: K_g = 70/1; torque constant: K_T = 0.00767 Nm/A; proportional constant: K_b = 0.00767 V/(rad/sec); motor constant: K_m = 0.00767 Nm/A; equivalent torsion spring constant: K_{stiff} = 2 Nm/rad; base inertia moment: J_{base} = 0.002 kgm^2 (Apkarian, 1997).

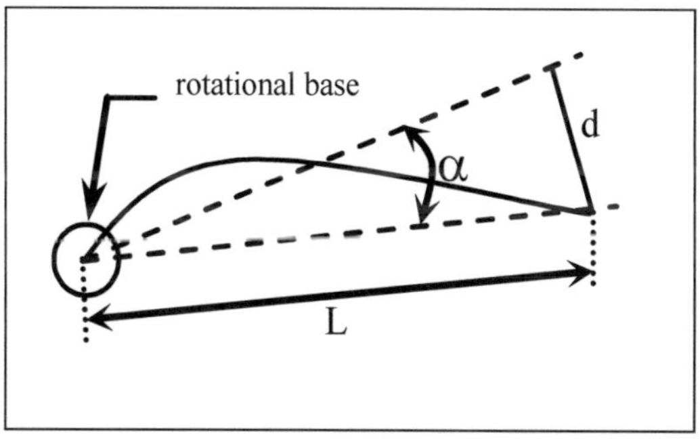

Fig. 4. Simplified model of flexible beam experiment

B. Rotary Inverted Pendulum Model

As a typical unstable nonlinear system, inverted pendulum system is often used as a benchmark for verifying the performance and effectiveness of a new control method because of the simplicity of the structure. Since the system has strong nonlinearity and inherent instability, it must to linearize the mathematical model of the object near upright position of the pendulum. To control both the angle of the pendulum and the position of the arm a robust controller will be tasted using a SMO to estimate the unmeasured states. The Quanser Rotary Inverted Pendulum module shown in Fig. 5.a consists of a rigid link (pendulum) rotating in a vertical plane. The rigid link is attached to a pivot arm, which is mounted on the load shaft of a DC-motor. The pivot arm can be rotated in the horizontal plane by the DC-motor. The DC-motor is instrumented with a potentiometer. In addition, a potentiometer is mounted on the pivot arm to measure the pendulum angle. The objective of the experiment is to design a control system that positions the arm as well as maintains the inverted pendulum vertical. This problem is similar to the classical inverted pendulum (linear) except that the trajectory is circular. The Quanser experimental set-up contains the following components: Quanser Universal Power Module UPM 2405/1503; Quanser MultiQ PCI data acquisition board; Quanser Rotary Inverted Pendulum; Quanser SRV02-E servo-plant; PC equipped with Matlab/Simulink and WinCon software.

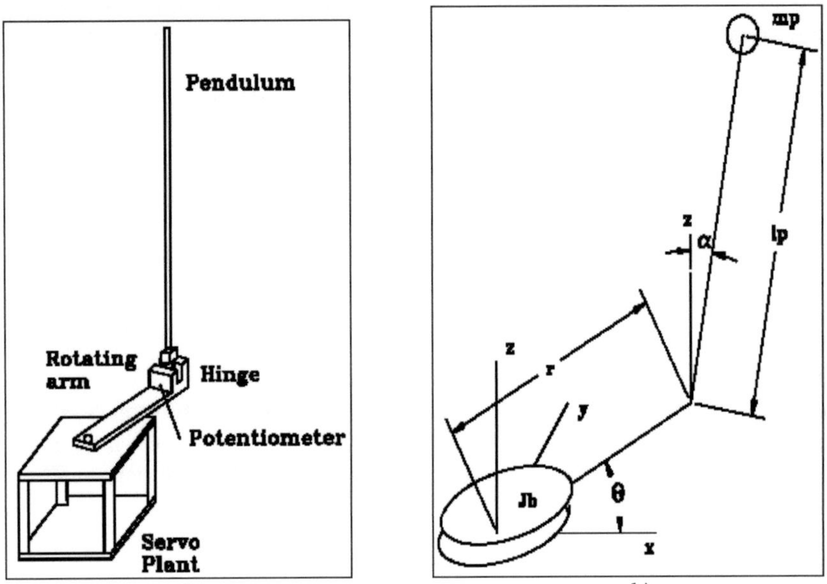

a) b)

Fig. 5. a) Schematic of Rotary Inverted Pendulum; b) Simplified model for rotary inverted pendulum

In order to obtain a useful model of the inverted pendulum, consider the simplified model in Fig. 5.b. Note that l_p is half L_p, the actual length of the pendulum ($l_p = 0.5L_p$). The kinetic and potential energies in the system are given by:

$$
\begin{aligned}
P_{pen} &= m_p g l_p \cos(\alpha) \\
T_{pen} &= 0.5 m_p [(\dot{\theta} r + \dot{\alpha} l_p \cos(\alpha))^2 + (\dot{\alpha} l_p \sin(\alpha))^2] \\
T_{base} &= 0.5 J_b \dot{\theta}^2
\end{aligned} \tag{16}
$$

where T is the kinetic energy of the system, P is the potential energy of the system. Using the above and the Lagrangian formulation one obtains the nonlinear differential equations of the system:

$$
\begin{cases}
\left(m_p r^2 + J_b\right)\ddot{\theta} + m_p r \ddot{\alpha} l_p \cos(\alpha) - m_p r \dot{\alpha}^2 l_p \sin(\alpha) = \tau \\
m_p l_p \cos(\alpha) \ddot{\theta} r - m_p l_p \sin(\alpha) \dot{\alpha} \dot{\theta} r + m_p \ddot{\alpha} l_p^2 - m_p g l_p \sin(\alpha) = 0
\end{cases} \tag{17}
$$

where: τ is the input torque from motor (Nm), m_p the mass of rod (kg), l_p the centre of gravity of rod (m), J_b the inertia of arm and gears (kgm), θ the deflection of arm from zero position (rad), α the deflection of pendulum from vertical up position (rad).
The linear equations resulting from (17) are:

$$\begin{bmatrix}\dot{\theta}\\ \dot{\alpha}\\ \ddot{\theta}\\ \ddot{\alpha}\end{bmatrix}=\begin{bmatrix}0 & 0 & 1 & 0\\ 0 & 0 & 0 & 1\\ 0 & -\dfrac{m_p rg}{J_b} & 0 & 0\\ 0 & g\dfrac{J_b+m_p r^2}{l_p J_b} & 0 & 0\end{bmatrix}\begin{bmatrix}\theta\\ \alpha\\ \dot{\theta}\\ \dot{\alpha}\end{bmatrix}+\begin{bmatrix}0\\ 0\\ \dfrac{1}{J_b}\\ -\dfrac{r}{l_p J_b}\end{bmatrix}\tau \qquad (18)$$

Note that the zero position for all the above equations is defined as the pendulum being vertical "up". The motor equations are:

$$V = I_m R_m + K_m K_g \dot{\theta} \qquad (19)$$

where: V (volts) is the voltage applied to motor, I_m (amp) is the current in motor, K_m (V/(rad·sec)) the back EMF constant, K_g the gear ratio in motor gearbox and external gears.
The torque generated by the motor is: $\tau = K_m K_g I_m = J_b \ddot{\theta}$. We have also $\dfrac{\theta(s)}{V(s)} = 1/s\left(\dfrac{J_b R_m}{K_m K_g}s + K_m K_g\right)$, where s is the complex variable from Laplace transform.
The linear model that was developed is based on a torque τ applied to the arm. The actual system however is voltage driven. From the motor equations derived above one get that $\tau = V\dfrac{K_m K_g}{R_m} - \dfrac{{K_m}^2 {K_g}^2}{R_m}\dot{\theta}$. Finally, one obtains the following linear model.

$$\begin{bmatrix}\dot{\theta}\\ \dot{\alpha}\\ \ddot{\theta}\\ \ddot{\alpha}\end{bmatrix}=\begin{bmatrix}0 & 0 & 1 & 0\\ 0 & 0 & 0 & 1\\ 0 & -\dfrac{m_p rg}{J_b} & -\dfrac{K_m^2 K_g^2}{J_b R_m} & 0\\ 0 & g\dfrac{J_b+m_p r^2}{l_p J_b} & \dfrac{rK_m^2 K_g^2}{l_p J_b R_m} & 0\end{bmatrix}\begin{bmatrix}\theta\\ \alpha\\ \dot{\theta}\\ \dot{\alpha}\end{bmatrix}+\begin{bmatrix}0\\ 0\\ \dfrac{K_m K_g}{J_b R_m}\\ -\dfrac{rK_m K_g}{l_p J_b R_m}\end{bmatrix}V \qquad (20)$$

The Quanser inverted pendulum parameters are: pendulum length: $L = 2l_p = 0.305\text{m}$; arm length r=0.145m; mass of pendulum m_p = 0.105 kg; resistance of motor circuit: R_m = 2.6 Ω; back EMF constant: K_m = 0.00767 V/(rad/sec); external gear ratio: K_g = 70:1; base inertia moment: J_b = 0.0044 kgm^2.

3. LQG/LTR control strategy

Nonlinear system model imprecision may come from actual uncertainty about the plant (e.g., unknown plant parameters), or from the purposeful choice of a simplified representation of the system's dynamics. Modeling inaccuracies can be classified into two major kinds: structured (or parametric) uncertainties and unstructured uncertainties (or unmodeled dynamics). The first kind corresponds to inaccuracies on the terms actually included in the model, while the second kind corresponds to inaccuracies on the system order. Modeling inaccuracies can have strong adverse effects on nonlinear control systems. One of the most important approaches to dealing with model uncertainty is robust control.

The LQG/LTR (Linear Quadratic Gaussian/Loop Control Recovery) theory is a powerful method for the control of linear systems in the state-space domain (Athans, 1986). The aim of these controllers is to achieve robust stability margins and good performance in step response of the system. LQG/LTR method is a systematic design approach based on shaping and recovering open-loop singular values. This LQG/LTR technique generates controllers with guaranteed closed loop stability robustness property even in the face of certain gain and phase variation at the plant input/output. In addition, the LQG/LTR controllers provide reliable closed-loop system performance despite of stochastic plant disturbance. The LQ control design framework is applicable to the class of stabilizable linear systems. Briefly, the LQG/LTR theory says that, given a nth order stabilizable system

$$\dot{x}(t) = Ax(t) + Bu(t),\ t \geq 0,\ x(0) = x_0 \tag{21}$$

where $x(t) \in \Re^n$ is the state vector and $u(t) \in \Re^m$ is the input vector, determine the matrix gain $K \in \Re^{mxn}$ such that the static, full-state feedback control law $u(t) = -Kx(t)$ satisfies the following criteria

1) The closed loop state space system is asymptotically stable;
2) The performance functional given by

$$J(K) \overset{\Delta}{=} \int_0^{\infty} \left[x^T(t)Qx(t) + u^T(t)Ru(t)\right] dt \tag{22}$$

is minimized.

The performance functional of equation (22) regulates the state trajectories of x close to the origin without excessive control demand through the design of the penalty weights of nonnegative definite matrices Q and R. The solution of the LQG/LTR problem can be obtained via a Lagrange multiplier-based optimisation technique and is given by $K = R^{-1}B^TP$, where $P \in \Re^{nxn}$ is a nonnegative-definite matrix satisfying the following algebraic Riccati equation

$$A^TP + PA + Q - PBR^{-1}B^TP = 0 \tag{23}$$

Note that it follows that the LQG/LTR-based control design requires the availability of all state variables for feedback purpose.

LQG/LTR strategy for the flexible beam. The objective for the rotary flexible link dynamic system is to achieve an asymptotically stable system response for flexible link. For the state variable of d(t) in (15), a LQG/LTR based controller drives the flexible dynamic response to zero asymptotically. For tracking the angular position, a new state variable is required to allow setpoint tracking. To achieve error regulation, an angular error and an angular velocity error are defined respectively as

$$e(t) \overset{\Delta}{=} \theta(t) - \theta_d, \; \dot{e}(t) = \dot{\theta}(t) \tag{24}$$

where θ_d is a desired constant angular position for the flexible link. In addition, an integral controller coupled in the rigid body dynamics is defined within the state space dynamics of (15), $\dot{\phi}(t) = e(t)$, so that the state space dynamics is augmented to give the final linear model. The under-actuated control objective involves error regulation for the absolute angular displacement of the rotary base and vibration control for the end of the flexible link. Using the above-described LQG/LTR controller design method and the model of the plant obtained with the identification procedure, we are able to get the state-feedback vector. For the Quanser flexible beam, the arm angle and the deflection are measured by a potentiometer and a strain gage respectively. Any physical sensor does not measure the flexible arm angular velocity and the deflection velocity; instead we compute these velocities using a modified Utkin sliding mode observer as a part of overall control scheme. The LQG/LTR strategy ensures a good behaviour with respect to angular reference tracking and has a good perturbation rejection capability.

LQR strategy for the inverted pendulum. The state variables used for the control experiment are $x(t) = \left[\theta(t) \;\; \alpha(t) \;\; \dot{\theta}(t) \;\; \dot{\alpha}(t)\right]^T$. For our laboratory model, the pivot arm angle θ and the pendulum angular position α are measured by two potentiometers. The pivot arm angular velocity $\dot{\theta}$ and pendulum angular velocity $\dot{\alpha}$ are not measured by any physical sensor, instead, we numerically compute $\dot{\theta}$ and $\dot{\alpha}$ by implementing a modified Utkin sliding mode observer. In order to regulate precisely the pendulum position, we introduce another state, the integral of the rotary arm error. So the state vector becomes: $x(t) = \left[\theta(t), \alpha(t), \dot{\theta}(t), \dot{\alpha}(t), \int \theta(t)dt\right]^T$. Then, the above described LQG/LTR strategy can be successfully applied.

4. Design of the sliding mode observers

A. Utkin sliding-mode observer

The sliding mode technique has been widely studied and developed for the control and state estimation problems since the works of Utkin. Observers based on sliding mode approach first were developed for linear systems (Jalili et al., 1997). Consider the following linear time-invariant system:

$$\begin{cases} \dot{x} = Ax + Bu \\ y = Cx \end{cases} \qquad A \in \Re^{n \times n}, \; B \in \Re^{n \times p}, \; C \in \Re^{p \times n} \tag{25}$$

The problem to be considered is that of reconstructing the state variables using only measured output information. Without loss of generality we assume that $\operatorname{rank} C = p$. It is also assume that the pair {C, A} is observable and matrices A, B, C are known. In this case, the observed vector y may be represented as:

$$\begin{aligned} & y = C_a x_a + C_b x_b,\ x = (x_a, x_b), \\ & C_a \in \Re^{p\times(n-p)}, C_b \in \Re^{p\times p},\ \det(C_b) \neq 0 \end{aligned} \tag{26}$$

Using the following linear transformation of state variable:

$$T_1 = \begin{bmatrix} I_{n-p} & 0 \\ C_a & C_b \end{bmatrix} \tag{27}$$

the system described by (25) can be written in the form:

$$\begin{aligned} & \dot{x}_a = A_{11} x_a + A_{12} y + B_1 u \\ & \dot{y} = A_{21} x_a + A_{22} y + B_2 u \end{aligned} \tag{28}$$

The corresponding sliding mode observer proposed by Utkin is given by:

$$\begin{cases} \dot{\hat{x}}_a = A_{11}\hat{x}_a + A_{12}\hat{y} + B_1 u + LM\operatorname{sgn}(\hat{y} - y) \\ \dot{\hat{y}} = A_{22}\hat{y} + A_{21}\hat{x}_a + B_2 u - M\operatorname{sgn}(\hat{y} - y) \end{cases} \tag{29}$$

where $(\hat{x}_a, \hat{y})$ are the estimates for (x_a, y), $L \in \Re^{(n-p)\times p}$ is a constant nonsingular feedback gain matrix and sgn is the signum function and M is a strictly positive gain. If one define $\varepsilon_y = \hat{y} - y$ and $\varepsilon_a = \hat{x}_a - x_a$ then, the following error system is obtained

$$\begin{cases} \dot{\varepsilon}_a = A_{11}\varepsilon_a + A_{12}\varepsilon_y + LM\operatorname{sgn}(\varepsilon_y) \\ \dot{\varepsilon}_y = A_{21}\varepsilon_a + A_{22}\varepsilon_y - M\operatorname{sgn}(\varepsilon_y) \end{cases} \tag{30}$$

Defining the following change of coordinates:

$$T_2 = \begin{bmatrix} I_{n-p} & L \\ 0 & I_p \end{bmatrix} \tag{31}$$

then the error system with respect to these new coordinates can be written as:

$$\dot{\tilde{\varepsilon}}_a = \tilde{A}_{11}\tilde{\varepsilon}_a + \tilde{A}_{12}\varepsilon_y \tag{32}$$

$$\dot{\varepsilon}_y = A_{21}\tilde{\varepsilon}_a + \tilde{A}_{22}\varepsilon_y - M\operatorname{sgn}(\varepsilon_y) \tag{33}$$

where:

$$\begin{aligned} & \tilde{A}_{11} = A_{11} + LA_{21};\ \tilde{A}_{12} = A_{12} + LA_{22} - \tilde{A}_{11}L; \\ & \tilde{A}_{22} = A_{22} - A_{21}L \end{aligned} \tag{34}$$

It can be shown that for large enough M>0 a sliding mode motion can be induced on the output error state in (33). It follows that, after some finite time $\varepsilon_y = 0$ and $\dot{\varepsilon}_y = 0$. Equation (32) then reduces to

$$\dot{\tilde{\varepsilon}}_a = \tilde{A}_{11}\tilde{\varepsilon}_a \tag{35}$$

which by choice of L represents a stable system and so $\tilde{\varepsilon}_a \to 0$ as $t \to \infty$. Consequently $\hat{x}_a \to x_a$ and the remaining states can be constructed in the original coordinate system as

$$\hat{x}_b = C_b^{-1}(y - C_a\hat{x}_a) \tag{36}$$

B. Modified Utkin sliding-mode observer

The major practical difficulty in the approach presented in subsection A is the selection of an appropriate gain M to induce a sliding motion in finite time (Edwards & Spurgeon, 1994). Consider the effect of adding a negative output error feedback term to each equation of the Utkin observer (29) (Xiong & Saif, 2000). This results in a new error system governed by:

$$\begin{cases} \dot{\tilde{\varepsilon}}_a = \tilde{A}_{11}\tilde{\varepsilon}_a + \tilde{A}_{12}\varepsilon_y - G_1\varepsilon_y \\ \dot{\varepsilon}_y = A_{21}\tilde{\varepsilon}_a + \tilde{A}_{22}\varepsilon_y - G_2\varepsilon_y - M\,\mathrm{sgn}(\varepsilon_y) \end{cases} \tag{37}$$

By selecting $G_1 = \tilde{A}_{12}$ and $G_2 = \tilde{A}_{22} - A_{22}^s$ where A_{22}^s is any stable design matrix of appropriate dimension, then

$$\begin{cases} \dot{\tilde{\varepsilon}}_a = \tilde{A}_{11}\tilde{\varepsilon}_a \\ \dot{\varepsilon}_y = A_{21}\tilde{\varepsilon}_a + A_{22}^s\varepsilon_y - M\,\mathrm{sgn}(\varepsilon_y) \end{cases} \tag{38}$$

In this form the (nominal) error system is asymptotically stable for any $M\,\mathrm{sgn}(\varepsilon_y)$ because the poles of the combined system are given by $\sigma(\tilde{A}_{11}) \cup \sigma(A_{22}^s)$ and so lie in the open left half complex plane. The two gain matrices G_1 and G_2 yields the potential to provide robustness against certain classes of uncertainty.

As it can be seen from relations (15) and (20), the system matrices for flexible link and inverted pendulum models have a similar structure of the following form:

$$A = \begin{bmatrix} 0 & 0 & 1 & 0 \\ 0 & 0 & 0 & 1 \\ 0 & a_{32} & a_{33} & 0 \\ 0 & a_{42} & a_{43} & 0 \end{bmatrix}, B = \begin{bmatrix} 0 \\ 0 \\ b_3 \\ b_4 \end{bmatrix}, C = \begin{bmatrix} c_1 & c_2 & 0 & 0 \end{bmatrix}, D = 0 \tag{39}$$

Choosing $C_a = [0 \;\; 0 \;\; c_2], C_b = c_1$ and using the linear transformation:

$$T_1 = \begin{bmatrix} 1 & 0 & 0 & 0 \\ 0 & 1 & 0 & 0 \\ 0 & 0 & 1 & 0 \\ 0 & 0 & c_2 & c_1 \end{bmatrix} \tag{40}$$

the matrices from (28) has the following form:

$$A_{11} = \begin{bmatrix} 0 & a_{43} & a_{42} \\ 0 & a_{33} & a_{32} \\ 1 & 0 & 0 \end{bmatrix}, A_{12} = \begin{bmatrix} 0 \\ 0 \\ 0 \end{bmatrix}, A_{21} = [c_2 \quad c_1 \quad 0], A_{22} = 0 \quad B_1 = \begin{bmatrix} b_4 \\ b_3 \\ 0 \end{bmatrix}, B_2 = 0 \tag{41}$$

and the matrices for the modified Utkin sliding-mode observer are:

$$\begin{aligned} G_1 &= A_{12} + LA_{22} - A_{11}L - LA_{21}L \\ G_2 &= A_{22} - A_{22}L - A_{22}^{s} \end{aligned} \tag{42}$$

i) Numerical values for the Flexible Beam case

For the flexible beam experiment we have the following numerical values for the parameters:

$$\begin{aligned} &a_{32} = \text{-}2035.9;\ a_{33} = \text{-}55.435;\ a_{42} = \text{-}2320.1;\ a_{43} = \text{-}55.435; \\ &b_3 = 103.25; b_4 = -103.25 \\ &G_1 = \begin{bmatrix} -237.59 \\ -209.16 \\ 0.067 \end{bmatrix} \quad G_2 = -0.677 \end{aligned} \tag{43}$$

ii) Numerical values for the Inverted Pendulum case

For the inverted pendulum experiment we have the following numerical values for the parameters:

$$\begin{aligned} &a_{32} = -33.95;\ a_{33} = -25.19;\ a_{42} = 96.60;\ a_{43} = 23.96; \\ &b_3 = 46.93; b_4 = -44.62 \\ &G_1 = \begin{bmatrix} 585.6 \\ -1065.6 \\ -195 \end{bmatrix} \quad G_2 = 29 \end{aligned} \tag{44}$$

5. Experimental results

A. Flexible beam case

The objective for the rotary flexible link dynamic system is to achieve an asymptotically stable system response for flexible link. This system is very sensitive to derivative feedback gains because the unmodelled higher modes will be excited if the bandwidth of the system is too high or if high frequency noise is present. Using the LQG/LTR design described in the previous section we obtain the optimal feedback gain K for the feedback law with the following components:

$$k_1 = 0.025; k_2 = -0.6; k_3 = 0.005; k_4 = 0.01 \tag{45}$$

The experimental results obtained to step reference for feedback gain matrix $L = [-0.1; -0.1; -0.1]$ and M=5 are presented in Fig. 6:

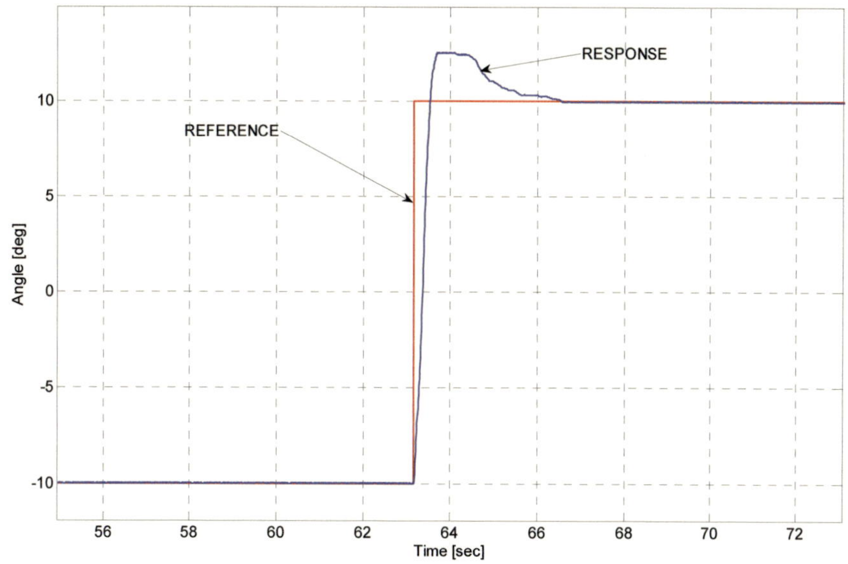

Fig. 6. Experimental step response of flexible link

In Fig. 7 the evolution of one measured state (arm angle velocity) and of its estimation is presented and in Fig. 8 the real and estimated arm angle evolution are depicted and it can be seen the good convergence of the sliding mode observer.

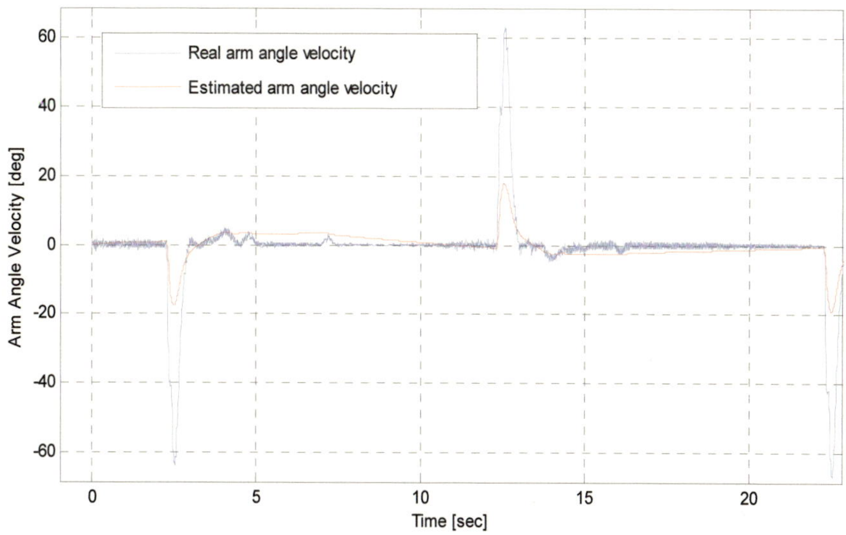

Fig. 7. Real and estimated arm angle velocity for flexible beam experiment

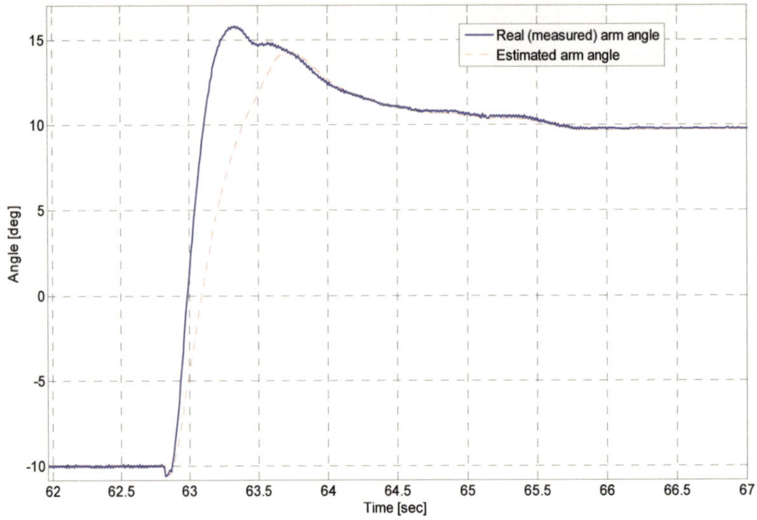

Fig. 8. Real and estimated arm angle for flexible beam experiment

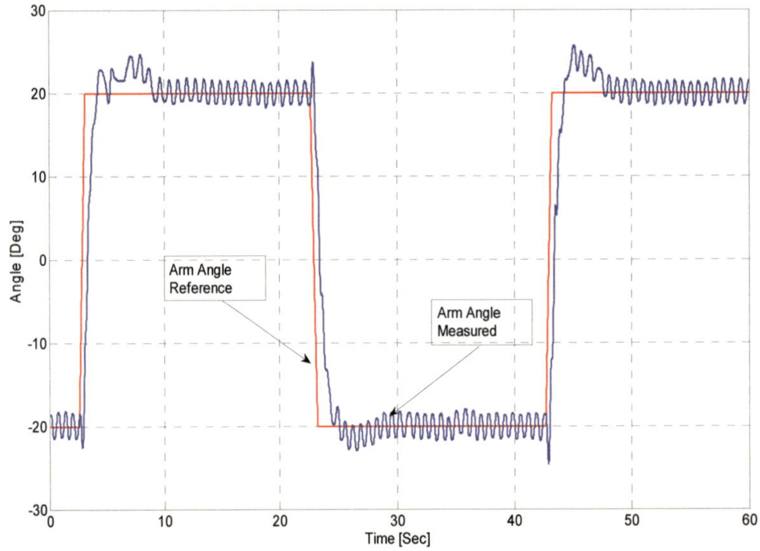

Fig. 9. Step response for real inverted pendulum experiment

B. Inverted pendulum case

The objective of the experiment is to design a control system that positions the arm as well as maintains the inverted pendulum vertical. The robust controller will be tested using a SMO to estimate the unmeasured states. Using the LQG/LTR design we obtain the optimal feedback gain K for the feedback law:

$$k_1 = -0.09; k_2 = -0.9; k_3 = -0.08; k_4 = -0.1 \tag{46}$$

The experimental results obtained to step references for feedback gain matrix $L=[-10;-10;-5]$ and M=20 are presented in Fig. 9.

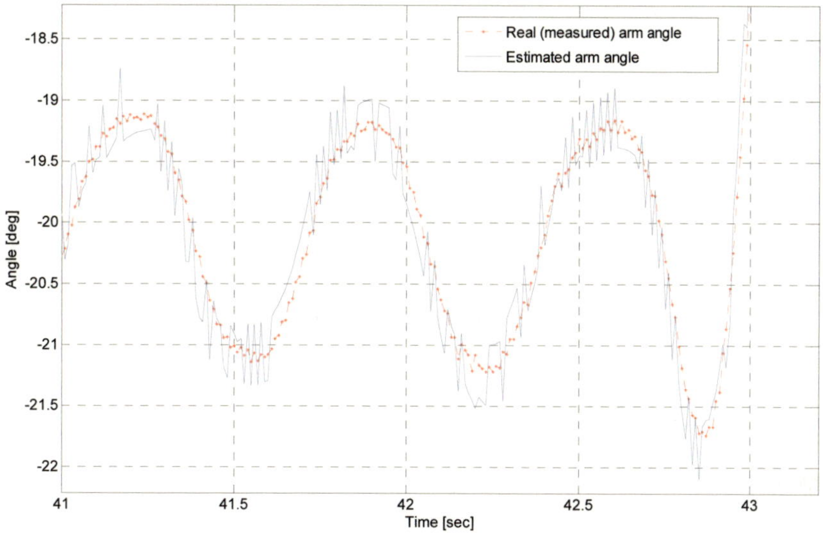

Fig. 10. Real and estimated arm angle for real inverted pendulum experiment

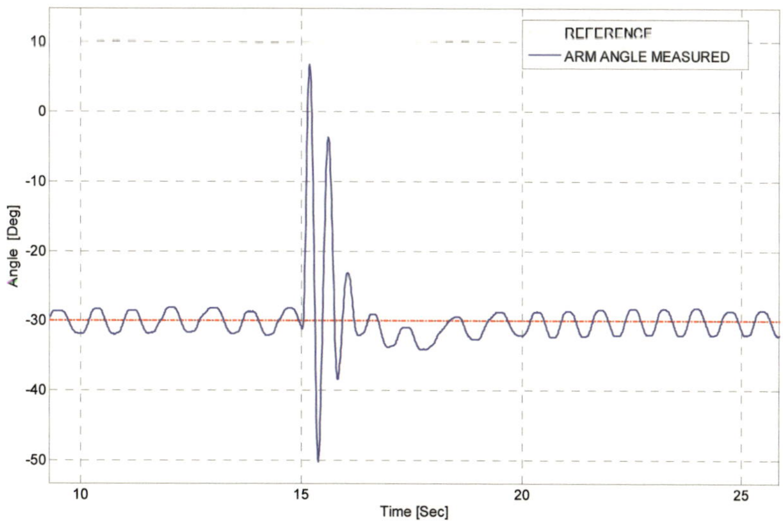

Fig. 11. The behaviour of the perturbed inverted pendulum

In Fig. 10 is presented the real and estimated arm angle evolution for the inverted pendulum system. It can be seen the small chattering due to the sliding mode estimations. In Fig. 11 the disturbance response of pendulum to a tap is presented. The pendulum is tapped such that it falls around 30 degree which causes the arm to move towards the falling direction. This results in the pendulum swinging to about 20 degree in the opposite direction. The system recovers in about 4 seconds. Advantages demonstrated by the SMO techniques for the inverted pendulum system include robustness in the presence of parameter uncertainties and disturbances plus ease of parameter selections for both the controller and observer.

6. Conclusion

This work presents some aspects regarding modelling and control of some robotics rotational experiments: flexible beam and inverted pendulum experiments. The experiments were realised using WinCon™ application that allows running code generated from a Simulink diagram in real-time. For the model describing the flexible beam experiment the control goal was to achieve the flexible beam position control and to damp the arm vibrations. The inverted pendulum experiment objective was to design a feedback control system that positions the arm as well as maintains the inverted pendulum vertical. Both experiments are highly nonlinear and consequently, the real mathematical models of the systems are very complicated, so for control purpose simplified models were used. Using the formulas of the kinetic and potential energies, from the generalized dynamic equations one obtained approximated linear models expressed by ordinary differential equations. Nonlinear systems model imprecision compensation and perturbations rejection were achieved using the robust controllers design. The LQG/LTR method was used in order to obtain feedback controllers for the benchmark robotic experiments. The aim of these controllers is to achieve robust stability margins and good performance in step response of the system. LQG/LTR method is a systematic design approach based on shaping and recovering open-loop singular values. The control strategies required the use of all state variables. Many of the proposed control strategies suppose that the state variables are available; this fact is not always true in practice so, it was necessary to design a state observer. The LQG/LTR control method and the modified Utkin SMO were designed and implemented. Sliding mode observers differ from more traditional observers e.g. Luenberger observers, in that there is a non-linear discontinuous term injected into the observer depending on the output estimation error. These observers are much more robust than Luenberger observers, as the discontinuous term enables the observer to reject disturbances. The Lyapunov based SMO (the so-called Walcott-Zak observer) provides exact estimation for certain class of nonlinear systems under existence of certain class of uncertainties. The difficulty in finding the design and gain matrices is the main drawback of this observer. A negative output feedback term was added to each equation of the Utkin observer and this result in a new error system. The addition of a Luenberger type gain matrix, feeding back the output error, yields the potential to provide robustness against certain classes of uncertainty. The problem considered was that of reconstructing the state variables using only measured output information.

For the flexible beam experiment a LQG/LTR controller was developed in order to achieve the flexible link position control and to damp the arm vibrations. The LQG/LTR controller uses the state estimations from a sliding-mode observer. A lot of experiments using the Quanser rotational experiments show that the modified Utkin sliding-mode observer provides better results than the classical Utkin sliding-mode observer. The results show also good angle reference tracking and vibration suppression. For the inverted pendulum experiment a LQG/LTR controller was developed also in order to maintain it upright. The non-measurable state variables are obtained using the modified Utkin SMO. The robustness of the controller is tested to some perturbations. The efficiency of the control-observer structure scheme has been successfully verified using the two experimental platforms. The proposed sliding mode observer-based control demonstrated very good performance; especially it is robust under external disturbances and it has good tracking references.

7. Acknowledgment

This work was supported by the National University Research Council - CNCSIS, Romania, under the research projects ID 786, 358/2007 (PNCDI II), and by the National Authority for Scientific Research, Romania, under the research projects SICOTIR, 05D7/2007 (PNCDI II).

8. References

Apkarian, J. (1997). A Comprehensive and Modular Laboratory for Control Systems Design and Implementation, Quanser Consulting.

Athans, M. (1986). A tutorial on the LQG/LTR method. In Proc. American Control Conf, Seattle, WA, pp. 1289-1296, 1986.

Drakunov, S.V. & Ozguner, U. (1992). Vibration suppression in Flexible Structures via the Sliding-Mode Control Approach, Proc. of 31st Conf. On Decision and Control, Tucson, USA, pp. 1365-1366, 1992.

Edwards, C. & Spurgeon, S. K. (1994). On the development of discontinuous observers, Int. J. Control, vol. 59, no. 5, pp. 1211-1229.

Gauthier, J. P., Hammouri, H. & Othman, S. (1992). A Simple Observer for Nonlinear Systems. Applications to Bioreactors, IEEE Trans. on Automatic Control, vol. 37, no. 6, pp. 875-880.

Gevers, M. & Bastin, G. (1986). A Stable Adaptive Observer for a Class of Nonlinear Second-Order Systems, in Analysis and Optimization of Systems, Bensoussan and Lions, Eds. New-York Springer-Verlag, pp. 143-155.

Gosavi S.V. & Kelkar, A.G. (2001). Passivity-based Robust Control of Piezo-actuated Flexible Beam, Proc. of American Control Conference, Arlington, USA, pp. 2492-2497, June 25-27, 2001.

Gu, H. & Song, G. (2004). Adaptive robust sliding-mode control of a flexible beam using PZT sensor and actuator, Proc. of 2004 IEEE Int. Symposium on Intelligent Control, Taipei, Taiwan, pp. 78-83, 2004.

Ionete, C. (2003). LQG/LTR Controller Design for Flexible Link Quanser Real-time Experiment, Proc. of Int. Symp. SINTES11, Craiova, Romania, vol. 1, pp. 49-54, 2003.

Jalili, N., Elmali, H., Moura, J.T. & Olgac, N. (1997). Tracking Control of a Rotating Flexible Beam using Modified Frequency-shaped Sliding Mode Control, Proc. of American Control Conference, Albuquerque, USA, pp. 2552-2556, 1997.

Kalman, R.E. (1976). On a New Approach to Filtering and Prediction Problems, ASME J. Basic Engineering, Vol. 24, pp. 705-718.

Selişteanu, D., Sendrescu, D. & Ionete, C. (2006). On Sliding Mode Control and Identification of a Flexible Beam, 12th IEEE International Conference on Method and Models in Automation and Robotics MMAR 2006, pp. 55-61, ISBN 83-60140-88-X , Miedzyzdroje, Poland, August 28-31, 2006.

Tan, C.P. & Edwards, C. (2000). An LMI Approach for Designing Sliding Mode Observers, IEEE Conference on Decision and Control, Australia, pp.2587-2592, 2000.

Thein, L.M-W. & Misawa, E. A. (1995). Comparison of the Sliding Observer to Several State Estimators Using a Rotational Inverted Pendulum, Proc. of the 34th Conference on Decision and Control, New Orleans, pp. 3385-3390, 1995.

Utkin, V.I. (1992). Sliding Modes in Control Optimization. Berlin: Springer Verlag.

Walcott, B. L. & Zak, S. H. (1986). Observation of dynamical systems in the presence of bounded nonlinearities/ uncertainties, Proc. of the 25th Conference on Decision and Control, pp. 961-966, 1986.

Xiong, Y. & Saif, M. (2000). Sliding-mode Observer for Uncertain Systems. Part I: Linear Systems Case, Proc. of the 39th IEEE Conference on Decision and Control, Sydney, pp. 316-321, 2000.

14

A Declarative Framework for Constrained Search Problems in Manufacturing

Sitek Pawek and Wikarek Jaroslaw
Technical University of Kielce
Poland

1. Introduction

Today's highly competitive business environment makes it an absolute requirement on behalf of the managers to continuously make the best decisions in the shortest possible time. *'Learning from mistakes'* has left its place to *'one strike and you're out'* reality. That is, there is no room for mistake in making decisions in this global environment. Success depends on quickly allocating the organizational resources towards meeting the actual needs and requirements of the customer. Decision problems involve various numeric and non-numeric constraints, some of which are conflicting with each other. Occasionally, decision-makers do not have complete information on the situation. Thus they perform *'what-if'* and goal-seeking analyses involving constraints. In order to succeed in such an unforgiving environment, managers and decision makers need integrated *'intelligent'* decision support systems (DSS) that are capable of using a wide variety of models along with data and information resources available to them at various internal and external repositories. In this chapter we present the use of constraint logic programming as a tool for such decision support systems in constrained search problems, focusing on the model representation and analyses.
The original contribution of our approach consists of a declarative framework for constrained search problems, developed within the constraint logic programming (CLP) paradigm together with relational SQL database, and the development of a constraint logic solver for scheduling problems with external resources and resource dependent processing times in different production organization environments.

2. Constrained search problems

Constrained search problems (e.g., scheduling, planning, resource allocation, placement, routing) appear frequently at different levels of decision in manufacturing. They are usually characterized by technical, environmental or manpower constraints, which make them unstructured, and in most of the cases are difficult to solve (NP-complete). Traditional mathematical programming approaches (linear programming, integer and mixed integer programming) are deficient in the following ways: their representation of constraints is artificial (commonly using 0-1 variables), their computing time in the presence of many constraints is very long (due to combinatorial explosion), and they cannot process various constraints applied to the main problem. Thus, the most used approach consists in developing specific software, written in a procedural language like PASCAL, BASIC or C, to solve each particular problem. However, the use of procedural languages brings the following well known disadvantages: the development time of the programs is very long and the programs are very complex, hence difficult to maintain and adapt to rapid changes of requirements.

Unlike traditional approaches, CLP provides for a natural representation of heterogeneous constraints and allows domain-specific heuristics to be used on top of generic solving techniques.

3. Declarative programming – SQL, CLP

Declarative programming is a term with two distinct meanings, both of which are in current use. According to one definition, a program is *'declarative'* if it describes *what* something is like, rather than *how* to create it. For example, HTML, XML web pages are declarative because they describe *what* the page should contain — title, text, images — but not *how* to actually display the page on a computer screen. This is a different approach from imperative programming languages such as PASCAL, C, and Java, which require the programmer to specify an algorithm to be run. In short, imperative programs explicitly specify an algorithm to achieve a goal, while declarative programs explicitly specify the goal and leave the implementation of the algorithm to the support software (for example, an SQL *select* statement specifies the properties of the data to be extracted from a database, not the process of extracting the data).

According to a different definition, a program is *'declarative'* if it is written in a purely functional programming language, logic programming language, or constraint programming language. The phrase "declarative language" is sometimes used to describe all such programming languages as a group, and to contrast them against imperative languages.

These two definitions overlap somewhat. In particular, constraint programming and, to a lesser degree, logic programming, focus on describing the properties of the desired solution (the *what*), leaving unspecified the actual algorithm that should be used to find that solution (the *how*). However, most logic and constraint languages are able to describe algorithms and implementation details, so they are not strictly declarative by the first definition.

Constraint Logic Programming (CLP) is a declarative modelling and procedural programming environment that integrates qualitative /heuristic knowledge representation of logic and quantitative/algorithmic reasoning into a single paradigm. Unlike traditional approaches, CLP provides for a natural representation of heterogeneous constraints and allows domain-specific heuristics to be used on top of generic solving techniques. The main issue for the constrained-based approach is CSP (Constraint Satisfaction Problem). In artificial intelligence and operation research, constraint satisfaction is the process of finding a solution to a set of constraints. Such constraints express allowed values for variables. A solution is therefore an evaluation of these variables that satisfies all constraints. Constraint Satisfaction Problems (on finite domains) are typically solved using a form of search. The most used techniques are variants of backtracking, constraint propagation and local search.

CLP as a declarative modelling and procedural programming environment is increasingly realized as an effective tool for decision support systems (Bisdorff & Laurent, 1995; Lamma et al., 1997; Lee & Lee 1996). Constraint Logic Programming is suitable for Decision Support Systems (DSS) because (Liao et al., 2002; Ryu, 1998):

- CLP is a very good tool for the development of knowledge base that has expertise and experience represented in terms of logic, rules and constraints. This tool allows the knowledge base to be built in an incremental and accumulating way (it is suitable for ill-structured or semi-structured decision analysis problems).
- Constraints naturally represent decisions and their inter-dependencies. Decision choices are explicitly modelled as the domains of constraint variables.
- CLP can serve as a good integrative environment for the decision analysis that has different kinds of model.

Decision analysis requires a number of computational facilities which this tool can provide.

4. Declarative framework for constrained search problems

There is a growing need for decision support tools capable of assisting a decision maker in the constrained search problems in manufacturing. The most important of them are scheduling problems and scheduling problems with resource allocation. The diversity of scheduling problems, the existence of many specific constraints (precedence, resource, capacity, etc.) in each problem and the efficient constraint based scheduling algorithms make constraint logic programming a method of choice for the resolution of complex practical problems. In constraint programming approach to decision support in scheduling problems, the problem to be solved is represented in terms of decision variables and constraints on these variables (Pape, 1995).

Depending on the particular applications, the variables of scheduling problems (job-shop, flow-shop, open-shop, and project shop) can be:

- The start time and the end time of each operation.
- The set of resources assigned to each operation (if this set is not fixed).
- The capacity of a resource that is assigned to an operation (e.g. the number of workers from a given team assigned to operation).
- The processing times (constant, variable increasing/decreasing function of starting times or allocated resources, etc.).

The constraints of a scheduling problem include:

- Temporal and precedence constraints which define the possible values for the start and end times of operations and the relations between the start and end time of two operations.
- Resource constraints which define the possible set of resources for each operation.
- Capacity constraints which limit the available capacity of each resource over time.
- Problem-specific constraint which correspond to particular features of operations and resources.

Additional variables and constraints can be included to represent optimization criteria, preferences of the user of scheduling system, etc.

4.1 Assumptions of DSS based on declarative framework

The presented in (section 3) advantages and possibilities of CLP environment for decision support make it interesting for decision support in constrained search problems. Building decision support system for scheduling, covering a variety of production organization forms, such as job-shop, flow-shop, project, multi-project etc., is especially interesting.

The following assumptions were adopted in order to design the presented scheduling processes of decision support system (see Fig. 1.):

- Problem-specific constraint which correspond to particular features of operations and resources.
- The system should possess data structures that make its use possible in different production organization environments (see Fig. 2.).
- The system should make it possible to schedule the whole set of tasks/jobs simultaneously, and after a suitable schedule has been found, it should be possible to add a new set of tasks later, and to find a suitable schedule for both sets without the necessity to change initial schedules.
- The decisions of the systems are the answers to appropriate questions formed as CLP predicates.
- The system should regard:
  - additional resource types apart from machines, e.g. people, tools, etc,
  - temporary inaccessibility of all resource types,
  - resource or time depending processing times, etc.

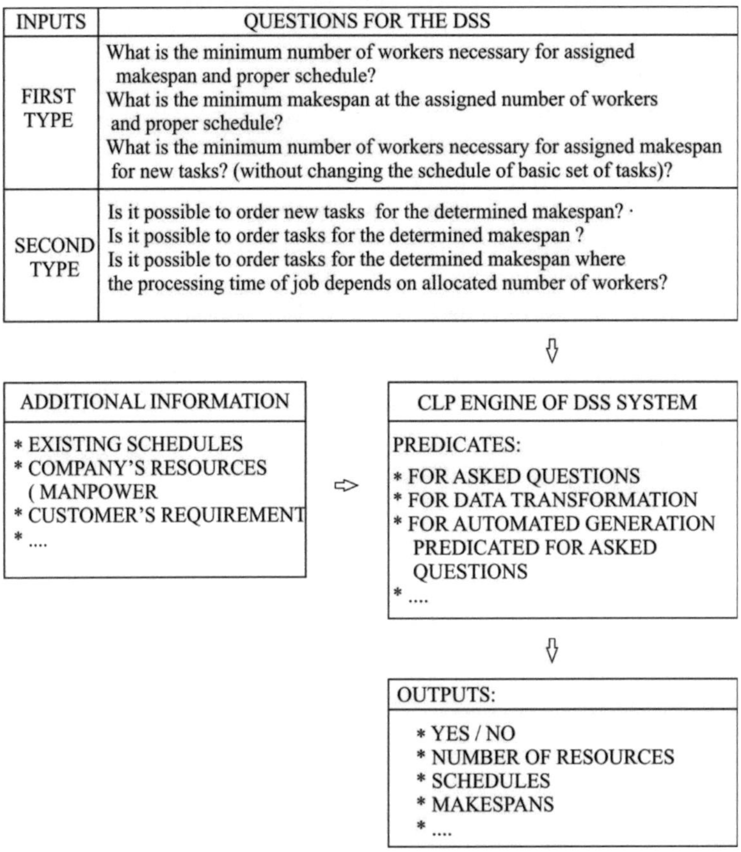

Fig. 1. Concept of DSS for scheduling problems based on declarative framework.

The range of the decisions made by the system depends on data structures and asked questions. Thus, the system is very flexible as it is possible to ask all kinds of questions (write all kinds of predicates). In this version of DSS the questions which can be asked are the following:

- What is the minimum number of workers necessary for assigned makespan and proper schedule? (predicate *opc_d(L,C)*).
- What is the minimum makespan at the assigned number of workers and proper schedule? (predicate *opc_g(L,C)*).
- Is it possible to order new tasks (both orders and projects) for the determined makespan? (predicate *opc_s(L,C))*.
- What is minimum makespan at the assigned number of workers for new tasks? (predicate *opcd_g(L,C)*).
- What is the minimum number of workers necessary for assigned makespan for new tasks? (without changing the schedule of basic set of tasks) (predicate *opcd_d(L,C)*).
- Is it possible to order tasks for the determined makespan ? (predicate *opcd_s(L,C)*).
- Is it possible to order tasks for the determined makespan where the processing time of task depends on allocated number of workers? (predicate *opcd_s1(L,C)*).

  L - number of workers (manpower), $C=C_{max}$ - makespan

These questions are just examples of questions that the present system can be asked. New questions are new predicates that need to be created in CLP environment. Two types of questions are asked in the system:

- About the existence of the solution (eg., is it possible to carry out a new task in the particular time?, etc.).
- About a particular kind of the solution: find a suitable schedule fulfilling the performance index, find the minimum scheduling length-makespan, find the minimum number of workers to carry out the task, etc.

The foregoing questions can include a random set of additional renewable resources (in this case, workers only) and refer a random number of production organization forms (job-shop, flow-shop, open-shop, project etc.). Additionally, the presented decision support system model implements an extra functionality which is resource dependent processing times. Scheduling problems literature gives the processing time as constant and defined before the tasks are realized. In practical applications the time is significantly dependent on the amount of the allocated resources for their realization. These dependencies are usually non-linear and can be presented as a relationship (relational database table) or function. The system implemented the possibility of changing the time of task/job realization in relation to the allocated number of workers. The functionality above does not call for the change of predicates; it requires suitably prepared data describing the problem and included in the relational database. The proposed structure of the relational database (see Fig. 2.) and the way CLP predicates are built allow the system to generate both schedules with determined parameters for different production organization forms, but also include allocation of additional resources (in general case resource sets) and effects they may have on the realized tasks.

4.2 Data structures

Data structures were designed in such a way that they could be easily used to decision problems in a variety of scheduling environments, which is job-shop, flow-shop, project or multi-project. The obtained flexibility resulted from the use of a relational data model.

Figure 2 presents the ERD (Entity Relationship Diagram) of the database that was designed to meet the requirements of cooperation with CLP environment and to have the following possibilities:

- Storing the data for scheduling problems and resource allocation for different types of production organisation.
- Storing information about additional resources (e.g. labour force, tools or AGV vehicles).
- Saving the content and parameters of CLP predicates calls.
- Generating ready scripts for a CLP engine on the basis of the existing data.
- Saving the results obtained with a CLP solver, necessary for further calculations, visualisations or creating reports.
- Saving data about other problems within the family of constrained search problems.

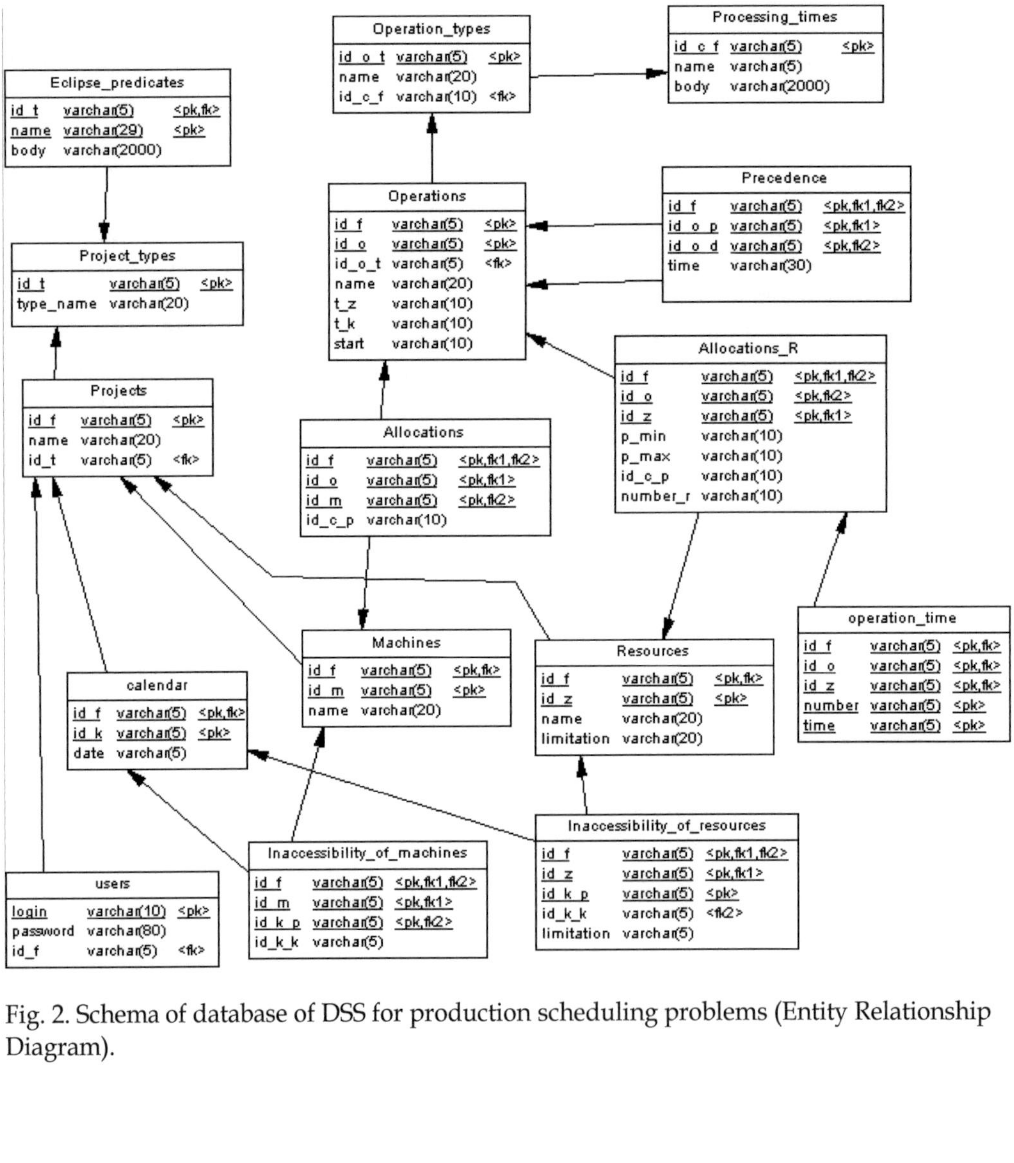

Fig. 2. Schema of database of DSS for production scheduling problems (Entity Relationship Diagram).

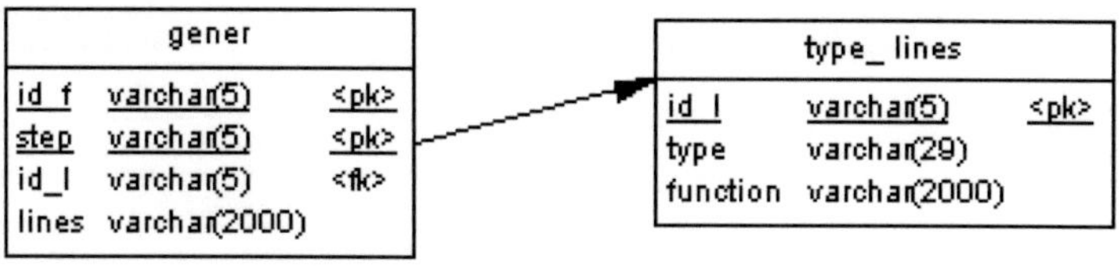

Fig. 2b. Schema of the part of database of DSS for an automatic generation CLP predicates (Entity Relationship Diagram).

Table 1 shows the description of database structure.

Table name	Table description	Column	Column description
Project_types	The types of possible projects for realization	id_t	project_type_id
		type_name	project_type_name
Projects	The specification of separate projects in enterprises	id_f	project_id
		name	project_name
		id_t	project_type_id
Processing_times	The list of functions of time calculation	id_c_f	function_id
		name	function_name
		body	function_body
Opertaion_types	The list of operation types	id_o_t	operation_type_id
		name	operation_type_name
		id_c_f	function_id
Operations	The list of operations to be realized	id_f	project_id
		id_o	operation_id
		id_o_t	operation_type_id
		name	operation_name
		t_z	release time
		t_k	critical time
		start	start time
Precedence	Defines the sequence of the realized operations	id_f	project_id
		id_o_p	operation_id
		id_o_d	operation_id
		time	time between operations
Machines	The specification of available machines for the operation realization	id_f	project_id
		id_m	machine_id
		name	machine_name
Allocations	The allocation of operation to machines	id_f	project_id
		id_o	operation_id
		id_m	machine_id
		id_c_p	parameters_of_function
Resources	The specification of renewable/external resources	id_f	project_id
		id_z	resource_id
		name	resource_name
		limitation	resource_limitation

Table name	Table description	Column	Column description
Allocations_R	The allocation of renewable/external/ additional resources to operations	id_f	project_id
		id_o	operation_id
		id_z	resource_id
		p_min	min number of allocated resource
		p_max	max number of allocated resource
		id_c_p	parameters_of_function
		number_r	number of allocated resource
Calendar	The specification of planning/scheduling periods	id_f	project_id
		id_k	period_number
		date	starting_date
Inaccessibility_ of_machines	The specification of inaccessibility of machines	id_f	project_id
		id_m	machine_id
		id_k_p	number of initial period
		id_k_k	number of final period
Inaccessibility_ of_resources	The specification of limitation/inaccessibilit y of resources	id_f	project_id
		id_z	resource_id
		id_k_p	number of initial period
		id_k_k	number of final period
		accessibility	number of accessible resources
Type_lines		id_l	line generation type
		type	type description
		function	function (in script language)
Gener	Describes the process of model generation for Eclipse	id_f	project_id
		step	number of generation step
		id_l	line generation type
		lines	line to be made
Eclipse_predicates	The codes for the ready predicates of Eclipse	id_f	project_id
		name	name of predicate
		body	code of predicate
Users		login	login
		password	password
		id_f	project_id

Table 1. Description of database structure.

5. Implementation of DSS based on declarative framework

We propose ECL^{i}PS^e (http://www.cs.kuleuven.ac.be, 2008, Apt & Wallace, 2007) and SQL database as a platform to decision support in scheduling problems. ECL^{i}PS^e is a software system - based on the CLP paradigm - for the development and deployment of constraint programming applications. It is also ideal for developing aspects of combinatorial problem solving, e.g. problem modelling, constraint programming, mathematical programming, and search techniques. Its wide scope makes it a good tool for research into hybrid problem solving methods. ECLiPSe comprises several constraint solver libraries, a high-level modelling and control language, interfaces to third-party solvers, an integrated development environment and interfaces for embedding into host environment. The ECLiPSe programming language is largely backward-compatible with Prolog and supports different dialects.

The novelty of the proposed approach is in the integration of the CLP methodology with a commonly used relational database model. The scripts started by a CLP engine are generated automatically on the basis of data in the database (numerical values and CLP predicates). The proposed solution makes it possible to easily develop the system (developing and saving in the database the content of additional CLP predicates) and to integrate it with other computer systems based on a relational SQL database (Fig. 3.). Owing to the developed database structure (see Fig. 2.) solving other problems of the constrained search problems class is possible. In order to ensure an automatic generation of the production scheduling problem model in the form of a script with CLP predicates, two additional tables were added to the database (Fig. 2b). The *gener* table describes the model schema as lines containing the model's identity (*id_f*), generating step (*step*) and the identity of the line type that is to be written in the CLP script (*id_l*) with its source (*lines*). The type of the generated line is determined from the entry in the table *type lines.* The model (CLP script) distinguishes lines created among others as inserting CLP predicate (line in the *eclipse_predicates* table), inserting data after SQL statement, inserting a comment, heading, etc; thus the relation between tables *gener* and *type_lines* is 1:N type (Fig. 2b.).

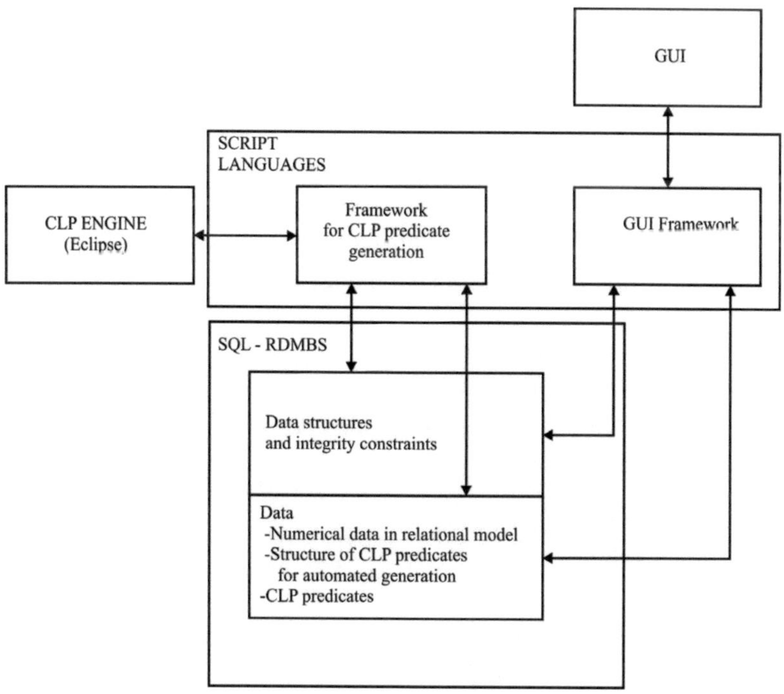

Fig. 3. Implementation of the declarative framework of DSS.

6. Illustrative examples

After the complete implementation of the DSS into ECL^{i}PS^e and SQL environments, computation experiments were carried out. The job-shop scheduling problem with manpower resources (Example 1) and project -building house (Example 2) were considered. The proposed illustrative examples cover a wide range of scheduling problems encountered in the SMEs (Small and Medium Sized Enterprises). The examples are selected in such a way that they how two extremely different forms of production organization; repetitive production in the job-shop environment and the unique production including the project. The presented methodology makes solving scheduling problems possible also in indirect methods of production organization. Moreover, the examples are larded with problems of constrained resources (e.g. manpower, specialized machines, etc.) and the dependence of particular jobs processing time on the amount of the allocated resources, for instance

6.1 Example 1- the job shop scheduling

In the classical scheduling theory job processing times are constant (Example_1a). However, there are many situations where processing time of a job depends on the starting time of the job in queue or the amount of allocated additional resources (e.g. people) (Example_1b) etc. The parameters of computational examples are presented in table 2. The job data structures are shown in Fig. 4a and Fig. 4b

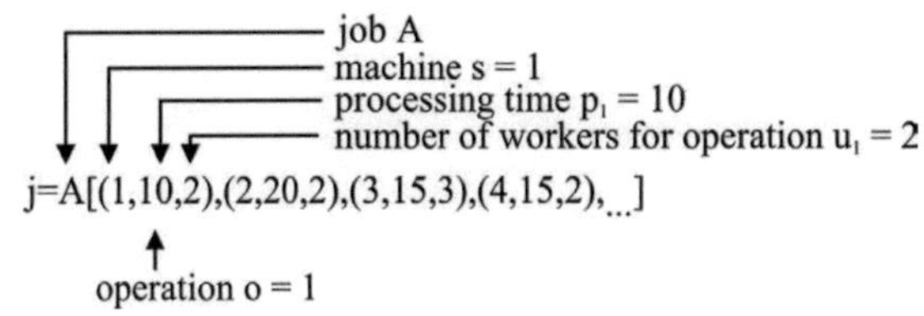

Fig. 4a. Description of task (job) data structure for job-shop computational example (Example_1a) - the constant processing times.

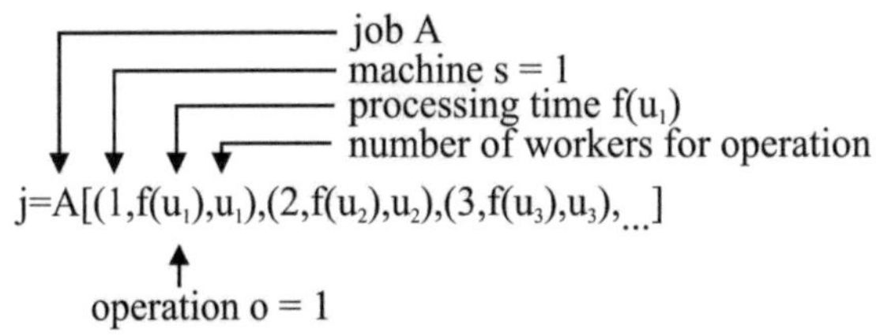

Fig. 4b. Description of task (job) data structure for job-shop computational example (Example_1b) - the processing times depend on allocated number of workers.

j∈{A,B,C,D,E}, o∈{1,2,3,4,5}, s∈{1,2,3,4,5}
j=A [(1,10,2), (2,20,2), (3,15,3), (4,15,2), (5,15,1)]
j=B[(1,10,1), (2,20,1), (3,15,2), (4,15,1), (5,20,1)]
j=C[(5,15,2), (4,20,2), (3,15,1), (2,10,2), (1,20,2)]
j=D[(1,10,3), (3,15,2), (2,20,2), (4,20,1), (5,10,2)]
j=E[(5,15,2), (4,10,1), (3,15,2), (2,10,2), (1,20,1)]

Table 2. (Example_1) - constant processing times

For the computational example (Example_1a) the following questions (write following predicates) were asked:

- *opc_g(_,_)* (see Fig. 5.).
- *opc_d(_, 120)* (see Fig. 6.).
- *opc_s(4,155)* (see Fig. 7.).
- *opc_s(4,180)* (see Fig. 8.).
- *opc_g(5,_)* (see Fig. 9.).

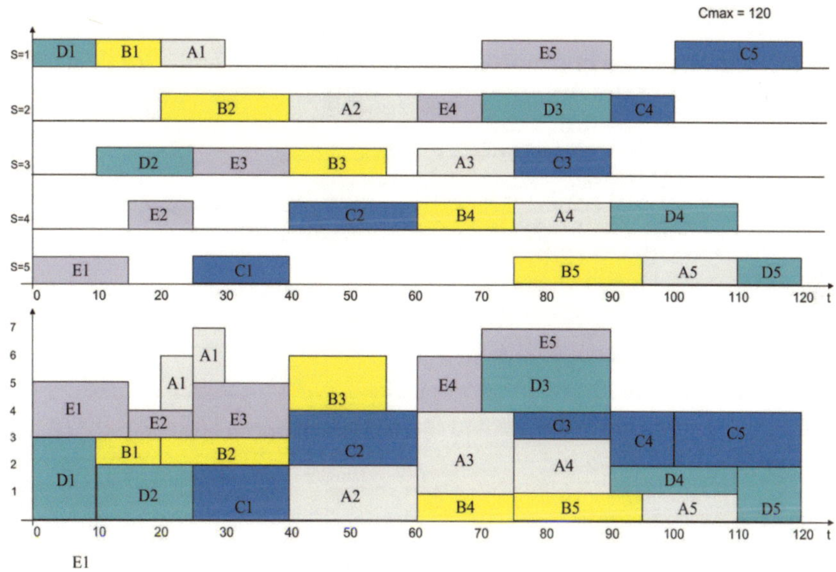

Fig. 5. Gantt's charts for the answer to the question implemented in predicate *opc_g(_,_)*, C_{max}*=120, L=7* (Example_1a).

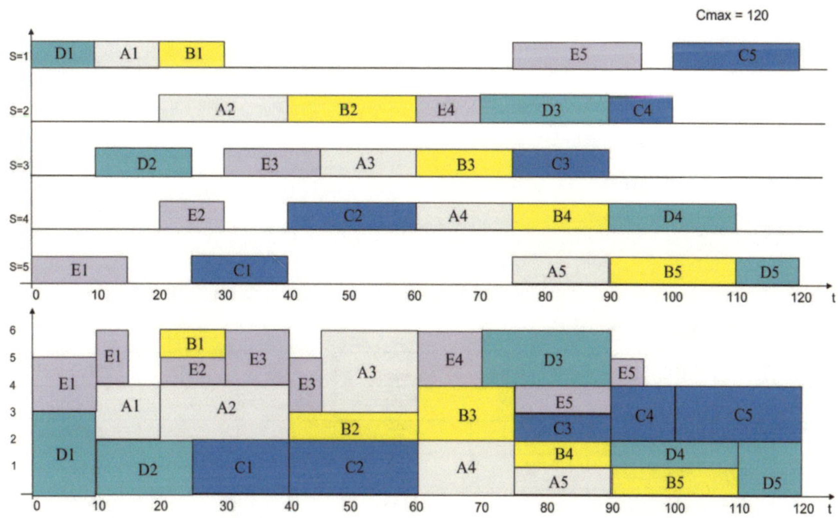

Fig. 6. Gantt's charts for the answer to the question implemented in predicate *opc_d(_,120)*, L_{min}*=6*, $C_{max}= C_{max}{}^{*}=120$ (Example_1a).

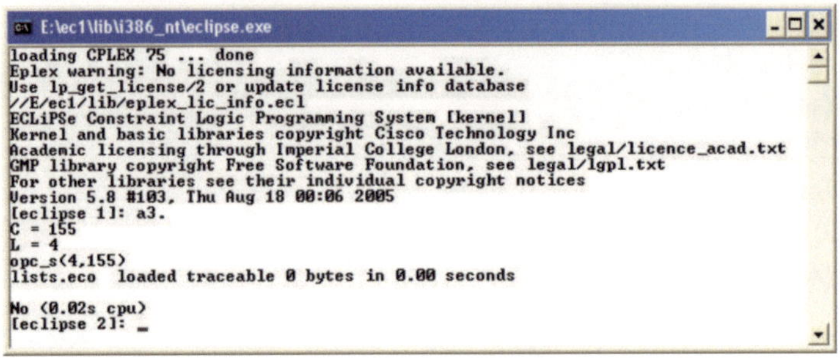

Fig. 7. Answer to the question implemented in predicate *opc_s(4,155)* – ***No*** (Example_1a).

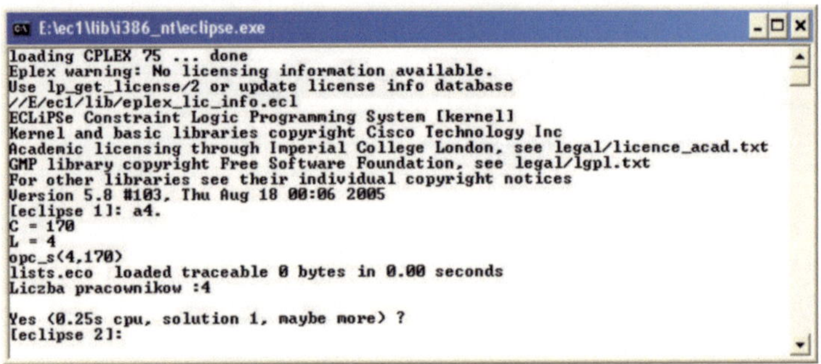

Fig. 8. Answer to the question implemented in predicate *opc_s(4,170)* – ***Yes*** (Example_1a).

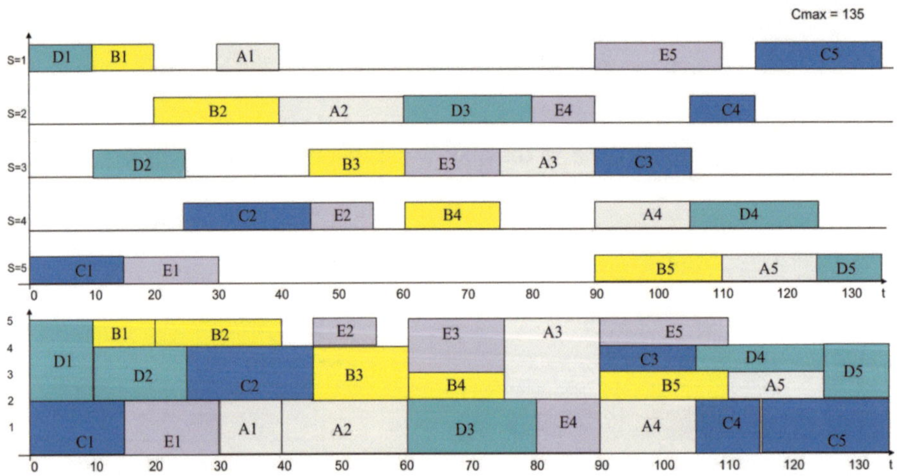

Fig. 9. Gantt's charts for the answer to the question implemented in predicate *opc_g(5,_)*, C_{max}*=135, L=5* (Example_1a).

	Predicate	L	C_{max}	Yes	No	Time (s)
1	*Opc_g(_,_)*	7	120	---	----	0,13
2	*Opc_d(_,120)*	6	120	---	---	0,35
3	*Opc_s(4,155)*	4	155	NO		0,02
4	*Opc_s(4,170)*	4	170	YES		0,25
5	*Opc_g(5,_)*	5	135	---	---	1,35

Table 3. (Example_1a) – Results of asked predicates (Fig.5-9).

The second version of computational example (Example_1b) was carried out with processing times of operation/activity dependent on allocated additional resource (workers). The parameters of computational Example_1b are presented in table 2 without processing times and number of allocated people. The processing time is a function of allocated workers $f(p_j,a_j,u_j)$ Fig. 10.

$$f(p_j,a_j,u_j) = p_j - a_j*(u_j - x_j)$$
and
$$f(p_j,a_j,u_j) > 0\ ,$$
$$a_j = 5,\ x_j \leq u_j \leq 2*x_j$$
where :
p_j - processing time from Example_1
u_j - number of allocated workers
x_j - number of allocated workers from Examle_1a
a_j - acceleration factor

Fig. 10. Processing time for Example_1b.

There is a simple linear function in this example. It can be any function in general case or relationship (relational database table). For the computational example (Example_1b) the following questions (write following predicates) were asked:

- *opc_g(_,_)* (see Fig. 11.).
- *opc_s(8,80)* (see Fig. 12.).
- *opc_d(_,60)* (see Fig. 13.).
- *opc_s(6,60)* (see Fig. 14.).

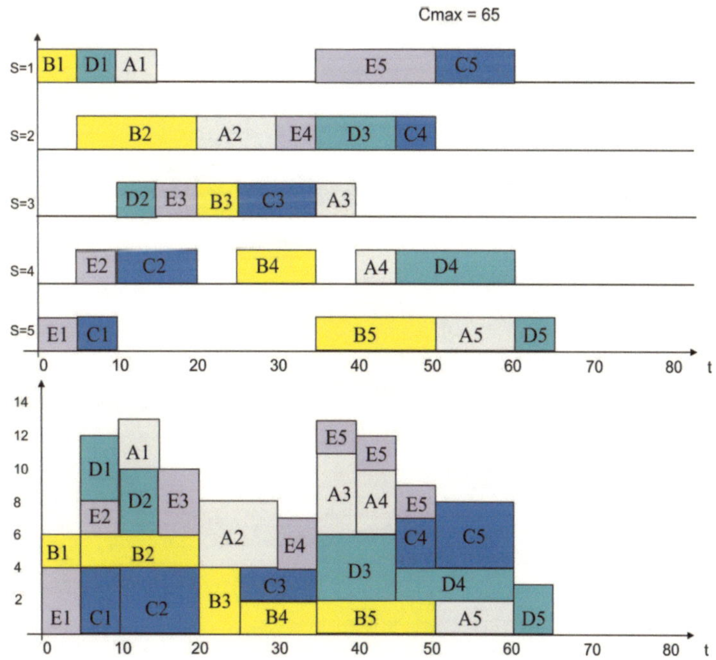

Fig. 11. Gantt's charts for answer to the question implemented in predicate *opc_g(_,_)*, C_{max}*=65, *L*=14 (Example_1b).

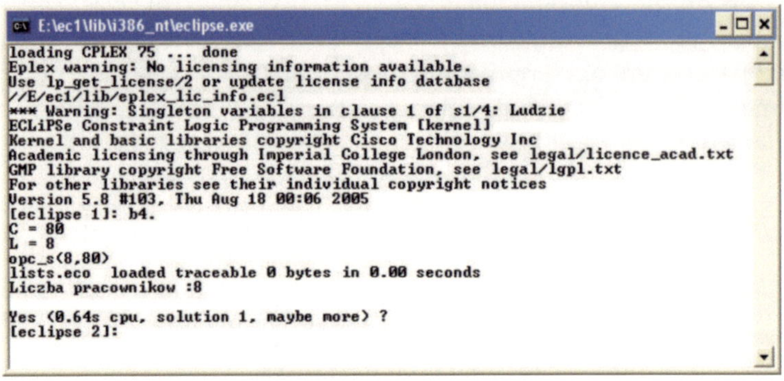

Fig. 12. Answer to the question implemented in predicate *opc_s(8,80)* – ***Yes*** (Example_1b).

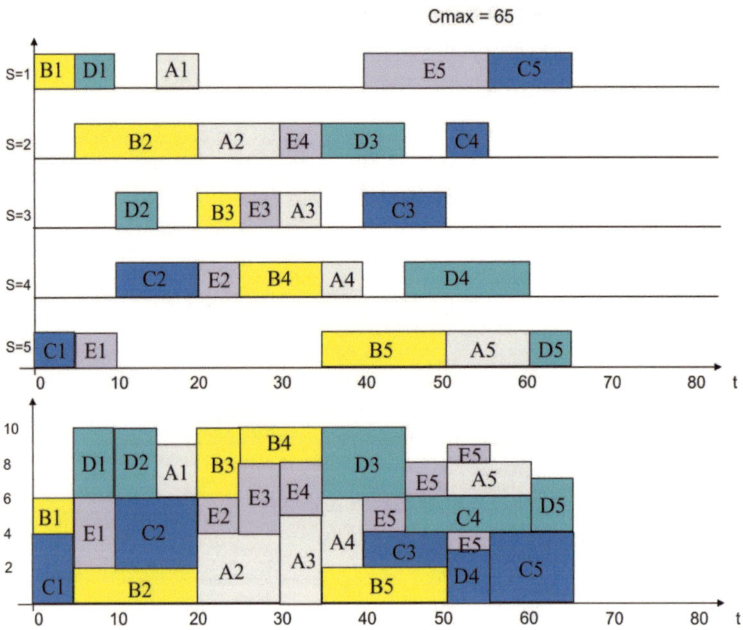

Fig. 13. Gantt's charts for answer to the question implemented in predicate *opc_d(_,65)*, $L_{min}=10$, $C_{max}= C_{max}{}^{*}=65$ (Example_1b).

Fig. 14. Answer to the question implemented in predicate *opc_s(6,60)* – ***No*** (Example_1b).

	Predicate	L	C_{max}	Yes	No	Time (s)
1	*Opc_g(_,_)*	13	65	---	---	0,14
2	*Opc_d(_,65)*	10	65	---	---	17,84
3	*Opc_s(8,80)*	8	80	YES		0,64
4	*Opc_s(6,60)*	6	60	NO		0,05

Table 4. (Example_1b) - Results of asked predicates (Fig.11-14).

6.1 Example 2- Project scheduling – building a house

A typical modern-day project has a variety of complications not considered in the original PERT/CPM methodology. There are three particular situations:

- You may be able to accelerate the completion of a project by speeding up or "crashing" some of the activities in the project.
- Your ability to finish a project quickly is hindered by limited resources (e.g., two activities that might otherwise be done simultaneously, in fact have to be done sequentially because they both require a crane and you have only one crane on site).
- How long it takes to do each activity is a random variable.

In table 5, we list the activities involved in a simple, but nontrivial, project of building a house. An activity cannot be started until all of its predecessors are finished. The network activity for this project has been shown in Fig. 15. To solve this example the DSS with declarative programming (section 4) was used. In this example the processing times of activities depend on allocated manpower resource.

On.	Activity Time	Min_MAN	Max_MAX	Name of activity
1	10	2	2	Dig Basement
2	12	4	6	Pour Foundation
3	6	1	3	Pour Basement
4	6	2	3	Install Floor Joists
5	6	1	3	Install Walls (ext)
6	4	2	8	Install Rafters
7	4	2	4	Install Walls (int)
8	4	2	2	Install Roof
9	16	4	8	Install Windows, Doors (ext)
10	12	4	8	Install Networks
11	12	6	8	Interior Plastering
12	4	2	4	Painting (int)
13	6	2	3	Finish Interior
14	18	6	9	Finish Terrace
15	4	2	4	Garden Arrangement
16	18	6	12	Exterior Plastering

MIN_MAN – minimum manpower (workers) for activity.
MAX_MAN – maximum manpower (workers) for activity.

Table 5. Parameters of Example_2

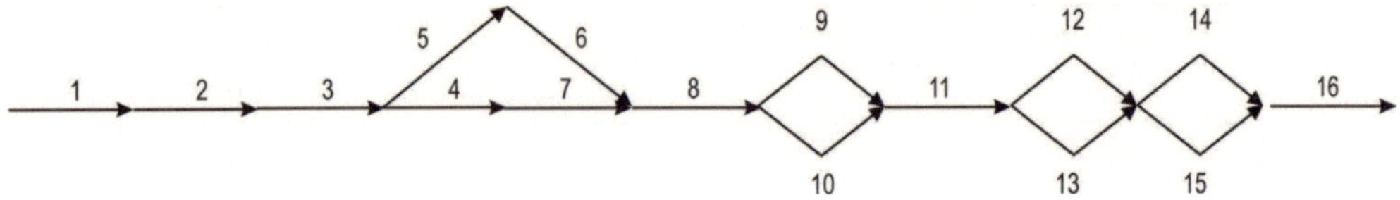

Fig. 15. Activity network for Example_2.

For the computational example the following questions (write following predicates) were asked (see section 4):

- *opc_g(150,200* (see Fig. 16., Table 6,7).
- *opc_g(5,400)* (see Fig. 17., Table 6,7).
- *opc_g(7,200)* (see Fig. 18., Table 6,7).
- *opc_g(12,200)* - processing times of jobs dependent on the allocated additional resource (workers) (see Fig. 19., Table 6,7).

Fig. 16. Answer to the question implemented in predicate *opc_g(150,200)* – ***Yes*** (Example_2).

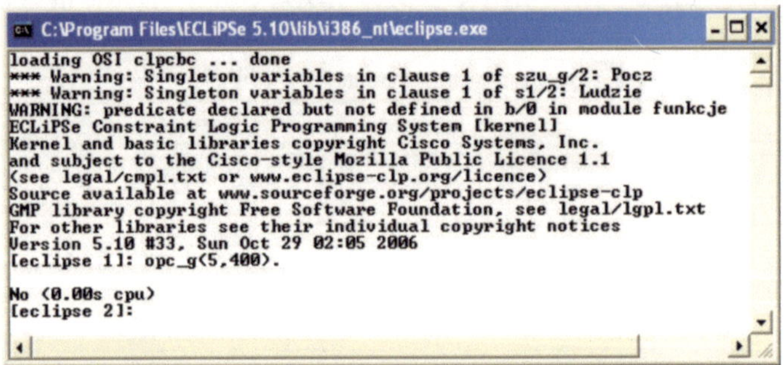

Fig. 17. Answer to the question implemented in predicate *opc_g(5,400)* – ***No*** (Example_2).

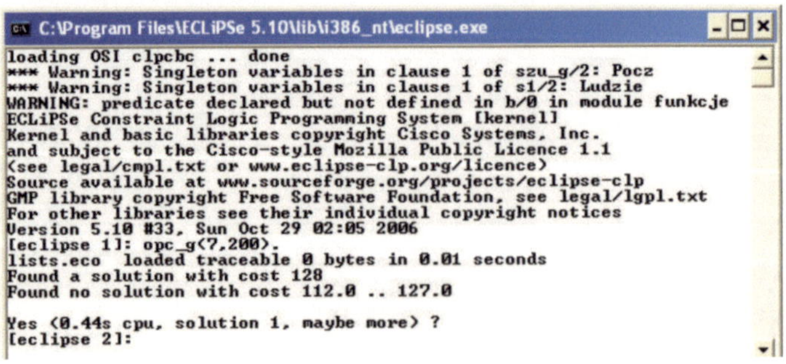

Fig. 18. Answer to the question implemented in predicate *opc_g(7,200)* – ***Yes*** (Example_2).

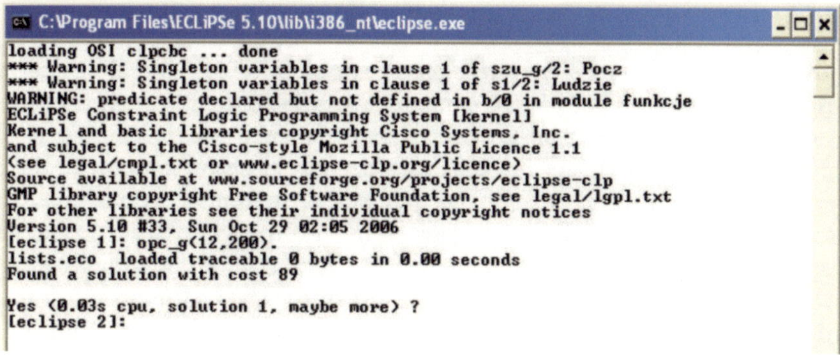

Fig.19. Answer to the question implemented in predicate *opc_g(12,200)*– ***Yes*** (Example_2).

On.	Predicate	L	C	Yes	No	Time (s)
1	*Opc_g(150,200)*	8	112	YES		0,05
2	*Opc_g(5,400)*	5	400	NO		0,00
3	*Opc_g(7,200)*	6	128	YES		0,44
4	*Opc_g(12,200)*	12	89	YES		0,03

Table 6 (Example_2) Results of asked predicates (Fig.16-19).

On.	Opc_g(150,200)	Opc_g(5,400)	Opc_g(7,200)	Opc_g(7,200)
1	0	----	0	0 (2)
2	10	----	10	10 (6)
3	22	----	22	20 (3)
4	28	----	2	24 (3)
5	28	----	28	24 (3)
6	34	----	34	28 (3)
7	34	----	34	29 (4)
8	38	----	38	31 (2)
9	42	----	42	35 (8)
10	42	----	58	35 (4)
11	58	----	70	47 (8)
12	70	----	82	57 (2)
13	70	----	82	57 (3)
14	76	----	88	62 (9)
15	76	----	106	62 (2)
16	94	----	110	77 (12)

Table 7 (Example_2) Result of asked predicates-start times of activities (additional number of allocated workers- only for predicate *Opc_g(7,200)*).

The results obtained for illustrative examples confirm suitability of the proposed framework for building decision support systems in constrained search problems. In scheduling problems the decision maker is provided with support related to possibilities of task accomplishment in the set time, necessary resources and their exploitation in time, possibilities of the realization of other tasks, decision optimization, etc.

7. Conclusions

The proposed approach can be considered to be a contribution to scheduling and especially to scheduling problems with additional/external resources. In many enterprises this kind of resources can have an influence on production and delivery schedules. That is especially important in the context of cheap, fast and user friendly decision support in SMEs. Great flexibility of the presented approach and practically unlimited possibilities of asking questions through creating predicates cannot be overestimated. What is more, the whole decision system can be built in one modeling and programming declarative environment, which lowers costs and adds to the solution effectiveness. The CLP-tools fulfill the need of intelligent production management structures and can be based successfully in cases of scheduling problems with external resources. The proposed approach seems to be a viable alternative option for supporting quite a number of decision making processes. The originality of our approach, which achieves the transition from custom imperative programming to declarative programming in a field of scheduling problems, consists in the data structure and CLP implementation. The presented framework can be implemented in many other constrained search problems apart from scheduling such as planning, routing, placement etc.

8. References

Liao S.Y., Wang H.Q., Liao L.J. "An extended formalism to constraint logic programming for decision analysis, Knowledge-based Systems" 15, 2002, pp 189-202.

Pape C.Le "Three Mechanisms for Managing Resource Constraints in a Library for Constraint-Based Scheduling Proceedings" INRIA/IEEE Conference on Emerging Technologies and Factory Automation, 1995.

Ryu U. Young ."Constraint logic programming framework for integrated decision supports" Decision Support Systems 22, 1998, pp 155-170.

Bisdorff R., Laurent S. "Industrial linear optimization problem solved by constraint logic programming", European Journal of Operational Research 84 (1), 1995, pp 82-95.

Lamma E., Mello P., Milano M. "A distributed constrained-based scheduler", Artificial Intelligence in Engineering 11,1997, pp 91-105.

Lee H.G., Lee G. Yu., "Constraint logic programming for qualitative and quantitative constraint satisfaction problems", Decision Support Systems 16 (1), 1996, pp 67-83. http://www.cs.kuleuven.ac.be/

Apt K.R., Wallace M.G. "Constraint Logic Programming using ECL^{i}PS^{e}", Cambridge, 2007

15

Derivation and Calculation of the Dynamics of Elastic Parallel Manipulators

Krzysztof Stachera and Walter Schumacher
Technical University of Braunschweig, Institute of Control Engineering
Germany

1. Introduction

Many algorithms for the modelling and calculation of the dynamics of rigid parallel manipulators already exist, and are based on two approaches: The Newton-Euler method and the Lagrangian principle. For the Newton-Euler method the dynamics equations are generated by the complete analysis of all forces and torques of each rigid body in the robot's structure (Featherstone & Orin, 2000, Spong & Vidyasagar, 1989). Therefore, the derivation of the equations of motion for complex systems becomes very complicated and laborious. However, due to the fact that all forces are explicitly regarded and analysed, this method supplies a very advanced understanding of the system's dynamics. The use of the Lagrangian principle is a much more elegant and efficient procedure. A scalar function called the Lagrangian is generated, and describes the entire kinetic, potential and dissipative energy of the system in generalized coordinates. For parallel manipulators, additional equations which describe the closed kinematic loop constraints, still have to be provided. The equation of motion for the parallel structure consists thus of the system of Lagrange and algebraic equations (DAE).

The Lagrangian method is very widely used in the area of parallel manipulators (Beyer, 1928, Kock, 2001). In particular, two procedures from this family are established here: Namely the Lagrangian equations of the first type (Kang & Mills, 2002, Miller & Clavel, 1992, Murray et al., 1994, Tsai, 1999) and the Lagrange-D'Alembert formulation (Nakamura, 1991, Nakamura & Ghodoussi, 1989, Park et al., 1999, Stachera, 2006a, Stachera, 2006b, Yiu et al., 2001). The use of generalized coordinates is employed in these procedures. Those being the coordinates of the active joints as well as an additional set of redundant coordinates of the passive non-actuated joints or end-effector coordinates. Active joints are the actuated joints of the machine. In the case of elastic manipulators a set of elastic degrees of freedom (DOF) will be introduced. In these generalized coordinates the energy function will be formulated. Additionally, the closed kinematic loop constraints of the parallel structure must also be considered. In the Lagrangian equations of the first type this is achieved by Lagrange multipliers. Contrary to these equations, for the Lagrange-D'Alembert formulation, the Jacobian matrices of the kinematic constraints parameterised by the non-redundant coordinates are used. The policy with the Jacobian matrix has the great advantage that the well known methods and techniques for the modelling of the manipulator's chain dynamics, which were already applied to serial elastic robots can be

used (Khalil & Gautier, 2000, Piedboeuf, 2001, Robinett et al., 2002). In this way, effects of friction, elasticities, etc. can be considered by the modelling of the dynamics without laborious modifications. This procedure provides compact equations of the manipulators dynamics, which is advantageous for system analysis and control design. The problem arises with the calculation of the direct dynamics of both presented approaches; it requires the inversion of the inertia matrix, which can be CPU-intensive for matrices of higher order and can thereby constitute a limitation in the real-time calculation for control purposes. The consideration of the manipulator's elasticities can introduce matrices of such high order. The partitioning of the dynamics equations into many groups and their calculation in parallel can reduce the computational effort. Approaches, which consider this problem can be found in the literature. A virtual spring approach has been proposed for this type of parallel processing (Wang & Gosselin, 2000, Wang et al., 2002). In this method, the modelling technique requires the modification of the model and the introduction of additional elements. In the case of elastic manipulators it seems to be a not desirable procedure.
Firstly this chapter presents a brief description of the two above mentioned Lagrangian based methods. It will be shown, how the equations of the inverse and direct dynamics can be obtained, subsequently, the main features of these methods are discussed. These formulations will be extended in comparison with previous research to consider the elastic degrees of freedom. The presentation of elasticities as discrete degrees of freedom does not introduce any limitations of the method and is a conventional method for the analysis of elastic robots (Beres & Sasiadek, 1995, Robinett et al., 2002). In addition to that, a new method for the derivation of the Jacobian matrix of the parallel manipulators will be presented (Stachera & Schumacher, 2007). This method allows the Jacobian matrix of the parallel manipulator to be derived systematically from the Jacobian matrices of the individual serial kinematic chains. Based on these procedures, the method - *Simultaneous Calculation of the Direct Dynamics* (SCDD) for elastic parallel manipulators will be presented. The idea of the "reduced system", which was already used to calculate the inverse dynamics, will be considered. The kinematic constraints of the closed loops are introduced here with the help of the forces and torques of the tree structure. Therefore the equations remain simple and their complexity should not rise. This feature is very important for simulations, for the application of an observer for complex systems or in a feedback control. The new method will then be compared with the existing one and the results will be discussed thereafter.

2. Lagrangian equations of the first type

The Lagrangian equations of the first type are formulated in a set of redundant coordinates (Kang & Mills, 2002, Miller & Clavel, 1992, Tsai, 1999). We assume that the manipulator possesses in all n joints, e and p of them are respectively discrete elastic DOF and passive joints as redundant coordinates. All of which joints have one degree of freedom. Coordinates of the end-effector or moving platform can be also used as redundant coordinates. The coordinates of the actuated joints n_a and the elastic DOF $n_e=e$ form a set of non-redundant coordinates. We assume the controllability of the manipulator structure in absence of elasticity. The coordinates of the structure are:

$$\mathbf{q}_t = \mathbf{q}_t(\mathbf{q}_a, \mathbf{q}_p, \mathbf{q}_e), \tag{1}$$

where $\mathbf{q}_a \in R^{(na\times1)}$, $\mathbf{q}_p \in R^{(np\times1)}$, $\mathbf{q}_e \in R^{(ne\times1)}$ and the dimension of $\mathbf{q}_t \in R^{(nt\times1)}$, where $n_t = n_a + n_p + n_e$. The $\mathbf{q}_t$ coordinates comprise the redundant degrees of freedom of the rigid movement of the manipulator augmented by degrees of freedom of the elastic deformation of the robot's structure. The redundant coordinates of the passive joints $\mathbf{q}_p$ depend on the remaining coordinates:

$$\mathbf{q}_p = \mathbf{q}_p(\mathbf{q}_a, \mathbf{q}_e). \tag{2}$$

Using (2) we can further write (1) as $\mathbf{q}_t = \mathbf{q}_t(\mathbf{q}_a, \mathbf{q}_e)$. In order to solve the dynamics equation, due to redundant coordinates, the formulation of dynamics requires a set of additional constraint equations. These can be determined by examining the structure of the system, with respect to the closed kinematic loop constraints of the parallel manipulator. The constraints equations and their derivatives supplement the original equations of the machine dynamics, so that the number of equations is equal to that of the unknowns. Therefore the Lagrangian equations of the first type are formulated as follows

$$\frac{d}{dt}\frac{\partial L_t}{\partial \dot{\mathbf{q}}_t} - \frac{\partial L_t}{\partial \mathbf{q}_t} + \frac{\partial Q_t}{\partial \dot{\mathbf{q}}_t} = \boldsymbol{\tau}_t + \sum_{i=1}^{np} \lambda_i \frac{\partial h_i}{\partial \mathbf{q}_t}, \tag{3}$$

where L_t is the Lagrange function consists of the kinetic and potential energy of the system, Q_t means the function of the dissipative energy, h_i denotes the ith constraint function, n_p is the number of constraints and at the same time number of redundant coordinates, $\boldsymbol{\tau}_t$ are the generalised torques and forces and λ_i are the Lagrange multipliers. In order to simplify the solution of these equations, they will be divided into two sets (Tsai, 1999).

2.1 Inverse dynamics

The first set of n_p equations refers to the redundant coordinates and is associated with the kinematic constraints of the closed loops. Here, the unknowns are the Lagrange multipliers $\lambda_i \in R^{(np\times1)}$. Hence, these equations take the form

$$\sum_{i=1}^{np} \lambda_i \frac{\partial h_i}{\partial \mathbf{q}_t} = \frac{d}{dt}\frac{\partial L_t}{\partial \dot{\mathbf{q}}_t} - \frac{\partial L_t}{\partial \mathbf{q}_t} + \frac{\partial Q_t}{\partial \dot{\mathbf{q}}_t} - \hat{\boldsymbol{\tau}}_t, \tag{4}$$

where $\hat{\boldsymbol{\tau}}_t$ represents generalised torques and forces. They represent the external potential and non-potential forces, acting on the manipulator, which are already known. Here, the torques of the actuators are not taken into account. From these n_p equations of the redundant coordinates the n_p Lagrange multipliers are calculated. The second set is related to the (n_a+n_e) non-redundant coordinates. The only unknowns in these equations are the forces and torques of the actuators, which can be computed from

$$\boldsymbol{\tau}_t = \frac{d}{dt}\frac{\partial L_t}{\partial \dot{\mathbf{q}}_t} - \frac{\partial L_t}{\partial \mathbf{q}_t} + \frac{\partial Q_t}{\partial \dot{\mathbf{q}}_t} - \sum_{i=1}^{np} \lambda_i \frac{\partial h_i}{\partial \mathbf{q}_t}. \tag{5}$$

With these two equation sets (4) and (5), the torques and forces of the actuators for a given trajectory are computed, and thus produce the desired movement of the elastic parallel manipulator.

2.2 Direct dynamics

For the given torques, the direct dynamics can be computed in a similar way. The n_p redundant coordinates and their derivatives are calculated from the closed kinematic loop constraints h_i and their derivatives. These redundant coordinates result from the non-redundant coordinates of the active joints and elastic DOF. The constraint forces of the structure are then computed (4). Finally, now that the input torques of the parallel manipulator and the constraint forces are known, (5) must be solved for the unknown accelerations of the non-redundant coordinates. Further, these equations can be solved by numerical integration, and the n_p Lagrange multipliers from (4) can also be computed on this way.

2.3 Features of the method of the Lagrangian equations of the first type

The coordinates of the active joints and elastic DOF form a subset of the selected generalised redundant coordinates. The remaining coordinates can be selected freely. These can be the coordinates of the platform, the end-effector or of the passive joints (Kang & Mills, 2002, Miller & Clavel, 1992, Tsai, 1999). Here the Lagrange multipliers might also have the meaning of generalised torques and forces, which determine the constraints of the closed loops for the serial kinematic chains. The disadvantage of this method is that, for the modelling of the manipulator, various simplifications must be made. In order to consider the Lagrange multipliers, the methods for the modelling of the dynamics that are used for the serial kinematic chains can require a modification. However, due to the equations' structures, a clear physical interpretation of the terms is not always possible, and therefore the employment of this method remains slightly complicated.

3. Lagrange-D'Alembert formulation (L-D'A)

3.1 Inverse dynamics

The Lagrange-D'Alembert formulation represents an elegant and effective consideration of the problem of manipulator's dynamics (Nakamura, 1991, Nakamura & Ghodoussi, 1989, Park et al., 1999, Yiu et al., 2001). Here, no additional multipliers are calculated. A set of independent and dependent generalized coordinates which satisfy the constraints of the mechanical system is chosen. The coordinates of the elastic DOF belong to the group of independent coordinates and are associated with the corresponding internal forces, resulting from the stress induced in the material. The procedure corresponds to the methods, which are known from the serial manipulators and consists of the following three steps:

1. *Transformation of the System:* Each closed kinematic loop of the parallel manipulator is separated at a passive joint, end-effector or link. The result is a tree structure as a reduced system (Nakamura & Ghodoussi, 1989). Consequently, only serial kinematics chains can be found in this system. Furthermore it is assumed that all remaining passive joints are equipped with virtual actuators.
2. *Computation of the Torques:* The torques and forces of the real and virtual actuators are computed for each kinematic chain. These torques and forces cause a movement in every chain, and these movements correspond to the movement of the original closed-link structure.
3. *Transformation of the Torques:* The torques and forces of the original parallel manipulator's actuators are calculated from the forces and torques of the tree structure by considering the additional closed kinematic loop constraints.

We assume that the manipulator consists of l closed kinematic loops. It possesses in all n joints, e and p of them are respectively discrete elastic DOF and passive joints. All of which joints have one degree of freedom. The coordinates of the active joints and elastic DOF form a set of non-redundant coordinates. We assume the controllability of the manipulator in absence of elasticity. According to the first step we divide this system into a tree structure. The number of active joints remains the same as in the original structure $n_a = (n-p-e)$. The number of passive joints amounts to $n_p = (p-l)$ and the number of the elastic DOF amounts to $n_e = e$. The coordinates of the tree structure are:

$$\mathbf{q}_t = \mathbf{q}_t(\mathbf{q}_a, \mathbf{q}_p, \mathbf{q}_e), \tag{6}$$

where $\mathbf{q}_e \in R^{(na\times 1)}$, $\mathbf{q}_p \in R^{(np\times 1)}$, $\mathbf{q}_e \in R^{(ne\times 1)}$ and the dimension of $\mathbf{q}_t \in R^{(nt\times 1)}$, where $n_t = n_a + n_p + n_e$. The redundant coordinates of the passive joints $\mathbf{q}_p$ depend on the coordinates of the active joints $\mathbf{q}_a$ and the elastic DOF $\mathbf{q}_e$:

$$\mathbf{q}_p = \mathbf{q}_p(\mathbf{q}_{ae}), \tag{7}$$

where $\mathbf{q}_{ae} \in R^{(nae\times 1)}$ and $n_{ae} = n_a + n_e$. Using (7) we can further write (6) as $\mathbf{q}_t = \mathbf{q}_t(\mathbf{q}_{ae})$. Generally, the relation represented in (7) does not exist analytically, but the quantity of redundant coordinates can always be determined by the consideration of the geometrical dependencies in the manipulator structure (Merlet, 2000, Stachera, 2005). Therefore, in order to determine the relationship between the velocities and accelerations of the active and passive joints, a more suitable solution must be derived (Yiu et al., 2001). For this purpose we introduce the closed kinematic loop constraints of the parallel manipulator:

$$h(\mathbf{q}_t) = h(\mathbf{q}_{ae}, \mathbf{q}_p) = 0. \tag{8}$$

By differentiation of (8) we obtain the constraints in the Pfaffian form:

$$\frac{\partial h}{\partial \mathbf{q}_{ae}^T}\dot{\mathbf{q}}_{ae} + \frac{\partial h}{\partial \mathbf{q}_p^T}\dot{\mathbf{q}}_p = 0. \tag{9}$$

Our goal is now to find the transformation between the tree structure and the original parallel manipulator. According to the D'Alembert principle the performed virtual work for both systems, the reduced and the original one, has to be equal:

$$\delta\mathbf{q}_c^T\boldsymbol{\tau}_c = \delta\mathbf{q}_t^T\boldsymbol{\tau}_t, \tag{10}$$

where $\boldsymbol{\tau}_t \in R^{(nt\times 1)}$ represents all forces and torques of the real and virtual drives of the tree system and $\boldsymbol{\tau}_c \in R^{(nae\times 1)}$ the drive torques of the original parallel manipulator. Hence, the Lagrange equations for the reduced system can be formulated:

$$\left(\frac{d}{dt}\frac{\partial L_t}{\partial \dot{\mathbf{q}}_t} - \frac{\partial L_t}{\partial \mathbf{q}_t} + \frac{\partial Q_t}{\partial \dot{\mathbf{q}}_t} - \boldsymbol{\tau}_t\right)^T \delta\mathbf{q}_t = 0, \tag{11}$$

where L_t is the Lagrange function of the tree structure and Q_t is the function of the dissipative energy. This Lagrange function consists of the kinetic and potential energy of the system $L_t = T_t - V_t$. We assume that the robot is normally actuated and away from actuator singularity. The matrix from (9) - $\frac{\partial h}{\partial \mathbf{q}_p^T}$ is square and invertible. The configuration space of the manipulator can be smoothly parameterised by the coordinates of the active joints and the elastic DOF $\mathbf{q}_{ae}$:

$$\dot{\mathbf{q}}_p = \left(\frac{\partial h}{\partial \mathbf{q}_p^T}\right)^{-1}\left(\frac{\partial h}{\partial \mathbf{q}_{ae}^T}\right)\dot{\mathbf{q}}_{ae} = \left(\frac{\partial \mathbf{q}_p}{\partial \mathbf{q}_{ae}^T}\right)\dot{\mathbf{q}}_{ae}\,. \tag{12}$$

Therefore the equations of the tree structure can be expressed in the non-redundant coordinates $\mathbf{q}_{ae}$. Considering (6), (11) and (12):

$$\begin{aligned}&\left(\frac{d}{dt}\frac{\partial L_t}{\partial \dot{\mathbf{q}}_{ae}} - \frac{\partial L_t}{\partial \mathbf{q}_{ae}} + \frac{\partial Q_t}{\partial \dot{\mathbf{q}}_{ae}} - \boldsymbol{\tau}_{ae}\right)^T \delta\mathbf{q}_{ae}\\ &+\left(\frac{d}{dt}\frac{\partial L_t}{\partial \dot{\mathbf{q}}_p} - \frac{\partial L_t}{\partial \mathbf{q}_p} + \frac{\partial Q_t}{\partial \dot{\mathbf{q}}_p} - \boldsymbol{\tau}_p\right)^T \delta\mathbf{q}_p = 0\end{aligned}, \tag{13}$$

and it is:

$$\begin{aligned}&\left(\frac{d}{dt}\frac{\partial L_t}{\partial \dot{\mathbf{q}}_{ae}} - \frac{\partial L_t}{\partial \mathbf{q}_{ae}} + \frac{\partial Q_t}{\partial \dot{\mathbf{q}}_{ae}}\right) + \left(\frac{\partial \mathbf{q}_p}{\partial \mathbf{q}_{ae}^T}\right)^T \cdot\\ &\left(\frac{d}{dt}\frac{\partial L_t}{\partial \dot{\mathbf{q}}_p} - \frac{\partial L_t}{\partial \mathbf{q}_p} + \frac{\partial Q_t}{\partial \dot{\mathbf{q}}_p}\right) = \boldsymbol{\tau}_{ae} + \left(\frac{\partial \mathbf{q}_p}{\partial \mathbf{q}_{ae}^T}\right)^T \boldsymbol{\tau}_p\end{aligned}. \tag{14}$$

The equations of motion of the entire parallel manipulator are similar to (11) and take the following form:

$$\left(\frac{d}{dt}\frac{\partial L_c}{\partial \dot{\mathbf{q}}_{ae}} - \frac{\partial L_c}{\partial \mathbf{q}_{ae}} + \frac{\partial Q_c}{\partial \dot{\mathbf{q}}_{ae}}\right) = \boldsymbol{\tau}_c\,. \tag{15}$$

Regarding (10), (14) and (15) we can finally write:

$$\begin{aligned}&\frac{d}{dt}\frac{\partial L_c}{\partial \dot{\mathbf{q}}_{ae}} - \frac{\partial L_c}{\partial \mathbf{q}_{ae}} + \frac{\partial Q_c}{\partial \dot{\mathbf{q}}_{ae}} =\\ &\left(\frac{d}{dt}\frac{\partial L_t}{\partial \dot{\mathbf{q}}_{ae}} - \frac{\partial L_t}{\partial \mathbf{q}_{ae}} + \frac{\partial Q_t}{\partial \dot{\mathbf{q}}_{ae}}\right)\\ &+\left(\frac{\partial \mathbf{q}_p}{\partial \mathbf{q}_{ae}^T}\right)^T \cdot \left(\frac{d}{dt}\frac{\partial L_t}{\partial \dot{\mathbf{q}}_p} - \frac{\partial L_t}{\partial \mathbf{q}_p} + \frac{\partial Q_t}{\partial \dot{\mathbf{q}}_p}\right)\end{aligned}, \tag{16}$$

$$\boldsymbol{\tau}_c = \boldsymbol{\tau}_{ae} + \left(\frac{\partial \mathbf{q}_p}{\partial \mathbf{q}_{ae}^T}\right)^T \boldsymbol{\tau}_p\,. \tag{17}$$

From these derivations, the transformation matrix between the tree structure and the original closed-link structure can be formulated:

$$\mathbf{W} = \frac{\partial \mathbf{q}_t}{\partial \mathbf{q}_{ae}^T} = \begin{bmatrix} \mathbf{I} \\ \frac{\partial \mathbf{q}_P}{\partial \mathbf{q}_{ae}^T} \end{bmatrix}. \tag{18}$$

Proofs of these derivations can be found in works (Nakamura, 1991, Nakamura & Ghodoussi, 1989).

Now, the equations of the manipulator's dynamics will be written in matrix form. The equations of motion of the tree structure are described by the following expression:

$$\begin{aligned} &\mathbf{M}_t(\mathbf{q}_t)\ddot{\mathbf{q}}_t + \mathbf{C}_t(\dot{\mathbf{q}}_t, \mathbf{q}_t)\dot{\mathbf{q}}_t + \boldsymbol{\eta}_t(\mathbf{q}_t) \\ &+ \mathbf{K}_t\mathbf{q}_t + \mathbf{D}_t\dot{\mathbf{q}}_t = \boldsymbol{\tau}_t \end{aligned}, \tag{19}$$

where the $\mathbf{M}_t(\mathbf{q}_t), \mathbf{C}_t(\dot{\mathbf{q}}_t, \mathbf{q}_t) \in R^{(nt \times nt)}$ are the inertia matrix and the Coriolis matrix of the tree structure respectively. These matrices satisfy the following structural properties:

1. $\mathbf{M}_t(\mathbf{q}_t)$ is symmetric and positive definite matrix,
2. $\dot{\mathbf{M}}_t(\mathbf{q}_t) - 2\mathbf{C}_t(\dot{\mathbf{q}}_t, \mathbf{q}_t)$ is a skrew-symmetric matrix.

$\boldsymbol{\eta}(\mathbf{q}_t) \in R^{(nt \times 1)}$ is the vector of the gravity force reflected in the joints' space. $\mathbf{K}_t \in R^{(nt \times nt)}$ and $\mathbf{D}_t \in R^{(nt \times nt)}$ represent the diagonal matrices of the lumped elasticities and lumped dampings in the joints' space. By using the matrix $\mathbf{W}$ from (18) the equations of the dynamics of the tree structure (19) can be transformed into the equations of the closed-link mechanism. Then, they are expressed only in dependence on the coordinates of the active joints $\mathbf{q}_a$ and the elastic DOF $\mathbf{q}_e$:

$$\begin{aligned} &\mathbf{M}_c(\mathbf{q}_t)\ddot{\mathbf{q}}_{ae} + \mathbf{C}_c(\dot{\mathbf{q}}_t, \mathbf{q}_t)\dot{\mathbf{q}}_{ae} + \boldsymbol{\eta}_c(\mathbf{q}_t) \\ &+ \mathbf{K}_c\mathbf{q}_{ae} + \mathbf{D}_c\dot{\mathbf{q}}_{ae} = \boldsymbol{\tau}_c \end{aligned}, \tag{20}$$

where:

$$\mathbf{M}_c = \mathbf{W}^T\mathbf{M}_t\mathbf{W} \in R^{(nae \times nae)}, \tag{21}$$

$$\mathbf{C}_c = \mathbf{W}^T\mathbf{M}_t\dot{\mathbf{W}} + \mathbf{W}^T\mathbf{C}_t\mathbf{W} \in R^{(nae \times nae)}, \tag{22}$$

$$\boldsymbol{\eta}_c = \mathbf{W}^T\boldsymbol{\eta}_t \in R^{(nae \times 1)}, \tag{23}$$

$$\mathbf{K}_c = \mathbf{W}^T\mathbf{K}_t\mathbf{W} \in R^{(nae \times nae)}, \tag{24}$$

$$\mathbf{D}_c = \mathbf{W}^T\mathbf{D}_t\mathbf{W} \in R^{(nae \times nae)}. \tag{25}$$

From these considerations, two methods for the computation of the inverse dynamics of the parallel manipulator result. In the first method, the real and virtual forces and torques of the tree structure (11) are computed. These torques are then transformed with (17) or (18) into the drive torques of the closed-link structure. In the second method, the equations of the dynamics of the tree structure (19) are transformed into the compact equations of the closed-link mechanism (20) and parameterised (21)-(25) by the non-redundant coordinates $\mathbf{q}_{ae}$. With these the drive torques can then be calculated.

3.2 Direct dynamics

In this method the equations of the direct dynamics are obtained from the compact equations (20) of the manipulator's inverse dynamics:

$$\begin{aligned}\ddot{\mathbf{q}}_{ae} = \mathbf{M}_c(\mathbf{q}_t)^{-1}(\boldsymbol{\tau}_c - \mathbf{C}_c(\dot{\mathbf{q}}_t, \mathbf{q}_t)\dot{\mathbf{q}}_{ae} \\ - \boldsymbol{\eta}_c(\mathbf{q}_t) - \mathbf{K}_c\mathbf{q}_{ae} - \mathbf{D}_c\dot{\mathbf{q}}_{ae})\end{aligned} \quad . \tag{26}$$

According to this, the complex equations of the direct dynamics, parameterized by the coordinates of the active joints and elastic DOF $\mathbf{q}_{ae}$ are obtained. The redundant coordinates of the passive joints, which are necessary for the computation of the matrices, result from the closed kinematic loop constraints of the parallel manipulator (7) as well as their first (12) and second derivatives.

3.3 Features of the Lagrange-D'Alembert formulation

In this method, for the modelling of the elastic parallel manipulators' dynamics one can use, without modifications, the well known methods and techniques from serial robotics (Khalil & Gautier, 2000, Piedboeuf, 2001, Robinett et al., 2002). The computations of the inverse dynamics can be carried out in parallel, and therefore can be faster, which is an advantage for the real time calculation of the manipulator's model. The method of the direct dynamics produces the compact equations of the elastic parallel manipulator. The disadvantage is that the computations cannot be executed in parallel. If more parameters are to be considered for the modelling, e.g. Finite-Element-Method (Beres & Sasiadek, 1995, Wang & Mills, 2004), the compact matrices of the system can reach such dimensions, that their calculation is simply not possible in real time.

4. New method for derivation of the Jacobian matrix of the parallel manipulator

In the conventional methods the Jacobian of the parallel manipulator will be derived from the velocity vector-loop method (Tsai, 1999) or from the analysis of the parallel manipulator's statics (Kock, 2001, Merlet, 2000). The Lagrange-D'Alembert Method (Nakamura, 1991, Nakamura & Ghodoussi, 1989, Park et al., 1999, Yiu et al., 2001) makes it possible to systematically convert between the single models of serial kinematic chains to the model of the compact parallel manipulator. In this method, however, it was not shown how the Jacobian matrices of the serial kinematic chains of the tree structure $\mathbf{J}_i$ can be transformed into the Jacobian of the parallel manipulator $\mathbf{G}$. An algorithm was developed because of that, in order to perform this transformation. For this purpose, the $\mathbf{W}$ matrix, representing the parameterisation of the configuration space from (18) and the static matrix $\mathbf{S}$ of the parallel manipulator are used. The static matrix $\mathbf{S}$ describes the relationship between the forces in the arms of the parallel manipulators $\mathbf{f}_B \in R^{(na \times 1)}$ and the force on its end-effector $\mathbf{f}_{XYZ}$. The external force $\mathbf{f}_{XYZ}$ acting on the end-effector is distributed into the corresponding branches, shown in the Fig. 1.
These forces in the branches can be calculated through the following relationship:

$$\mathbf{f}_B = \begin{bmatrix}\mathbf{s}_1 & \dots & \mathbf{s}_{na}\end{bmatrix}^{-1}\mathbf{f}_{XYZ} = \mathbf{S}^{-1}\mathbf{f}_{XYZ} \,. \tag{27}$$

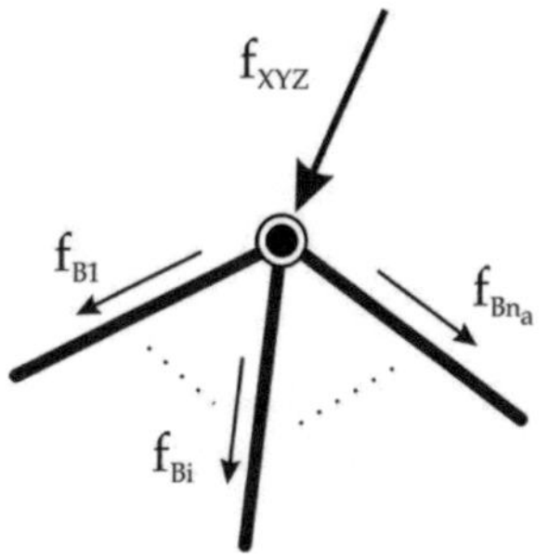

Fig. 1. Force distribution on the manipulator

If the matrix $\mathbf{S}$ is not square then $\mathbf{S}^{-1}$ is pseudo-inverse $\mathbf{S}^{+}$. The elements of the $\mathbf{S}$-Matrix $\mathbf{s}_i(\mathbf{q}_{ai}, \mathbf{q}_{pi}, \mathbf{q}_{ei})$ comprise the vector that relates $\mathbf{f}_{Bi}$, the force of the ith chain, and $\mathbf{f}_{XYZi}$, the Cartesian force, which is a result of this force. It can be described in the following formula:

$$\mathbf{f}_{XYZi} = \mathbf{s}_i \mathbf{f}_{Bi} \,. \tag{28}$$

In the matrix form with the matrix $\mathbf{U}$ takes this relation the form:

$$\mathbf{f}_{BXYZ} = \begin{bmatrix} \mathbf{s}_1 & \cdots & 0 \\ \vdots & \ddots & \vdots \\ 0 & \cdots & \mathbf{s}_{na} \end{bmatrix} \mathbf{f}_B = \mathbf{U}\mathbf{f}_B \,. \tag{29}$$

Now we introduce the Jacobian matrix $\mathbf{J}_t$ of the tree structure:

$$\mathbf{J}_t = \begin{bmatrix} \mathbf{J}_1 & \cdots & 0 \\ \vdots & \ddots & \vdots \\ 0 & \cdots & \mathbf{J}_{na} \end{bmatrix}, \tag{30}$$

where $\mathbf{J}_i(\mathbf{q}_{ai}, \mathbf{q}_{pi}, \mathbf{q}_{ei})$ are the n_a - Jacobian matrices of the serial kinematic chains. In order to eliminate the dependencies of the coordinates of the passive joint $\mathbf{q}_p$ for the calculation of the $\mathbf{G}$ Jacobian matrix of parallel manipulator, the matrix $\mathbf{J}_t$ will be parameterised with the matrix $\mathbf{W}$. After this parameterisation the new matrix no longer represents the mapping between the joint and Cartesian velocity and force space of the parallel manipulator. In order to obtain this mapping, the matrices $\mathbf{S}$ and $\mathbf{U}$ have to be introduced. The matrix $\mathbf{S}^{-1}$ represents the transformation between the forces from the Cartesian space into the branch forces. The matrix $\mathbf{U}$ constitutes the relation between the forces in the branches and these Cartesian components. With regards to this transformations, the Jacobian matrix of the parallel manipulator can be derived from the following relation:

$$\mathbf{G}^{+T} = \mathbf{W}^T \mathbf{J}_t^T \mathbf{U} \mathbf{S}^{-1} \,. \tag{31}$$

This pseudo-inverse Jacobian matrix $\mathbf{G}^{+T}$ represents the mapping between the Cartesian force $\mathbf{f}_{XYZ}$ on the end-effector of parallel manipulator and the forces/torques $\boldsymbol{\tau}_{ae} \in R^{(nae \times 1)}$ in the manipulator's structure in the joint space:

$$\boldsymbol{\tau}_{ae} = \mathbf{G}^{+T} \mathbf{f}_{XYZ} \,. \tag{32}$$

The presented method has the great advantage that the derivation of the serial Jacobian matrices is much easier than the derivation of the compact Jacobian matrix.

5. A new method for the calculation of the direct dynamics of elastic parallel manipulators

In this section, the formation of a system as a tree structure for the simultaneous calculation of the direct dynamics of the elastic parallel manipulator - SCDD is suggested. It is the same idea as the one used for the inverse dynamics of the Lagrange-D'Alembert formulation. However, in this system the closed kinematic loop constraints of the elastic parallel structure are represented by forces and torques, just like in the case of the Lagrangian equations of the first type. These forces and torques are distributed in the tree structure such that they cause motion and internal forces which match the motion and mechanical stress in the structure of the original parallel manipulator.

5.1 Simultaneous Calculation of the Direct Dynamics (SCDD)

The equations of the tree structure have the known form shown in (19). These equations will now be factored into the equations of motion of the individual serial kinematic chains:

$$\begin{aligned} &\mathbf{M}_{ti}(\mathbf{q}_{ti})\ddot{\mathbf{q}}_{ti} + \mathbf{C}_{ti}(\dot{\mathbf{q}}_{ti},\mathbf{q}_{ti})\dot{\mathbf{q}}_{ti} + \boldsymbol{\eta}_{ti}(\mathbf{q}_{ti}) \\ &+ \mathbf{J}_{ti}^{T}\mathbf{f}_{XYZi} + \mathbf{K}_{ti}\mathbf{q}_{ti} + \mathbf{D}_{ti}\dot{\mathbf{q}}_{ti} = \boldsymbol{\tau}_{ti} \end{aligned}, \tag{33}$$

for i=1 … n_a, where i designates one kinematic chain with the associated variables $\mathbf{q}_{ti} = [\mathbf{q}_{ai}\ \mathbf{q}_{pi}\ \mathbf{q}_{ei}]$ and torques $\tau_{ti} = [\tau_{ai}\ \tau_{pi}\ \tau_{ei}]$ of the active τ_{ai} and passive τ_{pi} joints and additionally structure torques τ_{ei}. $\mathbf{f}_{XYZi}$ represents an external force acting on the end of the ith-branches of the tree structure. The equations of the direct dynamics of each such chain can then be formulated:

$$\begin{aligned} \ddot{\mathbf{q}}_{ti} = \mathbf{M}_{ti}(\mathbf{q}_{ti})^{-1}\big(&\boldsymbol{\tau}_{ti} - \mathbf{C}_{ti}(\dot{\mathbf{q}}_{ti},\mathbf{q}_{ti})\dot{\mathbf{q}}_{ti} \\ &- \boldsymbol{\eta}_{ti}(\mathbf{q}_{ti}) - \mathbf{K}_{ti}\mathbf{q}_{ti} - \mathbf{D}_{ti}\dot{\mathbf{q}}_{ti} - \mathbf{J}_{ti}^{T}\mathbf{f}_{XYZi}\big)' \end{aligned} \tag{34}$$

for i=1 … n_a. Thus, the direct dynamics of each serial kinematic chain can be calculated. The input for each of these equations are the external forces acting on the end of the particular serial kinematic chain $\mathbf{f}_{XYZi}$ and the input torques τ_{ai} and τ_{pi}. The torques of the elastic DOF τ_{ei} result from the material properties like stiffness and damping. Additionally, they can be also produced by attached adaptronic actuators. They are independent. The input of the tree-structure (19) and of the compact parallel manipulator (20) is the torque vector τ_c. The virtual work of both systems is equal (10). The torques of the tree-structure are interdependent and result from the input torque vector. They represent the constraint torques/forces of the structure and the drive torques that induce the movement of the manipulator. The relation between these torques and the input torque vector is established in (17). However, before these torques can be calculated, one must first calculate the position (7), velocity (12) and after the differentiation of velocity, the acceleration of the redundant passive joints as a function of the active joints and the elastic DOF (Beyer, 1928, Stachera, 2005). This is done with the use of the closed kinematic loop constraints (8). Then from the equations of the reduced system (33) the partial matrices and vectors are taken, which are associated with the virtual torques of the passive joints:

$$\begin{aligned}\boldsymbol{\tau}_{pj} &= \mathbf{M}_{pj}(\mathbf{q}_{ti})\ddot{\mathbf{q}}_{ti} + \mathbf{C}_{pj}(\dot{\mathbf{q}}_{ti}, \mathbf{q}_{ti})\dot{\mathbf{q}}_{ti} \\ &+ \boldsymbol{\eta}_{pj}(\mathbf{q}_{ti}) + \mathbf{J}_{pj}^{T}\mathbf{f}_{XYZi} + \mathbf{D}_{pj}\dot{\mathbf{q}}_{ti}\end{aligned}, \tag{35}$$

for j=1 … n_p, i=1…n_a, where the jth passive joint belongs to the ith kinematic chains. Finally, the torques τ_a that arise from the computed virtual torques $\tau_p = [\tau_1 \ldots \tau_{np}]$ and from the drive torques τ_c of the original parallel structure can be calculated. For that, the Jacobian matrix (12) is used, which was already derived for the inverse dynamics (17) and (18). This matrix exists already in a symbolic form, which reduces the amount of work:

$$\boldsymbol{\tau}_a = \boldsymbol{\tau}_c - \left(\frac{\partial \mathbf{q}_P}{\partial \mathbf{q}_a^T}\right)^T \boldsymbol{\tau}_p . \tag{36}$$

Only the virtual torques (35) of the passive joints from all of the torques and forces in the robot's structure are used for the calculation of the torques τ_a of active joints. The influence of the torques and forces τ_e of the elastic DOF on the manipulator's movement is reflected in the coordinates of the elastic DOF and they were already used for the calculation of the virtual torques τ_p. These torques of the passive τ_p and active τ_a joints cause movement in the tree structure, that correspond to the movement of the original parallel manipulator, according to the D'Alembert principle of virtual work. In the compact equations of direct dynamics, the compact torques affect the active joints (20). These torques are accounted for by the torque and force distributions in the closed-link mechanism. For this reason, the compact torques should be applied to the active joints of the reduced tree structure in order to ensure the same operation conditions. Namely:

$$\begin{aligned}\boldsymbol{\tau}_a &= \boldsymbol{\tau}_{c,} \\ \boldsymbol{\tau}_p &= 0.\end{aligned} \tag{37}$$

In order to fulfill this condition, the new forces of the closed-loop constraints acting on the end of each ith -branch, must be calculated, and together with the drive torques supplied to the partial equations of direct dynamics (34). The difference between the acting torques of the compact manipulator and the acting torques of the tree structure amounts to:

$$\Delta\boldsymbol{\tau}_a = \boldsymbol{\tau}_c - \boldsymbol{\tau}_a = \left(\frac{\partial \mathbf{q}_P}{\partial \mathbf{q}_a^T}\right)^T \boldsymbol{\tau}_p . \tag{38}$$

The new constraints forces can be calculated:

$$\hat{\mathbf{f}}_{XYZi} = \mathbf{J}_{ti}^{-T}\left[\Delta\boldsymbol{\tau}_{ai} \quad -\boldsymbol{\tau}_{pi}\right], \tag{39}$$

for i=1 … n_a. Distribution of this force on the manipulator's structure imply the condition (37). Now the external forces acting on the end-effector of the manipulator have to be distributed between all the separate serial kinematic chains. The relation of static (27) and (29) will be used:

$$\mathbf{f}_{BXYZ} = \mathbf{U}\mathbf{S}^{-1}\mathbf{f}_{XYZ}\,, \tag{40}$$

where $\mathbf{f}_{BXYZ}=[\mathbf{f}_{XYZ1} \ldots \mathbf{f}_{XYZi} \ldots \mathbf{f}_{XYZna}]^T$. These forces (40) and the forces resulting from the constraints (39) form the common force acting on each serial kinematic chain. The final formulation for the forces takes the form:

$$\mathbf{f}_{XYZi} = \mathbf{f}_{XYZi} + \hat{\mathbf{f}}_{XYZi}, \tag{41}$$

for i=1 … n_a. The movement of the tree structure and the movement of the original parallel manipulator as well as the force and torques distribution in the structure are equal.

This algorithm can be summarized in the followings steps:

1. *Transformation of the system* in a reduced system and calculation of the direct dynamics for each serial kinematic chain separately - simultaneous (34). In order to compute these equations (in a calculation loop), the torques and forces resulting from the constraints and from the actuation have to be calculated first.
2. *Calculation of the trajectory* of the passive joints based on the non-redundant DOF (coordinates of the actuated joints and elastic DOF) and the constraints of the closed kinematic loops of the parallel structure.
3. *Calculation of the virtual torques* of the passive joints using the partial equations of the inverse dynamics of serial kinematic chains (35) and the difference between the torques of the actuated joints of the reduced system and the original manipulator (38).
4. *Calculation of the forces of constraints* for each serial kinematic chain from the virtual torques of the passive joints and the torque differences (39).
5. *Fusion of the forces of constraints* with the external forces acting on the end of each kinematic chain (41). Setting of the torques and forces of the reduced system (34) to those of the original parallel manipulator (37).

5.2 Features of the new method

In the Method - *Simultaneous Calculation of the Direct Dynamics*, SCDD - the system is segmented into a tree structure, as in the case of the inverse dynamics of Lagrange-D'Alembert formulation. This is done in order to accelerate the inversion of the inertia matrix. The most frequently used method, the LU-Gaussian elimination, has the complexity $0(n^3)$. For the symmetrical manipulator's structure with only the rotational joints the complexity can be written as $O((n_a+n_an_{ek})^3)$, where n_{ek} means the number of the elastic DOF in particular kinematic chain. In comparison, the complexity for the new distributed calculation performed for the same type of robots amounts to $O(n_a(1+n_{pk}+n_{ek})^3)$, where n_{pk} represents the number of the passive joints in one kinematic chain. For complex systems the relation $n_{pk} \ll n_{ek}$ is valid. The avoidance of the multiplication between n_a and n_{ek} under the power of three reduces the computational effort. Therefore, the computation speed of the direct dynamics in joint space of large scale systems can be significantly accelerated by using several small matrices instead of one complex matrix. Additionally, the computations of the direct dynamics with this decomposition can be performed in parallel. In the Table 1 the complexity of the matrix inversion, number of the necessary arithmetical operations, for three different robots from the *Collaborative Research Center 562* is shown (Hesselbach et al., 2005). These calculations were done, with the assumption that in each kinematic chain one elastic DOF n_{ek} exists.

These results show considerable reduction of the calculation complexity by using the proposed algorithm, even with only one additional elastic DOF in each kinematic chain. Therefore each kinematic chain can be modelled with more parameters, what is a common procedure for elastic manipulators.

	n_a	n_{pk}	n_{ek}	SCDD	L-D'A	Reduction
FIVE-BAR	2	1	1	54	64	16 %
HEXA	6	2	1	384	1728	78 %
TRIGLIDE	3	2	1	162	729	78 %

Table 1. Complexity of the matrix inversion

Also the calculation of the direct dynamics of rigid body parallel manipulators can benefit from this new method. The reduced form of the dynamics' equations can decrease the number of arithmetic operations needed for the calculation of the model. This problem was investigated on the base of rigid parallel manipulator FIVE-BAR (Stachera, 2006b). The model derived with this new method was compared with a model gained with the standard Lagrange-D'Alembert Formulation. Since it is a comparison study the exact form of the manipulator's model is here not important. The symbolic equations were derived and simplified with the use of Mathematica®. All the operations and transformations that are necessary for the computations of the direct dynamics have been considered.

Operation Type	Number of the operations		Reduction
	SCDD	L-D'A	
+	192	670	71 %
-	80	302	74 %
*	432	2482	83 %
/	38	36	-6 %

Table 2. Complexity of the arithmetic operations

The results presented in the Table 2 show a considerable reduction of the computational effort for each kind of operation excepting division (increasing about 6 %). A digital processor needs many machine steps for the multiplication, therefore the reduction of this operation's number is essential for the general reduction of the computational power for a model computation. In this case a reduction of 84 % was achieved. This confirms the applicability of this procedure for the effective reduction of computing power even for a rigid parallel manipulators.

5.3 Verification

The new SCDD method was compared with the L-D'A method in simulation. A model of elastic planar parallel manipulators FIVE-BAR was created. A lumped elasticity $c_L = c_R = 5.464 \cdot 10^6$ *N/m* was considered in the upper arms of the manipulator, shown in Fig. 2. M_L and M_R represent the motors. The other parameters of this model are not relevant, since it is a comparison study. A straight line trajectory between two points p^A and p^E was chosen. The models were then controlled by torques, which were created by a rigid body model without control. The black line represents the reference trajectory. The dark gray line is a result of the L-D'A model and the light gray line from the SCDD model. It can be seen, that the models both follow the trajectory with comparable accuracy.

For better comparison of these models, the same trajectories are expressed now with the help of the forces induced in the branches, F_L in the left branch and F_R in the right one, of the parallel manipulator, shown in Fig.3. A small difference between these forces can be noted. At the beginning of the simulation the differences are equal to zero, but with the time they change. Apart from the difference between these forces, a good agreement in the vibrations' behaviour of both systems, frequency, amplitude and phase, can be observed, which confirms the new proposed method.

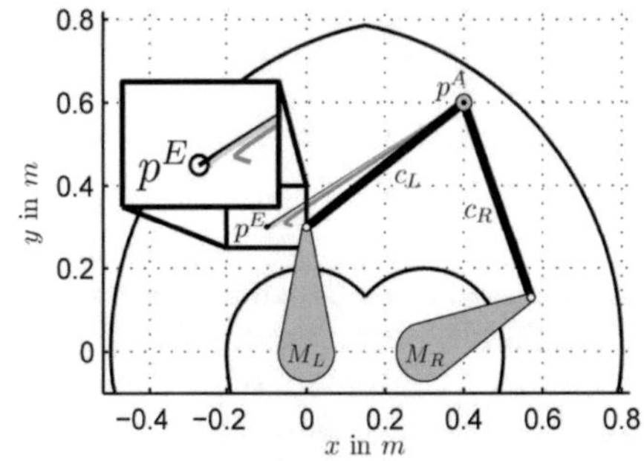

Fig. 2. Trajectory and workspace of elastic planar parallel manipulator FIVE-BAR

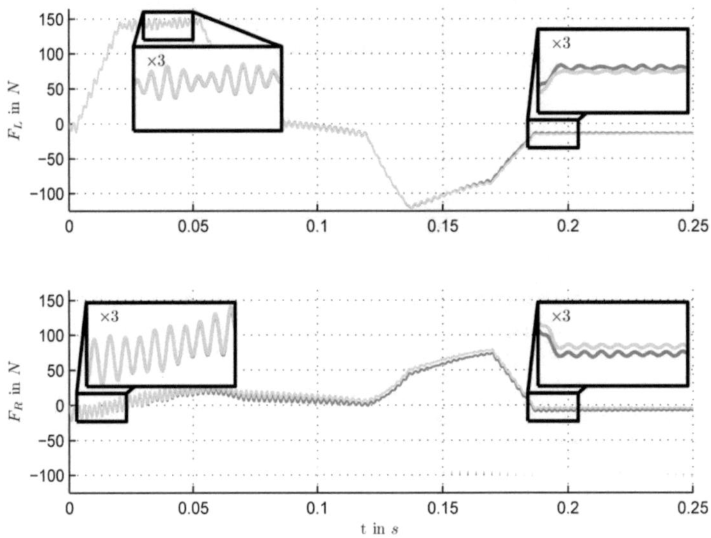

Fig. 3. Force in the active rods of the parallel manipulator - comparison

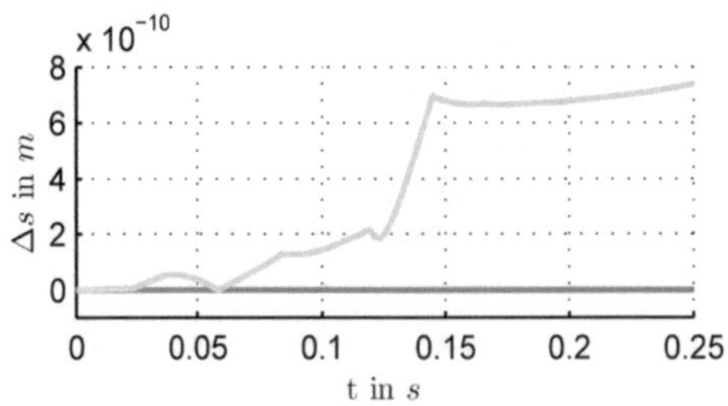

Fig. 4. Distance between two kinematic chains of FIVEBAR – numerical error of SCDD

The existing differences between the paths traveled by these two elastic models and the induced forces can be accounted for by the numerical precision. Fig. 4 shows the distance between the end points of both kinematic chains. This numerical precision causes the increase in time of the distance between two kinematic chains, that should have been equal to zero. The dark gray line $\Delta s = 1 \cdot 10^{-14}\ m$ shows the L-D'A and the light gray the SCDD model. The error is dependent on the sample interval of the simulation: the smaller the interval, the smaller the error. In the field of numerical methods algorithms are known that deal with the stabilization of the numerical calculation and increasing of the computation accuracy (Baumgarte, 1972), which will be the next step in the investigation of this new algorithm. Despite this numerical error, the analytical approach is confirmed by these presented results.

6. Conclusion

In this chapter, the Lagrange equation of the first type and Lagrange-D'Alembert Formulation were introduced around the consideration of elastic modes. To complete the standard method of Lagrange-D'Alembert, an algorithm for the derivation of the Jacobian matrix of the parallel manipulator based on the Jacobian matrices of the individual serial kinematic chains was presented. Originating from this knowledge, a new method was presented for the simultaneous calculation of the direct dynamics of the parallel and furthermore the elastic parallel manipulators. The new method shows a significant reduction of the complexity of the calculation, even for the rigid body manipulators. For the sophisticated systems this feature is a great advantage. The disadvantage of the presented method is the numerical stability over long periods of time, which will therefore be the topic of future researches.

7. References

Baumgarte, J. (1972). Stabilization of constraints and integrals of motion in dynamical systems. *Computer Methods in Applied Mechanics*, Vol.1, pp. 1–36

Beres, W. & Sasiadek, J. Z. (1995). Finite element dynamic model of multilink flexible manipulators. *Applied Mathematics and Computer Science*, Vol. 5, No. 2, pp. 231 - 262, Technical University Press Zielona Gora, Poland

Beyer, R. (1928). Dynamik der mehrkurbelgetriebe. In: *Zeitschrift fuer angewandte Mathematik und Mechanik*, Vol. 8, No. 2, pp. 122 - 133

Featherstone, R. & Orin, D. (2000). Robot dynamics: equations and algorithms. *Proceedings of the IEEE International Conference on Robotics and Automation*, pp. 826 - 834, San Francisco, USA

Hesselbach, J.; Bier, C.; Budde, C.; Last, P.; Maass, J. & Bruhn, M. (2005). Parallel robot specific control functionalities. In: *Robotic Systems for Handling and Assembly, 2nd International Colloquium of the Collaborative Research Center 562*, Last, P., Budde, C., and Wahl, F. M., (Ed.), pp. 93 - 108. Fortschritte in der Robotik Band 9, Shaker Verlag, Braunschweig, Germany

Kang, B. & Mills, J. K. (2002). Dynamic modeling of structurally-flexible planar parallel manipulator. *Robotica*, Vol. 20, pp. 329–339

Khalil, W. & Gautier, M. (2000). Modelling of mechanical system with lumped elasticity. *Proceedings of the IEEE International Conference on Robotics and Automation*,pp. 3965 - 3970, San Francisco, USA

Kock, S. (2001). Parallelroboter mit Antriebredundanz. *PhD thesis, Fortschritt - Berichte VDI*, Duesseldorf - Braunschweig, Germany

Merlet, J.-P. (2000). Parellel Robots. *Kluwer Academics Publishers*, Netherlands.

Miller, K. & Clavel, R. (1992). The lagrange-based model of delta-4 robot dynamics. *Robotersysteme*, Springer Verlag, Vol. 8, pp. 49–54., Germany

Murray, R. M.; Li, Z. & Sastry, S. S. (1994). A mathematical introduction to robotic manipulation. *CRC Press LLC*, USA

Nakamura, Y. (1991). Advanced robotics: redundancy and optimization. *Addison-Wesley Publishing Company*, USA

Nakamura, Y. & Ghodoussi, M. (1989). Dynamics computation of closed-link robot mechanisms with nonredundant and redundant actuators. *IEEE Transactions on Robotics and Automation*, Vol. 5, No. 3, pp. 294–302

Park, F. C.; Choi, J. & Ploen, S. R. (1999). Symbolic formulation of closed chain dynamics in independent coordinates. *Pergamon: Mechanism and Machine Theory*, Vol. 34, pp. 731 - 751

Piedboeuf, J.-C. (2001). Six methods to model a flexible beam rotating in the vertical plane. *Proceedings of the IEEE International Conference on Robotics and Automation*, pp. 2832 - 2839,Seul, Korea

Robinett, R. D.; Dohrmann, C.; Eisler, G. R.; Feddema, J.; Parker, G. G.; Wilson, D. G. & Stokes, D. (2002). Flexible robot dynamics and controls. *Kluwer Academic/Plenum Publishers: International Federation for System Research - IFSR*, New York, USA

Spong, M. W. & Vidyasagar, M. (1989). Robot dynamics and control. *John Wiley and Sons, Inc.*, USA

Stachera, K. (2005). An approach to direct kinematics of a planar parallel elastic manipulator and analysis for the proper definition of its workspace. *Proceedings of the 11th IEEE Conference on MMAR*, Miedzyzdroje, Poland

Stachera, K. (2006a). A new method for the direct dynamics' calculation of parallel manipulators. *Proceedings of the 6th IEEE World Congress on Intelligent Control and Automation*, Dalian, China

Stachera, K. (2006b). An approach for the simultaneous calculation of the direct dynamics of parallel manipulators. *Proceedings of the 12th IEEE Conference on MMAR*, Miedzyzdroje, Poland

Stachera, K. & Schumacher, W. (2007). Simultaneous calculation of the direct dynamics of the elastic parallel manipulators. *Proceedings of the 13th IEEE IFAC International Conference on Methods and Models in Automation and Robotics (MMAR)*, Szczecin, Poland

Tsai, L.-W. (1999). Robot analysis: the mechanics of serial and parallel manipulators. *John Wiley and Sons, Inc.*, USA

Wang, J. & Gosselin, C. (2000). Parallel computational algorithms for the simulation of closed-loop robotic systems. *Proceedings of the International Conference on Parallel Computing Applications in Electrical Engineering (PARELEC2000)*, IEEE Computer Society, pp. 34 - 38, Washington, DC, USA

Wang, J.; Gosselin, C. M. & Cheng, L. (2002). Modeling and simulation of robotic systems with closed kinematic chains using the virtual spring approach. *Kluwer Academic Publishers, Springer Netherlands*, Multibody System Dynamics, Vol. 7, No. 2, pp. 145 - 170

Wang, X. & Mills, J. K. (2004). A fem model for active vibration control of flexible linkages. *Proceedings of the IEEE International Conference on Robotics and Automation (ICRA)*, pp. 4308–4313, New Orleans, USA

Yiu, Y. K.; Cheng, H.; Xiong, Z. H.; Liu, G. F. & Li, Z. X. (2001). On the dynamics of parallel manipulators. *Proceedings of the IEEE International Conference on Robotics and Automation (ICRA)*, pp. 3766 - 3771, Seul, Korea

16

Orthonormal Basis and Radial Basis Functions in Modeling and Identification of Nonlinear Block-Oriented Systems

Rafał Stanisławski and Krzysztof J. Latawiec
Department of Electrical, Control and Computer Engineering
Opole University of Technology
Poland

1. Introduction

Nonlinear block-oriented systems, including the Hammerstein, Wiener and feedback-nonlinear systems have attracted considerable research interest both from the industrial and academic environments (Bai, 1998), (Greblicki, 1989), (Latawiec, 2004), (Latawiec et al., 2003), (Latawiec et al., 2004), (Pearson & Pottman, 2000).

It is well known that orthonormal basis functions (OBF) (Bokor et al., 1999) have proved to be useful in identification and control of dynamical systems, including nonlinear block-oriented systems (Gómez & Baeyens, 2004), (Latawiec, 2004), (Latawiec et al., 2003), (Latawiec et al., 2006), (Latawiec et al., 2004), (Stanisławski et al., 2006). In particular, an inverse OBF (IOBF) modeling approach has been effective in identification of a linear dynamic part of the feedback-nonlinear and Hammerstein systems (Latawiec, 2004), (Latawiec et al., 2004). On the other hand, regular OBF (ROBF) modeling approach has proved to be useful in identification of the Wiener system. The approaches provide the separability in estimation of linear and nonlinear submodels (Latawiec et al., 2004), thus eliminating the bilinearity issue detrimentally affecting e.g. the ARX-based modeling schemes (Latawiec, 2004), (Latawiec et al., 2003), (Latawiec et al., 2006), (Latawiec et al., 2004). The IOBF modeling approach is continued to be efficiently used here to model a linear dynamic part of the feedback-nonlinear and Hammerstein systems and regular OBF modeling approach is used to model a linear part of the Wiener system.

The problem of modeling of a nonlinear static part of the nonlinear block-oriented system can be classically tackled using e.g. the polynomial expansion (Latawiec, 2004), (Latawiec et al., 2004) or (cubic) spline functions. Recently, a radial basis function network (RBFN) has been used to model a nonlinear static part of the Hammerstein and feedback-nonlinear systems and a very good identification performance has been obtained (Hachino et al., 2004), (Stanisławski, 2007), (Stanisławski et al., 2007). The concept is extended here to cover the Wiener system.

This paper presents a new strategy for nonlinear block-oriented system identification, which is a combination of OBF modeling for a linear dynamic part and RBFN modeling for a nonlinear static element. The effective OBF approach is finally coupled with the RBFN modeling concept, giving rise to the introduction of a powerful method for identification of the nonlinear block-oriented system.

2. Regular and inverse OBF modelling concept

2.1 Regular OBF modeling

It is well known that an open-loop stable linear discrete-time system described by the transfer function $G(q)$ can be represented with an arbitrary accuracy by the model $\hat{G}(q)=\sum_{i=1}^{M} c_i L_i(q)$, including a series of orthonormal transfer functions $L_i(q)$ and the weighting parameters c_i, i=1,...,M, characterizing the model dynamics. Thus, the model of the system can be written as (Latawiec, 2004), (Latawiec et al., 2006), (Latawiec et al., 2004)

$$\hat{y}(t)=\sum_{i=1}^{M} c_i L_i(q) u(t) \tag{1}$$

Various OBF can be used in (1). Two commonly used sets of OBF are simple Laguerre and Kautz functions. These functions are characterized by the 'dominant' dynamics of a system, which is given by a single real pole (p) or a pair of complex ones (p, p^*), respectively.
In case of discrete Laguerre models to be exploited hereinafter, the orthonormal functions

$$L_i(q,p)=\frac{\sqrt{1-p^2}}{q-p}\left[\frac{1-pq}{q-p}\right]^{i-1} \quad i=1,\dots,M \tag{2}$$

consist of a first-order low-pass factor and (i-1)th-order all-pass filters. Dominant Laguerre pole p can be selected in an experimental way or can be determined with the aid of the stochastic gradient (SG) estimator (Boukis et al., 2006), (Oliveira, 2000).

2.1 Inverse OBF modeling

In case of use of the inverse OBF (IOBF) concept to model a linear dynamic part, the model equation can be presented in form

$$\hat{G}^{-1}(q)\,\hat{y}(t)=u(t) \tag{3a}$$

$$R(q)\,\hat{y}(t)=u(t) \tag{3b}$$

where FIR model $R(q)= r_0 q^d + r_1 q^{d-1} + \dots + r_d + r_{d+1} q^{-1} \dots + r_{L-1} q^{-L+d+1}$ is the inverse of the system model $\hat{G}(q)$. In the IOBF concept, the inverse $R(q)$ of the system is modeled using OBF. An OBF modeling approach can now be applied to equation (3b) instead of (3a) and finally we can present equation (1) in the following form (Latawiec et al., 2003)

$$y(t)+\sum_{i=1}^{M} c_i L_i(q,p) y(t)=\beta_0 u(t-d)+e_1(t) \tag{4}$$

where $e_1(t)$ is the equation error, d is the time delay of the system, β_0 and c_i i=1,…,M are the OBF model parameters.

3. RBF network

The nonlinear function approximated by a Radial Basis Functions Network (RBFN) consists of two layers of neurons (one hidden and one output layer). The hidden layer consists of m

neurons, where each neuron implements the radial activated function. The output layer consists of one linear neuron which realizes weighted sum of outputs of hidden layer neurons. The output of RBFN is described by the equation

$$x(t) = \sum_{i=1}^{m} w_i \phi_i(u(t)) \tag{5}$$

where w_i, i=1,…,m are the weighting coefficients and $\phi_i(u(t))$ are the outputs of hidden layer neurons. Typically, the Gaussian function is used as an activation function in RBFN. The Gaussian functions are modeled by two parameters characterizing their centers α_i and wides σ_i. In this case the $\phi_i(u(t))$ is given by the equation

$$\phi_i(u(t)) = \exp\left(-\left\|u(k) - \alpha_i\right\|^2 / \sigma_i^2\right) \text{ for } i=1,..,m \tag{6}$$

where ||.|| is the Euclidian norm.

Important advantage of the RBF network is that the weighting coefficients w_i, i=1,…,m can by estimated by using classical, linear estimation schemes e.g. recursive/adaptive least squares (RLS/ALS), or least mean squares (LMS). The centers α_i and wides σ_i (i=1,…,m) of the RBF can be determined with the aid of the stochastic gradient (SG) estimator (Kim et al., 2006), genetic algorithm (Hachino et al., 2004) or other optimization methods. However, in practical applications, the optimization of the α_i and σ_i is not absolutely necessary. It has been found in simulations (Stanisławski, 2007) that RBFN without optimization (with regular distribution of the centers and constant widths) can produce satisfactory solutions.

3. Nonlinear block-oriented systems

3.1 Hammerstein system

The Hammerstein system consists of two cascaded elements, where the first one is a nonlinear memoryless gain and the second one is a linear dynamic model. The whole Hammerstein system can be described by the equation

$$y(t) = G(q)\left[f(u(t)) + e_H(t)\right] = G(q)\left[x(t) + e_H(t)\right] \tag{7}$$

where $G(q)$ models a dynamic linear part, $f(.)$ describes a nonlinear function, $x(t)$ is the unmeasured output of the nonlinear part and $e_H(t)$ is the error/disturbance term. An alternative output error/disturbance formulation is also possible.

Combining equations (4),(5) and (7) we arrive at the equation describing the whole Hammerstein system

$$y(t) + \sum_{i=1}^{M} c_i L_i(q,p) y(t) = \beta_0 \sum_{i=1}^{m} w_i \phi_i(u(t-d)) + e_1(t) \tag{8}$$

Assuming that $\underline{w}_j = \beta_0 w_j$, i=1…m, the model output from the Hammerstein system can be finally given as

$$\hat{y}(t) = -\sum_{i=1}^{M} c_i L_i(q,p) y(t) + \sum_{j=1}^{m} \underline{w}_j \phi_j(t-d) \tag{9}$$

which can be presented in the linear regression form

$$\hat{y}(t) = \boldsymbol{\varphi}^T(t)\boldsymbol{\theta} \tag{10}$$

where $\boldsymbol{\varphi}^T(t) = [-v_1(t) \ \dots \ -v_M(t) \ \phi_1(t-d) \ \phi_2(t-d) \dots \ \phi_m(t-d)]$, $\theta = [c_1 \ \dots \ c_M \ w_1 \ w_2 \ \dots \ w_m]$ and $v_i(t)=L_i(q,p)y(t)$. Unknown parameters θ of the model can be estimated by the familiar recursive least squares (RLS) or least mean squares (LMS) algorithms.

3.2 Wiener system

In a single-input single-output Wiener system, a linear dynamic part is cascaded with a nonlinear static element. The output $\hat{y}(t)$ of the Wiener model, or the system output predictor, can be calculated as

$$\hat{y}(t) = \hat{f}[\hat{G}(q)u(t)] \tag{11}$$

Since a nonlinear static characteristic is invertible we can rewrite equation (11) in form

$$\hat{f}^{-1}[\hat{y}(t)] = \hat{G}(q)u(t) \tag{12}$$

The function $\hat{f}^{-1}[\hat{y}(t)]$ can be approximated with RBF network. Finally, we arrive at the linear regression function

$$\hat{y}(t) = \sum_{i=1}^{M} c_i L_i(q^{-1})u(t) - \sum_{i=1}^{m} \underline{w}_i \, \phi_i(y(t)) \tag{13}$$

where $\underline{w}_i = w_i - \alpha_i$ (i=1,..,m), which can be presented in the familiar form $\hat{y}(t) = \boldsymbol{\varphi}^T(t)\boldsymbol{\theta}$, with $\boldsymbol{\varphi}^T(t) = [\ v_1(t) \ \dots \ -v_M(t) \ -\phi_1(y(t)) \ -\phi_2(y(t)) \dots \ -\phi_m(y(t))]$, $\boldsymbol{\theta} = [c_1 \ \dots \ c_M \ \underline{w}_1 \ \underline{w}_2 \ \dots \ \underline{w}_m]$ and $v_i(t)=L_i(q,p)u(t)$, i=1,...,M.

3.3 Feedback-nonlinear system

In the block-oriented feedback-nonlinear system, the output of the linear dynamic part is fed (negatively) back to the input through the static nonlinearity, so that the whole system can be described by the equation

$$\begin{aligned} y(t) &= G(q)\left[u(t) - f(y(t)) + e_F(t)\right] \\ &= G(q)\left[u(t) - x(t) + e_F(t)\right] \end{aligned} \tag{14}$$

where $e_F(t)$ is the error/disturbance term. Combining equations (4),(5) and (14) we arrive at the equation describing the whole, IOBF-related feedback-nonlinear system (Stanisławski et al., 2007)

$$y(t) + \sum_{i=1}^{M} c_i L_i(q,p)y(t) = \beta_0 \left[u(t-d) - \sum_{j=1}^{m} w_j \, \phi_j(y(t-d)) \right] + e(t) \tag{15}$$

Putting $\underline{w}_j = \beta_0 w_j$, j=1…m, the output from the feedback-nonlinear system can be finally given as

$$y(t) = \beta_0 u(t-d) - \sum_{i=1}^{M} c_i L_i(q,p) y(t) - \sum_{j=1}^{m} \underline{w}_j \phi_j(y(t-d)) + e(t) \tag{16}$$

The equation (16) can be presented in the linear regression form, with $\boldsymbol{\varphi}^T(t) = [u(t-d)\ -v_1(t) \ldots -v_M(t)\ -\phi_1(y(t-d))\ -\phi_2(y(t-d)) \ldots -\phi_m(y(t-d))]$, $\boldsymbol{\theta} = [\beta_0\ c_1 \ldots c_M\ \underline{w}_1\ \underline{w}_2 \ldots \underline{w}_m]$ and $v_i(t) = L_i(q,p)y(t)$. Clearly, owing to the IOBF modeling approach applied, the linear and nonlinear submodels are separated from each other so that the bilinearity issue is eliminated here.

4. Simlation experiments

In the Matlab/Simulink environment, we comparatively analyze the three presented nonlinear block-oriented OBF/RBFN-related models consisting of 1) Hammerstein IOBF related model, 2) Wiener regular OBF related model and 3) feedback-nonlinear IOBF related model. For example, consider the magnetic levitation process which has been simulated as a demo in the Matlab/Simulink environment. Our main goal is to analyze efficiency of the approach in view of their possible use in on-line identification (and control). Performance of parameter estimation is evaluated by means of the mean square prediction error (MSPE). MSPE is described by the equation

$$MSPE = (1/N)\sum_{t=1}^{N}(y(t) - \hat{y}(t))^2 \tag{17}$$

The system is excited by a random number generator with regular distribution <0.5, 4>. Additionally, the system is corrupted with the input and output noises ($e_i(t)$ and $e_o(t)$), which are supplied from a Gaussian random number generators with $N(0, \delta_i)$ and $N(0, \delta_o)$, respectively. For estimation of weights of the RBFs and parameters of the dynamical model we use a classical RLS algorithm.

Table 1 specifies the results of a comparative analysis of the performance of the three models for M=6 and m=9.

δ_i	δ_o	Hammerstein system	Wiener system	Feedback-nonlinear system
0	0	8.851 e-6	0.2437	1.008 e-5
0.005	0	2.167 e-5	1.123	9.236 e-5
0.01	0	4.337 e-5	1.287	9.582 e-5
0	0.005	2.752	2.231	2.838
0	0.01	5.188	3.226	4.95
0.005	0.005	2.921	3.406	2.792

Table 1. MSPE of the Hammerstein, Wiener and feedback-nonlinear models

The results in Table 1 show that the high accuracy of identification has been obtained for the IOBF/RBFN-based models (Hammerstein and feedback-nonlinear models). The reasons are 1) the specific, structure of the IOBF-related model, 2) numerical conditioning of the covariance matrix for the IOBF-based estimation problem is essentially better than that for the OBF-based one. However, the inconvenience of IOBF-related models is the high sensitivity on the output error due to the equation error structure. Table 1 shows that the Wiener model cannot provide sufficiently high accuracy of the identification problem, causing that the RBF network in the Wiener system models the inversion of the nonlinear function *f*(.). The calculation of the original function on the basis of RBF network is ambiguous and badly numerical conditioned. Finally, only the Wiener model gives the satisfy results for the system corrupted with the high-level disturbances.
Plots of the actual output and its reconstruction by Hammerstein, Wiener and Feedback nonlinear models presented in Fig. 1 and Fig. 2 confirm very good performance of identification for Hammerstein and Feedback nonlinear models and poor performance for Wiener model, respectively.

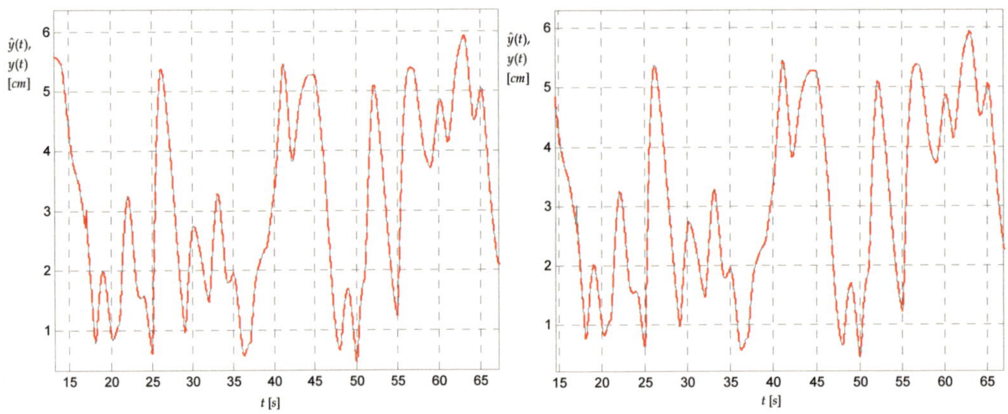

Fig. 1. Plots of actual (solid-black) vs. predicted (dashed-red) outputs of the Hammerstein system (left) and feedback-nonlinear system (right)

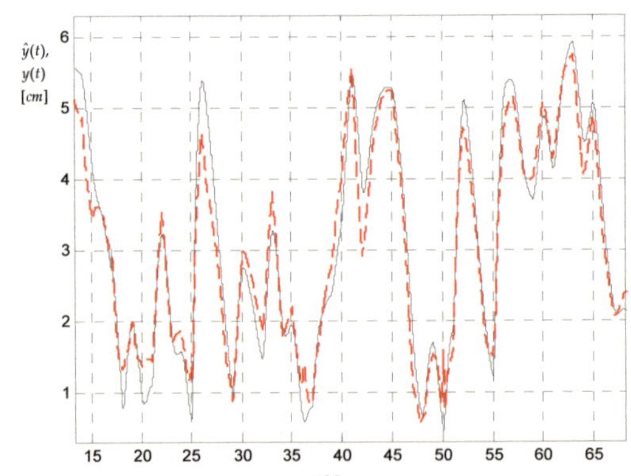

Fig. 2. Plots of actual (solid-black) vs. predicted (dashed-red) outputs of the Wiener system

7. Conclusion

The paper has presented the solutions to the nonlinear identification problem for the various nonlinear block-oriented systems using OBF-related models and RBF network. We have demonstrated that the Wiener model based on regular OBF modeling concept cannot provide sufficiently high performance of the identification problem. This is mainly to due with inversion problem of RBF network.

Results of a simulation analysis have shown that the strategy using the IOBF modeling concept in Hammerstein and feedback-nonlinear model can provide a very good performance, both in terms of low prediction errors and accurate reconstruction of the nonlinear characteristics, in addition to high computational efficiency.

8. References

Bai E.W. (1998). An optimal two-stage identification algorithm for Hammerstein-Wiener nonlinear systems. *Automatica,* Vol. 34, pp. 333-338.

Bokor J., Heuberger P., Ninness, B., Oliveira e Silva, T., Van den Hof P. & Wahlberg, B. (1999). Modelling and identification with orthogonal basis functions. *Proc. Preconference Workshop, 14th IFAC World Congress,* Beijing, P.R. China.

Boukis C., Mandic D.P., Constantinides A.G. & Polymenakos L.C. (2006). A Novel Algorithm for the Adaptation of the Pole of Laguerre Filters. *IEEE Signal Processing Letters,* Vol. 13, No. 7, pp. 429 - 432.

Greblicki W. (1989). Nonparametric orthogonal series identification of Hammerstein systems. *International Journal of Systems Science,* Vol. 20, No. 12, pp. 2355-2367.

Gómez J.C. & Baeyens E. (2004). Identification of block-oriented nonlinear systems using orthonormal bases. *Journal of Process Control,* Vol. 14, No. 6, pp. 685-697

Hachino T., Deguchi K. & Takata H. (2004). Identification of Hammerstein model using radial basis function networks and genetic algorithm. *Proc. 5th Asian Control Conference,* Vol. 1, pp. 124-129.

Kim N.Y., Byun H.G. & Kwon K.H. (2006). Learning Behaviors of Stochastic Gradient Radial Basis Function Network Algorithms for Odor Sensing Systems. *ETRI journal,* Vol. 28, No. 1.

Latawiec K.J. (2004) *The Power of Inverse Systems in Modeling and Control of Linear and Nonlinear Systems.* Vol. 167, Opole University of Technology Press, Opole, Poland.

Latawiec K.J., Marciak C., Hunek W. & Stanisławski R. (2003) A new analytical design methodology for adaptive control of nonlinear block-oriented systems. *Proc. 7th World Multi-Conference on Systemics, Cybernetics and Informatics,* Vol. XI, pp. 215-220, Orlando, Florida, USA.

Latawiec K.J., Marciak C. & Oliveira G.H.C.: (2006). A new control-oriented modeling methodology for a series DC motor. *Electromagnetic Fields in Mechatronics, Electrical and Electronic Engineering,* Wiak S., Krawczyk A. & Fernandez X.L.M. (Eds.), *IOS Press, Studies in Applied Electromagnetics and Mechanics,* Vol. 27, Chapter_B_13.

Latawiec K.J., Marciak C., Rojek R. & Oliveira G.H.C. (2003). Linear parameter estimation and predictive constrained control of Wiener/Hammerstein systems. *Proc. 13th IFAC Symposium on System Identification,* pp. 359-364, Rotterdam, The Netherlands.

Latawiec K.J., Marciak C., Stanisławski R. & Oliveira G.H.C. (2004) The mode separability principle in modeling of linear and nonlinear blockoriented systems. *Proc. the 10th IEEE MMAR Conference (MMAR'04)*, Vol. 1, pp. 479-484, Miedzyzdroje, Poland.

Oliveira S.T. (2000). Optimal pole conditions for Laguerre and two-parameter Kautz models: a survey of known results. *Proc. 12th IFAC Symp. on System Identification (SYSID'2000)*, pp. 457-462, Santa Barbara, CA, USA.

Pearson R.K. & Pottman M. (2000). Gray-box identification of block-oriented nonlinear models. *Journal of Process Control*, Vol. 10, pp. 301-315.

Stanisławski R., Latawiec K.J. & Stanisławski W. (2006). Modeling of a boiler proper using a complex structure model by means of multivariable orthonormal basis functions. *Proc. 12th IEEE MMAR Conference (MMAR'06)*, pp. 935-938, Miedzyzdroje, Poland.

Stanisławski R. (2007). Hammerstein system identification by means of orthonormal basis functions and radial basis functions. *Emerging Technologies, Robotics and Control Systems*, Pennacchio S. (Eds.), Internationalsar, Vol. 2, pp. 69-73, Palermo, Italy.

Stanisławski R., Latawiec K.J. & Hunek W.P. (2007). Identification of feedback-nonlinear systems by means of orthonormal basis and radial basis functions. *Proc. 13th IEEE IFAC IC MMAR 2007*, pp. 611-616, August 2007, Szczecin, Poland.

17

Control System of Underwater Vehicle Based on Artificial Intelligence Methods

Piotr Szymak and Józef Małecki
Polish Naval Academy
Poland

1. Introduction

One of the main development directions of an underwater technology are robots, which are working under the surface of a water. Using of these unmanned vehicles enables exploration at bigger depths and in more hazardous conditions (Kubaty & Rowiński, 2001). Correctness of realization of different underwater works requires precise control of robot's movement in underwater environment.

Fig. 1. Remotely operated vehicle called Ukwial

In the case of underwater robot is object of nonlinear dynamics and works in marine environment with different disturbances robust nonlinear control method may be applied. An example of this kind application is designed and verified automatic control system of underwater vehicle called Ukwial (fig. 1).
Problem of underwater vehicle's control is considered by several scientific centers (particularly in the United States - Florida Atlantic University, Massachusetts Institute of Technology, Naval Postgraduate School in Monterey; in Japan - Osaka University, in

Norway - University of Trondheim, in Poland - Szczecin University of Technology, Polish Naval Academy in Gdynia). Direct results of researches are usually inaccessible for the sake of their commercial or military application. While published results of researches are concerned mainly on basic problems: control of course and control of draught.
This chapter contribute into domain of underwater vehicle's control results of numerical and experimental researches of remotely operated vehicle Ukwial, which is used in Polish Navy. Using of presented robust nonlinear control method helps operators of Ukwial in their daily work.
In the chapter selected aspects of steering an underwater vehicle along desired trajectory have been developed. The fuzzy data processing has been applied for compensation of the nonlinear underwater vehicle's dynamics and influence of environmental disturbances. It has enabled to calculate command signals driving the vehicle with set values of movement's parameters. An architecture of the selected fuzzy logic controllers has been presented. Moreover, the results of computer simulations and experimental research of remotely operated vehicle Ukwial have been inserted.

2. Mathematical model of an underwater vehicle

Nonlinear model in six degrees of freedom has been accepted to simulate movement of the underwater vehicle (Fossen, 1994). This movement has been analyzed in two coordinate systems:
1. the body-fixed coordinate system, which is movable,
2. the earth-fixed coordinate system, which is immovable.

While for the aim of movement description, notation of physical quantities according to SNAME (*The Society of Naval Architects and Marine Engineers*) has been accepted. Underwater vehicle's movement is described with the aid of the six equations of motion, where the three first equations represent the translational motion and the three last equation represent the rotational motion. These six equations can be expressed in a compact form as:

$$M\dot{\nu} + C(\nu)\nu + D(\nu)\nu + g(\eta) + U(\nu)\nu = \tau \qquad (1)$$

Here $\nu=[u,v,w,p,q,r]$ is the body-fixed linear and angular velocity vector, $\eta=[x,y,z,\phi,\theta,\psi]$ is the earth-fixed coordinates of position and Euler angles vector and $\tau=[X,Y,Z,K,M,N]^T$ is the vector of forces and moments of force influenced on underwater vehicle. M is a inertia matrix, which is equal a rigid-body inertia matrix and added mass inertia matrix. C is a Coriolis and centripetal matrix, which is a sum of rigid-body and added mass Coriolis and centripetal matrixes. D is a hydrodynamic damping matrix and g is a restoring forces and moments matrix. U is a damping matrix generated by a cable called an umbilical cord. Underwater vehicle is supplied and can be controlled via the umbilical cord.
After making assumption that underwater vehicle has three planes of symmetry, it moves with small speed in a viscous liquid and an origin of movable coordinate system covers with vehicle's centre of gravity, specific form of matrixes with nonzero values of diagonal's elements has been obtained (Fossen, 1994). According to earlier researches (Szymak & Małecki, 2007) these elements were calculated on the base of geometrical parameters of remotely operated vehicle (abbr. ROV) Ukwial.
Whereas Coriolis and centripetal matrixes were omitted because of small numerical values, unimportant in computer simulation.

Nonlinear mathematical model of an underwater vehicle has been considered in more detail in (Fossen, 1994).

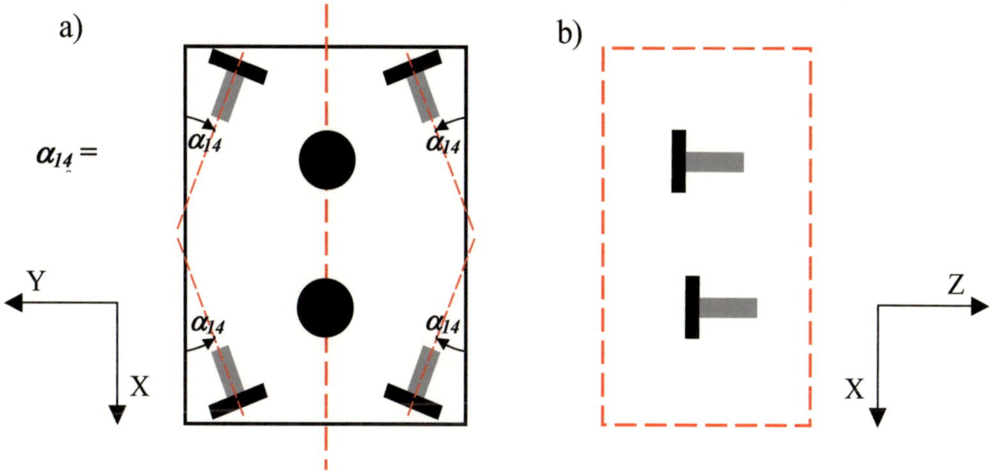

Fig. 2. Location of particular Ukwial's propellers in: a) horizontal and b) vertical plane

ROV Ukwial was designed in Underwater Technology Department from Gdansk University Of Technology. It is remotely operated and powered from board. A construction of Ukwial is based on cubicoid-shape frame, where all propulsion system and added equipment are mounted to the frame. This underwater vehicle has specific propulsion system, consisted of: four, three blade screw propellers in horizontal plane (fig. 2, here α_{14} = 29°) and two, three blade screw propellers in vertical plane. Each propeller is electrically driven.

Presented propulsion system enables to move underwater vehicle in water with average speed 0,5-1,0 m/s and allows to control ROV's movement in five degrees of freedom (three translations motions: in longitudinal axis of symmetry x_o, in lateral axis of symmetry y_o and in vertical axis of symmetry z_o, and two rotations around lateral axis of symmetry y_o and around z_o axis).

Moreover specific location of propellers in horizontal plane (at an angle of 29° to the longitudinal axis of symmetry) gives possibility of steering this ROV in case of one of propellers is out of order.

3. Architecture of Ukwial's control system

Designed automatic control system of underwater vehicle consists of (fig. 3):

1. supervisory control unit, which is responsible for setting values of movement's parameters, turning on and off individual controllers at the proper moments,
2. the four controllers of: course, displacement in X axis, displacement in Y axis and draught, which generate adequate control signals: moment of force *N*, force in X axis, force in Y axis and force *Z*.

Proportional-derivative action controllers based on the fuzzy logic have been applied to carry out control of course, displacement in X axis, displacement in Y axis and draught (fig. 4), where parameter *p* is adequate course, coordinate *x*, *y* or *z*.

Using of fuzzy logic method in FPD controllers depends on selection (Driankov et al., 1996):

1. number, type and position's parameters of membership function of the input and output variables,
2. fuzzy inference rules, which create base of rules.

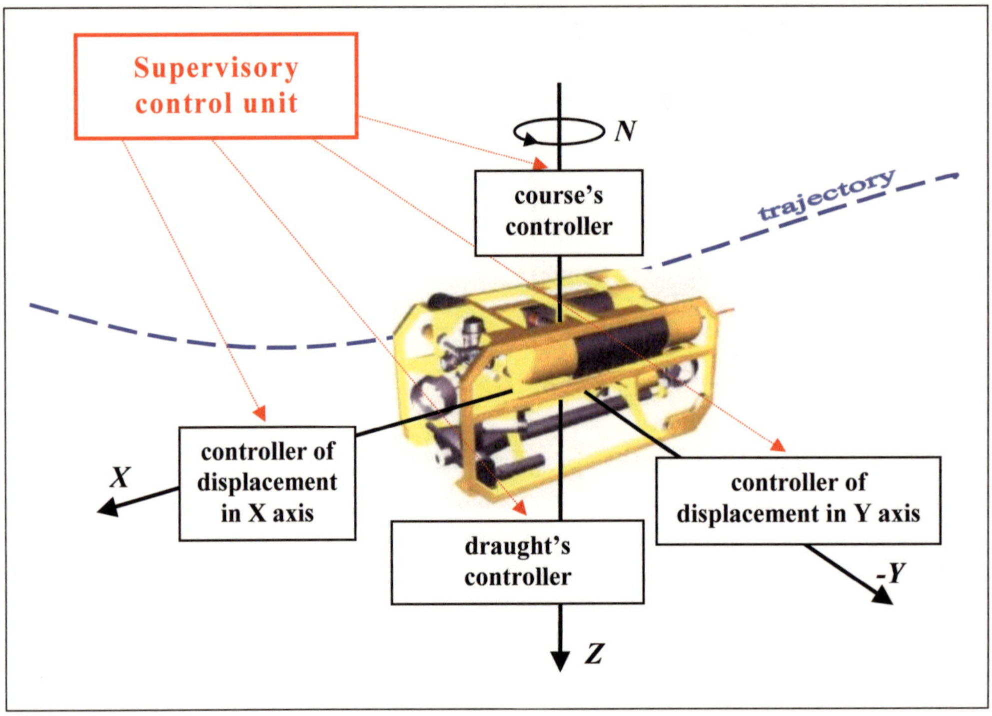

Fig. 3. Automatic control system of underwater vehicle called Ukwial

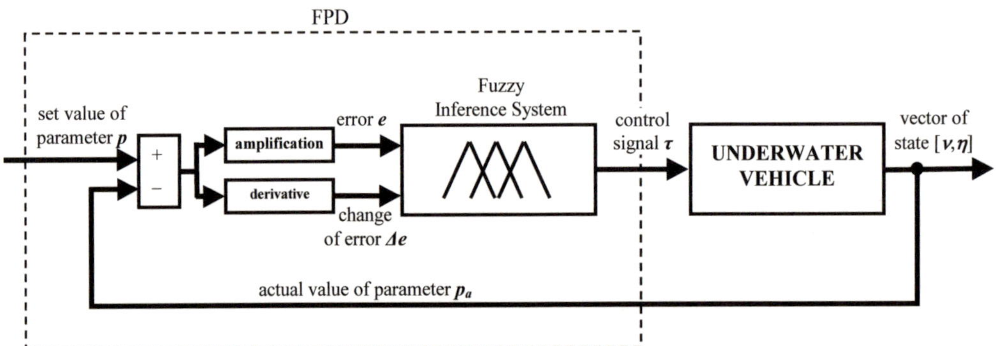

Fig. 4. Block diagram of fuzzy proportional-derivative controller FPD

Membership functions for linguistic input variables: error signal and derived change in error and output variable - control signal were tuned with the aid of the mathematical model simulation of the automatic controlled underwater vehicle. Direct and integral indexes were used to evaluate control quantity of designed control system. Results of this selection method for course controller have been presented in fig. 5.

Presented membership functions selection allow to create base of 35 rules (fig. 6). Particular rule could be read from the intersection of specified row and column. For the first row and first column following rule has been obtained:

If error of course **is** *Negative Large* **and** change in error of course **is** *Negative Large*
then moment of force *N* is *Negative Large*

Rules from the Mac Vicar-Whelan's standard base were chosen as the control rules (Garus & Kitowski, 2001).

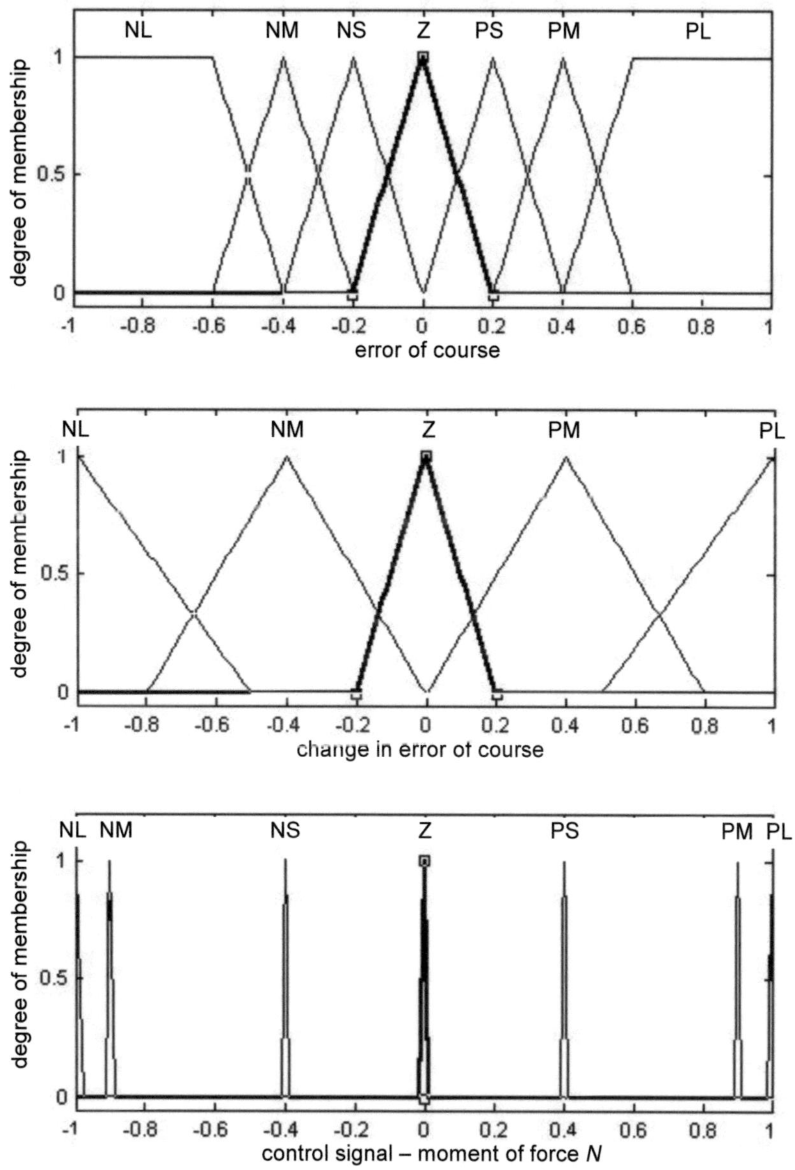

Fig. 5. Fuzzy partition of the universe of discourse of course

change in error of course		error of course						
		NL	NM	NS	Z	PS	PM	PL
	NL	NL	NL	NL	NM	Z	PS	PL
	NS	NL	NL	NM	NS	PS	PM	PL
	Z	NL	NM	NM	Z	PM	PM	PL
	PS	NL	NM	NS	PS	PM	PL	PL
	PL	NL	NS	Z	PM	PL	PL	PL
		control signal - moment of force N						

Fig. 6. Base of rules of course controller (NL - Negative Large, NM - Negative Mean, NS - Negative Small, Z - zero, PS - Positive Small, PM - Positive Mean, PL - Positive Large)

4. Results of numerical researches

Computer simulations were carried out in the Matlab environment on the platform computer PC / Windows XP. At the beginning each controller was tuned with the aid of direct and integral control quantity indexes.

Subsequently whole automatic control system of underwater vehicle Ukwial (fig. 3) was tested. Researches were carried out in simulated underwater environment with or without an influence of sea current with defined parameters: V_p (velocity) and α_p (an angle between magnetic north and direction of affecting in horizontal plane).

Tested task of designed control system was to steer the underwater vehicle along desired trajectory in vertical plane XZ (fig. 7).

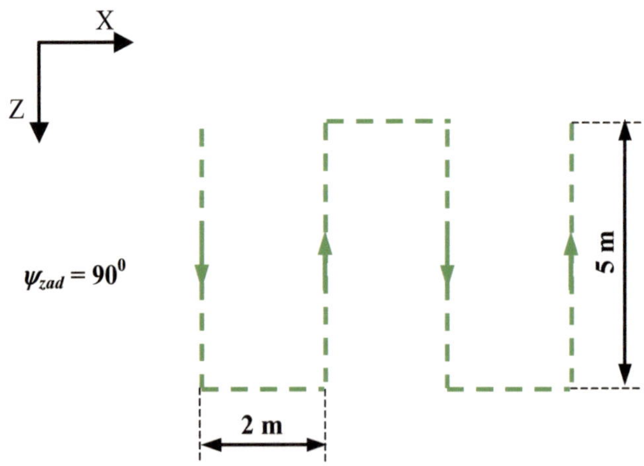

Fig. 7. Desired trajectory of Ukwial in vertical plane

Presented course of desired trajectory (fig. 7) comes from nature of the mission executed by the underwater vehicle, which is inspection of hull's part located below surface of water (fig. 8).

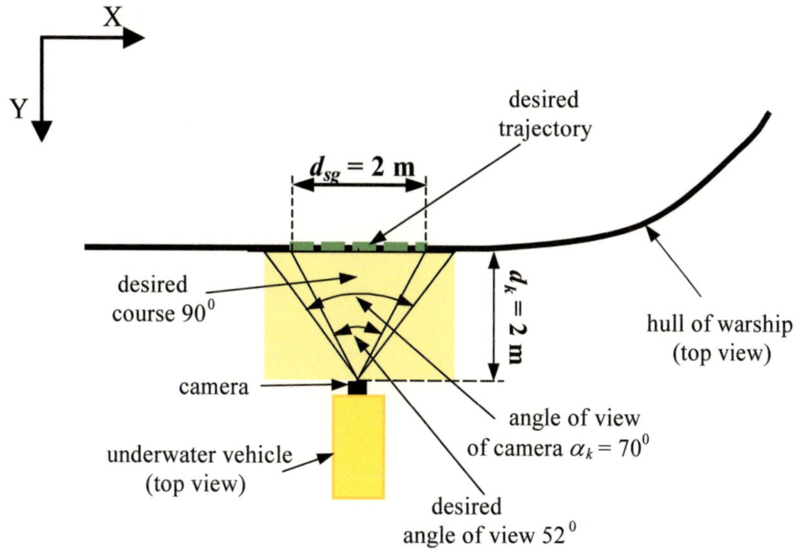

Fig. 8. Desired trajectory of Ukwial in vertical plane (top view)

From the fig. 8 results additional condition that a course of Ukwial should be controlled to the value of desired course 90°, what guarantees monitoring of whole underwater part of inspected hull.

Assuming that camera of an underwater vehicle is immovable and underwater vehicle moves along specified trajectory (fig. 7, fig. 8) following maximal errors of controlled parameters were calculated: maximal error in X axis $\Delta x = \pm\, 0{,}4$ m, maximal error in Y axis $\Delta y = \pm\, 0{,}5$ m, maximal error of course $\Delta\psi = \pm\, 9^{\circ}$.

To illustrate changes of 4 parameters (3 coordinates and an angle of course) on single figure following method has been accepted (fig. 9): changes of a course at the discrete points of trajectory are presented as line segments covering with longitudinal axis of symmetry. Additionally direction of affecting sea current was visualized in form of a red arrow, what helps to illustrate conditions of moving in an underwater environment.

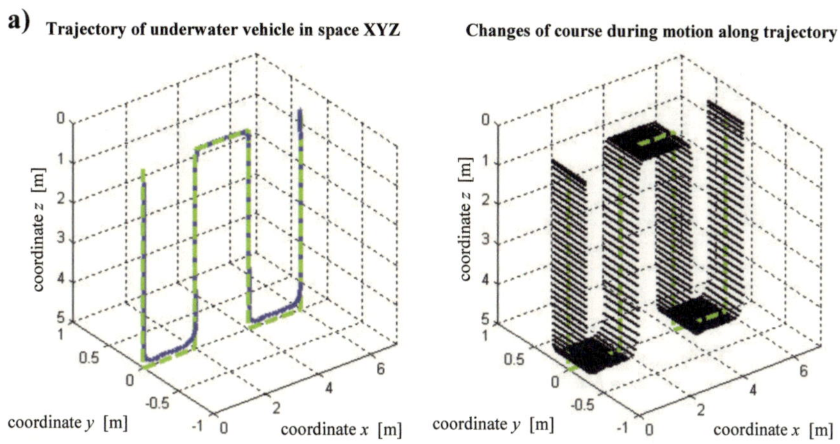

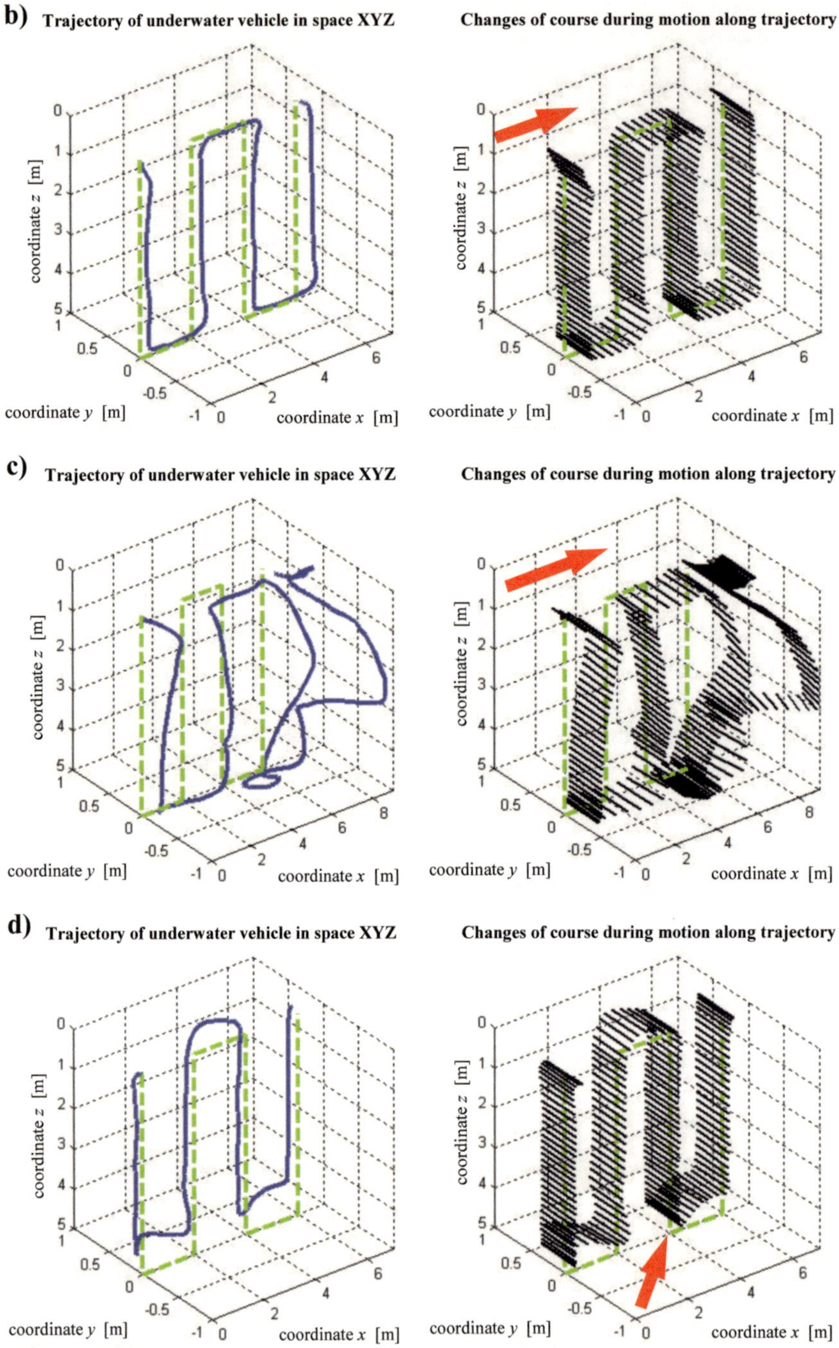

Fig. 9. Automatic steering of underwater vehicle along desired trajectory a) without sea current and with different sea currents: b) V_p= 0,5 m/s, $\alpha_p = 0^0$, c) V_p= 0,9 m/s, $\alpha_p = 0^0$ and d) V_p= 0,5 m/s, $\alpha_p = 45^0$

On the base of achieved results of numerical researches (time diagrams presented on fig. 9 and direct and integral control quantity indexes included in (Szymak, 2004)) following partial conclusions have been found:

1. in the case of sea current does not affect, control system precisely controls movement of underwater vehicle along desired trajectory,
2. in the case of sea current affects, underwater vehicle is "pushed out" from desired trajectory with force depended on velocity of sea current in direction of affecting (for velocity V_p= 0,9 m/s value of coordinate y exceeds the maximal error in Y axis),
3. action of sea current affects also stabilization of a course (for velocity V_p= 0,9 m/s value of a course exceeds the maximal error of course),
4. in other cases (below velocity V_p= 0,9 m/s) values of maximal errors are exceeded only in short time (1 or 2 second), what does not influence on quality of recorded video,
5. limitation of Ukwial control in the presence of stronger sea current (above 1 m/s) comes from limited value of thrust vector, which is generated by driving system.

5. Comparison of simulation and experiment

Experimental researches were carried out in the naval harbour Gdynia. Remotely operated vehicle Ukwial was launched from the warship "Flaming" (fig. 10). Computer simulation and experimental researches were executed without influence of sea currents. Selected results of computer simulations with influence of sea current have been presented in fig. 9. While experimental researches taking into account affect of sea current have not been carried out yet.

Fig. 10. Launching of remotely operated vehicle Ukwial

Selected results of course's fuzzy control have been presented on fig. 11. Results of other controller action have been inserted in (Szymak, 2004). Direct and integral indexes have been used to the evaluation of control quantity tested controllers.

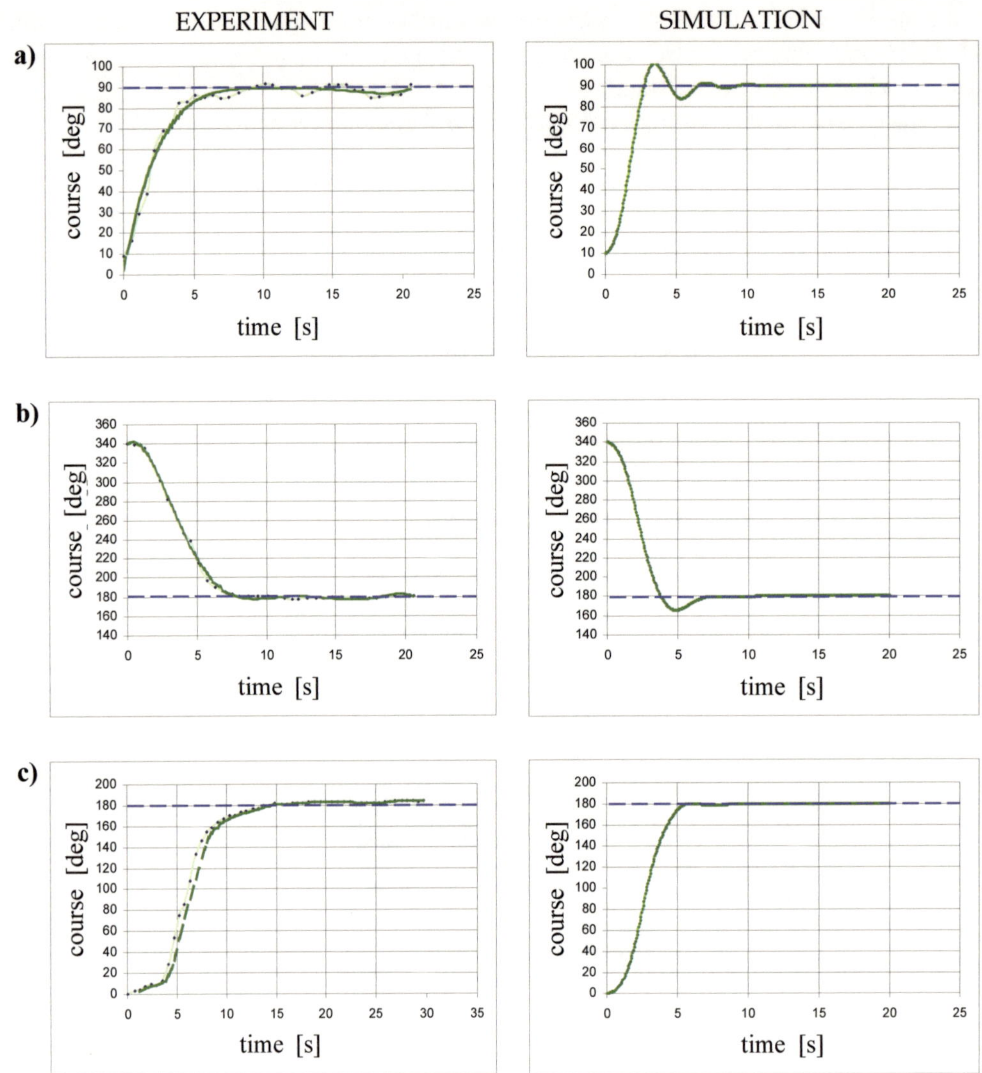

Fig. 11. Control of underwater vehicle's course: a) from initial value 10° to set value 90°, b) from initial value 340° to set value 180°, c) from initial value 0° to set value 180° with additional manoeuvre in X axis

Received results of researches allow to formulate the following conclusions for selected course FPD:

1. the better control quantity has been reached for underwater vehicle, which did not make additional manoeuvre; in that case total hydrodynamic thrust vector generated by propellers was used to change a course,
2. stabilizing influence of an umbilical cord on control of course can be observed on the base of experimental researches compare to oscillation achieved in simulation; it testifies that accepted model of an umbilical cord is not reliable,
3. designed course's controller carries out change of course 180° in average time 10s.

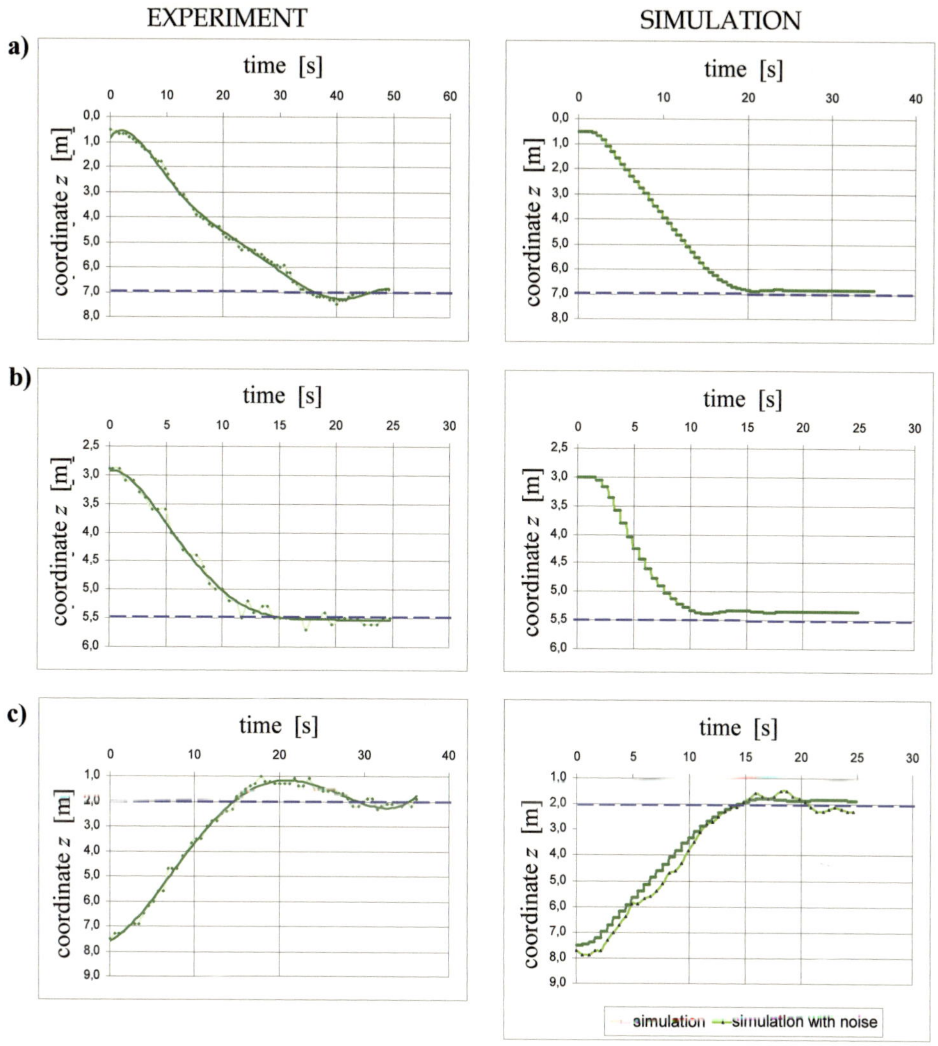

Fig. 12. Control of underwater vehicle's draught: a) from initial value 0,5m to set value 7m, b) from initial value 3m to set value 5,5m, c) from initial value 7,5m to set value 2m (additional simulation with noise)

During the experimental researches also draught's controller was verified correctly (fig. 12). On the base of received results it can be stated that:

1. signal coming from sensor of draught is less precise and has more added noise than signal of a course; it can be testified on the base of simulation with noise (curves received from experiment and simulation with noise are very similar, fig. 12c),
2. precise control of draught, which value is digitized with step 0,1m, is more difficult; the same control method gives worse results in control of draught than in control of course,
3. designed draught's controller carries out change of 1m in average time 5s.

Unfortunately controllers of displacement in X and Y axis were not verified because of incorrect operation of underwater positioning system.

6. Conclusion

Results of carried out numerical and experimental researches, which were presented partially in fig. 9, 11 and 12 confirmed that fuzzy data processing can be successfully used to steer the underwater vehicle with set values of movement's parameters.
Designed control system can be used to steer another underwater vehicles with different driving systems, because control signals were forces and moment of forces, which were processed to rotational speed of propellers with assistance of separate algorithm, specific for definite type of the underwater vehicle.
Positive verification of course's and draught's controllers enabled their implementation in the control desk of Ukwial.
Further researches should include: verification of controllers of displacement in X and Y axis, applying of other self-adopting to varying environmental conditions control methods.

7. References

Driankov, D.; Hellendoorn, H. & Reinfrank, M. (1996). *An introduction to Fuzzy Control,* WNT, ISBN 83-204-2030-X, Warsaw, in Polish

Fossen, T. I. (1994). *Guidance And Control Of Ocean Vehicles,* John Wiley & Sons Ltd., ISBN 978-0-471-94113-2, Norway

Garus, J. & Kitowski, Z. (2001). Fuzzy Control of Underwater Vehicle's Motion, In: *Advances in Fuzzy Systems and Evolutionary Computation,* Mastorakis N., pp. 100-103, World Scientific and Engineering Society Press, ISBN 960-8052-27-0

Kubaty, T. & Rowiński, L. (2001). *Mine counter vehicles for Baltic navy,* internet, http://www.underwater.pg.gda.pl/publikacje

Szymak, P. (2004). *Using of artificial intelligence methods to control of underwater vehicle in inspection of oceanotechnical objects,* PhD thesis, Naval Academy Publication, Gdynia, in Polish

Szymak, P. & Małecki, J. (2007). Neuro-Fuzzy Controller of an Underwater Vehicle's Trim. *Polish Journal of Environmental Studies,* Vol. 16, No 4B, 2007, pp. 171-174, ISSN 1230-1485

18

Automatization of Decision Processes in Conflict Situations: Modelling, Simulation and Optimization

Zbigniew Tarapata
Military University of Technology in Warsaw, Faculty of Cybernetics
Poland

1. Introduction

Military conflict is one of the types of conflict situations. The automation of simulated battlefield is a domain of Computer Generated Forces (CGF) systems or semi-automated forces (SAF or SAFOR) (Henninger et al., 2000; Lee & Fishwick, 1995; Longtin & Megherbi, 1995; Lee, 1996; Mohn, 1994; Petty, 1995). CGF or SAF (SAFOR) is a technique, which provides a simulated opponent using a computer system that generates and controls multiple simulation entities using software and possibly a human operator. In the case of Distributed Interactive Simulation (DIS) systems, the system is intended to provide a simulated battlefield which is used for training military personnel. The advantages of CGF are well-known (Petty, 1995): they lower the cost of a DIS system by reducing the number of standard simulators that must be purchased and maintained; CGF can be programmed, in theory, to behave according to the tactical doctrine of any desired opposing force, and so eliminate the need to train and retrain human operators to behave like the current enemy; CGF can be easier to control by a single person than an opposing force made up of many human operators and it may give the training instructor greater control over the training experience. One of the elements of the CGF systems is module for movement planning and simulation of military objects. In many of existing simulation systems there are different solutions regarding to this subject. In the *JTLS* system (JTLS, 1988) terrain is represented using hexagons with sizes ranging from 1km to 16km. In the *CBS* system (Corps Battle Simulation, 2001) terrain is similarly represented, but vectoral-region approach is additionally applied. In both of these systems there are manual and automatic methods for route planning (e.g. in the *CBS* controller sets intermediate points (coordinates) for route). In the *ModSAF (Modular Semi-Automated Forces)* system in module "SAFsim", which simulates the entities, units, and environmental processes the route planning component is located (Longtin & Megherbi, 1995). In the paper (Mohn, 1994) implementation of a *Tactical Mission Planner* for command and control of Computer Generated Forces in *ModSAF* is presented. In the work (Benton et al., 1995) authors describe a combined on-road/off-road planning system that was closely integrated with a geographic information system and a simulation system. Routes can be planned for either single columns or multiple columns. For multiple columns, the planner keeps track of the temporal location of each column and insures they will not occupy the same space at the same time. In the same paper the *Hierarchic Route*

Planner as integrate part of *Predictive Intelligence Military Tactical Analysis System (PIMTAS)* is discussed. In the paper (James et al., 1999) authors presented on-going efforts to develop a prototype for ground operations planning, the *Route Planning Uncertainty Manager (RPLUM)* tool kit. They are applying uncertainty management to terrain analysis and route planning since this activity supports the Commander's scheme of manoeuvre from the highest command level down to the level of each combat vehicle in every subordinate command. They extend the *PIMTAS* route planning software to accommodate results of reasoning about multiple categories of uncertainty. Authors of the paper (Campbell et al., 1995) presented route planning in the *Close Combat Tactical Trainer* (*CCTT*). Authors (Kreitzberg et al., 1990) have developed the *Tactical Movement Analyzer (TMA)*. The system uses a combination of digitized maps, satellite images, vehicle type and weather data to compute the traversal time across a grid cell. *TMA* can compute optimum paths that combine both on-road and off-road mobility, and with weather conditions used to modify the grid cost factors. The smallest grid size used is approximately 0.5 km. The author uses the concept of a signal propagating from the starting point and uses the traversal time at each cell in the array to determine the time at which the signal arrives to neighbouring cells. In the paper (Tarapata, 2004a) models and methods of movement planning and simulation in some simulation aided system for operational training on the corps-brigade level (Najgebauer, 2004) is described. A combined on-road/off-road planning system that is closely integrated with a geographic information system and a simulation system is considered. A dual model of the terrain ((1) as a regular network of terrain squares with square size 200mx200m, (2) as a road-railroad network), which is based at the digital map, is presented. Regardless of types of military actions military objects are moved according to some group (arrangement of units). For example, each object being moved in group (e.g. during attack, during redeployment) must keep distances between each other of the group (Tarapata, 2001). Therefore, it is important to recognize (during movement simulation) that objects inside units do not "keep" required distances (group pattern) and determine a new movement schedule. All of the systems presented above have no automatic procedures for synchronization movement of more than one unit. The common solution of this problem is when movement (and simulation, naturally) is stopped and commanders (trainees) make a new decision or the system does not react to such a situation. Therefore, in the paper (Tarapata, 2005) a proposition of a solution to the problem of synchronization movement of many units is shown. Some models of synchronous movement and the idea of module for movement synchronization are presented. In the papers (Antkiewicz et al., 2007; Tarapata, 2007c) the idea and model of command and control process applied for the decision automata on the battalion level for three types of unit tasks: attack, defence and march are presented.

The chapter is organized as follows. Presented in section 2 is the review of methods of environment modelling for simulated battlefield. An example of terrain model being used in the real simulator is described. Moreover, paths planning algorithms, which are being applied in terrain-based simulation, are considered. Sections 3 and 4 contain description of automatization methods of main battlefield processes (attack, defence and march) in simulation system like CGF. In these sections, a decision automata, which is a component of the simulation system for military training is described as an example. Presented in section 5 are some conclusions concerning problems and proposition of their solution in automatization of decision processes in conflict situations.

2. Environment modelling for simulation of conflict situations

2.1 An overview

The terrain database-based model is being used as an integrated part of route CGF systems. Terrain data can be as simple as an array of elevations (which provides only a limited means to estimate mobility) or as complex as an elevation array combined with digital map overlays of slope, soil, vegetation, drainage, obstacles, transportation (roads, etc.) and the quantity of recent weather. For example, in (Benton et al., 1995) authors describe HERMES (Heterogeneous Reasoning and Mediator Environment System) will allow the answering of queries that require the interrogation of multiple databases in order to determine the start and destination parameters for the route planner.

There are a few approaches in which the map (representing a terrain area) is decomposed into a graph. All of them first convert the map into regions of go (open) and no-go (closed). The no-go areas may include obstacles and are represented as polygons. A few methods of map representation is used, for example: visibility diagram, Voronoi diagram, straight-line dual of the Voronoi diagram, edge-dual graph, line-thinned skeleton, regular grid of squares, grid of homogeneous squares coded in a quadtree system, etc. (Benton et al., 1995; Schiavone et al., 1995a; Schiavone et al., 1995b; Tarapata, 2003).

The polygonal representations of the terrain are often created in database generated systems (DBGS) through a combination of automated and manual processes (Schiavone et al., 1995; Schiavone et al., 2000). It is important to say that these processes are computationally complicated, but are conducted before simulation (during preparation process). Typically, an initial polygonal representation is created from the digital terrain elevation data through the use of an automated triangulation algorithm, resulting in what is commonly referred to as a Triangulated Irregular Network (TIN). A commonly used triangulation algorithm is the Delaunay triangulation. Definition of the Delaunay triangulation may be done via its direct relation to the Voronoi diagram of set S with an N number of 2D points: the straight-line dual of the Voronoi diagram is a triangulation of S.

The *Voronoi diagram* is the solution to the following problem: given set S with an N number of points in the plane, for each point p_i in S what is the locus of points (x,y) in the plane that are closer to p_i than to any other point of S?

The *straight-line dual* is defined as the graph embedded in the plane obtained by adding a straight-line segment between each pair of points of S whose Voronoi polygons share an edge. Fig.1a depicts an irregularly spaced set of points S, its Voronoi diagram, and its straight-line dual (i.e. its Delaunay triangulation).

The *edge-dual graph* is essentially an adjacency list representing the spatial structure of the map. To create this graph, we assign a node to the midpoint of each map edge, which does not bound an obstacle (or the border). Special nodes are assigned to the start and goal points. In each non-obstacle region, we add arcs to connect all nodes at the midpoints of the edges, which bound the same region. The fact that all regions are convex, guarantees that all such arcs cannot intersect obstacles or other regions. An example of the edge-dual graph is presented in Fig.1b.

The *visibility graph,* is a graph, whose nodes are the vertices of terrain polygons and edges join pairs of nodes, for which the corresponding segment lies inside a polygon. An example is shown in Fig.2.

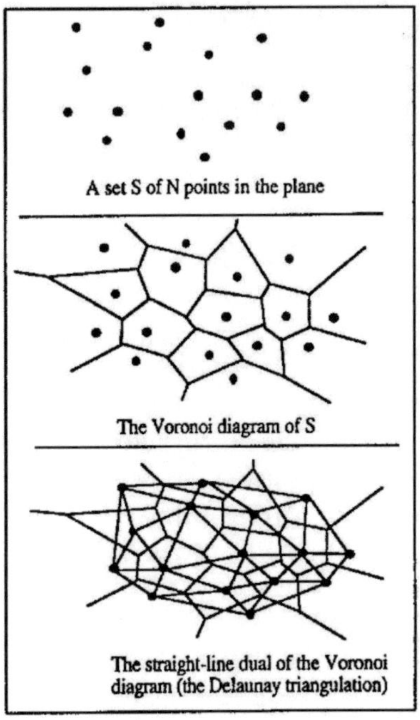

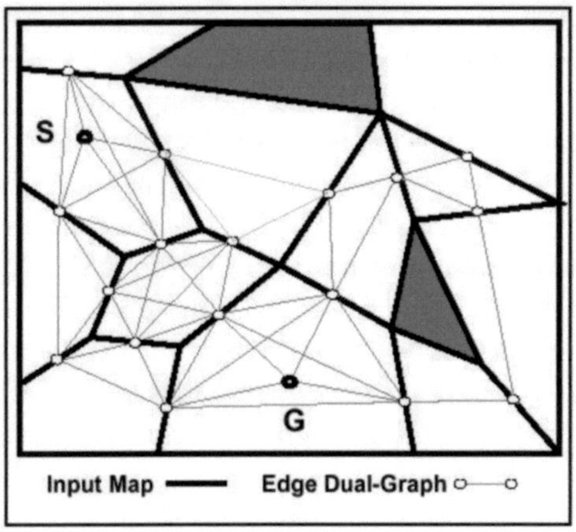

(a) (b)

Fig.1. (a) Voronoi diagram and its Delaunay triangulation (Schiavone et al., 1995); (b) Edge-dual graph. Obstacles are represented by filled polygons

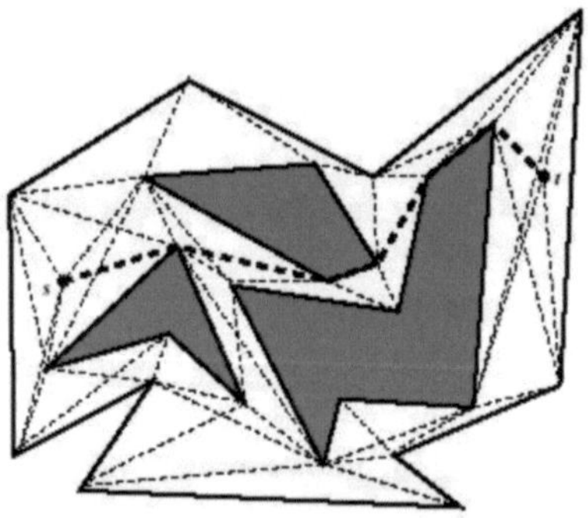

Fig.2. Visibility graph (Mitchell, 1999). The shortest geometric path is marked from source node s to destination t. Obstacles are represented by filled polygons

The *regular grid of squares* (or hexagons, e.g. in JTLS system (JTLS, 1988)) divides terrain space into the squares with the same size and each square is treated as having homogeneity from the point of view of terrain characteristics (Fig.3).

The *grid of homogeneous squares coded in quadtree system* divides terrain space into the squares with heterogeneous size (Fig.4). The size of square results from its homogeneity according to terrain characteristics. An example of this approach was presented in (Tarapata, 2000).

Advantages and disadvantages of terrain representations and their usage for terrain-based movement planning are presented in section 2.3.

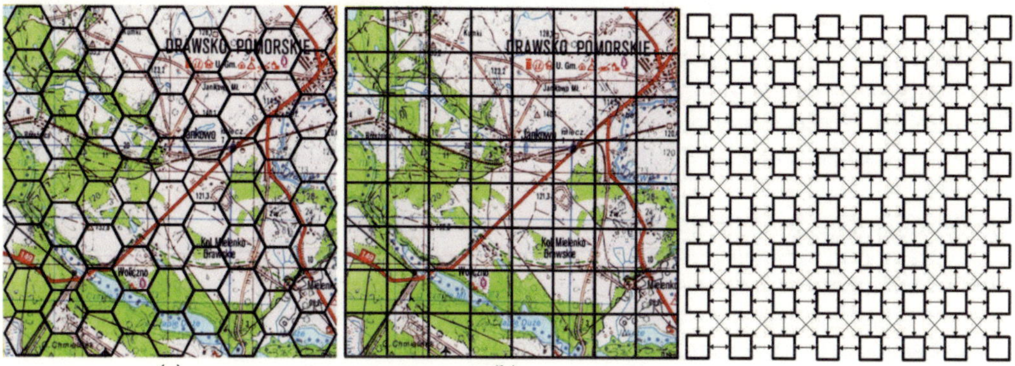

(a) (b)

Fig.3. Examples of terrain representation in a simulated battlefield: (a) regular grid of terrain hexagons; (b) regular grid of terrain squares and its graph representation.

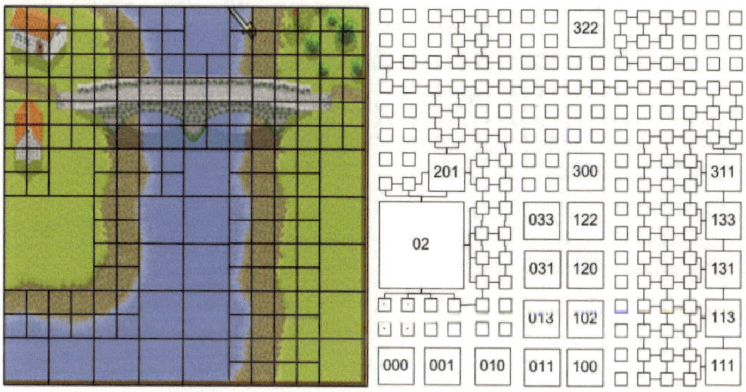

(a) (b)

Fig.4. (a) Partitioning of the selected real terrain area into squares of topographical homogeneous areas; (b) Determination of possible links between neighbouring squares and a description of selected vertices in the quadtree system for terrain area presented in (a)

In many existing simulation systems there are different solutions regarding terrain representation. In the *JTLS* system (JTLS, 1988) terrain is represented using hexagons with a size ranging from 1km to 16km. In the *CBS* system (Corps Battle Simulation, 2001) terrain is similarly represented, but an additional vectoral-region approach is applied. In the simulation-based operational training support system "Zlocien" (Najgebauer, 2004) a dual model of the terrain: (1) as regular network of terrain squares with square size 200mx200m, (2) as road-railroad network, which is based on a digital map, is used.

Taking into account multiresolution terrain modelling (Behnke, 2003; Cassandras et al., 2000; Davis et al., 2000; Pai & Reissell, 1994; Tarapata, 2001) the approach is also used for battlefield modelling and simulation. For example, in the paper (Tarapata, 2004b) a decomposition method, and its properties, which decreases computational time for path searching in multiresolution graphs has been presented. The goal of the method is not only computation time reduction but, first of all, using it for multiresolution path planning (to apply similarity in decision processes on different command level and decomposing-merging approach). The method differs from very effective representations of terrain using quadtree (Kambhampati & Davis, 1986) because of two main reasons: (1) elements of quadtree which represent a terrain have irregular sizes, (2) in majority applications quadtree represents only binary terrain with two types of region: open (passable) and closed (impassable). Hence, this approach is very effective for mobile robots, but it is not adequate, for example, to represent battlefield environment (Tarapata, 2003).

2.2 Terrain model for a battlefield simulation – an example

The terrain (environment) model S_0, which we use as a battlefield model for further discussions (sections: 3.4 and 4) is based on the digital map in VPF format. The model is twofold: (1) as a regular network Z_1 of terrain squares, (2) as a road-railroad network Z_2 and it is defined as follows (Tarapata, 2004a):

$$S_O(t) = \langle Z_1(t), Z_2(t) \rangle \qquad (1)$$

Regular grid of squares Z_1 (see Fig.3) divides terrain space into squares with the same size (200m×200m) and each square is homogeneous from the point of view of terrain characteristics (degree of slowing down velocity, ability to camouflage, degree of visibility, etc.). This square size results from the fact that the nearest level of modelled units in SBOTSS "Zlocien" (Najgebauer, 2004) is a platoon and 200m is approximately the width of the platoon front during attack. The Z_1 model is used to plan off-road (cross-country) movement e.g. during attack planning. In the Z_2 road-railroad network (see Fig.5) we have crossroads as network nodes and section of the roads linking adjacent crossroads as network links (arcs, edges). This model is used to plan fast on-road movement, e.g. during march (redeployment) planning and simulation.

These two models of terrain are integrated. This integration gives possibilities to plan movement inside both models. It is possible, because each square of terrain contains information about fragments of road inside this square. On the other hand each fragment of road contains information on squares of terrain, which they cross. Hence, route for any object (unit) may consist of sections of roads and squares of terrain. It is possible to get off the road (if it is impassable) and start movement off-road (e.g. omit impassable section of road) and next returning to the road. Conversely, we can move off-roads (e.g. during attack), access a section of road (e.g. any bridge to go across the river) and then return back off-road (on the other riverside). The characteristics of both terrain models depend on: time, terrain surface and vegetation, weather, the day and time of year, opponent and own destructions (e.g. destruction of the bridge which is element of road-railroad network) (see Table 1 and Table 2).

The formal definition of the regular network of terrain squares Z_1 is as follows (see Fig.3):

$$Z_1(t) = \langle G_1, \Psi_1(t) \rangle \qquad (2)$$

where G_1 defines Berge's graph defining structure of squares network, $G_1 = \langle W_1, \Gamma_1 \rangle$, W_1 - set of graph's nodes (terrain squares); $\Gamma_1 : W_1 \rightarrow 2^{W_1}$ - function describing for each nodes of G set of adjacent nodes (maximal 8 adjacent nodes); $\Psi_1(t) = \{\Psi_{1,0}(\cdot,t), \Psi_{1,1}(\cdot,t), \Psi_{1,2}(\cdot,t), \ldots, \Psi_{1,LW_1}(\cdot,t)\}$ - set of functions defined on the graph's nodes (depending on t).

One of the functions of $\Psi_1(t)$ is the function of slowing down velocity $FSDV(n,\ldots)$, $n \in W_1$ which describes slowing down velocity (as a real number from [0,1]) inside the n-th square of the terrain,

$$FSDV: W_1 \times T \times K\_Veh \times K\_Meteo \times K\_YearS \times K\_DayS \rightarrow [0,1] \quad (3)$$

where: T - set of times, K_Veh - set of vehicle types, K_Veh ={Veh_Wheeled, Veh_Wheeled-Caterpillar, Veh_Caterpillar}; K_Meteo - set of meteorological conditions, K_YearS - set of the seasons of year, K_DayS - set of the day of the season.
The function $FSDV$ is used to calculate crossing time between two squares of terrain. Other functions (as subset of $\Psi_1(t)$) described on the nodes (squares) of G_1 and essential from the point of view of trafficability and movement are presented in the Table 1.

Description of the function	**Definition of the function**
Geographical coordinates of node (centre of square)	$FWSP : W_1 \rightarrow R^3$
Ability to camouflage in the square	$FCam : W_1 \times T \rightarrow [0,1]$
Degree of terrain undulation in the square	$FUnd : W_1 \rightarrow [0,1]$
Subset of node's set of Z_2 network, which are located inside the square	$FW1OnW2: W_1 \rightarrow 2^{W_2}$

Table 1. The most important functions described on the terrain square (node of G_1)

Formal definition of the road-railroad network Z_2 is following (see Fig.5):

$$Z_2(t) = \langle G_2, \Psi_2(t), \zeta_2(t) \rangle \quad (4)$$

where G_2 describes Berge's graph defining structure of road-railroad network, $G_2 = \langle W_2, U_2 \rangle$, W_2 - set of graph's nodes (crossroads); $U_2 \subset W_2 \times W_2$ - set of graph G_2 arcs (sections of roads); $\Psi_2(t) = \{\Psi_{2,0}(\cdot,t), \Psi_{2,1}(\cdot,t), \ldots, \Psi_{2,LW_2}(\cdot,t)\}$ - set of functions defined on the graph's G_2 nodes (depending on t); $\zeta_2(t) = \{\zeta_{2,i}(\cdot,t)\}_{i=\overline{1,IG_2}}$ - set of functions defined on the graph's G_2 arcs (depending on t). Functions (as subset of $\Psi_2(t)$ and $\zeta_2(t)$) are presented, which are essential from the point of view of trafficability and movement, described on the nodes and arcs of G_2 in the Table 2. One of the most important functions is slowing down velocity function $FSDV2(u,\ldots)$, $u \in U_2$ which describes slowing down velocity (as real number from [0,1]) on the u-th arc (section of road) of the graph:

$$FSDV2: U_2 \times T \times K\_Veh \times K\_Meteo \times K\_YearS \times K\_DayS \rightarrow [0,1] \quad (5)$$

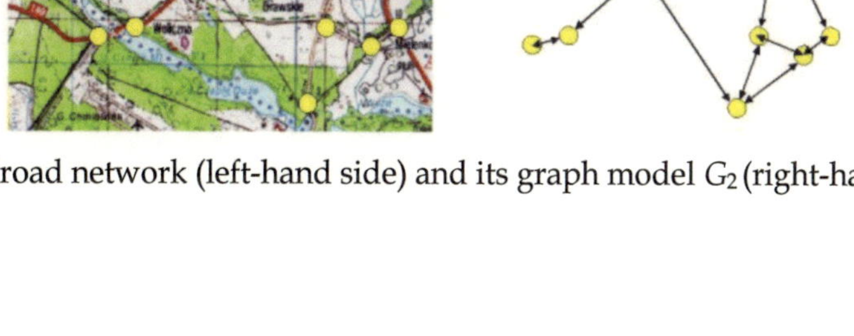

Fig.5. Road-railroad network (left-hand side) and its graph model G_2 (right-hand side)

Description of the function	Definition of the function
Geographical coordinates of node (crossroad)	$FWSP2 : W_2 \rightarrow R^3$
Node Z_1, which contains node Z_2	$FW2OnW1: W_2 \rightarrow W_1$
Subset of set of nodes of the Z_1 network, which contains the arc	$FU2OnW1: U_2 \rightarrow 2^{W_1}$
Degree of terrain undulation on the arc	$FUnd : U_2 \rightarrow [0,1]$
Arc length	$FLen : U_2 \rightarrow R^+$

Table 2. The most important functions described on the crossroads and on part of the roads (G_2)

2.3 Paths planning algorithms in terrain-based simulation

There are four main approaches that are used in a battlefield simulation (CGF systems) for paths planning (Karr et al., 1995): free space analysis, vertex graph analysis, potential fields and grid-based algorithms.

In the *free space approach*, only the space not blocked and occupied by obstacles is represented. For example, representing the centre of movement corridors with Voronoi diagrams (Schiavone et al., 1995) is a free space approach (see Fig.1). The advantage of Voronoi diagrams is that they have efficient representation. Disadvantages of Voronoi diagrams are as follows: they tend to generate unrealistic paths (paths derived from Voronoi diagrams follow the centre of corridors while paths derived from visibility graphs clip the edges of obstacles); the width and trafficability of corridors are typically ignored; distance is generally the only factor considered in choosing the optimal path.

In the *vertex graph approach*, only the endpoints (vertices) of possible path segments are represented (Mitchell, 1999). Advantages of this approach: it is suitable for spaces that have sufficient obstacles to determine the endpoints. Disadvantages are as follows: determining the vertices in "open" terrain is difficult; trafficability over the path segment is not represented; factors other than distance can not be included in evaluating possible routes.

In the *potential field approach*, the goal (destination) is represented as an "attractor", obstacles are represented by "repellors", and the vehicles are pulled toward the goal while being repelled from the obstacles. Disadvantages of this approach: the vehicles can be attracted into box canyons from which they can not escape; some elements of the terrain may simultaneously attract and repel.

In the *regular grid approach*, the grid overlays the terrain, terrain features are abstracted into the grid, and the grid rather than the terrain is analyzed. Advantages are as follows: analysis simplification. Disadvantages: "jagged" paths are produced because movement out of a grid cell is restricted to four (or eight) directions corresponding to the four (or eight) neighbouring cells; granularity (size of the grid cells) determines the accuracy of terrain representation.

Many route planners in the literature are based on the *off-line path planning algorithms*: a path for the object is determined before its movement. The following are exemplary algorithms of this approach: Dijkstra's shortest path algorithm, A* algorithm (Korf, 1999), geometric path planning algorithms (Mitchell, 1999) or its variants (Korf, 1999; Logan, 1997; Logan & Sloman, 1997; Rajput & Karr, 1994; Tarapata, 1999; 2001; 2003; 2004; Undeger et al., 2001). For example, A* has been used in a number of Computer Generated Forces systems as the basis of their component planning, to plan road routes (Campbell et al., 1995), to avoid moving obstacles (Karr et al., 1995), to avoid static obstacles (Rajput & Karr, 1994) and to plan concealed routes (Longtin & Megherbi, 1995). Moreover, the multicriteria approach to the path determined in CGF systems is often used. Some results of selected multicriteria paths problem and analysis of the possibility to use them in CGF systems are described, e.g. in (Tarapata, 2007a). Very extensive discussion related to geometric shortest path planning algorithms was presented by Mitchell in (Mitchell, 1999) (references consist of 393 papers and handbooks). The geometric shortest path problem is defined as follows: given a collection of obstacles, find an Euclidean shortest obstacle-avoiding path between two given points. Mitchell considers the following problems: geodesic paths in a simple polygon; paths in a polygonal domain (searching the visibility graph, continuous Dijkstra's algorithm); shortest paths in other metrics (L_p metric, link distance, weighted region metric, minimum-time paths, curvature-constrained shortest paths, optimal motion of non-point robots, multiple criteria optimal paths, sailor's problem, maximum concealment path problem, minimum total turn problem, fuel-consuming problem, shortest paths problem in an arrangement); on-line algorithms and navigation without map; shortest paths in higher dimensions.

The basic idea of the *on-line path planning algorithms* (Korf, 1999), in general, is that the object is moved step-by-step from cell to cell using a heuristic method. This approach is borrowed from robots motion planning (Behnke, 2003; Kambhampati & Davis, 1986; LaValle, 2006; Logan & Sloman, 1997; Undeger et al., 2001). The decision about the next move (its direction, speed, etc.) depends on the current location of the object and environment status. Examples of on-line path planning algorithms (Korf, 1999): RTA* (Real-Time A*), LRTA* (Learning RTA*), RTEF (Real-Time Edge Follows), HLRTA*, eFALCONS. For example, the idea of RTEF (real-time edge follow) algorithm (Undeger et al., 2001) is to let the object eliminate closed directions (the directions that cannot reach the target point) in order to decide on which way to go (open directions). For instance, if the object has a chance to realize that moving north and east won't let him reach the goal state, then it will prefer going south or west. RTEF finds out these open and closed directions by decreasing the number of choices the object has. However, the on-line path planning approach has one basic disadvantage: in this approach using a few criterions simultaneously to find an optimal (or acceptable) path is difficult and it is rather impossible to estimate, the moment of reaching the destination in advance. Moreover, it does not guarantee finding optimal solutions and even suboptimal ones may significantly differ from acceptable.

3. Automatization of main battlefield decision processes

3.1 Introduction

In this section the idea and model of command and control process applied for the decision automata for attack and defence on the battalion level are considered. In section 4 we will complete the description of the automata for the third type of unit task - march. As it was written in section 1 these problems are very rarely discussed in the literature; however some ideas we can come across in (Dockery & Woodcock et al., 1993; Hoffman H. & Hoffman M., 2000). The decision automata being presented replaces battalion commanders in the simulator for military trainings and it executes two main processes (Antkiewicz et al., 2003; Antkiewicz et al., 2007): decision planning process and direct combat control. The decision planning process (DPP) contains three stages: the identification of a decision situation, the generation of decision variants, the variants evaluation and the selection of the best variant, which satisfy the proposed criteria. The decision situation is classified according to the following factors: own task, expected actions of opposite forces, environmental conditions – terrain, weather, the day and season, current state of own and opposite forces in a sense of personnel and weapon systems. For this reason, we can define identification of the decision situation (the first stage of the DPP and the most interesting from the point of view of automatization process) as a multicriteria weighted graph similarity decision problem (MWGSP) (Tarapata, 2007b) and present it in sections 3.3 and 3.4 presenting them through a short overview of structural objects similarity (section 3.2). The remaining two stages of DPP (the variants evaluation and selecting the best variant) are described in detail in (Antkiewicz et al., 2003; Antkiewicz et al., 2007): for each class of decision situations a set of action plan templates for subordinate and support forces are generated. For example the proposed action plan contains (Antkiewicz et al, 2007): forces redeployment, regions of attack or defence, or manoeuvre routes, intensity of fire for different weapon systems, terms of supplying military materiel to combat forces by logistics units. In order to generate and evaluate possible variants the pre-simulation process based on some procedures: forces attrition procedure, slowing down rate of attack procedure, utilization of munitions and petrol procedure is used. In the evaluation process the following criteria: time and degree of task realization, own losses, utilization of munitions and petrol are applied.

3.2 Structural objects similarity – a short overview

Object similarity is an important issue in applications such as e.g. pattern recognition. Given a database of known objects and a pattern, the task is to retrieve one or several objects from the database that are similar to the pattern.

If graphs are used for object representation this problem turns into determining the similarity of graphs, which is generally referred to as graph matching. Standard concepts in graph matching include (Farin et al., 2003; Kriegel & Schonauer, 2003): graph isomorphism, subgraph isomorphism, graph homomorphism, maximum common subgraph, error-tolerant graph matching using graph edit distance (Bunke, 1997), graph's vertices similarity, histograms of the degree sequence of graphs. A large number of applications of graph matching have been described in the literature (Bunke, 2000; Kriegel & Schonauer, 2003; Robinson, 2004). One of the earliest applications was in the field of chemical structure analysis. More recently, graph matching has been applied to case-based reasoning, machine learning planning, semantic networks, conceptual graph, monitoring of computer networks, synonym extraction and web searching (Blondel et al., 2004; Kleinberg, 1999; Kriegel & Schonauer, 2003; Robinson, 2004; Senellart & Blondel, 2003). Numerous applications from the areas of pattern recognition and machine vision have been reported (Bunke, 2000; Champin & Solon, 2003; Melnik et al., 2002). They include recognition of graphical symbols, character recognition, shape analysis, three-dimensional object recognition, image and video indexing and others. It seems that structural similarity is not sufficient for similarity description between various objects. The arc in the graph gives only binary information concerning connection between two nodes. And what about, for example, the connection strength, connection probability or other characteristics? Thus, the weighted graph matching problem is defined, but in the literature it is relatively rarely considered (Almohamad et al., 1993; Champin & Solon, 2003; Tarapata, 2007b; Umeyama, 1988) and it is most often regarded as a special case of graph edit distance, which is a very time-complex measure

(Bunke, 2004; Kriegel & Schonauer, 2003). Therefore, in section 3.3 we will define a multicriteria weighted graph similarity decision problem (MWGSP) and we will show how to use it for pattern recognition (matching) of decision situations (PRDS) in decision automata, which replaces commanders in simulators for military trainings (Antkiewicz et al., 2007).

3.3 Definition of the multicriteria weighted graph similarity problem (MWGSP)

3.3.1 Structural and quantitative similarity measures between weighted graphs

Let us define weighted graph *WG* as follows:

$$WG = \left\langle G, \{f_i(n)\}_{\substack{i\in\{1,\dots,LF\}\\ n\in N_G}}, \{h_j(a)\}_{\substack{j\in\{1,\dots,LH\}\\ a\in A_G}} \right\rangle \tag{6}$$

where: G - Berge's graph, $G = \langle N_G, A_G \rangle$, N_G, A_G - sets of graph's nodes and arcs, $A_G \subset \{\langle n,n' \rangle : n,n' \in N_G\}$, $f_i : N_G \to R^n$ - the *i*-th function described on the graph's nodes, $i = 1,\dots LF$, (LF - number of node's functions); $h_j : A_G \to R^n$ - the *j*-th function described on the graph's arcs, $j = 1,\dots LH$ (LH – number of arc's functions).

Let two weighted graphs G_A and G_B be given. We propose to calculate two types of similarities of the G_A and G_B: structural and non-structural (quantitative). To calculate structural similarity between G_A and G_B it is proposed to use approach defined in (Blondel et al., 2004). Let A and B be the transition matrices of G_A and G_B. We calculate following sequence of matrices:

$$Z_{k+1} = \frac{BZ_kA^T + A^TZ_kB}{\left\| BZ_kA^T + A^TZ_kB \right\|_F}, \quad k \ge 0 \tag{7}$$

where Z_0=**1** (matrix with all elements equal 1); x^T – matrix x transposition; $\|x\|_F$ - Frobenius (Euclidian) norm for matrix x, $\|x\|_F = \sqrt{\sum_{i-1}^{n_B}\sum_{j-1}^{n_A} x_{ij}^2}$, n_B - number of matrix rows (number of nodes of G_B), n_A - number of matrix columns (number of nodes of G_A). Element z_{ij} of the matrix Z describes similarity score between the *i*-th node of the G_B and the *j*-th node of the G_A. The essence of the graph's nodes similarity is the fact that two graphs' nodes are similar if their neighbouring nodes are similar. The greater value of z_{ij} the greater the similarity between the *i*-th node of the G_B and the *j*-th node of the G_A. We obtain structural similarity matrix $S(G_A,G_B)$ between nodes of graphs G_A and G_B as follows (Blondel et al., 2004):

$$S(G_A, G_B) = [s_{ij}]_{n_B \times n_A} = \lim_{k\to+\infty} Z_{2k} \tag{8}$$

Some computation aspects of calculation $S(G_A,G_B)$ have been presented in (Blondel et al., 2004). We can write (7) more explicit by using the matrix-to-vector operator that develops a matrix into a vector by taking its columns one by one. This operator, denoted *vec*, satisfies the elementary property $vec(C\ X\ D)=(D^T \otimes C^T)\ vec(X)$ in which ⊗ denotes the Kronecker product (also denoted tensorial, direct or categorial product). Then, we can write equality (7) as follows:

$$z_{k+1} = \frac{(A \otimes B + A^T \otimes B^T) z_k}{\left\| (A \otimes B + A^T \otimes B^T) z_k \right\|_F} \tag{9}$$

Unfortunately, the iteration z_{k+1} does not always converge. Authors of (Melnik et al., 2002) showed that if we change the formula (9) for $z_{k+1} = \frac{(A \otimes B + A^T \otimes B^T) z_k + b}{\left\| (A \otimes B + A^T \otimes B^T) z_k + b \right\|_F}$, then the formula (9) converges for $b>0$. Having matrix $S(G_A,G_B)$, we can formulate and solve an optimal assignment problem (using e.g. Hungarian algorithm) to find the best allocation matrix $X = [x_{ij}]_{n_B \times n_A}$ of nodes from graph describing G_A, G_B:

$$d_S(G_A, G_B) = \sum_{i=1}^{n_B} \sum_{j=1}^{n_A} s_{ij} \cdot x_{ij} \to \max \tag{10}$$

with constraints:

$$\sum_{i=1}^{n_B} x_{ij} \le 1, \quad j = \overline{1, n_A} \tag{11}$$

$$\sum_{j=1}^{n_A} x_{ij} \le 1, \quad i = \overline{1, n_B} \tag{12}$$

$$\underset{i \in \{1,\dots,n_B\}}{\forall} \; \underset{j \in \{1,\dots,n_A\}}{\forall} \; x_{ij} \in \{0,1\} \tag{13}$$

The $d_S(G_A,G_B)$ describes the value of *structural similarity measure* of G_A and G_B (Fig.6).

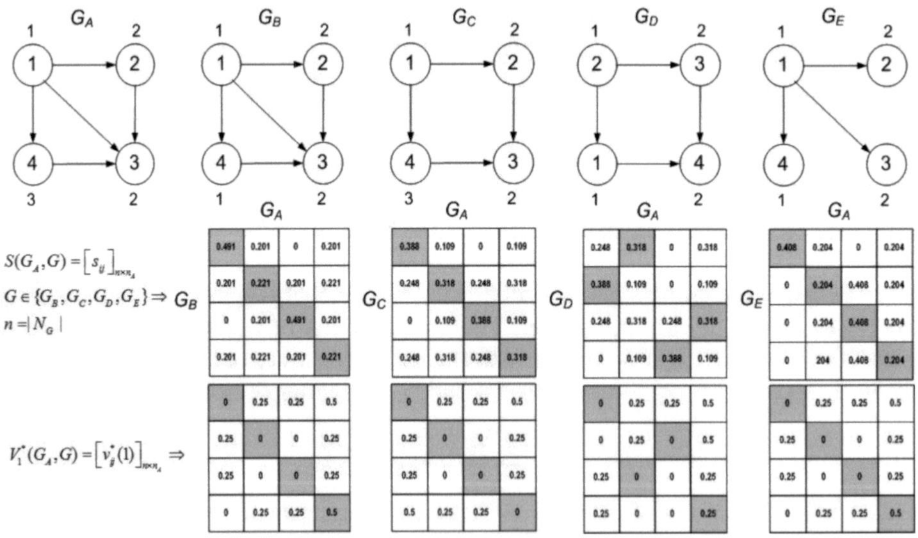

Fig.6. Examples of weighted graphs with a single function described on the nodes (set of functions described on the arcs is empty) and their structural (S(GA,G)) and quantitative ($V_1^*(G_A,G)$) similarity matrices. Filled cells describe ones, which create optimal assignment the nodes of GA to nodes of G.

To calculate non-structural (quantitative) similarity between G_A and G_B we should consider similarity between values of node's and arc's functions (*nodes and arcs quantitative similarity*). To compute nodes quantitative similarity we propose to create vector $\boldsymbol{v}(G_A,G_B)=\langle V_1,...,V_{LF}\rangle$ of matrices, where $V_k=\left[v_{ij}(k)\right]_{n_B\times n_A}$, k=1,…,LF, describing similarity matrix between nodes of G_A and G_B from the point of view of the k-th node's function ($f_k^A:N_{G_A}\to R^n$ for G_A and $f_k^B:N_{G_B}\to R^n$ for G_B) and $v_{ij}(k)=\left\|f_k^B(i)-f_k^A(j)\right\|$ describes "distance" between the i-th node of G_B and the j-th node of G_A from the point of view of f_k^B and f_k^A, respectively. We can apply a norm with parameter $p\geq 1$ as distance measure:

$$\left\|f_k^B(i)-f_k^A(j)\right\|=\left\|f_k^B(i)-f_k^A(j)\right\|_p=\left(\sum_{r=1}^{n}\left|f_{k,r}^B(i)-f_{k,r}^A(j)\right|^p\right)^{1/p} \tag{14}$$

where $f_{k,r}^A(\cdot)$, $f_{k,r}^B(\cdot)$ describe the r-th component of the vector being value of f_k^A and f_k^B, respectively. Next, we compute for each k=1,…,LF normalized matrix $V_k^*=\left[v_{ij}^*(k)\right]_{n_B\times n_A}$, where $v_{ij}^*(k)=v_{ij}(k)/\left\|V_k\right\|_F$. This procedure guarantees that each $v_{ij}^*(k)\in[0,1]$. Finally, we compute total quantitative similarity between the i-th node of G_B and the j-th node of G_A as follows:

$$\bar{v}_{ij}=\sum_{k=1}^{LF}\lambda_k\cdot v_{ij}^*(k),\quad \sum_{k=1}^{LF}\lambda_k=1,\quad \underset{k=1,...,LF}{\forall}\lambda_k\in[0,1] \tag{15}$$

The $d_{QN}(G_A,G_B)$ *nodes quantitative similarity measure* of G_A and G_B we compute solving assignment problem (10)-(12) substituting $-\bar{v}_{ij}$ for s_{ij} (because of that the smaller value of $\bar{v}_{ij}$ the better) and $d_{QN}(G_A,G_B)$ for $d_S(G_A,G_B)$ in (10). Example of calculations similarity matrices between nodes of some graphs and similarity measures d_S and d_{QN} between graphs are presented in the Fig.6 and in the Table 3. Let us note that the best structural matched graph to G_A is G_B ($d_S(G_A,G_B)$=1.423 is the maximal value among of values of this measure for other graphs) but the best quantitative matched graph to G_A is G_C ($d_{QN}(G_A,G_C)$=0 is minimal value among of values of this measure for other graphs). Question is: which graph is the most similar to G_A : G_B or G_C? Some method for solving the problem and to answer the question is presented in section 3.3.2: we have to apply multicriteria choice of the best matched graph to G_A. We can obtain *arcs quantitative similarity measure* $d_{QA}(G_A,G_B)$ by analogy to $d_{QN}(G_A,G_B)$: we build vector $\boldsymbol{e}(G_A,G_B)=\langle E_1,...,E_{LH}\rangle$ of matrices, where $E_k=[e_{ij}(k)]_{m_B\times m_A}$, k=1,…,LH (m_A, m_B – number of arcs in G_A and G_B) describing similarity matrix between arcs of G_A and G_B from the point of view of the k-th arc's function ($h_k^A:A_{G_A}\to R^n$ for G_A and $h_k^B:A_{G_B}\to R^n$ for G_B), $e_{ij}(k)=\left\|h_k^B(i)-h_k^A(j)\right\|_p$, next $e_{ij}^*(k)=e_{ij}(k)/\left\|E_k\right\|_F$ and $\bar{e}_{ij}=\sum_{k=1}^{LH}\mu_k\cdot e_{ij}^*(k)$, $\sum_{k=1}^{LH}\mu_k=1$, $\underset{k=1,...,LH}{\forall}\mu_k\geq 0$.

Substituting in (10) $-\bar{e}_{ij}$ for s_{ij}, $d_{QA}(G_A,G_B)$ for $d_S(G_A,G_B)$ and solving (10)-(12) we obtain $d_{QA}(G_A,G_B)$.

Graph G	$d_S(G_A,G)$	$d_{QN}(G_A,G)$	$0.5d_S(G_A,G) - 0.5d_{QN}(G_A,G)$
G_B	**1.423**	0.5	0.462
G_C	1.412	**0**	**0.706**
G_D	1.412	0.25	0.456
G_E	1.225	0.5	0.362

Table 3. Values of similarity measures between G_A and each of the four graphs from Fig.6

Let us note that it is possible to determine single quantitative similarity measure for G_A and G_B . To this end we use some transformation of graph $G=\langle N,A\rangle$ into temporary graph $G^*=\langle N^*,A^*\rangle$ as follows: $N^*=N\cup A$, $A^*\subset N^*\times N^*$ and

$$\underset{v\in N,a\in A}{\forall}\left(\underset{x\in N}{\exists}(v,x)=a\Rightarrow(v,a)\in A^*\right)\vee \left(\underset{x\in N}{\exists}(x,v)=a\Rightarrow(a,v)\in A^*\right) \tag{16}$$

If G was a weighted graph then in G^* we attribute the arc's and node's functions from G to appropriate nodes of G^* (that is to nodes and arcs from G). Using this procedure for G_A and G_B we obtain G_A^* and G_B^*. Next, for G_A^* and G_B^* we can calculate nodes quantitative similarity measure $d_{QN}(G_A^*,G_B^*)$. Example of constructing G^* from G is presented in the Fig.7.

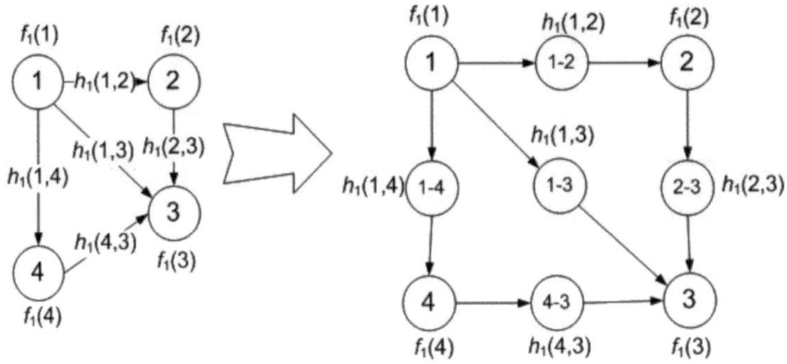

Fig.7. Transformation of G (left-hand side) into G* (right-hand side)

3.3.2 Formulation of multicriteria weighted graphs similarity problem (MWGSP)

Let us accept $SG=\{G_1,G_2,...,G_M\}$ as a set of weighted graphs defining certain objects. Moreover, we have weighted graph P that defines a certain pattern object. The problem is to find such a graph G^o from SG that is the most similar to P. We define this problem as a multicriteria weighted graphs similarity problem (*MWGSP*), which is a multicriteria optimization problem in the space SG with relation R_D:

$$MWGSP=\left(SG,F,R_D\right) \tag{17}$$

where $F:SG\rightarrow R^3$, $F\left(G\right)=\left(d_S(P,G),d_{QN}(P,G),d_{QA}(P,G)\right)$ and

$$R_D = \left\{ \begin{array}{r} (Y,Z) \in SG \times SG : d_S(P,Y) \geq d_S(P,Z) \wedge \\ d_{QN}(P,Y) \leq d_{QN}(P,Z) \wedge \\ d_{QA}(P,Y) \leq d_{QA}(P,Z) \end{array} \right\} \quad (18)$$

Domination relation R_D (Pareto relation between elements of *SG*) gives possibilities to compare graphs from *SG*. Weighted graph *Z* is more similar to *P* than *Y* if structural similarity between *P* and *Y* is not smaller than between *P* and *Z* and, simultaneously, both quantitative similarities between *P* and *Y* are not greater than between *P* and *Z*. There are many methods for solving the problem (17) (Eschenauer et al., 1990): weighted sum (scalarization of set of objectives), hierarchical optimization (the idea is to formulate a sequence of scalar optimization problems with respect to the individual objective functions subject to bounds on previously computed optimal values), trade-off method (one objective is selected by the user and the other ones are considered as constraints with respect to individual minima), method of distance functions in L_p-norm ($p \geq 1$) and others. We propose to use scalar function $H(G): SG \rightarrow R$ as weighted sum of objectives:

$$\begin{array}{l} H(G) = \alpha_1 \cdot d_S(P,G) + \alpha_2 \cdot \left(-d_{QN}(P,G)\right) + \alpha_3 \cdot \left(-d_{QA}(P,G)\right) \\ \alpha_1, \alpha_2, \alpha_3 \geq 0, \quad \alpha_1 + \alpha_2 + \alpha_3 = 1 \end{array} \quad (19)$$

Taking into account (19) the problem of finding the most matched G^o to pattern *P* can be formulated as follows: to determine such a $G^o \in SG$, that $H(G^o) = \max_{G \in SG} H(G)$. In the last column of the Table 3 the scalar function *H*(*G*) is defined as follows:

$$H(G) = \alpha_1 \cdot d_S(P,G) + \alpha_2 \cdot (-d_{QN}(P,G)) + \alpha_3 \cdot (-d_{QA}(P,G)) \quad (20)$$

where $\alpha_1 = \alpha_2 = 0.5$, $\alpha_3 = 0$, $P = G_A$, $SG = \{G_B, G_C, G_D, G_E\}$. Let us note that the best matched graph to G_A being solution of *MWGSP* with scalar function *H*(*G*) is G_C ($H(G^o{=}G_C)=0.706$).
In the paper (Tarapata, 2007b) epsilon-similarity of weighted graphs as another view on quantitative similarity between weighted graphs is additionally considered.

3.4 Application of weighted graphs similarity to pattern recognition of decision situations

For the identification of the decision situation described in section 3.1 we define decision situations space as follows:

$$DSS = \left\{ SD : SD = [SD_{ij}]_{\substack{i=1,...,X \\ j=1,...,Y}} \right\} \quad (21)$$

where *SD* denotes net of terrain squares as a model of activities (interest) area $SD_{ij} = (SD_{ij}^k)_{k=1,..,8}$. For the terrain square with the indices (*i,j*) each of elements denotes: SD_{ij}^1 - the degree of terrain passability, SD_{ij}^2 - the degree of forest covering, SD_{ij}^3 - the degree of water covering, SD_{ij}^4 - the degree of terrain undulating, SD_{ij}^5 - armoured power (potential) of opposite units deployed in the square, SD_{ij}^6 - infantry power (potential) of opposite units deployed in the square, SD_{ij}^{7} - artillery power (potential) of opposite units deployed in the square, SD_{ij}^{8} - coordinates of square, X - the width of an activities (interest) area (number of squares), Y - the depth of an activities (interest) area (number of squares) and $SD_{ij}^{k} \in [0,1]$, $k = 1,...,7$, $SD_{ij}^{8} \in R_{+}^{2}$. Moreover, we have set *PDSS* of decision situations patterns written in the database, $PDSS = \{PS : PS \in DSS\}$ and current situation $CS \in DSS$. The problem is: to find the most similar $PS \in PDSS$ to current situation $CS \in DSS$.

In the presented proposition the weighted graphs similarity approach to identification of decision situation is used. It consists of three stages:

1. Building weighted graphs *WGT*(*CS*), *WGD*(*CS*) and *WGT*(*PS*), *WGD*(*PS*) representing decision situations: current (*CS*) and pattern (*PS*) for topographical conditions (*WGT*) and units (potential) deploying (*WGD*);
2. Calculation of similarity measures between pairs: *WGT*(*CS*), *WGT*(*PS*) and *WGD*(*CS*), *WGD*(*PS*) for each $PS \in PDSS$;
3. Selecting the most similar *PS* to *CS* using calculated similarity measures.

Stage 1

The first stage is to build weighted graphs *WGT* and *WGD* as follows:

$$WGT = \left\langle GT = \langle N_{GT}, A_{GT} \rangle, \{f_k^T(n)\}_{\substack{k\in\{1,...,5\} \\ n\in N_{GT}}} \right\rangle,\ WGD = \left\langle GD = \langle N_{GD}, A_{GD} \rangle, \{f_k^D(n)\}_{\substack{k\in\{1,...,4\} \\ n\in N_{GD}}} \right\rangle$$

where *G* (*GT* or *GD*) – Berge's graphs, $G = \langle N_G, A_G \rangle$, N_G, A_G – sets of graph's nodes and arcs, $A_G \subset \{\langle n, n' \rangle : n, n' \in N_G\}$. Weighted graphs *WGT* and *WGD* describe decision situations (current *CS* and pattern *PS*). Each node *n* of *GT* and *GD* describes terrain cells (*i,j*)=*n* with non-zero values of characteristics defined as components of SD_{ij} from (21) and $\forall_{k\in\{1,...,4\}} f_k^T(n) = SD_{ij}^k$, $f_5^T(n) = SD_{ij}^8$, $\forall_{k\in\{1,...,3\}} f_k^D(n) = SD_{ij}^{4+k}$, $f_4^D(n) = SD_{ij}^8$. Two nodes $x, y \in N_{GD}$ (for $x, y \in N_{GT}$ by analogy) are linked by an arc, when cells represented by *x* and *y* are adjacent (more precisely: they are adjacent cells that taking into account the direction of action, see Fig.8). For example, the terrain can be divided into 15 cells (3 rows and 5 columns, left-hand side, see Fig.8). The units are located in some cells (denoted by circles and Xs). Structural representation of deployment of units is defined by the graph *GD*. Let us note that similar representation can be used for topographical conditions (single graph for one of the topographical information layer: waters, forests, passability or single graph *GT* for all of this information, see Fig.8, right-hand side).

Stage 2

Having weighted graphs *WGD*(*CS*) and *WGD*(*PS*) (*WGT*(*CS*) and *WGT*(*PS*)) representing current *CS* and pattern *PS* decision situations (for units deploying) we use the procedure described in section 3.3.1 to calculate structural and quantitative similarity measures for both graphs. We obtain for *WGD*: d_S(*WGD*(*CS*), *WGD*(*PS*))= $d_S^D(CS, PS)$, d_{QN}(*WGD*(*CS*), *WGD*(*PS*))= $d_{QN}^D(CS, PS)$ and for *WGT*: d_S(*WGT*(*CS*),*WGT*(*PS*))= $d_S^T(CS, PS)$, d_{QN}(*WGT*(*CS*),*WGT*(*PS*))= $d_{QN}^T(CS, PS)$.

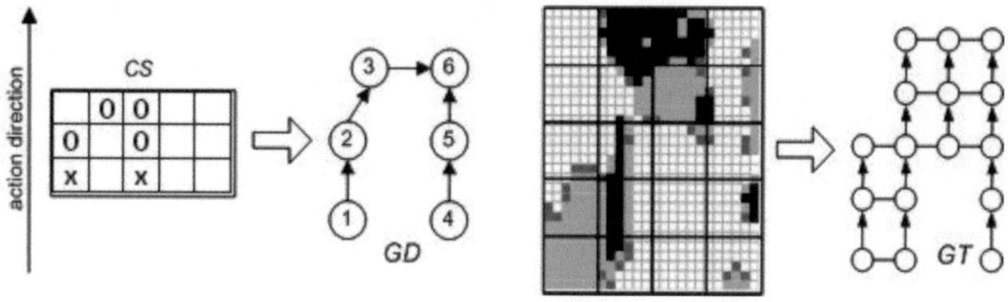

Fig.8. Deployment of units and their structural (graph *GD*) representation (left-hand side) and terrain covering (growth) and its structural (*GT*) representation (right-hand side). Circle (O) and sharp (X) describe two types of units

Stage 3

We formulate problem (17), separately for *WGT* and *WGD*, where: *SG*:=*PDSS*, $F(G):=F_D(PS)$, $d_S(P,G):=d_S^D(CS,PS)$, $d_{QN}(P,G):=d_{QN}^D(CS,PS)$ for *WGD* and $F(G):=F_T(PS)$, $d_S(P,G):=d_S^T(CS,PS)$, $d_{QN}(P,G):=d_{QN}^T(CS,PS)$ for *WGT*. Next, we define scalar functions (19) to solve the problem (17) for *WGD* and *WGT*:

$$H_D(\cdot)=\alpha_1\cdot d_S^D(\cdot,\cdot)+\alpha_2\cdot(-d_{QN}^D(\cdot,\cdot))$$

and

$$H_T(\cdot)=\gamma_1\cdot d_S^T(\cdot,\cdot)+\gamma_2\cdot(-d_{QN}^T(\cdot,\cdot)).$$

Having $H_D(PS)$ and $H_T(PS)$ we can combine these criteria (like in (19)) or set some threshold values and select the most matched pattern situation to the current one.

An example of using the presented approach to find the most matched pattern decision situation to current one is presented in the Fig.9 and in the Table 4. Results of calculations $H_D(PS)$ are presented for each $PS\in PDSS=\{PS_1,...,PS_8\}$. Only function $f_4^{D(CS)}(n)=SD_{ij}^8$ ($f_4^{D(PS)}(n)$ for pattern *PS*) is used from *WGD* to compute nodes quantitative similarity (see section 3.3.1) because all units have the same type. Thus, vector $v(WGD(CS),WGD(PS))$ of matrices has one component $V_1=[v_{ij}(1)]_{|N_{GD(PS)}|\times|N_{GD(CS)}|}$. Function $f_4^{D(CS)}(n)$ describes coordinates of node *n* (left-lower cell has coordinates (1,1)). The norm from (14) has the form of: $\left\|f_4^D(i)-f_4^D(j)\right\|_{p=2}=\left(\sum_{r=1}^{2}\left|f_{4,r}^D(i)-f_{4,r}^D(j)\right|^2\right)^{1/2}$ and it describes the geometric distance between nodes $i\in N_{GD(PS)}$ and $j\in N_{GD(CS)}$. Let us note that for weights $\alpha_1=0,\ \alpha_2=1$ value in Table 4 (for the row PS_i) describes $d_{QN}^D(CS,PS_i)$ and for $\alpha_1=1,\ \alpha_2=0$ describes $d_S^D(CS,PS_i)$. The best matched *PS* to *CS* is PS_2 (taking into account d_S^D and d_{QN}^D).

The process of optimal selection of weights can be organized as follows: we build a learning set $\{CS_i,PDSS_i\}_{i=1,...,LS}$ and for different values of weights experts estimate whether, in their subjective opinion, CS_i is similar to $PS^*\in PDSS_i$ determined from the procedure. Combination of weight values, which are indicated by majority of experts is the optimal combination.

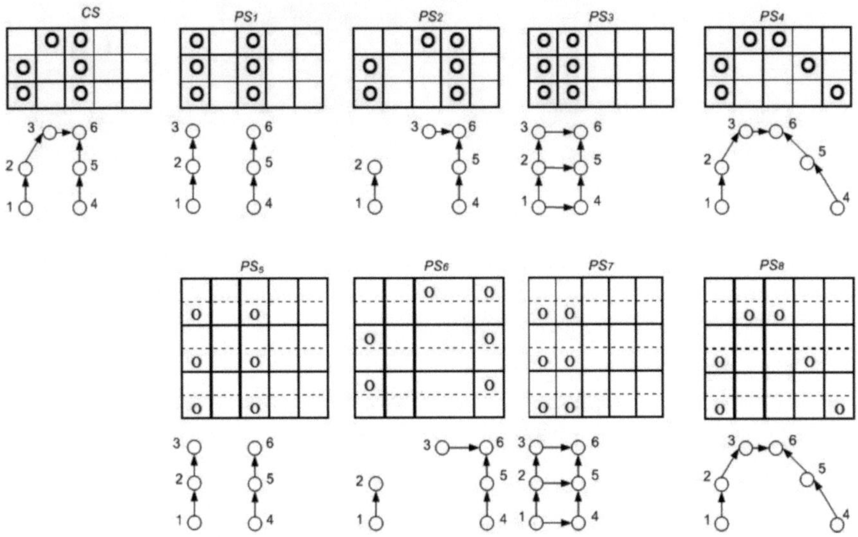

Fig.9. Current situation *CS* with graph *GD*(*CS*) and eight pattern situations PS_i (i=1,…,8) with graphs $GD(PS_i)$ describing structure of units deployment. Patterns 1-5, 2-6, 3-7 and 4-8 have the same structure but cells for patterns 5,..,8 have a greater size than for patterns 1,…,4

Pattern	Weights (α_1 ; α_2)				
PS_i	(0; 1)	(0.33; 0.67)	(0.5; 0.5)	(0.67; 0.33)	(1; 0)
PS_1	**-0.094**	**0.283**	0.463	0.800	**1.527**
PS_2	-0.370	**0.283**	**0.593**	**0.870**	1.504
PS_3	-0.478	0.157	0.360	0.726	1.254
PS_4	-0.233	0.176	0.467	0.827	**1.527**
PS_5	-0.474	0.120	0.461	0.824	**1.527**
PS_6	-0.706	0.032	0.378	0.761	1.504
PS_7	-0.63	0.070	0.279	0.631	1.254
PS_8	-0.508	0.047	0.415	0.793	**1.527**

Table 4. Values of scalar function $H_D(PS_i)$ combining structural (weight α_1) and quantitative (weight α_2) similarity measures between *GD*(*CS*) and $GD(PS_i)$ from Fig.9. The best (maximal) value in the columns are denoted in bold

4. Automatization of march process

4.1 Introduction

The automata for march executes two main processes (Tarapata, 2007c): march planning process and direct march control. The march planning process relating to the automata includes the determination of: march organization (unit order in march column, count and place of stops and rests), paths for units and detailed march schedule for each unit in the column. The direct march control process contains such phases like command, reporting and reaction to fault situations during the march simulation. The automata is implemented in the ADA language and it represents a commander of battalion level (the lowest level of trainees is brigade level). It is a component of distributed interactive simulation system SBOTSS "Zlocien" for CAX (Computer Assisted Exercises) (Najgebauer, 2004).

4.2 The march planning process

4.2.1 Description of the problem

The march planning process relating to the automata contains the determination of such elements as: march organization (units order in march column, count and place of stops), paths for units and detailed march schedule for each unit in the column. Algorithms, which carry out the decision planning process described below, are presented in the section 4.4.
The decision process for march starts in the moment t, when the battalion id receives the march order $SO(id, t)$ from a superior (brigade) unit. Structure of the $SO(id, t)$ is as follows:

$$SO(id,t) = \left(t_0(id,t), t_S(id,t), MD(id,t)\right) \tag{22}$$

where: $SO(id, t)$ – superior order to march for battalion id; $t_0(id,t)$ - readiness time for the unit id; $t_S(id,t)$ - starting time of the march for the unit id; $MD(id,t)$ - detailed description of march order. Definition of the $MD(id)$ (we omit t) is as follows:

$$MD(id) = \left\langle S(id), D(id), RP(id), IP(id) = \left(in_p(id), it_p(id)\right)_{p=\overline{1,NIP}} \right\rangle \tag{23}$$

where: $S(id), D(id)$ - source and destination areas for id, respectively; $RP(id)$ – rest area for the id unit (after twenty-four-hours of march), optional; $IP(id)$ – vector of checkpoints for the id unit (march route must cross these points), $in_p(id)$ – the p-th checkpoint, $in_p(id) \in W_1 \cup W_2$, $in_1(id)=PS(id)$ is the starting point of the march (at this point the head of the march column is formed) and it is required, other checkpoints are optional, $it_p(id)$ – time of achieving the p-th checkpoint (optional); NIP – number of checkpoints. After the id unit (battalion) receives the brigade commander's order to march, the decision automata starts planning the realization of this task. Taking into account $SO(id,t)$, for each unit id' (of company level and equivalent) directly subordinate to id the march order, $MDS(id')$ is determined as follows:

$$MDS(id') = \left\langle S(id'), D(id'), PS(id'), PD(id'), RP(id'), \mu\left(id', S(id'), D(id')\right)\right\rangle \tag{24}$$

where: $S(id'), D(id')$ - source and destination areas for id', respectively, $S(id') \subset S(id)$, $D(id') \subset D(id)$; $RP(id')$ – rest area for the id' unit (after twenty-four-hours of march), $RP(id') \subset RP(id)$, optional parameter; $PS(id')$ – starting point for the id' unit, the same for all $id' \in id$ and $PS(id') = in_1(id) \in W_1 \cup W_2$; $PD(id')$ – ending point of the march for the id' unit, the same for all $id' \in id$ and $PD(id') \in W_1 \cup W_2$; $\mu(id', S, D)$ - the route for the unit id' from the region $S(id')=S$ to region $D(id')=D$, $\mu(id',S,D) = \left(w(id',m), v(id',m)\right)_{m=\overline{1,LW(\mu(id',S,D))}}$, $w(id',m)$ - the m-th node on the path for id', $w(id',m) \in W_1 \cup W_2$, $S,D \subset W_1 \cup W_2$ and $w(id',1) \in S$, $w\left(id', LW\left(\mu(id',S,D)\right)\right) \in D$; $LW(\mu(id', S, D))$ – number of nodes (squares or crossroads) on the path $\mu(id',S,D)$ for id' unit; $v(id',m)$ - velocity of the id' unit on the arc starting in the m-th node. It is important to note that path $\mu(id',S,D)$ may consist of sequences of nodes from $Z_1(t)$ and $Z_2(t)$ (when we accept descending from the road on the squares (if it is possible) and vice versa).

4.2.2 March organization determination

March organization includes the determination of such elements as: number of columns, order of units in march columns and number and place of stops.

Number (#) of columns results from tactical rules and depends on the tactical level of the unit: for the battalion level #columns=1, for the brigade level #columns=1÷3; for the division level #columns=3÷5. Order of units in march column results from tactical rules as well (algorithm *Units_Order_In_March_Column_Determ(id')*, see Table 6). Number of stops $c_{stops}(id)$ is calculated as follows (algorithm *Number_of_Stops_Determ(id')*, see Table 6):

$$c_{stops}(id) = \max\left\{\left\lfloor \frac{\left(t_D(id,t)-t_S(id,t)-t_{rest}(id)\right)\cdot v_{avg}(id)-L_{path}(id)}{v_{avg}(id)\cdot\left(t_{stop}(id)+\Delta s\right)}\right\rfloor, 0\right\} \tag{25}$$

where: $t_D(id,t)$ - demanded ending time of the march for the *id* unit, $t_S(id,t)$ - starting time of the march for the *id* unit (like in (22)), $t_D(id,t) > t_S(id,t) \geq 0$, $t_{rest}(id)$ - duration time of the rest for the *id* unit, $v_{avg}(id)$ - average march velocity for the *id* unit, $L_{path}(id)$ - length of the path determined for the *id* unit (in km), $t_{stop}(id)$ - duration time of the stop for the *id* unit, Δs - time interval between stops. In practice, values of parameters are as follows: $t_{rest}(id)\approx 24$h, $v_{avg}(id)\in[30\div 40]$ km/h, $t_{stop}(id)\approx 1$ h, $\Delta s\in[3,4]$ h.

Place of stops are fixed after path determination and algorithm *Place_Of_Stops_Determ(id')* (see Table 6) takes into account $c_{stops}(id)$ and the *FCam* function (see Table 1) to find optimal positions of stops.

4.2.3 Detailed march schedule determination

Detailed movement schedule for *id'* unit is defined as follows:

$$H(id',t_0) = \langle S, D, \mu(id',S,D), T(id',S,D)\rangle \tag{26}$$

where: t_0 – starting moment of schedule realization; $T(id',S,D)$ - vector of moments of achieving nodes on the path, $T(id',S,D) = \langle t(id',m)\rangle_{m=\overline{1,LW(\mu(id',S,D))}}$, $t(id',m)$ - moment of achieving the m-th node on the path,

$$t(id',m) = t_0 + \sum_{j=1}^{m-1}\frac{L\left(w(id',j), w(id',j+1)\right)}{v(id',j)} \tag{27}$$

and $L(w(id',j),w(id',j+1))$ describes geometric distance between the j-th and the $(j+1)$-st nodes on the path, $LW(\mu(id',S,D))$ - number of nodes on the path for *id'* unit. After determining $MDS(id')$ for each unit *id'* subordinates to battalion *id*, the order is sent by automata to each of the *id'* units. The idea of determining march route for the unit *id* is presented in the Fig.10.

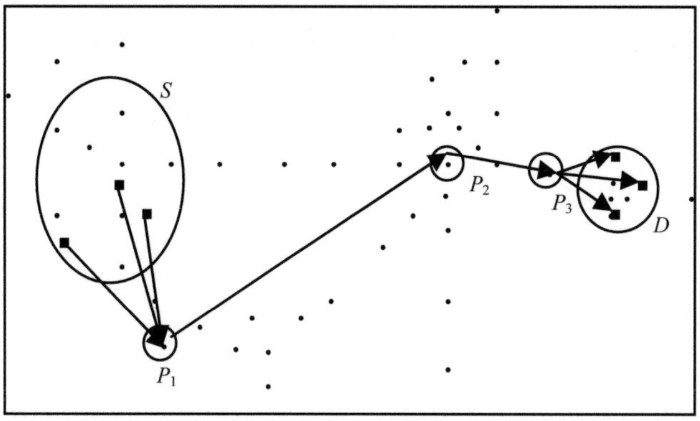

Fig.10. An example of a march route (path) for three units $id' \in id$ (filled squares) from the S source area to the D destination area (dots represent crossroads from a digital map). We have three checkpoints: P_1=*PS*, P_2 and P_3=*PD* (the path for all units must follow these points). P_1 is the starting point of the march (in this point the head of the march column consisting of three units is formed), P_3 is the ending point of the march (at this point the march column is resolved), P_2 is the intermediate point of the march. The path between P_1 and P_3 is common for all units, however each unit has its own path from subarea of S to P_1 and from P_3 to subarea of D.

In general, the automata uses two categories of criteria for synchronous movement scheduling of the K object (unit) columns. To simplify further considerations, let unit *id* be equivalent to the k-th column, k=1,...,K, that is $k \equiv id$. Moreover, let us accept following descriptions: $I_k(s_k,t_k) = I_k = \left(i^0(k) = s_k,\ i^1(k),...,i^r(k),...,\ i^{R_k}(k) = t_k \right)$ - vector of nodes describing path for the k-th object, $s_k \in S, t_k \in D$, $i^r(k)$ - the r-th node on the path for the k-th object, $\tau^r(k)$ - time instance of achieving node $i^r(k)$ by the head of the k-th object, $v_{i^r(k),i^{r+1}(k)}$ - velocity of the k-th object on the arc $\left(i^r(k), i^{r+1}(k)\right)$ of its path, $d_{i^r(k),i^{r+1}(k)}$ - terrain distance between the graph nodes $i^r(k)$ and $i^{r+1}(k)$, R_k - number of arcs belonging to the path I_k.

The first category of criteria is time of movement of K objects with two basic measures of this category:

$$\max_{k\in\{1,...,K\}} \tau^{R_k}(k) \quad \text{or} \quad \sum_{k=1}^{K} \tau^{R_k}(k) \qquad (28), (29)$$

The second category is "distance" between times of achieving alignment points by all of K objects. We can define three main measures of this category:

$$\sum_{p=1}^{NIP}\sum_{k=1}^{K} \tau_p^{\max} - \tau_p(k) \quad \text{or} \quad \min_{p\in\{1,...,NIP\}} \max_{k\in\{1,...,K\}} \left(\tau_p^{\max} - \tau_p(k)\right) \quad \text{or} \quad \sum_{p=1}^{NIP}\sum_{k=1}^{K} \left|\tau_p^{avg} - \tau_p(k)\right| \qquad (30), (31), (32)$$

where: $\tau_p(k)$ moment of achieving the p-th alignment node ($in_p(id)$ from (23)),

$$\tau_p(k) = \tau^0(k) + \sum_{\substack{r\in\{0,...,R_k-1\} \\ r \le r_p(k)}} \frac{d_{i^r(k),i^{r+1}(k)}}{v_{i^r(k),i^{r+1}(k)}}, \quad r_p(k) = r \in \{1,...,R_k\} \Leftrightarrow in_p(k) = i^r(k), \quad \tau_p^{\max} = \max_{k\in\{1,...,K\}} \tau_p(k),$$

$\tau_p^{avg} = \frac{1}{K}\sum_{k=1}^{K}\tau_p(k)$. Taking into account that unit *id* is equivalent to the *k*-th column we can write as follows: $v_{i^r(k),i^{r+1}(k)} \equiv v(k,r)$, $i^r(k) \equiv w(k,r)$, $d_{i^r(k),i^{r+1}(k)} \equiv L(w(k,r),w(k,r+1))$.

One of the formulations of the optimization problem for movement synchronization of *K* objects using measures (28)-(32) can be defined as follows: for fixed paths I_k of each *k*-th object to determine such $v_{i^r(k),i^{r+1}(k)}$, $r=\overline{0,R_k-1}$, $k=\overline{1,K}$ that

$$\sum_{p=1}^{NIP}\sum_{k=1}^{K}\tau_p^{\max}-\tau_p(k)\rightarrow \min \tag{33}$$

with the constraints :

$$v_{i^r(k),i^{r+1}(k)} \le v^{\max}(k), \qquad r=\overline{0,R_k-1},\ k=\overline{1,K} \tag{34}$$

$$v_{i^r(k),i^{r+1}(k)} > 0, \qquad r=\overline{0,R_k-1},\ k=\overline{1,K} \tag{35}$$

where $v^{\max}(k)$ describes maximal velocity of the *k*-th object resulting from its technical properties.

4.2.4 Path determination for march

To find paths for units, modified shortest path algorithms (SPA) such as Dijkstra's, A*, geometric SPA are used in SBOTSS "Zlocien" (Najgebauer, 2004). Geometric SPA supplements two algorithms presented above (the hybrid shortest path algorithm is obtained) and it is used in case the size of the network is large (default is 10000 nodes, but it is a parameter set in a so-called calibrator of the simulation system (Antkiewicz et al., 2006)). Modifications of mentioned algorithms deal with the following details: (a) paths determination in different configurations - (a1) from point (region) to point (region), (a2) visiting selected points (regions), (a3) omitting selected points (regions, obstacles), (a4) inside or outside selected region, (a5) off-roads only, (a6) on-roads only, (a7) combined on- and off-roads and others; (b) if we do not set the region inside where we want to find the path then the algorithm itself, iteratively determines the rectangular region, which is based on a line linking the beginning and end points (nodes) of movement, to minimize computational time; (c) if we want to find an on-road path only, and there are no nodes of the road network inside the intermediate squares, then the algorithm may optionally find crossroads (nodes of the road network), which are nearest to squares inside that the path must cross. Detailed description of the movement planning algorithms used in SBOTSS "Zlocien" is presented in (Tarapata, 2004a).

In general, modelling and optimization of multi-convoy redeployment (for simultaneous movement of many columns) are very complicated processes. Complexity of these processes depends on the following conditions: number of convoys (the greater the number of convoys the more complicated is the scheduling of redeployment); number of objects in each convoy (the longer the convoy the more complicated is the scheduling of redeployment); Have convoys been redeployed simultaneously? Can convoys be destroyed during redeployment? Can the terrain-based network be destroyed during redeployment? Have convoys been redeployed through disjoint routes? Have convoys achieved selected positions (nodes) at a fixed time? Do convoys have to start at the same time? Have convoys determined any action strips for moving? Can convoys be joined and separated during redeployment? Do convoys have to cross through fixed nodes?, etc. Some of these aspects are considered in section 4.2.3 and in the papers: (Benton et al., 1995; Cassandras et al. 1995; Karr et al., 1995; Kreitzberg et al., 1990; Logan & Sloman, 1997; Logan, 1997; Longtin & Megherbi, 1995; Mohn, 1994; Pai & Reissell, 1994; Schrijver & Seymour, 1992; Rajput & Karr, 1994; Tarapata, 1999; 2000; 2001; 2003; 2004a; 2005).

4.3 The direct march control

4.3.1 Identifying fault situations during a march simulation and automata reactions

The direct march control process contains such phases as: command, reporting and reaction to fault situations during march simulation (Tarapata, 2007c). Let us remember that automata replaces battalion commander and manages subordinate units (company or/and platoons and equivalent).
The automata for march react to some fault situations during the march simulation presented in the Table 5.

Fault situation during march simulation	Automata reaction
Current velocity of a subordinate unit differs from scheduled velocity	- If the unit is at the head of the column and it does not move at planned velocity then increase the velocity (in case of delay) or decrease it (in case of acceleration); - If the unit is not at the head of column then adapt velocity to velocity of the preceding unit in the column
Achieving critical fuel level in one of the subordinate units	Reporting to automatic commander. Attempt to refuel at the next stop or refuel as soon as possible
Detection of an opponent unit	If opponent forces are overwhelming (opponent combat potential is greater then a threshold value) and distance between own and the opponent units is relatively small then unit is to be stopped, make defence and report to commander. Otherwise, report to commander only
Detection of a minefield	stop and report to commander
Loss of capability to carry out the march (destruction of part of the march route (e.g. bridge, river crossing) or other cause of impassability)	- If part of the route is impassable due to destruction of part of the march route then attempt to find a detour. Report to commander; - If there is another cause of impassability then make defence and report to commander
Contamination of part of the march route or subordinate unit	Report to commander. If degree of contamination is low then run chemical defence and continue march, otherwise try to exit from the contaminated area

Table 5. Fault situations during march simulation and automata reactions

Situations, which require reporting to the superior of the battalion, are as follows: achieving checkpoints, stop area or rest area; slowing down velocity, which causes delays; encountering contamination; encountering a minefield; achieving a fuel level of 75% and 50% of the normative level; loss capability of carrying out the march (reporting cause of capability loss); detection of opponent units. A detailed description of movement synchronization is presented in section 4.3.2.

4.3.2 Velocity calculation

We "see" the unit on the road twofold: (1) as occupying arcs (part of the roads) and nodes (crossroads) of the Z_2 network, (2) as sequence of squares of the Z_1 network by which the arc cross. In the (1) case we move the head and the tail of the column and we register arcs of the Z_2 in which the head and the tail are located with degrees of crossing these arcs. In the (2) case we locate the head and the tail of the column on small squares and we move the "snake" of small squares (from the head to the tail). Movement of the unit on the road (deployed in the column) is done by determining the sequence of nodes (crossroads) and arcs (part of the roads) of the Z_2 network using algorithms presented in section 4.2 and then we realize movement from crossroad to crossroad.

The important problem during simulation is to set the current velocity of the unit *id*. Procedure of setting the velocity inside the *j*-th square taking into account two cases: (a) when the unit *id* does not fight in the *j*-th square; (b) when the unit *id* fights in the *j*-th square.

In the (a) case the current velocity $v_{cur}(id, j)$ of the unit *id* in the *j*-th square is calculated as follows:

$$v_{cur}(id,j)=\min\{v^{slowd}(id,j), v_{dec}(id,j)\} \tag{36}$$

where: $v^{slowd}(id,j)$ - maximal velocity of the unit *id* in the *j*-th square taking into account topographical conditions,

$$v^{slowd}(id,j)=v^{\max}(id)\cdot FOP(id,\bullet) \tag{37}$$

$v^{\max}(id)$ - maximal possible velocity of the unit *id* resulting from technical parameters of the vehicles belonging to this unit, $v^{\max}(id)=\min_{p\in ZVeh(id)} v^{tech}(p)$, $ZVeh(id)$ – set of vehicles belonging to the *id* unit, $v^{tech}(p)$ – maximal velocity of vehicle p (resulting from technical parameters), $FOP(id,\bullet)$ - slowing down velocity function for the *id* unit in the *j*-th square, $FOP(id,\bullet)$ is equal (3) or (5); $v_{dec}(id, j)$ – velocity resulting from commander decision (equals $v(id,j)$ in (27)). If the unit *id* is a head of a column and it does not move with planned velocity $v_{dec}(id, j)$ then the velocity is increased (in case of delay) or decreased (in case of acceleration). If the unit *id* is not at the head of column then velocity of the unit *id* is adapted to velocity of the preceding unit in the column.

In the (b) case the current velocity $v_{cur}(id, j)$ of the unit *id* in the *j*-th square is calculated as follows:

$$v_{cur}(id,j)=\min\left\{f\left(v^{slowd}(id,\bullet),U_A,U_B,dist\right),v_{dec}(id,j)\right\} \tag{38}$$

where: $f(\bullet,\bullet,\bullet,\bullet)$ – function describing velocity in the square depending on $v^{slowd}(id,\bullet)$, potentials of the unit *id* of side A (U_A) and B (U_B) which fight, distance (*dist*) between fighting sides.

Some results of velocity calculations in real scenario for brigade march are presented in the Table 7.

4.3.3 Fuel consumption calculation

Fuel consumption *FC(id, veh, u)* on the *u* part of a path for the type of vehicle *veh* belonging to the *id* unit is calculated as follows:

$$FC(id,\ veh,\ u) = FLen(u) \cdot FCC(u,veh) \cdot \frac{NFC(veh)}{100} \cdot N(id,veh) \tag{39}$$

where: *FLen*(*u*) describes the length of the *u* part of a path, *FCC*(*u*,*veh*) – fuel consumption coefficient for the *u* part of a path and for vehicle type *veh*, *NFC*(*veh*) – normative average fuel consumption for the *veh* type of vehicle (per 100km), *N*(*id, veh*) – number of vehicles of *veh* type in the *id* unit. Fuel consumption coefficient *FCC* is calculated as follows:

$$FCC(u,veh)=(1.0+MTC(veh))*(1.0+UC(u)) \tag{40}$$

where *MTC*(*veh*) describes mechanical-tactical coefficient and *UC*(*u*) - utilization coefficient, $veh \in K\_Veh$ resulting from logistic calculations.

4.4 Automata implementation

The automata are implemented in the Ada language and it represents a part of an automatic commander on the battalion level (Antkiewicz et al., 2007). They realize their own tasks and pass on tasks to subordinate units. Simulation objects and their methods are managed by dedicated simulation kernel (extension of Ada language). Object methods are divided into two sets: (1) non-simulation methods – designed in order to set and get attributes values, specific calculations and database operations; (2) simulation methods – prepared in order to synchronous ("wait-for" methods) and asynchronous ("tell" methods) data sending. Procedures implemented and used for decision planning and direct march control processes are presented in the Table 6.

Procedures implemented and used for each unit $id' \in id$ for the decision planning process	Procedures implemented and used for each unit $id' \in id$ for the direct march control process

Units_Order_In_March_Column_Determ(id')
Column_Length_Determ(id')
Number_of_Stops_Determ(id')
Place_Of_Stops_Determ(id')
Ending_Point_PD_Determ(id')
March_Schedule_Determ(id')
    Paths_Determ(id')
        Path_ S_To_PS_Determ(id')
        Common_Path_PS_To_PD(id')
        Path_ PD_To_D_Determ(id')
    Detailed_Schedule_Determ(id')
	March_Simulation(id')
	    Simulate_Unit_Movement(id')
	    React_To_Fault_Situations(id')
	    Fuel_Consumption_Determ(id')
	    Adapt_March_Velocity(id')
	    Report_To_Commander(id')

Table 6. Procedures implemented and used for decision planning and direct march control processes in the march automata

4.5 Practical example

In this section a practical example of march planning and simulation is presented. In Fig.11a initial tactical situation is shown. In our example 2 mechanized brigades (121BZ and 123BZ: each of the brigades consists of 4 mechanized battalion x 4 mechanized companies) of the blue side receive order to march.

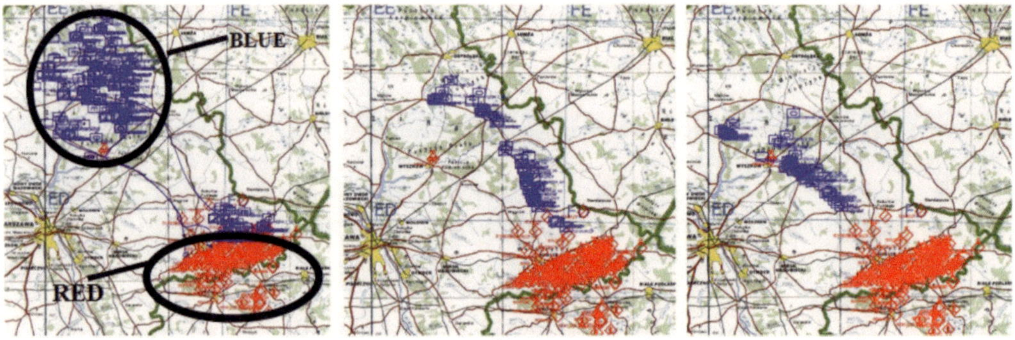

(a) (b) (c)

Fig.11. (a) Initial tactical situation, 4:00am: two mechanized brigades of the "blue" side (121BZ and 123BZ) receive an order to march; (b) Location of the 121 BZ on the road, 5:50am; (c) Location of the 123 BZ on the road, 5:50am

In the superior order (22): destination area for 121BZ and 123BZ is set to about 30 km to the north of the northern edge of the location area of the red side; distance from source area S to destination area D is equal about 110km; 5 checkpoints is set.

In the Fig.11b and Fig.11c location of 121BZ and 123BZ, respectively, after nearly 2 hours of march are presented.

Initial redeploying of the blue side is presented in Fig.12a. 121BZ is redeployed on the northern-east of the blue force redeploying area. 123 BZ is redeployed on the south of 121 BZ. The location of 121BZ and 123BZ at 5.50am is shown in Fig.12b.

Fig.12. (a) Initial redeployment of the blue side, 4:00am; (b) Location of 121 BZ and 123 BZ, 5:50am

Presented in Table 7 are the average velocities between selected march checkpoints for 121BZ and 123BZ. Average march velocity is equal to about 30km/h.

Unit	S=>P_S	P_S=>P_D	P_D=>D	S=>D
121BZ	12.32	39.65	18.24	29.54
123BZ	14.07	27.84	22.57	24.65

Table 7. Average velocities between selected march checkpoints for 121BZ and 123BZ (in km/h)

5. Conclusions

The models and methods described in the chapter are used in real simulation support system for military operational training (Antkiewicz et al., 2007) and/or can be used in Computer Generated Forces systems. The presented methods and their implementations are very promising in the context of Computer Assisted Exercises management and effectiveness. By using, for example, decision automata on the battalion level we can save a lot of time and training participants, so even very complex exercises can be organized and carried out by analyzing and go through different scenarios of military conflicts. One of the aspects of automatization of the decision processes - movement planning, synchronization and simulation is essential not only in CGF systems. Simulation systems for military trainings should have modules for management (planning, synchronization) multi-objects movement. The quality of this management has an effect on accuracy, effectiveness and other characteristics of simulated battlefield systems. A very important problem, which deals with automatization of decision processes, is the calibration of simulation models of complex processes (Antkiewicz et al., 2006; Dockery & Woodcock, 1993; Hoffmann, 2005). It enables the tuning of these models. This process has an influence on one of the most important features of simulation models as is adequateness.

6. Acknowledgement

This work was supported in part by the Military University of Technology in Warsaw under Grant PBW-571 and GW-AD 604.

7. References

Almohamad H. & Duffuaa S. (1993): A Linear Programming Approach For The Weighted Graph Matching Problem, *IEEE Trans. Pattern Anal. Mach. Intelligence* 15(5), 522–525.

Antkiewicz R., Najgebauer A. & Tarapata Z. (2003): The decision automata for command and control simulation on the tactical level, *Proceedings of the NATO Regional Conference on Military Communication and Information Systems*, 07-10 October, Zegrze (Poland) 2003, ISBN 83-920120-0-3 , (CD-ROM publication).

Antkiewicz R., Najgebauer A., Rulka J. & Tarapata Z. (2006): Calibration of simulation models of selected battlefield processes, *Proceedings of the 1st Military Communication and Information Systems Conference*, ISBN 83-920120-1-1, 18-19.09.2006, Gdynia (Poland).

Antkiewicz R., Najgebauer A., Tarapata Z., Rulka J., Kulas W., Pierzchala D. & Wantoch-Rekowski R. (2007): The Automation of Combat Decision Processes in the Simulation Based Operational Training Support System, *Proceedings of the IEEE Symposium on Computational Intelligence for Security and Defense Applications (CISDA'07)*, 01-05.04.2007, ISBN 1-4244-0698-6, Honolulu (Hawaii).

Behnke S. (2003): Local Multiresolution Path Planning, In B. Browning, D. Polani, A. Bonarini, and K. Yoshida (editors): *RoboCup-2003: Robot Soccer World Cup VII, Lecture Notes in Computer Science 3020*, Springer-Verlag (2004), 332-343.

Benton J.R., Iyengar S.S., Deng W., Brener N. & Subrahmanian V.S. (1995): Tactical route planning: new algorithms for decomposing the map, *Proceedings of the IEEE International Conference on Tools for AI*, 6-8 November, Herndon 1995, pp. 268-277.

Blondel V., Gajardo A., Heymans M., Senellart P., Van Dooren P. (2004): A Measure Of Similarity Between Graph Vertices: Applications To Synonym Extraction And Web Searching. *SIAM Review*, vol.46(4), (2004), 647–666.

Bunke H. (1997): On A Relation Between Graph Edit Distance And Maximum Common Subgraph, *Pattern Recognition Letters*, vol. 18, (1997), 689–694.

Bunke H. (2000): Graph Matching: Theoretical Foundations, Algorithms, And Applications, in *Proceedings Vision Interface 2000*, Montreal, (2000), 82–88.

Campbell C., Hull R., Root E., Jackson L. (1995): Route planning in CCTT, in *Proceedings of the 5th Conference on Computer Generated Forces and Behavioural Representation*, Technical Report, Institute for Simulation and Training, pp. 233-244, 1995.

Cassandras C.G., Panayiotou C.G., Diehl G., Gong W-B., Liu Z. & Zou C. (2000): Clustering methods for multi-resolution simulation modeling, *Proceedings of the Conference on Enabling Technology for Simulation Science*, The International Society for Optical Engineering, 25-27 April, Orlando (USA) 2000, pp. 37-48.

Champin P., Solnon Ch. (2003): Measuring The Similarity Of Labeled Graphs, *Proc. 5th International Conference on Case-Based Reasoning (ICCBR 2003), Lecture Notes in Artificial Intelligence 2689*, Springer-Verlag, (2003), 80–95.

Corps Battle Simulation (CBS) (2001): Version 1.6.0, Analyst's Guide, Volume 1, Ground, *U.S. Army Simulation, Training, and Instrumentation Command* Orlando, Florida, June 2001.

Davis P.K., Bigelow J.H. & McEver J. (2000): Informing and calibrating a multiresolution exploratory analysis model with high resolution simulation: the interdiction problem as a case history, *Proceedings of the 2000 Winter Simulation Conference*, pp. 316-325.

Dockery J. & Woodcock A.E.R. (1993): The Military Landscape, Mathematical Models of Combat, *Published by Woodhead Publishing Ltd.*, Cambridge, England, 1993.

Eschenauer H., Koski J. & Osyczka A. (1990): Multicriteria Design Optimization, *Springer Verlag*, Berlin-Heidelberg-New York, (1990).

Farin D., With P., Effelsberg W. (2003): Recognition of User-Defined Video Object Models using Weighted Graph Homomorphisms, *Proc. Image and Video Communications and*

Processing (IVCP 2003), Proc. SPIE 5022, Bhaskaran Vasudev, T. Russell Hsing, Andrew G. Tescher, and Touradj Ebrahimi, ed., (2003), 542–553.

Henninger A.E., Gonzalez A.J., Georgipoulos M., DeMara R.F. (2000): Modeling Semi-Automated Forces with Neural Networks: Performance Improvement through a Modular Approach, *The Ninth Conference on Computer Generated Forces and Behavioral Representation Proceedings*, Orlando, FL, 2000.

Hofmann H.W. & Hofmann M. (2000): On the Development of Command & Control Modules for Combat Simulation Models on Battalion down to Single Item Level. In: *Proceedings of the NATO/RTO Information Systems Technology Panel (IST) Symposium "New Information Processing Techniques for Military Systems"*. NATO AC/329 (IST-017) TP/8, Istanbul, Turkey, 9-11 Oct. 2000, pp. 85-96.

Hofmann M. (2005): On the Complexity of Parameter Calibration in Simulation Models, *JDMS, The Society for Modeling and Simulation International*, Volume 2, Issue 4, pp.217–226, October 2005.

James J., Sayrs B., Benton J. & Subrahmanian V.S. (1999): Uncertainty management: keeping battlespace visualization honest, *ATRIP Conference Proceedings*, February 1999, *http://citeseer.nj.nec.com/ 386770.html.*

JTLS (1988): The Analyst Guide, Joint Theater Level Simulation (JTLS), Version 1.65, Modern Aids to Planning Program (MAPP), *Force Structure and Assessment Directorate (J-8), Joint Staff, The Pentagon*, September 1988.

Kambhampati S. & Davis L.S. (1986): Multiresolution Path Planning for Mobile Robots, *IEEE Journal of Robotics and Automation*, Vol. RA-2, No. 3 (1986), 135-145.

Karr C.R., Craft M.A. & Cisneros J.E. (1995): Dynamic obstacle avoidance, *Proceedings of the Conference on Distributed Interactive Simulation Systems for Simulation and Training in the Aerospace Environment*, The International Society for Optical Engineering, 19-20 April, Orlando (USA) 1995, pp. 195-219.

Kleinberg J. (1999): Authoritative Sources In Hyperlinked Environment, *Journal of the ACM*, vol.46(5), (1999), 604–632.

Korf R.E. (1999): Artificial intelligence search algorithms, in *Algorithms Theory Computation Handbook*, Boca Raton, FL: CRC Press (1999).

Kreitzberg T., Barragy T. & Nevin B. (1990): Tactical movement analyzer: a battlefield mobility tool, *Proceedings of the 4th Join Tactical Fusion Symposium*, Laurel, 1990.

Kriegel H.P. & Schonauer S. (2003): Similarity Search in Structured Data, *Proc. 5th Int. Conf. on Data Warehousing and Knowledge Discovery (DaWaK'03)*, Prague, Czech Republic, 2003, in: *Lecture Notes in Computer Science (LNCS)*, vol.2737, (2003), 309–319.

LaValle S. (2006): Planning algorithms, *Cambridge University Press*, 2006.

Lee J.J. & Fishwick P.A. (1995): Simulation-based real-time decision making for route planning, *Proceedings of Winter Simulation Conference*, 1995, 1087-1095.

Lee J.J. (1996): A Simulation-Based Approach for Decision Making and Route Planning, *PhD Thesis, University of Florida*, August 1996.

Logan B. & Sloman A. (1997): Agent route planning in complex terrains, *Technical Report CSRP-97-30, University of Birmingham,* School of Computer Science, Birmingham 1997.

Logan B. (1997): Route planning with ordered constraints, *Proceedings of the 16th Workshop of the UK Planning and Scheduling Special Interest Group,* 17-18 December, Durham (UK), 1997.

Longtin M. & Megherbi D. (1995): Concealed routes in ModSAF, in *Proceedings of the 5th Conference on Computer Generated Forces and Behavioural Representation,* Technical Report, Institute for Simulation and Training, pp. 305-314, 1995.

Melnik S., Garcia-Molina H. & Rahm E. (2002): Similarity Flooding: A Versatile Graph Matching Algorithm And Its Application To Schema Matching, *Proceedings of the 18th International Conference on Data Engineering,* San Jose, California, (2002), 117-128.

Mitchell J.S.B. (1999): Geometric shortest paths and network optimization, in J.R. Sack and J. Urrutia: Handbook of Computational Geometry, *Elsevier Science Publishers,* B.V. North-Holland, Amsterdam 1999.

Mohn H. (1994): Implementation Of A Tactical Mission Planner For Command And Control Of Computer Generated Forces In ModSaf, *Master's Thesis,* Monterey, CA: Naval Postgraduate School.

Najgebauer A. (1999): Decision Support Systems for Conflict Situations. Models, Methods and the Interactive Simulation Environments (in Polish). *Ed. Biuletyn WAT,* Warsaw 1999, Poland (294 p.), ISBN 83-908620-6-9.

Najgebauer A. (2004): Polish Initiatives in M&S and Training. Simulation Based Operational Training Support System (SBOTSS) Zlocien, *Proceedings of the ITEC'2004,* London, UK, April 20-22, 2004.

Pai D.K., Reissell L.M. (1994): Multiresolution rough terrain motion planning, Department of Computer Sciences, University of British Columbia, *Technical Report TR 94-33,* Vancouver 1994.

Petty M.D. (1995): Computer generated forces in Distributed Interactive Simulation, *Proceedings of the Conference on Distributed Interactive Simulation Systems for Simulation and Training in the Aerospace Environment,* The International Society for Optical Engineering, 19-20 April, Orlando (USA) 1995, pp. 251-280.

Rajput S. & Karr C. (1994): Unit Route Planning, *Technical Report IST-TR-94-42,* Institute for Simulation and Training, Orlando (USA) 1994.

Robinson S. (2004): The Ongoing Search for Efficient Web Search Algorithms, *SIAM News,* vol.37(9), (2004).

Schiavone G.A., Nelson R.S. & Hardis K.C. (1995): Interoperability issues for terrain databases in distributed interactive simulation, *Proceedings of the Conference on Distributed Interactive Simulation Systems for Simulation and Training in the Aerospace Environment,* The International Society for Optical Engineering, 19-20 April, Orlando (USA) 1995, pp. 89-120.

Schiavone G.A., Nelson R.S. & Hardis K.C. (2000): Two surface simplification algorithms for polygonal terrain with integrated road features, *Proceedings of the Conference on Enabling Technology for Simulation Science*, The International Society for Optical Engineering, 25-27 April, Orlando (USA) 2000, pp. 221-229.

Schrijver A. & Seymour P. (1992): Disjoint paths in a planar graph – a general theorem, *SIAM Journal of Discrete Mathematics* 5 (1992), pp. 112-116.

Senellart P. & Blondel V. (2003): Automatic Discovery Of Similar Words, in: *Survey of Text Mining, Springer-Verlag* Berlin Heidelberg New York (2003).

Tarapata Z. (1999): Simulation method of aiding and estimation of transportation columns movement planning in stochastic environment, *Proceedings of the 13th European Simulation Multiconference*, The Society For Computer Simulation International, 01-04 June, Warsaw 1999, pp. 613-619.

Tarapata Z. (2000): Some aspects of multi-convoy redeployment modelling and simulation, *TechNet Europe 2000 - Proceedings of the 21st AFCEA Europe Symposium & Exposition*, 18-20 October, Prague (Czech Republic), 2000 (CD publication).

Tarapata Z. (2001): Modelling, optimisation and simulation of groups movement according to group pattern in multiresolution terrain-based grid network, *Proceedings of The NATO Regional Conference on Military Communication and Information Systems*, 10-12 October, Zegrze (Poland) 2001, vol.I, 241-251.

Tarapata Z. (2003): Military route planning in battlefield simulation: effectiveness problems and potential solutions, *Journal of Telecomm. and Information Technology*, N°° 4 (2003), pp. 47-56.

Tarapata Z. (2004a): Models and methods of movement planning and simulation in simulation aided system for operational training, *Proceedings of the 6th NATO Regional Conference on Military Communication and Information Systems*, 06-08 October, Zegrze (Poland) 2004, pp. 152-161.

Tarapata Z. (2004b): Decomposition algorithm for finding shortest paths in grid networks of large size, *Proceedings of the 15th International Conference on Systems Science*, 7-10 September, Wroclaw (Poland) 2004, vol.III, pp. 209-216.

Tarapata Z. (2005): Synchronization method of many objects movement in Computer Generated Forces systems, *Proceedings of the 7th NATO Regional Conference on Military Communication and Information Systems*, 04-05 October, Zegrze (Poland) 2005, pp. 93-99.

Tarapata Z. (2007a): Selected multicriteria shortest path problems: an analysis of complexity, models and adaptation of standard algorithms, *International Journal of Applied Mathematics and Computer Science*, Vol.17, No.2 (2007), 269-287.

Tarapata Z. (2007b): Multicriteria weighted graphs similarity and its application for decision situation pattern matching problem, *Proceedings of the 13th IEEE/IFAC International Conference on Methods and Models in Automation and Robotics*, ISBN 978-83-751803-3-6, 27-30 August 2007, Szczecin, Poland, 1149-1155.

Tarapata Z. (2007c): The decision automata for manoeuvre planning and control in simulation aided system for operational training, *Proceedings of the Military*

Communications and Information Systems Conference MCC'2007, ISBN 978-3-934401-16-7, 25-26 September 2007, Bonn, Germany (CD publication).

Umeyama S. (1988): An Eigen Decomposition Approach To Weighted Graph Matching Problems. *IEEE Trans. Pattern Analysis and Machine Intelligence*, vol.10(5), (1988), 695–703.

Undeger C., Polat F. & Ipekkan Z. (2001): Real-time edge follow: a new paradigm to real-time path search, *Annual European Game-On Conference*, London, UK, Nov.30-Dec.1, 2001.

19

Fuzzy Knowledge Representation Using Probability Measures of Fuzzy Events

Anna Walaszek-Babiszewska
Opole University of Technology
Poland

1. Introduction

The concepts of *Soft Computing* introduced by Lotfi A. Zadeh in 1991 has integrated different methodologies and approaches, as: fuzzy set theory, fuzzy logic, approximate reasoning, linguistic expression of knowledge, probabilistic reasoning, and others for solving problems of complex systems in the way similar to human perception, recognition and solving problem methods. Linguistic fuzzy modelling gives the formal, mathematical instruments for expressing human knowledge described in natural language. Probability of fuzzy meanings of linguistic variables determines a frequency of the occurrence the imprecisely expressed events.

This work presents the methods of applications linguistic modelling and probability measures of fuzzy events for creating models compatible to the features of real systems, and more flexible than traditional rule-based models derived from linguistic knowledge.

In Section 2. we remind the notions of a linguistic variable and a probability of fuzzy events, formulated by Zadeh, which have become fundamental for the development of fuzzy systems. We define probability distributions of a linguistic variable and a linguistic vector as well as a mean fuzzy value (a mean fuzzy set) of the linguistic variable. The conditional probability of fuzzy events will be the base for the inference procedure.

Section 3. shows an exemplary probabilistic modelling for the characteristics representing features of particles in a certain population, formulated in fuzzy categories.

The created knowledge representation states a collection of weighted rules (Section 4.) Weights of rules represent probabilities of fuzzy events of input and output system variables. Construction of fuzzy models is presented for different stochastic systems. The weights are involved in the inference procedures.

2. Linguistic and probabilistic modelling - basic definitions and concepts

2.1 Linguistic variable

Linguistic fuzzy modelling with a linguistic knowledge representation gives us the formal, mathematical way for expressing the human linguistic perception of real world. A linguistic variable is the main notion in such modelling. The variable whose values are words, can be defined by the quadruplet $<X,L(X),U,M_x>$, where X means the name of the variable, $L(X)$ is a set of linguistic values (words) which X takes, U is an universe of discourse, and M is a semantic function, that assigns the fuzzy meaning (fuzzy subsets A_i, $i=1,\ldots,I$ in U) to each linguistic value from $L(X)$ (Zadeh, 1975).

As an example let us consider a linguistic variable *X=diameter of particles,* which takes the linguistic values *L(X)={fine, middle size, coarse}*. A semantic function M associates fuzzy meanings (fuzzy sets) A_i, $i=1,2,3$ to each linguistic value. Fuzzy sets are given by membership functions $\mu_A(u)$ determined in the universe of discourse $U \subset R$ (an interval of real numbers), as follows:

$$\mu_{A_1}(u) = \begin{cases} 1, & u \in [0,0.2) \\ \dfrac{0.35-u}{0.15}, & u \in [0.2,0.35] \end{cases} \tag{1}$$

$$\mu_{A_2}(u) = \begin{cases} \dfrac{u-0.2}{0.15}, u \in [0.2,\, 0.35) \\ 1, u \in [0.35,\, 0.65] \\ \dfrac{0.8-u}{0.15}, u \in (0.65,\, 0.8] \end{cases} \tag{2}$$

$$\mu_{A_3}(u) = \begin{cases} \dfrac{0.65-u}{0.15}, & u \in [0.65,0.8) \\ 1, u \in [0.8,\, 1] \end{cases} \tag{3}$$

where A_1: *fine,* A_2: *middle size,* A_3: *coarse.*

2.2 Probability of fuzzy events and distributions of linguistic variables

A fuzzy event A, in compliance with Zadeh's definition, is a fuzzy subset $A = \{(\mu_A(u),\, u)\}$ in the elementary events domain (U,Ω), with the membership function $\mu_A(u) \in [0,1]$ measurable in Boreal sense (Zadeh, 1968). In another notation, a fuzzy event can be expressed as $A = \sum_{u \in U} (\mu_A(u)/u)$, where the sum sign is considered as set character, not arithmetical.

Let p be the probability function, which assigns to each Borel set in the domain $U = \{u_1, \ldots u_N\}$ the real number $p \in [0,1]$. A probability $P(A)$ of a fuzzy event A is defined in the way:

$$P(A) = \sum_{u \in U} p(u)\mu_A(u) \tag{4}$$

where $p(u) \in [0,1]$ is a probability function in (U,Ω).

If the domain U is infinite, and $f(u)$ is a probability density function in (U,Ω), then a probability $P(A)$ of a fuzzy event A can be calculated by the following integral:

$$P(A) = \int_{u \in U} \mu_A(u) f(u) du \tag{5}$$

Probability values of fuzzy events, calculated according to (4) and (5) are real numbers, $P(A) \in [0,1]$.

Let fuzzy subsets $A_i, i = 1,...,I$ of the linguistic variable X are defined by their membership functions $\mu_{A_i}(u) \in [0,1]$ in such way, that for every $u \in U$, the relationship $\sum_{i=1}^{I} \mu_{A_i}(u) = 1$ is fulfilling. Then, the set of probabilities $\{P(A_i)\}, i = 1,..,I$ calculated for fuzzy subsets $A_i, i = 1,...,I$ according to (4) or (5) and fulfilling the relation

$$\sum_{i=1}^{I} P(A_i) = 1 \tag{6}$$

states a probability distribution of the linguistic variable X.

A mean fuzzy value of the linguistic random variable X, signed as $\overline{A}$, in a probability distribution $P(A_i)$, $i=1,\ldots,I$ given above, is a fuzzy set with the membership function defined as follows:

$$\mu_{\overline{A}}(u) = P(A_1)\mu_{A_1}(u) + ... + P(A_I)\mu_{A_I}(u), \ \forall u \in U \tag{7}$$

The mean fuzzy value is the convex combination fuzzy set (Kacprzyk, 1986). It will be used in the aggregation procedure (Section 4).

For the linguistic variable whose fuzzy meanings of linguistic values are given by (1) - (3), assume that probability density function is constant over the domain $U=[0, 1]$, $f(u)=1$. Probability of fuzzy events A_1: *fine*, A_2: *middle size*, A_3: *coarse* can be calculated by the integrals

$$P(A_1) = \int_0^{0.35} \mu_{A_1}(u) f(u) du = 0.275, \tag{8}$$

$$P(A_2) = \int_{0.2}^{0.8} \mu_{A_2}(u) f(u) du = 0.450, \tag{9}$$

$$P(A_3) = \int_{0.65}^{1} \mu_{A_3}(u) f(u) du = 0.275. \tag{10}$$

The calculated probability values fulfil (6), so the mean fuzzy value of events A_1, A_2, A_3 can be calculated according to the dependence (7).

Let us consider, as it is usually assumed in industrial practice, that for disjoint intervals $\Delta u_m = a_m, m = 1,...,M$ the empirical probability is constant and equal to the quotient

$$p(\Delta u_m) = P(u \in \Delta u_m) = \frac{n_m}{n} \tag{11}$$

where n_m is the number of particles whose a feature x takes the values from the proper intervals, and n is the total number of particles, $n = \sum_{m=1,...,M} n_m$. Fuzzy sets $A_i, i = 1,...,I$ representing linguistic values of a linguistic variable X can be determined on the disjoint intervals a_m as follows

$$A_i = \sum_{m=1,...,M} \mu_{A_i}(a_m) / a_m \tag{12}$$

where the membership functions fulfill the condition $\sum_{i=1,...,I} \mu_{A_i}(a_m) = 1, \forall a_m \in U$.

Probabilities of the events (12) can be expressed by the relationship

$$P(A_i) = \sum_{m=1,...,M} \mu_{A_i}(a_m) p_m \tag{13}$$

where $p_m = P(u \in a_m)$. If the set of probabilities $\{P(A_i)\}$ of fuzzy events, calculated according to (12) and (13) is fulfilling the relationship $\sum_{i=1,...,I} P(A_i) = 1$ then it states a probability distribution of the linguistic variable X.

Let us consider two linguistic variables: $<X,L(X),U,M_x>$ and $<Y,L(Y),V,M_y>$, where X means the name of the input (reason) variable, Y is the name of the output (result) variable of a SISO system, $L(X)$ and $L(Y)$ are sets of linguistic values, $U \subset R$ and $V \subset R$ are universes of discourse of particular variables, M_x, M_y are semantic functions, that assign fuzzy meaning (fuzzy subsets $A_i, i = 1,...,I$ in $U \subset R$ and $B_j, j = 1,...,J$ in $V \subset R$) to each linguistic value from $L(X)$ and $L(Y)$, respectively.

Fuzzy sets $A_i, i = 1,...,I$ and $B_j, j = 1,...,J$ state the numeric descriptions of particular linguistic values of variables X and Y, respectively. Let fuzzy sets are defined by membership functions in the way

$$\mu_{A_i}(u) \in [0,1], i=1,\ldots,I \text{ and } \sum_{i=1}^{I} \mu_{A_i}(u) = 1, \forall u \in U; \tag{14}$$

$$\mu_{B_j}(v) \in [0,1], , j=1,\ldots,J \text{ and } \sum_{j=1}^{J} \mu_{B_j}(v) = 1, \forall v \in V. \tag{15}$$

A new term set of a linguistic vector (X,Y) can be created in the space $L(X) \times L(Y)$ by the numeric description $\mu_{A_i \times B_j}(u,v)$ in the universe $U \times V$. The membership function $\mu_{A_i \times B_j}(u,v)$ is a Borel function, which can be defined as a t-norm

$$\mu_{A_i \times B_j}(u,v) = T(\mu_{A_i}(u), \mu_{B_j}(v)) \tag{16}$$

e.g., as a product t-norm $\mu_{A_i \times B_j}(u,v) = \mu_{A_i}(u) \mu_{B_j}(v)$.

A set of probability values $\{P(A_i \times B_j)\}$, of fuzzy events (fuzzy relations) $A_i \times B_j$, i=1,…,I, j=1,…,J can be calculated using the basic definition (4), as follows

$$P(A_i \times B_j) = \sum_{(u,v)\in U\times V} p(u,v)\mu_{A_i \times B_j}(u,v) \tag{17}$$

where $p(u,v) \in [0,1]$ is a joint probability function.
If the set of probabilities of fuzzy events $\{P(A_i \times B_j)\}$ fulfils the relationship

$$\sum_{i=1}^{I}\sum_{j=1}^{J} P(A_i \times B_j) = 1 \tag{18}$$

then, it states a joint probability distribution *P(X,Y)* of the linguistic vector variables *(X,Y)*. The marginal probability distributions $P(X) = \{P(A_i)\}, i = 1,...,I$, and $P(Y) = \{P(B_j)\}$, j=1,…,J can be calculated for particular linguistic variables, as follows:

$$P(A_i) = \sum_{j=1}^{J} P(A_i \times B_j) \tag{19}$$

$$P(B_j) = \sum_{i=1}^{I} P(A_i \times B_j) \tag{20}$$

The marginal distributions *P(X)* and *P(Y)* defined above are normalized.

$$\sum_{i=1}^{I} P(A_i) = 1, \quad \sum_{j=1}^{J} P(B_j) = 1 \tag{21}$$

Conditional probability distributions of particular linguistic variables can be derived from the joint probability distribution *P(X,Y)* given by (17) and a marginal probability distributions (19) or (20). The conditional probability distribution *P(Y/X)* of the linguistic variable *Y*, under the condition that *X* takes fuzzy values $A_i, i = 1,...,I$, is a set of probability values $P(Y/X) = \{P(B_j / A_i)\}$,j=1,…,J; i=*const*, calculated as follows:

$$P(B_j / A_i) = P(A_i \times B_j) / P(A_i), \; j=1,\ldots,J;\; i=const. \tag{22}$$

Taking into account the normalization of probability distributions (see (18) and (21)), the total probability of the result B_j can be calculated, similarly to Bayes' formula, and assuming, that the conditional probabilities $P(B_j / A_i)$, i=1,…,I, calculated under the condition of the reasons A_i are known (Walaszek-Babiszewska, 2008):

$$P(B_j) = \sum_{i=1}^{I} P(B_j / A_i) P(A_i). \tag{23}$$

Let us note, that fuzzy sets $A_i, i = 1,..., I$ are not disjoint in *U*.

3. Exemplary linguistic and probabilistic modelling

3.1 Particle characteristics as results of measurements

In chemical and biochemical research, in many industrial processes such as mineral preparation processes or in numerous food processes, the material to be prepared consists of a population of different types of particles.

There are basic characteristics of material utilised by process engineers and automation engineers:

- a characteristic of the size composition presenting portions of particles belonging to different size fractions,
- a densimetric characteristic presenting portions of particles belonging to different density fractions,
- a characteristic of tested chemical components.

The two first characteristics are often considered as an empirical probability distribution of a two-dimensional random variable: volume x and density y of particles

$$p_{ij}(x,y) = P(x \in a_i, y \in b_j) = N_{ij} / N, \quad i = 1,2,...,I; \quad j = 1,2,...,J \tag{24}$$

where a_i, $i=1,\dots, I$ are disjoint intervals of the particle size (size classes) in a domain X, and b_j, $j=1,\dots,J$ are disjoint intervals of the particle density (density fractions) in a domain Y, N_{ij} is a number of that particles in the parent population, whose volume belongs to *i-th* interval a_i and the density belongs to *j-th* interval b_j, N is a total number of particles in the population, and $N = \sum_{i=1}^{I}\sum_{j=1}^{J} N_{ij}$.

In engineering practice a different measure of the probability is being more often applying, the quotient of the respective masses:

$$\pi_{ij}(x,y) = M_{ij} / M \quad \text{i=1,2,..., I;} \quad \text{j =1,2,...,J;} \tag{25}$$

where M_{ij} is a mass of that particles in the parent population, whose volume belongs to *i-th* interval a_i and the density belongs to *j-th* interval b_j, and $M_{ij} = x_{m,i}y_{m,j}N_{ij}$, where $x_{m,i}$, $y_{m,j}$ are mean values of particle volume and density in the intervals a_i and b_j, respectively; M is a total mass of the population, $M = x_m y_m N$, where x_m, y_m are mean values of volume and density of particles in the population, and $M = \sum_{i=1}^{I}\sum_{j=1}^{J} M_{ij}$.

There is a relation between two expressions of empirical probabilities (Walaszek-Babiszewska, 2004):

$$\pi_{ij} = a_{ij} p_{ij}, \quad i=1,2,..., I; \quad j=1,2,...,J; \tag{26}$$

where:

$$a_{ij} = \frac{x_{m,i} y_{m,j}}{x_m y_m}. \tag{27}$$

Table 1 presents the values of an empirical joint probability distribution $p(x_i,y_j)=p_{ij}$, calculated on the base of measurements (Walaszek-Babiszewska, 2004). Each of the ranges of volume and density of particles has been divided into 4 intervals. The smallest value of indexes *i,j* concerns to the smallest value of density and volume:

$$x_1 < x_2 < x_3 < x_4; \quad y_1 < y_2 < y_3 < y_4.$$

The marginal probabilities $p_{i.}(x)$ and $p_{.j}(y)$ are also given in Table 1.

Density fraction number	Probability $p_{ij}(x, y)$				Marginal probability $p_{.j}(y)$
	Size class number				
j	i=1	i=2	i=3	i=4	
1	0.6290	0.0304	0.0074	0.0020	0.6688
2	0.1338	0.0044	0.0011	0.0003	0.1396
3	0.0534	0.0050	0.0010	0.0002	0.0596
4	0.1198	0.0092	0.0025	0.0005	0.1320
Marginal probability $p_{i.}(x)$	0.9360	0.0490	0.0120	0.0030	$\sum_i p_{i.} = \sum_j p_{.j} = 1$

Table 1. The empirical joint probability distribution $p_{ij}(x,y)$ and marginal probability distributions $p_{.j}(y)$, $p_{i.}(x)$ of particle features

3.2 Linguistic characteristics of particles

Perception-based information of human experts, expressing in natural language a quantity-quality characteristic of particles features, can be verified on the base of linguistic and probabilistic modelling presented above.
Let us assume two linguistic variables considered above:
x_{name} : *'volume of particles'* and the set of linguistic values *L(X)={small(A₁), middle(A₂), large(A₃)}* with the membership functions determined over the disjoint intervals a_i, $i=1,\ldots, I$ as follows:

$$A_1 = 1/a_1 + 0.2/a_2; \quad A_2 = 0.8/a_2 + 0.8/a_3; \quad A_3 = 0.2/a_3 + 1/a_4$$

y_{name} : *'density of particles'* and the set of linguistic values $L(Y)=\{light(B_1), middle(B_2), heavy(B_3)\}$ with the membership functions determined over the disjoint intervals b_j , $j=1,\ldots, J$, as follows:

$$B_1 = 1/b_1 + 0.5/b_2; \quad B_2 = 0.5/b_2 + 0.5/b_3; \quad B_3 = 0.5/b_3 + 1/b_4$$

For these two linguistic variables and the empirical joint probability distribution given in Table 1. we can calculate the probability of the simultaneous events, e.g.

P{ (x is small) and (y is light)}

using (16) i (17) as follows:

$$P(A_1 \times B_1) = p_{11}(x,y)\mu_{A_1}(a_1)\mu_{B_1}(b_1) + p_{12}(x,y)\mu_{A_1}(a_1)\mu_{B_1}(b_2) + p_{21}(x,y)\mu_{A_1}(a_2)\mu_{B_1}(b_1) + p_{22}(x,y)\mu_{A_1}(a_2)\mu_{B_1}(b_2)$$

$$P(A_1 \times B_1) = 0.6290 \cdot 1 \cdot 1 + 0.1338 \cdot 1 \cdot 0.5 + 0.0304 \cdot 0.2 \cdot 1 + 0.0044 \cdot 0.2 \cdot 0.5 = 0.7024$$

In the similar way we can compute the values of probabilities $P(A_i \times B_j)$, i,j=1,2,3 (Table 2.).

	A_1	A_2	A_3	$P(B_j)$
B_1	0.7024	0.0324	0.0037	0.7385
B_2	0.0946	0.0046	0.0005	0.0997
B_3	0.1488	0.0118	0.0012	0.1618
$P(A_i)$	0.9458	0.0488	0.0054	$\Sigma P(A_i)=$ $\Sigma P(B_j)=1$

Table 2. The probability distributions of linguistic variables *(x,y)* representing probability of fuzzy events $P(A_i \times B_j)$ and marginal probabilities

Probability distributions of linguistic variables (Table 2.) could be used for the validation of experts' opinion:
'The contents of the light and small particles is very high'; $P(A_1 \times B_1) = 0.7024$;
'The contents of the light fraction is high'; $P(B_1)=0.7385$;
'The contents of large particles is low'; $P(A_3)=0.0054$.
The values of probability of fuzzy events calculated according to (16) and (17) depend on a choice of a t-norm. The problem is important for creating the inference procedure in knowledge-based systems.

3.3 Quality parameters of particles as a mean value of a fuzzy event

Characteristics of tested chemical components in population of particles are usually called the quality characteristics. Suppose the quality parameter $\beta_{ij} = \beta(x_i, y_j)$ in every elementary fraction of particles, where x_i, y_j are mean values of particle volume and density in the intervals a_i and b_j, respectively. The mean value of a tested substance in the population of particles whose features are determined by a fuzzy event e.g. "C: small and light particles" can be calculated by using the notion of a mean value of fuzzy event, as follows (Walaszek-Babiszewska, 2004):

$$\beta_C = \frac{\sum_{i=1}^{I} \sum_{j=1}^{J} \beta_{ij} p_{ij} \mu_C(x_i, y_j)}{\sum_{i=1}^{I} \sum_{j=1}^{J} p_{ij} \mu_C(x_i, y_j)} \qquad (28)$$

4. Knowledge representation

4.1 General form of a fuzzy model

A fuzzy model represented a MISO system, consisting of the collection of fuzzy rules in a form 'IF *x is A* THEN *y is B'* is considered (Yager and Filev, 1995). The propositions *x is A* in antecedents and *y is B* in consequents of rules are based on the partition of the input-output space, given by experts. The exemplary *i-th* file rule includes *J* elementary rules, in a form:

$$R_i: w_i(IF\ x_1\ is\ A_{1,i}\ AND\ x_2\ is\ A_{2,i} ... AND\ x_p\ is\ A_{p,i}$$
$$THEN\ y\ is\ B_1\ (w_{1/i})$$
$$------------$$
$$ALSO\ y\ is\ B_j\ (w_{j/i}) \tag{29}$$
$$------------$$
$$ALSO\ y\ is\ B_J\ (w_{J/i}))$$

where $x^T = (x_1,...,x_p)$ is a linguistic vector of system inputs (antecedent variables), y is a linguistic output variable. The linguistic values (term sets) $L(x_1),...,L(x_p),L(y)$ of the input and output variables are predefined by process experts. Fuzzy sets $A_{1,i},..., A_{p,i}$, $i=1,...,I$ represent linguistic values of the input vector, and are defined by membership functions $\mu_{A_{1,i}}(u_1),...,\mu_{A_{p,i}}(u_p)$ in the domains $U_1,...,U_p$, $U_i \subset R, i=1,...,p$. The linguistic output (consequent) variable y has the family of fuzzy subsets B_j with membership functions $\mu_{B_j}(v)$, $j=1,...,J$ in the numeric space $V \subset R$.

The rule weights w_i and $w_{j/i}$ $i=1,...,I$, $j=1,...,J$ represent probabilities of fuzzy events occurring in the antecedents and consequence of the model $w_i = P(A_i)$, $w_{j/i} = P(B_j / A_i)$ (Walaszek-Babiszewska, 2007). The weight w_i of a file rule represents a joint probability of fuzzy events $A_{1,i} \times ... \times A_{p,i}$ in the antecedent domain, calculated according to (16) and (17):

$$P(A_i) = \sum_{u \in U} p(u_1,...,u_p) T(\mu_{A_{1,i}}(u_1),...,\mu_{A_{p,i}}(u_p)) \tag{30}$$

where T means a t-norm, membership functions $\mu_{A_{1,i}}(u_1),...,\mu_{A_{p,i}}(u_p)$ are defined in a such way, that for every numeric value $u^{T*} = (u_1^*,...,u_p^*) \in U$ the relationship $\sum_{i=1,2,...,I} \mu_{A_i}(u^*) = 1$ is fulfilled, and $p(u_1,...,u_p)$ is a probability distribution which assigns to each Borel set in U a real number $p \in [0,1]$.

Elementary rule weights $w_{j/i}$, $i=const$, $j=1,...,J$ state the conditional probabilities of the events (y is B_j) of the consequent variable, under the condition of the input variable (x is A_i). It can be calculated from Bayesian formula (see (22)), as follows

$$w_{j/i} = P(B_j / A_i) = \frac{P(A_i \times B_j)}{P(A_i)}, \quad j=1,...,J,\ i=const \tag{31}$$

where the probability of fuzzy events (fuzzy relations) $A_i \times B_j$, $i=1,...,I$, $j=1,...,J$, determined by the formula

$$P(A_i \times B_j) = \sum_{(u,v) \in U \times V} p(u,v) T(\mu_{A_i}(u), \mu_{B_j}(v)) = w_{ij} \tag{32}$$

states the joint probability distribution of linguistic input-output vector $P(X,Y)=\{P(A_i \times B_j)\}$, i=1,...,I, j=1,...,J . The joint probability distribution $p(u,v) \in [0,1]$ determined in the input-output universe $U \times V \subset R^{p+1}$ is understood in the sense of the probability theory.

The weights w_i , w_{ij} and $w_{j/i}$ i=1,...,I, j=1,...,J of the model can be estimate by using a set of input-output measurements $\{(u^m, v^m)\}$,m=1,...,M and as probability distributions should fulfil the relationships

$$\sum_{i=1}^{I} w_i = 1, \quad \sum_{i=1}^{I}\sum_{j=1}^{J} w_{ij} = 1, \quad \sum_{j=1}^{J} w_{j/i} = 1, \; i = const. \tag{33}$$

4.2 Inference and aggregation procedure

The approximate reasoning is based on a fuzzy logic and fuzzy sets theory (Zadeh, 1979). The generalized *modus ponens* permits to deduce an imprecise conclusion from imprecise premises. A great number of works in the literature dealt with fuzzy reasoning, e.g. (Pedrycz, 1984), (Yager & Filev, 1994), (Hellendoorn & Driankov, 1997).

When the proposition x *is* A_i^* is given, then from the *ij-th* elementary rule of the model (29), a proposition y *is* $B_{j/i}^*$ can be computed. The membership function $\mu_{B_{j/i}^*}(v)$ of the inferred fuzzy output is given by the formula:

$$\mu_{B_{j/i}^*}(v) = \sup_{u \in U} T(\mu_{A_i^*}(u), \mu_{R_{ij}}(u,v)) \tag{34}$$

where T means a t-norm, R_{ij} is a fuzzy relation determined in the input-output space $U \times V$ with the membership function $\mu_{R_{ij}}(u,v)$ expressed as an implication operator or as a t-norm (*min* or *product*) derived from membership functions $\mu_{A_i}(u)$ and $\mu_{B_{j/i}}(v)$. Inferred fuzzy set $B_{j/i}^*$ depends on a t-norm as well as the chosen type of the fuzzy relation R_{ij}.

Let us check the inferring procedure from the model (29), taking into account the rule weights representing probabilities of fuzzy events defined above (according to (Walaszek-Babiszewska, 2007a and 2008). Assuming a crisp value (singleton) of input variables $u^* = (u_1^*,...,u_p^*)$ with the degree of fitting u^* to the input fuzzy set A_i , calculated by

$$\mu_{A_i}(u^*) = T(\mu_{A_{1,i}}(u_1^*),..., \mu_{A_{p,i}}(u_p^*)) = \tau_i \tag{35}$$

the output fuzzy set $B_{j/i}^*$ can be found as follows:

$$\mu_{B_{j/i}^*}(v) = T(\mu_{A_i}(u^*), \mu_{B_{j/i}}(v)) \tag{36}$$

where the t-norm determines the relation R_{ij} . Using the product t-norm (according to Larsen's rule) in (36), we have the output fuzzy set $B^*_{j/i}$ inferred from *ij-th* elementary rule, determined by a membership function

$$\mu_{B^*_{j/i}}(v) = \tau_i \mu_{B_{j/i}}(v) \tag{37}$$

Fuzzy outputs $B^*_{j/i}$ computed from elementary rules *j=1,…,J*, at the same value of the antecedent (*i=const*), can be aggregated by using weights $w_{j/i}$:

$$\mu_{B^*_i}(v) = \tau_i \sum_{j=1}^{J} w_{j/i} \mu_{B_{j/i}}(v) \tag{38}$$

The fuzzy set B^*_i derived in such way is a fuzzy conditional mean value (see (7) in paragraph 2.2) of the conclusion (37), calculated under the condition (x is A^*_i).
If the crisp value of input variables $u^* = (u^*_1,...,u^*_p)$ belongs also to another input fuzzy sets A_i , and $\tau_i \neq 0$, *i=1,…,I* then fuzzy outputs of the file rules B^*_i , *i=1,…,I* can be aggregated using weights w_i of all switched rules. Then the aggregated fuzzy set B^* states a total mean fuzzy value of the conclusion (37), with the membership function calculated according to:

$$\mu_{B^*}(v) = \sum_{i=1}^{I} w_i \tau_i \sum_{j=1}^{J} w_{j/i} \mu_{B_{j/i}}(v) \tag{39}$$

or in the way:

$$\mu_{B^*}(v) = \frac{\sum_{i=1}^{I} w_i \tau_i \sum_{j=1}^{J} w_{j/i} \mu_{B_{j/i}}(v)}{\sum_{i=1}^{I} w_i} \tag{40}$$

The relationships (33) have been taken into account in formulas (38) and (39).

4.3 Knowledge representation of stochastic systems

Stochastic systems are often described by the ordered pair *(x,y)* of input and output variables:

$$\{(x(t,\omega), y(t,\omega)) : t \in T, x \in X, y \in Y, \omega \in \Omega\} \tag{41}$$

where X is the system input domain, Y is the output domain of the system, T represents a time domain, and Ω is an elementary events domain. There is a certain probabilistic, reason-result relationship between variables x and y, where x plays the role of a reason, and y - the result.

In paragraph 4.2 we considered the linguistic fuzzy model of the MISO system, assuming that x and y are linguistic variables (vector) with linguistic values determined by suitable fuzzy sets in the input and output numerical domain. Moreover, the probabilistic measure *p(x,y)* on a set of realizations of the processes have been given. The model (29) can be treated as a joint probability of linguistic vector variable in the input-output domain.
Let us assume now, that the probabilistic measure *p(x,y)* on a set of realizations of the processes $\{x(t), y(t)\}, t = t_k, k = 1,2,...K$ observed at the discrete moments, is given.
There are many models of stochastic systems discrete in a time domain *T*, for example an input-output dynamic model:

$$y(t_k) = f[x(t_k), x(t_{k-1}),..., x(t_{k-n}),..., y(t_{k-1}),..., y(t_{k-m})] \tag{42}$$

where *f()* can be a multivariable regression function. These types of models are well known as Box-Jenkins' time series models and are modelled by using Takagi-Sugeno type fuzzy models (Yager, and Filev, 1994), (Hellendoorn, and Driankov, 1997).
We are interested in other types of models, which take into account a multivariable distribution function of the processes $\{x(t), y(t)\}, t = t_k, k = 1,2,...K$ observed at the discrete moments, e.g.

$$p(x, y) = p[x(t_k), x(t_{k-1}),..., x(t_{k-n}),..., y(t_k), y(t_{k-1}),..., y(t_{k-m})] \tag{43}$$

These models are used in more simple forms, as the first order models (e.g. white noise) or the second order models (e.g. Markov's process, known also as a *short memory process*).
The general form of the fuzzy model of a stochastic process discrete in a time domain T, can be expressed as a set of weighted rules:

$$\begin{aligned} & w_i[IF\ x(t_k)\ is\ A_{i,k}\ AND\ x(t_{k-1})\ is\ A_{i,k-1} ... AND\ x(t_{k-n})\ is\ A_{i,k-n} ... \\ & \quad AND\ y(t_{k-1})\ is\ B_{i,k-1} ... AND\ y(t_{k-m})\ is\ B_{i,k-m} \\ & THEN\ \ y(t_k)\ is\ B_{i,k}] \end{aligned} \tag{44}$$

where
i=1,…,I - number of rules, determined by the partition of the input-output space $X^{n+1} \times Y^{m+1}$;
x,y -linguistic variables, $x \in X$, $y \in Y$ with linguistic values sets *L(X), L(Y),* determining linguistic states of the system,
$A_{i,k}, A_{i,k-1},..., A_{i,k-n}$ - fuzzy subsets corresponding to linguistic values of variables $x(t_k), x(t_{k-1}),..., x(t_{k-n})$, $x \in X$;
$B_{i,k}, B_{i,k-1},..., B_{i,k-m}$ - fuzzy subsets corresponding to linguistic values of variables $y(t_k), y(t_{k-1}),..., y(t_{k-m})$, $y \in Y$;
w_i - weight of *i-th* rule, a joint probability of the fuzzy event (fuzzy relation R_i) in the input-output space $X^{n+1} \times Y^{m+1}$ (according to (Walaszek-Babiszewska, 2007b))

$$w_i = P(R_i) = P(A_{i,k} \times A_{i,k-1} \times ... \times A_{i,k-n} \times B_{i,k} \times B_{i,k-1} \times ... \times B_{i,k-m}) \tag{45}$$

The weighted rule (44) can be easily written in a form of a rule with two weights, corresponding to a probability of the antecedent events and to a conditional probability of the consequent event, similarly to model (29).

4.4 Exemplary knowledge representation of a stochastic process

The data $\{x_{t_k}\}$ of the euro/Polish zloty exchange rate, observed daily in the first year of involving it into 12 countries of the EU, has been recognized as a realization of a certain stochastic process. The process has been modelled to predict some linguistic value of the process and the probability of its occurrence.

Two variables $x_{t_{k-1}}, x_{t_{k-2}}$ have been assumed as antecedent variables. From the point of view of fuzzy modelling, the created model represents a fuzzy relation $R(x_{t_k}, x_{t_{k-1}}, x_{t_{k-2}})$ of the linguistic variables in a form of weighted rules. Three linguistic states of the process have been distinguish: *L(X)={low(*A_1*), middle(*A_2*), high(*A_3*)}* and the fuzzy meaning have been defined, based on disjoint intervals in the process domain X.

The joint empirical probability distribution $p(x_{t_k}, x_{t_{k-1}}, x_{t_{k-2}})$ has been calculated, using disjoint cube intervals $a_i \times a_j \times a_k \in X^3$, *i,j,k*=1,…,4. The empirical probability distribution $P(x_{t_k}, x_{t_{k-1}}, x_{t_{k-2}})$ of linguistic variables, taking the fuzzy states A_1, A_2, A_3 observed at the moments t_k, t_{k-1}, t_{k-2}, has been computed. Then, the marginal and conditional probability distributions have been calculated.

The linguistic fuzzy model consists of 7 file rules. Table 3. presents all file rules of the model in a form of a decision table (Walaszek-Babiszewska, 2007b).

x_{t-2} \ x_{t-1}	A_1	A_2	A_3
A_1	$0.365\begin{cases} x_t \text{ is } A_1/0.84 \\ x_t \text{ is } A_2/0.16 \\ x_t \text{ is } A_3/0 \end{cases}$	$0.06\begin{cases} x_t \text{ is } A_1/0.42 \\ x_t \text{ is } A_2/0.55 \\ x_t \text{ is } A_3/0.03 \end{cases}$	0
A_2	$0.07\begin{cases} x_t \text{ is } A_1/0.4 \\ x_t \text{ is } A_2/0.43 \\ x_t \text{ is } A_3/0.17 \end{cases}$	$0.07\begin{cases} x_t \text{ is } A_1/0.10 \\ x_t \text{ is } A_2/0.85 \\ x_t \text{ is } A_3/0.05 \end{cases}$	$0.025\begin{cases} x_t \text{ is } A_1/0 \\ x_t \text{ is } A_2/0.48 \\ x_t \text{ is } A_3/0.52 \end{cases}$
A_3	0	$0.03\begin{cases} x_t \text{ is } A_1/0 \\ x_t \text{ is } A_2/0.30 \\ x_t \text{ is } A_3/0.70 \end{cases}$	$0.380\begin{cases} x_t \text{ is } A_1/0 \\ x_t \text{ is } A_2/0.07 \\ x_t \text{ is } A_3/0.93 \end{cases}$

Table 3. The rule-based fuzzy model of the stochastic process $\{x_{t_k}\}$

5. References

Zadeh, L.A. (1975). The concept of a linguistic variable and its application to approximate reasoning. *Information Sciences*, Part I, Vol. 8, pp. 199-240

Zadeh, L.A. (1968). Probability measures of fuzzy events. *Journal of Mathematical Analysis and Applications*, Vol.23, No.2, pp. 421-427

Kacprzyk, J. (1986) *Fuzzy Sets in System Analysis* (in Polish), PWN, Warsaw

Walaszek-Babiszewska, A. (2008). Probability measures of fuzzy events and linguistic fuzzy modelling -forms expressing randomness and imprecision, *Proc. WSEAS Conf. 'Art. Intell., Knowledge Eng., and Data Bases'*, pp. 207-212, Cambridge, UK, February 2008, WSEAS

Walaszek-Babiszewska, A. (2004). *Statistical and Fuzzy Modeling of Grain Material Sampling and Operations; Selected Approaches*. Publishing House of the Silesian University of Technology, Gliwice, Poland

Yager, R. R. & Filev, D.P. (1995). *Essentials of Fuzzy Modelling and Control* (in Polish), WNT and Wiley, Warsaw

Walaszek-Babiszewska, A. (2007a). Construction of fuzzy models using probability measures of fuzzy events, *Proc.13th IEEE/IFAC Int.. Conf. on Methods and Models in Automation and Robotics, MMAR 2007*, pp. 661-667, August 2007, Szczecin, Poland

Zadeh, L.A. (1979). A theory of approximate reasoning, *Machine Intelligence*, Vol.9, J.E Hayes, D. Michie and L.I. Mikulich, (Ed.), Elsevier, New York, pp. 149-194.

Pedrycz, W. (1984). An identification algorithm in fuzzy relational systems. *Fuzzy Sets and Systems*, Vol.13, pp. 153-167

Yager, R. R. & Filev, D.P. (1994). Template based fuzzy systems modelling. *Journal of Intelligent Systems*, Vol. 2, pp. 39-54

Hellendoorn, H. & Driankov, D. (Ed.) (1997). *Fuzzy Model Identification; Selected Approaches*, Springer, Berlin - Heidelberg

Walaszek-Babiszewska, A. (2007b). Linguistic knowledge representation for stochastic systems. *Proc. of the Int. Multiconference on Computer Science and Information Technology IMCSIT 2007 (in cooperation with IEEE), Wisła, Poland; Vol. 2, pp. 141-150*

20

Multiple Multi-Objective Servo Design - Evolutionary Approach

Piotr Wozniak
Institute of Automatic Control, Technical University of Lodz
Poland

1. Introduction

Design of control systems is characterised by many targets, therefore the methods enabling optimisation of several objectives have received more and more attention over the past years. When dealing with multi-objective optimisation problems the notion of the scalar function optimality was extended. The most common approach was originally proposed in 19th century by Edgeworth and later generalised by Pareto. This trade-off approach means no element of the vector of optimal solution, so called Pareto optimal solution, can be improved without making some other criteria worse. There are many different notions of dominance. One of them is so called weak Pareto dominance relation which is defined as follows :

$$\preceq_{\mathcal{F}'} := \{(\mathbf{x}, \mathbf{y}) \mid \mathbf{x}, \mathbf{y} \in X \wedge \forall f_i \in \mathcal{F}' : f_i(\mathbf{x}) \leq f_i(\mathbf{y})\} \tag{1}$$

where $\mathcal{F}'$ is a set of objectives with

$$\mathcal{F}' \subseteq \mathcal{F} := \{f_1, \ldots, f_k\}$$

A solution $x^* \in X$ is called Pareto optimal if there is no other $x \in X$ that weakly dominates x^* with respect to the set of all objectives taking into account all constraints. The set of all optimal solutions form the Pareto set.

Most of the research in the multi-objective optimisation has concentrated on tracing the Pareto front. Often this solution, which is non-dominated in the objective space, cannot be described analytically especially when the complexity of the problem makes exact methods unsuitable. The Pareto set is the projection of the Pareto front to the decision space.

In the last 20 years meta-heuristics approach to the multi-objective optimisation problems proved it can be applied even when only little is known about the underlying problems. From these methods, evolutionary algorithms are, without a doubt, the most widely used today mainly due to their flexibility while dealing with non-linear, non-quadratic, non-convex problems and thanks to their ease of use (for extensive presentation of the state-of-the-art research results see (Coello Coello, et al., 2007)). Also in engineering design formulated as multi-objective optimisation problems the evolutionary algorithms (MOEA) achieve popularity (Fleming et al., 2005) although generating Pareto front approximation is computationally expensive.

At the moment, thanks to rapid progress in computing technologies, novel algorithms of population-based optimisation may now be run on multiprocessor computing platforms in shorter time.

On the other hand, the designer, as well as the decision maker, may not be interested in having an excessively large number of Pareto optimal solutions (vectors from the decision space) to deal with due to overflow of information. Therefore, many multi-objective optimisation problems are reformulated to find a manageable number of Pareto optimal vectors which are evenly distributed along the Pareto front, and thus good representatives of the entire set of decisions. In real problems, a single solution must be selected.

Preferably, unique solution must belong to the non-dominated solutions set and must take into account the preferences of a designer and the decision maker.

Evolutionary methods are extensively applied for multi-objective optimisation problems mostly with two or three objectives only (Coello Coello, et al., 2007). On the other hand designers may prefer to put every performance index related to the problem as an objective, rather than as a constraint, thereby increasing number of criteria. The problems with a high number of objectives cause additional challenges with respect to low-dimensional problems. Current algorithms, developed for problems with a low number of objectives, have difficulties to find a good Pareto front approximation for higher dimensions. Even with the availability of sufficient computing resources, some methods are practically not useable for a high number of objectives. It has been investigated, whether it is possible to effectively solve optimisation problems with a large number of objectives where most of solutions generated become incomparable (Brockhoff & Zitzler, 2006). In the complex design it is not clear whether any two given objectives are nonconflicting. That is, although a conflict exists elsewhere, some objectives may behave in a non-conflicting manner near the Pareto front. In such cases, the trade-off curve may be of dimension lower than the number of objectives.

The problem of dimensionality reduction multi-objective optimisation is defined as the question of finding a minimum objective subset, maintaining the given dominance structure (1) and good approximation of the Pareto front.

There are increasing number of research recently on influence of the objectives reduction on quality of the Pareto front approximation. In the literature dominates the a posteriori approach, where reduction is performed after preliminary solution to the multi-objective optimisation problems, (Deb & Saxena, 2005), (Brockhoff & Zitzler, 2006), (Woźniak, 2007a). Alternatively, a reduction in the complexity of most design problems is typically achieved by the problem decomposition based on the designer/decision maker's knowledge (Engau & Wiecek, 2007), or the transformation of the multi-objective optimisation problem into the set of single-objective optimisation problems (Qingfu & Hui, 2007).

The objective of this study is twofold. First, aim is to find a new coordination mechanism which guarantees that the final selection leads to a design that is Pareto optimal for the overall multiple Multi-Objective Optimisation Problem (mMOOP). The second aim is to propose a procedure for the mMOOP with many objectives solution under the changing environment conditions.

The methodology presented in this study integrates several multi-objective optimisation problems, while steering clear of the high dimensionality problems.

The issues of multi-objective optimisation are highlighted in Section 2. The multiple multi-objective optimisation problem is outlined in Section 3 while the proposed algorithm for the mMOOP solution is proposed in Section4. In Section 5 the application of the mMOOP design is presented for the servo design as a future field of interest. The Section 6 summarizes the study.

2. Dimensionality issues in multi-objective optimisation

The majority of the existing multi-objective evolutionary algorithms for approximating the Pareto front have been designed for, and tested on, low dimensional examples (Coello Coello, et al. 2007). However, for complex optimisation problems often a higher number of dimensions occur. Increased number of criteria cause difficulties in terms of the quality of the Pareto front approximation and running time (e.g. algorithms based on the hypervolume indicator (Brockhoff & Zitzler, 2006) lead to running times exponential in the number of objectives). Additionally there is a greater probability of having any two arbitrary solutions to be non-dominated to each other. Consequently the proportion of such solutions in the population increases. Since multi-objective evolutionary algorithms put more emphasis on the non-dominated solutions, a significant part of the old population is preserved in the elite (Coello Coello, 2007). Therefore growing elite leaves no much room for new solutions to be included in the population when the constant size of pool is assumed. This, in consequence, reduces the selection pressure for the better solutions in the population and the search process slows down.

When the Pareto dominance-based ranking procedures become ineffective determining the quality of solutions, new measures and relations are introduced to guide the optimisation process. Recent results on using preference order-based approach as an optimality criterion in the ranking stage of multi-objective evolutionary algorithms (Engau & Wiecek, 2007) proved convergence improvement.

In general dimension reduction aims at keeping those objectives that can explain most of the variance in the objective space. However, it is not clear :

i. how the objective reduction alters the dominance structure,
ii. what is the quality of a generated objective subset.

The most accepted method is aggregation of the vector objectives into the single criterion by introducing the weighted sums. The multi-objective problem is therefore reduced to single function optimisation which is easy to solve even in the presence of local optima and, on a first sight, scale well.

But for high dimensions these techniques reach their limits, since :

i. it is hard (or even impossible) to determine good weights,
ii. such approaches lack the desired parallel search ability.

Another prospective ways of solving this type of problems includes reduction in the number of objectives (Brockhoff & Zitzler, 2006), (Woźniak & Witczak, 2007), (Woźniak, 2007a) or discovering objectives, which are entirely unrelated by the divide-and-conquer strategy (Purshouse & Fleming, 2003). The later method is based on splitting multi-objective optimisation problem into sub-problems. The main limitation of this approach is excessive number of pair-wise comparisons at the merge step after solution of sub-problems.

Decomposition methods are particularly well suited for design optimisation as most of complex engineering systems usually consist of many subsystems and components having smaller complexity. Dividing large and complex systems into several smaller entities is done to enable local optimisation and decision-making. In general, however, these subsystems will still be coupled so that the solution of each subsystem is dependent upon information from the others. Hence, along with the benefit of reduced complexity, comes the issue of exchange of the separate design decisions (i.e. values of the criteria arguments) to eventually arrive at a single overall design solution that is feasible. To solve this coordination problems the concept of the multiple multi-objective optimisation is introduced in Section 3.

3. Problem definition

The mathematical background of the multiple multi-objective optimisation problem remains the same as of a classic multi-objective optimisation problem.
We consider the common formulation of the multi-objective optimisation problem in its general form :

$$\begin{aligned} &\text{min. } f(x), \\ &\text{s.t. } \quad x = [x_1, x_2, \ldots, x_m] \quad , \\ &x \in X \subseteq S \subseteq R^m \\ &f(x) = \left[f_1(x), f_2(x), \ldots, f_n(x) \right] \quad ; n \geq 2 \end{aligned} \tag{2}$$

$$\text{subject to. } g(x) = \left[g_1(x), g_2(x), \ldots, g_m(x) \right] \leq 0,$$
$$h(x) = \left[h_1(x), h_2(x), \ldots, h_l(x) \right] = 0,$$

where x is the vector of the decision variable, which might be subject to inequality $g(x)$ and/or equality constraints $h(x)$.
A solution which satisfies all the constraints is called a feasible one. Due to contradicting objectives there is no single solution to (2). Instead there is a set of alternative solutions.

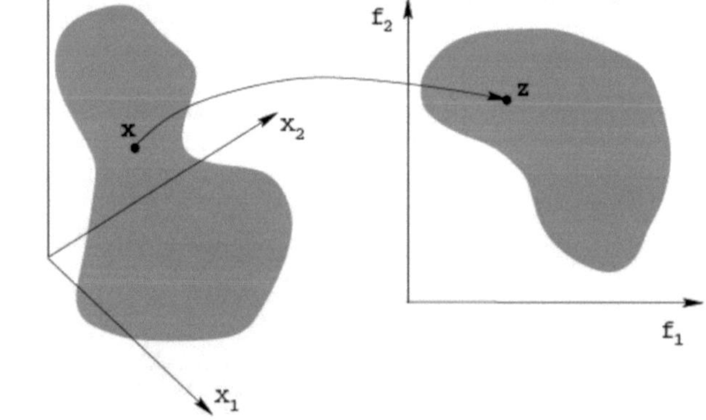

Fig. 1. Representation of the decision space and the corresponding objective space.

These solutions are optimal in the sense that no other solutions dominate (are superior to) them when all objectives are considered. They are known as Pareto-optimal solutions.
The interest, in the classical multi-objective optimisation problem, is therefore on the trade-offs with respect to the objectives (Shukla & Deb, 2007). Each objective function maps

the input decision vector (point in the m dimensional decision space) (see Fig. 1) to the target vector in the n dimensional objective space.

The domination relation defined in the objective space is used to identify

i. the Pareto set in the decision space,
ii. the Pareto front in objective space and
iii. the Pareto rank of each solution.

The main difference between approach introduced in this study and classical single multi-objective optimisation problem lies in the synchronised consideration of simultaneous multi-objective optimisation problems sharing the same decision space, but with the environment changes. Distinct environment conditions may be introduced when variations in the multi-objective optimisation problem formulation is needed to describe discrepancy between the physical plant and the mathematical model with constraints used for the design.

Every vector of the environment changes form the context which therefore is identified by its parameters, and is denoted *c*. The context belongs to the permissible environment conditions space C^o.

There are several possible ways to integrate environment conditions $c \in C^o$ into a classical multi-objective optimisation problem. In each case the vector of objective functions (results in Fig.2) changes.

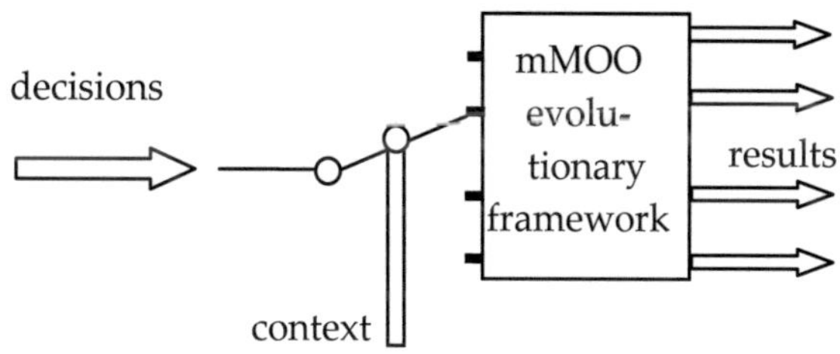

Fig. 2. The changes of environment conditions for the plant leading to multiple multi-objective optimisation problem (mMOOP).

The alternatives may be obtained by :

i. extending the decision (input) vector by the context *c*. Now we consider the resulting mapping with extended (comparing to (2)) arguments $f^*(x,c)$. A common algorithm for a multi-objective optimisation problem is used to find all optimal solutions in the decision space of the higher dimension. Since the decision space of the problem and the context space C^o are unified, just the optimal solutions x^*_c over the new input space will be found. For this reason such integration of the environment conditions is not suitable for the control system design.
ii. extending the objective vector by the context c. The resulting mapping will be $f_c(x)$ with $f_c \in FC^{n+o}$ in higher dimensional space. A common algorithm for a single multi-objective optimisation problem is used to find all optimal solutions in the objective space of the higher dimension. For this reason, as discussed in details in Section 3, such an integration of the context is not preferred.

iii. treating every context as a single multi-objective optimisation problem. This corresponds to an exhaustive a-posteriori search in every o approximated Pareto fronts (for all possible contexts). It is obvious that such an approach is not efficient, because it leads to optimisation in the set of o fronts $f_c(x_c)$.
iv. The multiple multi-objective optimisation problem mapping. The characteristic is that all different multi-objective optimisation problems share the input space, and the outputs are generated concurrently $f_c(x)$.

The key observation is that in the multi-objective optimisation problem framework iv. finding Pareto optimal solutions is equivalent to a search for a trade-off solution with variation within some parameters.

In this study variations included in the multiple multi-objective optimisation problem mapping formulation iv. are considered as distinct working conditions of the system (see Fig.2).

Directly from the above definitions of the multiple multi-objective optimisation problem mapping follows that there are multiple outputs for a single decision input (one for every context). After collecting a set of solutions, the Pareto rank for every solution in each context can be calculated.

To compress this information to a single value only the highest Pareto rank value (the lowest from the calculated $Prank_{c^i}$) is selected and further defined as

$$bPrank = min\left\{Prank_{c^1}, Prank_{c^2}, \dots, Prank_{c^o}\right\} \tag{3}$$

This value bundles the quality of a solution into a single value. As a result its value is crucial for multi-objective optimisation algorithms, because they are based on ranking comparisons of different solutions.

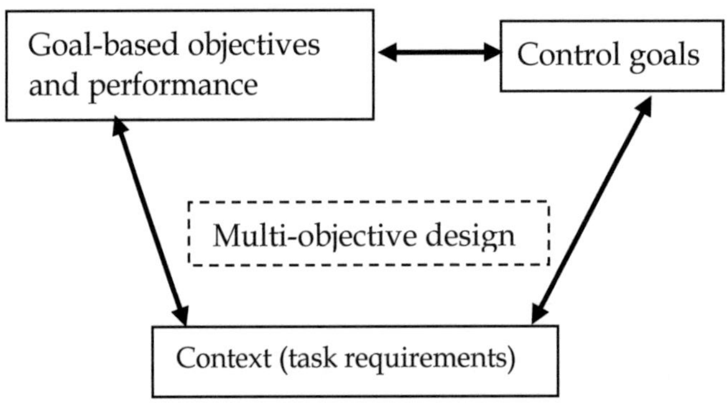

Fig. 3 Multi-objective control design framework with task requirements - context.

In this work, we propose a procedure of transferring some performance criteria of the control system into the context variables. The approach is motivated by the real-life problem of having a large number of potential objectives in the redundant robot manipulators control based upon the existing multi-criteria inverse kinematics, and will be discussed in details in Section 5.

The task-based controller is a controller that unifies position and force control of redundant manipulators and takes task requirements as the central component of the multi-objective control design framework, with context presented in Fig. 3.

4. Evolutionary methodology of the multiple multi-objective optimisation problem solution

Since evolutionary algorithms deal with a number of population members in each generation, they are ideal for finding multiple Pareto-optimal solutions in of the multi-objective optimisation problem. All of these methods emphasize :

i. non-dominated solutions for progressing towards the Pareto-optimal front,
ii. less-crowded solutions for maintaining a good diversity among obtained solutions,
iii. elites to provide a faster and reliable convergence near the Pareto-optimal front.

There are numerous approaches for solving multi-objective optimisation problems. The salient features of multi-objective evolutionary algorithms are :

i. the convergence of solutions in the objective space to the Pareto front,
ii. support for diversity of the solutions along the front,
iii. efficiency characterised by the processing time or the number of evaluations required.

New algorithms introduced every year aim to improve on one or more of the above mentioned issue. Some of the most well-known algorithms are: VEGA, MOGA, PAES, NSGA-II and SPEA2. For comprehensive description see (Konak et al., 2006) and (Coello Coello et al., 2007).

Essential parameters to be fixed in an evolutionary algorithm:

i. population size,
ii. number of generations,
iii. parameters related to selection,
iv. recombination (crossover probability, crossover operator),
v. mutation (mutation probability, mutation operator).

Population size is a crucial parameter in a successful application of each algorithm. Even in the case of an adequate population size optimisation the algorithm must be run for a critical number of generations in order to obtain convergence near the optimal solution (Coello Coello et al., 2007).

In case where context can be configured concurrently, a single evaluation run delivers several results, each consisting of multiple objective values, for each instance of the multi-objective optimisation problem.

The presented approach is based on sequential calculations of MOO sub-problems of the multiple multi-objective optimisation problem. After selecting one, leading multi-objective optimisation problem, its Pareto set is henceforth considered as constant for all remaining multi-objective optimisation problems.

The idea behind this approach is presented in Fig. 4 for two contexts of a bi-objective problem (denoted $f_1^1 f_2^1$ in Fig. 4a and $f_1^2 f_2^2$ in Figs. 4b and 4c, respectively).

After four elements of the Pareto front for the first context are found and designated with different symbols in Fig. 4a, their arguments in the decision space are passed to the second context. Using each of the values may result in a front shown in Fig. 4b, when the next, second, multi-objective optimisation problem is solved. This means that for each point in the objective space of the first multi-objective optimisation problem there may be more than one solution in the second objective space. These are designated by the same symbols like in Fig. 4a.

In the next step the results are sorted for non-dominancy and lead to the front depicted in Fig. 4c (dominated solutions are discarded).

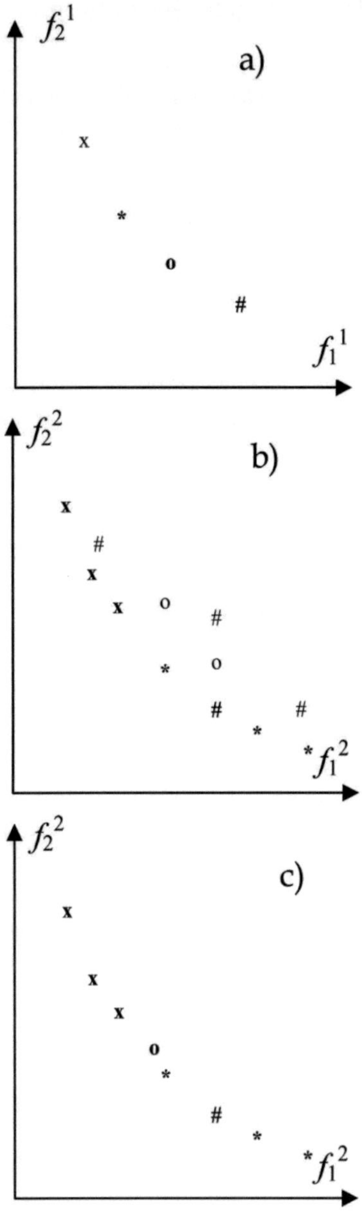

Fig. 4 Outline of Pareto front derivation for two contexts of bi-objective optimisation problems

Considering the above mentioned approach, the pseudo-code of the proposed sequential optimisation may be formulated as presented in Fig. 5.

For this specific multiple multi-objective optimisation problem design the order of the considered sequences of contexts is far less important than in the similar multiple multi-objective optimisation problem s proposed in (Avigad, 2007) and (Ponweiser & Vincze, 2007). It is possible to make it robust to the order of the multi-objective optimisation problems by introducing epsilon tolerances to reflect the implicit trade-off between solutions of two different contexts.

```
1. Decision Making step - identify all contexts
   c_i , i=1,..,o, and introduce the order in the C
   set.

2. Initialise parameters of MOEA and search space.

3. Apply MOEA with non-dominated sorting to solve
   C_1. Store results in form of the Pareto set x_1
   and the Pareto front c_1, i.e. (x_1,t_1).

4. For j:= i+1 to o do
     a. Initialise c_j^th MOEA parameters taking into
        account Pareto solutions (x_j-1,c_j-1)
     b. Apply MOEA with non-dominated sorting to
        solve c_j. Store results in form of
        the Pareto set x_j and the Pareto front c_j,
        i.e. (x_j,c_j)
     c. Reject from (x_j-1,c_j-1) solutions, which
        became dominated in the j^th step

5. IF the maximal number of populations is reached
   THEN STOP ELSE goto STEP 3
```

Fig. 5 Pseudo-code of the proposed mMOOP algorithm.

Solving the individual MOO sub-problems before selecting a final design generally may overemphasize one context, while significantly degrading the performances of others. Moreover, it is shown that the best compromise solution is not necessarily optimal for any MOO sub-problem, and thus remains unknown to the designer who follows the traditional decomposition - integration approach. We plan to consider this issue in the near future.

The first and probably the most important property that needs to be considered for the design of optimiser for a multiple multi-objective optimisation problem are multiple instances of the objective space. There exists one for every context. Although any of averaging technique can be used to operate in these spaces (e.g. mean, standard deviation, minimum or maximum value), a careful selection of values from each one is needed. Furthermore, the computational effort increases enormously because the calculations have to be done for every context separately. Out of these insights it is advisable to avoid performing any operations in the objective space.

In classical multi-objective evolutionary algorithms methods the objective space is intuitively used to calculate the density of solutions (for example in SPEA2 or NSGA-II). A solution for the multiple multi-objective optimisation problem is to relocate the density calculations from the objective space to the decision space. The placement of these measures, either in the decision space or in the objective space, was subject to a long scientific discussion (Coello Coello et al., 2007). In most of the implementations the objective space is used. Therefore, at this stage of research on multiple multi-objective optimisation problem, the NSGA-II (Deb, 2001) state-of-art algorithm is considered as the most prospective.

Another effect that needs to be considered is the extension of the Pareto rank to the best Pareto rank (3). In the NSGA-II the Pareto rank is the main selection criteria. A drawback of the best Pareto rank is its computational effort, but so far no better approach may be put forward. The complexity of a single Pareto rank calculation is multiplied by the number of contexts. This issue still lacks a computationally effective solution.

5. Multiple multi-objective optimisation problem of servo control - an outline

We will consider the so-called mechatronic servo system, i.e. the servo system adopted in the numerical control machine or industrial robot with many joints. Generally, dynamic characteristics of robot actuators and sensors are highly nonlinear with constraints, and these factors cause trajectory control errors. Feeding back the difference between the robot servomechanism velocities enables force adjustment.

The performance criteria for robot control optimisation may be broadly divided into two categories :

i. constraint-based criteria,

ii. operational goal-based criteria.

The constraint-based criteria, as its name implies, are directly associated with system constraints (e.g. joint limits, obstacles, singularities, etc.). Therefore, in general they have clear physical meanings that the user can easily relate to. They are task-dependent and usually give more insight to the operator on the task at hand.

Operational goal-based criteria, on the other hand, are concerned with the ability of the robot to perform the task better. They are functions of only manipulator configuration and states, and are not tied to any specific task. This makes the criteria very useful for the system designer, who cannot foresee all the possible tasks the robot could perform in the future.

The comprehensive description of the objectives, and performance criteria, for optimisation of redundant robot system presented hereafter was published in the Ph.D. thesis (Pholsiri, 2004). Redundancy, in this context, is defined as having more inputs than those required to create the desired output. As such, traditionally non-redundant robots, e.g. most 6 degrees of freedom (DOF) commercial robots, can be considered redundant too if their tasks at hand require fewer DOFs than the robots possess. Redundancy implies an ability to change configuration of the joint without changing the position of the robot's end-effector.

The main criteria are listed hereafter, and will enable the introduction and formulation of the multiple multi-objective optimisation problem :

C1 Criteria for Joint Range Availability (JRA).

Every joint in a manipulator has its travel limits which cannot be exceeded. Any attempt to move a joint over its limit can potentially damage the robot.

$$\gamma_{JRA} = \frac{1}{n}\sum_{i=1}^{n}\left(\frac{\left|\theta_i - \theta_{i,mid}\right|}{\theta_{i,max}}\right)^p \tag{4}$$

where :

θ_i is the joint displacement,

$\theta_{i,mid}$ is the displacement at the midpoint of the travel range,

$\theta_{i,max}$ is the displacement at the travel limits.

C2 Criteria for Velocity Limit Avoidance.

The joint Velocity Limit Avoidance (VLA) tries to minimise the velocity of each joint or the sum of the velocities of all joints. The velocity limit can be avoided by minimizing the norm of the joint velocity vector. It is crucial to keep VLA from approaching 0. The pseudo inverse solution minimises the VLA criterion.

C3 Criteria for Peak Torque Avoidance.

Although their formulation is simple and straightforward, their use in practice is limited for various reasons. First of all, the torque readings require that torque sensors be present at all actuators, which is not common (due to their cost). Secondly, even with the torque information available, this criterion can only be used to monitor the torque states of the robot but generally cannot be used in redundancy resolution to prevent the robot from exceeding their joint torque limits because most, if not all, redundancy resolution techniques do not work in the force domain.

C4 Criteria for Obstacle Avoidance.

When a manipulator is utilised in a cluttered environment or in a multi-arm system, the need to avoid obstacles or contacts with other manipulators arises. This may be formulated in the form that it is independent of the number of links and the number of obstacles.

C5 Criteria for Mathematical Singularity Avoidance.

Physically, at singularities, a manipulator loses one or more degrees of freedom. The robot may not be able to move along the desired direction. To avoid mathematical software failure, it is crucial to keep MSA from approaching zero.

The objectives mentioned above (C1 - C5) represent constraint-based criteria and may compose the context for operational goal-based objectives (Gi).

The most important goal-based objectives are :

G1 Criteria for Manipulator Precision.

A manipulator's joints are expected to have some amount of error, including position sensor error (encoder resolution or noise), control error, and deflection due to joint compliance. These joint errors are propagated through the links and to the end effector. Minimizing the effect of this error propagation is essential in applications requiring precise manipulation.

G2 Criteria for Speed of Operation.

Maximising Velocity Transmission Ratio (VTR) will minimise the joint velocity required to produce a given end effector speed in the direction, in general or for any given joint velocity.

G3 Criteria for Load Carrying Capacity.

Maximizing Force Transmission Ratio (FTR) will increase the end effector force capability in the desired direction. Looking at formulations of the VTR and the FTR, it can be concluded that they are not independent.

G4 Criteria for Energy Minimisation.

Kinetic energy minimisation is one of the early criteria used in redundancy resolution because kinetic energy is directly associated with the power consumed by the system during its operation. It is desirable to minimise the energy-based objective, especially for repetitive tasks.

A quick look at the list of performance criteria (G1 - G4) reveals that most, if not all, of these criteria are coupled. It is therefore not possible to optimise one criterion without affecting another. Hereafter there is a list of the major interaction between criteria. For example, maximising the JRA (4) criterion will likely have an impact on the VTR criterion. Even though the intention of adding the JRA to the redundancy resolution process is merely to avoid the joint limits, we may unintentionally decrease the ability of the robot to move in a desired direction. These couplings also make it impossible to completely separate the purposes of these criteria, making the task of choosing criteria for a given optimisation very difficult.

These couplings result in conflicts among criteria. The best example is the conflict between the speed and force capabilities of the robot. When considering them independently one would like to maximise both of them. However, because of the conflicting nature of these two quantities, it is physically impossible to do so at the same time. A closer look at the VTR and the FTR criteria shows that these two criteria are tightly coupled. As a matter of fact in some special cases they are the reciprocals of each other. It was investigated whether the VTR can be used to either increase the end effector speed or the end effector precision (Pholsiri, 2004). However, while increasing the speed requires that VTR be increased, improving the end effector precision demands the opposite.

These conflicts also cause difficulty when choosing appropriate criteria for a given task. The problems of couplings and conflicts among performance criteria are one of the main motivations behind the multi-objective optimisation research in the robot's servo control design.

In the considered redundant robot control problem the context is defined by constraint-based criteria (C1-C5).

While it is essential to keep the system from violating constraints (C1-C5) during operation, their values are not objectives of optimisation. Instead, their values may differ from one context to another. The most straightforward approximation is to keep every constraint constant during optimisation in each context.

At the present moment the investigation on the proposed novel multiple multi-objective optimisation problem is at its early stage of development. First simulation experiments showed that there is still significant potential for improvement, especially in the development of metrics measuring the performance of optimisation algorithms for multiple multi-objective optimisation problem in decision space, instead of using evaluation in the objective spaces (one space per context).

5. Case study – servo design

The mechatronic servo system, i.e. the servo system adopted in the numerical control machine or industrial robot is considered. In this system, there are two types of control. One is position control (PTP: point to point) emphasizing the arriving time and stop position from any position without considering the response route. Another is the contour control emphasizing the motion trajectory from the current position to the next position (position at each moment and its motion velocity).

The typical system includes the servo system of each axis, which is consists of the following parts :

- the motor ,
- the power amplifier ,
- the current control ,
- the velocity control ,
- the position control.

The structure of the system is generally different from the servo system introduced in textbooks of automatic control and is presented in Fig. 5 (Woźniak, 2007b).

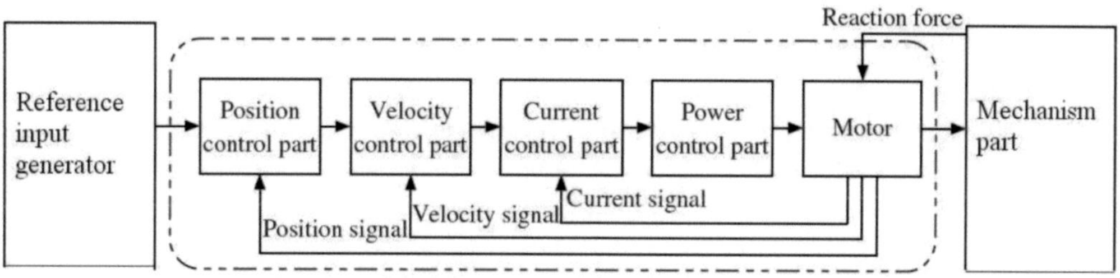

Fig. 5. Mechatronic servo system structure

5.1 The comprehensive presentation of three multi-objective problems

The overall design problem may be considered mMOOP with divided into three MOOPs as outlined in Fig.6.

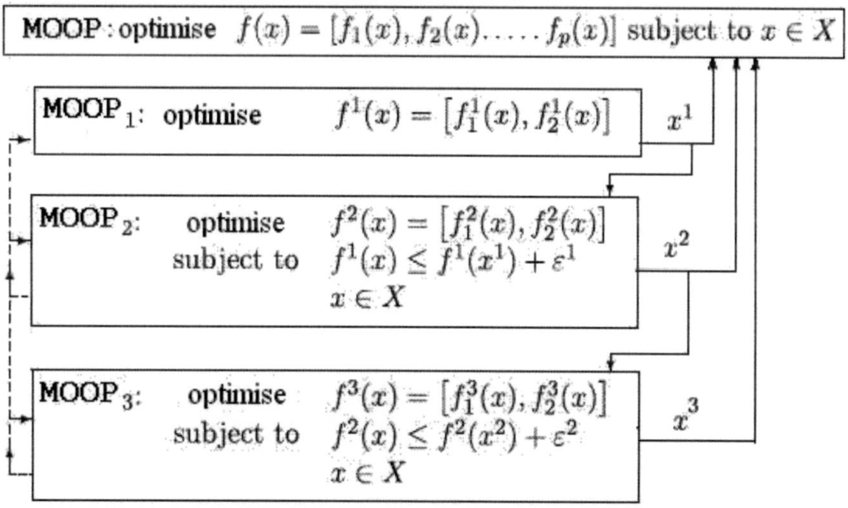

Fig. 6 The epsilon tolerance integration of the mMOOP with distinct contexts

The control goals may be easily organised in the same manner as presented in Fig.5. It is realistic, from engineering point of view, to consider position control part of the design as the most important one. This loop is responsible for the following the reference path with at last two conflicting targets - fast transients and small overshoot combined with the zeroing steady-state error. The position control loop supervises velocity signal control. The dynamics of this subsystem also has at least two conflicting objectives.

The most inner part of the presented in Fig. 5 servo system structure has the most complex dynamics forced by the pulse-width modulation control of the permanent magnet synchronous motor. Unlike the mechanical control loops(i.e. Velocity signal, and Position signal), this one has to be modeled by discrete-time model with time constants of several microseconds.
The mMOOP interaction between multi-objective designs takes into account some tolerance ε, which improves robustness of the solution (Engau & Wiecek, 2007) and is realised according to the coordination scheme outlined in Section 4 (see Fig.4).

6. Conclusions

This study contributed a novel formulation to the emerging research area of the optimisation methods - the multiple multi-objective optimisation problem. It is an extension of the multi-objective optimisation ideas to the set of concurrent multi-objective optimisation problems defined by changing the environment conditions - the context.
In this study, the burden of high dimensional multi-objective optimisation problem (as discussed in Sect. 3) is relaxed by considering aggregation of the constraint-based criteria with conditions for operational goal-based objectives.
The Pareto optimal solutions of the multiple multi-objective optimisation problem are evaluated without introducing ordering of the multi-objective optimisation problems. The shared decision space of multi-objective optimisation problems is considered as a connecting bridge between all multi-objective optimisation problems.
As an example from the control servo system design, the redundant robot design problem is outlined for further research.
In the future work, we intend to further investigate the information that can be obtained from the proposed trade-off and sensitivity analysis. In view of the current approach, we are aware of the remaining weakness that this information only allows a local trade-off assessment, and thus cannot be used for more accurate estimates in a larger region of the outcome space.
We would also like to address remaining issues such as computational benchmarking or further analysis of effects from grouping and ordering of objectives using examples from the industry. We believe that such future efforts will further improve the recognised features of the current method and eventually provide an effective and flexible decision-making tool for multi-objective design optimisation.

7. References

Avigad, G. (2007). multi-Multi-Objective Optimization Problem and Its Solution by a MOEA, *Proceedings of the 4th Conference on Evolutionary Multi-Criterion Optimization - EMO 2007*, Obayashi S. et al. (Eds.), pp.847–861, ISBN 978-3-540-70927-5, Matsushima, Japan, March 5-8, 2007, Springer, Berlin

Brockhoff, D. & Zitzler E. (2006). Are All Objectives Necessary? On Dimensionality Reduction in Evolutionary Multiobjective Optimization, *Proceedings of the 9th Conference on Parallel Problem Solving from Nature-PPSN IX*, Runarsson, T.P. et al.

(Eds.), pp. 533–542, ISBN 978-3-540-38990-3, Reykjavik, Iceland, September 9-13 2006

Coello Coello, C.A. ; Lamont, G.B. & Van Valdhuizen, D.A. (2007). *Evolutionary Algorithms for Solving Multi-Objective Problems (2nd Ed.)*, ISBN 978-0-387-332549-3, Springer, Berlin

Deb, K. (2001) *Multi-Objective Optimization Using Evolutionary Algorithms*, Wiley, ISBN 978-0-471-87339-6, Chicester, UK

Deb, K. & Saxena, D.K. (2005) On finding pareto-optimal solutions through dimensionality reduction for certain large-dimensional multi-objective optimization problems. Technical Report KanGAL Report No. 2005011, Kanpur Genetic Algorithms Laboratory, 2005

Engau, A. & Wiecek, M.M. (2007). 2D decision-making for multicriteria design optimization, *Structural and Multidisciplinary Optimization*, Vol.34, No.4, (Oct. 2007), pp. 301-315, ISSN 1615-147X

Fleming, P. J.; Purshouse, R. C. & Lygoe, R. J. (2005). Many-Objective Optimization:An Engineering Design Perspective, *Proceedings of the 3rd. Conference on Evolutionary Multi-Criterion Optimization - EMO 2005*, Coello Coello, C. A. et al. (Eds.), pp. 14–32, ISSN 0302-9743 Guanajuato, Mexico, March 2005

Konak, A. ; Coit, D.W. & Smith, A.E. (2006). Multi-objective optimization using genetic algorithms: A tutorial, *Reliability Engineering and System Safety*, Vol.91, pp.992-1007, Sept.2006

Pholsiri, C. (2004). Task-based decision making and control of robotic manipulators *Ph.D. Thesis*, University of Texas at Austin, 2004, Available at: https://www.lib.utexas.edu/etd/d/2004/pholsirid74234/pholsirid74234.pdf

Ponweiser, W. & Vincze, M. (2007) "The Multiple Multi Objective Problem - Definition, Solution and Evaluation, *Proceedings of the 4th Conference on Evolutionary Multi-Criterion Optimization - EMO 2007*, Obayashi, S. et al. (Eds.), pp. 877–892, ISBN 978-3-540-70927-5, Matsushima, Japan, March 5-8, 2007, Springer, Berlin

Purshouse, R. C. & Fleming, P. J. (2003) An adaptive divide-and-conquer methodology for evolutionary multi-criterion optimisation, *Proceedings of the 2nd Conference on Evolutionary Multi-Criterion Optimization EMO 2003*, Fonseca, C.M. et al. (Eds.), pp. 133–147, ISBN 978-3-540-01869-8, Faro, Portugal, April 8–11, 2003, Springer, Berlin

Qingfu, Z. & Hui, L. (2007) MOEA/D: A Multiobjective Evolutionary Algorithm Based on Decomposition, *IEEE Trans on Evolutionary Computation*, Vol. 11, No. 6, (Dec. 2007), pp.712-731, ISSN 1089-778X

Shukla, P.K. & Deb, K. (2007) On finding multiple Pareto-optimal solutions using classical and evolutionary generating methods, *European Journal of Operational Research*, Vol.181, No. 3, (Sept 2007), pp.1630-1652, ISSN 0377-2217

Woźniak, P. (2007a) Dimensionality Reduction in Evolutionary Multiobjective Design: Case Study, *Proceedings of the 9th annual conference on Genetic and evolutionary computation GECCO-2007*, Thierens et al. (Eds.), pp. 913-915, ISBN 978-1-59593-697-4

Woźniak, P. (2007b) Multiple Multi-Objective Optimisation of Servomechanism Control Systems Design - Evolutionary Approach, *Proceedings of the 13th IEEE International*

Conference on Methods and Models in Automation and Robotics MMAR 2007, Emirsajłow, Z. (Ed.), pp. 379-385, Szczecin, Poland, August 27-30, 2007

Woźniak, P. & Witczak, P. (2007). Dimensionality Reduction in Evolutionary Multiobjective Design of Permanent Magnet Generator, *Proceedings of the 4th Conference on Evolutionary Multi-Criterion Optimization EMO 2007,* Obayashi S. et al. (Ed.), pp. 63-68, LBP, Matsushima, Japan, March 5-8, 2007

21

Model-Based Control of a Nonlinear One Dimensional Magnetic Levitation with a Permanent-Magnet Object

Zhenyu Yang, Gerulf K.M. Pedersen and Jørgen H. Pedersen
Esbjerg Institute of Technology, Aalborg University
Denmark

1. Introduction

The Electromagnet levitation technique has been popularly used in transport and industrial felds in recent decades, such as high-speed levitation trains, frictionless magnetic bearings, and high precision control in semiconductor manufacturing (CST (1996); Kim et al. (1998)). Due to its high efficiency and good environmental orientation, the application of this technique is extensively growing. For instance, the attitude of a small-sized satellite can be efficiently controlled by using the electromagnetic force generated from the interaction between the on- board (controlled) electrical field and the earth magnetic field (Wisniewski & Stoustrup (2004)).

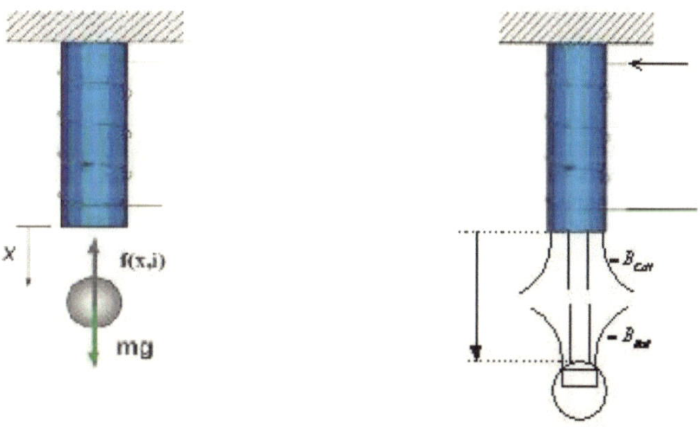

(a) Conventional structure (b) Considered structure

Fig. 1. Principles of conventional and considered levitation systems

The principle of electromagnetic levitation can be illustrated by a simple one-dimensional system as shown in Fig.1 (a). By controlling the electric current flowing through coils around a solenoid, a conductible object, e.g., an iron or a steel ball, can be possibly levitated by the generated magnetic force. However, to develop a reliable and efficient levitation system is far from easy with respect to the fact that this kind of system is featured by

complexity, nonlinearities, natural instability and large electromagnetic uncertainties (Gentili & Marconi (2003); Kim (1997); Thompson (2000); Varella et al. (2004)).
A planar levitation system was investigated in (Kim (1997); Kim et al. (1998); Thompson (2000)). By conducting AC current through a disk-shaped insulated coil, the coil can be lift-off above a wide aluminum plate. The realized system is stable but under-damped without feedback control. The thermal problem is also investigated in (Thompson (2000)), and it turned out that the coil resistance increased significantly with the increase of temperature, which means that the system required more power in order to keep the levitated object at the same height when the temperature increases. As a consequence, the test setup can only be run for a few second at a time (Thompson (2000)). In order to control the levitated object's position and overcome the under-damping issue, a feedback mechanism is often required. The feedback control of a laboratory-sized one-dimensional levitation system is discussed in (Wong (1986)), and an analog lead compensator was developed using standard frequency response methods. Some application of advanced control methods such as the robust control and integrator back- stepping for magnetic bearing control can be found in (CST (1996)) and references therein. As we observed that most existing controllers are designed based on some kind of linear/linearized models and therefore linear. Measurements of the levitated object position and the current through the coil are often required by these controllers.
By focusing on the one-dimensional levitation, the comparison of system performances under a linear controller and a nonlinear controller was investigated in (Barie & Chiasson (1996)). The nonlinear controller was developed by using feedback linearization based on a nonlinear model (Isidori (1989)). It showed that both controllers resulted more or less same system performances in terms of tracking capability for step-type references. However, the nonlinear controller is more sensitive to quantization error (e.g., 8 bit or 12 bit A/D convertors) in the current measurement. Regarding the sinusoid-type references, it turned out that the nonlinear controller resulted much better tracking performance than the linear controller did. However, the development of nonlinear controller heavily depends on the precision of available mathematical model. From practice point of view, no matter what kind of controller will be used, the thermal dynamic (heating coil) is always a critical concerning issue (Sønderskov & Østerö (2007); Thompson (2000); Yang & Pedersen (2006); Yang et al. (2007)).
Different from most existing one-dimensional levitation systems which use a conductible ball or coil as the levitated object (Barie & Chiasson (1996); Gentili & Marconi (2003); Oliveira et al. (1999); Wong (1986); Yang & Pedersen (2006), here we consider a one-dimensional levitation system with a permanent magnet object instead, i.e., a small NIB (Neodymium, Iron, Boron) magnet is glued at the inside top of a plastic ball as shown in Fig.0 (b). The main benefits of this configuration lie in the following perspectives:

- The solenoid's overheating problem is moderated. It is known that a large magnetic field is often required to levite a conductible object even with a relatively small operating range. It means that the coils must provide a large amount of current which directly leads to the heat dissipation problem (Thompson (2000)). Instead of purely depending on the coils, the magnetic field generated in the proposed configuration consists of contributions from the permanent NIB magnet as well as the contribution from coils around the solenoid.
- The system's operating range is enlarged under the same solenoid condition compared with the standard configuration (with conductible object). The magnetic field is

considerably enhanced due to the contribution from the NIB magnet. In our constructed system the NIB contributes 4-5 times more flux density than the solenoid operating at the maximal current (Sønderskov & Østerö (2007); Yang et al. (2007)).

However, the payoff of the above benefits is the complexity. The proposed configuration makes modeling and control of this kind of levitation system much more complicated regarding the fact that a permanent magnet is attached on a moving object (Simpson (1999)). This paper will explore the modeling, control and implementation of the proposed levitation system. First of all, the magnetic field generated by the moving NIB is experimentally investigated and modeled. Then a nonlinear model of the entire system is derived. System parameters are identified using some experimental ways. Afterwards a set of PID controllers are designed via trial-and-error method and automatic tuning using genetic algorithms, respectively. The developed controllers are implemented in the PC-supported LabView environment. The experimental tests show some good system performances. The rest of the paper is organized as: Section 2 gives a brief description of our benchmark system; Section 3 derives the nonlinear model of the considered system and then identifies the system coefficients by experiments; Section 4 analyzes the PID control design, automatic tuning and implementation issues; Section 5 discusses experimental results and we conclude the paper in Section 6.

2. Experimental apparatus

A one-dimensional levitation system is constructed using an aluminium framework as shown in Fig. 2. The electromagnet device consists of a solenoid with an iron core which is composed of thin steel plates riveted together. The levitated object is a plastic ball with diameter of 2 cm. There is a small NIB magnet glued to the top inside the ball, and a M4 nut glued to the bottom acting as the counterweight to the NIB magnet. On the sides of the framework, slits are milled for ease of mounting and adjustment of the optical sensor system.

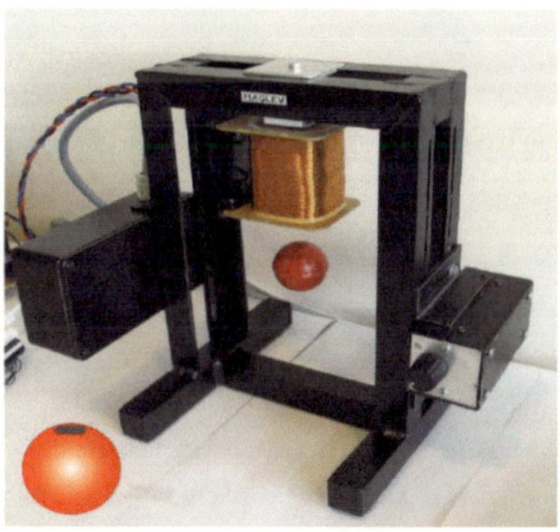

Fig. 2. Experimental laboratory setup

2.1 Position sensor

An optical sensor system for measuring the distance between the solenoid bottom and the levitated ball is developed using two LEDs (IR333-A) and a photodiode array (Hamamatsu 16- element Si photodiode array, type S5668-1). The sensor system is mounted inside an aluminium house with a milled slit facing to the possible operating range. As shown in Fig. 3., when the ball enters the detectable area, it casts a shadow on the photodiode array which leads to changes of currents. By measuring these currents, the position can be estimated by $x = \frac{L}{2}\frac{I_2 - I_1}{I_2 + I_1}$ where I_1 and I_2 are the currents through the photodiodes as shown in Fig. 3. x is the upper boundary of the shadow on the position sensor, and L is the length of the detectable area, which is 6mm in our case. The measured current is converted to a voltage through the diagram as shown in Fig. 4.

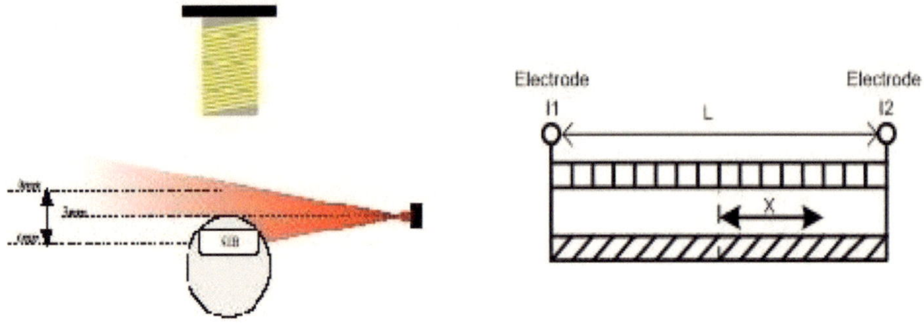

Fig. 3. Principle of the position detection

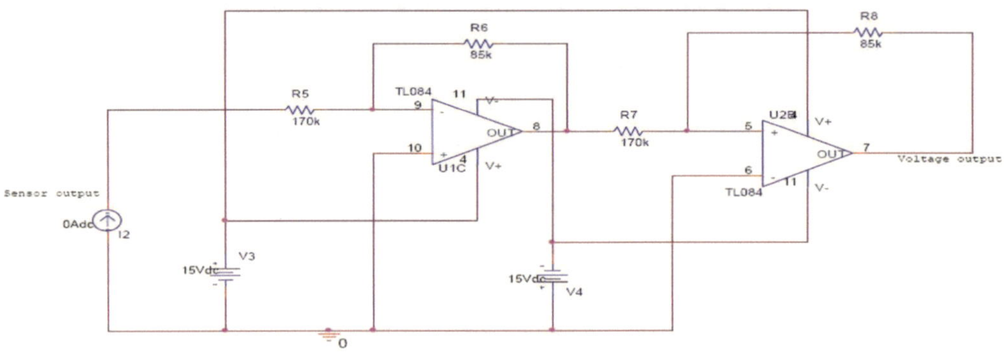

Fig. 4. Current-to-voltage conversion of the sensor measurement

2.2 Current generator

The current control scheme (Yang & Pedersen (2006)) is employed for the control purpose instead of the conventional voltage control (Barie & Chiasson (1996); Oliveira et al. (1999); Wong (1986)), such that the current drifting problem due to the thermal dynamic of the solenoid can be avoided. The basic scheme of the proposed current control is shown in Fig. 5. A digital- to-analog converter named AD7523 (Intersil) is used to converter the digital control signal into a analog voltage signal with a span of $200mV$. Through the opamp U3B (TL082) a new voltage signal with a span of $5V$ is generated and used to control the open and close of the MOSFET transistor IRFZ44. In order to protect the MOSFET transistor IRFZ44 from the high voltage peaks, a varistor S14K30AUTO is placed between the drain and ground (Sønderskov & Østerö (2007)).

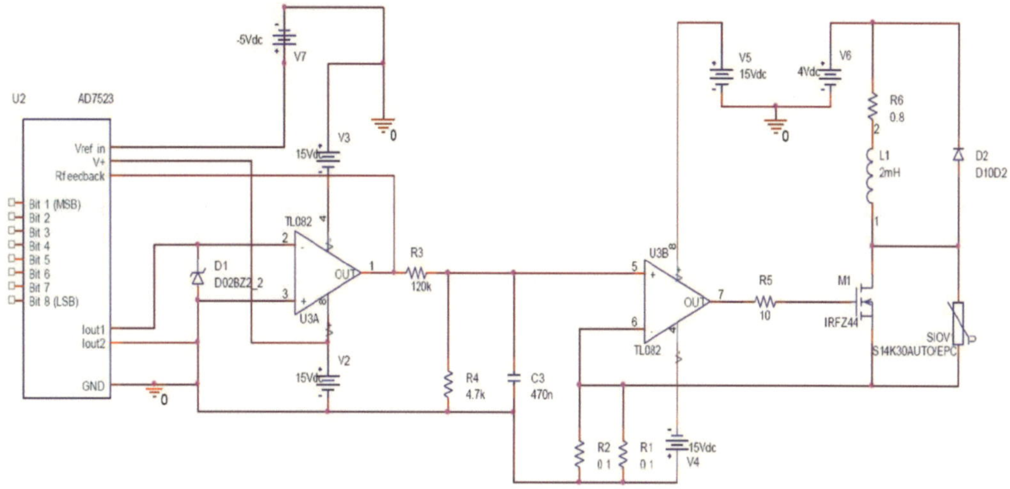

Fig. 5. Diagram of the current generator

2.3 LabView environment

The control algorithm is implemented in the National Instruments (NI) LabView environment for Windows XP. A Data Acquisition (DAQ) card typed NI PCI 6229 is used as the interface between the physical hardware and the LabView software. More information can be found in (Sønderskov & Østerö (2007)).

3. Modeling and identification

The entire magnetic field in the considered setup consists of two distinguished parts: contribution from the permanent NIB magnet attached on the ball, and contribution from the solenoid when electric current flows through it. This magnetic field can be expressed as

$$\vec{B}_t = \vec{B}_c + \vec{B}_b. \tag{1}$$

where $\vec{B}_t$ is the total magnetic field, $\vec{B}_c$ is the magnetic field induced by the solenoid, and $\vec{B}_b$ is the field induced by the NIB magnet. In the following, the feature of $\vec{B}_b$ is first investigated based on the setup. Then the total field $\vec{B}_t$ is analyzed using a theoretical approach. System parameters are identified through experiments.

3.1 NIB magnetic field $\vec{B}_b$

The NIB magnetic field is investigated through an experiment way. It is obvious that the magnetic field $\vec{B}_b$ will be influenced if the distance between the solenoid and the ball becomes smaller even without any current running in the coils around the solenoid (Woodson & Melche (1968)). Thereby we define the magnetic field generated by the NIB magnet as a function of the distance between the bottom of the solenoid and the top of the ball, denoted as $\vec{B}_b(x)$, where x is the mentioned distance. This magnetic field function can be measured by attaching a Hall Effect sensor at the top of the ball and manually moving the ball up or down within the possible working range. One measurement is shown in Fig. 6. By using the curve fitting technique, a 4th order polynominal is obtained as

$$B_b(x) = a_4x^4 + a_3x^3 + a_2x^2 + a_1x + a_0, \quad (2)$$

with coefficients listed in Table. 1. In the following, equation (2) is used as the model of NIB magnetic field.

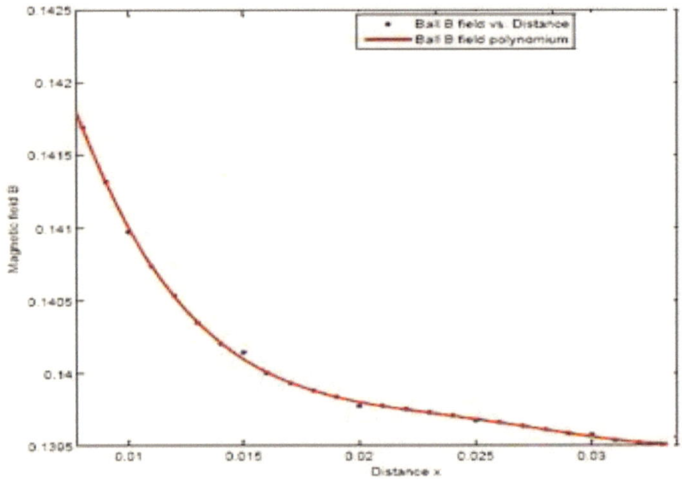

Fig. 6. Measured magnetic field generated by NIB via distance

a_0	0.1417
a_1	-0.1196×10^{-1}
a_2	0.6905×10^{2}
a_3	-0.1794×10^{4}
a_4	0.1734×10^{5}

Table.1. Coefficients of $B_b(x)$ induced by NIB magnet

3.2 Nonlinear system model

Under assumption that the used material has a linear characteristic, i.e., the magnetization density only depends on the magnetic field density (Woodson & Melcher (1968)), the magnetic flux of the entire field, denoted as $\lambda(t)$, can be approximated by

$$\lambda(t) \hat{=} L(x(t))i(t) + \lambda_B(x(t)), \quad (3)$$

where $i(t)$ denotes the current through the solenoid, and $x(t)$ denotes the displacement of the levitated object to the solenoid bottom. $L(x)$ denotes the inductance when the levitated object is assumed to be iron/steel and it can be regarded as a function of $x(t)$ (Wong (1986); Yang & Pedersen (2006)). $\lambda_B(x)$ is the flux introduced by the NIB magnet, and it also is a function of $x(t)$ as we find out in eq.(2). By using the proposed approximation in (Wong (1986); Oliveira et al. (1999); Yang & Pedersen (2006)), $L(x)$ can be expressed as

$$L(x) = L_1 + \frac{L_0}{1 + (\frac{x}{a})}, \tag{4}$$

where $L_0 = L(0) - L(\infty)$, $L_1 = L(\infty)$ and a is a constant coefficient.
According to the electromagnetic theory (Woodson & Melcher (1968)), the magnetic co-energy, denoted as W, can be calculated as

$$W(t) = \int_0^{i(t)} \lambda(\bar{i}, x(t)) d\bar{i}. \tag{5}$$

By inserting (3) and (4) into (5), there is

$$W(t) = \frac{1}{2}(L_1 + \frac{L_0}{1 + (\frac{x(t)}{a})}) i^2(t) + \lambda_B(x(t)) i(t). \tag{6}$$

The introduced magnetic force, denoted as $f(t)$, is determined from the magnetic co-energy according to

$$f(t) = \frac{\partial W(t)}{\partial x_a},$$

where x_a represents the force acting axis, which is equal to the $x(t)$ axis. Then from (6) we have

$$f(t) - -\frac{1}{2}\frac{L_0 i^2(t)}{a(1 + \frac{x(t)}{a})^2} + \frac{d\lambda_B(x(t))}{dx} i(t). \tag{7}$$

Assume that the magnetic flux $\lambda_B(x)$ and the magnetic flux density have a constant linear relationship. It could be reasonable if the considered system only has small moving distance. There is

$$\lambda_B(x) \hat{=} \beta_B B_b(x), \tag{8}$$

where $B_b(x)$ is the value calculated from equation (2). Therefore, $\frac{d\lambda_B(x)}{dx}$ can be approximated by

$$\frac{d\lambda_B(x)}{dx} = 4a_4 x^3 + 3a_3 x^2 + 2a_2 x + a_1, \tag{9}$$

with coefficients given in Table 1.
Denote the mass of the levitating object as m and the gravity acceleration as g. By neglecting the air drag friction, the dynamic of the levitating object can be obtained from Newton's Second Law as

$$m\frac{d^2x(t)}{dt^2} = mg + f(t).$$

By inserting (7) into the above equation, there is

$$m\frac{d^2x(t)}{dt^2} = mg - \frac{1}{2}\frac{L_0 i^2(t)}{a(1+\frac{x(t)}{a})^2} + \frac{d\lambda_B(x(t))}{dx}i(t). \tag{10}$$

Compared with models used in (Barie & Chiasson (1996); Oliveira et al. (1999); Pedersen & Yang (2006); Wong (1986); Yang & Pedersen (2006)), the third term on the right side of equation (10) is new and it is due to the existing of the permanent NIB magnet.
Through circuit analysis, the electrical perspective of the solenoid can be modeled as

$$u(t) = Ri(t) + \frac{d(L(x(t))i(t))}{dt} + \frac{d\lambda_B(x(t))}{dt}, \tag{11}$$

where R is the coil resistance, and $u(t)$ is the input voltage to the coil. Compared with models used in (Barie & Chiasson (1996); Oliveira et al. (1999); Pedersen & Yang (2006); Wong (1986); Yang & Pedersen (2006)), the second term on the right side of (11) is new, and it is the EMF induced by the permanent NIB magnet.
By taking relationship (8) and substituting (4) and (2) into (11), there is

$$\frac{di(t)}{dt} = \frac{aR + Rx(t)}{aL(0) + L_1x(t)}i(t) + \frac{aL_0}{(a+x(t))(aL(0)+L_1x(t))}i(t)\frac{dx(t)}{dt}$$
$$+\frac{a+x(t)}{aL(0)+L_1x(t)}u(t)$$

$$-\frac{\beta_B(a+x(t))}{aL(0)+L_1x(t)}(4a_4x^3(t) + 3a_3x^2(t) + 2a_2x(t) + a_1)\frac{dx(t)}{dt}. \tag{12}$$

Without triviality, if a small operating range is considered, the inductance (4) can be approximated by a constant value (L = 0.1398H). In addition, by taking the linear part of $\lambda_B(x)$, a linear version of equation (12) can be derived as

$$u(t) = Ri(t) + L\frac{di(t)}{dt} + \beta_B a_1\frac{dx(t)}{dt} \tag{13}$$

which is similar to a simplified linear DC-motor model (Woodson & Melcher (1968)).
Equations (10) and (12) constitute of a nonlinear model of the considered levitation system.

Compared with models used in (Barie & Chiasson (1996); Oliveira et al. (1999); Pedersen & Yang (2006); Wong (1986); Yang & Pedersen (2006)), here the influence of the NIB magnet is reflected by the extra force in (10) and the EMF part in (12), respectively.

3.3 Coefficient identification

System coefficients L_0, $L(0)$ and L_1 used in (4) can be directly measured or estimated. However, coefficients a and β_B in (10) need to be identified through an experimental approach similar to those used in (Oliveira et al. (1999); Yang & Pedersen (2006)). A set of experiments is organized to find the currents required to levitate the object at different equilibrium positions. The result is plotted in Fig. 7.

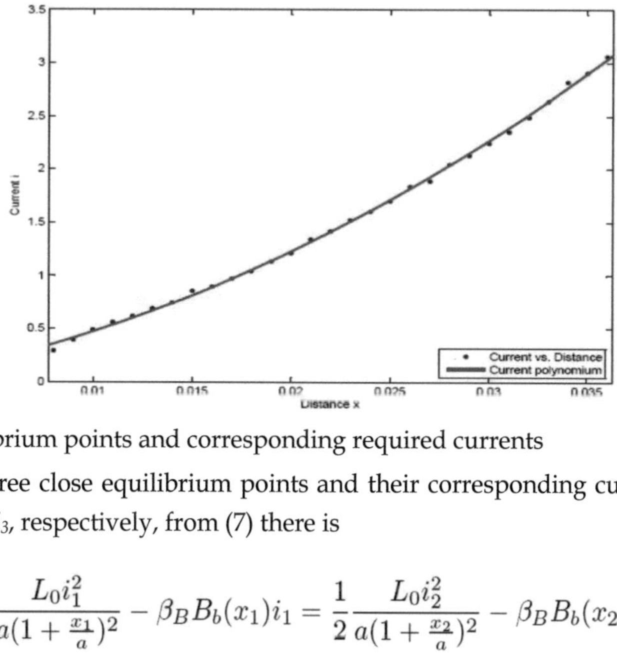

Fig. 7. The equilibrium points and corresponding required currents

By picking up three close equilibrium points and their corresponding currents, denoted as x_1, x_2,x_3 and i_1, i_2, i_3, respectively, from (7) there is

$$\frac{1}{2}\frac{L_0 i_1^2}{a(1+\frac{x_1}{a})^2} - \beta_B B_b(x_1) i_1 = \frac{1}{2}\frac{L_0 i_2^2}{a(1+\frac{x_2}{a})^2} - \beta_B B_b(x_2) i_2,$$

and

$$\frac{1}{2}\frac{L_0 i_1^2}{a(1+\frac{x_1}{a})^2} - \beta_B B_b(x_1) i_1 = \frac{1}{2}\frac{L_0 i_3^2}{a(1+\frac{x_3}{a})^2} - \beta_B B_b(x_3) i_3.$$

Coefficient a can be calculated by combining the above two equations. After a is determined, β_B can be determined based on any set, e.g., set (x_1, i_1). A simple way to determine a is to assume the term $\beta_B B_b(x_k) i_k$ is almost constant for k = 1, 2, 3. This assumption is reasonable for a small operating range, so a can be determined by

$$a = \frac{i_2 x_1 - i_1 x_2}{i_1 - i_2}, \tag{14}$$

Correspondingly, β_B can be determined by

$$\beta_B = \frac{mg + \frac{1}{2}\frac{L_0 i_1^2}{a(1+\frac{x_1}{a})^2}}{B_b(x_1)i_1}. \tag{15}$$

Average values of obtained a and β_B and other directly measured coefficients are listed in the Table 2.

Description	Symbol	Value	Unit
Coil inductance	L_1	2.0×10^{-3}	H
Coil resistance	R	0.8	Ω
Inductance	L_0	0.99×10^{-3}	H
Mag. ind. coeff.	a	1.18	m
Mass of object	m	4.27×10^{-3}	kg
Flux coeff.	β	0.065	

Table 2. Parameters used in the considered system

Due to the considered levitation system being naturally unstable and having a very fast response, it is difficult to validate the developed model directly. Therefore, a simple PID feedback controller is developed to keep the considered system operating properly. The mathematical model is validated by comparing the simulated closed-loop control system and the real controlled system afterwards (Yang et al. (2007)).

4. Design and implementation of PID controllers

4.1 Empirical PID controller

By using the obtained nonlinear model, an analog PID controller is developed and manually tuned based on the Ziegler-Nichols PID tuning method. Then the developed PID controller is discretized with a sampling frequency of 480 Hz, which is determined by the NI DAQ card used for the digital implementation. The implemented controller has the form

$$\begin{aligned} u(k) &= u(k-1) + K_p\left(1 + \frac{T}{T_i} + \frac{T_d}{T}\right)e(k) \\ &-K_p\left(1 + 2\frac{T_d}{T}\right)e(k-1) + K_p\frac{T_d}{T}e(k-2)\ , \end{aligned} \tag{16}$$

where T, K_p, T_i and T_d are sampling period, P, I, and D coe±cients, respectively. $e(k)$ is the displacement tracking error. The simulation of the closed-loop control system using the empirical PID controller is shown in Fig.8. It can be observed that the controlled system has a reasonable response time and good tracking capacity.

4.2 Automatic tuning of PID controller using GA algorithms

From our preliminary investigation (Pedersen & Yang (2006); Yang & Pedersen (2006)), it turned out that the PID controller can be automatically tuned using the multi-objective non-dominated sorting genetic algorithm (NSGA-II) based on the nonlinear system model.

The performance induced by different PID-controller parameters are evaluated by the following criteria based on the step response:

- Overshoot (M_p);
- Rise time (t_r);
- Settling time (t_s); and
- Integrated absolute error (IAE).

An illustration of the performance measures is given in Fig. 9. Each of these performance measures will be included as objectives to be minimized as their inter-dependence will depend highly on the nonlinear system expressed by (10) and (12).

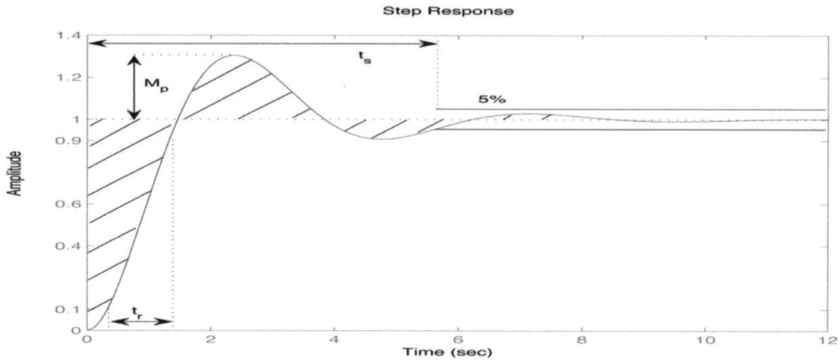

Fig. 9. Performance measures for step response

The non-dominated sorting genetic algorithm (NSGA-II) developed in (Deb et al. (2000)) is a multi-objective algorithm, which can evolve a set of non-dominated solutions that are all equally well suited for solving the specific problem given the performance measures specified. Many of the NSGA-II run-time parameters used for here are the same as the NSGA-II default values (Pedersen & Yang (2006); Yang & Pedersen (2006)), such as

Description	setting
Crossover probability	0.9
Mutation probability	0.33
SBX parameter	10
Mutation parameter	50
Rigid bounds	1 (yes)

Table. 3. Parameters used for running NSGA-II

In the simulation, The range for K_p is set to [-1000,0]. The ranges for T_i and T_d are both set to [0,15]. With respect to the computational complexity of the simulations, a population size of 50 individuals was chosen along with a maximum number of generations of 150. Besides from the use of the 4 objectives a constraint on the allowable amount of overshoot has also been formulated as only values below 100% was allowed. The distribution of K_p, T_i and T_d for the case where the outliers have been removed is illustrated in Fig. 10.
It is quite obvious that there is a large grouping of individuals for small values of T_i and K_p values below -800. A simulation of a typical controller from this cluster, with parameters as K_p = -800.46, T_i = 0.021 and T_d = 0.06, is shown in Fig. 11.

The corresponding performance measures for this individual are IAE=$5 \cdot 10^{-4}$, M_p = 84.82%, t_r = $21ms$ and t_s = 0.425s. It can be observed that the system response consists of a fast oscillation on top of a slower one. The fast rise time is mainly due to the size of K_p which is obviously very aggressive towards positional errors.

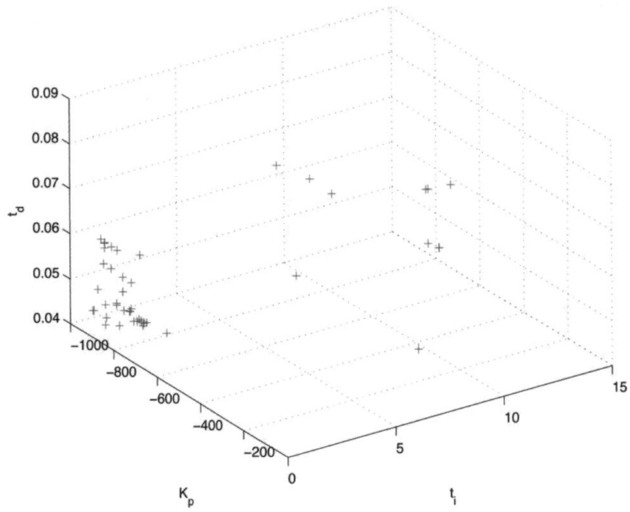

Fig. 10. Plot of parameters K_p, T_i and T_d for last generation

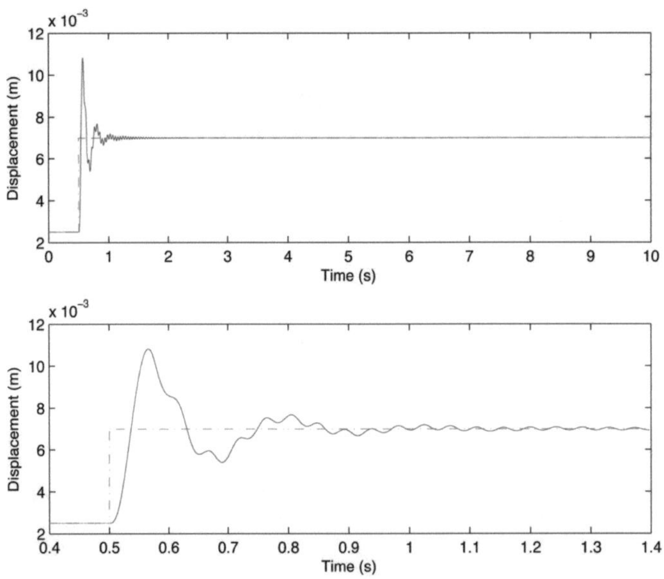

Fig. 11. System step response in simulation

4.3 LabView Implementation

The developed controllers are implemented in NI LabView environment on a PC running Windows XP. Therefore some attention needs to be paid on the real-time issues. For instance, the connection between the external devices and the LabView environment is setup manually, even though the DAQ assistant in LabView could more easily create the communication line. However, our experiences showed that the DAQ Assistant is quite time consuming, no matter if it is used inside or outside the timed loop (Sønderskov & Østerö (2007); Yang et al. (2007)). Another real-time issue relevant to the Windows XP operating system. It is well known that Windows XP gives priority to different processes that are executed. For example, just moving the mouse is sometimes enough to slow down the execution of LabView code. In order to solve this real-time problem, the timed loop structure is used in the LabView program, which guarantees that the LabView code should be executed within the defined time period. Furthermore, In order to check the sampling rate issues, a sampling frequency calculator is constructed as shown in Fig. 12. A front panel of the developed controller is shown in Fig.13.

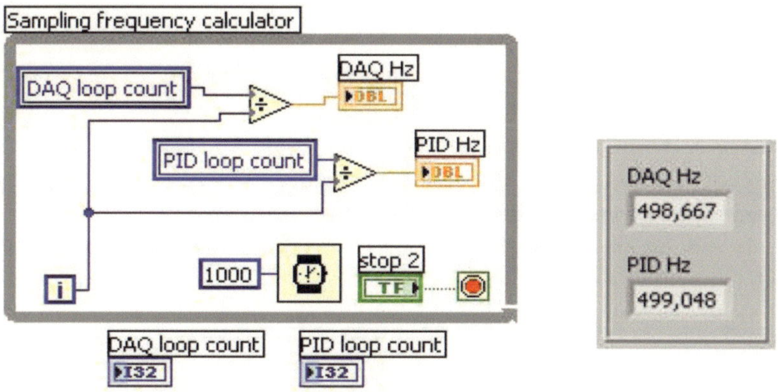

Fig. 12. Sampling frequency calculator with front panel indicators

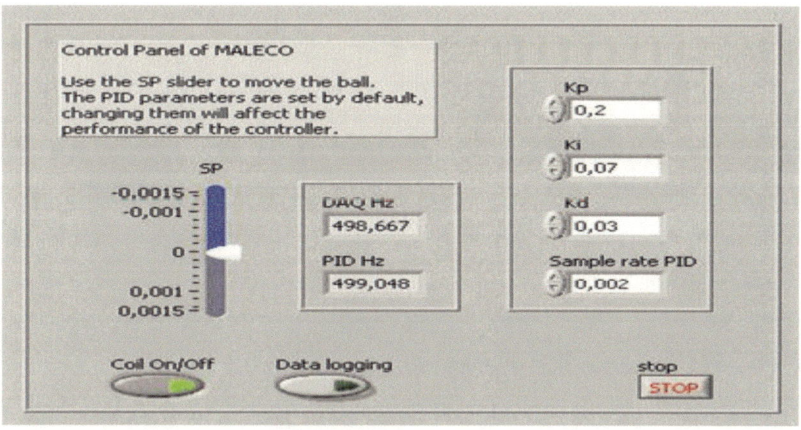

Fig. 13. Front panel of the developed controller

5. Testing results and discussions

The simulated performance of the closed-loop control system using the empirical PID controller is shown in Fig. 8. The same controller is implemented in the LabView program and tested with the physical setup. One test result based on the same set of set-points as for simulation is shown in Fig. 14. It can be observed that in principle the controlled physical system has quite similar performance as the simulation model. However, it is also obvious that the controlled physical system has much shorter response time and much larger overshot and oscillation compared with the simulated system performance. The reasons for these deviations could be explained in the following perspectives:

- Imprecise sensor measurement. The optical position sensor is very sensitive to light disturbances;
- Frequent switchings of the MOSFET IRFZ44. The frequent on-off switchings of current due to this MOSFET can directly lead to oscillations in real tests (Yang et al. (2007));
- Imprecise sampling rates of DAQ card and PID computation due to the real-time problem of Windows XP operating system. This could cause synchronization problems in data acquisition and control computation;
- the approximation of system coefficients. For example, in a strict sense, the system coefficient β_B should be displacement dependent. However, we assume it is always constant due to simplicity.

The consistency between simulation and real tests could be improved if above problems could be solved or moderated. By softly changing the set-points, e.g., filtering the rectangular set- points, the controlled physical system shows a better performance as shown in Fig. 15. It can be observed that the large overshot that appeared in Fig. 14 has disappeared.

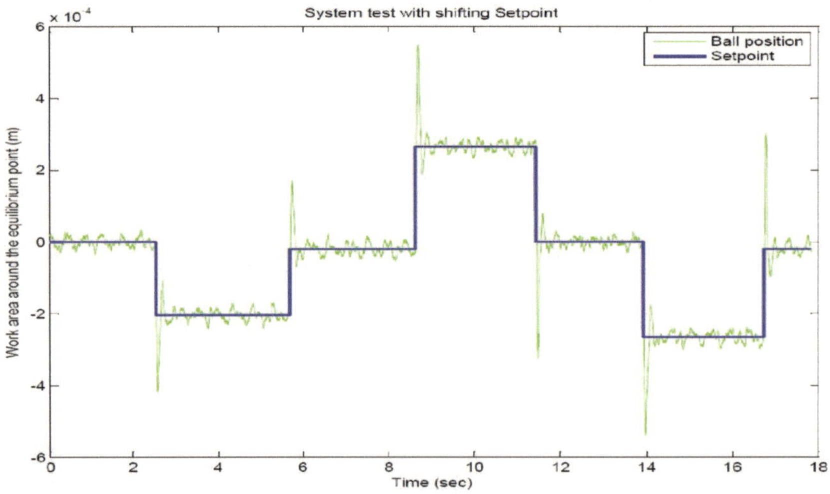

Fig. 14. Response of the controlled physical setup

One test result using the same control coefficients directly from NSGA-II tuning is shown in Fig. 16. Compared with the simulation result shown in Fig. 11, this implemented controller has quite similar behavior as simulation study. However, it is also obvious that the fast dynamic has much larger amplitude than it does in simulation, which could be due to the following facts:

- The designed closed-loop system is obviously under-damped;
- The influence from the external disturbances, e.g., the air flow around the ball etc;
- Model uncertainties and unprecise position measurements.

More analysis of these issues will be one part of our future work.

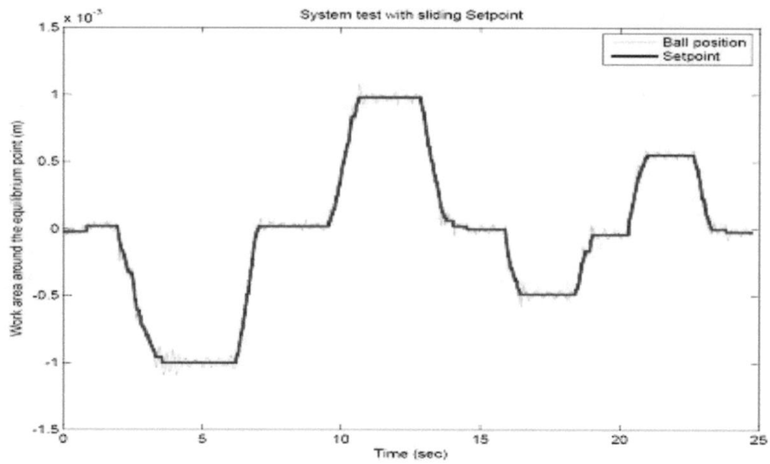

Fig. 15. Response of the controlled physical setup with soft changes

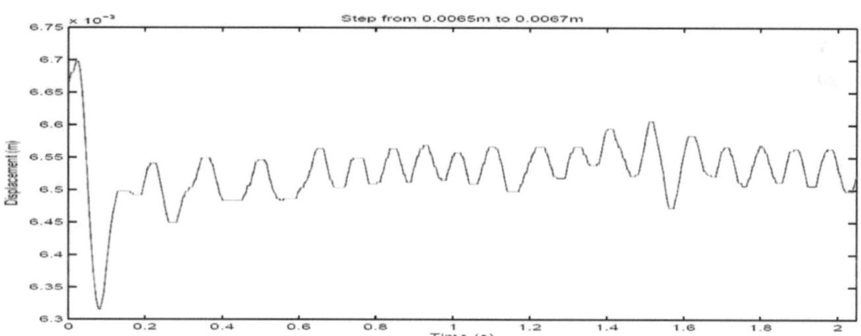

Fig. 16. Step response of the controlled setup using the NSGA-II tuned controller

6. Conclusion

The modeling and control of a 1-D magnetic levitation system with a permanent magnet object is investigated. The feature of the moving permanent magnet is explored using an experimental method and it is modeled through curve fitting technique. The entire system model is derived based on the electromagnetic theory and afterward system coefficients are identified through designed experiments. The developed model is validated through performance comparison of the closed-loop model and the controlled physical system.

The PID control is chosen as the control structure at this stage regarding the fact: (1) it is simple and require few computation resources; (2) The developed PID controllers only need the position information, with no need for the current measurement and speed estimation, such that the potential degradation of the system performance due to quantization (Barie & Chiasson (1996)) can be minimized;

The developed controllers are implemented in the LabView environment based on a PC running Windows XP. The real-time issues are managed by additional programs. Both simulation and real tests showed a clear consistency and a good system performance. Furthermore, The investigation of using genetic algorithms to automatically tune PID controller shows a potential to use this artificial intelligence method for supporting the control design for complicated nonlinear systems.

7. Acknowledgement

The authors would like to thank René M. Sønderskov, Kim S. Østerö, Niels A. Pedersen, Stefan K. Greisen and Jette R. Hansen for their contributions in system development and laboratory tests.

8. References

Special issue on magnetic bearing control. IEEE Control Systems Technology, Sept 1996.

W. Barie and J. Chiasson. Linear and nonliear state-space controllers for magnetic levitation. Int. J. of Systems Science, 27(11):1153-1163, 1996.

K. Deb, A. Pratap, and S. Moitra. A fast elitist non-dominated sorting genetic algorithm for multi-objective optimization: Nsga-ii. Parrallel Problem Solving from Nature - PPSN VI, pages 849-858, 2000. NSGA-II code available at KanGAL website: http://www.iitk.ac.in/kangal.

L. Gentili and L. Marconi. Robust nonlinear disturbance suppression of a magnetic levitation system. Automatica, (39):735-742, 2003.

A. Isidori. Nonlinear Control Systems. New York: Springer-Verlag, 1989.

W. Kim. High-Precision Planar Magnetic Levitation. Phd thesis, Massachusetts Institute of Technology, June 1997.

W. Kim, D.L. Trumper, and J.H. Lang. Modeling and vector control of planar magnetic levitator. IEEE Trans. on Industry Applications, 34(6):1254-1262, Nov/Dec 1998.

V.A. Oliveira, E.F. Costa, and J.B. Vargas. Digital implementation of a megnetic suspension control system for laboratory experiments. IEEE Trans. on Education, 42(4):315-322, Nov. 1999.

G.K.M. Pedersen and Z. Yang. Multi-objective pid-controller tuning for a magnetic levitation system using nsga-ii. In Maarten Keijzer, editor, Proceedings of Genetic and Evolutionary Computation Conference - GECC0 2006, pages 1737-1744, Seattle, Washington, USA, Jul 2006. ACM.

T.L. Simpson. Effect of a conducting shield on the inductance of an air-core solenoid. IEEE Trans. on Magnetics, 35(1):508-515, Jan 1999.

R.M. Sønderskov and K.S. Østerö. Malecos: Magnetic levitation control systems. 7th semester project report, Aalborg University Esbjerg, Denmark, Jan 2007.

M.T. Thompson. Electrodynamic magnetic suspension - models, scaling laws, and experimental results. IEEE Trans. on Education, 43(3):336-342, Aug. 2000.

M. Varella, E. Calloni, L.Di Fiore, L. Milano, and N. Arnaud. Feasibility of a magnetic suspension for second generation gravitational wave interferometers. Astroparticle Physics, (21):325-335, 2004.

R. Wisniewski and J. Stoustrup. Periodic h-2 synthesis for spacecraft attitude control with magnetorquers. Journal of Guidance Control and Dynamics, 27(5):874-881, 2004.

T.H. Wong. Design of a magnetic levitation control system - an undergraduate project. IEEE Trans. on Education, E-29(4):196-200, Nov 1986.

H. Woodson and J. Melcher. Electromechanical Dynamics - part I: Discrete Systems. Wiley, New York, 1968.

Z. Yang and G.K.M. Pedersen. Automatic tuning of pid controller for a 1-d levitation system using a genetic algorithm: a real case study. In Proceedings of the 2006 IEEE International Symposium on Intelligent Control, pages 3098-3103, Munich, Germany, Oct 2006. IEEE.

Z. Yang, G.K.M. Pedersen, and J.H. Pedersen. Modeling and control of one-dimensional magnetic levitation system with a permanent-magnet object. In Proceedings of the 13th IEEE/IFAC International Conference on Methods and Models in Automation and Robotics, pages 723-729, Szczecin, Poland, Aug 2007. IEEE.

22

Nonlinear Adaptive Tracking-Control Synthesis for General Linearly Parametrized Systems

Zenon Zwierzewicz
Department of Applied Mathematics
Szczecin Maritime University
Poland

1. Introduction

A common problem of engineering practice is to cope with mathematical models of objects with only partly known structure. The model may e.g. involve some unknown (linear or nonlinear) functions that depend on the kind of object (of a given class to which the model refers) and/or of its operation conditions. As an example we take an affine model of SISO system

$$\dot{\boldsymbol{x}} = \boldsymbol{\alpha}(\boldsymbol{x}) + \boldsymbol{\beta}(\boldsymbol{x}) \cdot u \tag{1a}$$

$$y = h(\boldsymbol{x}) \tag{1b}$$

where y, x, u denote output, state and control variables respectively, $\boldsymbol{\alpha}$ and $\boldsymbol{\beta}$ are smooth vector fields on R^n and $h: R^n \to R$ a smooth function. It is assumed here also that the functions $\boldsymbol{\alpha}$ and $\boldsymbol{\beta}$ are unknown or may be estimated with a considerable inaccuracy.
Considering the system (1) it is possible (under certain conditions (Fabri & Kadrikamanathan, 2001; Sastry & Isidori, 1989)) to obtain a direct input-output relation between u and y, by successive differentiation y with respect of time having

$$y^{(r)} = f(\boldsymbol{x}) + g(\boldsymbol{x})u \tag{2}$$

where r denotes a system relative degree. The whole approach could be well systematized and explained using the concept of Lie derivatives (Isidori, 1989) .
In this chapter the system (1) is uncertain in the sense it is linearly parametrized, or in other words, the unknown functions $\boldsymbol{\alpha}_i$ and $\boldsymbol{\beta}_i$ are assumed to be linear combinations of some known model related functions which represents our elementary knowledge on the model. It is easy to prove (see appendix) that if the functions $\boldsymbol{\alpha}_i$ and $\boldsymbol{\beta}_i$ of system (1a) are of the form of linear combinations of some known functions $\boldsymbol{\alpha}_i$ and $\boldsymbol{\beta}_i$ i.e.

$$\boldsymbol{\alpha}(\boldsymbol{x}) = \sum_{i=1}^{m_1} a_i \boldsymbol{\alpha}_i(\boldsymbol{x}); \qquad \boldsymbol{\beta}(\boldsymbol{x}) = \sum_{i=1}^{m_2} b_i \boldsymbol{\beta}_i(\boldsymbol{x}) \tag{3}$$

where a_i, b_i are real unknown parameters then the scalar functions f, g of system (2) may be represented in similar form:

$$f(\boldsymbol{x})=\sum_{i=1}^{n_1}\theta_i^1 f_i(\boldsymbol{x})+f_0(\boldsymbol{x}) \;;\quad g(\boldsymbol{x})=\sum_{i=1}^{n_2}\theta_i^2 g_i(\boldsymbol{x})+g_0(\boldsymbol{x}) \tag{4}$$

with θ_i^1, θ_i^2 unknown parameters and f_i, g_i (called here *model basis functions*) again known trough the $\boldsymbol{\alpha}_i$ and $\boldsymbol{\beta}_i$ (see appendix).

There are a huge amount of nonlinear systems that might be modeled in general form (1),(3). Using described above model transformation one can obtain a parametric model of the form (2),(4) in relative easy way (see section 3.2). The model in this form, referred below as a transformed model, was considered in many papers. One of the known method of tracking control synthesis in the case when we have a rough estimate of the model (2) functions, is a sliding mode control law (Slotine & Li, 1991). The alternative is to use adaptation (for model in the form (2),(4)) which offers more subtle policy but requires more advanced theory.

In our approach the unknown functions f and g of the transformed model are, as it turned out, linear combinations of some known model related *basis functions* i.e. some elementary knowledge of the model is assumed. The assumption above may, however, be substantially relaxed via applying, as basis functions, some sort of known approximators (Fabri & Kadrikamanathan, 2001; Tzirkel-Hancock & Fallside, 1992). As an example one may adopt a neuro-approximator with Gaussian radial basis functions (Sanner & Slotine, 1992). Systems of this sort are referred to as *functional adaptive* (Fabri & Kadrikamanathan, 2001) and represent a new branch of intelligent control systems. In the real-world applications, however, it seems purposeful to assume that we have at our disposal some (often very limited) knowledge, on the considered plant or process, that should be exploited in reasonable way. In this paper the accent is put-on the later issue.

This chapter is concerned with the problem of adaptive tracking system control synthesis for the described above class (1),(3) of uncertain systems. It has been proven that proportional state feedback plus parameters adaptation via the model basis function concept are able to assure system asymptotic stability. This form of controller permits on-line compensation of unknown model nonlinearities which leads to satisfactory tracking performance. The presented theory is illustrated by the example of ship path-following control system (Zwierzewicz, 2007ab).

It is worth to observe that affine model description (1) is taken here without loss of generality. The general nonlinear system

$$\dot{\boldsymbol{x}}=\boldsymbol{F}(\boldsymbol{x},u) \tag{5a}$$

$$y=h(\boldsymbol{x}) \tag{5b}$$

may be easy expressed in this form by augmenting it with input integrator $\dot{u}=v$ which leads to new state $\boldsymbol{x}_a=\begin{bmatrix}\boldsymbol{x}^T & u\end{bmatrix}^T$. Now considering v as a new input the above system is in the form (1).

The chapter is organized as follows. In section 2., an appropriate portion of the theory is shortly presented, which utility (in the next section) is then verified via an example of ship path-following control system. The next sections contain results of the relevant system simulations, remarks and conclusion.

2. Adaptive tracking control synthesis

The control objective is to force the plant (1) output vector $\boldsymbol{y}=[y,\dot{y},\cdots,y^{(r-1)}]^T$ to follow a specified desired trajectory $\boldsymbol{y}_d=[y_d,\dot{y}_d,\cdots,y_d^{(r-1)}]^T$ with state vector $\boldsymbol{x}$ remaining bounded. It is moreover assumed that reference input y_d and its r derivatives are bounded and known as well as that the system zero dynamics is globally exponentially stable (minimum phase condition) .

As the model (1),(3) can be transformed to the form (2),(4) thus, in what follows, our considerations will be referred to the later form.

2.1 The case of exact model

It is assumed in this section that the nonlinear functions f and g of model (2) are known and $g(\boldsymbol{x})\neq 0,\ \ \forall \boldsymbol{x}\in R^n$. A substitution of control law

$$u=\frac{-f(\boldsymbol{x})+v}{g(\boldsymbol{x})} \tag{6}$$

in the system (2) results in exact cancellation of both nonlinearities ($f(\boldsymbol{x})$ and $g(\boldsymbol{x})$) which yields

$$y^{(r)}=v \tag{7}$$

To find control $v(t)$ stabilizing this linear system, a standard poles location technique can be used. If v is chosen as

$$v=y_d^{(r)}-\mu_r e^{(r-1)}-\cdots-\mu_1 e \tag{8}$$

where y_d denotes the reference input which y is required to track, $e:=y-y_d$ denotes the output tracking error and coefficients μ_i are chosen such that $\Gamma(s)=: s^r+\mu_r s^{r-1}+\cdots+\mu_1 s=0$ is Hurwitz polynomial in the Laplace variable s, then the tracking error and its derivatives converge to zero asymptotically, because the closed-loop dynamics reduce to the equation

$$e^{(r)}+\mu_r e^{(r-1)}+\cdots+\mu_1 e=0 \tag{9}$$

which, by virtue of the choice of coefficients μ_i is asymptotically stable (Fabri & Kadrikamanathan, 2001; Sastry & Isidori, 1989; Tzirkel-Hancock & Fallside 1992).

2.2 The case with functional uncertainty

Let us consider now the case when functions f and g are unknown but have the form (4) with $\theta_i^1,\ \ i=1,\cdots n_1$, $\theta_i^2,\ \ i=1,\cdots n_2$ unknown 'true' parameters and the $f_i(\boldsymbol{x})$, $g_i(\boldsymbol{x})$ known model basis functions. At time t our estimates of the functions f and g are respectively

$$\hat{f}(\boldsymbol{x}) = \sum_{i=1}^{n_1} \hat{\theta}_i^1(t) f_i(\boldsymbol{x}) + f_0(\boldsymbol{x}) \; ; \quad \hat{g}(\boldsymbol{x}) = \sum_{i=1}^{n_2} \hat{\theta}_i^2(t) g_i(\boldsymbol{x}) + g_0(\boldsymbol{x}) \tag{11}$$

with $\hat{\theta}_i^1, \hat{\theta}_i^2$ standing for the estimates of the parameters θ_i^1, θ_i^2 respectively at time t. Since substitution in the system (2) the control law

$$u = \frac{-\hat{f}(\boldsymbol{x}) + v}{\hat{g}(\boldsymbol{x})} \tag{12}$$

no longer guarantees exact cancellation and whereby a resulting system linearity (like in the former case (6)), we will proof below a useful here theorem. Prior to its formulation let us define a sliding surface (Slotine & Li, 1991) which represents some (aggregate) measure of the tracking error

$$\varepsilon(t) = \eta_1 e + \cdots + \eta_{r-1} e^{(r-2)} + e^{(r-1)} := \Psi(e) \tag{13}$$

as well as introduce some notations

$$f - \hat{f} = \sum_{i=1}^{n_1} (\theta_i^1 - \hat{\theta}_i^1) f_i(\boldsymbol{x}) = \boldsymbol{\theta}^{1T} \boldsymbol{w}_1 ; \quad (g - \hat{g})u = \sum_{i=1}^{n_1} (\theta_i^2 - \hat{\theta}_i^2) g_i(\boldsymbol{x}) u = \boldsymbol{\theta}^{2T} \boldsymbol{w}_2 \tag{14}$$

where

$$\boldsymbol{w}_1 = \begin{bmatrix} f_1 & f_2 & \cdots & f_{n_1} \end{bmatrix}^T ; \qquad \boldsymbol{w}_2 = \begin{bmatrix} g_1 & g_2 & \cdots & g_{n_2} \end{bmatrix}^T u \tag{15}$$

are model *basis functions* and

$$\boldsymbol{\theta}^1 = [(\theta_1^1 - \hat{\theta}_1^1) \cdots (\theta_{n_1}^1 - \hat{\theta}_{n_1}^1)]^T ; \; \boldsymbol{\theta}^2 = [(\theta_1^2 - \hat{\theta}_1^2) \cdots (\theta_{n_2}^2 - \hat{\theta}_{n_2}^2)]^T \tag{16}$$

are vectors of parameters.
Moreover $\boldsymbol{\theta} = \begin{bmatrix} \boldsymbol{\theta}^{1T} & \boldsymbol{\theta}^{2T} \end{bmatrix}^T$; $\boldsymbol{w} = [\boldsymbol{w}_1^T \; \boldsymbol{w}_2^T]^T$.

Theorem

The closed-loop system (2), (12) and (8) after introduction of parameter update law,

$$\dot{\boldsymbol{\theta}} = -\varepsilon \boldsymbol{w} \tag{17}$$

yields bounded $y(t)$ asymptotically converging to $y_d(t)$.
Proof:
Differentiating (13) and multiplying by a scalar k_d we have

$$\begin{aligned} \dot{\varepsilon}(t) + k_d \varepsilon(t) &= k_d \eta_1 e + (k_d \eta_2 + \eta_1)\dot{e} + \cdots + (k_d + \eta_{n-1}) e^{(r-1)} + e^{(r)} = \\ &= \mu_1 e + \mu_2 \dot{e} + \cdots \mu_r e^{(r-1)} + y^{(r)} - y_d^{(r)} = y^{(r)} - v \end{aligned} \tag{18}$$

The coefficients η_i as well as k_d should be selected so that μ_i should have the property mentioned earlier, i.e. that they should ensure an asymptotically stable solution to equation (9).

Transforming now (12) and substituting in (2) yields

$$y^{(r)} - v = f + gu - v \tag{19}$$

$$y^{(r)} - v = f + gu - \hat{f} - \hat{g}u = f - \hat{f} + (g - \hat{g})u \tag{20}$$

so we get the following error equation

$$\dot{\varepsilon}(t) = -k_d\varepsilon(t) + f - \hat{f} + (g - \hat{g})u \tag{21}$$

Making use of (14) the error equations (21) will take a form

$$\dot{\varepsilon}(t) + k_d\varepsilon(t) = \boldsymbol{\theta}^{1T}\boldsymbol{w}_1 + \boldsymbol{\theta}^{2T}\boldsymbol{w}_2 = \boldsymbol{\theta}^T\boldsymbol{w} \tag{22}$$

We prove that the error equation (22) along with the update law (17) yields a bounded $y(t)$ asymptotically converging to $y_d(t)$.
Let us take the Lapunov-like (Slotine & Li, 1991) function of the form

$$V(\varepsilon, \boldsymbol{\theta}) = \frac{1}{2}\varepsilon^2 + \frac{1}{2}\boldsymbol{\theta}^T\boldsymbol{\theta} \tag{23}$$

hence

$$\dot{V} - \varepsilon \cdot \dot{\varepsilon} + \boldsymbol{\theta}^T\dot{\boldsymbol{\theta}} - \varepsilon(-k_d\varepsilon + \boldsymbol{\theta}^T\boldsymbol{w}) - \varepsilon\boldsymbol{\theta}^T\boldsymbol{w} = -k_d\varepsilon^2 \leq 0 \tag{24}$$

If we assume that $k_d > 0$ we have proved that Lapunov function is decreasing along trajectories of (22); thereby establishing bounded ε and $\boldsymbol{\theta}$. However, to verify that $\varepsilon \to 0$ as $t \to \infty$ we use Barbalat's lemma (Slotine & Li, 1991) To check the uniform continuity of $\dot{V}$ it is enough to prove that the second derivative of V i.e.

$$\ddot{V} = -2k_d\varepsilon\dot{\varepsilon} = -2k_d\varepsilon(-k_d\varepsilon + \boldsymbol{\theta}^T\boldsymbol{w}) \tag{25}$$

is bounded. This in turn needs $\boldsymbol{w}$, a continuous function of $\boldsymbol{x}$ to be bounded. Note that if ε and $\boldsymbol{y}_d$ are bounded, it is implied that $\boldsymbol{y}$ is bounded. These facts and assumed stable zero dynamics imply that the state $\boldsymbol{x}$ is bounded. Now (if we could guarantee that $\hat{g}(\boldsymbol{x})$ of (12) is bounded away from zero) it follows that $\boldsymbol{w}$ is bounded. □

Remarks:

Note that, although ε converges to zero the system (22), (17) is not asymptotically stable because $\boldsymbol{\theta}$ is only guaranteed to be bounded.

Prior bounds on the parameters θ_i^2 are frequently sufficient to guarantee that $\hat{g}(\boldsymbol{x})$ is bounded away from zero (Sastry & Bodson, 1989).

One can now observe that adaptive reconstruction of functions f and g in the formula (11) may be interpreted as an extra control leading to much more exact cancellation of system (2) nonlinearities, which in turn make the resulting system closer to linear (see Fig. 1)

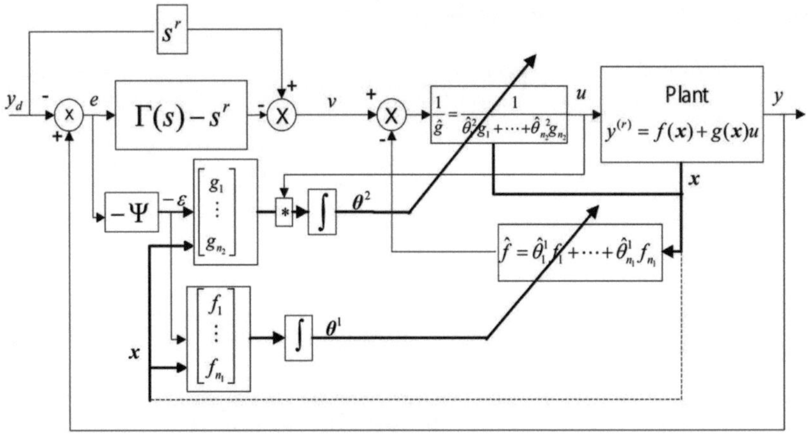

Fig. 1. Model basis functions adaptive control scheme.

3. Adaptive ship path-following control synthesis

Prior to introduction a model that represents further a base for controller synthesis we define some preliminary notions.

3.1 Path-following errors definition

Assume that a path to be followed (preset) is composed of broken line segments defined by a sequence of vertexes (turning points) $P_1(x_1,y_1)$, $P_2(x_2,y_2)$, ... , $P_i(x_i,y_i)$, ..., $P_n(x_n,y_n)$. Let us introduce also the following coordinate systems (Fig.2):
earth-fixed coordinate system (X_g, Y_g) (these coordinates can be measured directly via GPS).
relative (transformed) coordinate system (X_r, Y_r) whose center is located at the point $P_i(x_i,y_i)$ and with the axis OX_r directed along a segment P_iP_{i+1} (i=1,2,...,n)
The relative ship position (x_r,y_r) as well as its relative heading ψ_r can be obtained through the following simple transformation:

$$\begin{bmatrix} x_r \\ y_r \\ \psi_r \end{bmatrix} = \begin{bmatrix} \cos\varphi_{ro} & \sin\varphi_{ro} & 0 \\ -\sin\varphi_{ro} & \cos\varphi_{ro} & 0 \\ 0 & 0 & 1 \end{bmatrix} \begin{bmatrix} x_g - x_i \\ y_g - y_i \\ \psi - \varphi_{ro} \end{bmatrix} \tag{26}$$

which express the successive translation and then rotation of the earth-fixed system where $\varphi_r o$ is an angle of its rotation

$$\tan\varphi_{ro} = \frac{y_{i+1} - y_i}{x_{i+1} - x_i} \tag{27}$$

Now it is reasonable to treat the coordinate y_r and the heading ψ_r as the path-following errors corresponding to the given segment.
For curvilinear reference path the local (relative) coordinate system should be tangent to the path at the point that is closest to the actual ship position. This system has to be then shifted and rotated from time step to time step in such a way, that it remains tangent to the reference path and that the x-coordinate represents the arc length along the path.

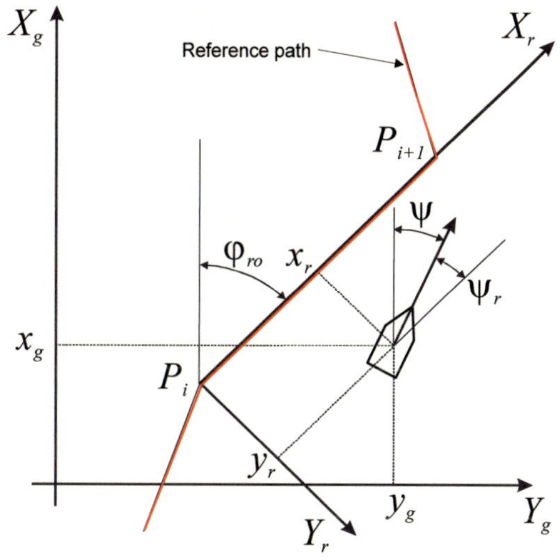

Fig. 2. Earth-fixed and relative coordinate systems

3.2 The case with functional uncertainty

In order to synthesize a path-following controller we apply the adaptive control concepts, presented in the section 2., to the following (partially known), ship motion model presented in the form of so-called error equation

$$\begin{cases} \dot{y}_r = u \sin \psi_r + v \cos \psi_r & (28a) \\ \dot{\psi}_r = r & (28b) \\ \dot{r} = \Phi(r) + c\delta & (28c) \end{cases}$$

with the output

$$y = y_r \tag{28d}$$

where

y_r - relative abscissa of the ship position (cross-track error)
ψ_r - relative heading (course-error)
r - angular velocity
u - longitudinal velocity
v - transversal velocity
y - system output
δ - rudder deflection as a control variable
c - unknown model parameter
$\Phi(\cdot)$ - unknown function

The equation (28a) is a second equation of the ship kinematical model (compare the first two equations of model (39)) while (28b) and (28c) are in fact the Norrbin ship model (Fossen, 1994; Lisowski, 1981) whose standard form

$$T\ddot{\psi} + F(\dot{\psi}) = k\delta \tag{29}$$

can be transformed into the relevant equations of (28) via definition $\dot{\psi}_r = r$ and substitution of

$$\Phi = -\frac{F(\cdot)}{T} \text{ and } c = k/T \tag{30}$$

The first equation of kinematics, in the model (28), is omitted as x_r represents movement along the path - which is irrelevant here. It is also assumed, for simplicity, that transversal velocity v is of the form $v = -r_1 r$ (compare the last equation of model (39)) where r_1 is unknown.

The double differentiation (which in fact represents a formalism delivered in appendix) of output y with respect to time leads to

$$\ddot{y} = f(\boldsymbol{x}) + g(\boldsymbol{x})\delta \tag{31}$$

where

$$f(\boldsymbol{x}) = ru\cos\psi_r + r_1 r^2 \sin\psi_r - r_1 \cos\psi_r \cdot \Phi(r) \tag{32a}$$

$$g(\boldsymbol{x}) = cr_1 \cos\psi_r \tag{32b}$$

and the state vector $\boldsymbol{x} = [y_r \;\; \psi_r \;\; r]^T$ is assumed to be accessible to measurement.

Simple analysis of this system as well as physical limitations indicate its stable internal (zero) dynamics.

Remark:

In the 'classical' approach to ship control the structure of function F is (according to Norrbin model) often adopted in different ways. Generally it may be assumed in the form

$$F(\dot{\psi}) = a_3\dot{\psi}^3 + a_2\dot{\psi}^2 + a_1\dot{\psi} + a_0 \tag{33}$$

or ignoring the terms of third or second degree we have for example

$$F(\dot{\psi}) = a_3\dot{\psi}^3 + a_1\dot{\psi} + a_0 \tag{34}$$

Now, assuming that a structure of the function F has been predetermined, the coefficients a_i are usually identified via sea trials (Lisowski, 1981).

Owing to that as well as taking into account that Φ has a similar structure as F (below we take the case (33)), it is natural to estimate the (partially) unknown functions (32) of model (31) as follows

$$\begin{aligned}\hat{f}(\boldsymbol{x}) = \sum_{i=1}^{4}\hat{\theta}_i^1 f_i + f_0 = \hat{\theta}_1^1 r^3 \cos\psi_r + \hat{\theta}_2^1 r^2 \cos\psi_r + \\ + \hat{\theta}_3^1 r\cos\psi_r + \hat{\theta}_4^1 \cos\psi_r + \hat{\theta}_5^1 r^2 \sin\psi_r + ru\cos\psi_r\end{aligned} \tag{35a}$$

$$\hat{g}(\boldsymbol{x}) = \sum_{i=1}^{1} \hat{\theta}_i^2 g_i + g_0 = \hat{\theta}_1^2 \cos\psi_r \tag{35b}$$

defining thereby a set of model basis functions f_i, g_i.
It can be seen from (35) that to implement our algorithm besides of the state vector measurements the longitudinal velocity u is also required.
To complete the employing of the theory introduced earlier to our specific case we also need:
the measure of the error

$$\varepsilon(t) = \dot{e} + \eta e = \dot{y}_r + \beta y_r \tag{36}$$

rudder control law

$$\delta = \frac{-\hat{f}(\boldsymbol{x}) + v}{\hat{g}(\boldsymbol{x})} \tag{37}$$

where

$$v(t) = \ddot{y}_d - \mu_2 \dot{e} - \mu_1 e = -\mu_2 \dot{y}_r - \mu_1 y_r \tag{38}$$

and the parameter update law (17).
Note that in our setting above (coordinate transform) $y_d = 0$, so a main task for our controller is to bring output i.e. cross-track error to zero. In fact bringing at the same time ψ_r to zero, in presence of disturbances (e.g. transversal current), is (for the considered here ship (39)) not always possible (Zwierzewicz, 2003) This way the path-following process may be, in our case, accomplished only in the presence of a course error (nonzero drift angle).

4. Ship model and simulations

4.1. Ship motion model

As a simulation model that represents further a real ship dynamics we adopt here the following de Wit-Oppe's (W-O) ship dynamical model (Wit & Oppe, 1979-80).

$$\begin{aligned}
\dot{x} &= u\cos\psi - v\sin\psi \\
\dot{y} &= u\sin\psi + v\cos\psi \\
\dot{\psi} &= r \\
\dot{r} &= -a\,r - br^3 + c\delta \\
\dot{u} &= -f\,u - Wr^2 + S \\
v &= -r_1\, r - r_3 r^3
\end{aligned} \tag{39}$$

where
(x, y) - Cartesian coordinates
ψ - course (heading)
r - angular velocity

u - longitudinal velocity
v - transversal velocity
δ - rudder deflection as a control variable
S - propelling force
Compared to the model (28) one can see that the structure of function Φ adopted there takes the form $\Phi(r) = -br^3 - ar$. Note that this ship characteristic is obviously unknown to the control system designer and has to be adaptively reconstructed.
As the ship model parameters the dynamic maneuvering parameters of the m.s. Compass Island model are adopted. The units of time, length and angle are respectively one minute, one nautical mile and one radian. The parameters were determined as follows a = 1.084 /min, b=0.62min, c = 3.553 rad/min, r_1 = -0.0375 nm/rad, r_2=0, f = 0.86 /min, W= 0.067 nm/rad^2, S=0.215 nm/min^2. The maximum speed of rudder and rudder angle are 3.8 deg/s, and 35 deg, respectively. The ship has got the following characteristics, gross register tonnage 9214 t, deadweight, 13498 t, length, 172 m, draught, 9.14 m, one propeller, and maximum speed, 20 knots. Notice that the adopted parameters make the ship directionally stable (Fossen, 1994; Lisowski, 1981) and that other ship dynamic model (parameters) could be used here as well.

4.2 Simulation results

The *Simulink* simulations are based on the *nonlinear* W-O model of ship dynamics (34) including the controller (37) together with the main feedback linear control component (38), while the adaptation mechanism is realized by *aggregate* tracking error (36), model basis functions (35) as well as parameters update law (17) (Fig. 1).
In Fig. 3 the path to be followed (preset) is a broken line defined by the *way points* (0,0); (0,10); (4,12) and (4, 20). The original ship position, its heading and angular velocity are (0,-0.5), 60° and 0 rad/min respectively. The adopted distance scale is 1 nm while the nominal ship velocity is 0.25 nm/min. In the simulation a transversal current has been, as a load disturbance, introduced (d_y=0.04 nm/min).
To evaluate the accuracy of adaptive process control there is depicted here also a trajectory (blue) driven by controller (37) with fully known dynamics (exact model functions). As we can see the differences are practically negligible.
Fig. 4. describes plots of ship heading versus time. The blue line refers to the case of the fully known ship dynamic model. As one can observe the ship heading, during straight line path segments, is about -10 deg, which in fact indicate a course-error. Such a behavior is, on the other hand, necessary to compensate an effect of currents action. These simulations comply thereby with the relevant comment of section 3.2.
In Fig. 5. it can be seen, that in the case of limited ship model knowledge, the rudder action is substantially more intensive (red line), as compared to the case of full model familiarity.
The last Fig. 6. depicts the plots of cross-track errors versus time. As before the red plot refers to the limited knowledge of the ship dynamics. It proves once more that the differences are relatively small.
An interesting feature of the adaptation process is that the steering process is performed without asymptotic convergence of parameters errors $\boldsymbol{\theta} = \left[\boldsymbol{\theta}^{1T} \quad \boldsymbol{\theta}^{2T}\right]$ to zero (we have proved, at the most, their boundedness). This fact reflects an idea that the main goal of the adaptive system is to drive the error $e := y - y_d$ to zero which does not necessarily imply

that the controller parameters approach their correct values. In fact, the input signal must have certain properties, for the parameters to converge, related to the notion of *persistent excitation* (Astrom & Wittenmark, 1995). This concept, in reference to the closed-loop signals, may be formulated as a requirement of sufficient richness of functions $\boldsymbol{w}$ (15). It is, however, impossible to verify this condition explicitly ahead of time (Sastry & Isidori, 1989; Wang & Hill, 2006).

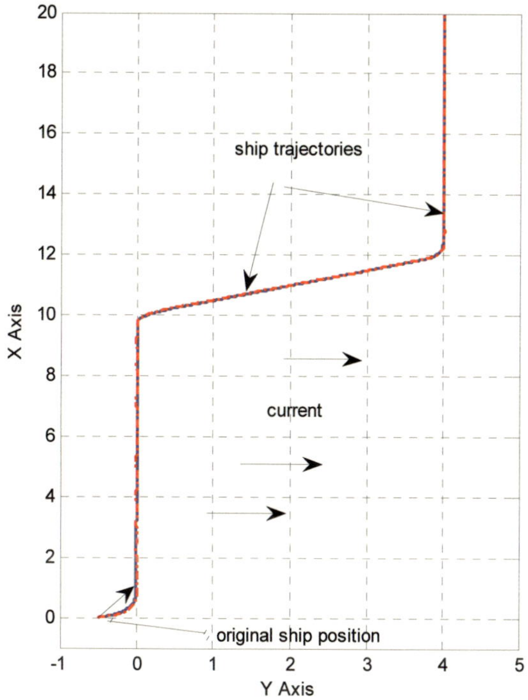

Fig. 3. Ship trajectories, constant current.

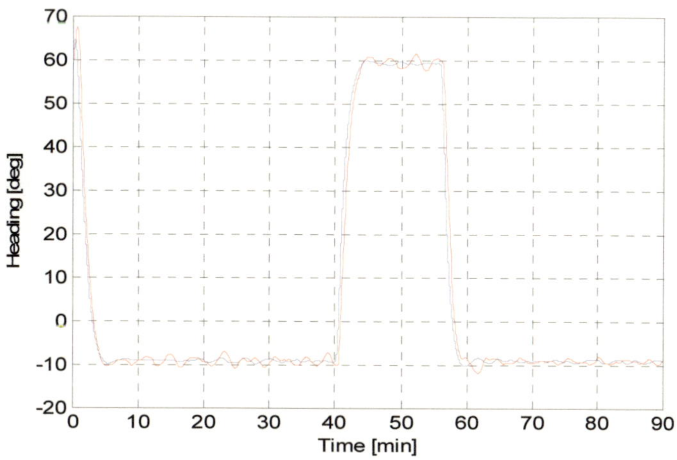

Fig. 4. Ship headings versus time.

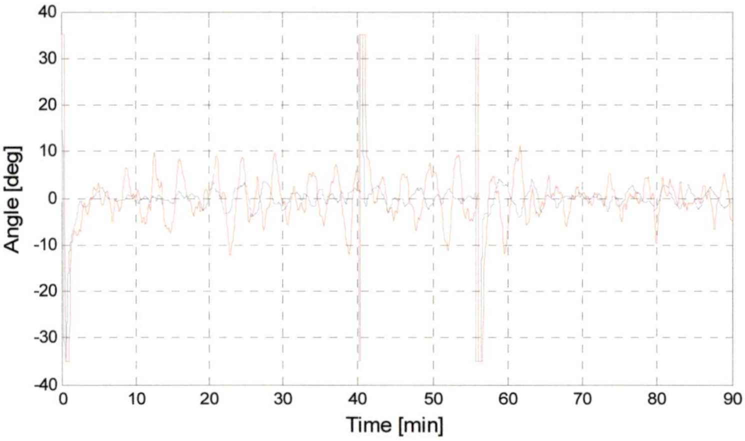

Fig. 5. Rudder deflections versus time.

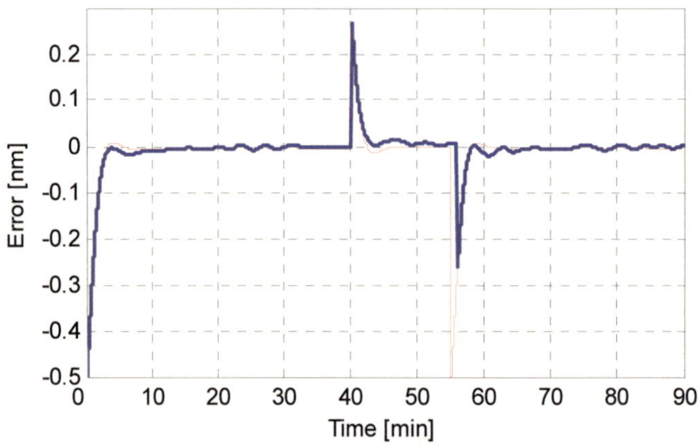

Fig. 6. Cross-track errors versus time.

As a reference input comprises stepwise signals (path) changes, to fulfill the assumptions of its differentialability it has been initially prefiltered. Similarly the wave disturbances were modeled in the form of a white noise driven shaping filter (Fossen, 1994; Zwierzewicz, 2003).
During conducted here simulations, the system performance turned out to be especially sensitive for initial guess of parameter θ_1^2 that had to be picked up in some vicinity of its true value (true value 0.133; picked up 0.5). In this respect, to ensure robustness for the disturbances that arise due, e.g., to the initial guess of parameters and thus inherent approximation errors the system should be additionally augmented with a sliding mode control. This technique is often applied to force the system global stability (Fabri & Kadrikamanathan, 2001; Sanner & Slotine, 1992; Tzirkel-Hancock & Fallside, 1992).

5. Conclusion

In the paper a general class of uncertain, linearly parametrized, nonlinear SISO plants was considered. It has been proven that proportional state feedback plus adaptation via *model basis functions* are able to assure their asymptotic stability. As a result of presented theory an adaptive ship path-following system has been proposed. The presented simulations confirm that the system is insensitive for object (ship) model unfamiliarity.

6. References

Astrom, K. & Wittenmark, B. (1995). *Adaptive Control.* Addison Weseley.

De, C. Wit & Oppe, J. (1979-80). Optimal collision avoidance in unconfined waters *Journal of the Institute of Navigation,* Vol. 26, No. 4, pp. 296-303.

Fabri, S. & Kadrikamanathan, V. (2001). *Functional Adaptive Control. An Intelligent Systems Approach.* Springer-Verlag.

Fossen, T. I. (1994). *Guidance and control of ocean vehicles.* John Wiley.

Lisowski, J. (1981). *Statek jako obiekt sterowania automatycznego.* Wyd. Morskie Gdańsk, , (in Polish).

Isidori, A. (1989). *Nonlinear Control Systems. An Introduction.* Springer –Verlag, Berlin.

Sanner, R. & Slotine, J.E. (1992). Gaussian networks for direct adaptive control *IEEE Transations on Neural Networks* vol. 3, no. 6, pp.837-863, Nov. 1992,

Sastry, S. & Bodson, M. (1989) *Adaptive control: Stability, Convergence and Robustness.* Prentice-Hall, ch. 7.

Sastry, S. & Isidori, A. (1989). Adaptive control of linearizable systems *IEEE Transations on Automatic Control* vol. 34, no. 11, pp. 1123-1131.

Slotine, J. E. & Weiping, Li. (1991). *Applied Nonlinear control.* Prentice Hall.

Spooner, J. T. & Passino, K. M. (1996). Stable adaptive control using fuzzy systems and neural networks" *IEEE Transactions on Fuzzy Systems* Vol. 4, No. 3, pp. 339- 359.

Tzirkel-Hancock, E. & Fallside, F. (1992). Stable control of nonlinear systems using naural networks *International Journal of Robust and Nonlinear Control,* vol. 2, pp. 63-86,

Wang C. & Hill, D. J. (2006). Learning from neural control *IEEE Transations on Neural Networks* Vol. 17, No. 1, pp.130-146.

Zwierzewicz, Z. (2003). On the ship guidance automatic system design via lqg-integral control in *Proc. 6th Conference on Manoeuvring and Control of Marine Crafts (MCMC2003),* Girona, Spain, pp. 349-353.

Zwierzewicz, Z. (2007a). Ship course-keeping via nonlinear adaptive control synthesis, In: *Emerging Technologies, Robotics and Control Systems,* Int. Society for Advanced Research, Ed. Salvatore Pennacchio, Palermo, Italy.

Zwierzewicz, Z. (2007b). *Ship guidance via nonlinear adaptive control synthesis* IFAC Conference on Control Applications in Marine Systems, 19-21, Sept., Bol, Croatia.

7. Appendix

We will prove that the system (1),(3) may be easy transformed to the form (2),(4). To this end we recall to the concept of Lie derivative.

Lie derivative of scalar function $h(\boldsymbol{x})$ with respect to a vector $\boldsymbol{\alpha}(\boldsymbol{x})$, denoted by $L_a h(\boldsymbol{x})$ is defined as:

$$L_a h(\boldsymbol{x}) = \nabla h(\boldsymbol{x}) \boldsymbol{\alpha}(\boldsymbol{x}) \tag{40}$$

where ∇h denotes the gradient of $h(x)$ i.e. $[\partial h / \partial x_1 ... \partial h / \partial x_n]$. Lie derivative is scalar so the process of taking Lie derivatives could be chained and is denoted as follows

$$L_{\boldsymbol{\alpha}}^{i} h(\boldsymbol{x}) = \nabla(L_{\boldsymbol{\alpha}}^{i-1} h(\boldsymbol{x}))\boldsymbol{\alpha}(\boldsymbol{x}) \tag{41}$$

$$L_{\boldsymbol{\beta}} L_{\boldsymbol{\alpha}}^{i} h(\boldsymbol{x}) = \nabla(L_{\boldsymbol{\alpha}}^{i} h(\boldsymbol{x}))\boldsymbol{\beta}(\boldsymbol{x}) \tag{42}$$

Differentiating y in eqation (1) with respect to time and using Lie derivatives we get e.g.

$$y^{(1)} = \frac{\partial y}{\partial \boldsymbol{x}} \dot{\boldsymbol{x}} = L_{\boldsymbol{\alpha}} h(\boldsymbol{x}) + L_{\boldsymbol{\beta}} h(\boldsymbol{x}) u \tag{43}$$

where $y^{(i)}$ denotes te ith derivative of y with respect to time.
Assume that the system (1) has relative degree equal to r i.e. after r differentiations the following conditions are satisfied

$$L_{\boldsymbol{\beta}} L_{\boldsymbol{\alpha}}^{i-1} h(\boldsymbol{x}) = 0 \qquad \text{for } i = 1, \ldots, (r-1) \tag{44a}$$

$$L_{\boldsymbol{\beta}} L_{\boldsymbol{\alpha}}^{r-1} h(\boldsymbol{x}) \neq 0 \tag{44b}$$

Calculating now the Lie derivatives of r-th order to the system (1),(3) yields

$$L_{\boldsymbol{\alpha}}^{r} h(\boldsymbol{x}) = \sum_{i_r=1}^{m_1} \cdots \sum_{i_2=1}^{m_1} \sum_{i_1=1}^{m_1} a_{i_1} a_{i_2} \cdots a_{i_r} \nabla(\cdots \nabla(\nabla h \cdot \boldsymbol{\alpha}_{i_1})\boldsymbol{\alpha}_{i_2} \cdots)\boldsymbol{\alpha}_{i_r}(\boldsymbol{x}) = \sum_{i=1}^{n_1} \theta_i^1 f_i(\boldsymbol{x}) \tag{45}$$

and

$$L_{\boldsymbol{\beta}} L_{\boldsymbol{\alpha}}^{r-1} h(\boldsymbol{x}) = \sum_{j=1}^{m_2} \sum_{i_{r-1}=1}^{m_1} \cdots \sum_{i_1=1}^{m_1} a_{i_1} \cdots a_{i_r} b_j \cdot \nabla(\nabla(\cdots(\nabla h \cdot \boldsymbol{\alpha}_{i_1}) \cdots)\boldsymbol{\alpha}_{i_{r-1}})\boldsymbol{\beta}_j(\boldsymbol{x}) = \sum_{i=1}^{n_2} \theta_i^2 g_i(\boldsymbol{x}) \tag{46}$$

So the system (1) can be written in the form

$$y^{(r)} = L_{\alpha}^{r} h(\boldsymbol{x}) + L_{\beta} L_{\alpha}^{r-1} h(\boldsymbol{x}) u = \sum_{i=1}^{n_1} \theta_i^1 f_i(\boldsymbol{x}) + \sum_{i=1}^{n_2} \theta_i^2 g_i(\boldsymbol{x}) u \tag{47}$$

which is in fact system (2), (4).
Observe that the free terms $f_0(\boldsymbol{x})$ and $g_0(\boldsymbol{x})$ in formula (4) may be easy obtained by treating one of the coefficients in each sum of (3) as equal to one e.g. $a_1 = 1$ and $b_1 = 1$. This way one of the terms in the formula (45) will take a form $L_{\boldsymbol{\alpha}_1}^{r} h(\boldsymbol{x}) = f_0(\boldsymbol{x})$ or respectively $L_{\boldsymbol{\beta}_1} L_{\boldsymbol{\alpha}_1}^{r-1} h(\boldsymbol{x}) = g_0(\boldsymbol{x})$ - in relation to (46).